ASPEN PUBLISHER

EMPLOYER'S GUIDE TO

Health Care Reform

2010

Brian M. Pinheiro
Jean C. Hemphill
Clifford J. Schoner
Jonathan M. Calpas

Ballard Spahr LLP

Wolters Kluwer

Law & Business

AUSTIN   BOSTON   CHICAGO   NEW YORK   THE NETHERLANDS

This publication is designed to provide accurate and authoritative information in regard to the subject matter covered. It is sold with the understanding that the publisher is not engaged in rendering legal, accounting, or other professional services. If legal advice or other professional assistance is required, the services of a competent professional person should be sought.

—From a *Declaration of Principles* jointly adopted by
a Committee of the American Bar Association and
a Committee of Publishers and Associations

Printed in the United States of America

ISBN 978-0-7355-9894-2

1 2 3 4 5 6 7 8 9 0

About Wolters Kluwer Law & Business

Wolters Kluwer Law & Business is a leading provider of research information and workflow solutions in key specialty areas. The strengths of the individual brands of Aspen Publishers, CCH, Kluwer Law International and Loislaw are aligned within Wolters Kluwer Law & Business to provide comprehensive, in-depth solutions and expert-authored content for the legal, professional and education markets.

CCH was founded in 1913 and has served more than four generations of business professionals and their clients. The CCH products in the Wolters Kluwer Law & Business group are highly regarded electronic and print resources for legal, securities, antitrust and trade regulation, government contracting, banking, pension, payroll, employment and labor, and healthcare reimbursement and compliance professionals.

Aspen Publishers is a leading information provider for attorneys, business professionals and law students. Written by preeminent authorities, Aspen products offer analytical and practical information in a range of specialty practice areas from securities law and intellectual property to mergers and acquisitions and pension/benefits. Aspen's trusted legal education resources provide professors and students with high-quality, up-to-date and effective resources for successful instruction and study in all areas of the law.

Kluwer Law International supplies the global business community with comprehensive English-language international legal information. Legal practitioners, corporate counsel and business executives around the world rely on the Kluwer Law International journals, loose-leafs, books and electronic products for authoritative information in many areas of international legal practice.

Loislaw is a premier provider of digitized legal content to small law firm practitioners of various specializations. Loislaw provides attorneys with the ability to quickly and efficiently find the necessary legal information they need, when and where they need it, by facilitating access to primary law as well as state-specific law, records, forms and treatises.

Wolters Kluwer Law & Business, a unit of Wolters Kluwer, is headquartered in New York and Riverwoods, Illinois. Wolters Kluwer is a leading multinational publisher and information services company.

ASPEN PUBLISHERS SUBSCRIPTION NOTICE

This Aspen Publishers product is updated on a periodic basis with supplements to reflect important changes in the subject matter. If you purchased this product directly from Aspen Publishers, we have already recorded your subscription for the update service.

If, however, you purchased this product from a bookstore and wish to receive future updates and revised or related volumes billed separately with a 30-day examination review, please contact our Customer Service Department at 1-800-234-1660 or send your name, company name (if applicable), address, and the title of the product to:

ASPEN PUBLISHERS
7201 McKinney Circle
Frederick, MD 21704

Important Aspen Publishers Contact Information

- To order any Aspen Publishers title, go to *www.aspenpublishers.com* or call 1-800-638-8437.

- To reinstate your manual update service, call 1-800-638-8437.

- To contact Customer Care, e-mail *customer.care@aspenpublishers.com*, call 1-800-234-1660, fax 1-800-901-9075, or mail correspondence to Order Department, Aspen Publishers, PO Box 990, Frederick, MD 21705.

- To review your account history or pay an invoice online, visit *www.aspenpublishers.com/payinvoices*.

Wolters Kluwer
Law & Business

PREFACE

"What does health care reform really mean?" This is the question we heard over and over again in the summer of 2009 from clients, friends, neighbors and family members, and even from total strangers calling and e-mailing in to television and radio shows. Media reports focused on some of the more scandalous rumors, including the now infamous "death panel" debate among national politicians. Somehow, new legislation that meant so much for so many seemed to be understood by so few.

We undertook an effort, beginning in the summer of 2009, to educate ourselves and to explain to our clients (many of whom are employers) exactly how and why health care reform is relevant. Along the way, we discovered that health care reform will have a significant impact on virtually every employer, and even presents some cost-savings opportunities upon which employers who are paying attention can capitalize.

We wrote this book as a guide to health care reform for employers. We tried to be comprehensive while still providing practical pointers. We hope you find this book to be as helpful as we found the process of writing it to be interesting.

Brian Pinheiro
Jean Hemphill
Cliff Schoner
Jonathan Calpas

ABOUT THE AUTHORS

Brian M. Pinheiro is the chair of the Employee Benefits and Executive Compensation Group at Ballard Spahr LLP and a member of the Health Care Group and the Health Care Reform Initiative. Mr. Pinheiro represents clients on matters relating to employer-sponsored health and welfare benefit plans; executive compensation, including Section 409A and the Section 280G golden parachute rules; and tax-qualified retirement plans, including cash balance pension plans and section 401(k) plans and section 403(b) tax-sheltered annuity programs. Prior to joining Ballard, he was a tax law specialist for the Employee Plans Division of the Internal Revenue Service (National Office).

Mr. Pinheiro is a frequent lecturer on employee benefits and executive compensation issues and an adjunct professor of law at Temple University James F. Beasley School of Law. *Chambers USA: America's Leading Lawyers for Business* named Mr. Pinheiro a leader in the field of benefits and compensation law in the 2006 through 2009 editions. He also is the co-editor of *ERISA: A Comprehensive Guide, Third Edition* (Aspen Publishers).

Mr. Pinheiro graduated with distinction from Georgetown University Law Center with an LL.M. in tax law and a Certificate in Employee Benefits. He is also a graduate of Boston College (B.A. 1992), and Catholic University of America Columbus School of Law (J.D., *magna cum laude*, 1995), where he served as Production Editor for the Catholic University Law Review.

Jean C. Hemphill is a partner in the Business and Finance Department of Ballard Spahr. She is the chair of the Health Care Group and a member of the Employee Benefits and Executive Compensation, Mergers and Acquisitions/Private Equity, CCRC Financing and Workout, Corporate and Government Investigations and White Collar Defense, Nonprofit Organizations, and Higher Education Groups. She concentrates her practice in the areas of general corporate, health care, employee benefits, and nonprofit, health care, and church plan laws.

Before joining Ballard Spahr in 1997, Ms. Hemphill was Vice President and General Counsel of the Board of Pensions of the Presbyterian Church (U.S.A.). She continues to serve as General Counsel for the Board and legal counsel to numerous other denominational benefits programs. She is a director of the National Health Law Project and a frequent lecturer on nonprofit law.

Ms. Hemphill is a graduate of the University of Pennsylvania and Temple University's James E. Beasley School of Law. She has received an AV Peer Review Rating from Martindale-Hubbell.

Clifford J. Schoner is of counsel in the Employee Benefits and Executive Compensation Group at Ballard Spahr. He concentrates his practice in employee benefits law, including the treatment of executive compensation and benefits in mergers and acquisitions and all fiduciary aspects of plan operation and investment.

Before joining Ballard Spahr, Mr. Schoner worked with Union Pacific Railroad Company as ERISA counsel for more than 17 years. He serves on the Executive Committee and Board of Directors of the ERISA Industry Committee (ERIC) and also chairs ERIC's Legal Committee.

Mr. Schoner is a graduate of Syracuse University (B.A. 1974), Rutgers School of Law—Camden (J.D. 1977), and New York University School of Law, Graduate Division (LL.M. 1982).

Jonathan M. Calpas is an associate in the Employee Benefits and Executive Compensation Group. Mr. Calpas represents for-profit, tax-exempt, church, and government employers on matters related to tax-qualified retirement plans and employer-sponsored health and welfare plans. He focuses on compliance with the statutory and regulatory rules relating to such plans, including rules arising out of the Internal Revenue Code, ERISA, and HIPAA.

Before joining Ballard Spahr, Mr. Calpas spent five years working for a large cable communications company as a financial accountant, and also worked for a major public accounting firm assisting clients with corporate and partnership tax compliance issues. Mr. Calpas is a Certified Public Accountant in the Commonwealth of Pennsylvania.

Mr. Calpas is a graduate of Penn State (B.S., *with distinction*, 2002) and Temple University James E. Beasley School of Law (J.D. 2008), where he was a member of the Temple Journal of Science, Technology & Environmental Law.

ACKNOWLEDGMENTS

Putting together a comprehensive review of health care reform from an employer's point of view within eight weeks of enactment is not an easy task. We could not have produced this text without a tremendous amount of assistance and support. We wish to thank everyone in the Employee Benefits and Executive Compensation Group and the Labor and Employment Group at Ballard Spahr LLP, with particular thanks to Marla Roshkoff (our intrepid proofreader), Ed Leeds, Samantha McMillan, Jacquelyn Gray, Brian Pedrow, John Langel, Dan Johns, Shannon Farmer, Steve Suflas, Denise Keyser, Pat Harvey, John McLaughlin, Isaac Hernandez, Bob Krauss, Kristin McCarthy, Beth Shea, Robin Ireland, Eileen Kenney, Maryanne Barrett, Barbara Stokes, and Randee Borasky.

For editorial guidance, encouragement, and support throughout this project, we thank May Wu and the rest of the professional staff at Wolters Kluwer Law & Business.

We also wish to thank our families and friends who have tolerated interminable discussions about health care reform during the past weeks and months.

TABLE OF CONTENTS

APPENDICES

INDEX

LIST OF ACRONYMS

ACIP	Advisory Committee on Immunization Practices
ACO	Accountable care organizations
AD&D	Accidental death & dismemberment insurance
AHRQ	HHS Agency for Healthcare Research and Quality
AWP Statutes	Any willing provider statutes
CBO	Congressional Budget Office
CDC	Centers for Disease Control
CHIP	Children's Health Insurance Program
CLAS	Culturally and linguistically appropriate services
CMS	HHS Centers of Medicare and Medicaid Services
COBRA	Consolidated Omnibus Budget Reconciliation Act of 1985
DOL	U.S. Department of Labor
DRG	Diagnostic related group
EMTALA	Emergency Medical Treatment and Labor Act
EPSDT	Early and Periodic Screening, Diagnostic and Treatment
ERISA	Employee Retirement Income Security Act of 1974
FEHBP	Federal Health Benefits Program
FICA	Federal Insurance Contributions Act
FLSA	Fair Labor Standards Act of 1938
FMLA	Family and Medical Leave Act of 1993
FPL	Federal poverty level
FSA	Flexible spending account
FTE	Full-time equivalent employee
FUTA	Federal Unemployment Tax Act
GDP	Gross domestic product
HCERA[*]	Health Care and Education Reconciliation Act of 2010
HDHP	High-deductible health plan
HELP	U.S. Senate Health, Education, Labor and Pension Committee
HHS	U.S. Department of Health and Human Services
HI	Hospital Insurance (portion of FICA)
HIPAA	Health Insurance Portability and Accountability Act of 1996
HMO	Health maintenance organization
HRA	Health reimbursement account
HRSA	Health Resources and Services Administration
HSA	Health savings account
IPPS	Inpatient Prospective Payment System
IRS	Internal Revenue Service
MEWA	Multiple employer welfare arrangement
MMA	Medicare Prescription Drug, Improvement and Modernization Act of 2003

MSA	Medical savings account
NAIC	National Association of Insurance Commissioners
OBRA	Omnibus Budget Reconciliation Act
OTC	Over the counter
PHSA	Public Health Service Act
POS	Point of service
PPA	Pension Protection Act of 2006
PPACA*	Patient Protection and Affordable Care Act of 2010
PPO	Preferred provider organization
QHP	Qualified health plan
RDS	Retiree drug subsidy
SAFRA	Student Aid and Fiscal Responsibility Act
SECA	Self-Employment Contribution Act
SMM	Summary of material modifications
SPD	Summary plan description
SSA	Social Security Act
TPA	Third-party administrator
TRICARE	TRICARE military service plans
UCR	Usual, customary, and reasonable
VBID	Value-Based Insurance Design
VEBA	Voluntary Employees' Beneficiary Association

*For convenience, when we intend to refer to both the PPACA and the HCERA, we refer to the "2010 Health Care Reform Act" or simply the "Act."

CHAPTER 1

INTRODUCTION

What does health care reform mean for employers? That is the simple and straightforward question which this book, the *Employer's Guide to Health Care Reform,* attempts to address. While the question may be simple and straightforward, the answer is not. Health care reform presents different opportunities and challenges for different types of employers. How an employer will react to health care reform depends on a number of variables, including:

- The size of the employer's workforce;
- The average income level of employees;
- The extent to which the employer's workforce is unionized;
- Whether the employer provides group health coverage to pre-Medicare and/or post-Medicare retirees;
- The types of group health plans provided to employees, including traditional indemnity, preferred provider organizations (PPOs), point-of-service (POS) arrangements, health maintenance organizations (HMOs), high-deductible and consumer-driven health plans, health reimbursement accounts (HRAs), health flexible spending accounts (Health FSAs), and health savings accounts (HSAs);
- Whether the costs incurred under those plans are "self-funded" by the employer out of its operating assets, or funded through insurance (or a combination of both);
- The design of the employer's group health plan and the terms and conditions of coverage;
- Whether the employer is for-profit or nonprofit; and
- The degree to which health benefits continue to be viewed as an important benefit for the recruiting and retention of employees in the employer's industry.

The health care reform effort is a once-in-a-generation overhaul of about one-sixth of the United States economy.[1] In its current form, health care reform could fundamentally alter the manner in which health care benefits are provided to Americans, potentially shifting from an employment-based system to an individual-based system run through "Exchange" marketplaces organized at the state level. Shortly after signing the health care reform law on March 23, 2010, President Obama said:

> I said this once or twice, but it bears repeating: If you like your current insurance, you will keep your current insurance. No government takeover; nobody is changing what you've got if you're happy with it. If you like your doctor, you will be able to keep your doctor. In fact, more people will

---

[1] *See* Patient Protection and Affordable Care Act of 2010 § 1501(a)(2)(B) (finding that "[n]ational health spending is projected to increase from [$2.5 trillion], or 17.6 percent of the economy, in 2009 to [$4.7 trillion] in 2019"). *See also* Executive Office of the President, Council of Economic Advisors, *The Economic Case for Health Care Reform, http://www.whitehouse.gov/assets/documents/ CEA_Health_Care_Report.pdf,* p. 1 (June 2009) (providing that health care expenditures represent almost 18% of GDP in 2009 and are projected to rise to 34% of GDP by 2040); Congressional Budget Office, *The Long Term Outlook for Health Care Spending, http:// www.cbo.gov/ftpdocs/87xx/doc8758/MainText.3.1.shtml,* p. 3 (indicating the total spending on health care for 2007 equaled about 16% of the United States gross domestic product for that year).

keep their doctors because your coverage will be more secure and more stable than it was before I signed this legislation.[2]

While the new law does not force individuals to drop or change their coverage, it remains to be seen whether employers, through which many individuals currently have health insurance coverage, decide to continue to provide the same type of coverage in light of the health care reform changes. Because health care reform will be implemented in pieces over the next decade, subject to several intervening federal and state election cycles, it is difficult to predict what the health care system will look like in future years. Legislative changes, regulatory interpretations, and marketplace reactions all will serve to shape the manner in which health care reform is implemented.

The breadth and depth of the changes, along with the protracted and divisive political process that led to the changes, have created substantial confusion among the employers who will be affected by health care reform. This guide addresses employer concerns as follows:

- Chapter 2 provides the context for health care reform by describing the relevant aspects of the United States health care system prior to reform and explaining the objectives that health care reform is intended to address. It also discusses the legislative process that resulted in health care reform, the structure of the new law and how it relates to other laws affecting human resources and employee benefits, and how the changes in the new law will be enforced.

- Chapter 3 introduces some of the basic concepts of the new law and defines key terms used throughout the statute. Among other things, this chapter explains the subtle yet important differences between a "group health plan" and "health insurance coverage."

- Chapter 4 describes in detail a key exemption from the health care reform requirements—grandfathered health plans—as well as the special grandfathered treatment afforded certain collectively bargained plans. Neither exemption will allow an employer to avoid all of the health care reform changes; employers will need to carefully consider whether they can or should take advantage of the exemption.

- Chapter 5 introduces health care reform changes that are designed to make health coverage more accessible and more affordable to Americans.

- Chapter 6 addresses the programs being adopted immediately to preserve, extend, or expand coverage to the demographic groups most likely to be uninsured: high-risk individuals, early retirees, employees of small business, and young adults. These programs include some of the very first issues that employers will need to tackle in implementing health care reform. Among the changes is an immediate opportunity for employers to receive reimbursements from the federal government for providing certain health coverage to retirees.

- Chapter 7 discusses the basic changes to health plan design that must be implemented prior to 2014 under the new law. Most of the design changes will be effective for 2011 (or earlier), and employers will need to amend their plan documents and communications materials to reflect the changes.

- Chapter 8 discusses additional changes to health plan design that must be implemented beginning with the 2014 plan year. Employers will have a bit more time to determine how to update their plan documents and communications materials to reflect these changes.

- Chapter 9 summarizes the transparency and accountability reporting that the 2010 Health Care Reform Act imposes on group health plans and health insurance issuers as well as the information that will become available to individuals about their health coverage options either directly from

---

[2] President Obama, remarks at the U.S. Department of the Interior, March 23, 2010; *http://www.whitehouse.gov/blog/2010/03?page=3.*

their employer plan sponsor or through a United States Department of Health and Human Services (HHS) Web portal.

- Chapter 10 focuses on the "meat and potatoes" of the health care reform law, explaining the obligation of individuals to enroll in certain health coverage or pay a penalty, as well as the obligation of employers to provide certain health coverage or pay a penalty. It also describes the "Exchanges" created by the new law, and how certain individuals can obtain subsidized health insurance coverage through an Exchange.

- Chapter 11 explains operational changes in the new law that will have a direct or indirect effect on employers, including a series of changes that will affect the Medicare Part D retiree drug subsidy (RDS) payable to employers that offer certain retiree prescription drug coverage.

- Chapter 12 examines some of the new taxes and revenue-raisers that will have a direct or indirect impact on employers. Employers will need to amend certain plans, including Health FSAs, to reflect these changes.

- Chapter 13 summarizes the most relevant changes from different points of view. For example, it identifies which changes large employers should be considering and compares them to the changes in which small employers would be most interested. It also discusses the changes that are most significant for full-time and part-time employees, union and non-union groups, modest- and high-income employees, and self-funded and insured group health plans.

CHAPTER 2
EVOLUTION OF HEALTH CARE REFORM

§ 2.01   Reasons for Health Care Reform

While there has been widespread debate and disagreement about how to reform the health care system in the United States, there does not seem to be much of a dispute about the basic problems that need to be addressed:

- Improving access to and the quality of care,

- Reining in the ever-increasing cost of health care, and

- Finding a way to pay for any reforms that are enacted.

Improving access to and quality of care. For 2008, the U.S. Census Bureau determined that 46.3 million people in the United States, or more than 15 percent of the total population, did not have health insurance coverage.[1] An estimated 87 million people were uninsured at some point in 2007 or 2008.[2] Young adults represent approximately 33 percent of the uninsured population.[3] People who do not have insurance tend not to receive preventive care and often fail to treat small health problems before they turn into chronic or high-cost problems. Failure to receive timely and proper care leads to lost workplace productivity and higher rates of serious illness and death.[4]

Reining in the ever-increasing cost of health care. Employers certainly do not need to be reminded of the need to rein in increasing health care costs. Premiums for health coverage have more than doubled in the last decade, which is more than three times the rate of wage increases over the same period.[5] Many employers have faced double-digit increases in the cost of health coverage in recent years, even as they have seen their revenues shrink in a recessionary economy.

Finding a way to pay for any reforms that are enacted. Nearly everyone involved in the health care reform debate seemed to agree that if any reforms were enacted, they needed to be accompanied by enough tax increases and other revenue raisers to have a net positive effect on the federal budget. On March 20, 2010, the Congressional Budget Office released its final cost estimate on the new health care reform law, in which it projected that the law would produce a net $143 billion reduction in federal deficits over the 2010–2019 period.[6] Much of the savings comes from provisions in the new law to address Medicare fraud, waste, and abuse, and to otherwise streamline the health care system. However, the law also includes tax increases for certain high earners, as well as an array of fees and penalties on individuals, employers, and other constituents in the health care system.[7]

After more than a year of intense political debate about how to solve the problems of the United States health system, Congress passed and President Obama signed two bills: the Patient Protection

---

[1] U.S. Census Bureau, *Income, Poverty and Health Insurance Coverage in the United States: 2008, http://www.census.gov/prod/2009pubs/p60-236.pdf,* p. 20 (September 2009); *see also* Peter R. Orszag, Director of Office of Management and Budget, *Counting the Uninsured: 46 Million or "More Than 30 Million?" http://www.whitehouse.gov/omb/blog/09/09/10/CountingtheUninsured46MillionorMorethan30Million/* (explaining that the 46.3 million figure includes about 10 million illegal aliens).

[2] Meena Seshamani, M.D., Ph.D., *The Costs of Inaction, the Urgent Need for Health Reform, http://www.healthreform.gov/reports/inaction/diminishing/index.html.*

[3] Meena Seshamani, M.D., Ph.D., *Young Americans and Health Insurance Reform: Giving Young Americans the Security and Stability They Need, http://www.healthreform.gov/reports/youngadults/youngamericans.pdf.pdf.*

[4] Meena Seshamani, M.D., Ph.D., *The Costs of Inaction, the Urgent Need for Health Reform, http://www.healthreform.gov/reports/inaction/diminishing/index.html.*

[5] *Lower Premiums, Stronger Businesses: How Health Insurance Reform Will Bring Down Costs for Small Businesses, http://www.healthreform.gov/reports/smallbusiness2/index.html* (citing Kaiser Family Foundation, Employer Health Benefit Survey (Menlo Park, CA: Kaiser Family Foundation, 2009). http://ehbs.kff.org/).

[6] Letter from Douglas W. Elmendorf, Director of the Congressional Budget Office, to the Honorable Nancy Pelosi, Speaker of the United States House of Representatives, dated March 20, 2010, *http://www.cbo.gov/ftpdocs/113xx/doc11379/Manager'sAmendmentto ReconciliationProposal.pdf.*

[7] *See* **Chapter 12,** *infra,* for a discussion of the new taxes and revenue raisers.

and Affordable Care Act (enacted on March 23, 2010)[8] and the Health Care and Education Reconciliation Act of 2010 (enacted on March 31, 2010).[9] We refer to the laws throughout this book as the "PPACA" and the "HCERA," or together as the "2010 Health Care Reform Act" or "the Act."

§ 2.02   The Employer-Based Health Care Coverage Landscape Prior to Health Care Reform

Approximately 177 million Americans (59 percent of the total population) now obtain their health care coverage through an employer-based arrangement.[10] Ninety-six percent of employers with 50 or more employees offer health care coverage; 43 percent of employers with fewer than 50 employees offer coverage.[11] Under an employer-based arrangement, an individual may potentially be covered as an employee; a former employee (either under COBRA coverage or as a retiree under an active or retiree plan); a spouse of a current or former employee; a child or stepchild of a current or former employee, including adopted children, a grandchild being raised by an employee, a legal ward or a foster child of the employee; a domestic partner; or a child of a domestic partner.

[A]   Group Health Plans

When an employer offers coverage to more than one employee, a "group health plan" is established.[12] A group health plan may be insured, self-funded (sometimes referred to as self-insurance), or both.

An "insured" group health plan is one that is funded through the purchase of insurance. The employer (and possibly the current and former employees) pay a premium to an insurance company, and any benefits payable under the plan are paid by the insurance company out of its assets. A "self-funded" group health plan is one that is funded out of the employer's general assets. The employer may hire an insurance company to decide and pay claims, but the benefits payable under the plan are paid out of the employer's general assets. Self-funded plans tend to be less expensive, because employers do not have to pay premium taxes or fund insurance company reserves, but the costs may be more volatile depending on the experience of covered employees and their dependents. Some employers that sponsor self-funded plans purchase stop-loss insurance to cap their individual or aggregate claims exposure. Approximately 55 percent of workers are covered by self-funded employer-based plans.[13]

While most small employers offer coverage through the group health insurance market, smaller employers sometimes join together in various arrangements to obtain better rates for coverage as a group or an association. Employers with a unionized labor workforce may, as an alternative to offering coverage directly, contribute on behalf of their union employees to health plans sponsored or operated by a union, including Taft-Hartley trust arrangements. As discussed in more detail in Chapter 10, the 2010 Health Care Reform Act maintains existing employer-based group health plan coverage principles. At the same time, it creates a new independent infrastructure for individuals and their dependents to access affordable, quality health care coverage separate from their employment.

[B]   Plan Design

There are many different types of health plan designs offered by employers in their group health plans. Different coverage offerings may include, for example, traditional indemnity plans; managed

---

[8] Pub. L. No. 111-148, 124 Stat. 119.

[9] Pub. L. No. 111-152, 124 Stat. 1029.

[10] U.S. Census Bureau, *Income, Poverty and Health Insurance Coverage in the United States* (2007).

[11] Executive Office of the President, Council of Economic Advisors, *The Economic Case for Health Care Reform*, *http://www.whitehouse.gov/assets/documents/CEA_Health_Care_Report.pdf*, page 8 (June 2009).

[12] 42 U.S.C. § 300gg-91(a)(1); I.R.C. § 5000(b)(1).

[13] Kaiser/HRET Survey of Employer-Sponsored Health Benefits, 1999–2007.

care plans such as health maintenance organizations (HMOs); preferred provider organizations (PPOs) and point-of-service (POS) arrangements; high-deductible and consumer-driven arrangements; and account-based arrangements, such as health reimbursement arrangements (HRAs), health savings accounts (HSAs), health flexible spending accounts (FSAs), and Archer medical spending accounts (Archer MSAs).

Some employers offer a single health plan that provides medical, behavioral health, and prescription drug benefits through a single insurance carrier or third-party administrator (TPA). Other employer plans carve out basic medical coverage from care or services offered by specialty providers, such as a separate prescription drug plan or a separate behavioral health benefits plan that provides mental health and substance abuse benefits. To cover out-of-pocket expenses that may not otherwise be covered by the plan, an employer may offer a supplemental HRA or Health FSA so that its employees can pay those costs with pretax dollars.

An employer may provide a single health care coverage package or a variety of options from which employees can choose through a cafeteria plan offered by an employer.[14] The employee's choice of coverage may result in a higher contribution amount toward the premium for the coverage or different levels of deductibles, copays, and cost-sharing. In some cafeteria plans, employees may opt out of coverage altogether and receive the amounts they otherwise would have paid as pretax premiums for health coverage as additional cash compensation.

Under the 2010 Health Care Reform Act, these plan designs may continue but they may not qualify as health care coverage that an individual or employer must offer to avoid paying a tax or penalty. Many will qualify if their benefit coverage provisions are amended to conform with the requirements for qualified coverage.

[C] Regulation of Health Care Plans

Most, but not all, employer-sponsored health plans are subject to regulation by the United States Department of Labor (the DOL) under the Employee Retirement Income Security Act, as amended (ERISA).[15] Also, since most employer-sponsored health plans are provided on a pretax basis to employees and former employees and their spouses and dependents, the plans are subject to rules set forth in the Internal Revenue Code of 1986, as amended (Code) and corresponding U.S. Treasury regulations.[16] Health plans sponsored by government and church employers are exempt from ERISA,[17] but are subject to the tax laws as well as federal health care laws and regulations in the Code and the Public Health Service Act (the PHSA)[18] that are administered by the Department of Health and Human Services (HHS).

Insurance companies, often referred to as health insurance carriers or issuers, are licensed by the individual states and regulated by the state departments of insurance. An employment-based group health plan that is insured (as opposed to self-funded) may be subject to federal mandates under ERISA and state law mandates that govern the insurance industry.

Most self-funded plans are not subject to regulation by the states. If the self-funded plan is subject to ERISA, the plan will be exempt from most state regulation under the ERISA preemption clause.[19]

Under the 2010 Health Care Reform Act, the same regulatory entities continue to preside over the provision of health coverage by employers and insurance companies. However, HHS, the administrative agency currently responsible for Medicare, Medicaid, and other federal government health

---

[14] *See* I.R.C. § 125 (providing the cafeteria plan design requirements).

[15] Pub. L. No. 93-406, 88 Stat. 829.

[16] I.R.C. §§ 105, 106.

[17] 29 U.S.C. § 1003(b). A church plan may elect to be subject to ERISA, and such an election is irrevocable. I.R.C. § 410(d).

[18] PHSA, 42 U.S.C. Ch. 6A.

[19] 29 U.S.C. § 1144(a) (pre-empting any and all state laws insofar as they relate to any employee benefits plan covered by ERISA).

care programs, takes on a new and vastly expanded role with respect to employment-based and individual health care coverage and becomes the predominant regulatory agency. Currently, the DOL and state insurance departments are the primary regulators of employer-based health care coverage.

[D]   Coverage Other Than Employment-Based Coverage

Those who do not receive their health coverage through their employer may be covered by one of the existing government health care programs—for example, Medicare, a state Medicaid plan under Title XIX of the Social Security Act, a state children's health insurance program (CHIP), active military and veterans' coverage under TRICARE, or the Indian Health Service. Those who do not have access to coverage through an employer or a government program may purchase coverage in the private individual insurance market. There are also some states that offer coverage under Medicaid or other programs to individuals who have income in excess of the federal government's income eligibility guidelines or who are unable to obtain affordable insurance through the private market due to a pre-existing condition or serious health issue.

[E]   Taxation of Employment-Based Health Care Coverage

Most employment-based health care coverage is a tax-free benefit for employees and their eligible dependents. Under the Code, a taxpayer may exclude from gross income employer-provided health coverage for the employee, the employee's spouse or the employee's qualified dependents[20] or direct or indirect reimbursement for medical care.[21]

For these purposes, each dependent child must meet certain relationship, residency, support, and age requirements set forth in Section 152 of the Code.[22] A dependent child includes an individual who is the son, daughter, stepson, or stepdaughter of the employee, and a child includes both an individual who is legally adopted by the employee and an individual who is lawfully placed with the employee for legal adoption by the employee.[23] A child also includes an eligible foster child, defined as an individual who is placed with the employee by an authorized placement agency or by judgment, decree, or other court order.[24] A married child is not a dependent beginning with the calendar year in which the individual files a joint income tax return.[25] To be an eligible dependent, the dependent child (1) must have the same principal place of residence as the taxpayer for at least half the year, (2) must have not provided more than one-half of his or her own support in the calendar year, and (3) must have not attained age 19 (age 24 if a student) as of the close of the calendar year.[26]

Most employment-based group health plans have adopted dependent eligibility requirements that are consistent with the requirements of the Code for tax-free benefits for the employee. The exception is coverage provided to a domestic partner (and the domestic partner's dependent children). To the extent that an employer provides coverage for domestic partners who do not otherwise qualify as dependents for tax purposes, the value of the coverage is subject to federal income tax. The 2010 Health Care Reform Act eliminates the dependent child residency and support requirements and raises the age limit for tax-free health care benefits from employers.[27]

---

[20] I.R.C. § 106.

[21] I.R.C. § 105(b).

[22] I.R.C. § 105.

[23] I.R.C. § 152.

[24] I.R.C. § 152(f)(1).

[25] I.R.C. § 152(b)(2).

[26] I.R.C. § 152(c).

[27] *See infra* **§ 7.04**, notes 30–56 and accompanying text (discussing the extended coverage requirement for adult children and the broadened tax exclusion for child coverage).

§ 2.03   The Legislative Process: Making Sausage

The unusual two-law structure of the 2010 Health Care Reform Act is the result of a tortured legislative process spanning almost a full calendar year.

[A]   Legislative History

In the U.S. House of Representatives, the health care reform legislation was originally set forth in different versions of H.R. 3200, the "America's Affordable Health Care Choices Act," that were adopted by the House Ways and Means Committee and the House Education and Labor Committee on July 17, 2009. The House Energy and Commerce Committee released its markup of H.R. 3200 on this same date. The result of these bills was H.R. 3962, the "Affordable Health Care for America Act," which the House passed on November 7, 2009.

The first congressional committee to propose legislation was the United States Senate's Health, Education, Labor, and Pension (HELP) Committee, which reported out its bill (S. 1679, the Affordable Health Choices Act) on July 15, 2009. Two months later, on September 16, 2009, Senate Finance Committee Chairman Max Baucus (D-Mont.) released his chairman's mark for health care reform legislation. After eight days of meetings during which 135 amendments were considered and 79 roll call votes were held, the Senate Finance Committee issued a report.[28] This bill then went through a reconciliation process with the HELP Committee bill that resulted in the Senate's passage of H.R. 3950, the "Patient Protection and Affordable Care Act," on December 24, 2009. Although this is the bill that ultimately became the basis for the PPACA, as described below, the final legislation differs from the bill passed by the Senate on December 24, 2009.

Once the House and the Senate had passed different versions of the health care reform legislation, the Senate used its budget reconciliation process as the vehicle for reconciling the two versions. The first step in this cumbersome process required the House of Representatives to adopt verbatim the Senate's version of the legislation contained in H.R. 3590 and then separately adopt provisions (H.R. 4872) amending this law to reflect the desires of the House, which the House did in successive votes taken on March 21, 2009. H.R. 3590, now having been passed by both the House and the Senate, went to the president for signature. President Obama signed the PPACA on March 23, 2010.

The Senate then took up for consideration H.R. 4872 under its budget reconciliation process, which is a process not subject to filibuster under the rules of the Senate and thus permits the Senate to pass legislation by a majority vote. Because the Senate parliamentarian ruled that two provisions in H.R. 4872 concerning student loans were not eligible for the budget reconciliation process, the Senate passed H.R. 4872, without these two provisions, on March 25, 2010. On the same day, the House passed the Senate's amended version of H.R. 4872, which is the version of the HCERA signed by the president on March 30, 2010.

To a large extent the provisions set forth in the two laws reflect measures on which the House and Senate were in agreement in principle. Both congressional chambers seemed to agree on the importance of an individual mandate, mechanisms to encourage employers to continue providing health benefits to their employees, the need to subsidize coverage for low-income individuals and families, market reforms (e.g., the elimination of pre-existing conditions, guaranteed issue and renewal, limits on lifetime and annual maximums, restrictions on waiting periods, understandable and consistent explanations of coverage), and benefit improvements (e.g., expansion of dependent coverage, first-dollar availability of preventive care, wellness incentives).

Two fault lines that emerged at the end of the legislative process concerned the major health care policy issue of whether there should be a public option and the equally, if not more, prominent social

---

[28] S. Rep. No. 111-89, Report to Accompany S. 1796 on Providing Affordable, Quality Health Care for All Americans and Reducing the Growth in Health Care Spending and for Other Purposes, together with Additional and Minority Views.

policy issue about the use of federal funds to pay for abortions.[29] The House ultimately backed away from its insistence on a public option and, after President Obama agreed to issue a Presidential Order reaffirming the administration's commitment to not using federal funds to pay for abortions,[30] enough House members overcame their reservations on the abortion issue to ensure the passage of H.R. 3950 by the House.

[B] Laws Affected by the PPACA and the HCERA

The 2010 Health Care Reform Act amends a variety of federal laws, including the PHSA, the Code, ERISA, the Fair Labor Standards Act of 1938 (the FLSA),[31] the Social Security Amendments Act,[32] and the Indian Health Care Improvement Act.[33] The 2010 Health Care Reform Act also enacts a number of new laws, such as the Catalyst to Better Diabetes Care Act of 2009,[34] the Cures Acceleration Network Act of 2009,[35] the Establishing a Network of Health-Advancing National Centers of Excellence for Depression Act of 2009,[36] the Congenital Heart Futures Act,[37] and the Young Women's Breast Health Education and Awareness Requires Learning Young Act of 2009;[38] Finally, in what may be a first, the 2010 Health Care Reform Act amends itself.[39]

As if the foregoing were not overwhelming enough, the HCERA, in turn, amends parts of provisions set forth in PPACA as if such amendments were included in PPACA in the first place,[40] adds new provisions to PPACA,[41] independently amends the provisions of federal laws,[42] and enacts at least one new law of its own—the Student Aid and Fiscal Responsibility Act (SAFRA).[43]

The end result of the legislative process is an Act that is broad in scope and uniquely complex. This should not be surprising, given the difficulty of the subject matter, the competing governing philosophies of the two major political parties, the myriad interest groups affected, the lack of any consensus for reform among the public, and the fact that three committees of the House and two committees of the Senate were involved in developing the legislative proposals.

[C] Architecture of the 2010 Health Care Reform Act

The 2010 Health Care Reform Act is made up of ten titles.[44] A crucial building block for understanding the Act's impact on employment-based group health plans is understanding the architecture of Title I of the Act, which is captioned "Quality, Affordable Health Care for All Americans." In broad brush, the relevant portions of Title I of the Act, which will be discussed in substantial detail in this guide, are:

---

[29] See Lois Montgomery & Paul Kane, *House health-care vote Sunday may hinge on abortion issues*, WashingtonPost.com, March 21, 2010.

[30] *Id.*

[31] Pub. L. No. 75-718, 52 Stat. 1060.

[32] Pub. L. No. 98-21, 97 Stat. 65.

[33] Pub. L. No. 94-437, 90 Stat. 400.

[34] PPACA § 10407.

[35] PPACA § 10409.

[36] PPACA § 10410.

[37] PPACA § 10411.

[38] PPACA § 10413.

[39] PPACA, tit. X, pt. 1.

[40] *See, e.g.,* HCERA § 1001.

[41] HCERA § 1102.

[42] *See, e.g.,* HCERA § 1103.

[43] HCERA § 2001.

[44] They are: Title I—Quality, Affordable Health Care For All Americans; Title II—Role of Public Programs; Title III—Improving the Quality and Efficiency of Health Care; Title IV—Prevention of Chronic Disease and Improving Public Health; Title V—Health Care Workforce; Title VI—Transparency and Program Integrity; Title VII—Improving Access to Innovative Medical Therapies; Title VIII—CLASS Act; Title IX—Revenue Provisions; and Title X—Strengthening Quality, Affordable Health Care for All Americans.

- Subtitle A of Title I of the Act[45] and Part 1 of Subtitle C of Title I of the Act,[46] which impose new substantive and reporting requirements on employment-based group health plans through amendments to the PHSA;

- Section 1251 of Part 2 of Subtitle C of Title I of the Act, which modifies the application of Subtitles A and C of Title I of the Act for employment-based group health plans that are either grandfathered plans[47] or collectively bargained insured plans;[48]

- Subtitle F of Title I of the Act, which imposes the individual enroll-or-pay rules[49] and the pay-or-play penalty on large employers that do not provide their full-time employees with minimum essential coverage;[50] and

- The "conforming amendments" contained in Subtitle G of Title I of the Act, which, along with existing provisions of the PHSA,[51] allocate responsibility for enforcing Part A of the PHSA among the DOL,[52] the IRS,[53] and the HHS.[54]

§ 2.04   Enforcement Responsibility

The 2010 Health Care Reform Act's new substantive requirements incorporated into the PHSA apply to health coverage provided on an insured and self-funded basis and on an individual and group basis.[55] The three agencies of the federal government historically involved in administering laws applying to such coverage—the DOL, IRS, and HHS—will all be involved in enforcing these requirements.

The 2010 Health Care Reform Act incorporates the PHSA enforcement provisions, which authorize HHS to enforce the terms of the PHSA with respect to individual health insurance coverage and employment-based group health plans sponsored by government employers (other than the federal government), into ERISA and the Code.[56] However, the incorporation of the PHSA enforcement provisions is limited to their application to "group health plans" and "health insurance issuers issuing providing health insurance coverage in connection with group health plans."

---

[45] Section 1001(5) of Subtitle A of Title I of the Act adds the following new sections to Part A of the PHSA (42 U.S.C. §§ 300gg et seq.): No Lifetime or Annual Limits (PHSA § 2711); Prohibition on Rescission (PHSA § 2712); Coverage of Preventive Health Services (PHSA § 2713); Extension of Dependent Coverage (PHSA § 2714); Development and Utilization of Uniform Explanations of Coverage Documents and Standardized Definitions (PHSA § 2715); Provision of Additional Information (PHSA § 2715A); Prohibition on Discrimination in Favor of Highly Compensated Individuals (PHSA § 2717); Ensuring the Quality of Care (PHSA § 2717); Bringing Down the Cost of Health Care Coverage PHSA § 2718); Appeals Process (PHSA § 2719); Patient Protections (PHSA § 2719A).

[46] Section 1201(4) of Part 1 of Subtitle C of Title I of the Act adds the following new sections to Part A of the PHSA: Prohibition of Preexisting Condition Exclusions or other Discrimination Based on Health Status (PHSA § 2704); Fair Health Insurance Premiums (PHSA § 2701); Guaranteed Availability of Coverage (PHSA § 2702); Guaranteed Renewability of Coverage (PSA § 2703); Prohibiting Discrimination Against Individual Participants and Beneficiaries Based on Health Status (PHSA § 2705); Non-Discrimination in Health Care (PHSA § 2706); Comprehensive Health Insurance Coverage (PHSA § 2707); Prohibition on Excessive Waiting Periods (PHSA § 2708); and Coverage for Individuals Participating in Approved Clinical Trials (PSA § 2709).

[47] PPACA § 1251(a).

[48] PPACA § 1251(d).

[49] PPACA § 1501.

[50] PPACA § 1513.

[51] 42 U.S.C. § 300gg-22.

[52] PPACA § 1562(e).

[53] PPACA § 1562(f).

[54] PPACA § 1562(c)(14).

[55] 42 U.S.C. §§ 300gg et seq.

[56] PPACA §§ 1562(e), (f). The provisions of the PHSA are incorporated into Subpart B of Part 7 of subtitle A of title I of ERISA, which generally includes portability, access, and renewability requirements applicable to group health plans. The provisions of the PHSA are incorporated into Subchapter B of Chapter 100 of the Code, which generally includes portability, access, and renewability requirements applicable to group health plans.

Thus, it appears that the DOL and the IRS are responsible for enforcing Part A of the PHSA with respect to group health plans that provide coverage on a self-funded or insured basis, other than with respect to such coverage provided by an employment-based group health plan sponsored by a government employer (other than the federal government). HHS retains enforcement authority over non–federal government employment-based group health plans and health insurance issued to individuals by insurance companies.

This analysis is consistent with the following statement by the HHS in its interim final and proposed rule jointly issued by the three agencies regarding dependent coverage of children to age 26 under the Act:

> We are soliciting public comment on the following sections of this document that contain information collection requirements (ICR) regarding the Affordable Care Act—ICR Relating to Enrollment Opportunity Notice—Dependent Coverage. As discussed earlier in this preamble, the Affordable Care Act and these interim final regulations require issuers in the individual market and group health plans sponsored by State and local governments to notify participants regarding an enrollment opportunity related to the extension of dependent coverage.[57]

---

[57] 75 Fed. Reg. 27122, 27132 (May 13, 2010).

CHAPTER 3

HEALTH CARE COVERAGE KEY TERMS

The 2010 Health Care Reform Act's coverage reforms address both employment-based group health plans and individual insurance coverage. When considering a health care reform provision, it is critically important to carefully identify the entity or type of coverage that is subject to the provision. The applicability of each provision may vary depending on whether the plan is insured or self-funded, large or small market, and so forth. To assist employers and HR professionals in understanding these important differences, we define the key terms as follows:

A *health plan* means both health insurance coverage and a group health plan.[1] The term "health plan" does not include a group health plan or multiple-employer welfare arrangement (MEWA) if the plan or the MEWA is not subject to state insurance regulation under the ERISA pre-emption provision.[2] In other words, a health plan does not include a self-funded employment-based group health plan. The term "health plan" generally is used in the 2010 Health Care Reform Act when referring to Exchange-provided coverage.[3]

Health insurance coverage is defined as "benefits consisting of medical care (provided directly through insurance or reimbursement or otherwise and including items and services paid for as medical care) under any hospital or medical service policy or certificate, hospital or medical service plan contract, or health maintenance organization contract offered by a health insurance issuer."[4]

A *group health plan* is an employee welfare benefit plan (as defined in Section 3(1) of ERISA) that provides medical care services and supplies for employees or their dependents (as defined under the terms of the plan) directly or through insurance, reimbursement, or otherwise.[5] A group health plan includes both insured and self-funded arrangements.

A *health insurance issuer* (also referred to as an "issuer") is an entity licensed to engage in the business of insurance in a state and which is subject to state law that regulates insurance.[6]

The *group health insurance market* is health insurance coverage sold to group health plans.[7] The market is divided into the large-group market and the small-group market. For purposes of an insurance market, a small employer is defined as an employer that employed, on average, at least one but no more than 100 employees on business days during the preceding calendar year.[8] A state may elect the option of defining a small employer as an employer that employed on average at least one but not more than 50 employees beginning on January 1, 2016.[9]

Individual health insurance coverage is health insurance coverage offered to individuals in the individual market, but does not include short-term limited-duration insurance.[10]

The *individual market* means the market for health insurance coverage offered to individuals other than in connection with a group health plan.[11]

---

[1] PPACA § 1301(b)(1).

[2] PPACA § 1301(b)(1)(B) (referencing 29 U.S.C. § 1144).

[3] *See infra* § 10.04, notes 44–56 and accompanying text (discussing Exchanges).

[4] PPACA § 1301(b)(2) (referencing 42 U.S.C. § 300gg-91(b)(1)).

[5] PPACA § 1301(b)(3) (referencing 42 U.S.C. § 300gg-91(a)(1)).

[6] PPACA § 1301(b)(2) (referencing 42 U.S.C. § 300gg-91(b)(1)).

[7] PPACA §§ 1304, 1551 (referencing 42 U.S.C. § 300gg-91(e)).

[8] PPACA §§ 1304(b)(1), 1562(c)(16) (amending 42 U.S.C. § 300gg-91(e)(2)).

[9] PPACA § 1304(b)(2).

[10] PPACA §§ 1304, 1551 (referencing 42 U.S.C. § 300gg-91(b)(5)).

[11] PPACA §§ 1304, 1551 (referencing 42 U.S.C. § 300gg-91(e)(1)(A)).

A *health insurance product* is not defined in the Act, but HHS defines it as a package of benefits that an issuer offers that is reported to state regulators in an insurance filing.[12]

A *grandfathered plan* is a group health plan or individual health insurance coverage in existence on March 23, 2010.[13]

Essential health benefits consist of coverage for items and services in a comprehensive list of categories set forth in the 2010 Health Care Reform Act under such terms and conditions as shall be determined by HHS pursuant to guidelines set forth in the Act.[14]

Minimum essential coverage includes coverage under (i) specified government programs; (ii) health insurance coverage obtained in the individual market that provides for essential health benefits; (iii) health insurance coverage obtained in the small group market that provides for essential health benefits; (iv) health insurance coverage obtained in the large group market; (v) grandfathered coverage, whether or not it is provided through health insurance coverage; and (vi) coverage under a governmental plan, whether or not it is provided through health insurance coverage.[15] It appears that the latter three types of coverage provide minimum essential coverage as long as they provide any coverage that is not an excepted benefit.[16] Absent from the list is coverage provided on a self-funded basis through a group health plan.[17] This may, and should, be remedied by HHS exercising its authority to designate other health benefits coverage as minimum essential coverage. HHS could limit its designation to self-funded coverage that provides essential health benefits.

An *Exchange plan* is a "qualified health plan," which is described at length in **Chapter 10**.

Retiree-only plans are defined after the enactment of the 2010 Health Care Reform Act in the Code and ERISA as any group health plan covering fewer than two active employees on the first day of the plan year.[18] The 2010 Health Care Reform Act deletes the subsection of the PHSA that contained a comparable exclusion for such plans subject to the provisions of the PHSA. This curious deletion is discussed in the preamble to the interim final regulations for group health plans and health insurance coverage relating to grandfathered health plan status under the 2010 Health Care Reform Act jointly issued by HHS, DOL and IRS on June 14, 2010.[19] The preamble affirms that the deletion of the provision from the PHSA does not affect group health plans subject to the Code and ERISA, which means such plans are not subject to Parts A and C of Title I of the 2010 Health Care Reform Act. For group health plans subject to the PHSA (i.e., group health plans that provide their benefits through health insurance and nonfederal government group health plans that provide their benefits on a self-funded basis), the preamble announces a no-enforcement policy at the federal level. Recognizing that the states have independent authority to regulate group health insurance issuers, the preamble "encourages" the states to adopt the same position. As a result, it is currently unclear if retiree-only plans that provide benefits through health insurance will be required by one or more states to conform such coverage to the requirements of Parts A and C of Title I of the 2010 Health Care Reform Act.

---

[12] 45 C.F.R. § 159.110.

[13] PPACA § 1251. *See infra* § 4.01, for a detailed discussion of grandfathered plans.

[14] PPACA § 1302(b).

[15] PPACA § 1401(a) (adding Section 36B to the Code and referencing I.R.C. §§ 5000A(f)(1), (2) and PHSA § 2707).

[16] I.R.C. § 5000A(f)(3).

[17] I.R.C. § 5000A(f)(2)(B). The term "large group market" as used in this provision is defined in Section 1304 of the Act as "the health insurance market under which individuals obtain health insurance coverage." "Health insurance coverage" is coverage purchased through a health insurance issuer that is subject to state insurance law (*i.e.*, not a self-funded plan).

[18] The Act deletes the current subsection of the PHSA that excludes from the scope of the portion of the PHSA amended by Parts A and C of Title I of the Act any group health plan covering less than two active employees on the first day of its plan year. The Act does not delete the comparable exclusions in the Code (section 9832(a)(2)) and ERISA (section 732(a)), which laws have also been amended by the Act to include these provisions of the PHSA. PPACA §§ 1562(e), (f).

[19] Group Health Plans and Health Insurance Coverage Relating to Status as a Grandfathered Health Plan Under the Patient Protection and Affordable Care Act; Interim Final Rule and Proposed Rule, 75 FR 34538–34570, amending 26 CFR Parts 54 and 602, 29 CFR Part 2590 and 45 CFR 147. The relevant discussion appears on pages 34539–34540.

CHAPTER 4

GRANDFATHERED AND COLLECTIVELY BARGAINED PLANS

§ 4.01 Grandfathered Health Plans: "If You Like Your Current Insurance, You Will Keep Your Current Insurance"

In March 2010, at the time health care reform became a reality, close to 85 percent of Americans had some form of health care coverage either through their employer, a government program like Medicare, Medicaid or military coverage, or private health care insurance.[1] While the cost of coverage has steadily increased, perhaps unsustainably, for most employees, employers, or other plan sponsors, many individuals were satisfied with the terms and conditions of their coverage. President Obama and the congressional leadership promised those individuals that nothing in the law would prohibit them from continuing their existing coverage arrangements.[2]

That promise was incorporated into the 2010 Health Care Reform Act, which provides in part that "[n]othing in this Act (or an amendment made by the Act) shall be construed to require that an individual terminate coverage under a group health plan or health insurance coverage in which such individual was enrolled on the date of enactment of the Act."[3] Further, the individual may continue to renew the existing coverage for subsequent periods.[4] These existing group health plans and individual health insurance coverages are defined in the law as "grandfathered health plans."[5] The government estimates that there will be approximately 2.2 million grandfathered health plans in 2011.[6]

Grandfathered health plans are exempt from some, but not all, of the coverage improvements and market reforms that the 2010 Health Care Reform Act imposes on group health plans and individual insurance issuers and, after January 1, 2014, plans offered through the exchange option.[7] A chart listing the PPACA group health plan coverage improvement provisions and their applicability to grandfathered health plans is shown in **Appendix A.**

The 2010 Health Care Reform Act restricts changes to grandfathered health plans after the date of enactment but allows for new entrants into the plan. The law limits enrollment in a grandfathered plan to individuals enrolled on March 23, 2010, family members of those individuals,[8] and new employees (and their families).[9]

Based on the language of the statute, many employers and plans were hesitant to make any change to their plans, lest their coverage be de-grandfathered. Such fears were alleviated in part on June 14, 2010, when HHS, Treasury, and the DOL jointly published interim final regulations for group health plans and health insurance coverage relating to grandfathered health plan status under the 2010 Health Care Reform Act.[10] Attempting to balance the objective of preserving the ability of employers

---

[1] *See supra* **§ 2.01**, notes 3–5 (providing statistics on access to health coverage).

[2] *See supra* **Chapter 1**, note 2 and accompanying text (quoting President Obama).

[3] PPACA § 1251(a). The date of enactment of the PPACA is March 23, 2010.

[4] PPACA § 1251(b).

[5] PPACA § 1251(e).

[6] 75 Fed. Reg. 34555.

[7] When the grandfathered health plan provision (PPACA § 1251) was drafted and approved by the Senate HELP Committee, grandfathered health plans were exempted from subtitles A (the coverage improvement provisions) and C (the market reforms that begin in January 2014). The Senate Finance Committee's sections of the bill, Titles IX and X, amended the provision to subject grandfathered health plans to sections 2715 and 2718. PPACA § 10103(d). In the HCERA, Section 1251(a) was further amended to extend certain of the insurance market reforms to grandfathered plans, including the provisions relating to excessive waiting periods (PHSA § 2708), the prohibitions on lifetime and annual limits (PHSA § 2711), the extension of dependent coverage (PHSA § 2714), and pre-existing condition exclusions (PHSA § 2704). HCERA § 2301. Also, the dependent coverage provisions application to grandfathered plans was clarified. HCERA § 2301.

[8] PPACA § 1251(b).

[9] PPACA § 1251(c).

[10] 75 Fed. Reg. 34538-70, amending 26 C.F.R. Parts 54 and 602, 29 C.F.R. Part 2590, and 45 C.F.R. § 147, See **Appendix B** for grandfathered health plan regulations.

and individuals to maintain existing coverage with the goal of expanding access to quality health coverage, the regulations delineate very broadly at what point changes to an existing plan are significant enough to cause the plan or health insurance coverage to cease to be a grandfathered health plan.

It is important to note that the regulations are written as "negative rules" which, according to Obama administration officials, means that changes that are not expressly prohibited are permitted, subject to the anti-abuse provisions in the regulations. In general, a material reduction in benefits, a substantial increase in the employee's financial responsibility for costs through cost-sharing and/or premium contribution increases, or a change in the insurance issuer will cause a plan to lose its grandfathered status. Plan changes that improve benefits or reduce costs for employees and beneficiaries are permitted without cessation of grandfathered status.

[A] Grandfathered Health Plan Defined

A *grandfathered health plan* is coverage provided by a group health plan (self-funded or insured) or a health insurance issuer in which an individual was enrolled on March 23, 2010 (for as long as it maintains its status under the grandfather rules).[11] A grandfathered health plan does not cease to be such a plan merely because one or more (or even all) of the individuals enrolled as of March 23, 2010, are no longer enrolled, provided that someone has been enrolled continuously in the plan since March 23, 2010.

The grandfathered health plan determination must be made for each separate benefit package made available under the plan.

[B] New Enrollees in Grandfathered Health Plans After March 23, 2010

The 2010 Health Care Reform Act permits a grandfathered health plan to enroll "new employees" and "family members" of existing and new enrolled employees.[12] However, the terms "new employee" and "family member" are not defined in the statute.

[1] New Employees

The regulations clarify that new employees include both newly hired and newly enrolled employees and their families.[13] By clarifying that "new employees" includes "newly enrolled employees," the regulations accommodate routine employer plan enrollment practices, as well as legally required enrollments. For example, under current law employers permit existing employees who deferred enrollment because they had other coverage available through another source (typically through a spouse or other employer on more favorable terms) to enroll in the employer's coverage when they lose the other coverage. When an employee loses the other coverage for reasons specified in the law and regulations, the employer is required under the Health Insurance Portability and Accountability Act of 1996 (HIPAA) to maintain a special enrollment period for that employee.[14] The grandfathered health plan regulations now permit the enrollment after March 23, 2010, of any employee entitled under the HIPAA special enrollment rules to enroll in the employment-based plan.[15]

Likewise, an existing employee who did not enroll in a group health plan offered by an employer prior to March 23, 2010, because he or she was working in an employment classification that was ineligible for coverage under the plan may be enrolled in the plan without loss of grandfathered health

---

[11] 26 C.F.R. § 54.9815-1251T; 29 C.F.R. § 2590.715-1251; 45 C.F.R. § 147.140.

[12] PPACA §§ 1251(b), (c).

[13] 26 C.F.R. § 54.9815-1251(b); 29 C.F.R. § 2590.715-1251(b); 45 C.F.R. § 147.140.

[14] 29 U.S.C. § 1181(f).

[15] 26 C.F.R. § 54.9815-1251T(b)(1); 29 C.F.R. § 2590.715-1251(b)(1); 45 C.F.R. § 147.140(b)(1).

plan status.[16] For example, the employee may have been working on a part-time basis prior to March 23, 2010, and is now working in a full-time position with eligibility for health care benefits. When the employment classification changes and renders the employee eligible to enroll, the employee will be deemed a "new employee" for purposes of enrolling in a grandfathered health plan.

The regulations also address new employees who became employed in connection with a merger or acquisition. Existing employees of the newly acquired company are "new employees" for purposes of health care coverage in a grandfathered health plan.

There are two anti-abuse provisions in the regulations relating to the definition of new employee. First, if the principal purpose of the merger, acquisition, or business restructuring is to cover new individuals under the grandfathered health plan, the plan ceases to be a grandfathered health plan.[17] This anti-abuse rule is to prevent grandfathered status from being bought and sold as a commodity in commercial transactions.

The second anti-abuse rule relates to employees transferred into the plan or health insurance coverage (transferee plan) from a plan or health insurance coverage under which the employees were covered on March 23, 2010 (the transferor plan).[18] Under the second rule, one must first compare the terms of the transferee plan with those of the transferor plan (as in effect on March 23, 2010), then consider the terms of the transferee plan as an amendment to the transferor plan. If the amendment would have caused the transferor plan to lose grandfathered health plan status and there was no bona fide employment-based reason for the transfer of the employees into the transferee plan, then the enrollment of the transferee plan employees into the transferor plan would cause the plan to cease being a grandfathered health plan. Changing the terms or cost of coverage is not a bona fide employment-based reason.

[2] Family Members

Who is a "family member" for purposes of the grandfathered health plan provision? Neither the statute nor the interim final regulations answers that question. Many employment-based group health plans define eligible family members as the spouse and the dependent children of the employee. Some plans incorporate by reference the Code's definition of a dependent child.[19] Other plans define the term more broadly and include coverage for domestic partners.

Notwithstanding the absence of express guidance in the regulations, representatives of HHS and the DOL have explained at various briefings following the release of the grandfather regulations that, subject to the anti-abuse rules, any changes to a group health plan or health insurance coverage that are not prohibited in the regulations would be permissible. When asked expressly whether an amendment to a plan after March 23, 2010, to provide coverage for domestic partners and their families as dependents would result in the loss of grandfathered status, an Obama administration representative responded that an expansion of access to or an increase in benefits for employees would not result in the loss of a plan's grandfathered status.[20]

[C] Reforms Imposed on Grandfathered Health Plans

When the 2010 Health Care Reform Act was originally drafted, grandfathered health plans were exempt from all of the coverage improvement requirements imposed on group health plans and individual insurance coverage. However, as the bills moved through Congress, amendments were made that subjected grandfathered plans to most of the key immediate coverage improvement requirements.

---

[16] 26 C.F.R. § 54.9815-1251T(b)(1); 29 C.F.R. § 2590.715-1251(b)(1); 45 C.F.R. § 147.140(b)(1).

[17] 26 C.F.R. § 54.9815-1251T(b)(2)(i); 29 C.F.R. § 2590.715-1251(b)(2)(i); 45 C.F.R. § 147.140(b)(2)(i).

[18] 26 C.F.R. § 54.9815-1251T(b)(2)(ii); 29 C.F.R. § 2590.715-1251(b)(2)(ii); 45 C.F.R. § 146.140(b)(2)(ii).

[19] *See* I.R.C. § 152 (defining "dependent" for tax purposes).

[20] 26 C.F.R. §§ 54.9815-1251T(c), (d), & (e); 29 C.F.R. §§ 2590.715-1251(c), (d), & (e); 45 C.F.R. §§ 147.140(c), (d), & (e).

Effective for the first plan year[21] that begins on or after September 23, 2010 (except as otherwise noted), grandfathered health plans are subject to the following coverage improvements and additional requirements described in more detail in Chapters 7 and 8:

- Extended dependent coverage;[22]

- Pre-existing condition exclusion prohibitions (beginning with the first plan year on or after September 23, 2010, for children under age 19, and in 2014 for older individuals);

- Prohibitions on lifetime maximum dollar limits on benefits;

- Prohibitions on annual dollar limits for essential medical benefits;

- Prohibitions on eligibility waiting periods in excess of 90 days (beginning in 2014);

- Prohibitions on rescission or non-renewal of coverage, except for fraud or intentional misrepresentations of material fact;

- Provision of uniform benefit summaries to all eligible enrollees and participants; and

- Requirements for insured plans to spend at least 85 percent of their premium revenues on medical claims costs for large-employer plans and 80 percent for small-employer plans, or rebate a portion of the premium revenues.[23]

By contrast, grandfathered health plans are exempt from the following coverage improvements and additional requirements described in more detail in Chapters 7 and 8:

- Coverage of preventive health services with no cost-sharing;

- Provision of information on plan design to HHS;

- Prohibition on discriminating in favor of highly paid employees in insured plans;

- Reporting to HHS on quality-of-care and wellness programs;

- Requirement to implement a claims appeals process, including external review;

- For insured plans, limits on variances in premium costs, guaranteed availability and renewability, and provision of essential health benefits (beginning in 2014);

- Prohibition against discrimination among health care providers (beginning in 2014); and

- Limits on annual cost-sharing (beginning in 2014).[24]

[D] Maintenance of Grandfathered Status

The grandfathered health plan regulations identify specific types of changes the adoption of which will cause a grandfathered health plan to forfeit its grandfathered status.[25] These changes are:

---

[21] The term "plan year" means the year that is designated as the plan year in the plan document of an employment-based group health plan. If the plan document does not designate a plan year, if the plan year is not a 12-month plan year, or if there is no plan document, the plan year is: (1) the deductible or limit year used under the plan; (2) the policy year, if the plan does not impose deductibles or limits on a 12-month basis; (3) the sponsor's taxable year, if the plan does not impose deductibles or limits on a 12-month basis, and either the plan is not insured or the insurance policy is not renewed on a 12-month basis; or, (4) the calendar year, in any other case. 45 C.F.R. § 149.2.

[22] Grandfathered health plans can exclude adult children who are eligible for other employment-based group health plan coverage. *See infra* § 7.04, notes 29–55 and accompanying text (discussing the extended dependent coverage provision).

[23] PPACA § 1251(a).

[24] PPACA § 1251(a).

[25] 26 C.F.R. § 54.9815-1251T(g); 29 C.F.R. § 2590.715-1251(g); 45 C.F.R. § 147.140(g).

- The elimination of substantially all benefits to diagnose or treat a particular condition;

- Any increase in a percentage cost-sharing requirement;

- Any increase in a fixed-amount cost-sharing requirement, other than a copayment, in excess of the maximum percentage increase permitted under the regulation;

- Any increase in a fixed-amount copayment in excess of the greater of the allowable maximum percentage or a fixed dollar amount increase established by the regulation;

- Certain decreases in the premium contribution rate by employers; and

- Certain additions or modifications of overall annual or lifetime limits on the dollar value of benefits.

[1] Elimination of Coverage for a Particular Condition

If a grandfathered health plan or health insurance coverage is amended to eliminate all or substantially all benefits to diagnose or treat a particular condition, the plan will cease to be a grandfathered plan.[26] For example, if a plan is amended to eliminate benefits for cystic fibrosis, the plan will cease to be a grandfathered health plan (even if the number of participants with the condition is small).

Likewise, the elimination of any necessary element to diagnose or treat a condition is considered the elimination of all or substantially all benefits. For example, if a plan covered a mental health condition, the accepted treatment plan for which is prescription medication and counseling, and the plan eliminates the counseling benefit, the elimination would trigger the loss of grandfathered health plan status.

[2] Increasing Cost-Sharing Requirements

The regulations limit the amount that a participant's cost-sharing requirements may be increased without causing the grandfathered health plan or health insurance coverage to cease being a grandfathered health plan. Cost-sharing requirements include deductibles, copayments, or co-insurance amounts.

[a] *Increases in Percentage Cost-Sharing Requirements Prohibited*

The rules prohibit any increase, measured from March 23, 2010, in a percentage cost-sharing requirement.[27]

The regulations include the following example:

Example. On March 23, 2010, a grandfathered health plan has a co-insurance requirement of 20 percent for inpatient surgery. The plan is subsequently amended to increase the co-insurance requirement to 25 percent.

In this example, the increase in the co-insurance requirement from 20 percent to 25 percent causes the plan to cease to be a grandfathered health plan.

This restriction may preclude certain plan changes that have become fairly routine. For example, if a plan's prescription drug plan has a copayment of 20 percent for each generic drug, 30 percent for

---

[26] 26 C.F.R. § 54.9815-1251T(g)(1)(i); 29 C.F.R. § 2590.715-1251(g)(1)(i); 45 C.F.R. § 147.140(g)(1)(i).

[27] 26 C.F.R. § 54.9815-1251T(g)(1)(ii); 29 C.F.R. § 2590.715-1251(g)(1)(ii); and 45 C.F.R. § 147.140(g)(1)(ii).

each brand-name formulary drug, and 40 percent for any non-formulary prescription drug, the copayment percentages may not be increased if the plan wants to maintain its grandfathered status.

[b]   Limits on Fixed-Amount Cost-Sharing Increases (Other Than a Copayment)

Any increase in a fixed-amount cost-sharing requirement (other than copayments) in excess of a maximum percentage increase, determined as of the effective date of the increase, will cause the plan to cease being a grandfathered health plan.[28] The "maximum percentage increase" is defined as medical inflation, expressed as a percentage, plus 15 percentage points.[29] The 15-percentage-point increase is a one-time aggregate addition, not an annual allowance.

"Medical inflation" means the increase since March 2010 in the overall medical care component of the Consumer Price Index for All Urban Consumers (CPI-U) (unadjusted) published by the DOL using the 1982–1984 base of 100. The March 2010 CPI-U is 387.142.[30] For purposes of determining the medical inflation percentage at a future date, identify the index amount for any month in the 12 months before the new change is to take effect, subtract 387.142 from that number, and then divide that amount by 387.142.

[c]   Limits on Fixed-Amount Copayment

Fixed-amount copayments (deductibles or out-of-pocket limits) are limited to a total increase in the copayment measured from March 23, 2010, of no more than the greater of (i) $5.00 (adjusted by medical inflation) or (ii) the maximum percentage increase described in the preceding paragraph.[31]

The regulations provide a number of examples, including the following:

Example 1. On March 23, 2010, a grandfathered health plan has a copayment requirement of $30 per office visit for specialists. The plan is subsequently amended to increase the copayment requirement to $40. Within the 12-month period before the $40 copayment takes effect, the greatest value of the overall medical care component of the CPI-U (unadjusted) is 475.

In this example, the increase in the copayment from $30 to $40, expressed as a percentage, is 33.33 percent. Medical inflation from March 2010 is 0.2269 (475 − 387.142 = 87.858; 87.858 ÷ 387.142 = 0.2269, or 22.69%). The maximum percentage increase permitted is 37.69 percent (22.69% + 15% = 37.69%). Because 33.33 percent does not exceed 37.69 percent, the change in the copayment requirement at that time does not cause the plan to cease to be a grandfathered health plan.

Example 2. Same facts as the example above, except the grandfathered health plan subsequently increases the $40 copayment requirement to $45 for a later plan year. Within the 12-month period before the $45 copayment takes effect, the greatest value of the overall medical care component of the CPI-U (unadjusted) is 485.

In this example, the increase in the copayment from $30 (the copayment that was in effect on March 23, 2010) to $45, expressed as a percentage, is 50 percent. Medical inflation (as defined in the regulations) from March 2010 is 0.2527 (485 − 387.142 = 97.858; 97.858 ÷ 387.142 = 0.2527 or 25.77%). The increase that would cause a plan to cease to be a grandfathered health plan is the greater of the maximum percentage increase of 40.27 percent (25.27% + 15% = 40.27%), or $6.26 ($5.00 × 25.27% = $1.26; $1.26 + $5.00 = $6.26).

---

[28] 26 C.F.R. § 54.9815-1251T(g)(1)(iii); 29 C.F.R. § 2590.715-1251(g)(1)(iii); 45 C.F.R. § 147.140(g)(1)(iii).

[29] 26 C.F.R. § 54.9815-1251T(g)(3)(ii); 29 C.F.R. § 2590.715-1251(g)(3)(ii); 45 C.F.R. § 147.140(g)(3)(ii).

[30] 26 C.F.R. § 54.9815-1251T(g)(3)(i); 29 C.F.R. § 2590.715-1251(g)(3)(i); 45 C.F.R. § 147.140(g)(3)(i).

[31] 26 C.F.R. § 54.9815-1251T(g)(1)(iv); 29 C.F.R. § 2590.715-1251(g)(1)(iv); 45 C.F.R. § 147.140(g)(1)(iv).

Because 50 percent exceeds 40.27 percent and $15 exceeds $6.26, the change in the copayment requirement at that time causes the plan to cease to be a grandfathered health plan.

Example 3. On March 23, 2010, a grandfathered health plan has a copayment of $10 per office visit for primary care providers. The plan is subsequently amended to increase the copayment requirement to $15. Within the 12-month period before the $15 copayment takes effect, the greatest value of the overall medical care component of the CPI-U (unadjusted) is 415.

In this example, the increase in the copayment, expressed as a percentage, is 50 percent. Medical inflation from March 2010 is 0.0720 (415.0 − 387.142 = 27.858; 27.858 ÷ 387.142 = 0.0720, or 7.20%). The increase that would cause a plan to cease to be a grandfathered health plan is the greater of the maximum percentage increase of 22.20 percent (7.20% + 15% = 22.20%), or $5.36 ($5.00 × 7.20% = $0.36; $0.36 + $5.00 = $5.36). The $5.00 increase in copayment would not cause the plan to cease to be a grandfathered health plan because the maximum percentage increase would permit an increase in the copayment of up to $5.36.

Example 4. The same facts as in Example 3, except on March 23, 2010, the grandfathered health plan has no copayment for office visits for primary care providers. The plan is subsequently amended to increase the copayment requirement to $5.

In this example, medical inflation from March 2010 is 0.0720 (415.0 − 387.142 = 27.858; 27.858 ÷ 387.142 = 0.0720, or 7.20%). The increase that would cause a plan to cease to be a grandfathered health plan is $5.36 ($5.00 × 7.20% = $0.36; $0.36 + $5.00 = $5.36). The $5.00 increase in copayment in this example is less than $5.36. Thus, the $5.00 increase in copayment does not cause the plan to cease to be a grandfathered health plan.

[3] Increasing Employees' Contribution Rate To Premiums

A plan or health insurance coverage will lose its grandfathered status if the employer decreases its contribution rate based on the cost of coverage any more than five percentage points below the contribution rate for the coverage period that includes March 23, 2010.[32] Cost of coverage equals the applicable premium for the coverage for COBRA purposes.

Likewise, an employer may not decrease its contribution rate based on a formula by more than 5 percent below the contribution rate for coverage as of March 23, 2010.[33]

The regulations include the following examples:

Example 1. On March 23, 2010, a self-funded group health plan provides two tiers of coverage—self-only and family. The employer contributes 80 percent of the total cost of coverage for self-only and 60 percent of the total cost of coverage for family. Subsequently, the employer reduces the contribution to 50 percent for family coverage, but keeps the same contribution rate for self-only coverage.

The decrease of 10 percentage points for family coverage in the contribution rate based on cost of coverage causes the plan to cease to be a grandfathered health plan. The fact that the contribution rate for self-only coverage remains the same does not change the result.

Example 2. On March 23, 2010, a self-funded grandfathered health plan has an annual COBRA premium for the 2010 plan year of $5,000 for self-only coverage and $12,000 for family coverage. The required employee contribution for the coverage is $1,000 for self-only coverage and

---

[32] 26 C.F.R. § 54.9815-1251T(g)(1)(v)(A); 29 C.F.R. § 2590.715-1251(g)(1)(iv)(A); 45 C.F.R. § 147.140(g)(1)(v)(A).

[33] 26 C.F.R. § 54.9815-1251T(g)(1)(v)(A); 29 C.F.R. § 2590.715-1251(g)(1)(iv)(A); 45 C.F.R. § 147.140(g)(1)(v)(A).

$4,000 for family coverage. Thus, the employer's contribution rate based on cost of coverage for 2010 is 80 percent (($5,000 – $1,000) ÷ $5,000) for self-only coverage and 67 percent (($12,000 – $4,000) ÷ $12,000) for family coverage. For a subsequent plan year, the COBRA premium is $6,000 for self-only coverage and $15,000 for family coverage. The employee contributions for that plan year are $1,200 for self-only coverage and $5,000 for family coverage. Thus, the contribution rate based on cost of coverage is 80 percent (($6,000 – $1,200) ÷ $6,000) for self-only coverage and 67 percent (($15,000 – $5,000) ÷ $15,000) for family coverage.

Because there is no change in the contribution rate based on cost of coverage, the plan retains its status as a grandfathered health plan. The result would be the same if all or part of the employee contribution was made on a pretax basis through a cafeteria plan under Code section 125.

[4]   Changes in Limits on the Dollar Value of Benefits

If a plan or health insurance coverage did not impose an overall annual or lifetime limit on dollar value of all benefits as of March 23, 2010, it may not add such a limit and continue to maintain a grandfathered health plan status.[34]

If a plan or health insurance coverage had an overall lifetime limit on dollar value of all benefits but no overall annual limit as of March 23, 2010, it will lose its grandfathered health plan status if it adopts an overall annual limit at a dollar value that is lower than the dollar value of the lifetime limit as of March 23, 2010.[35]

Finally, if a plan or health insurance coverage imposed an overall annual limit on dollar value of all benefits as of March 23, 2010, it may not decrease the dollar value of the annual limit (regardless of whether the plan or coverage also imposed an overall lifetime limit on March 23, 2010) and continue to maintain its grandfathered plan status.[36]

[E]   Plan Design Changes That Will Not Result in Forfeiture of Grandfather Status

The preamble to the grandfathered plan regulations sheds some light on the HHS, Treasury, and DOL's rationale for the negative rule approach to the regulations and provides some broad guidance for plan administrators. Generally, the regulations are designed to take into account "reasonable changes routinely made by plan sponsors or issuers without the plan or health insurance coverage relinquishing its grandfather status."[37]

The agencies acknowledged that "plan sponsors and issuers of grandfathered health plans should be permitted to take steps within the boundaries of the grandfather definition to control costs, including limited increases in cost-sharing and other plan changes not prohibited by these interim final regulations."[38]

Premiums can be raised as long as the contribution rate of the employees is not increased disproportionately in relation to the employer's share as described in Section 4.01[D] above.

In addition, changes other than the prohibited changes described in the regulation "will not cause a plan or coverage to cease to be a grandfathered health plan. Examples include changes to premiums, changes to comply with Federal or tate legal requirements, changes to voluntarily comply with provisions of the [2010 Health Care Reform Act], and changing third-party administrators, provided these

---

[34] 26 C.F.R. § 54.9815-1251T(g)(1)(vi)(A); 29 C.F.R. § 2590.715-1251(g)(1)(vi)(A); 45 C.F.R. § 147.140(g)(1)(vi)(A).
[35] 26 C.F.R. § 54.9815-1251T(g)(1)(vi)(B); 29 C.F.R. § 2590.715-1251(g)(1)(vi)(B); 45 C.F.R. § 147.140(g)(1)(vi)(B).
[36] 26 C.F.R. § 54.9815-1251T(g)(1)(vi)(C); 29 C.F.R. § 2590.715-1251(g)(1)(vi)(C); 45 C.F.R. § 147.140(g)(1)(vi)(C).
[37] 75 Fed. Reg. 34546.
[38] 75 Fed. Reg. 34547.

changes are made without exceeding the standards established by paragraph (g)(1)" (the actions that cause a cessation of grandfathered status described in **Section 4.01[D]** above).[39]

While the preamble expressly provides that a change in a third-party administrator by a self-funded plan would not necessarily cause the plan to be so different from the plan in effect on March 23, 2010, that it should forfeit its grandfathered status, the regulation provides that the change of an insurance issuer in an insured plan would result in the loss of grandfathered status for the employer's plan.[40]

The seemingly broad license to make any changes other than those that are specifically prohibited may not continue indefinitely. In the preamble to the regulations, the agencies invite comments as to whether other changes should be added to the list of prohibited changes. Specifically, they ask whether the following actions should result in cessation of grandfathered health plan status:

(1)   Any changes to plan structure (such as switching from a health reimbursement arrangement to major medical coverage or an insured product to a self-funded product);

(2)   Changes in a network plan's provider network, and if so, what magnitude of change would be prohibited;

(3)   Changes to a prescription drug formulary, and if so, what magnitude of changes would be prohibited; or

(4)   Any other substantial change to the overall benefit design.[41]

Importantly, the agencies indicate that any new standards published in the final regulations that are more restrictive than the final interim regulations would only apply prospectively after the publication of the final rules.[42]

[F]   Document Retention and Disclosure Requirements

A plan or health insurance issuer must maintain records that document the plan or policy terms in effect on March 23, 2010, and any other documents that are necessary to verify the continuing status of the grandfathered health plan. The records must be made available for examination by participants, beneficiaries, individual policy subscribers, or state or federal agency officials.[43]

Grandfathered health plans and health insurance coverage must include a statement in any plan materials provided to participants or beneficiaries describing the benefits provided under the plan or coverage that discloses that the plan is a grandfathered plan and provides contact information for questions and complaints.[44] See **Appendix B** for the model notice published with the regulations.

[G]   Analyzing the Benefits of Maintaining a Grandfathered Plan

Weighing the benefits versus the burdens of maintaining a grandfathered health plan is a plan-specific exercise. Each plan or employer must consider both the 2010 Health Care Reform Act coverage reform exemptions available to grandfathered health plans and the restrictions imposed on reductions in benefits and cost-shifting to plan participants.

With respect to the exemptions from the coverage and insurance market reforms, the most substantial exemption for insured plans may be the exemption from the Act's rating restrictions. While

---

[39] 75 Fed. Reg. 34544.

[40] 26 C.F.R. § 54.9815-1251T(a)(1)(ii); 29 C.F.R. § 2590.715-125(a)(1)(ii); 45 C.F.R. § 147.140(a)(1)(ii).

[41] 75 Fed. Reg. 34544.

[42] 75 Fed. Reg. 34545.

[43] 26 C.F.R. § 54.9815-1251T(a)(3); 29 C.F.R. § 2590.715-1251(a)(3); 45 C.F.R. § 147.140(a)(3).

[44] 26 C.F.R. § 54.9815-1251T(a)(2); 29 C.F.R. § 2590.715-1251(a)(2); 45 C.F.R. § 147.140(a)(2).

the 2010 Health Care Reform Act rating rules will not apply to insured grandfathered health plans, state rating rules (if any) will still apply. For an employer with a younger workforce (typically a lower-risk group under conventional rating rules), remaininga grandfathered health plan may mean lower premiums than entering the larger, high-risk non-grandfathered risk pool. The converse may be true for a plan with a demographic profile of older or more high-risk individuals.

For those employers that have already imposed substantial cost-sharing and premium contribution obligations on employees, the regulatory restrictions on cost increases may not be a major concern because the permitted medical inflation maximum increases may be acceptable from a cost standpoint. If a plan has not yet adopted an employee contribution amount or has very limited cost-sharing provisions, the inability to adopt those changes now may outweigh the benefits of remaining a grandfathered health plan. Many cost-sharing benefit structures are designed to modify plan members' utilization of high-cost drugs, providers, or facilities. In addition to the first-dollar financial savings that such provisions produce for the plan, the additional costs saved by changing utilization patterns may be even more substantial. Weighing the benefits of being a grandfathered health plan versus capturing those cost savings may lead an employer to elect to forgo the grandfathered status. Plan changes to promote utilization improvements and quality care initiatives, particularly in disease management programs, can still be implemented but may need to be restructured to provide positive incentives for plan members rather than financial penalties in the form of increased copays or co-insurance.

Aside from the economic and regulatory impact on an employer-based group health plan, there are likely to be human resource considerations, such as the value that the employees place on the benefit and the competition for labor in the industry, which an employer must factor into the decision.

[H] Transitional Rules

Certain changes to terms of the plan or health insurance coverage that are not effective until after March 23, 2010, are deemed to be considered part of the plan as of March 23, 2010. Namely:

- Changes effective after March 23, 2010, pursuant to a legally binding contract entered into on or before March 23, 2010;

- Changes effective after March 23, 2010, pursuant to a filing on or before March 23, 2010, with a state insurance department; and

- Changes effective after March 23, 2010, pursuant to written amendments to a plan that were adopted on or before March 23, 2010.[45]

If a plan or health insurance issuer made changes to the terms of the plan or coverage that were adopted prior to June 17, 2010, the plan or coverage will not cease to be a grandfathered health plan under the rules if the changes are revoked or modified to conform with the regulations effective as of the first day of the first plan year beginning on or after September 23, 2010.[46]

The preamble also indicates that for purposes of enforcement, "the Departments will take into account good-faith efforts to comply with a reasonable interpretation of the statutory requirements and may disregard changes to plan and policy terms that only modestly exceed those changes described in [the grandfathered health plan regulations] and are adopted before the date the regulations were made publicly available."[47]

---

[45] 26 C.F.R. § 54.9815-1251T(g)(2)(i); 29 C.F.R. § 2590.715-1251(g)(2)(i); 45 C.F.R. § 147.140(g)(2)(i).
[46] 26 C.F.R. § 54.9815-1251T(g)(2)(ii); 29 C.F.R. § 2590.715-1251(g)(2)(ii); 45 C.F.R. § 147.140(g)(2)(ii).
[47] 75 Fed. Reg. 34544.

§ 4.02 Exemption for Retiree-Only Plans

The preamble to the grandfathered health plan regulations indicates that "retiree-only plans" are not subject to Parts A and C of Title I of the 2010 Health Care Reform Act, which set forth various plan design and operational changes for employment-based group health plans and group health insurance coverage.[48] A *retiree-only plan* is defined after the enactment of the 2010 Health Care Reform Act in the Code and ERISA as any group health plan covering fewer than two active employees on the first day of the plan year.[49] The 2010 Health Care Reform Act deletes the subsection of the PHSA that contained a comparable exclusion for such plans subject to the provisions of the PHSA (i.e., group health plans that provide their benefits through health insurance, and state and local government group health plans that provide their benefits on a self-funded basis). Thus, for the plans subject to the PHSA, the preamble announces a no-enforcement policy at the federal level.[50] Recognizing that the states have independent authority to regulate group health insurance issuers, the preamble "encourages" the states to adopt the same position. As a result, it is currently unclear whether retiree-only plans that provide benefits through health insurance will be required by one or more states to conform such coverage to the requirements of Parts A and C of Title I of the 2010 Health Care Reform Act.

§ 4.03 Exemption for Excepted Benefits

Along the same lines as the exemption for retiree-only plans, the preamble to the grandfathered health plan regulations provides that "excepted benefits" generally are not subject to Parts A and C of Title I of the 2010 Health Care Reform Act.[51] Excepted benefits generally include dental-only and vision-only plans, Health FSAs, Medigap policies, and AD&D coverage.[52] Again, the 2010 Health Care Reform Act deletes the subsection of the PHSA that contained a comparable exclusion for excepted benefits subject to the provisions of the PHSA (i.e., group health plans that provide their benefits through health insurance and state and local government group health plans that provide their benefits on a self-funded basis), and the preamble announces a similar non-enforcement position.[53]

§ 4.04 Collectively Bargained Insured Plans

The 2010 Health Care Reform Act contains a special rule applicable to certain insured employment-based group health plans that are subject to collective bargaining. The special rule applies to "health insurance coverage maintained pursuant to one or more collective bargaining agreements . . . ratified before [March 23, 2010]."[54] For purposes of determining whether a collective bargaining agreement ratified before the enactment of the 2010 Health Care Reform Act has been terminated, the Act disregards any amendments that implement the Act's coverage improvement requirements.

---

[48] 75 Fed. Reg. 34539–40.

[49] The Act deletes the current subsection of the PHSA that excludes from the scope of the portion of the PHSA amended by Parts A and C of Title I of the Act any group health plan covering fewer than two active employees on the first day of its plan year. The Act does not delete the comparable exclusions in the Code (§ 9832(a)(2)) and ERISA (§ 732(a)), which laws have also been amended by the Act to include these provisions of the PHSA. PPACA §§ 1562(e), (f).

[50] 75 Fed. Reg. 34539–40.

[51] 75 Fed. Reg. 34539–40.

[52] 26 C.F.R. § 9831-1; 29 C.F.R. § 2590.732; 45 C.F.R. §§ 146.145, 148.220.

[53] 75 Fed. Reg. 34539–40.

[54] PPACA § 1251(d). The interim final regulations confirm that the special rule only applies to health insurance maintained under one or more collective bargaining agreements. 29 C.F.R. 54.9815-1251T(f)(1); 29 C.F.R. § 2590.715-1251(f)(1); 45 C.F.R. § 147.140(f)(1).

If such insured coverage exists, "the provisions of [subtitles A and C] (and the amendments made by such subtitles) shall not apply until the date on which the last of the collective bargaining agreements relating to the coverage terminates."[55] The interim final regulations on grandfathered health plans limit the effect of this seemingly broad language to the preservation of grandfathered health plan status for such plans when they enter into new insurance arrangements while the special rule is applicable to the group health plan.[56]

Interpretational challenges presented by the special rule for collectively bargained insured plans not resolved by the interim final regulations are as follows:

• *When is a plan "maintained" pursuant to one or more collective bargaining agreements?*

    This issue arises when a plan covers both union and non-union employees. The traditional rule applied to this situation is that a plan is maintained pursuant to a collective bargaining agreement if at least 25 percent of the covered group is participating in the plan pursuant to a collective bargaining agreement.[57] It is unclear whether the 25 percent rule will apply for purposes of the special rule.

• *If a plan provides coverage on both an insured and a self-funded basis, how does one determine if the plan provides insured or self-funded coverage for purposes of the special rule?*

    For example, if a plan provides medical benefits on an insured basis and prescription drug benefits on a self-funded basis, will the whole plan (medical plus prescription) be treated as an insured plan no matter what percentage of its total benefits are provided on an insured basis, or will the benefits provided by the respective portions of the plan be considered different benefit packages?

• *When does a collective bargaining agreement "terminate" for purposes of this section?*

    Under the Railway Labor Act and certain state laws governing collective bargaining between a public-sector employer and labor unions representing employees, an employer cannot unilaterally change the status quo at the expiration of a collective bargaining agreement.[58] Instead, the terms of the expired agreement remain in effect. It is not clear in these circumstances on which date the collective bargaining agreement would terminate for purposes of the temporary exemption.

---

[55] PPACA § 1251(d).

[56] 26 C.F.R. § 54.9815-1251T(a)(1)(ii); 29 C.F.R. § 2590.715-1251(a)(1)(ii), 45 C.F.R. § 147.140(a)(1)(ii).

[57] *See, e.g.,* I.R.S. Priv. Ltr. Ruls. 9610025 (March 8, 1996), 8618043 (February 4, 1986), 8605032 (November 5, 1985) (applying the 25 percent rule).

[58] *See, e.g.,* Detroit & Toledo Shore Line R.R. v. United Trans. Union, 396 U.S. 142 (1969) (regarding the Railway Labor Act); Philadelphia Housing Auth. v. PLRB, 620 A.2d 594 (Pa. Commw. Ct. 2003) (applying Pennsylvania public sector labor law).

CHAPTER 5

QUALITY, AFFORDABILITY, AND ACCESSIBILITY

Congress recognized that while universal access to affordable, quality health care coverage could not be implemented immediately, preliminary measures could be adopted to begin the transition and improve access to coverage. The major reforms, such as prohibitions on pre-existing condition exclusions for adults,[1] guaranteed availability and renewability of individual insurance coverage, and the state Exchanges, do not begin until January 1, 2014. The period from the date of enactment of the 2010 Health Care Reform Act, March 23, 2010, through January 1, 2014, is sometimes referred to as the "transition period."

The changes that become effective during the transition period generally are interim measures intended to preserve or improve access to affordable coverage by demographic groups that currently represent significant portions of the underinsured—young adults, early retirees, and high-risk individuals. The 2010 Health Care Reform Act also imposes a number of immediate coverage and reporting requirements on existing group health plans and individual insurance coverage. Premiums charged by insurance issuers begin to be regulated and limited. Finally, new reporting requirements begin the process of providing more consumer information about available options and costs, premium transparency, and quality information. Each of these measures is described in detail in subsequent chapters. A quick list of the reforms that begin during the transition period follows.

§ 5.01 Immediate Steps to Expand and Preserve Coverage[2]

Effective as of March 23, 2010, HHS is directed to take steps immediately to establish the following programs and activities:

- A high-risk health insurance pool program to provide health insurance coverage for eligible individuals beginning no later than June 21, 2010 (90 days after enactment), and ending on January 1, 2014;[3]

- A temporary reinsurance program to provide reimbursement for employer-sponsored group health plans for a portion of the cost of providing health insurance coverage to early retirees (including their eligible spouses, surviving spouses, and dependents) for the period June 21, 2010, through January 1, 2014;[4]

- A small-employer tax credit to subsidize part of a small employer's cost of coverage for employees;[5]

- An Internet portal through which a resident of any state may identify affordable health insurance options in that state, including Medicaid coverage, any high-risk pool offered by a state, and the new federal high-risk pool described above (beginning July 1, 2010).[6]

§ 5.02 Transition Period Coverage Improvements Applicable to Group Health Plans[7]

Effective for plan years beginning on or after September 23, 2010 (six months after the date of enactment), the 2010 Health Care Reform Act amends the PHSA to prohibit certain practices and add

---

[1] Prohibitions on pre-existing condition exclusions for children under age 19 apply for the first plan year beginning on or after September 23, 2010. PPACA § 1255(2) (amending PHSA § 2704).

[2] These steps are found primarily in Subtitle B of Title I of the Act.

[3] PPACA § 1101.

[4] PPACA § 1102.

[5] PPACA § 1421.

[6] PPACA § 1103.

[7] The immediate changes applicable to health plans are found primarily in Subtitle A of Title I of the Act. Also, these requirements are subject to the discussion of grandfathered health plans and collectively bargained plans in **Chapter 4**.

new coverage requirements for group health plans and health insurance issuers offering group or individual health insurance coverage, including:

- A prohibition on lifetime or annual limits on the dollar value of benefits;[8]
- A prohibition on pre-existing condition exclusion provisions for children under age 19;[9]
- Minimum preventive health services coverage requirements without cost-sharing by the enrollee;[10]
- The extension of coverage for children until age 26;[11]
- Requirements for an appeals process of coverage determinations and claims which must include, at a minimum, an internal process and an external review process that is binding on the plan;[12]
- Restrictions on rescissions of plan coverage of an enrollee, other than for fraud or an intentional misrepresentation of material fact, and subject to notice of cancellation;[13]
- A required standardized summary of benefits and coverage to be provided to applicants, enrollees, and policy holders prior to enrollment and upon renewal of coverage;[14] and
- A prohibition on eligibility rules for insured group health plans that have the effect of discriminating in favor of higher-wage employees.[15]

§ 5.03 Coverage Improvements Applicable to Employment-Based Coverage Effective January 1, 2014[16]

Some coverage improvements are deferred until January 1, 2014, when the Exchanges begin and the insurance issuer market reforms become effective. These include:

- Prohibitions on pre-existing coverage exclusions for adults;[17]
- Underwriting of premiums for insured coverage is limited to certain ratios for age and tobacco use;[18]
- All insured plans must guarantee availability and renewability of coverage;[19]
- Prohibitions on discrimination in benefits against individual participants and beneficiaries based on health status;[20]
- Annual cost-sharing limits for comprehensive benefits;[21]
- Prohibitions on discrimination against health care provider participation;[22]

---

[8] PPACA § 1001 (adding PHSA § 2711).
[9] PPACA §§ 1201 (adding PHSA § 2704), 1255(2).
[10] PPACA § 1001 (adding PHSA § 2713).
[11] PPACA § 1001 (adding PHSA § 2714).
[12] PPACA § 1001 (adding PHSA § 2719).
[13] PPACA § 1001 (adding PHSA § 2712).
[14] PPACA § 1001 (adding PHSA § 2715).
[15] PPACA § 1001 (adding PHSA § 2716).
[16] These provisions are found primarily in Subtitle C of Title I of the Act.
[17] PPACA § 1201 (adding PHSA § 2704).
[18] PPACA § 1201 (adding PHSA § 2701).
[19] PPACA § 1201 (adding PHSA §§ 2702, 2703).
[20] PPACA § 1201 (adding PHSA § 2705).
[21] PPACA § 1201 (adding PHSA § 2707(b)).
[22] PPACA § 1201 (adding PHSA § 2706).

- No waiting periods in excess of 90 days;[23] and

- Coverage of medical services in clinical trials.[24]

§ 5.04   New Reporting Obligations

Insurers and group health plans will be subject to new reporting obligations to HHS:

- To facilitate the introduction of the Web portal for consumers beginning on July 1, 2010 (described above), insurers must submit plan background information to HHS for posting starting with basic summary information as early as May 21, 2010, and continuing with more specific pricing and benefit information later in the year.[25]

- Insurers will be required to report on the percentage of total premium revenue that is expended on clinical service, health care quality improvement, and non-claims costs.[26] Insurers will be required to provide an annual rebate to each enrollee, on a pro rata basis, if the non-claims costs exceed 20 percent of the premium for the group market and 25 percent of the premium for the individual market.[27]

- Group health plans and insurance coverage will be required to report on their benefits and reimbursement provisions that improve health outcomes, prevent medical errors and improve patient safety, and implement wellness and health promotion activities.[28]

- Group health plans and health insurance issuers must submit certain information regarding plan design to HHS.[29]

- Each hospital must publish annually a list of its standard charges for items and services it provides.[30]

§ 5.05   Additional Electronic Transaction Standards

To advance the financial transactions that will be necessary to implement and operate the exchanges, HHS also is charged with the adoption of additional uniform standards and business operating rules under HIPAA for the electronic exchange of information by health plans with respect to eligibility, electronic funds transfers, enrollment and disenrollment, health care premium payments, and claims-related transactions.[31]

---

[23] PPACA § 1201 (adding PHSA § 2708).
[24] PPACA § 1201 (adding PHSA § 2709).
[25] 45 C.F.R. 159.120. See **Appendix C.**
[26] PPACA § 1001 (adding PHSA § 2718(a)).
[27] PPACA § 1001 (adding PHSA § 2718(b)).
[28] PPACA § 1001 (adding PHSA § 2717).
[29] PPACA § 1001 (adding PHSA § 2715A).
[30] PPACA § 1001 (adding PHSA § 2718(c)).
[31] PPAC § 1104.

CHAPTER 6

PRESERVING AND EXPANDING IMMEDIATE ACCESS TO COVERAGE

The changes that become effective during the transition period (i.e., the period between March 23, 2010, and January 1, 2014) generally are interim measures intended to preserve or improve access to affordable coverage by demographic groups that currently represent significant portions of the underinsured—young adults, early retirees, employees of small employers, and high-risk individuals. This chapter reviews the immediate transition period reforms and subsidies relating to preserving and expanding coverage and discusses their implications for employment-based group health plans.

§ 6.01   Temporary Reinsurance Program for Early Retirees

One of the first health care reform decisions that an employer will need to make is whether to apply to HHS for reimbursement of expenses relating to the provision of employment-based health coverage to early retirees.[1] The PPACA directs HHS to establish a temporary Early Retiree Reinsurance Program (the Program) no later than June 21, 2010.[2] HHS has indicated, in the form of interim final regulations, that to better align the Program with plan years, the Program and the regulations are effective on June 1, 2010.[3] Funding is limited, and the Program is scheduled to end on January 1, 2014, to coincide with the commencement of the Exchanges.

The Program is designed to encourage employers to continue providing retiree health coverage to pre-Medicare retirees.[4] According to the White House, employer-provided retiree health coverage is a valuable benefit because early retirees, as compared to the general population, have greater health risk, incur greater health costs, and have relatively less access to adequate and affordable health coverage.[5]

An employer that maintains a retiree health plan for early retirees may apply to HHS under the Program to receive reinsurance payments for certain costs incurred.[6] A draft copy of the application and the accompanying instructions is set forth in **Appendix E**. The 2010 Health Care Reform Act defines an "early retiree" as an individual age 55 or older who is not Medicare-eligible (either by reason of attaining age 65 or being disabled), and is not an active employee of the employer that has made substantial contributions to fund the employment-based retiree health plan.[7]

To be approved for reinsurance under the Program, the employer's retiree health plan must implement programs and procedures to generate cost savings with respect to participants with chronic and high-cost conditions.[8] HHS defines "chronic and high-cost conditions" as any condition for which $15,000 or more in health benefit claims is likely to be incurred during a plan year by any one plan participant.[9] A plan is not required to have programs and procedures in place for all chronic and high-cost conditions. It is sufficient for plans and plan sponsors to take a reasonable approach in identifying such conditions and selecting programs and procedures to lower the cost of care and improve the quality of care for those conditions.[10] According to HHS, examples of programs and procedures to generate cost savings for plan participants with chronic and high-cost conditions include a diabetes

---

[1] PPACA § 1102.

[2] PPACA § 1102(a)(1).

[3] Preamble to 45 C.F.R. pt. 149 § III.B (p. 49).

[4] Preamble to 45 C.F.R. pt. 149 § I.A (p. 5). *See* **Appendix D**.

[5] The White House, *Fact Sheet: Early Benefits from the Affordable Care Act of 2010—Reinsurance Program for Early Retirees*, May 4, 2010, *http://www.whitehouse.gov/the-press-office/fact-sheet-early-retiree-reinsurance-program*.

[6] The application process is intended to be consistent with the process for applying for Medicare Part D RDS payments. *See infra* § 11.01[C] notes 21–30 and accompanying text (discussing the RDS payment process). One significant difference, however, is that only one application is required under the Program for all years (through the end of 2013). 45 C.F.R. § 149.40(d). Application for RDS payments under Medicare Part D must be made annually. *See http://www.rds.cms.hhs.gov/app_deadline.htm* (providing information about RDS application deadlines).

[7] PPACA § 1102(a)(2)(C).

[8] PPACA § 1102(b)(2)(A); 45 C.F.R. § 149.35.

[9] 45 C.F.R. § 149.2.

[10] Preamble to 45 C.F.R. pt. 149 § II.A.2 (p. 10).

management program that features aggressive monitoring and behavioral counseling, as well as reduced deductibles, co-insurance, and copayments for treatments and health care provider visits related to cancer.[11]

In addition, plan sponsors must have written agreements with health insurers or their group health plans to require the insurer or plan, as applicable, to disclose information on behalf of the plan sponsor to HHS in support of the Program application and reinsurance claims.[12] This requirement arises out of a concern under the HIPAA privacy rules that plan sponsors may not have direct access to the necessary claims information generated by the group health plan to support requests for reinsurance under the Program.[13] Plan sponsors should ensure that their agreements with health insurers are updated to satisfy this requirement for insured group health plans, and that the HIPAA plan amendment and business associate agreements are updated for self-funded group health plans.

Plan sponsors applying under the Program must attest that there are policies in place with respect to their group health plans to detect and reduce fraud, waste, and abuse.[14] The policies must be available to be produced to HHS to substantiate their implementation and effectiveness.[15] Such policies might include internal and external eligibility and claims audits. Plan sponsors should discuss whether it may be possible to incorporate the policies of their health insurers and third-party administrators by reference.

Finally, the plan sponsor must provide a summary in its Program application of how it proposes to use the reinsurance amounts.[16] In general, the reinsurance amounts must be used to lower costs under the plan.[17] The 2010 Health Care Reform Act specifies that the reinsurance amounts "may be used to reduce premium costs for [an employer providing the coverage]," as well as to reduce premium contributions, deductibles, copayments, co-insurance and other out-of-pocket costs for plan participants.[18] The payments cannot be used as general revenues for employers or other plan sponsors.[19] HHS regulations clarify that plan sponsors may use the reinsurance amounts to reduce their own costs with respect to the plan, but they must maintain their level of support for the plan.[20] Thus, reinsurance amounts may be used by the plan sponsor to offset any cost increases that would otherwise be paid by the plan sponsor (including increased premiums in an insured arrangement), but may not reduce the level of the plan sponsor's "support" or funding of the plan at the time application to the Program is made. Significantly, reinsurance amounts paid under the Program may be used to reduce all plan costs, including costs incurred under the plan for active employees.[21]

Once approved, HHS is authorized to reimburse up to 80 percent of the costs associated with the provision of retiree health coverage between $15,000 and $90,000 per year.[22] Both dollar amounts are adjusted each year based on the percentage increase in the Medical Care Component of the Consumer

---

[11] Preamble to 45 C.F.R. pt. 149 § II.B.2 (p. 17).

[12] 45 C.F.R. § 149.35(b)(2).

[13] Preamble to 45 C.F.R. pt. 149 § II.B.2 (p. 20). *See* 45 C.F.R. §§ 164.500 *et seq.* (setting forth the HIPAA privacy rules applicable to HIPAA-covered entities, such as employer-sponsored group health plans).

[14] 45 C.F.R. § 149.35(b)(3).

[15] 45 C.F.R. § 149.35(b)(3).

[16] 45 C.F.R. § 149.40(f)(5). In addition, the plan sponsor's application must include a projected amount of reinsurance to be received under the Program for each of the first two plan years. 45 C.F.R. § 149.40(f)(6).

[17] PPACA § 1102(c)(4); 45 C.F.R. § 149.200.

[18] PPACA § 1102(c)(4).

[19] PPACA § 1102(c)(4); 45 C.F.R. § 149.200(b).

[20] 45 C.F.R. §§ 149.40(f)(5); .300.

[21] 45 C.F.R. § 149.300; Preamble to C.F.R. pt. 149 § II.D (p. 32).

[22] PPACA § 1102(c); 45 C.F.R. § 149.100. Coverage for which reinsurance is available under the Program includes costs for medical, surgical, hospital prescription drug and other types of health coverage, but not for "excepted benefits" (such as long-term care) as described in HIPAA. 45 C.F.R. § 149.2 (defining claim or medical claim). Also, a "dependent" means an individual covered as a dependent under the plan, regardless of whether such individual is a dependent for tax purposes under Section 152 of the Code. 45 C.F.R. § 149.2.

Price Index for all urban consumers (rounded to the nearest multiple of $1,000).[23] The costs subject to reinsurance include costs incurred with respect to the early retiree, his or her spouse, surviving spouse and dependents, net of discounts, and other negotiated price concessions.[24] Significantly, such costs may include costs actually paid by the early retiree, spouse, surviving spouse or dependent in the form of deductibles, copayments, and co-insurance.[25] If the group health plan is insured, the actual net costs incurred by the insurer and the early retiree may be counted, but the premium costs paid by the plan sponsor or the early retiree are excluded.[26]

Because the Program starts on June 1, 2010, plan sponsors likely will be eligible for reinsurance for only part of their 2010 plan year. Only costs incurred on or after June 1, 2010, can be reimbursed under the Program.[27] However, HHS will allow plan sponsors to count costs incurred prior to June 1, 2010 (but during the 2010 plan year), against both the $15,000 threshold and the $90,000 maximum limit.[28] Thus, if at least $15,000 in costs has been incurred with respect to an early retiree in the 2010 plan year prior to June 1, 80 percent of costs incurred from June 1, 2010, through the end of the 2010 plan year are eligible for reinsurance (subject to the $90,000 limit).

The reinsurance payments received under the Program are not treated as income to the employer maintaining the employment-based retiree health plan.[29] Thus, the reinsurance payments appear to create a double tax benefit for employers that can deduct the cost of providing retiree health benefits and receive tax-free reimbursements for those same costs under the Program. Ironically, this is the same type of inequitable double tax benefit that the 2010 Health Care Reform Act unwinds with respect to the RDS payments under Medicare Part D.[30]

If an employer wishes to seek reimbursement under the Program, it must act quickly. The 2010 Health Care Reform Act allocates only $5 billion to the Program, and that amount is likely to be used up long before the Program's scheduled ending date in 2013. Both applications for the Program and claims submitted under the Program are evaluated on a first-come, first-served basis.[31]

§ 6.02   Temporary High-Risk Pools

As described above, the most far-reaching health care reforms, relating to the establishment of Exchanges and the implementation of the individual "enroll or pay" and the employer "pay or play" requirements, are not scheduled to occur until 2014.[32] In order to implement the policy goal of providing universal access to health coverage, the 2010 Health Care Reform Act calls for the prompt establishment of temporary high-risk insurance pools to provide health insurance coverage to uninsured eligible individuals who have pre-existing conditions.[33] The Act indicates that these temporary high-risk pools should be up and running by late June 2010, and would last through 2013, at which

---

[23] PPACA § 1102(c); 45 C.F.R. § 145.115(c).

[24] Spouses, surviving spouses, and dependents are not subject to the age 55, non–Medicare eligible and retired conditions applicable to early retirees. 45 C.F.R. § 149.2 (definition of "early retiree"). Negotiated price concessions include any direct or indirect remuneration offered to a plan sponsor, health insurer or plan that would serve to decrease the costs incurred under the plan. 45 C.F.R. § 149.2 (definition of "negotiated price concession").

[25] PPACA § 1102(c)(1).

[26] 45 C.F.R. § 149.100.

[27] 45 C.F.R. § 149.105.

[28] 45 C.F.R. § 149.105.

[29] PPACA § 1102(c)(5).

[30] See infra § 11.01[C] notes 21–30 and accompanying text (discussing the Act provision which eliminates the employer's deduction for retiree prescription drug costs that are reimbursed through RDS payments).

[31] 45 C.F.R. §§ 149.310; .315. Denied claims may be appealed to HHS within 15 days of the claim denial, and only one level of appeal is permitted. 45 C.F.R. § 149.500.

[32] See Chapter 10 for a discussion of Exchanges, individual "enroll or pay," and employer "pay or play."

[33] PPACA § 1101. Only U.S. citizens and nationals are eligible for the temporary high-risk pools. PPACA § 1101(d)(1).

point the individuals receiving health insurance coverage through the pools would be able to enroll in health insurance coverage through the Exchanges.[34]

The 2010 Health Care Reform Act directs HHS to establish the temporary high-risk pools directly, or to work with states and nonprofit entities to set up the pools. On April 5, 2010, HHS Secretary Kathleen Sebelius sent a letter to each state seeking expressions of state interest in participating in the establishment of temporary high-risk pools.[35] In her letter, the secretary outlined five possible options for states to participate:

- Operate a new high-risk pool alongside an existing high-risk pool maintained by the state;

- Establish a new high-risk pool, where the state does not currently offer such a pool;

- Build upon existing coverage programs designed to cover high-risk individuals;

- Contract with an insurance carrier to provide subsidized coverage for uninsured individuals with pre-existing conditions; or

- Do nothing, in which case HHS would establish the temporary high-risk pool for the state.[36]

The 2010 Health Care Reform Act appropriates $5 billion in funding for the state-based temporary high-risk pools.[37] HHS intends to allocate the funding among the states using a formula similar to what it uses to allocate Children's Health Insurance Program (CHIP) funds.[38] To avoid abuse, the Act provides that states entering into an arrangement with HHS to provide temporary high-risk pools cannot reduce the annual amount expended by the state on existing state high-risk pools during the year prior to the year in which the arrangement is established.[39] Given the tight time frame, the secretary asked for states to respond with their expressions of interest no later than April 30, 2010. States vary greatly in the manner and extent to which they provide coverage for uninsured, high-risk individuals, and it is expected that all of the above-outlined options, as well as others, will be implemented throughout the United States to satisfy the Act's mandate.

Once established, the temporary high-risk pools must provide coverage to eligible individuals that (1) does not impose any pre-existing condition exclusions; (2) covers at least 65 percent of eligible costs; (3) has out-of-pocket expense limits that do not exceed, for 2010, $5,950 for self-only coverage or $11,900 for family coverage; (4) meets certain premium limitations (including a limitation that premiums cannot vary based on age by a ratio of more than four to one); and (5) satisfies any other requirements imposed by HHS.[40]

While the establishment of temporary high-risk pools does not directly affect employment-based group health plans, employers need to be aware of the rules prohibiting the dumping of risk on the temporary high-risk pools. The 2010 Health Care Reform Act directs HHS to establish criteria for determining whether insurers and employment-based group health plans have discouraged individuals from remaining in prior coverage based on that individual's health status (the "anti-dumping rule").[41] The determination will be based in part on whether the employer, the plan, or the insurer provided money or other financial incentives to the individual to disenroll from the employment-based group

---

[34] PPACA § 1101(a).

[35] *See http://www.hhs.gov/news/press/2010pres/04/20100402b.html.*

[36] *See http://www.hhs.gov/news/press/2010pres/04/20100402b.html.*

[37] PPACA § 1101(g).

[38] *See* Fact Sheet—Temporary High Risk Pool Program, *http://www.hhs.gov/ociio/initiative/hi_risk_pool_facts.html.* California, the most populous state, would receive the most funding—approximately $761 million.

[39] PPACA § 1101(e).

[40] PPACA § 1101(c); *see also* I.R.S. Rev. Proc. 2009-29, 2009-3 I.R.B. 321 (providing the out-of-pocket expense limits for 2010).

[41] PPACA § 1101(e).

health plan. The sanction for violating the anti-dumping rule is to reimburse the medical expenses incurred by the temporary high-risk pool.[42]

Many employers offer "opt-out" arrangements pursuant to which employees may elect to decline coverage under the employer's group health plan in exchange for some monetary or other incentive. Such arrangements usually are offered to all employees or broad-based portions of the total employee population. So long as such arrangements are broad-based, it would seem that they would not run afoul of the anti-dumping rule because they would not be basing eligibility for the opt-out payment on an individual's health status.

§ 6.03 Small-Employer Incentives

[A] Employer Eligibility

Because employees of small employers make up a substantial portion of the ranks of the uninsured, the 2010 Health Care Reform Act includes incentives for small employers to make health insurance coverage available to employees. Beginning in 2010, employers that employ fewer than 25 full-time equivalent employees (FTEs) and have an average payroll of less than $50,000[43] per FTE will be eligible for tax credits if they maintain a "qualifying arrangement"[44] for their employees.[45] The tax credits only apply to eligible small employers that provide medical benefits through health insurance coverage (i.e., the tax credits are not available to self-funded plans) prior to January 1, 2014, at which point the Exchanges become operational.[46] Once the Exchanges become operational, the tax credits are available only to eligible small employers who provide medical benefits through a QHP (i.e., a plan offered through the Exchange).

[B] Employer Limitations

Employers may not treat any premiums paid pursuant to a salary reduction arrangement under a Section 125 cafeteria plan as an employer contribution.[47] An additional limitation for employers is that the controlled group rules under Code Sections 414(b), (c), (m), and (o) will apply when determining the size of an employer.[48] Thus, all employees of a controlled group or affiliated service group (except employees not taken into account as described above), and all wages paid to, and premiums paid for, employees by the members of the controlled group or affiliated service group (except employees not taken into account as described above), are taken into account in determining who is an eligible small employer.

[C] Form and Amount of Credit

These tax credits will come in the form of general business tax credits for for-profit employers.[49] As such, they may be carried forward if the for-profit entity does not have enough tax liability in a

---

[42] PPACA § 1101(e)(2).

[43] The $50,000 wage limit will be adjusted for inflation beginning in 2014. I.R.C. § 45R(d)(3)(B)(ii).

[44] A "qualifying arrangement" is an arrangement under which the employer non-electively pays premiums for each employee enrolled in health insurance coverage offered by the employer in an amount equal to a uniform percentage (but not less than 50 percent) of the premium cost of the coverage. I.R.S. Notice 2010-44, § II(A).

[45] PPACA § 1421 (adding I.R.C. § 45R(d)). Although the term "eligible small employer" is defined in section 45R(d)(1) to include employers with "no more than" 25 FTEs and average annual wages that "do not exceed" $50,000, the phase-out of the credit amount under section 45R(c) operates in such a way that an employer with exactly 25 FTEs or with average annual wages exactly equal to $50,000 is not in fact eligible for the credit. I.R.S. Notice 2010-44 § II(A).

[46] I.R.C. § 45R(b).

[47] I.R.C. § 45R(e)(3).

[48] I.R.C. § 45R(e)(5).

[49] I.R.C. § 38(b)(36).

given year to use the full amount of the tax credit.[50] Nonprofit employers will use these tax credits to offset payroll (FICA) taxes.[51] For the 2010 through 2013 taxable years, the credit amount is equal to 35 percent (25 percent for tax-exempt entities) of the aggregate amount of non-elective employer contributions made on behalf of employees to an insured health plan.[52] For taxable years beginning on or after January 1, 2014, the amount of the credit increases to 50 percent (35 percent for tax-exempt entities) of the aggregate amount of non-elective employer contributions made on behalf of employees to a qualified health plan (QHP).[53]

[D]   Proration of Credit

The credit is prorated based on the number of employees and the average salary base. If the number of FTEs exceeds ten, the reduction is determined by multiplying the otherwise applicable credit amount by a fraction, the numerator of which is the number of FTEs in excess of 10 and the denominator of which is 15. If average annual wages exceed $25,000, the reduction is determined by multiplying the otherwise applicable credit amount by a fraction, the numerator of which is the amount by which average annual wages exceed $25,000 and the denominator of which is $25,000.[54] In both cases, the result of the calculation is subtracted from the otherwise applicable credit to determine the credit to which the employer is entitled.[55] See the following tables for specific detail on credit proration.

---

[50] I.R.S. Notice 2010-44 § IV.
[51] I.R.C. § 45R(f).
[52] I.R.C. § 45R(g).
[53] I.R.C. § 45R(b).
[54] I.R.S. Notice 2010-44 § III(C).
[55] I.R.S. Notice 2010-44 § III(C).

Table 6-1. Small Employer Tax Credit as a Percent (Maximum of 35%) of Employer Contribution to Premiums, For-Profit Firms in 2010–2013 and Nonprofit Firms in 2014 and Beyond[56]

# of employees	Average Wage					
	Up to $25,000	$30,000	$35,000	$40,000	$45,000	$50,000
Up to 10	35%	28%	21%	14%	7%	0%
11	33%	26%	19%	12%	5%	0%
12	30%	23%	16%	9%	2%	0%
13	28%	21%	14%	7%	0%	0%
14	26%	19%	12%	5%	0%	0%
15	23%	16%	9%	2%	0%	0%
16	21%	14%	7%	0%	0%	0%
17	19%	12%	5%	0%	0%	0%
18	16%	9%	2%	0%	0%	0%
19	14%	7%	0%	0%	0%	0%
20	12%	5%	0%	0%	0%	0%
21	9%	2%	0%	0%	0%	0%
22	7%	0%	0%	0%	0%	0%
23	5%	0%	0%	0%	0%	0%
24	2%	0%	0%	0%	0%	0%
25	0%	0%	0%	0%	0%	0%

---

[56] Congressional Research Service, *Summary of Small Business Health Insurance Tax Credit Under PPACA (P.L. 111-148)*, April 5, 2010, available at *http://www.ncsl.org/documents/health/SBtaxCredits.pdf.*

Table 6-2. Small Employer Tax Credit as a Percent (Maximum of 50%) of Employer Contribution to Premiums, For-Profit Firms in 2014 and Beyond[57]

# of employees	Average Wage					
	Up to $25,000	$30,000	$35,000	$40,000	$45,000	$50,000
Up to 10	50%	40%	30%	20%	10%	0%
11	47%	37%	27%	17%	7%	0%
12	43%	33%	23%	13%	3%	0%
13	40%	30%	20%	10%	0%	0%
14	37%	27%	17%	7%	0%	0%
15	33%	23%	13%	3%	0%	0%
16	30%	20%	10%	0%	0%	0%
17	27%	17%	7%	0%	0%	0%
18	23%	13%	3%	0%	0%	0%
19	20%	10%	0%	0%	0%	0%
20	17%	7%	0%	0%	0%	0%
21	13%	3%	0%	0%	0%	0%
22	10%	0%	0%	0%	0%	0%
23	7%	0%	0%	0%	0%	0%
24	3%	0%	0%	0%	0%	0%
25	0%	0%	0%	0%	0%	0%

---

[57] Congressional Research Service, *Summary of Small Business Health Insurance Tax Credit Under PPACA (P.L. 111-148)*, April 5, 2010, available at *http://www.ncsl.org/documents/health/SBtaxCredits.pdf*.

Table 6-3. Small Employer Tax Credit as a Percent (Maximum of 25%) of Employer Contribution to Premiums, Nonprofit Firms in 2010–2013[58]

# of employees	Average Wage					
	Up to $25,000	$30,000	$35,000	$40,000	$45,000	$50,000
Up to 10	25%	20%	15%	10%	5%	0%
11	23%	18%	13%	8%	3%	0%
12	22%	17%	12%	7%	2%	0%
13	20%	15%	10%	5%	0%	0%
14	18%	13%	8%	3%	0%	0%
15	17%	12%	7%	2%	0%	0%
16	15%	10%	5%	0%	0%	0%
17	13%	8%	3%	0%	0%	0%
18	12%	7%	2%	0%	0%	0%
19	10%	5%	0%	0%	0%	0%
20	8%	3%	0%	0%	0%	0%
21	7%	2%	0%	0%	0%	0%
22	5%	0%	0%	0%	0%	0%
23	3%	0%	0%	0%	0%	0%
24	2%	0%	0%	0%	0%	0%
25	0%	0%	0%	0%	0%	0%

[E] Calculation of Employees

The calculation to determine the number of FTEs for the tax credit is different from similar calculations used for other purposes under the 2010 Health Care Reform Act. For this purpose, FTEs are determined by dividing the total number of hours of service[59] for which wages were paid by the employer to employees, including leased employees, during the taxable year, by 2,080.[60] The resulting number is

---

[58] Congressional Research Service, *Summary of Small Business Health Insurance Tax Credit Under PPACA (P.L. 111-148)*, April 5, 2010, available at *http://www.ncsl.org/documents/health/SBtaxCredits.pdf.*

[59] An employee's hours of service for a year include the following: (1) each hour for which an employee is paid, or entitled to payment, for the performance of duties for the employer during the employer's taxable year; and (2) each hour for which an employee is paid, or entitled to payment, by the employer on account of a period of time during which no duties are performed due to vacation, holiday, illness, incapacity (including disability), layoff, jury duty, military duty or leave of absence (except that no more than 160 hours of service are required to be counted for an employee on account of any single continuous period during which the employee performs no duties). In calculating the total number of hours of service, the employer may use any of the following methods: (1) determine actual hours of service; (2) use a days-worked equivalency whereby the employee is credited with 8 hours of service for each day for which the employee would be required to be credited with at least one hour of service; or (3) use a weeks-worked equivalency whereby the employee is credited with 40 hours of service for each week for which the employee would be required to be credited with at least one hour of service. I.R.S. Notice 2010-44 § II(C).

[60] I.R.C. § 45R(d)(2)(A).

then rounded to the next lowest whole number. If an employee works more than 2,080 hours of service during any taxable year, any hours over 2,080 are not included.[61] All FTEs are considered in this analysis, not just the ones who are enrolled in the health insurance coverage or QHP.[62]

Certain employees are excluded from consideration, including:[63]

- Self-employed individuals (e.g., partners and sole proprietors);
- A 2 percent shareholder, if the small employer is a Subchapter S corporation;
- Any 5 percent owner of the small employer;
- An individual who satisfies the dependent eligibility criteria under Section 152 of the Code; and
- Seasonal workers, unless the seasonal worker works for the employer for at least 121 days during the taxable year.

[F] Calculation of Average Annual Wages

Average annual wages are determined by dividing (1) the aggregate amount of wages that were paid to *all* employees (not just FTEs) by the employer during the taxable year, by (2) the number of FTEs of the employer[64] for the taxable year.[65] This amount is rounded to the next lowest multiple of $1,000.[66] While the hours worked by an employee in excess of 2,080 hours are not taken into consideration for the purpose of calculating FTEs, the wages paid to an employee who works in excess of 2,080 hours per year are taken into consideration.[67] Therefore, if an employee works 2,200 hours and earns $10 per hour, only 2,080 of the 2,200 hours are considered for determining employer size, but all wages paid ($22,200) are factored into the calculation for average annual wages.

[G] Employer Premiums

To be considered for the tax credit, an employer must pay premiums for health insurance coverage under a qualifying arrangement.[68] The amount of an employer's premium payments that are considered for purposes of the credit is limited to lesser of (1) the actual premiums paid by the employer; or (2) the average premium for the small group market in the state in which the employer offers coverage. For 2010, premiums that were paid during the 2010 taxable year but prior to the date of enactment of the 2010 Health Care Reform Act may be included for purposes of the credit.[69]

For purposes of this credit prior to January 1, 2014, health insurance coverage includes, but is not limited to, limited-scope dental or vision, long-term care, nursing home care, home health care, community-based care, coverage for specific diseases, hospital indemnity or other fixed indemnity insurance, Medicare supplements, and other supplemental coverage. Premium payments made pursuant to any of these plans can be counted as being paid under a qualifying arrangement.[70] However,

---

[61] I.R.C. § 45R(d)(2)(B).

[62] I.R.S. Notice 2010-44, Section II(D) Ex. 4.

[63] I.R.C. §§ 45R(d)(5), (e)(1).

[64] The Act as drafted provides "the number of full-time equivalent employees of the employee," which is clearly a typographical error and will likely be corrected via a technical correction. I.R.C. § 45R(d)(3)(A)(ii).

[65] I.R.C. § 45R(d)(3)(A).

[66] I.R.C. § 45R(d)(3)(A).

[67] I.R.S. Notice 2010-44 § II(E).

[68] A special transitional rule for the 2010 taxable year provides that in the case of an employer who pays a non-elective amount equal to at least 50 percent of the premium for single (employee-only) coverage for each enrolled employee, such employer will be deemed to satisfy the uniformity requirement for a qualifying arrangement, even if the employer does not pay the same percentage of the premium for each such employee who has more expensive coverage (e.g., family coverage). I.R.S. Notice 2010-44 § V.

[69] I.R.S. Notice 2010-44 § II.F.

[70] I.R.S. Notice 2010-44 § II.G.

different types of health insurance plans cannot be aggregated to satisfy the requirements for a qualifying arrangement.[71] Each type of coverage must separately satisfy the requirements for a qualifying arrangement.[72] Therefore, if an eligible small employer paid 60 percent of the premium cost for medical coverage but only 40 percent of the premium cost for dental coverage, the employer would be eligible for the tax credit only with respect to the medical coverage since it did not pay at or above the 50 percent threshold for dental coverage.

[H] Recap

An employer should follow these steps[73] to determine if it is eligible for a tax credit under Section 45R of the Code:

Step 1: Determine the employees who are taken into account for purposes of the tax credit.

Step 2: Determine the number of hours of service performed by the employees in Step 1.

Step 3: Calculate the number of FTEs.

Step 4: Determine the average annual wages paid per FTE.

Step 5: Determine the premiums paid by the employer that are taken into account for purposes of the credit (i.e., paid under a qualifying arrangement).

---

[71] I.R.S. Notice 2010-44 § II.G.
[72] I.R.S. Notice 2010-44 § II.G.
[73] I.R.S. Notice 2010-44 § II.A.

CHAPTER 7

COVERAGE IMPROVEMENTS DURING THE TRANSITION PERIOD

This chapter discusses coverage improvements that become effective during the transition period, subject to the discussion in Chapter 4 of grandfathered health plans and certain collectively bargained plans.

§ 7.01 Prohibitions on Lifetime and Annual Dollar Limits on Benefits

Group health plans and health insurers offering group health or individual insurance coverage are prohibited from imposing lifetime limits on the dollar value of benefits for any participant or beneficiary, and most annual limits on essential health benefits.[1] The ban on lifetime and annual dollar benefits starts for plan years beginning on after September 23, 2010.[2] HHS, Treasury and the DOL issued interim final regulations published in the *Federal Register* on June 28, 2010 further explaining these restrictions.[3]

The elimination of dollar limits and restrictions on annual limits will place a premium on a plan's medical necessity and case management activities to avoid ineffective over-utilization of services by providers and plan beneficiaries.

[A] Lifetime Limits

Effective for plan years beginning on or after September 23, 2010, a group health plan and health insurance issuer offering group or individual health insurance coverage may not establish lifetime limits on the dollar value of benefits for a participant or beneficiary.[4] While the law prohibits a lifetime limit on dollar benefits, it does not require a plan to cover all benefits. A plan may exclude all benefits for a condition.[5] An exclusion is not considered an annual or lifetime limit.[6]

If an employee or beneficiary lost coverage due to a lifetime maximum dollar limit prior to the effective date of the regulations but is still otherwise eligible for the coverage, the plan must notify the individual in writing that the lifetime limit on the dollar value of all benefits no longer applies and that the individual, if covered, is once again eligible for benefits. If the individual is not enrolled in the plan, the individual must be given an opportunity to enroll for at least 30 days (including written notice).[7] Notice to the employee, on behalf of a dependent, satisfies the notice obligation. The previously covered individual re-enrolls into the plan as a special enrollee.[8] This means that the enrollee must be offered all of the benefit packages available to similarly situated individuals who did not lose coverage by reason of reaching the lifetime limit. The enrollee cannot be required to pay more for coverage than similarly situated individuals.

[B] Annual Limits

[1] Restricted Annual Limits on Essential Benefits

During the transition period prior to January 1, 2014, group health plans and health insurers offering group health or individual insurance coverage may impose restricted annual limits with respect to

---

[1] PPACA § 1001 (adding PHSA § 2711).

[2] PPACA § 1001 (adding PHSA § 2711).

[3] 75 Fed. Reg. 37188–37241 and 37242–37243, amending 26 C.F.R. Pts 54 and 602, 29 C.F.R. 2590 and 45 C.F.R. Pts 144, 146 and 147.

[4] PHSA § 2711.

[5] Under the grandfather plan rules, the elimination of all benefits for a condition would result in the forfeiture of the plan's grandfather status. *See* § **4.01**, *infra*.

[6] 26 C.F.R. 54.9815-2711T(b), 29 C.F.R. § 2590.715-2711(b) and 45 C.F.R. § 147.126(b).

[7] 26 C.F.R. 54.9815-2711T(e), 29 C.F.R. § 2590.715-2711(e) and 45 C.F.R. § 147.126(e)

[8] 26 C.F.R. 54.9815-2711T(e)(4), 29 C.F.R. § 2590.715-2711(e)(4) and 45 C.F.R. § 147.126(e)(4).

the scope of benefits that are essential health benefits to the extent permitted by HHS.[9] The regulations impose a three-year phased-in approach to the annual limit restriction:

- For plan years beginning after September 23, 2010, and before September 23, 2011, the minimum annual limit on benefits is $750,000.

- For plan years beginning after September 23, 2011, and before September 23, 2012, the minimum annual limit on benefits is $1,250,000.

- For plan years beginning after September 23, 2012, and before December 31, 2013, the minimum annual limit on benefits is $2,000,000.[10]

Only essential benefits are to be taken into account in determining whether an individual has received the applicable amount.[11] The regulations define "essential health benefits" by cross-reference to Section 1302(b) of the 2010 Health Care Reform Act and note that further regulations will be forthcoming. Section 1302(b) defines "essential health benefits" as including at least the following general categories: ambulatory patient services; emergency services; hospitalization; maternity and newborn care; mental health and substance use disorder services, including behavioral health treatment; prescription drugs; rehabilitative and habilitative services[12] and devices; laboratory services; preventive and wellness services; chronic disease management; and pediatric services, including oral and vision care.[13]

[2]   Non-Essential Benefits

A group health plan or health insurance issuer offering group health or individual insurance coverage may impose lifetime or annual limits on coverage of specific benefits that are not essential health benefits, or exclude all benefits for a condition.[14]

[C]   Account-Based Plans

The prohibition on annual dollar limits for benefits under a group health plan do not apply to account-based plans, including Health Flexible Spending Accounts (Health FSAs), Medical Savings Accounts (MSAs) established under Section 220 of the Code, Health Savings Accounts (HSAs) established under Section 223 of the Code, and certain Health Reimbursement Accounts (HRAs).[15]

In the preamble to the regulations, it is noted that the annual limits do not apply to MSAs and HSAs because they are not group health plans. Amounts in those arrangements are available for medical and non-medical expenses. With respect to HRAs, the regulators comment that the annual limit prohibition will not apply if the HRA is integrated with a group health plan and the group health plan complies with the regulations, or if the HRA is for a retiree-only plan.[16]

---

[9] 26 C.F.R. 54.9815-2711T(a)(2), 29 C.F.R. § 2590.715-2711(a)(2) and 45 C.F.R. § 147.126(a)(2).

[10] 26 C.F.R. 54.9815-2711T(d)(1), 29 C.F.R. § 2590.715-2711(d)(1) and 45 C.F.R. § 147.126(d)(1).

[11] 26 C.F.R. 54.9815-2711T(d)(2), 29 C.F.R. § 2590.715-2711(d)(2) and 45 C.F.R. § 147.126(d)(2).

[12] "Habilitative services" includes various therapies used to treat autism. Numerous state laws currently mandate coverage of such services, but several state laws allow annual dollar limits on those benefits. Unless HHS clarifies this provision in the essential benefit regulations, the state law annual limits may not be permissible under PPACA.

[13] *See* PPACA § 1302(b) (defining essential health benefits).

[14] 26 C.F.R. 54.9815-2711T(b), 29 C.F.R. § 2590.715-2711(b) and 45 C.F.R. § 147.126(b).

[15] 26 C.F.R. 54.9815-2711T(a)(2)(ii), 29 C.F.R. § 2590.715-2711(a)(2)(ii) and 45 C.F.R. § 147.126(a)(2)(ii).

[16] 75 Fed. Reg. 37190–37191.

§ 7.02   Prohibition on Pre-Existing Condition Exclusion Provisions for Children Under Age 19

The 2010 Health Care Reform Act generally extends the group health plan prohibition on pre-existing condition exclusion provisions to the individual insurance market as one of the market reforms that begins in January 1, 2014.[17] However, the Act accelerates the prohibition for enrollees who are under age 19 for plan or coverage years beginning on and after September 23, 2010.[18] No coverage or enrollment limitations may be imposed, regardless of the child's previous coverage status. The terms and conditions applicable to pre-existing condition provisions are explained in detail in **Section 8.01**.

§ 7.03   Coverage of Preventive Health Services

The 2010 Health Care Reform Act requires any group health plan or health insurance company offering group or individual health insurance coverage to provide, at a minimum and without the imposition of any cost-sharing requirements, coverage for specific items or services in four separate and distinct areas.[19]

First, the preventive health benefit must cover all evidence-based items or services that have in effect a rating of "A" or "B" in the current recommendations of the United States Preventive Services Task Force (Task Force).[20]

Second, the preventive health benefit must cover immunizations recommended by the Advisory Committee on Immunization Practices (ACIP) of the Centers for Disease Control and Prevention (CDC) with respect to the individual involved.[21]

Third, preventive health benefits for infants, children, and adolescents must include preventive care and screenings set forth in comprehensive guidelines supported by the Health Resources and Services Administration (HRSA). The Early and Periodic Screening, Diagnostic, and Treatment (EPSDT) service is Medicaid's comprehensive and preventive child health program for individuals under age 21. EPSDT includes periodic screening, vision, dental, and hearing services.[22] In addition, the Social Security Act (SSA) requires that any medically necessary health care service (as defined in the SSA) be provided to an EPSDT recipient even if the service is not available under the state's Medicaid plan to the rest of the Medicaid population.[23] The goal of the EPSDT program is to assess the child's health needs through initial and periodic examinations and evaluations, and to assure that the health problems found are diagnosed and treated early, before they become more complex and their treatment more costly.

Fourth, for women, in addition to the preventive care and screenings identified by the Task Force, the preventive health benefit must also include any other preventive care and screenings for in comprehensive guidelines supported by the HRSA. The 2010 Health Care Reform Act provides that while the current recommendations of the Task Force regarding breast cancer screening, mammography, and prevention apply, the controversial Task Force recommendations regarding the recommended frequency of screening mammographies released in November 2009 are to be disregarded.[24]

---

[17] PPACA § 1201 (adding PHSA § 2704), 26 C.F.R. 54.9815-2704T, 29 C.F.R. § 2590.715-2704 and 45 C.F.R. § 147.108.

[18] 26 C.F.R. 54.9815-2704T(b)(2), 29 C.F.R. § 2590.715-2704(b)(2) and 45 C.F.R. § 147.108(b)(2).

[19] PPACA § 1001 (adding PHSA § 2718).

[20] The 2009 Guide to Clinical Preventive Services can be accessed at *http://www.ahrq.gov/clinic/pocketgd.htm.*

[21] The schedules are available from the CDC's Web site at *http://www.cdc.gov/vaccines/recs/schedules/default.htm.* Copies of the 2009 schedules for children, adolescents, and adults are reprinted in **Appendix G**.

[22] Adopted in the Omnibus Budget Reconciliation Act of 1989, Pub. L. No. 101-239, 103 Stat. 2106.

[23] 42 U.S.C. § 1396d(r)(5) (referencing 42 U.S.C. § 1396d(a) for the definition of health care service).

[24] PHSA § 2713(a)(5).

The Task Force, the CDC, and the HRSA update their recommendations from time to time. The 2010 Health Care Reform Act provides that HHS may establish a minimum interval between the date on which a recommendation or guideline is issued and the plan year with respect to which the requirement must be adopted. The minimum interval is to be at least one year.[25]

HHS also may develop guidelines that permit a group health plan or health insurance issuer offering group individual health insurance coverage to utilize value-based insurance designs (VBIDs).[26] VBID programs adjust the plan participant's cost-sharing to correlate it with the clinical benefit that the particular item or service may have for the individual. Thus, the more clinically beneficial the therapy for the patient, the lower that patient's cost-sharing obligation. Higher cost-sharing obligations apply to interventions with little or no proven benefit.[27]

The University of Michigan Center for Value-Based Insurance Design, established in 2005 to develop, evaluate, and promote value-based insurance initiatives, has a list of papers and other resources on this subject available on its Web site.[28]

§ 7.04   Extension of Coverage for Children Up to Age 26

[A]   General Rules

As noted in **Chapter 2**, young adults represent a significant portion (30 percent) of the Americans who lacked health insurance coverage prior to health care reform. Young adults have the lowest rate of access to employer-based coverage and lack the financial resources to cover health care bills when and if they should be incurred. Children also need coverage: one in six young adults has a chronic illness like cancer, diabetes, or asthma.[29]

The 2010 Health Care Reform Act addresses that need in several ways. First, it requires all group health plans and all health insurance issuers offering group or individual health insurance coverage that provide coverage for dependent children to continue to make that coverage available to adult children (regardless of the child's marital status) until the child attains age 26.[30] Second, the Act amends the Code to make the extended dependent coverage a pretax benefit for an employee or a deductible benefit for self-employed taxpayers.[31] Third, the Act provides for a high-deductible catastrophic coverage option for adults under age 30 participating in the Exchanges beginning in 2014. This section will discuss the extension of coverage requirements for group health plans and the corresponding tax implications. The Exchange plan for adults under age 30 is covered in **Chapter 10**.[32]

Effective for the first plan year beginning on or after September 23, 2010, any group health plan (insured or self-funded), including grandfathered health plans, and any individual insurance coverage that offers dependent coverage for children must make such coverage available to the employee or individual until the child attains age 26.[33] The 2010 Health Care Reform Act does not require a plan or policy to provide coverage for dependents, but, if coverage is available to dependents, the coverage must also be extended to older children.[34] Thus, if a group health plan or individual insurance policy does not offer coverage for anyone other than the employee or the individual, the requirement does

---

[25] PHSA § 2713(b).

[26] PHSA § 2713(c).

[27] *Health Affairs*, February 2010.

[28] *http://www.sph.umich.edu/vbidcenter/index.htm*.

[29] Young Adults and the Affordable Care Act: Protecting Young Adults and Eliminating Burdens on Families and Businesses, DOL briefing paper released with Dependent Coverage Interim Final Rules on May 9, 2010.

[30] PPACA § 1001 (adding PHSA § 2714), as amended by PPACA § 10103(d) and HCERA § 2301(b).

[31] HCERA § 1004(d) (amending I.R.C. §§ 105(b), 163(l), 501(c)(9), 401(h)).

[32] *See infra* **§ 10.04**.

[33] PHSA § 2714.

[34] PHSA § 2714(a).

not apply. This provision applies to all employment-based coverage, including grandfathered health plans.[35]

HHS, Treasury, and DOL have jointly issued interim final regulations interpreting the extended coverage requirement.[36] The agencies announced that surcharges for coverage of children under age 26 are not allowed except where the surcharges apply regardless of the age of the child. Plans cannot vary benefits or other terms of the plan or insurance coverage based on the age of the child.[37]

The tri-agency regulations also confirm that plans and issuers cannot limit dependent coverage to unmarried children.[38] However, a plan or issuer is not required to cover the spouse or the child of a covered child.[39] The regulations provide that conditioning coverage on whether a child is a tax dependent or a student, or resides with or receives financial support from the parent or is married, is no longer an appropriate factor for a child at any age under age 26 and plans or coverage may not use those requirements to deny coverage to children.[40]

The value of medical coverage or reimbursement of medical expenses provided by an employer to its employees and their spouses and dependent children is treated as tax-free compensation for employees for federal income tax purposes.[41] The 2010 Health Care Reform Act amends the Code to extend pretax treatment for employment-based health coverage provided to adult children of an employee up to the calendar year in which the child reaches age 27.[42] The amendments to the Code, which are effectively immediately, now base the tax-free treatment of dependent heath coverage solely on relationship and age.

Under Section 105(b) of the Code,[43] an employee may exclude from gross income the amounts paid to reimburse the employee for qualified medical expenses of the taxpayer, his spouse and his dependents as defined in Section 152 of the Code.[44] To be a dependent for purposes of receiving

---

[35] PPACA § 1251(a), as amended by HCERA § 2301(a).

[36] 45 C.F.R. §§ 147.000 et seq. Treas. Reg. §§ 54.9815-2714T et seq. (Treasury regulations); 29 C.F.R. §§ 2590.715-2714 et seq. (DOL regulations). See **Appendix H**.

[37] 45 C.F.R. § 147.120(d); Treas. Reg. § 54.9815-2714T(d); 29 C.F.R. § 2590.715-2714(d).

[38] 45 C.F.R. § 147.120(b); Treas. Reg. § 54.9815-2714T(b); 29 C.F.R. § 2590.715-2714(b).

[39] 45 C.F.R. § 147.120(c); Treas. Reg. § 54.9815-2714T(c); 29 C.F.R. § 2590.715-2714(c).

[40] 45 C.F.R. § 147.120(b); Treas. Reg. § 54.9815-2714T(b); 29 C.F.R. § 2590.715-2714(b).

[41] I.R.C. § 105(b).

[42] HCERA § 1004(d); see I.R.S. Notice 2010-38, 2010-20 I.R.B. 682 (addressing the tax treatment of extended coverage for dependents).

[43] Section 105(b) provides as follows:

"(b) Amounts expended for medical care. Except in the case of amounts attributable to (and not in excess of) deductions allowed under section 213 (relating to medical, etc., expenses) for any prior taxable year, gross income does not include amounts referred to in subsection (a) if such amounts are paid, directly or indirectly, to the taxpayer to reimburse the taxpayer for expenses incurred by him for the medical care (as defined in section 213(d)) of the taxpayer, his spouse, and his dependents (as defined in section 152, determined without regard to subsections (b)(1), (b)(2), and (d)(1)(B) thereof). Any child to whom section 152(e) applies shall be treated as a dependent of both parents for purposes of this subsection." I.R.C. § 105(b).

[44] Section 152 of the Code provides, in relevant part:

(c) Qualifying Child.—For purposes of this section—(1) In general.—The term "qualifying child" means, with respect to any taxpayer for any taxable year, an individual—(A) who bears a relationship to the taxpayer described in paragraph (2), (B) who has the same principal place of abode as the taxpayer for more than one-half of such taxable year, (C) who meets the age requirements of paragraph (3), (D) who has not provided over one-half of such individual's own support for the calendar year in which the taxable year of the taxpayer begins, and (E) who has not filed a joint return (other than only for a claim of refund with the individual's spouse under section 6013 for the taxable year beginning in the calendar year in which the taxable year of the taxpayer begins.

(2) Relationship.—For purposes of paragraph (1)(A), an individual bears a relationship to the taxpayer described in this paragraph if such individual is—(A) a child of the taxpayer or a descendant of such a child, or (B) a brother, sister, stepbrother, or stepsister of the taxpayer or a descendant of any such relative.

(3) Age requirements.—(A) In general.—For purposes of paragraph (1)(C), an individual meets the requirements of this paragraph if such individual is younger than the taxpayer claiming such individual as a qualifying child and—(i) has

tax-free health benefits, the individual must meet both a relationship and age test. The individual must be a child or descendent of such a child or a brother, sister, stepbrother, or stepsister of the taxpayer or a descendant of any such relative.[45] An adopted child stands in the same position as a natural child of the taxpayer.[46] The age test, prior to the enactment of the 2010 Health Care Reform Act, was under age 19, or for students, under age 24 as of the close of such calendar year.[47]

The 2010 Health Care Reform Act adds a new category of individuals eligible for tax-free employment-based coverage—"any child of the taxpayer who as of the end of the taxable year has not attained age 27."[48] Parallel amendments were also made to provide an equivalent deduction for self-employed taxpayers under Section 162(l)(1) of the Code.[49] The Act does not limit the tax-advantaged treatment of employment-based health coverage to "dependent" children, i.e., the residency and support requirements no longer apply.

To further address the tax issues associated with extended coverage for adult children, the Internal Revenue Service has issued guidance, in the form of Notice 2010-38, on the tax treatment of health coverage for children up to age 27.[50] The IRS guidance indicates that, effective March 30, 2010, employment-based health coverage for an employee's child who has not attained age 27 as of the end of the employee's taxable year is excluded from the employee's gross income for federal income tax purposes.[51] The IRS guidance provides five examples illustrating the new rule, including the following:

Example 1:   Employer X provides health care coverage for its employees and their spouses and dependents and for any employee's child (as defined in § 152(f)(1)) who has not attained age 26. For the 2010 taxable year, Employer X provides coverage to Employee A and to A's son, C. C will attain age 26 on November 15, 2010. During the 2010 taxable year, C is not a full-time student. C has never worked for Employer X. C is not a dependent of A because prior to the close

---

not attained the age of 19 as of the close of the calendar year in which the taxable year of the taxpayer begins, or (ii) is a student who has not attained the age of 24 as of the close of such calendar year. (B) Special rule for disabled.—In the case of an individual who is permanently and totally disabled (as defined in section 22(e)(3)) at any time during such calendar year, the requirements of subparagraph (A) shall be treated as met with respect to such individual."

I.R.C. §§ 152(c)(1), (2), (3).

Section 152(f) defines "child" as follows:

(f) Other Definitions and Rules.—For purposes of this section—(1) Child defined.—(A) In general.—The term "child" means an individual who is—(i) a son, daughter, stepson, or stepdaughter of the taxpayer, or (ii) an eligible foster child of the taxpayer. (B) Adopted child.—In determining whether any of the relationships specified in subparagraph (A)(i) or paragraph (4) exists, a legally adopted individual of the taxpayer, or an individual who is lawfully placed with the taxpayer for legal adoption by the taxpayer, shall be treated as a child of such individual by blood. (C) Eligible foster child.—For purposes of subparagraph (A)(ii), the term "eligible foster child" means an individual who is placed with the taxpayer by an authorized placement agency or by judgment, decree, or other order of any court of competent jurisdiction. (2) Student defined.—The term "student" means an individual who during each of 5 calendar months during the calendar year in which the taxable year of the taxpayer begins—(A) is a full-time student at an educational organization described in section 170(b)(1)(A)(ii), or (B) is pursuing a full-time course of institutional on-farm training under the supervision of an accredited agent of an educational organization described in section 170(b)(1)(A)(ii) or of a State or political subdivision of a State.

I.R.C. § 152(f).

[45] I.R.C. § 152(c)(2).

[46] I.R.C. § 152(f)(1)(B).

[47] I.R.C. § 152(c)(3).

[48] HCERA § 1004(d) (amending I.R.C. §§ 105(b), 162(l), 501(c)(9), 401(h) to include children of the taxpayer who had not attained age 27 before the close of the tax year).

[49] HCERA § 1004(d)(2).

[50] I.R.S. Notice 2010-38, 2010-20 I.R.B. 682. See **Appendix I**.

[51] I.R.S. Notice 2010-38, § II.

of the 2010 taxable year C had attained age 19 (and was also not a student who had not attained age 24).

C is a child of A within the meaning of § 152(f)(1). Accordingly, and because C will not attain age 27 during the 2010 taxable year, the health care coverage and reimbursements provided to him under the terms of Employer X's plan are excludible from A's gross income under §§ 106 and 105(b) for the period on and after March 30, 2010, through November 15, 2010 (when C attains age 26 and loses coverage under the terms of the plan).[52]

The examples affirm that status as a tax dependent (as defined in Section 152 of the Code) is not required to qualify for the tax exemption.

A grandfathered health plan is subject to the requirement to extend coverage to adult children up to age 26.[53] However, for plan years prior to January 1, 2014, grandfathered health plans may exclude an adult child from coverage if the adult child is eligible to enroll in another employer-sponsored health plan.[54] This special exclusion does not apply where the child is eligible for coverage under the plans of the employers of both parents to avoid a situation where each plan excludes the child based on eligibility for the other.[55] For plan years beginning on or after January 1, 2014, a grandfathered health plan can no longer use this special exclusion and must comply with all requirements of the extended coverage provision.[56] Employers will need to weigh whether the benefits of the special exclusion from the extended coverage requirement and other grandfathered health plan advantages outweigh the limited flexibility that employers will have to make changes to grandfathered health plans.

[B] Transitional Relief

When President Obama signed the 2010 Health Care Reform Act, many individuals with children graduating from school or reaching the current age limits of their plans in 2010 were surprised to learn that the extended coverage provision does not take effect until the first plan year beginning on or after September 23, 2010. While coverage is available for these children under COBRA or private health insurance, the cost is prohibitive for many. Due to overwhelming demand from the administration, HHS, and plan members, many insurance carriers have announced that they would voluntarily provide extended coverage for adult children as of May 1, 2010.[57]

Other children whose coverage had expired previously, but who are under age 26, want to re-enroll in their parents' coverage. The tri-agency regulations published on May 10, 2010, formalize the transitional procedures for children to return to coverage under the plan.[58] The transitional rules apply to individuals whose coverage ended or was denied and never started because their eligibility for dependent coverage ended before age 26. The coverage availability is required to be effective on the first day of the first plan year beginning on or after September 23, 2010.[59] For calendar year plans, this means no later than January 1, 2011.

---

[52] I.R.S. Notice 2010-38 § 11, Ex. 1.

[53] PPACA § 1251(a)(4)(A)(iv).

[54] PPACA § 1251(a)(4)(B)(ii).

[55] Preamble to tri-agency regulations on extended dependent coverage, pp. 11–12.

[56] PPAC § 1251(d)(4)(B)(ii).

[57] For For a list of the insurance companies, see *http://www.hhs.gov/ociio/regulations/adult_child_faq.html*.

[58] 45 C.F.R. § 147.120(f); Treas. Reg. § 54.9815-2714T(f); 29 C.F.R. § 2590.715-2714(f).

[59] PHSA § 2714.

[1] Notice of Enrollment Opportunity

Under the transitional rules, the plan or issuer is required to give the child a special opportunity to enroll that continues for at least 30 days.[60] The opportunity (including a written notice describing the enrollment opportunity) must be provided beginning not later than the first day of the first plan year beginning on or after September 23, 2010.[61] The written notice must include a statement that children whose coverage ended or who were denied coverage because the availability of the dependent coverage ended before the child attained age 26 are eligible to enroll for coverage.[62] It is unclear whether a child who was previously dropped from coverage for reasons other than expiration of eligibility is entitled to the special enrollment opportunity. The obligation to provide the notice of enrollment opportunity can be satisfied for both the plan and the issuer if the notice is provided to the employee or the individual on behalf of the child.[63] The notice may be included with other enrollment materials that a plan distributes to its employees, as long as the statement is prominent.[64]

[2] Terms of Enrollment

Any child who enrolls through the special enrollment opportunity must be treated as if enrolled under the HIPAA special enrollment rules, which means that the child will not be treated as a late enrollee.[65] The child must be offered all the benefit packages available to similarly situated individuals who did not lose coverage by reason of loss of dependent eligibility status.[66] There can be no difference in benefits or cost-sharing requirements, and the child cannot be required to pay more for coverage than similarly situated individuals who did not lose coverage by reason of cessation of dependent status.[67]

§ 7.05 Mandated Appeals Process

Group health plans and health insurance issuers offering group or individual health insurance coverage, other than grandfathered health plans and certain collectively bargained insured health plans, are required to implement appeals processes that comply with the 2010 Health Care Reform Act no later than the first day of the first plan year beginning on or after September 23, 2010.[68] The Act requires the appeals process to provide:

- An internal claims appeal process during which an enrollee may review his or her file, present evidence and testimony, and continue receiving coverage during the pendency of the internal appeals process.[69]

- An external claims appeal process during which an enrollee may review his or her file, present evidence and testimony, and continue receiving coverage during the pendency of the external appeals process.[70]

---

[60] 45 C.F.R. § 147.120(f)(2); Treas. Reg. § 54.9815-2714T(f)(2); 29 C.F.R. § 2590.715-2714(f)(2).

[61] 45 C.F.R. § 147.120(f)(2); Treas. Reg. § 54.9815-2714T(f)(2); 29 C.F.R. § 2590.715-2714(f)(2).

[62] 45 C.F.R. § 147.120(f)(2)(ii); Treas. Reg. § 54.9815-2714T(f)(2)(ii); 29 C.F.R. § 2590.715-2714(f)(2)(ii).

[63] 45 C.F.R. § 147.120(f)(2)(ii); Treas. Reg. § 54.9815-2714T(f)(2)(ii); 29 C.F.R. § 2590.715-2714(f)(2)(ii).

[64] 45 C.F.R. § 147.120(f)(2)(ii); Treas. Reg. § 54.9815-2714T(f)(2)(ii); 29 C.F.R. § 2590.715-2714(f)(2)(ii).

[65] 45 C.F.R. § 147.120(f)(4); Treas. Reg. § 54.9815-2714T(f)(4); 29 C.F.R. § 2590.715-2714(f)(4).

[66] 26 C.F.R. 54.9815-2714T(f)(4), 29 C.F.R. 2590.715-2714(f)(4), 45 C.F.R. 147.120(f)(4).

[67] 26 C.F.R. 54.9815-2714T(f)(4), 29 C.F.R. 2590.715-2714(f)(4), 45 C.F.R. 147.120(f)(4).

[68] PPACA § 1001 (adding PHSA § 2719), as amended by PPACA § 10101(g).

[69] PHSA § 2719(a).

[70] PHSA § 2719(b).

- Notice of the appeals process and the availability of any office of health insurance consumer assistance or ombudsman established under the 2010 Health Care Reform Act to assist enrollees with the appeals process, in a manner that is culturally and linguistically appropriate.[71]

These requirements are discussed separately below.

[A] Internal Claims Appeal Process

The internal claims appeal process required of a group health plan or health insurance issuer of group health coverage covered by ERISA is a process for filing and resolving claims and appeals that meets the standards issued from time to time by the DOL.[72] For employment-based group health plans that are insured and subject to both ERISA and state law, the 2010 Health Care Reform Act may require an insured group health plan to ignore any state law that imposes an internal claims appeal process that is different from the ERISA procedures. Further, there may be conflicts between DOL's current standards and the enrollee's rights under the Act to review his or her file and present testimony during the internal claims appeal review process. It seems that any such conflicts will not be considered violations of the Act, pending a DOL update of its claims procedure regulations.

Any health insurance issuer of individual health coverage and any other issuer that is not subject to standards issued by DOL under ERISA (e.g., group health plans of government and church employers) satisfy the internal claims appeals process requirement by complying with the process for filing and resolving claims and appeals in effect under the law applicable to these respective arrangements at the time of the 2010 Health Care Reform Act's enactment, until HHS updates such standards.[73] As with the current standards issued by DOL, it appears that any conflicts between the current laws, if any, applicable to these arrangements and the Act's requirements are permissible pending updates issued by HHS.

One potential concern is that the requirement that an enrollee continue to receive coverage during the pendency of an appeal could make the internal appeal process irrelevant when an adverse benefit determination relates to a service or treatment not currently provided to the enrollee. This concern will be alleviated if HHS interprets the continued coverage requirement to mean that the enrollee's right to receive other coverage (i.e., coverage unrelated to the subject of the internal appeal) provided by the plan is not interrupted during the pendency of any appeal.

[B] External Claims Appeal Process

An employment-based group health plan that is self-funded and that does not have to comply with state insurance regulations (e.g., a plan subject to ERISA) is required to implement an external review process that meets standards issued by HHS.[74] These standards are intended to be similar to state external review processes and at a minimum to reflect the consumer protections contained in the Uniform External Review Model Act issued by the National Association of Insurance Commissioners (NAIC External Review Act).[75] The most recent version of the NAIC External Review Act was issued by

---

[71] PHSA § 2719(a) (referencing PPACA § 1002, which adds PHSA § 2793, to award grants to states to establish offices of health insurance consumer assistance or health insurance ombudsman programs); *see infra* **§ 7.05[C]** notes 83–85 and accompanying text (addressing the consumer assistance and ombudsman provisions).

[72] 29 C.F.R. § 2560.503-1.

[73] PHSA § 2719(a)(2)(B).

[74] PHSA § 2719(b).

[75] PHSA § 2719(b).

NAIC in April 2010.[76] HHS presumably will issue guidance about the external review process standards that these plans can rely upon sufficiently in advance of September 23, 2010, for such guidance to be reflected in open enrollment materials provided to enrollees.

All other plans and health insurance issuers are required to comply with their applicable state external review processes, provided such processes reflect the consumer protections contained in the NAIC External Review Act.[77] Otherwise, such plans and health insurance issuers are required to implement an external review process that meets the standards issued by HHS for a self-funded plan that does not have to comply with state insurance regulations.[78] HHS presumably will provide guidance sufficiently in advance of September 23, 2010, for these plans and issuers to know which external review process is applicable to them and to communicate this process in the open enrollment materials provided to enrollees.

Employment-based group health plans that are self-funded generally do not have to comply with state insurance regulations and likely will be affected the most by the new external review requirement. These plans have rarely provided for any external review process, apart from an enrollee's right to challenge an adverse benefit determination in court.[79] Adverse benefit determinations by ERISA plans of this type generally are reviewed by a court based on the record developed during the plan's internal review process under a deferential review standard.[80] These plans, subject to the exceptions noted above, will now be required to provide an external review process under which, according to the NAIC External Review Act, the external reviewer is not limited to considering the information on which a plan administrator or claims administrator reached its adverse determination during the internal review process and cannot defer to the decisions or conclusions reached during the internal review process.

This represents, in the ERISA context, a fundamental shift of authority from the fiduciaries of a self-funded plan charged with the obligation to administer the plan to a third party chosen by HHS. Further, if the NAIC External Review Act is controlling in this respect, while it seems that the sponsor of a self-funded plan generally continues to have the right to determine the terms and conditions of coverage, this right may not extend to provisions that can be used to deny coverage based upon a service or treatment being experimental or investigational. Adverse benefit determinations of this type are evaluated on the basis of whether the service or treatment in question is more likely to be beneficial to an enrollee than a standard service or treatment, without substantially increasing the adverse risks of the enrollee.

The extent of a plan's ability to challenge a determination resulting from the external review process is unclear. Under the NAIC External Review Act, the rights of a health carrier and a participant or beneficiary are limited to the remedies available to them under state law.[81] A participant or beneficiary has a right under ERISA to bring a civil action for benefits payable under a plan.[82] Neither a plan nor a fiduciary of an ERISA plan has any right to challenge the benefits awarded to a participant or a beneficiary under an external review process, unless such action can be characterized as one that seeks to enjoin an act that violates the terms of the plan or to enforce the terms of the plan. Also unclear is the standard of review that a court reviewing the results of the external review process will apply. If the court is reviewing a determination upholding the result reached by the plan's internal review process, a deferential review standard appears appropriate. On the other hand, if a plan can

---

[76] See http://www.naic.org/documents/committees_b_uniform_health_carrier_ext_rev_model_act.pdf.

[77] PHSA § 2719(b).

[78] PHSA § 2719(b).

[79] ERISA § 502(a)(1)(B).

[80] See Firestone Tire & Rubber Co. v. Bruch, 489 U.S. 101 (1989) (discussing the deferential standard of review provided to plan administrators who decide claims).

[81] NAIC External Review Act, § 11; see supra note 76 for the Web site at which the Act is available.

[82] ERISA § 502(a)(1)(B).

bring a civil action challenging an external determination that overturns the results of a plan's internal review process, a deferential standard of review may not be appropriate.

[C] Office of Health Insurance Consumer Assistance or Ombudsman Established

The 2010 Health Care Reform Act provides funding for states to establish offices of health insurance consumer assistance or ombudsman.[83] To receive such funding, a state must create an independent position that deals with issues concerning "health insurance coverage with respect to federal health insurance requirements and under State law."[84] The Act generally uses the term "health insurance coverage" when referring to health insurance offered by insurance carriers.[85] One of this position's duties is provide assistance to enrollees filing internal appeals with group health plans or health insurance issuers. Whether such a position must or will be permitted to assist enrollees in self-funded plans with internal claims remains to be seen.

§ 7.06 Prohibitions on Rescissions

Another coverage improvement added by the 2010 Health Care Reform Act is a prohibition on the cancellation or rescission of coverage by a group health plan or a health insurance issuer offering group or individual health insurance coverage of an enrollee once the enrollee is covered under the plan or coverage.[86] There is an exception where a covered individual has performed an act or practice that constitutes fraud or an intentional misrepresentation of material fact.[87]

Coverage under a group health plan or health insurance generally may be cancelled only with notice and only as permitted under the law.[88] Generally, coverage may only be nonrenewed or discontinued by a health insurance issuer for the following reasons:

- Nonpayment of premiums.

- Fraud.

- Termination of the plan, where the issuer is ceasing to offer coverage in the individual market in accordance with applicable state law.

- Movement outside service area—where an individual no longer resides, lives, or works in the service area (or in an area for which the issuer is authorized to do business), but only if such coverage is terminated uniformly without regard to any health status–related factor of covered individuals.

- Association membership ceases—in the case of health insurance coverage that is made available in the individual market only through one or more bona fide associations, the membership of the individual in the association (on the basis of which the coverage is provided) ceases, but only if such coverage is terminated uniformly without regard to any health status–related factor of covered individuals.[89]

---

[83] PPACA § 1002 (adding PHSA § 2793).

[84] PHSA § 2793.

[85] *See supra* **Chapter 3** note 4 and accompanying text (defining health insurance coverage).

[86] PPACA § 1001 (adding PHSA § 2712).

[87] PHSA § 2712.

[88] PHSA § 2702.

[89] PHSA § 2712 (citing PHSA § 2741(b) for cancellation with notice provisions); 26 C.F.R. § 54.9815-2712T; 29 C.F.R. § 2590.715-2712; 45 C.F.R. § 147.128.

This provision will affect mostly individual health insurance coverage, as most group health plans are already subject to such prohibitions under HIPAA.[90]

The statute and regulations clarify that only an intentional misrepresentation will justify rescission. This may be a more protective standard than state law or federal common law previously provided.[91]

7.07   Patient Protections

[A]   Designation of Primary Care Physician

The 2010 Health Care Reform Act imposes upon group health plans (self-funded and insured) and individual health insurance coverage offered through an issuer, new requirements relating to a participant's choice of health care professional.[92] Three requirements relate to plans with network designs. A fourth requirement, relating to emergency services, applies to any type of plan. None of these requirements applies to grandfathered health plans.[93]

If a plan or policy requires a participant or beneficiary to designate a primary care provider, then the plan or issuer must permit each participant or beneficiary to designate any participating primary care provider who is available to accept such individual. The interim final regulations expand upon the statutory provision and provide that a plan or issuer must permit the designation of a primary care physician specializing in pediatrics if the covered person is a child.[94]

Likewise, if a plan or policy provides coverage for obstetrical or gynecological care and requires the designation of an in-network primary care provider, the plan may not require authorization or referral by the plan or primary care provider for a female participant or beneficiary to seek obstetrical or gynecological care by a physician specializing in obstetrics or gynecology. This provision is not intended to preclude a plan or issuer from requiring the obstetrician or gynecologist to comply with the policies and procedures of the plan or policy relating to pre-authorizations or referrals for certain items and services. The regulations also make it clear that these patient rights apply to health care professionals, a definition that includes any individual who is authorized under applicable state law to provide obstetrical or gynecological care, and not limited to a physician.[95]

Notice must be provided to each participant or beneficiary describing each of their rights with respect to the designation of a physician. The regulation includes model language:[96]

(A)   For plans and issuers that require or allow for the designation of primary care providers by participants or beneficiaries:

> *[Name of group health plan or health insurance issuer] generally [requires/ allows] the designation of a primary care provider. You have the right to designate any primary care provider who participates in our network and who is available to accept you or your family members. [If the plan or health insurance coverage designates a primary care provider automatically, insert: Until you make this designation, [name of group health plan or health insurance issuer] designates one for you.] For information on how to select a primary care provider, and*

---

[90] PHSA §§ 2731 (as renumbered by PPACA § 1001(3)) (guaranteeing availability of insurance coverage in the small-group market); 2742 (guaranteeing availability of insurance coverage for certain individuals).

[91] 75 Fed. Reg. 37192.

[92] PHSA § 2719A.

[93] 26 C.F.R. § 54.9815-2719AT, § 29 C.F.R. 2590.715-2719A, 45 C.F.R. § 147.138.

[94] 26 C.F.R. § 54.9815-2719AT(a)(2), § 29 C.F.R. 2590.715-2719A(a)(2), 45 C.F.R. § 147.138(a)(2).

[95] 26 C.F.R. § 54.9815-2719AT(a)(3)(i)(B), § 29 C.F.R. 2590.715-2719A(a)(3)(i)(B), 45 C.F.R. § 147.138(a)(3)(i)(B).

[96] 26 C.F.R. § 54.9815-2719AT(a)(4)(iii), 29 C.F.R. § 2590.715-2719A(a)(4)(iii), 45 C.F.R. § 147.138(a)(4)(iii).

for a list of the participating primary care providers, contact the [plan adminis-trator or issuer] at [insert contact information].

(B) For plans and issuers that require or allow for the designation of a primary care provider for a child, add:

> *For children, you may designate a pediatrician as the primary care provider.*

(C) For plans and issuers that provide coverage for obstetric or gynecological care and require the designation by a participant or beneficiary of a primary care provider, add:

> *You do not need prior authorization from [name of group health plan or issuer] or from any other person (including a primary care provider) in order to obtain access to obstetrical or gynecological care from a health care professional in our network who specializes in obstetrics or gynecology. The health care professional, however, may be required to comply with certain procedures, including obtaining prior authorization for certain services, following a pre-approved treatment plan, or procedures for making referrals. For a list of participating health care professionals who specialize in obstetrics or gynecology, contact the [plan administrator or issuer] at [insert contact information].*

[B] Coverage of Emergency Services

If a group health plan (self-funded or insured) provides any benefits with respect to an emergency department of a hospital, coverage must be provided:

- Without the need for any prior authorization determination, even if provided on an out-of-network basis;
- Without regard to whether the health care provider furnishing the emergency services is a participating provider;
- Without imposing any administrative requirement or limitation on coverage that is more restrictive than the requirements that apply to an in-network provider;
- Without imposing cost-sharing requirements (copayments and co-insurance amounts) that exceed the cost-sharing requirements applicable to an in-network provider (although the participant may be required to pay the excess of charges over the amount the plan or policy pays the out-of-network provider, i.e., balance billing is permitted); and
- Without regard to any other term or condition of coverage other than exclusion of or coordination of benefits, applicable waiting period and cost-sharing.

The regulations require a plan or policy to pay an out-of-network provider a reasonable amount for its services. A plan or issuer satisfies the copayment and co-insurance provisions if it pays an out-of-network provider an amount equal to the greater of (1) the negotiated contract rate with in-network providers (or the median thereof), (2) the amount calculated using the same method that the plan generally uses to determine payments for out-of-network services but substituting the in-network cost-sharing provisions for the out-of-network cost-sharing provisions, or (3) the amount Medicare would pay for the service.[97]

---

[97] 26 C.F.R. § 54.9815-2719AT(b)(3), 29 C.F.R. § 2590.715-2719A(b)(3), 45 C.F.R. § 147.138(b)(3).

The regulations define the terms *emergency medical condition, emergency services*, and *stabilize*, consistent with the definitions found in the Emergency Medical Treatment and Labor Act (EMTALA),[98] except that the definition of an emergency medical condition is based on the judgment of a prudent layperson, whereas the standard in EMTALA is based on the judgment of qualified hospital medical personnel. "Emergency medical condition" is defined as a medical condition manifesting itself by acute symptoms of sufficient severity (including severe pain) so that a prudent layperson who possesses an average knowledge of health and medicine could reasonably expect the absence of immediate medical attention to result in placing the health of the individual in serious jeopardy, serious impairment of bodily functions or serious dysfunction of any bodily organ or part.[99] "Emergency services" includes emergency screening and treatment sufficient to stabilize the patient.

---

[98] Section 1867 of the Social Security Act, 42 U.S.C. § 1395dd.
[99] 26 C.F.R. § 54.9815-2719AT(b)(4)(i), 29 C.F.R. § 2590.715-2719A(b)(4)(i), 45 C.F.R. § 147.138(b)(4)(i).

IMPROVEMENTS EFFECTIVE JANUARY 1, 2014

A number of the most important coverage reforms become effective as of January 1, 2014,[1] i.e., when the Exchanges become available for individuals and certain small employers, and the employer and individual coverage mandates also become effective.[2] These reforms include prohibitions on pre-existing conditions for individuals age 19 and older, guaranteed issue and renewability, fair insurance premium pricing requirements, health status discrimination prohibitions, and limitations on annual cost-sharing and deductible requirements. In coordinating the timing of the reforms with the mandates, Congress acknowledged that without the mandates, the insurance market reforms may lead to unsustainable adverse selection, particularly for the individual insurance market. If you prohibit pre-existing condition exclusion provisions and require guaranteed eligibility for enrollment in the individual insurance market, but do not mandate continuous coverage, individuals would only buy coverage when they need it. This is contrary to sound insurance principles and financing of risk.

Most of the market reforms discussed in this chapter apply to coverage offered by health insurance issuers, either in individual or group health plan coverage. Some of the reforms also apply to self-funded group health plans and a few of the reforms apply to grandfathered health plans. In the detailed descriptions of the reforms that follows, we make note of the types of plans subject to the requirements.

§ 8.01 Prohibitions on Pre-Existing Coverage Exclusions and Other Health Status Discrimination

The 2010 Health Care Reform Act prohibits all pre-existing condition exclusions by group health plans and individual health coverage offered by health insurance issuers.[3] By so doing, health insurers as well as group health plans are now prohibited from imposing certain pre-existing condition exclusions and establishing eligibility based on health status–related factors of the individual or a dependent of an individual. These provisions apply to grandfathered health plans.

[A] Prohibition on Pre-Existing Condition Exclusions

Pre-existing condition exclusions generally have been limited for employment-based health care coverage since the adoption of HIPAA in 1986.[4] As discussed in Chapter 7, no pre-existing exclusion limitation is applicable to enrollees in the individual or group insurance markets who are under age 19 for plan years beginning on or after September 23, 2010.[5] As of January 1, 2014, pre-existing condition exclusions are prohibited even after age 19 in group health plans and the individual insurance market.

[B] Prohibitions on Discrimination Based on Health Status

The 2010 Health Care Reform Act extends health status discrimination prohibitions to the individual health insurance coverage market.[6] This change imposes on issuers of individual health insurance coverage the health status discrimination, premium contribution restrictions, genetic information discrimination, genetic testing limitations, and genetic data collection prohibitions currently applicable to group health plans.[7]

---

[1] These reforms are found in Subtitle C of Title I of the Act.
[2] See **Chapter 10** for a discussion of the Exchanges and the individual and employer coverage mandates.
[3] PPACA § 1201 (adding PHSA § 2704).
[4] 42 U.S.C. § 300gg(a).
[5] See **§ 7.02**, *supra*.
[6] PPACA § 1201 (adding PHSA § 2705).
[7] 42 U.S.C. § 300gg-1.

The PHSA currently specifies the following health status–related factors:

- Health status;
- Medical condition;
- Claims experience;
- Receipt of health care;
- Medical history;
- Genetic information;
- Evidence of insurability (including conditions arising out of acts of domestic violence); and
- Disability.[8]

The 2010 Health Care Reform Act authorizes HHS to add any other health status factor determined appropriate.

[C] Employer Health and Wellness Programs

The 2010 Health Care Reform Act provides that health promotion and disease prevention programs offered by an employer that meet certain requirements will not violate the prohibition on discrimination on the basis of health status.[9]

An employer may offer a premium discount, rebate, or other reward for participation in a wellness program if the reward is not conditioned upon an individual satisfying a standard that is related to a health status factor.[10] A reward may be in the form of a discount or rebate of a premium or contribution, a waiver of all or part of a cost-sharing obligation (such as deductibles, copayments, or co-insurance), the absence of a surcharge, or the value of a benefit that would otherwise not be provided by the plan.[11] If the employer desires to condition the reward upon an individual satisfying a standard that is related to a health status factor, additional requirements are imposed. They include:

- The reward may not exceed 30 percent of the cost of employee-only coverage or, if dependents are fully eligible for the wellness program, 30 percent of the cost of such coverage (the total of the employer and employee contributions) under the plan;

- The program must be reasonably designed to promote health or prevent disease (i.e., has a reasonable chance of improving health or preventing disease and is not a subterfuge for discriminating based on health status);

- Eligible individuals must be given the opportunity to qualify for the reward at least once each year;

- The full reward must be made available to all similarly situated individuals; and

- The plan or issuer involved must describe the availability of the reasonable alternative (or possibility of a waiver) in any plan materials that describe the terms of the wellness program.[12]

To be available to all similarly situated individuals, the reward program must include a reasonable alternative standard (or waiver of the applicable standard) for obtaining the reward for any individual for whom it is unreasonably difficult or medically inadvisable, due to a medical condition, to

---

[8] PHSA § _____.
[9] PPACA § 1201 (adding PHSA § 2705(j)).
[10] PHSA § 2705(j)(2).
[11] PHSA § 2705(j)(2).
[12] PHSA § 2705(j)(3).

satisfy the conditions of the reward.[13] The plan or issuer may seek verification from the individual's physician to substantiate the unreasonableness or medical inadvisability of the condition.[14]

Existing employer wellness programs that meet all applicable regulations may continue for as long as the regulations remain in effect.

[D] Wellness Program Demonstration Projects for Health Insurance Issuers

HHS is directed to establish a 10-state demonstration project by July 1, 2014, under which states may apply the employer wellness program provisions to insured plans.[15]

§ 8.02 Fair Health Insurance Premiums

To make coverage more affordable for everyone, the 2010 Health Care Reform Act includes prohibitions on "discriminatory premium rates" charged by health insurance issuers for health insurance issued in the individual or small-group market and defines certain underwriting restrictions on the rate-setting of premiums.[16] For the large-group market (defined as more than 100 employees unless a state elects to define the small-group market as no more than 50 employees, in which case the large-group market would be more than 50 employees), these requirements apply to any coverage offered through a state Exchange to the large group market.[17]

Under the 2010 Health Care Reform Act, the premium rates for individual and small group health insurance coverage may vary with respect to a particular plan or coverage only by:

- Whether such plan covers an individual or family;

- Geographical rating areas to be established by each state;

- Permissible age bands to be established by HHS in consultation with the NAIC (except that the rate may not vary by more than 3 to 1 for adults); and

- Tobacco use (except that the rate may not vary by more than 1.5 to 1).[18]

Underwriting of premiums cannot be based on any other factor, including the claims experience of a small group.

The impact of these reforms on small insured employer group health plans will depend on the demographics and claims experience of the group. If the group is younger and healthier than the average small group, the cost of coverage may increase. On the other hand, a small group of older participants with more medical needs or a small group with one or more individuals with substantial claims experience should be able to purchase coverage on a more affordable and stable premium basis. These provisions do not apply to grandfathered health plans.

§ 8.03 Guaranteed Issue and Renewability

Throughout the course of the health care reform debate, terrible stories were featured in the media about individuals losing their jobs and being uninsurable thereafter or having their coverage cancelled when the insurance company learned that the participant or a dependent now had a chronic or serious medical condition. The insurance market reforms are designed to end those insurance practices.

---

[13] PHSA § 2705(j)(3)(D).

[14] PHSA § 2705(j)(3)(D).

[15] PPACA § 1201 (adding PHSA § 2705(l)).

[16] PPACA § 1201 (adding PHSA § 2701).

[17] PHSA § 2701; *see supra* **Chapter 3** notes 7–9 (defining large- and small-group markets).

[18] PHSA § 2701(a).

Beginning in 2014, each health insurance issuer that offers health insurance in the individual or group market in a state must accept every employer and every individual who applies for coverage.[19] The issuer may restrict enrollment to open or special enrollment periods as described in regulations to be published by HHS. Likewise, the 2010 Health Care Reform Act requires each issuer to renew or continue in force the coverage at the option of the employer or the individual.[20] These provisions apply to grandfathered health plans.

§ 8.04   Prohibiting Discrimination Against Health Care Providers

Another provision of the 2010 Health Care Reform Act that applies to both group health plans and health insurance issuers offering group or individual health insurance coverage, other than grandfathered health plans and certain collectively bargained plans, prohibits discrimination against any health care provider who is acting within the scope of the provider's license or certification under applicable state law.[21] An example of the application of this provision is benefits coverage that covers acupuncture services only if provided by a licensed physician. If the state where the coverage is offered licenses acupuncturists and the services that are covered under the plan if provided by a physician are within the scope of the acupuncturist's license, the coverage would have to include services performed by the acupuncturist as well as the physician. This is a significant change for employment-based group health plans because they can no longer limit reimbursements to only certain types of providers (e.g., doctor vs. chiropractor).

This is not an "any willing provider" provision;[22] the 2010 Health Care Reform Act specifies that a group health plan or insurance issuer shall not be required to contract with any health care provider willing to abide by the terms and conditions for participation established by the plan.[23] Thus, a plan can limit the number of participating providers in the network. A plan or issuer may also establish varying reimbursement rates based on quality or performance measures.

§ 8.05   Quality Coverage Provisions

[A]   Comprehensive Benefits Coverage in Individual and Small-Group Markets

The 2010 Health Care Reform Act's market reforms also require a health insurance issuer who offers health insurance coverage in the individual or small-group market to ensure that the coverage includes the essential health benefits package required for Exchange plans.[24] For a full description of those requirements, see **Section 10.04**.

[B]   Cost-Sharing Limits on Group Health Plans

Group health plans, other than grandfathered health plans and certain collectively bargained plans, are required to ensure that any annual cost-sharing imposed under the plan does not exceed the limits imposed on Exchange plans.[25] Beginning in 2014, the cost-sharing limit is $2,000 for single coverage and $4,000 for family coverage.[26] See **Section 10.04[E]** for a more complete description of the annual cost-sharing limitations.

---

[19] PPACA § 1201 (adding PHSA § 2702).

[20] PPACA § 1201 (adding PHSA § 2703).

[21] PPACA § 1201 (adding PHSA § 2706).

[22] *See* Kentucky Ass'n of Health Plans v. Nichols, 227 F.3d 352 (6th Cir. 2000) (considering ERISA pre-emption of the Kentucky AWP statute).

[23] PHSA § 2706.

[24] PPACA § 1201 (adding PHSA § 2702(a)).

[25] PPACA § 1201 (adding PHSA § 2707(b)).

[26] PHSA § 2707(b) (referencing the deductible limit for HSAs, as set forth in Section 223(c)(2)(A)(ii) of the Code).

§ 8.06 Limits on Waiting Periods

Group health plans and health insurers, other than certain collectively bargained plans, offering group health insurance coverage may not impose any waiting period for coverage in excess of 90 days.[27] The impact of this requirement will be felt most acutely by employers with high-turnover workforces, which may currently have longer waiting periods to avoid the cost of coverage for short-term employees. In addition to increasing the cost of coverage for the employer, it may also increase the administrative burden on a group health plan with respect to COBRA continuation administration and elections by short-term employees to opt out of coverage initiated under the large-employer automatic enrollment provisions. See **Section 11.03** for more information on large-employer automatic enrollment requirements.

§ 8.07 Coverage for Individuals Participating in Approved Clinical Trials

Coverage for medical services provided to a participant in a clinical trial has long been a subject of debate and dispute. The 2010 Health Care Reform Act clarifies the obligation of a group health plan or a health insurance issuer, other than grandfathered health plans and certain collectively bargained plans, offering group or individual health coverage to cover routine patient costs that would be covered if the participant were not in a study.[28] The requirements are effective beginning January 1, 2014.

The clinical trial must be an approved phase I, II, III, or IV clinical trial that is a federally funded trial, an investigational new drug application subject to FDA review, or a drug trial that is exempt from having an investigational new drug application.[29] The clinical trial must be conducted in relation to the prevention, detection or treatment of cancer or other life-threatening disease or condition, i.e., any disease or condition from which the likelihood of death is probable unless the course of the disease or condition is interrupted.[30]

A plan or insurance policy may not deny or impose additional conditions upon coverage of a qualified individual's routine patient costs for items or services furnished in connection with a study.[31] The individual must be eligible according to the trial protocol, and either the individual must be referred to the clinical trial by a participating health care provider or the participant or beneficiary must provide medical and scientific information establishing that the individual's participation in the study would be appropriate.[32]

The plan is not required to cover the cost of the investigational item, device, or service itself, items that are provided solely to satisfy data collection and analysis needs and that are not used in direct clinical management of the patient, or any service that is clearly inconsistent with widely accepted standards of care.[33]

If a participating provider is participating in a clinical trial, a plan or issuer may require the participant to participate through a participating provider, if the provider will accept the participant in the study. If the study is conducted outside the state in which the participant resides, the plan or issuer must provide the coverage. If a plan or issuer does not provide coverage for out-of-network benefits, the plan or issuer is not obligated to provide benefits provided outside the coverage's health care provider network.[34]

---

[27] PPACA § 1201 (adding PHSA § 2708).

[28] PPACA § 10103(c) (adding PHSA § 2709).

[29] PHSA § 2709(d).

[30] PHSA § 2709(e).

[31] PHSA § 2708(a)(2).

[32] PHSA § 2709(b).

[33] PHSA § 2709(b)(2)(B).

[34] PHSA § 2709(c).

TRANSPARENCY AND ACCOUNTABILITY

The 2010 Health Care Reform Act imposes numerous reporting and disclosure requirements on group health plans and health insurance issuers to make information about coverage options available to consumers. It also directs HHS to make most of that information available to the public on Web sites and a portal established for this purpose. Many of the data reporting and communication requirements begin during the transition period (March 23, 2010–January 1, 2014).

§ 9.01   Uniform Summary of Benefits and Coverage

Within 24 months of enactment (i.e., by March 23, 2012), every health insurance issuer and, in the case of an employment-based group health plan that is self-funded, the plan sponsor or designated administrator of each plan (e.g., a third-party administrator), must provide to each applicant, enrollee, and policyholder a summary of benefits and coverage.[1]

The 2010 Health Care Reform Act sets forth, in great detail, the standards for the summary, which must not exceed four pages in length and not include print smaller than 12-point type.[2] The purpose is to have each plan uniformly summarized so that an individual consumer can use the summary to compare health insurance coverage and understand the terms of his or her coverage.

[A]   Culturally and Linguistically Appropriate Communication

Each summary must be presented in a culturally and linguistically appropriate manner and utilize terminology understandable by the average plan enrollee.[3] HHS has issued national standards for culturally and linguistically appropriate services (CLAS) in health care.[4] CMS commissioned a paper on the subject, which defines these terms as follows.[5]

Linguistic Competence: Providing readily available, culturally appropriate oral and written language services to limited English proficiency (LEP) members through such means as bilingual/bicultural staff, trained medical interpreters, and qualified translators.

Cultural Competence: A set of congruent behaviors, attitudes, and policies that come together in a system or agency or among professionals that enables effective interactions in a cross-cultural framework.

Cultural and Linguistic Competence: The ability of health care providers and health care organizations to understand and respond effectively to the cultural and linguistic needs brought by the patient to the health care encounter.

Cultural competence requires organizations and their personnel to:

value diversity;
assess themselves;
manage the dynamics of difference;
acquire and institutionalize cultural knowledge; and
adapt to diversity and the cultural contexts of individuals and communities served.

There are currently 14 CLAS standards, of which four are mandated standards for all health care organizations and other recipients of federal funds.[6] The mandated standards include providing competent language assistance services, including interpreter services, at no cost to each patient/consumer

---

[1] PPACA § 1001 (adding PHSA § 2715).

[2] PHSA § 2715(b)(1).

[3] PHSA § 2715(b)(2).

[4] *See http://minorityhealth.hhs.gov/templates/browse.aspx?lvl=2&lvlID=15* (for health care organizations) and *www.ahrq.gov/about/cods/planclas.htm* (for managed care plans).

[5] *What Is Cultural and Linguistic Competence?* (February 2003), Agency for Healthcare Research and Quality, Rockville, Md. *http://www.ahrq.gov/about/cods/cultcompdef.htm.*

[6] http://minorityhealth.hhs.gov/templates/browse.aspx?lvl=2&lvlID=15.

with limited English proficiency at all points of contact in a timely manner during all hours of operation; verbal offers and written notices in the preferred language of the patients/consumers informing them of their right to receive language assistance; and providing patients/consumers with easily understood patient-related materials and signage in the languages of commonly encountered groups.[7] While these standards are applicable to health care providers, they are instructive to health plans as well. For example, the summary should advise participants of the availability of language assistance or written notices in their preferred language.

[B]　Use of Uniform Definitions of Standard Insurance Terms and Medical Terms

HHS is directed to issue, within 12 months of the enactment of the law, standard definitions of insurance-related and medical terms to be used in the summary and other communications with individuals.[8]

The insurance-related terms will include terms such as:

- Premium;
- Deductible;
- Co-insurance;
- Copayment;
- Out-of-pocket limit;
- Preferred provider;
- Non-preferred provider;
- Out-of-network copayments;
- Usual, customary, and reasonable (UCR) fees;
- Excluded services;
- Grievance and appeals;

and other terms that HHS determines are important to define.

The medical terms to be defined include:

- Hospitalization;
- Hospital outpatient care;
- Emergency room care;
- Physician services;
- Prescription drug coverage;
- Durable medical equipment;
- Home health care;
- Skilled nursing care;
- Rehabilitation services;

---

[7] See http://minorityhealth.hhs.gov/templates/browse.aspx?lvl=2&lvlID=15. See also Compendium of Cultural Competence, Initiatives in Health Care, The Henry J. Kaiser Family Foundation, January 2003, at http://www.kff.org/uninsured/loader.cfm?url=/commonspot/security/getfile.cfm&PageID=14365.

[8] PHSA § 2715(a).

- Hospice services;
- Emergency medical transportation;

and such other terms as HHS determines are important to define.[9]

[C] Benefits Description

The summary must describe the benefits coverage, including:

1. Cost-sharing for each of the categories of the essential health benefits[10] and other benefits, as identified by HHS;

2. Any exceptions, reductions, and limitations on coverage;

3. The cost-sharing provisions, including deductible, co-insurance, and copayment obligations;

4. The renewability and continuation of coverage provisions;

5. A coverage facts label that includes examples to illustrate common benefits scenarios, including pregnancy and serious or chronic medical conditions and related cost-sharing, with such scenarios based on recognized clinical practice guidelines;

6. A statement of whether the plan or coverage provides minimum essential coverage (as defined under Section 5000A(f) of the Code), and ensures that the plan or coverage share of the total allowed costs of benefits provided under the plan or coverage is not less than 60 percent of costs;

7. A statement that the outline is a summary of the plan, policy, or certificate and that the plan or coverage document itself should be consulted to determine the governing contractual provisions; and

8. A contact number for the individual to call with additional questions and an Internet Web address where a copy of the actual plan document, individual coverage policy, or group certificate of coverage can be reviewed and obtained.[11]

If a plan makes any material modifications in any of the terms involved, the summary must be updated to provide notice of the modification to enrollees not later than 60 days prior to the date that the modification becomes effective.[12] By way of comparison, the current requirement applicable to employment-based group health plans subject to ERISA is that notice of any material reduction in coverage must be provided not later than 60 days *after* its date of adoption.[13]

Any entity that willfully fails to provide the notice shall be subject to a fine of not more than $1,000 for each such failure. A failure with respect to each enrollee shall constitute a separate offense for purposes of this fine.[14]

§ 9.02 Reporting on Claims Practices and Plan Financing

Another transparency provision requires group health plans and health insurers in the group health and individual markets (other than grandfathered health plans and certain collectively bargained

---

[9] PHSA § 2715(g).

[10] Essential health benefits are defined in Section 1302(b) of the PPACA. *See* **§ 10.04[C][1]**.

[11] PHSA § 2715(b)(3).

[12] PHSA § 2715(d)(4) (referencing ERISA § 102 for a description of what constitutes a material modification).

[13] 29 C.F.R. § 2520.104b-3(d).

[14] PHSA § 2715(f).

plans) to submit accurate and timely disclosures to participants of group health plans of plan terms and conditions, periodic financial disclosures, and other information required by standards to be established by HHS.[15] The information covers such items as claims payment policies and practices, cost-sharing and claims payments information, and information on enrollee and participant rights.[16] The information must be submitted to HHS and the state insurance commission, and made available to the public.[17]

§ 9.03   Quality-of-Care Reporting

For years, the federal government has attempted to drive various quality-of-care initiatives through Medicare reimbursement policies. Under the 2010 Health Care Reform Act, these measures are expanded to the group health plan and health insurance market (other than grandfathered health plans and certain collectively bargained plans). By March 23, 2012, HHS must issue regulations providing criteria for determining whether the reimbursement structures of a group health plan or health insurance coverage improve health outcomes, prevent hospital readmissions, improve patient safety, reduce medical errors, and promote health and wellness activities.[18] Thereafter, each group health plan and health insurance issuer will be required to report annually regarding the extent to which the design of its plan or coverage satisfies the criteria.[19]

The reports are to be filed with HHS and made available to enrollees or potential enrollees during each open enrollment period.[20] HHS is also directed to make the reports available to the public through an Internet Web site.[21] The regulations may include appropriate penalties for noncompliance with the reporting obligation.

HHS must develop the reporting criteria by March 2012 in consultation with experts in health care quality and stakeholders. The criteria must address implementation activities such as quality reporting, effective case management, care coordination, chronic disease management, and medication and care compliance initiatives, including the use of the medical homes model[22] for treatments and services under the plan or coverage.[23]

In addition, the 2010 Health Care Reform Act suggests that health plans should also have reimbursement structures that address provider performance by implementing activities to prevent hospital readmissions through a comprehensive program for hospital discharge that includes patient-centered education and counseling, comprehensive discharge planning, and post-discharge reinforcement by an appropriate health care professional.[24] Likewise, plans will have to report on their activities addressing patient safety and medical error reduction through the appropriate use of best clinical practices, evidence-based medicine, and health information technology. For health plans, these provisions are designed to encourage the private payer market (employer plans and insured plans) to adopt programs similar to those initiated by Medicare. For example, with respect to medical error reduction, in 2008

---

[15] PPACA § 10101(c) (adding PHSA § 2715A).

[16] PHSA § 2715A (referencing PPACA § 1311(e)(3)).

[17] PHSA § 2715A.

[18] PPACA § 1001 (adding PHSA § 2717).

[19] PHSA § 2717(a)(2).

[20] PHSA § 2717(a)(2).

[21] PHSA § 2717(a)(2)(C).

[22] A medical home is an evolving approach to managing the medical care of patients through their primary care physician. A new generation of the gatekeeper model of reimbursement, focused on quality outcomes and chronic disease management, it is a team-based model of care led by a personal physician who provides continuous and coordinated care throughout a patient's lifetime to maximize health outcomes. American Academy of Family Physicians, American Academy of Pediatrics, American College of Physicians, and American Osteopathic Association, *Joint principles of the patient-centered medical home (March 2007)*, http://www.acponline.org/advocacy/where_we_stand/medical_home/approve_jp.pdf.

[23] PHSA 2717(a)(1)(A).

[24] PHSA § 2717(a)(1).

Medicare stopped reimbursing claims of health care providers for services related to incidents that Medicare classified as medical errors that are "serious, largely preventable and of concern to both the public and health care providers."[25] Commonly referred to as "never events," the medical errors so classified in 2010 include such non-reimbursable conditions as:

- Wrong surgical or other invasive procedures performed on a patient;
- Surgical or other invasive procedures performed on the wrong body part;
- Surgical or other invasive procedures performed on the wrong patient;
- Objects left in after surgery;
- Air embolisms;
- Blood incompatibility;
- Pressure ulcers;
- Falls in the hospital;
- Catheter-associated urinary tract infections;
- Catheter-associated vascular infections;
- Mediastinitis after CABG;
- Inadequate glycemic control;
- Surgical site infections;
- Deep vein thrombosis and pulmonary embolism; and
- Drug-induced delirium.[26]

Medicare has also initiated various pay-for-performance and other reimbursement programs to provide financial incentives for improved health quality outcomes. These are the types of reimbursement structures that HHS will most likely address when it issues the quality reporting regulations.

Finally, each plan or issuer will have to report on its health and wellness programs.[27] The 2010 Health Care Reform Act defines health and wellness programs as including:

- Smoking cessation;
- Weight management;
- Stress management;
- Physical fitness;
- Nutrition;
- Heart disease prevention;
- Healthy lifestyle support; and
- Diabetes prevention.[28]

---

[25] Centers for Medicare and Medicaid Services, Inpatient Prospective Payment System (IPPS) FY 2009, 73 Fed. Reg. 49796 (Aug. 22, 2008).

[26] Medicare Benefit Policy Manual, *http://www.cms.gov/manuals/Downloads.*

[27] PHSA § 2717(b).

[28] PHSA § 2717(b).

The 2010 Health Care Reform Act's health and wellness provision includes an express protection of each individual health plan member's Second Amendment right to own or possess a gun.[29] The Act prohibits a health and wellness program provided under a plan or coverage from collecting any data relating to the presence or storage of a lawfully possessed firearm or ammunition in the residence or on the property of an individual or the lawful use, possession, or storage of a firearm or ammunition by an individual.[30] Accordingly, no health risk assessment program can include questions about firearms or ammunition in the home. HHS is prohibited from collecting any such information and the Act shall not be construed as authorizing the collection of any data or maintenance of any records or data banks with any such information. Further, a premium rate may not be increased on the basis of an individual's ownership or residency in a home where firearms or ammunition are possessed or stored.

The first quality outcomes reports will need to be filed by health plans shortly after the publication of the regulations, as the 2010 Health Care Reform Act calls for an independent report on the impact of the reporting six months later.[31] Not later than 180 days after the publication of the regulations, the Government Accountability Office is supposed to report to committees of the U.S. Senate and House of Representatives on the impact that the activities have had on the quality and cost of health care.

§ 9.04　　The Cost of Care

To spur immediate change in the health insurance markets in advance of the introduction of the Exchanges in 2014, there are three measures that take effect immediately. Two address health insurance issuers only (and not employment-based group health plans that are self-funded) and relate to the use of premium revenues. The third relates to the transparency of hospital charges.

[A]　Insurance Company Reporting to HHS for Clear Accounting

To promote "clear accounting" for costs by health insurance issuers, each insurance issuer offering group or individual health insurance coverage (including group coverage offered as a grandfathered health plan) will be required to submit to HHS a report regarding the ratio of the incurred loss (or incurred claims) plus the loss adjustment expense (or change in contract reserves) to earned premiums.[32] The report must include the percentage of total premium revenue for the coverage, after accounting for collections or receipts for risk adjustment and risk corridors and payments of reinsurance, that the insurer spends on (1) reimbursement for clinical services, (2) health care quality improvement and (3) non-claims costs.[33] For non-claims costs, the report must include an explanation of the nature of the costs, excluding state taxes and licensing or regulatory fees.

By December 31, 2010, the National Association of Insurance Commissioners (NAIC) is directed to establish uniform definitions of the types of activities that may be included in each expenditure category and standardized methods for calculating measures of such activities.[34] The NAIC is also to define what activities constitute health care quality improvement costs. In doing so, the NAIC must address special circumstances that may exist for smaller plans, different types of plans, and newer plans. The NAIC's standards are subject to certification by HHS.

The reports will be made available to the public on an HHS Web site.

---

[29] Section 2717(c) of the Public Health Services Act.
[30] PHSA § 2717(b).
[31] PHSA § 2717(e).
[32] PPACA § 1001 (adding PHSA § 2718).
[33] PHSA § 2718(a).
[34] PHSA § 2718(c).

[B] Health Insurance Rebates When Non-Claims Costs Are Too High

Another key provision of PPACA aimed at containing the cost of health insurance coverage that begins immediately relates to the amount of premium revenue spent by a health care insurer on costs other than medical claims reimbursement.[35] Beginning not later than January 1, 2011, a health insurance issuer offering group or individual health insurance coverage (including group coverage offered as a grandfathered health plan) must clearly account for the amount of premium revenues spent on reimbursement for clinical services, activities for health care quality improvement, and all other non-claims costs.[36] If the total amount of the premium revenue expended for clinical claims and health improvement activities is less than 85 percent for plans in the large-group market or 80 percent for plans in the small-group market and individual market, then the insurer must rebate on a pro rata basis, with respect to each plan year, an amount equal to the product of the amount by which the non-claims costs expenditures exceed the 15 percent or 20 percent, respectively, and the amount of the total premium revenue (excluding federal and state taxes and licensing or regulatory fees and after accounting for certain risk adjustments, risk corridors, and reinsurance) for such plan year.[37] The states may set a higher percentage for insurers, but HHS may adjust the percentages if the application of the higher percentage may destabilize the individual market in the state.[38] HHS may also adjust the rates if appropriate to avoid volatility in the individual markets due to the establishment of the state Exchanges.[39]

Beginning in January 1, 2014, the determination of the rebate will be based on the previous three-year average for the plan.[40]

[C] Hospital Rate Transparency

Another measure adopted for early implementation with the intent of bringing down the cost of coverage is a requirement that each hospital establish (and update annually) and make public a list of the hospital's standard charges for items and services, including diagnostic related groups (DRGs) charged under the Medicare program.[41] HHS is to develop guidelines for the publication of this information.

§ 9.05   Ensuring That Consumers Get Value for Their Dollars

Beginning with the 2010 plan year, the 2010 Health Care Reform Act directs HHS to develop a process for an annual review of "unreasonable" health insurance coverage premium increases.[42] Insurers will be required to provide justification to HHS and the related state for the increase. The justification also must be posted on the insurance company's Web site.

The 2010 Health Care Reform Act also authorizes funds for grants to establish medical reimbursement data centers to provide better information to plans and consumers about the actual cost of coverage.[43] The centers are to be established at academic or other nonprofit institutions to collect medical reimbursement information from health insurance issuers, to analyze and organize such information, and to make such information available to such issuers, health care providers, health researchers, health care policy makers, and the general public.[44]

---

[35] PHSA § 2718(b).

[36] PHSA § 2718(a).

[37] PHSA § 2718(b).

[38] PHSA § 2718(b)(2).

[39] PHSA § 2718(d).

[40] PHSA § 2718(b)(1)(B)(ii).

[41] PPACA § 1001 (adding PHSA § 2718(e)).

[42] PPACA § 1003.

[43] PPACA § 10101(i)(2) (adding PHSA § 2794(d)). The law authorizes $250 million for these expenditures.

[44] PHSA § 2794(d).

§ 9.06   Empowering Consumers With Information

A major thrust of the health care reform law is to empower health care consumers through access to information. Throughout the 2010 Health Care Reform Act, HHS is charged with the responsibility of making information available to the public. This will be accomplished through a Web portal to be developed by HHS. The portal will enable consumers to access information gathered from group health plans and insurance issuers by HHS under the Act and to link to Web sites of state-organized offices and programs. The intent is that, beginning as early as July 1, 2010, through the HHS-established Internet portal, any resident of any state may identify affordable health insurance coverage options in that state.[45]

The Web site or Web portal is to provide, at a minimum, information on the following coverage options:

- Health insurance coverage offered by insurers;

- Medicaid coverage;

- CHIP coverage;

- State high-risk pool coverage;

- Federal high-risk pool; and

- Coverage within the small-group market for small businesses and their employees, including reinsurance for early retirees, tax credits available under Section 45R of the Code, and other information specifically for small businesses regarding affordable care options.[46]

On May 5, 2010, HHS published an interim final rule with comment period[47] describing the information that will be collected and displayed on the Web portal. HHS intends to release initial summary information that is available as of July 1, 2010, with a second release to follow on October 1, 2010. The first release will include basic information provided by insurance issuers and states on issuers and their products in the individual and small-group markets. Detailed pricing and benefit information for individual and small-group coverage will not be available until the second release date.

Beginning during the transition period and continuing even after the Exchanges are accessible, a wealth of information will be collected and made available to the regulators and the public about:

- The cost and availability of coverage;

- The quality of care being paid for by that coverage;

- The quality, efficiency, and integrity of the providers; and

- The research trends in quality care and other related topics.

See **Appendix C** for a list of the HHS information-reporting and Web site posting mandates.

§ 9.07   State Health Insurance Consumer Information

The 2010 Health Care Reform Act appropriates $30 million for HHS to award grants to the states to establish offices of health insurance consumer assistance or health insurance ombudsman programs.[48] Future appropriations for subsequent years are authorized in the Act. The office must be

---

[45] PPACA § 1103(a).
[46] PPACA § 1103.
[47] 75 Fed. Reg. 86, 24470 *et seq.* (May 5, 2010).
[48] PPACA § 1002 (adding PHSA § 2793).

independent of, but work in coordination with, the state insurance regulators and consumer assistance offices to receive and respond to inquiries and complaints regarding federal health insurance requirements and state law.[49]

Each office must provide consumer assistance and data collection for HHS. The office is directed to assist with the filing of complaints and appeals in both the initial and external appeal stages; to collect, track, and quantify problems and inquiries encountered by consumers; to provide consumer education about the rights and responsibilities of group health plans and health insurers; to provide information, referral, and enrollment assistance for consumers; and to resolve problems relating to an individual's obtaining the premium tax credit available under the Exchanges beginning in 2014.[50]

In addition, as a condition of receiving the grant, the office will be required to collect and report data requested by HHS on the types of problems consumers are encountering.[51] HHS is to use the information to identify areas where more enforcement is necessary and shall share the information with the state insurance regulators, the DOL, and Treasury.[52]

States also have obligations to post information publicly on the Internet and to link to some of the provider comparison Web sites[53] being established by HHS and CMS for state-licensed facilities such as skilled nursing facilities and nursing homes.

By far the largest new Internet obligation on states will be the Exchange site. The Exchange Internet portal will include plan rating, enrollee satisfaction information, and enrollment information.[54] See **Chapter 10** for more information about the Exchange information to be posted on the Internet for consumers.

States are also required to facilitate Medicaid enrollment through the Internet Exchange portal beginning in 2014.[55]

---

[49] PHSA § 2793.
[50] PHSA § 2793(3). See **§ 10.04[E]** for a description of the premium tax credit available for individuals beginning January 1, 2014.
[51] PHSA § 2793(d).
[52] PHSA § 2793(d).
[53] See **Appendix C**, PPACA.
[54] PPACA § 1311.
[55] PPACA § 2401.

CHAPTER 10
MANDATES AND EXCHANGES

§ 10.01   Individual Enroll-or-Pay

A cornerstone of national health care reform is that all American citizens should have access to health care coverage, regardless of their health status and income level. The group market reforms discussed earlier in Chapters 7 and 8 revealed many of the changes that will expand access to health care coverage for millions of Americans who are currently uninsured or grossly underinsured. Increased access is only effective if the uninsured segment of the population actually enrolls in coverage. Therefore, along with these changes comes a requirement for individuals to enroll in health care coverage. Beginning on January 1, 2014, "applicable individuals" will be required to enroll in "minimum essential coverage" or pay a tax penalty to the federal government.[1] We refer to this concept as "enroll or pay."

[A]   Applicable Individuals

The term *applicable individuals* encompasses all American citizens except those who qualify for a religious exemption or are incarcerated.[2] Also specifically exempted from the enroll-or-pay requirement are non–U.S. citizens and U.S. nationals.[3]

[B]   Minimum Essential Coverage

Currently, the definition of *minimum essential coverage* is very simplistic but this term may change over time. An individual can satisfy the minimum essential coverage requirement by obtaining health care coverage through one of the following sources:

- Government-sponsored programs, including Medicare, Medicaid, TRICARE, and the Children's Health Insurance Program;[4]

- Eligible employer-sponsored health plans,[5] which may include governmental plans or any other plans or coverage offered in the small- or large-group market within a state; (As the 2010 Health Care Reform Act is drafted, it appears that self-funded employment-based group health plans (other than those sponsored by government employers) are not included in the definition of an eligible employer-sponsored health plan. However, it seems likely that the omission of self-funded plans from the definition of an eligible employer-sponsored health plan was an oversight that would result in unintended consequences for tens of millions of Americans who receive health care coverage through the nation's largest employers. This oversight will likely be corrected either through a technical amendment or HHS will craft regulations that interpret this provision to include self-funded plans.);

- Grandfathered health plans,[6] including those that are self-funded; or

- Individual health plans, including a plan purchased through an Exchange or outside an Exchange.[7]

Minimum essential coverage will not include coverage for excepted benefits, which include:

- Coverage only for accident, or disability income insurance;

---

[1] PPACA § 1501(b) (adding I.R.C. § 5000A(b)).

[2] I.R.C. § 5000A(d).

[3] I.R.C. § 5000A(d); *see supra* § **2.01** note 1 and accompanying text (regarding the subtraction of illegal aliens from the uninsured statistics).

[4] I.R.C. § 5000A(f).

[5] I.R.C. § 5000A(f).

[6] *See supra* **Chapter 4** for a discussion of grandfathered health plans.

[7] I.R.C. § 5000A(f).

- Coverage issued as a supplement to liability insurance;
- Liability insurance;
- Workers' compensation or similar insurance;
- Automobile medical payment insurance;
- Credit-only insurance;
- Coverage for on-site medical clinics; and
- Other similar insurance under which benefits for medical care are secondary or incidental to other benefits.[8]

[C] Penalties

Effective January 1, 2014, any individual who is required to enroll in minimum essential coverage but chooses not to do so must pay a penalty to the federal government, subject to a few exemptions.[9] Those who are exempted include the following:

- Individuals whose required contribution for the lowest-cost plan option would be in excess of 8 percent of household income.[10]
- Individuals who do not file Form 1040 tax returns because they do not earn enough income. The filing threshold comprises two numbers—the personal exemption amount plus the standard deduction amount. For the 2009 taxable year, the sum of these amounts is $9,350 for individuals filing as "single" and $18,700 for individuals filing as "married filing jointly."[11]
- Individuals who were not covered by minimum essential coverage for a continuous period of less than three months. Once the continuous period without minimum essential coverage reaches a period of three months or more, this exemption expires and the penalty applies retroactively for the entire period.[12]
- Individuals who do not have an affordable coverage option, either through an employment-based group health plan or a qualified health plan offered through an Exchange.[13]
- Members of Indian tribes.[14]

The penalty for not having minimum essential coverage will be calculated on a monthly basis and is based on the annual amounts set forth in Table 10-1. The penalty is calculated as the greater of (1) a set dollar amount, or (2) a percentage of household income that exceeds the dollar threshold required to file a Form 1040 tax return.[15] For 2009, those thresholds are $9,350 for single filers and $18,700 for married taxpayers filing jointly. The thresholds will be adjusted for cost-of-living increases for future years.

---

[8] I.R.C. § 5000A(f).

[9] I.R.C. § 5000A(e).

[10] I.R.C. § 5000A(e)(1).

[11] I.R.C. § 5000A(e)(2). The 2009 threshold is $9,350 for married taxpayers filing separately and at least $12,000 for taxpayers filing as head of household.

[12] I.R.C. § 5000A(e)(4).

[13] I.R.C. § 5000A(e)(5); PPACA § 1311(d)(4)(H).

[14] I.R.C. § 5000A(e)(3).

[15] I.R.C. § 5000A(c).

Table 10-1. Annual Enroll-or-Pay Penalties for Individuals

Year	Individual Dollar Penalty	Individual % of Income Penalty
2014	$95	1.0%
2015	$325	2.0%
2016 (and after)	$695 (as indexed)	2.5%

The individual dollar penalty in Table 10-1 is for individuals who have attained age 18 at the beginning of a month. For individuals who have not attained age 18 at the beginning of a month, the individual dollar penalties are reduced by 50 percent. For a family, the sum of the individual dollar penalties cannot exceed 300 percent of the values in the table. For example, the annual individual dollar penalty for a family comprising two parents and six children would be no more than $285 ($95 × 300%) for 2014. However, because there is no cap on the percentage of household income penalty, the enroll-or-pay penalty could be significantly more than $285 for the 2014 calendar year.

Example: Joe and Jen Jones are married adults with three dependent children (Amber, age 14; Brad, age 16; Cindy, age 19). For the 2014 calendar year, Joe and Jen decide not to enroll in minimum essential coverage. The standard deduction and personal exemptions for their family total $29,650 (based on 2009 figures). The *annual* individual dollar penalties are calculated as follows.

Name	2014 Annual Individual Dollar Penalty
Joe	$95.00
Jen	$95.00
Amber	$47.50
Brad	$47.50
Cindy	$95.00
Total	380.00*

* Penalty would be capped at $285.00 (300% of the individual penalty).

If the combined income for Joe and Jen's family in 2014 is $40,000, the monthly percent of household income penalty would be $103.50 (1 percent of the household income that exceeds the sum of the applicable standard deduction and personal exemptions). The $103.50 is calculated as follows:

$40,000 − $29,650 = $10,350

$10,350 × 1% = $103.50

Thus, the family would be subject to the $285 maximum individual dollar penalty, which is greater than the $103.50 percent of household income penalty.

However, if the combined family income is $100,000, the family would be subject to an annual penalty of $703.50 because 1 percent of household income that exceeds the sum of the applicable standard deduction and personal exemptions is greater than the maximum individual dollar penalty of $285.

[D] Payment of Penalty

Individuals subject to the enroll-or-pay penalty must remit payment to the IRS. While the penalty is assessed on a monthly basis, payment will be made annually and will be administered through the Form 1040 tax return, which will have to be redesigned to accommodate this change. Taxpayers who fail to remit an enroll-or-pay penalty will be subject to interest and the traditional IRS penalties for underpayments of tax.[16] However, such taxpayers will not be subject to criminal charges for tax underpayments[17] or to liens or levies on property.[18] These limitations on the collectability of enroll-or-pay penalties strips away some of the effectiveness of the provision.

§ 10.02   Employer Pay-or-Play

Complementing the requirement that individuals enroll in minimum essential coverage or pay a tax penalty is a requirement that certain employers offer minimum essential coverage or pay a tax penalty.[19] We refer to this concept as "pay or play." Beginning January 1, 2014, certain employers will be required to offer full-time employees the chance to enroll in employment-based group health plan coverage that satisfies the definition of minimum essential coverage and that is both adequate and affordable. "Applicable employers" that fail to provide minimum essential coverage to any "full-time employee" eligible to receive a subsidy for coverage obtained through an Exchange will be subject to a nondeductible federal tax penalty. The calculation of this penalty will vary depending upon whether the employer is offering minimum essential coverage to all its full-time employees, including full-time employees covered by a collective bargaining agreement. These defined terms and penalties are discussed below.

[A] Applicable Employers

Pay-or-play is applicable only to large employers.[20] Large employers are employers that employed, on average, 50 or more full-time employees on business days during the preceding calendar year.[21] For a new business or one that was not in existence for the entire *preceding* calendar year, the large employer determination will be based on the average number of employees the business reasonably expects to employ on business days during the *current* calendar year.[22] An employer will not be subject to the pay-or-play rules if during the preceding calendar year it (1) employed 50 or more full-time employees for 120 days or less; and (2) the employees in excess of 50 for such period were

---

[16] I.R.C. § 5000A(g)(1); *see* I.R.C. § 6651(a)(2) (providing penalties for tax underpayments).

[17] I.R.C. § 5000A(g)(2)(A).

[18] I.R.C. § 5000A(g)(2)(B).

[19] PPACA § 1513 (adding I.R.C. § 4980 H).

[20] I.R.C. § 4980H(a) and (b).

[21] I.R.C. § 4980H(c)(2)(A).

[22] I.R.C. § 4980H(c)(2)(C)(ii).

seasonal workers.[23] The controlled group rules under Code Sections 414(b), (c), (m), and (o) will apply when determining the size of an employer.[24]

[B] Calculation of Employees

Because only large employers are subject to the pay-or-play rules, employers must pay careful attention to how a "full-time employee" is defined. *Full-time employees* are employees who work, on average, at least 30 hours of service per week.[25] For purposes of determining which employers are large employers, full-time equivalent employees also must be included in the employee count.[26] *Full-time equivalent employees* are determined by adding all the hours worked by non–full-time employees in a given month and dividing that number by 120.[27]

The following example illustrates how full-time employees are calculated in determining whether an employer is a "large employer" for purposes of the pay-or-play rules.

Example 1: November Pain Corp. (NPC), which sells guns and roses, employs 45 employees who each work, on average, 37.5 hours per week for the entire year and an additional 100 part-time sales employees who work 12 hours per week for the entire year. Based solely on the total of 45 full-time employees, NPC would not be a large employer because it does not meet the requisite 50 full-time-employee threshold. However, full-time equivalent employees must be taken into consideration. For purposes of this example, assume that each month contains four weeks. NPC would calculate its full-time equivalent employees as follows:

[(100 employees × 12 hours ÷ week × 4 weeks) ÷ 120] = 40

Therefore, once the part-time employees are factored in, NPC is a large employer for purposes of determining employer size under the pay-or-play rules, because it employs 85 full-time employees.

[C] Penalties

There are two types of penalties that may be assessed under the pay-or-play rules—penalties for employers that choose not to provide minimum essential coverage (i.e., employers who are no longer in the business of providing health benefits to their employees),[28] and penalties for employers that provide minimum essential coverage (e.g., employer-sponsored health coverage) that is inadequate or unaffordable.[29] A large employer may be subject to only one of these penalties, not both, and the latter penalty cannot exceed the amount that would have been payable under the former penalty had the employer not offered minimum essential coverage. These penalties are excise taxes and are not deductible for federal tax purposes.

---

[23] I.R.C. § 4980H(c)(2)(B)(i). Work is done on a seasonal basis where, ordinarily, the employment pertains to or is of the kind exclusively performed at certain seasons or periods of the year and which, from its nature, may not be continuous or carried on throughout the year. A worker who moves from one seasonal activity to another, while employed in agriculture or performing agricultural labor, is employed on a seasonal basis even though he may continue to be employed during a major portion of the year. 29 U.S.C. § 500.20(s)(1). Seasonal workers also include retail employees.

[24] I.R.C. § 4980H(c)(2)(C)(i). The controlled group rules require certain related companies under common control to be treated as a single employer.

[25] I.R.C. § 4980H(c)(4).

[26] I.R.C. § 4980H(c)(2)(E).

[27] I.R.C. § 4980H(c)(2)(E).

[28] I.R.C. § 4980H(a).

[29] I.R.C. § 4980H(b).

[1] Penalty for No Minimum Essential Coverage

An employer that chooses not to provide minimum essential coverage to its full-time employees and has at least one full-time employee who receives a premium tax credit or cost-sharing reduction related to enrollment in a qualified health plan through an Exchange will be subject to a penalty of $166.67 per month per full-time employee.[30] The monthly penalty amount will be adjusted for inflation beginning in 2015. The first 30 full-time employees are excluded from the penalty calculation.[31]

The following example illustrates how the pay-or-play penalty is calculated for employers that do not offer minimum essential coverage.

> **Example 2:** Let's continue with November Pain Corp. which was introduced in Example 1. As we established in Example 1, NPC is subject to pay-or-play. Because of rising health care premiums and the market for guns and roses not being what it used to be, NPC eliminates its employment-based group health plan. In turn, all NPC employees enroll in a qualified health plan through a state Exchange. Many of NPC's employees are lower paid; as a result, all of its 100 part-time employees and 10 of its 45 full-time employees receive a premium tax credit to help defray the cost of coverage under an Exchange-provided qualified health plan. Because NPC does not offer minimum essential coverage and has *at least one full-time employee* enrolled in a qualified health plan through a state Exchange who receives a premium tax credit, it must pay a monthly penalty of $166.67 for *each full-time employee* after the first 30 full-time employees. This translates into a penalty of $2,500.05 per month: [(45 full-time employees − 30 full-time employees) × $166.67]. Again, this penalty is not deductible for federal tax purposes.

Because pay-or-play penalties are assessed on a monthly basis, an employer that begins the calendar year without offering minimum essential coverage could change its mind at any point during the year and begin to offer minimum essential coverage (either through an employment-based group health plan or an Exchange plan, in certain cases). Thus, an employer that had been paying the penalties under pay-or-play from January 1, 2014, through June 30, 2014, could, effective July 1, 2014, begin offering minimum essential coverage that is adequate and affordable to eliminate future monthly pay-or-play penalties.

[2] Penalty for Inadequate or Unaffordable Coverage

An employer that offers minimum essential coverage that is either inadequate or unaffordable will be subject to a pay-or-play penalty of $250 per month per full-time employee who receives a premium tax credit or cost-sharing reduction related to enrollment in a qualified health plan through a state Exchange.[32] Minimum essential coverage is inadequate if the plan's share of the total cost of benefits is less than 60 percent, and it is unaffordable if the employee premium constitutes more than 9.5 percent of the employee's household income.[33] The monthly penalty amount will be adjusted for inflation beginning in 2015. However, unlike employers that choose not to offer minimum essential coverage, employers that offer inadequate or unaffordable minimum essential are *not* able to exclude the first 30 full-time employees from the penalty calculation.

---

[30] I.R.C. § 4980H(a).

[31] I.R.C. § 4980H(d)(2)(D).

[32] I.R.C. § 4980H(b)(1).

[33] I.R.C. § 36B(c)(2)(C). *Household income* is determined by adding an individual's "modified adjusted gross income" plus the aggregate modified gross income of all other individuals who are taken into account in determining the taxpayer's family size that were required to file a tax return for the taxable year. *Modified adjusted gross income* means gross income *decreased* by (1) trade and business deductions; (2) losses from sale or exchange of property; (3) rents and royalties deductions; and (4) alimony, and *increased* by (1) tax-exempt interest and income earned by U.S. citizens living abroad (Code § 911 income). I.R.C. § 36B(d)(2).

The following example illustrates how the pay-or-play penalty is calculated for employers that offer minimum essential coverage that is inadequate or unaffordable.

Example 3: As we established in Example 1, NPC is subject to pay-or-play. To avoid negative publicity, NPC decides that it will provide its employees with minimum essential coverage for the 2014 calendar year. However, because of rising health care costs, NPC decides that it can only contribute 30 percent of the total health insurance premium, leaving employees to pay the other 70 percent, which would cost most employees more than 9.5 percent of their household income. In turn, all NPC employees enroll in a qualified health plan through an Exchange. As indicated in Example 2, many of NPC's employees are lower paid, and all of its part-time employees and 10 of its full-time employees receive a premium tax credit to help defray the cost of coverage under a qualified health plan. Because NPC does not offer minimum essential coverage that is affordable and has at least one full-time employee enrolled in a qualified health plan through a state Exchange who receives a premium tax credit, it must pay a monthly penalty of $250 for *each* full-time employee receiving a subsidy. This translates into a penalty of $2,500 per month [(10 full-time employees receiving a subsidy) × $250]. Again, this penalty is not deductible for federal tax purposes.

§ 10.03 Free Choice Vouchers

While large employers are subject to the pay-or-play rules, all "offering employers" will be required to provide free choice vouchers to their "qualified employees" beginning on January 1, 2014.[34] Offering employers that provide qualified employees with a free choice voucher will be able to deduct the amount of the voucher for federal income tax purposes and will not be subject to pay-or-play penalties with respect to any employee receiving a free choice voucher.[35] Employees receiving a free choice voucher will not be subject to the enroll-or-pay penalties, so long as they use their voucher to obtain health care coverage through an Exchange.[36]

[A] Offering Employer

An *offering employer* is any employer that (1) offers minimum essential coverage through an eligible employer-sponsored plan, and (2) pays any portion of the costs of such plan.[37] There is no requirement that an offering employer have 50 or more employees, so small businesses may be classified as offering employers.

[B] Qualified Employee

A *qualified employee* is any employee (1) whose required contribution for minimum essential coverage through an eligible employer-sponsored plan is at least 8 percent but does not exceed 9.8 percent[38] of the employee's household income for the applicable taxable year (as indexed for years beginning after 2014); (2) whose household income for the applicable taxable year is not greater than 400 percent of the federal poverty level for the appropriate family size; and (3) who does not participate in the health plan offered by the offering employer.[39]

---

[34] PPACA § 10108 (this provision does not amend an existing law or add a new provision to any law).

[35] I.R.C. § 162(a).

[36] I.R.C. § 4980H(b)(3).

[37] PPACA § 10108(b).

[38] This likely should have been changed to 9.5%, corresponding with the change made to premium tax credits. It may be corrected through a technical correction.

[39] PPACA § 10108(c).

[C] Voucher Amounts

The amount of a free choice voucher provided by an offering employer to a qualified employee will be equal to the monthly portion of the cost of the eligible employer-sponsored plan that would have been paid by the offering employer if the qualified employee were covered under the plan.[40] The qualified employee will be able to apply the amount of the voucher toward the purchase of a qualified health plan through an Exchange.[41] The offering employer is responsible for remitting the amount of the voucher to the Exchange on behalf of the employee. If the amount of the voucher exceeds the premium of the qualified health plan, the employee is entitled to the difference.[42] The portion of a voucher that is used to reduce the premiums associated with a qualified health plan purchased through an Exchange is not taxable to the qualified employee.[43] The portion of a voucher, if any, that is not used to defray the cost of premiums associated with a qualified health plan is includible in the qualified employee's gross income and treated as taxable compensation.

The following example illustrates how free choice vouchers work.

Example 4: As previously noted in Examples 1, 2, and 3, NPC has 45 full-time employees. Assume also that NPC continues to offer minimum essential coverage but requires employees to pay a share of the premium. Ten of the full-time employees who have household income between 100 percent and 400 percent of the federal poverty level (and who therefore may be eligible for subsidies under an Exchange plan) decline participation in NPC's health plan because they would rather purchase coverage through the Exchange. Let's assume that if these 10 employees had enrolled in NPC's plan, each of them would have to pay a share of the premium in an amount that is between 8 percent and 9.8 percent of household income. The other 35 full-time employees (whose household income exceeds 400 percent of the federal poverty level) enroll in the NPC plan.

In this example, because NPC is an offering employer, it must provide the 10 qualified employees with a free choice voucher. Because these employees would receive a free choice voucher, they would not be eligible for subsidies under an Exchange plan. The 35 full-time employees who enrolled in minimum essential coverage provided through NPC's health plan are not, by definition, qualified employees and are not eligible for a voucher. Because free choice vouchers are not limited to only full-time employees, whether or not NPC is required to provide part-time employees with a free choice voucher depends on the terms of the employment-based group health plan. If part-time employees are eligible to enroll in NPC's plan, NPC would have to provide a free choice voucher to any part-time employee who is a qualified employee. If part-time employees are not eligible to enroll in the NPC plan, NPC would not have to provide a free choice voucher to part-time employees.

---

[40] PPACA § 10108(d)(1).

[41] PPACA § 10108(d)(2).

[42] PPACA § 10108(d)(3). It is not clear whether the difference must be paid to the employee by the Exchange or by the employer, and if paid by the Exchange, whether the Exchange or the employer is responsible for tax reporting.

[43] I.R.C. § 139D.

§ 10.04 Health Care Exchanges

Traditionally, most individuals with health care coverage in the United States receive that coverage through an employment-based group health plan.[44] Employer-sponsored plans still play a significant role in providing health care coverage, but their role has begun to diminish due to a number of factors.[45] First, the recession of the last few years has added millions of Americans to the ranks of the unemployed, many of whom are eligible for COBRA continuation coverage for only 18 months after termination of employment. Second, over the past decade, health care costs have grown at rates far eclipsing the rise in the consumer price index and the growth in real wages, causing many small employers to eliminate or cut back their health plans. Third, systemic changes in the American workforce have pushed more workers employed in non-agricultural pursuits than ever before to enter the ranks of the self-employed.[46] These three significant changes, among others, have left millions of Americans with only one option to obtain health care coverage—the individual insurance market. Because high quality comes with high costs in the individual insurance market, it is not uncommon to see individuals purchasing coverage through the individual insurance market take out "catastrophic" policies that do not provide for preventive care or prescription drug benefits, which ultimately can lead to higher use and more expensive treatment down the road.

To help solve this growing problem, the 2010 Health Care Reform Act introduces a new concept called the American Health Benefit Exchange (more commonly known as an "Exchange"). An Exchange is a marketplace of health insurance issuers composed of traditional for-profit insurance companies and nonprofit cooperatives that will sell a type of health plan called a qualified health plan (QHP), defined more fully in **Section 10.04[C]**, below. States, acting through a state governmental agency or nonprofit entity established and operated by the state, will establish the Exchanges using $6 billion in federal grant funds.[47] Because each state operates its own Exchange, each state may require QHPs sold through its Exchange to offer additional benefits other than those required by HHS.[48] After January 1, 2015, each Exchange is expected to be self-sustaining and will not receive aid from the federal government.[49] Funds used to operate and maintain the Exchange will likely come from fees on health insurance issuers or individuals enrolling in an Exchange plan.

The goals of an Exchange are as follows:

1. To enhance consumer choice;

2. Create single risk pools based on community ratings that are subject to strict underwriting requirements;[50]

3. Lessen the reliance on employer-sponsored health care coverage; and

4. Allow consumers to make "apples to apples" comparisons of available health plans. To accomplish these goals and more, each Exchange will feature an Internet Web site through which comparative information may be obtained, a rating system that rates QHPs based on

---

[44] *See http://www.bls.gov/ncs/ebs/sp/ebnr0015.pdf.*

[45] *See supra* **§ 2.02** notes 10–11 and accompanying text (providing statistics on health plan coverage).

[46] *http://www.bls.gov/opub/mlr/2004/07/art2full.pdf.*

[47] PPACA § 1322(g).

[48] PPACA § 1311(d)(3)(B). However, the state is required to make payments either to the individual or to the QHP to defray their cost. PPACA § 1311(d)(3)(B)(ii).

[49] PPACA § 1311(d)(5).

[50] Insurers will not be able to charge tobacco users more than 1.5 times the rate of non–tobacco users and premiums may not vary by a ratio of more than 3 to 1 based on age.

quality and price, and annual enrollee satisfaction surveys for each QHP that has more than 500 enrollees. Each Exchange will be responsible for preparing, maintaining, and updating this information.

[A] Eligibility

Beginning January 1, 2014, individuals and small employers will be able to purchase health insurance coverage through an Exchange.[51] Small employers are employers with at least one but not more than 100 employees on business days during the preceding calendar year and who employ at least one employee on the first day of the plan year.[52] Large employers are not eligible to purchase a QHP through an Exchange until 2017, at the earliest.[53] Large employers are employers that have employed on average at least 101 employees on business days during the preceding calendar year and who employ at least one employee on the first day of the plan year.[54] For purposes of determining the size of an employer, the controlled group rules set forth in Code Sections 414(b), (c), (m), and (o) of the will apply.[55] Beginning in 2016, each state may opt to reduce the maximum employee limit for small employers from 100 employees to 50 employees and large employers from 101 employees to 51 employees.[56]

[B] Special Eligibility Rules

There are a couple of special eligibility rules for new employers and small employers. A new employer that was not in existence during the preceding calendar year will determine whether it is a small or large employer based on the average number of employees it reasonably expects to employ on business days during the current calendar year.[57] A small employer that makes coverage available to its employees through a QHP in the Exchange will continue to be treated as a small employer, even if it would otherwise cease to be a small employer due to an increase in the number of its employees, for the period beginning with the increase in employees and ending with the first day on which the employer does not make such QHP available to its employees.[58] Essentially, small employers whose businesses grow can keep their existing QHP.

[C] Qualified Health Plans

A *QHP* is defined as a health plan offered through an Exchange that (1) provides for an "essential health benefits package"; (2) has a certificate of approval signifying its compliance with the certification criteria established by HHS; and (3) is offered by an "approved" health insurance issuer.[59]

[1] Essential Health Benefits Package

An *essential health benefits package* must (1) provide a level of coverage described in Table 10-2; (2) limit cost-sharing (deductibles, co-insurance, copayments, etc.) for essential health benefits to the

---

[51] PPACA § 1312(f).

[52] PPACA § 1304(b)(2).

[53] PPACA § 1312(f)(2)(B).

[54] PPACA § 1304(b)(1).

[55] PPACA § 1304(b)(4)(A). The controlled group rules require related companies under common control to be treated as a single employer.

[56] PPACA § 1304(b)(3).

[57] PPACA § 1304(b)(4)(B).

[58] PPACA § 1304(b)(4)(D).

[59] PPACA § 1301(a)(1).

annual HSA contribution limit ($5,950 and $11,900 for 2010) and cap annual deductibles on health plans offered through the small group market to $2,000 for self-only coverage and $4,000 for family coverage, as adjusted beginning in 2015; and (3) provide essential health benefits in at least the following general categories:[60]

- Ambulatory patient services;

- Emergency services;

- Hospitalization;

- Maternity and newborn care;

- Mental health and substance abuse, including behavioral health treatment (it is unclear whether this would include autism coverage);

- Prescription drugs;

- Preventive and wellness services;

- Chronic disease management;

- Pediatric services, including dental and vision care;

- Rehabilitative and habilitative services; and

- Laboratory services.

When defining the specific services covered under each essential health benefit listed above, HHS will ensure an appropriate balance among the categories, not unduly weighting coverage toward any one category.[61] HHS will take into account the health care needs of the entire population, including women, children, and persons with disabilities and ensure that essential benefits will not be denied to individuals against their wishes on the basis of age, life expectancy, quality of life, etc. (i.e., there will be no "death panels," at least not as suggested by various opponents of the legislation).[62] HHS will not make coverage decisions, determine reimbursement rates, establish incentive programs or design benefits in ways that discriminate based on age, disability, or life expectancy.[63] HHS will periodically review and revise the essential health benefits listed above and the services covered under each benefit.[64]

Table 10-2. Coverage Tiers for Plan Offered Through an Exchange

Tier	Includes Essential Benefits?	Percentage of Covered Benefit Costs	Out-of-Pocket Limit for Individual/Family
Bronze	Yes	60%	$5,950 / $11,900
Silver	Yes	70%	$5,950 / $11,900
Gold	Yes	80%	$5,950 / $11,900
Platinum	Yes	90%	$5,950 / $11,900

---

[60] PPACA §§ 1302(a), (b).

[61] PPACA § 1302(b)(4).

[62] PPACA § 1302(b)(4). While there are no "death panels," an argument can be made that health care could be rationed.

[63] PPACA § 1302(b)(4).

[64] PPACA § 1302(b)(4).

[2] HHS Certification Criteria

At a minimum, a QHP must be certified to satisfy the following criteria[65] established by HHS:

- Meets marketing requirements and does not employ marketing practices that discourage individuals with significant health needs from enrolling in health care coverage.[66]

- Ensures a sufficient choice of providers, both in-network and out-of-network.[67]

- Includes within health plan networks those essential community providers that service predominantly low-income and medically underserved individuals.[68]

- Implements a quality improvement strategy that provides increased reimbursement or other incentives for:[69]

  —Implementation of wellness and health promotion activities;

  —Quality reporting, effective case management, care coordination, chronic disease management, and care compliance initiatives;

  —Implementation of activities to prevent hospital readmissions; and

  —Implementation of activities to improve patient safety and reduce medical errors.

- Uses a standardized enrollment form.[70]

- Uses a standard format for presenting health benefit options.[71]

- Provides information to enrollees and prospective enrollees on quality measures for each health plan offered in each Exchange.[72]

[3] Approved Health Insurance Issuer

An *approved health insurance issuer* is a health insurance issuer that:

- Is licensed and in good standing in each state where the issuer offers health insurance coverage through an Exchange;

- Offers at least one QHP at the "silver level" and "gold level" in each state Exchange in which the issuer participates;

- Charges the same premium rate for a QHP purchased through an Exchange as it does for the same plan purchased outside of an Exchange or through a broker; and

- Complies with other applicable HHS regulations and other requirements an Exchange may establish.

[D] Catastrophic Plan

In addition to QHPs, health insurance issuers may offer a catastrophic plan through an Exchange.[73] A catastrophic plan would be available only to (1) individuals who have not yet attained

---

[65] PPACA § 1301(a)(1)(A).

[66] PPACA § 1311(c)(1)(A).

[67] PPACA § 1311(c)(1)(B).

[68] PPACA § 1311(c)(1)(C).

[69] PPACA § 1311(c)(1)(E).

[70] PPACA § 1311(c)(1)(F).

[71] PPACA § 1311(c)(1)(G).

[72] PPACA § 1311(c)(1)(H).

[73] PPACA § 1302(e).

age 30 (determined at the beginning of the plan year), (2) individuals who are exempt from the enroll-or-pay penalties because of a hardship, and (3) individuals who would not otherwise have access to affordable coverage.

A catastrophic plan provides coverage for at least three primary care visits per year and the essential health benefits listed above.[74] However, no reimbursement will occur for essential health benefits (other than primary care visits) in a given plan year until the individual has incurred cost-sharing expenses in excess of the annual HSA contribution limit ($5,950 for single coverage and $11,900 for family coverage for 2010).

[E] Exchange Subsidies

Beginning in 2014, applicable taxpayers will be allowed a refundable tax credit for the premiums paid to purchase a QHP through an Exchange during a taxable year. An *applicable taxpayer* is a taxpayer whose household income for the taxable year is between 100 percent and 400 percent of the FPL for the appropriate family size. Table 10-3 shows the applicable FPL income thresholds (for 2009).

Table 10-3. 2009 Federal Poverty Level (FPL)

Family Size	100% of FPL	200% of FPL	300% of FPL	400% of FPL
1	$10,830	$21,660	$32,490	$43,320
2	$14,570	$29,140	$43,710	$58,280
3	$18,310	$36,620	$54,930	$73,240
4	$22,050	$44,100	$66,150	$88,200

The amount of premium tax credit an applicable taxpayer receives depends on the taxpayer's household income and is the lesser of (1) the total amount of premiums payable by the taxpayer for a QHP; or (2) the excess of the adjusted monthly premium based on the second-lowest-cost silver plan over an amount equal to one-twelfth of the product of the applicable percentage provided in Table 10-4 below times the taxpayer's household income.[75]

An example best illustrates how the premium tax credit is calculated.

Example 1: William and his wife Erin are married and have no children. Both work at Paradise City Pools, a small employer that does not offer any health care coverage. Their household income is $58,280 per year. Both William and Erin are enrolled in a QHP through an Exchange that provides them with health care coverage. The adjusted monthly premium for the second-lowest-cost silver plan is $500 per month. William and Erin pay a $600 monthly premium for their QHP. Because William and Erin have household income between 100 percent and 400 percent of the FPL, they may be eligible for a premium tax credit. The calculation of their annual premium tax credit is shown below.

1. Multiply $58,280 by 9.5%, which equals $5,536.60.
2. Divide $5,536.60 by 12 months, which equals $461.38.
3. Subtract $461.38 from $500, which equals $38.62.
4. Take the lesser of $600 and $38.62.

---

[74] PPACA § 1302(e)(1)(B).
[75] I.R.C. § 36B(b).

Result: The monthly premium tax credit for William and Erin is $38.62.

Table 10-4. Exchange Premium Limits for Eligible Individuals

Income Level (in terms of FPL)	Max. % of Income Paid Toward Health Care Coverage
Up to 133%	2%
133–150%	3–4%
150–200%	4–6.3%
200–250%	6.3%–8.05%
250–300%	8.05%–9.5%
300–400%	9.5%

Table 10-5. Exchange Cost-Sharing Subsidies for Eligible Individuals

Income Level (in terms of FPL)	Out-of-Pocket Spending Limits
100–200%	$1,983 (I) / $3,967 (F)
200–300%	$2,975 (I) / $5,950 (F)
300–400%	$3,987 (I) / $7,973 (F)

Table 10-6. Exchange Cost-Sharing Subsidies for Eligible Individuals

EXCHANGE COST-SHARING SUBSIDIES FOR ELIGIBLE INDIVIDUALS	
Income Level (in terms of FPL)	Cost-Sharing Limits
100–150%	6%
>150–200%	13%
>200–250%	27%
>250–400%	30%

The 2010 Health Care Reform Act provides for two other subsidies—reductions in out-of-pocket spending limits and reductions in cost-sharing limits—for an "eligible insured" who is enrolled in a QHP through an Exchange and whose household income is between 100 percent and 400 percent of the FPL.[76] The issuer of the QHP will be notified by HHS if an eligible insured is eligible for a reduction in the out-of-pocket spending limits and cost-sharing limits, and such issuer must reduce the

---

[76] PPACA § 1402(a).

cost-sharing accordingly. See Table 10-5 for a graphical illustration of the reductions in out-of-pocket spending limits and Table 10-6 for a graphical illustration of the reductions in cost-sharing limits.

[F] Special Rules

Cost-sharing subsidies are not available to individuals who are not lawfully present in the United States. To be lawfully present, an individual must be a citizen or national of the United States or an alien lawfully present in the United States.[77]

An American Indian who has household income of not more than 300 percent of the FPL will be classified as an eligible insured and the issuer of the plan will eliminate any cost-sharing under the QHP.[78]

Cost-sharing subsidies are not available to an individual who receives a free choice voucher from his or her employer.[79]

---

[77] PPACA § 1402(e).
[78] PPACA § 1402(d).
[79] I.R.C. § 36B(c)(2)(D).

CHAPTER 11

OPERATIONAL CHANGES FOR HEALTH PLANS

§ 11.01   Medicare Part D

[A]   Background

In 2003, President Bush signed the Medicare Prescription Drug, Improvement and Modernization Act of 2003 (the MMA),[1] which at the time was the most significant overhaul of the federal Medicare program since its inception nearly 40 years before. The MMA created Medicare Part D, which, effective January 1, 2006, extended the Medicare entitlement to prescription drug coverage for the first time.[2] Whereas Medicare Part A (hospitalization coverage) and Part B (outpatient and doctor visit coverage) are run almost entirely by the federal government, Part C (Medicare Advantage) and Part D are based on a system where private insurers provide coverage subject to certain federal minimum requirements and receive significant subsidies from the federal government.

A Medicare Part D plan offered by a private insurer must offer enrollees "qualified prescription drug coverage," which satisfies the standard requirements outlined below, or coverage that is actuarially equivalent to the standard prescription drug coverage.[3] The insurer must submit the proposed Medicare Part D plan to the Centers for Medicare and Medicaid Services (CMS) and receive CMS approval before the plan can be offered as a Medicare Part D plan entitling the insurer to a federal subsidy.[4] Qualified prescription drug coverage in a standard Medicare Part D plan consists of the following elements:

- An annual deductible, which for 2010 is $310. An individual who enrolls in the standard Medicare Part D plan must pay 100 percent of the first $310 in annual prescription drug costs incurred during 2010.[5]

- An initial corridor of coverage, which for 2010 runs from $310 to $2,830 in annual prescription drug costs. An individual who incurs prescription drug costs in this corridor pays only 25 percent of the costs. The Medicare Part D plan picks up the remaining 75 percent as a cost-sharing benefit.[6]

- A coverage gap (commonly known as the "donut hole") for annual prescription drug costs between $2,830 and $4,550 in 2010. The $4,550 is referred to as the "out-of-pocket expense limit." An individual who incurs prescription drug costs within the donut hole will have to pay 100 percent of such costs. No cost-sharing is available in the donut hole under the original version of the Medicare Part D program.[7]

- Catastrophic coverage for annual prescription drug costs in excess of $4,550 for 2010. An individual who incurs prescription drug costs at this level is deemed to have incurred catastrophic costs, and is only required to pay 5 percent of such costs. The Medicare Part D plan picks up the remaining 95 percent as a cost-sharing benefit.[8]

Viewing all of the elements together graphically, the standard Medicare Part D plan coverage for 2010 would look like this:

---

[1] Pub. L. No. 108-173, 117 Stat. 2066 (2003).

[2] 42 U.S.C. §§ 1395w-101 *et seq.*

[3] 42 U.S.C. § 1395w-101(a). Qualified prescription drug coverage must be available for covered Part D prescription drugs, and must include access to negotiated prices. 42 U.S.C. § 1395w-102.

[4] 42 U.S.C. § 1395w-101(b).

[5] 42 U.S.C. § 1395w-102(b)(1).

[6] 42 U.S.C. §§ 1395w-102(b)(2), (3).

[7] 42 U.S.C. § 1395w-102(b)(3).

[8] 42 U.S.C. § 1395w-102(b)(4). Once an eligible individual reaches the out-of-pocket expense limit for a year, the individual is only required to pay the greater of 5% of the cost, or a $5 copay for any prescription drug ($2 for generics and preferred multiple source drugs). *Id.*

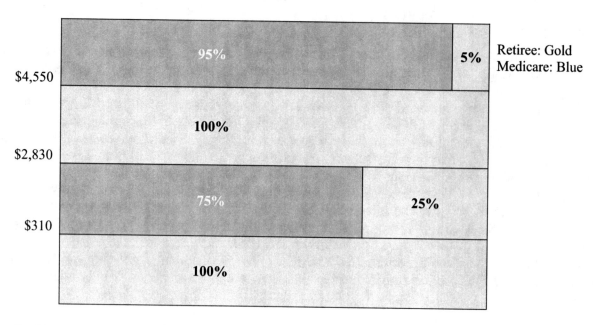

Or like this (assuming $7,500 in annual prescription drug costs):

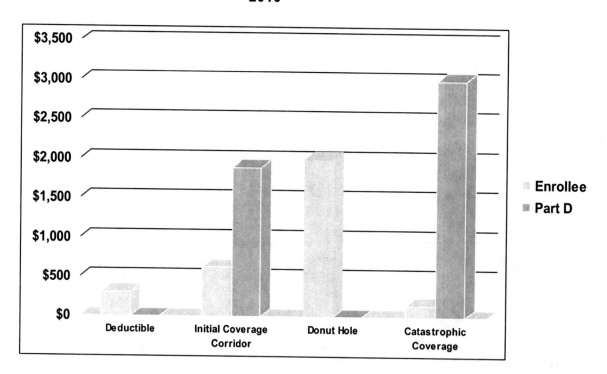

The total out-of-pocket expenses for an individual enrolled in a standard Medicare Part D plan for 2010 at various levels of annual prescription drug costs are as follows:

Prescription Drug Cost	Average Monthly Premium	Medicare Pays	Enrollee Pays (Including Premium)
$1,000	$30	$517.50	$842.50 (84%)
$5,000	$30	$2,317.50	$3,042.50 (61%)
$10,000	$30	$7,067.50	$3,292.50 (33%)

[B] Closing the Donut Hole

Notwithstanding a significant narrowing of the donut hole since 2006, when it spanned annual prescription drug costs from $2,250 to $5,100, Medicare Part D was viewed by many as incomplete coverage. Those with donut hole expenses received no cost-sharing benefits for those expenses, unless the Medicare Part D plan in which they were enrolled provided coverage in excess of the standard coverage or on some actuarially equivalent basis. Congress addressed this perceived problem in the 2010 Health Care Reform Act.

[1] 2010 Rebate

The 2010 Health Care Reform Act closes the donut hole by adding Part D cost-sharing at every level of cost (except the deductible) through 2020.[9] For 2010, the donut hole relief will take the form of a rebate. Any individual who is enrolled in a Medicare Part D plan as of the last day of a calendar quarter in 2010, and who has incurred costs for covered Part D prescription drugs in excess of the initial coverage limit of $2,830 for 2010 (which is the cap on the initial coverage corridor described above) is entitled to receive a rebate payment of $250 no later than the 15th calendar day of the third month following the end of the quarter.[10] An individual may receive only one such payment, and individuals who are already receiving income-related subsidies or reduction in premium subsidies under Medicare Part D are not eligible for the rebate.[11] Thus, if an eligible individual is covered under a Part D plan and incurs prescription drug costs in excess of $2,830 in the first calendar quarter of 2010 (ending March 31, 2010), that individual is entitled to receive a $250 rebate check from HHS by June 15, 2010.

[2] 2011 and Forward

After 2010, the 2010 Health Care Reform Act creates a Medicare Coverage Gap Discount Program, which will provide eligible individuals with access to manufacturers' discounts for certain drugs, the cost of which would fall into the donut hole.[12] In addition, the Act modifies the definition of qualified prescription drug coverage in a standard Medicare Part D plan to include coverage for generic and certain other non-generic drugs in the donut hole.[13] However, individuals who are already receiving income-related subsidies or reduction in premium subsidies under Medicare Part D are not eligible for the new donut hole coverage.[14]

---

[9] HCERA § 1101.

[10] HCERA § 1101(a) (adding new subsection (c) to 42 U.S.C. § 1395w-152).

[11] HCERA § 1101(a). Section 1101(a) of the HCERA amends Section 3301(b) of the PPACA, which had added a new Section 1395w-114A, entitled "Medicare Coverage Gap Discount Program." Individuals with income up to 150% of the federal poverty level are eligible to receive income-related subsidies under Medicare Part D.

[12] PPACA § 3301.

[13] HCERA § 1101(b) (adding new subparagraph (C) to 42 U.S.C. § 1395w-102(b)(2)).

[14] HCERA § 1101(b) (adding new subparagraph (C) to 42 U.S.C. § 1395w-102(b)(2)); see 42 U.S.C. 1395w-114A(g)(1), as added by Section 3301(b) of the PPACA, for a definition of an "applicable individual" who is eligible to receive the new donut hole coverage.

For generic drugs, an individual enrolled in a standard Medicare Part D plan will have "generic-gap co-insurance" for annual prescription drug costs incurred in the donut hole equal to 93 percent in 2011.[15] The generic-gap co-insurance is reduced by seven percentage points each year through 2019.[16] In 2020 and future years, the generic-gap co-insurance will be 25 percent.[17]

If we incorporate the 2010 Health Care Reform Act's changes into the standard Medicare Part D coverage, the coverage will look like this for 2011 (assuming all drug costs relate to generic drugs and all other thresholds remain the same as 2010):

2011—Generic Only

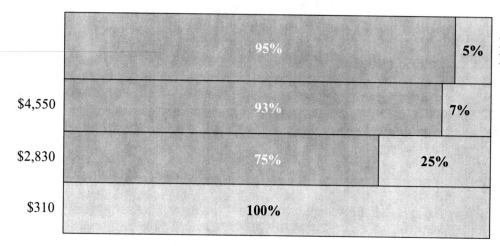

Or like this (assuming $7,500 in annual prescription drug costs):

2011—Generic Only

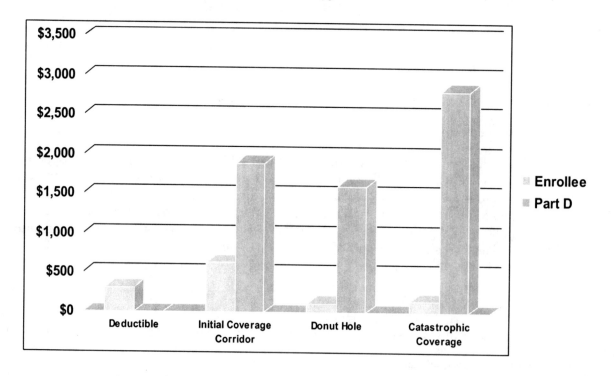

---

[15] HCERA § 1101(b) (adding new subparagraph (C)(ii)(I) to 42 U.S.C. § 1395w-102(b)(2)).

[16] HCERA § 1101(b) (adding new subparagraph (C)(ii)(II) to 42 U.S.C. § 1395w-102(b)(2)).

[17] HCERA § 1101(b) (adding new subparagraph (C)(ii)(III) to 42 U.S.C. § 1395w-102(b)(2)).

The total out-of-pocket expenses for an individual enrolled in standard Medicare Part D coverage for 2011, after incorporating the 2010 Health Care Reform Act's changes, at various levels of annual prescription drug costs for generic drugs are as follows:

2011—Generic Only

Prescription Drug Cost	Average Monthly Premium	Medicare Pays	Enrollee Pays (Including Premium)
$1,000	$30	$517.50	$842.50 (84%)
$5,000	$30	$3,917.10	$1,442.90 (29%)
$10,000	$30	$8,667.10	$1,692.90 (17%)

For non-generic drugs, an individual enrolled in a standard Medicare Part D plan will have co-insurance for annual prescription drug costs (based on the negotiated price) incurred in the donut hole equal to the difference between the "applicable gap percentage" and the discount percentage.[18] The applicable gap percentage is 97.5 percent for 2013 and 2014, 95 percent for 2015 and 2016, 90 percent for 2017, 85 percent for 2018, 80 percent for 2019, and 75 percent for 2020 and each year thereafter.[19] The discount percentage is a flat 50 percent.[20]

Again, if we incorporate the 2010 Health Care Reform Act's changes into the standard Medicare Part D coverage, the coverage will look like this for 2013 (assuming all drug costs relate to non-generic drugs and all other thresholds remain the same as 2010):

2013—Non-Generic Only

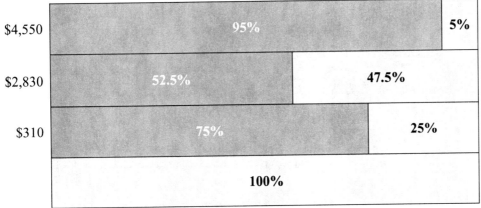

---

[18] HCERA § 1101(b) (adding new subparagraph (D) to 42 U.S.C. § 1395w-102(b)(2)).

[19] HCERA § 1101(b) (adding new subparagraph (D)(ii) to 42 U.S.C. § 1395w-102(b)(2)).

[20] HCERA § 1101(b) (adding new subparagraph (D) to 42 U.S.C. § 1395w-102(b)(2)). *See* 42 U.S.C. § 1395w-114A(g)(4)(A), as added by Section 3301(b) of the PPACA (providing the discount percentage).

Or like this (assuming $7,500 in annual prescription drug costs):

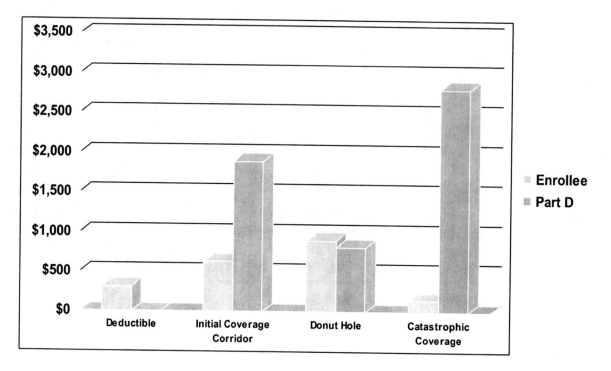

2013—Non-Generic Only

The total out-of-pocket expenses for an individual enrolled in standard Medicare Part D coverage for 2013, after incorporating the 2010 Health Care Reform Act's changes, at various levels of annual prescription drug costs for non-generic drugs, are as follows:

2013—Non-Generic Only

Prescription Drug Cost	Average Monthly Premium	Medicare Pays	Enrollee Pays (Including Premium)
$1,000	$30	$517.50	$842.50 (84%)
$5,000	$30	$3,134.50	$2,225.50 (46%)
$10,000	$30	$7,884.50	$2,475.50 (25%)

[C] Nondeductibility of Retiree Drug Subsidy Payments

While Congress envisioned a Medicare Part D prescription drug coverage program based on the private insurance system, it did not want to discourage employers from providing or continuing to provide prescription drug coverage for their Medicare-eligible retirees. To incentivize employers to maintain such coverage, the MMA authorized the payment of a retiree drug subsidy (RDS) to employers that maintained retiree prescription drug plans that were at least actuarially equivalent to the standard

Medicare Part D plan.[21] On an annual basis, employers can apply electronically to CMS for the RDS and provide an actuarial certification that their plans are actuarially equivalent to the standard Medicare Part D plan.[22]

If approved, plan sponsors will receive RDS payments from CMS on an annual, quarterly, or monthly basis equal to 28 percent of each qualifying retiree's allowable prescription drug costs incurred within a certain corridor.[23] For 2010, the RDS applies to allowable prescription drug expenses between $310 and $6,300.[24] Allowable prescription drug costs are actual incurred expenses for any Part D drugs, net of any discounts, rebates or other price concessions.[25] Thus, to the extent that a qualifying retiree incurs $6,300 in allowable prescription drug costs in 2010, the plan sponsor may be eligible to receive an RDS payment for that qualifying retiree of $1,677.20 (28% × ($6,300 − $310)).

One significant benefit of the RDS for companies subject to federal income tax was that, under the MMA, RDS payments were tax-exempt.[26] Thus, for-profit employers received a double tax benefit. They could deduct any expenses incurred by the employer to pay for retiree prescription drug costs,[27] and then receive an RDS payment from CMS for those same expenses without including the RDS payment in taxable income. This double tax benefit made the RDS payments more valuable for employers subject to tax than for government, church, and other tax-exempt employers.

The 2010 Health Care Reform Act addresses and eliminates the double tax benefit associated with RDS payments for tax years beginning after December 31, 2012.[28] The Act amends section 139A of the Code to provide that an employer's tax deduction for allowable prescription drug expenses is reduced to the extent the employer is reimbursed for such expenses through the receipt of RDS payments. Even though the Act changes do not become effective until 2013,[29] for-profit employers receiving RDS payments were required to recognize the full accounting impact of this change in the employer's financial statements for the first quarter of 2010 (the quarter in which the 2010 Health Care Reform Act was enacted). For example, Verizon Communications announced shortly after the Act was enacted that it would post a one-time accounting charge of $970 million in the first quarter of 2010 due to the 2013 change in the tax treatment of the RDS payments.[30] Ultimately, the Act puts for-profit employers back on equal footing with tax-exempt employers with respect to the value of the RDS payments.

§ 11.02 Nondiscrimination Rules Applicable to Insured Health Benefits

Sections 105 and 106 of the Code provide the basis for an employee to exclude from gross income for federal income tax purposes the value of employer-provided health coverage.[31] Section 105 allows an employee to exclude from income the amounts actually reimbursed by an employer for the

---

[21] 42 U.S.C. § 1395w-132. The changes made by the 2010 Heath Care Reform Act to Medicare Part D will make the standard Medicare Part D plan more valuable on an actuarial basis, which will make it more difficult for employer-sponsored retiree prescription drug plans to qualify for RDS payments. *See supra* **§ 11.01** notes 1–20 and accompanying text for a discussion of the Act's changes to the standard Medicare Part D plan.

[22] *See http://www.cms.gov/EmployerRetireeDrugSubsid/Downloads/OviewoftheRDSrev1.pdf* for information on how an employer can apply for RDS payments.

[23] 42 U.S.C. § 1395w-132(a)(3).

[24] *See http://rds.cms.hhs.gov/reference_materials/threshold_limit.htm.*

[25] 42 U.S.C. § 1395w-132(a)(3)(C).

[26] I.R.C. § 139A (as added by the MMA § 1202(a)).

[27] I.R.C. § 162 (providing a deduction for trade or business expenses).

[28] PPACA § 9012.

[29] HCERA § 1407 (delaying the effective date of Section 9012 of the PPACA from tax years beginning after December 31, 2010, to tax years beginning after December 31, 2012).

[30] James A. White, *Corporate Charges Pegged to New Health Law Keep Adding Up*, WSJ. April 2, 2010.

[31] I.R.C. §§ 105, 106.

medical care of an employee, his or her spouse, and dependents.[32] Section 106 allows an employee to exclude from income the cost of group health plan coverage paid by the employer.[33] Together, they house the single largest tax expenditure in the Internal Revenue Code and incentivize employers to provide health care coverage to employees.[34]

As with any tax expenditure, there are limits on the incentive. Section 105(h) of the Code provides that benefits made available in a self-funded group health plan will qualify for the Section 105 tax exclusion only if the plan does not discriminate in favor of highly com-pensated individuals.[35] A "highly compensated individual," for this purpose, means one of the five highest paid officers, a shareholder who owns more than 10 percent of the employer, or an individual who is among the highest-paid 25 percent of all employees.[36] Certain employees are excluded from the eligibility portion of the nondiscrimination analysis (as described below), including employees who have completed less than three years of service, employees who have not attained age 25, part-time or seasonal employees, collectively bargained employees, and employees who are non-resident aliens who receive no U.S.-source earned income.[37] This definition of "highly compensated individual" tends to be broader than the definition of "highly compensated employee" used for purposes of the nondiscrimination requirements applicable to tax-qualified retirement plans.[38]

The Section 105(h) nondiscrimination requirement applies in two ways. First, a self-funded group health plan cannot discriminate in favor of highly compensated individuals as to eligibility to participate. This requirement can be satisfied by passing a percentage test that is similar to the minimum coverage test applicable to tax-qualified retirement plans under Section 410(b) of the Code. Second, the benefits provided under a self-funded group health plan cannot discriminate in favor of highly compensated individuals. This requirement is satisfied only if all benefits provided under the plan to highly compensated individuals are also provided to other plan participants. To the extent that a self-funded health plan provides benefits to retirees, the nondiscrimination requirements will apply separately to the retiree population.[39]

Notwithstanding the existence of the Section 105(h) nondiscrimination limitation, employers that wish to provide additional health benefits to top executives and other highly compensated individuals have been undeterred. Employers can provide discriminatory health benefits either on an insured basis, thereby avoiding Section 105(h) (which only applies to self-funded group health plans), or by imputing the cost of the additional health benefits as income for federal income tax purposes. Employers often use these techniques to enhance incentive or retention compensation packages for executives, to provide additional coverage to certain highly compensated retirees, and to equalize benefits for highly compensated expatriates.

The 2010 Health Care Reform Act closes what may be viewed as a loophole in the existing tax law by extending the nondiscrimination requirements of Section 105(h) to insured group health plans.[40] Therefore, for plan years beginning on or after September 23, 2010, employers are prohibited from providing discriminatory health coverage to highly compensated individuals on an insured basis. However, if the discriminatory health coverage is provided as part of a grandfathered health plan,[41]

---

[32] I.R.C. § 105(b).

[33] I.R.C. § 106(a).

[34] *See www.taxpolicycenter.org/briefing-book/background/expenditures/largest.cfm* (comparing tax expenditures for the 2008 tax year).

[35] I.R.C. § 105(h).

[36] I.R.C. § 105(h)(5).

[37] I.R.C. § 105(h)(3)(B).

[38] *Compare* I.R.C. § 105(h)(5) *with* I.R.C. § 414(q) (providing a definition of highly compensated employee that generally is limited to 5% shareholders and employees who earn compensation in the previous year in excess of a dollar threshold ($110,000 for 2010)).

[39] Treas. Reg. § 1.105-11(c)(3)(iii).

[40] PPACA § 1001(5) (adding PHSA § 2716).

[41] *See* **Chapter 4** for a discussion of grandfathered health plans.

the prohibition will not apply unless and until the plan loses its grandfathered status.[42] Employers that make significant use of insured arrangements that discriminate in favor of highly compensated individuals should consider whether it is possible and desirable to take advantage of the grandfathering exemption.

Curiously, the penalties for providing discriminatory health coverage appear to be different based on whether the coverage is provided through a self-funded or an insured plan. Because the new provision does not apply to self-funded plans, the provision of discriminatory health coverage in violation of Section 105(h) of the Code continues to result in the inclusion of the value of the discriminatory benefits in the gross income of the affected highly compensated individuals.[43] Employers and highly compensated individuals may be able to reduce the tax exposure by designing the arrangement to impute the cost of the discriminatory coverage in income, as opposed to the value of the actual benefits provided.

On the other hand, the penalty for providing discriminatory health coverage through an insured arrangement is a civil money penalty of $100 per day per individual affected by the violation.[44] Because the penalty is provided under the PHSA and not the Code, imputing the amount of discriminatory benefits or the cost of the discriminatory coverage in income for the covered highly compensated individuals would not seem to be sufficient to avoid the civil monetary penalty. If this is the case, employers may shift back to self-funded arrangements to provide discriminatory health coverage to highly compensated individuals on an after-tax basis.

§ 11.03   Auto-Enrollment

In the Pension Protection Act of 2006 (PPA),[45] Congress paved the way for most employers to institute automatic enrollment arrangements in their Section 401(k) and 403(b) retirement savings programs. The PPA amended ERISA to supersede any state wage payment laws that would otherwise prohibit automatic enrollment arrangements for ERISA-covered plans.[46] By encouraging employers to establish automatic enrollment arrangements in their retirement plans, Congress hoped to increase retirement savings among American workers by leveraging employee inertia.

In a retirement plan automatic enrollment arrangement, new employees (and sometimes existing employees) are deemed to have elected to participate in the plan and to make contributions at a level set by the employer (e.g., 3 percent of pay).[47] The employer must provide sufficient advance notice of the automatic enrollment arrangement to employees, and employees must have the ability to opt out of the arrangement.[48] Employees can opt out by affirmatively electing not to participate in the retirement plan, or to participate at a different contribution level (e.g., 1 percent or 5 percent of pay).

The 2010 Health Care Reform Act extends the automatic enrollment concept to employment-based group health plans. The Act adds a new Section 18A to the Fair Labor Standards Act of 1938, as amended (FLSA),[49] which requires large employers that offer enrollment in one or more group health plans to automatically enroll new full-time employees in one of the plans (subject to any waiting periods authorized by law) and to continue enrollment of current employees.[50] "Large employers"

---

[42] PPACA § 1251(a).

[43] I.R.C. § 105(h).

[44] PHSA § 2723(b)(2).

[45] Pub. L. No. 109-280, 120 Stat. 780.

[46] PPA § 902(f) (adding Section 514(e)(1) of ERISA). The ERISA preemption provision does not apply to non-ERISA plans, such as those sponsored by church and governmental employers.

[47] See I.R.C. § 401(k)(13), as added by PPA § 902(a) (providing a safe harbor from section 401(k) plan nondiscrimination testing for certain plans with qualified automatic contribution arrangements).

[48] I.R.C. § 401(k)(13).

[49] Pub. L. No. 75-718, 52 Stat. 1060; see 29 U.S.C. § 201 et seq.

[50] PPACA § 1511.

are defined, for this purpose, as having more than 200 full-time employees.[51] Further guidance will be necessary to determine whether the threshold number of employees is determined as an average over some period and whether full-time equivalents are counted.

Large employers subject to the new requirement must provide adequate advance notice to employees regarding the automatic enrollment arrangement, and an opportunity to opt out of any coverage in which the employee is automatically enrolled.[52] Following in the footsteps of the PPA, the 2010 Health Care Reform Act specifically supersedes any state wage payment law that would prevent an employer from implementing an automatic enrollment arrangement in a group health plan.[53]

Curiously, the 2010 Health Care Reform Act does not include a specific effective date for the automatic enrollment provision. The lack of a specific effective date suggests that the requirement becomes effective on the PPACA's date of enactment, March 23, 2010. However, the requirement must be satisfied in accordance with regulations to be issued by the DOL, which have not yet been issued.[54]

§ 11.04   Employer Notice of Coverage Options

While employers are busy figuring out exactly how their employment-based group health plans compare to the Exchange options that will be available beginning in 2014, they need to be cognizant of a new employee notice requirement that requires disclosure of information relating to the employer's plan(s) and the Exchange. The 2010 Health Care Reform Act adds a new Section 18B to the FLSA, which sets forth the details of the new notice requirement.[55] All employers subject to the FLSA must disclose, in a written notice, the following:

- Information regarding the existence of an Exchange, including a description of the services provided by the Exchange as well as information regarding how employees can contact the Exchange for assistance and further information;[56]

- If the employment-based group health plan is deemed to be "inadequate," i.e., the plan's share of total allowed costs under the plan is less than 60 percent of such costs, information regarding the employees' possible eligibility for a premium tax credit or cost-sharing reduction for coverage purchased through the Exchange;[57] and

- If an employee purchases a QHP through the Exchange and the employer does not offer a free choice voucher, information regarding the possibility that the employee may lose the benefit of any tax-free employer contribution to the employment-based group health plan.[58]

The new notice requirement becomes effective on March 1, 2013, which is slightly less than three years following the enactment of the 2010 Health Care Reform Act.[59] Employers must provide the notice to all then-current employees by March 1, 2013, and to all new hires thereafter at the time of hiring.

---

[51] FLSA § 18A.

[52] FLSA § 18A.

[53] FLSA § 18A; see also PPA § 902(f) (adding Section 514(e)(1) of ERISA relating to pre-emption of state laws inhibiting automatic enrollment for retirement plans).

[54] FLSA § 18A.

[55] PPACA § 1512 (adding FLSA § 18B).

[56] FLSA § 18B(a); see Chapter 10 (discussing Exchanges).

[57] FLSA § 18B(a); see supra § 6.03 notes 43–73 and accompanying text (premium tax credits and cost-sharing reductions).

[58] FLSA § 18B(a); see supra § 10.03 notes 35–36 and accompanying text (free choice vouchers).

[59] FLSA § 18B(b).

§ 11.05 Nursing Mothers

The 2010 Health Care Reform Act also amends the FLSA to require employers to make certain accommodations for nursing mothers. The Act adds new Section 7(r) to the FLSA to require employers to provide:

- A "reasonable break time" for an employee to express breast milk for a nursing child for one year following the child's birth each time the employee has the need to express milk; and

- A place, other than a bathroom, that is shielded from view and intrusion by the public and co-workers, where the employee can express breast milk.[60]

The new provision does not require employers to compensate an employee for the breaks, notwithstanding the fact that many rest periods or breaks of short duration are treated as "working time" by employers.

An employer with fewer than 50 employees may be exempt from the requirements for nursing mothers if such requirements would impose an undue hardship on the employer.[61] The 2010 Health Care Reform Act defines "undue hardship" as imposing on the employer "significant difficulty or expense when considered in relation to the size, financial resources, nature or structure of the employer's business."[62] Significantly, the Act does not pre-empt the laws in several states that may provide equivalent or greater protections to employees who are nursing mothers.[63]

§ 11.06 Reporting Cost of Coverage on Form W-2

Beginning with the 2011 tax year, the 2010 Health Care Reform Act requires all employers that provide an employment-based group health plan to employees to report, on each employee's Form W-2, the aggregate cost of the plan.[64] The "aggregate cost," for this purpose, is determined in the same manner as the "applicable premium" for COBRA purposes.[65] However, the aggregate cost to be reported on Form W-2 does not include any employee salary reduction contributions to a health flexible spending account (Health FSA), or any contributions to an HSA or an Archer MSA.[66] Because Forms W-2 are due on January 31 following a tax year, employers need to be prepared to report the aggregate cost of their group health plans on 2011 Forms W-2 by January 31, 2012.[67]

§ 11.07 Simple Cafeteria Plans for Small Businesses

[A] Background

Many employers that provide employment-based group health plans and charge a portion of the cost of the group health plan to employees offer employees an opportunity to pay that cost on a pretax basis through a "cafeteria plan" that satisfies the requirements of Section 125 of the Code. A cafeteria plan is a written plan document under which participating employees may choose to receive cash or one or more qualified benefits.[68] A "qualified benefit" is any benefit that is not includible in the gross

---

[60] PPACA § 4207 (adding FLSA § 7(r)).

[61] FLSA § 7(r).

[62] FLSA § 7(r).

[63] *See, e.g.*, N.J. Rev. Stat. § 26:4B-4/5 (entitling a nursing mother to breastfeed in any place of public accommodation).

[64] PPACA § 9002 (adding I.R.C. § 6051(a)(14)).

[65] I.R.C. § 6051(a)(14) (citing the definition of applicable premium set forth in Section 4980B(f)(4) of the Code).

[66] I.R.C. § 6051(a)(14).

[67] I.R.C. § 6051(a).

[68] I.R.C. § 125(d).

income of an employee by reason of a specific provision of the Code.[69] Qualified benefits generally include employer-provided health coverage, group term life and accidental death and dismemberment (AD&D) insurance, disability benefits, Health FSAs, and dependent care flexible spending accounts.[70] Employees who elect to receive qualified benefits under a cafeteria plan generally make pretax salary reduction contributions to pay for those benefits.

Cafeteria plans are subject to certain nondiscrimination requirements under Section 125 of the Code. Generally, a cafeteria plan cannot discriminate in favor of highly compensated individuals as to eligibility to participate in the plan or with respect to contributions and benefits provided under the plan.[71] If the cafeteria plan is discriminatory, highly compensated individuals will be treated as being in constructive receipt (for tax purposes) of a cash benefit.[72] A "highly compensated individual" is defined as an officer, 5 percent shareholder, or highly compensated employee of the employer.[73] In addition, the benefits provided to key employees in a cafeteria plan cannot exceed 25 percent of the aggregate of such benefits provided to all employees under the plan.[74]

A cafeteria plan does not discriminate as to eligibility to participate if (i) the plan benefits a classification of employees that does not discriminate in favor of officers, shareholders, or highly compensated individuals, (ii) no more than three years of employment are required to participate in the plan and the employment requirement is uniform for all employees, and (iii) eligible employees begin participation by the first day of the first plan year after the employment requirement is satisfied.[75] Under proposed Treasury regulations, a cafeteria plan does not discriminate as to eligibility if the plan satisfies certain nondiscriminatory classification tests based on the tests that apply to tax-qualified retirement plans.[76]

A cafeteria plan that offers group health plan benefits does not discriminate with respect to contributions and benefits if (i) contributions for each participant equal 100 percent of the cost of the health benefit coverage under the plan of the majority of highly compensated participants similarly situated, or 75 percent of the cost of the most expensive health benefit coverage of the similarly situated participant having the highest-cost health benefit coverage under the plan, and (ii) contributions and benefits in excess of those described in clause (i) bear a uniform relationship to compensation.[77] Many view these rules as unworkable, and it is expected that Treasury will issue new regulations to provide guidance as to how the cafeteria plan nondiscrimination rules should be applied.

[B] New Option for Small Businesses

Beginning in 2011, the 2010 Health Care Reform Act provides small employers with a means of establishing a cafeteria plan that is automatically exempt from the Section 125 nondiscrimination requirements.[78] A "small employer" means an employer that employed, on average, 100 or fewer employees on business days during either of the two preceding years.[79] If the employer was not in existence in a preceding year (and throughout the whole preceding year), the calculation is based on

---

[69] I.R.C. § 125(f).

[70] I.R.C. § 125(f).

[71] I.R.C. § 125(b)(1).

[72] I.R.C. § 125(b)(1); Prop. Treas. Reg. § 1.125-7(m)(2).

[73] I.R.C. § 125(e). Spouses and dependents of highly compensated individuals are themselves considered highly compensated individuals. I.R.C. § 125(e)(1)(D).

[74] I.R.C. § 125(b)(2). "Key employees" are defined in the same manner as under the top-heavy rules and the rules regarding nonqualified deferred compensation under Section 409A of the Code. *See* I.R.C. § 416(i).

[75] I.R.C. § 125(g)(3); Prop. Treas. Reg. § 1.125-7.

[76] Prop. Treas. Reg. § 1.125-7(b)(1). *See generally* I.R.C. § 410(b); Treas. Reg. §§ 1.410(b)-2 *et seq.* (discussing the minimum coverage rules applicable to tax-qualified retirement plans).

[77] I.R.C. § 125(g)(2); Prop. Treas. Reg. § 1.125-7(e).

[78] PPACA § 9022 (adding I.R.C. § 125(j)).

[79] I.R.C. § 125(j)(5).

the number of employees that the employer reasonably expects to employ on business days in the current year.[80] If a small employer establishes a "simple cafeteria plan" described in this section, and subsequently increases its employee base such that it can no longer satisfy the 100-employee test, the employer is deemed to remain a small employer until such time as it employs, on average, 200 or more employees in any preceding year.[81] All affiliates that are in the employer's controlled group are treated as a single employer for purposes of the determining whether the employer is a small employer.[82]

The simple cafeteria plan contemplated by the 2010 Health Care Reform Act must meet both an employer contribution requirement and minimum eligibility and participation requirements. To satisfy the employer contribution requirement, the employer must contribute, on behalf of each qualified employee (i.e., those who are not highly compensated individuals or key employees), an amount (i) equal to a uniform percentage (at least 2 percent) of the employee's compensation for the plan year, or (ii) that is at least equal to the lesser of 6 percent of the employee's compensation or two times ($2\times$) the amount of the employee's salary reduction contributions for the plan year.[83] If the employer seeks to satisfy the contribution requirement using matching contributions, the rate of matching contributions for any highly compensated or key employee cannot be greater than the rate of matching contributions for any other non–highly compensated or non-key employee.[84]

To satisfy the minimum eligibility and participation requirements, any employee who completes at least 1,000 hours of service for the employer for the preceding plan year must be eligible to participate in the plan, and any eligible employee must be permitted to elect any benefit available under the plan, subject to any terms and conditions of the plan applicable to all participants.[85] Certain employees may be excluded for this purpose, such as employees who have not attained age 21 by the end of the plan year, have less than one year of service with the employer, are covered by a collective bargaining agreement, or are nonresident aliens with no U.S.-source income.[86]

---

[80] I.R.C. § 125(j)(5)(B). Any predecessor employer is treated as the employer for purposes of applying the 100-employee test. I.R.C. § 125(j)(5)(D)(i).

[81] I.R.C. § 125(j)(5)(C).

[82] I.R.C. § 125(j)(5)(D)(ii) (referencing the controlled group rules set forth in Section 414 of the Code).

[83] I.R.C. § 125(j)(3). The contribution rule is similar to the contribution obligation applicable to safe harbor Section 401(k) plans that are exempt from the annual nondiscrimination tests. *See* I.R.C. §§ 401(k)(12), (13).

[84] I.R.C. § 125(j)(3)(B).

[85] I.R.C. § 125(j)(4).

[86] I.R.C. § 125(j)(4)(B).

CHAPTER 12
NEW TAXES AND OTHER REVENUE-RAISERS

§ 12.01 "Cadillac" Tax

One way to control the rising cost of health coverage is to incentivize employees (and their dependents) to use only the necessary and appropriate health-related products and services. Requiring employees to pay for a portion of such products and services may provide such an incentive. However, if an employee has very valuable "Cadillac" health coverage for which he or she pays little or nothing, the incentive to act as a rational consumer of health-related products and services vanishes.

The 2010 Health Care Reform Act attempts to address this issue (and raise revenue to help pay for health care reform) by adding a new nondeductible tax on "Cadillac" health coverage. The Act adds Section 4980I to the Internal Revenue Code, which imposes a 40 percent excise tax on the "excess benefit" in "applicable employer-sponsored coverage."[1] The excise tax is imposed on the insurance company in an insured health plan and on the employer/plan sponsor in an employment-based group health plan that is self-funded.[2]

The excess amount, determined on a monthly basis, is equal to the aggregate monthly cost of employer-sponsored coverage over one-twelfth of the annual limitation.[3] The cost of a plan is determined in the same manner as the COBRA premium.[4] Beginning in 2018, the annual limitation is $10,200 for self-only coverage and $27,500 for family coverage.[5] Both figures are adjusted, beginning in 2018, by the "health cost adjustment percentage," which basically measures the growth in health insurance costs, adjusted by age and gender factors, by reference to the growth in the cost of the standard benefit option in the Federal Employees Health Benefit Plan after 2010.[6]

The threshold for determining excess amounts is higher for qualified retirees and those participating in a plan sponsored by an employer where the majority of the employees covered by the plan are engaged in a high-risk profession or are employed to repair or install electrical or telecommunication lines.[7] Beginning in 2018, the annual limitation for these individuals is $11,850 for self-only coverage and $30,950 for family coverage, adjusted in each case for cost-of-living increases.[8] A qualified retiree is an individual who is receiving retiree coverage, is over age 55, and is not Medicare eligible.[9] High-risk professions include police and fire personnel, emergency medical technicians and other first responders, longshoremen, and individuals engaged in the construction, mining, agriculture (not including food processing), forestry, and fishing industries.[10] Retirees of high-risk professions are included if they have at least 20 years of employment in the profession.[11]

The term "applicable employer-sponsored coverage" includes any employment-based group health plan provided to any employee, former employee, or surviving spouse (or any other primary insured individual) on a pretax basis, other than a plan providing certain "excepted" benefits, long-term care,

---

[1] PPACA § 9001 (adding I.R.C. § 4980I).

[2] I.R.C. § 4980I(c)(2).

[3] I.R.C. § 4980I(b)(2).

[4] I.R.C. § 4980I(d)(2) (citing the COBRA premium calculation rules located at Section 4980B(f)(4) of the Code).

[5] I.R.C. § 4980I(b)(3)(C)(i).

[6] I.R.C. §§ 4980I(b)(3)(C)(ii), (iii).

[7] I.R.C. § 4980I(b)(3)(C)(iv). This is the substantially identical to the definition of "early retiree" that is applicable to the temporary early retiree reinsurance program. *See supra* § **6.01** notes 2–31 for a discussion of the reinsurance program. Therefore, to some extent the Act creates conflicting incentives for employers. Through the end of 2013, the reinsurance program encourages employers to continue to provide early retiree health coverage by providing reimbursements of 80% of the health expenses between $15,000 and $90,000. However, beginning in 2018, employers are penalized for providing retiree health coverage with a value in excess of $11,850 (self) or $30,950 (family), as adjusted.

[8] I.R.C. § 4980I(b)(3)(C)(iv).

[9] I.R.C. § 4980I(f)(2).

[10] I.R.C. § 4980I(f)(3).

[11] I.R.C. § 4980I(f)(3).

dental or vision benefits.[12] Applicable employer-sponsored coverage is determined without regard to whether the employee pays for all or a portion of the coverage, and includes Health FSAs and plans covering government employees.[13]

In the event that the insurer or employer/plan sponsor underpays the excise tax for any month, a penalty equal to 100 percent of any underpayment amount is imposed, plus interest calculated at the IRS tax underpayment rate.[14] However, the penalty may not apply if the employer/plan sponsor can show that it neither knew, nor by exercising reasonable diligence would have known, that an underpayment existed, if the underpayment is corrected within 30 days, and in such other circumstances as may be specified in regulations.[15]

§ 12.02   Health FSAs

[A]   Background

In the 1980s, after about a decade of administering defined benefit pension plans in accordance with the ERISA rules, employers and employees started to look for ways to supplement the standard pension benefits. Section 401(k) plans, which had first appeared in the late 1970s, started to become a popular addition to employer retirement benefits packages because they allowed employees to supplement their employer-funded pensions with their own contributions on a pretax basis.[16] As defined benefit pension plans fell out of favor in the 1990s due to their complexity and unpredictable costs, Section 401(k) plans and their progeny ultimately became the primary retirement benefits vehicle for most employers.[17] Thus, for better or for worse, there has been an evolutionary shift in the manner in which retirement benefits are provided, from the paternalistic employer-funded defined benefit pension plans to the more flexible employer and employee-funded defined contribution Section 401(k) plans.

A similar evolutionary cycle is under way for employment-based group health plans. In the years following ERISA's enactment, many employers provided health benefits to employees through traditional indemnity arrangements funded entirely or almost entirely by employers. Employees (and their spouses and dependents) could go to any health care provider to receive treatment, and the insurance company would pay most or all of the expenses. As health care costs rose in the 1980s, 1990s, and 2000s, employers started to adopt arrangements with cost-containment structures, such as PPOs, HMOs, and POS arrangements. Employers also introduced the concept of employee co-insurance and cost-sharing to shift a portion of the increasing costs to employees.

To supplement the traditional employment-based group health plans, employers began to make health flexible spending accounts (Health FSAs) available to employees. Like Section 401(k) plans on the retirement side, Health FSAs are accounts to which employees (and employers) can make contributions on a pretax basis to reimburse the employee for medical expenses incurred by the employee

---

[12] I.R.C. § 4980I(d)(1). Excepted benefits, for this purpose, include coverage only for accident or disability income insurance, liability insurance or coverage issued as a supplement to liability insurance, workers' compensation or similar insurance, automobile medical payment insurance, credit-only insurance and other similar coverage. I.R.C. § 9832(c)(1). However, coverage for on-site medical clinics may be applicable employer-sponsored coverage. I.R.C. § 4980I(d)(1)(B)(i). Applicable employer-sponsored coverage also does not include coverage for a specified disease or illness, or hospital indemnity or fixed indemnity insurance if such coverage is not excludable from gross income. I.R.C. § 4980I(d)(1)(B)(iii).

[13] I.R.C. § 4980I(d)(1).

[14] I.R.C. § 4980I(e).

[15] I.R.C. § 4980I(e)(2).

[16] I.R.C. § 401(k), as added by the Revenue Act of 1978, Pub. L. No. 95-600, 92 Stat. 2763, § 135.

[17] Over the years, Section 403(b) tax-sheltered annuity plans, which are available only for public school and nonprofit employers, and Section 457(b) eligible deferred compensation plans, which are available for government and nonprofit employers, have become subject to many of the same requirements and principles as apply to Section 401(k) plans.

(or former employee), spouse or dependent that are not otherwise covered by health insurance.[18] Unlike Section 401(k) plans, contributions to Health FSAs do not have to be held in trust. A Health FSA can simply be recorded as an unfunded liability in the employer's bookkeeping records.

[B] New Contribution Limit of Health FSAs

Prior to the 2010 Health Care Reform Act, there was no limit on the amount that an employee could elect to contribute to a Health FSA on a pretax basis. However, Health FSAs are subject to a "use it or lose it" rule, whereby any amounts remaining in the Health FSA at the end of the plan year (or at the end of a grace period following the plan year) after all claims are incurred must be forfeited to the employer.[19] In addition, Health FSAs are subject to a uniform coverage rule, whereby the maximum amount of reimbursement elected by the employee must be available at all times during the plan year.[20] For example, if prior to the plan year an employee elects to contribute $5,000 on a pretax basis to a Health FSA for the plan year, the entire $5,000 must be available to the employee as reimbursement on the first day of the plan year. If the employee incurs $5,000 in reimbursable expenses on the first day of the plan year, receives the full reimbursement from the Health FSA, and then terminates employment before contributing the full $5,000 to the Health FSA, the employer is liable for the loss and cannot seek recovery from the terminated employee. Thus, as a practical matter, most employers have implemented an annual limit of $5,000 or less to avoid material exposure to employees under the use-it-or-lose-it rule, or to the employer under the uniform coverage rule.

Beginning in 2013, annual contributions to Health FSAs are limited to $2,500.[21] The limit applies to the aggregate of employer and employee contributions to Health FSAs, and is adjusted for cost-of-living increases after 2013.[22] Employers will need to amend their Health FSA plan documents and summary plan descriptions to reflect this change before the end of the 2013 plan year. This change, which obviously does not expand health coverage, is one of the revenue-raisers intended to provide a small part of the funding for health care reform.

[C] Prohibition of Reimbursement of OTC Drug Expenses

Amounts held in Health FSAs can be used to reimburse an employee for expenses incurred for "medical care" of the employee (or former employee), spouse and dependents.[23] In 2003, the Internal Revenue Service ruled, for the first time, that expenses incurred for medicines and drugs purchased "over the counter" (i.e., without a prescription of a physician) could constitute expenses for medical care that can be reimbursed from a Health FSA.[24] Such "OTC" expenses might include purchases of allergy medicine, pain relievers, antacids, and cold medicine. However, expenses for dietary supplements and similar items that are merely beneficial to the general health of the employee, spouse, and dependents are not expenses for medical care and cannot be reimbursed from a Health FSA.[25] While many employer-sponsored Health FSAs now provide for reimbursements of OTC medicines and drugs, it remains a challenge for employees, employers and third-party administrators to substantiate

---

[18] I.R.C. § 105(b); Prop. Treas. Reg. § 1.125-5(a).

[19] I.R.C. § 125(d)(2); Prop. Treas. Reg. § 1.125-5(c). A Health FSA plan may provide a grace period following the plan year during which claims may be incurred and reimbursed from the Health FSA for the plan year just ended. I.R.S. Notice 2005-42, 2005-23 I.R.B. 1204; Prop. Treas. Reg. § 1.125-1(e). The grace period can extend for up to 2½ months following the end of the plan year. I.R.S. Notice 2005-42, 2005-23 I.R.B. 1204; Prop. Treas. Reg. § 1.125-1(e).

[20] I.R.C. § 125(d)(2); Prop. Treas. Reg. § 1.125-5(d)(1).

[21] PPACA § 9005 (adding I.R.C. § 125(i)).

[22] I.R.C. § 125(i).

[23] I.R.C. § 105(b).

[24] I.R.S. Rev. Rul. 2003-102, 2003-2 C.B. 559.

[25] I.R.S. Rev. Rul. 2003-102, 2003-2 C.B. 559.

the differences between OTC expenses for medical care (which may be reimbursed) and OTC expenses for the general health of the employee, spouse, or dependent (which may not).

In another effort to raise revenue for health care reform, the 2010 Health Care Reform Act adds Section 106(f) to the Code to provide that, beginning in calendar year 2011, OTC medicines and drugs are no longer eligible for reimbursement from Health FSAs.[26] Calendar year Health FSAs that feature grace periods may permit reimbursement of OTC medicines and drugs purchased in 2011, but only to the extent that costs are incurred during the grace period for the 2010 plan year (which cannot extend for more than two and one-half months after the end of the 2010 plan year), and are charged against the 2010 Health FSA balances.[27] Only prescription drug and insulin costs will be considered medical expenses eligible for reimbursement.[28] This change will require employers and third-party administrators that offer Health FSAs, and particularly those that have implemented debit card features for their Health FSAs, to redesign the structure of their Health FSAs. Employers that offer Health FSAs based on fiscal years other than the calendar year should advise employees who have already made Health FSA elections for the fiscal year ending in 2011, that OTC medicine and drug expenses are not reimbursable if they are incurred after December 31, 2010.

§ 12.03   HSAs

[A]   Background

Another vehicle that employees may use to supplement their employer-sponsored health plan coverage is a health savings account (HSA). HSAs, which first became available in 2004, are trust or custodial accounts that may be established by eligible individuals who have coverage under a high-deductible health plan (HDHP).[29] Eligible individuals (and their employers) may contribute to the HSA on a pretax basis, and the HSA account may be used by the individual for reimbursement of certain medical expenses of the individual or his or her spouse or dependents.[30]

HSAs have certain advantages as compared to Health FSAs. HSAs are not subject to the use-it-or-lose-it rules that apply to Health FSAs, so unused account balances can be carried forward from year to year, and eligible individuals can never be reimbursed in an amount greater than the then-current HSA account balances.[31] Also, HSAs are portable, which means that an employee who switches jobs does not need to set up multiple HSAs.[32] All contributions can be made to the same HSA. Finally, whereas Health FSA balances must be used to reimburse medical expenses, an individual can withdraw funds from an HSA for any reason, provided that the individual pays federal income taxes (and possibly an excise tax) if funds are withdrawn from an HSA other than as reimbursement for qualified medical expenses.[33]

HSAs have some disadvantages as well. Unlike Health FSAs (at least until 2013),[34] monthly contributions to an HSA are capped at one-twelfth of $3,150 (for those individuals with single coverage under an HDHP for 2010) and $6,150 (for those individuals with family coverage under an

---

[26] PPACA § 9003(c) (adding I.R.C. § 106(f)). A similar rule applies for HSAs and Archer MSAs. PPACA §§ 9003(a), (b); *see infra* **§ 12.03** notes 29–37 discussing HSAs.

[27] *See* I.R.S. Notice 2005-42, 2005-23 I.R.B. 1204 (discussing Health FSA grace periods).

[28] I.R.C. § 106(f).

[29] Medicare Prescription Drug, Improvement, and Modernization Act of 2003, Pub. L. No. 108-173, 117 Stat. 2066, § 1201(a).

[30] I.R.C. §§ 223(d), (f). Investment earnings held within the HSA are not taxed until they are distributed to the individual I.R.C. § 223(e).

[31] *See supra* **§ 12.02[B]** notes 19–20 (discussing use-it-or-lose-it and uniform coverage rules applicable to Health FSAs).

[32] I.R.C. § 223(d) (indicating that the individual is the owner of the account).

[33] I.R.C. § 223(f); *see infra* **§ 12.03[C]** notes 42–45 for a discussion of the Act's change to the additional tax on HSA withdrawals used for purposes other than the reimbursement of qualified medical expenses.

[34] *See supra* **§ 12.02[B]** notes 19–22 for a discussion of the Act's limit on annual Health FSA contributions.

HDHP for 2010).[35] For individuals who will attain age 55 before the end of the year, those limits are increased by $1,000.[36] Also, an individual is eligible to contribute to an HSA only if he or she is covered under an HDHP that meets certain requirements. For 2010, an HDHP must have a deductible of at least $1,200 (for single coverage) or $2,400 (for family coverage) and an out-of-pocket expense limit of no more than $5,950 (for single coverage) or $11,900 (for family coverage).[37]

[B] Prohibition of Reimbursement of OTC Drug Expenses

If HSA funds are used to reimburse an individual for "qualified medical expenses," the reimbursements are not subject to federal income tax for the individual.[38] Qualified medical expenses are defined in the same fashion as "expenses for medical care" in the Health FSA context.[39] Therefore, the provisions of the 2010 Health Care Reform Act that exclude expenses for OTC medicines and drugs from being eligible medical expenses that can be reimbursed from Health FSAs apply equally to HSAs.[40] Accordingly, beginning in 2011, the only medicine and drug expenses that will be treated as qualified medical expenses for purposes of tax-free reimbursement from an HSA are prescription drug and insulin expenses.[41]

[C] Tax Increase for Non-Qualified Medical Expense Reimbursements

As indicated above, HSA reimbursements for qualified medical expenses are tax-free to the individual. However, the HSA rules permit individuals to withdraw funds from their HSAs for reasons other than qualified medical expenses. In such cases, the amounts withdrawn are subject to federal income tax at the individual's normal tax rate.[42] However, if the individual is not yet Medicare eligible (which generally means that the individual has not yet reached age 65), there is an additional 10 percent tax applied to the amount withdrawn for purposes other than qualified medical expenses.[43] The additional tax does not apply if the withdrawal is made after the individual has become disabled or has died.[44]

Under the 2010 Health Care Reform Act, beginning in 2011, the additional tax applicable to HSA distributions used for purposes other than qualified medical expenses is increased to 20 percent.[45] The existing exceptions for withdrawals after Medicare eligibility, death or disability continue to apply.

§ 12.04 Administrative Fees for Self-Funded and Insured Plans

The 2010 Health Care Reform Act generally provides funding for new studies and research on how the quality and efficiency of the United States health care system can be improved. One example

---

[35] I.R.C. § 223(b)(2).

[36] I.R.C. § 223(b)(3).

[37] I.R.C. § 223(c)(2).

[38] I.R.C. § 223(f)(1).

[39] I.R.C. § 223(d)(2)(A) (defining qualified medical expenses as amounts paid by an HSA beneficiary for medical care (as defined in Section 213(d) of the Code) of the individual, his or her spouse, and his or her dependents, provided that such expenses have not be reimbursed by insurance or otherwise).

[40] PPACA § 9003(a) (amending I.R.C. § 223(d)(2)(A)); see supra § 12.02[C] notes 23–28 for a discussion of the change to reimbursements of OTC medicines and drugs from Health FSAs.

[41] I.R.C. § 223(d)(2)(A).

[42] I.R.C. § 223(f)(2).

[43] I.R.C. § 223(f)(4)(C). An individual also may become eligible for Medicare by reason of certain disabilities prior to age 65.

[44] I.R.C. § 223(f)(4)(B).

[45] PPACA § 9004(a) (amending I.R.C. § 223(f)(4)(A)). A similar excise tax for Archer MSAs is increased from 15% to 20%. PPACA § 9004(b).

is Section 6301 of the PPACA, which provides for comparative clinical effectiveness research.[46] Basically, this means research to compare health outcomes and the clinical effectiveness, risks and benefits of two or more medical treatments, services or items.[47] The research will be conducted by a new nonprofit organization called the Patient-Centered Outcomes Research Institute (the Institute), and funding for the Institute will be generated, in part, from new fees imposed upon insured and self-funded health plans.[48]

For insured health plans, the 2010 Health Care Reform Act imposes a new fee on each health insurance policy for each policy year ending after September 30, 2012.[49] The new fee, which is payable by the insurance company that issues the policy, is equal to $2.00 multiplied by the average number of lives covered under the policy.[50] Note that the fee is based on the number of covered lives, which would include spouses, surviving spouses, dependents, and others eligible for coverage. However, for calendar years ending in fiscal year 2013, the fee is reduced from $2.00 to $1.00 per covered life.[51] The fee is adjusted for policy years beginning in fiscal years ending after September 30, 2014, by the percentage increase in the projected per capita amount of National Health Expenditures, as published by the U.S. Treasury Department.[52]

For self-funded health plans, the 2010 Health Care Reform Act imposes a similar new fee to fund the Institute. Again, the fee is equal to $2.00 multiplied by the average number of lives covered under the plan, with a similar reduction to $1.00 for plan years ending during fiscal year 2013, and similar adjustments for the percentage increase in the projected per capita amount of National Health Expenditures.[53] The major difference is that the fee for self-funded health plans must be paid by the plan sponsor, which generally is the employer in the case of a single-employer plan.[54] Also, unlike the case in other areas, the Act makes clear that a self-funded health plan includes any portion of a health plan that is not insured.[55]

In both cases, the fees to fund the Institute are applied on a temporary basis. The 2010 Health Care Reform Act specifies that new fees will not apply for policy years (in the case of insured health plans) and plan years (in the case of self-funded health plans) that end after September 30, 2019.[56]

§ 12.05   Additional Taxes on High Earners

[A]   Increase in Basic HI Tax

One of the obvious challenges in crafting the new health care reform law was to find ways to pay for the changes to the system. While much of the funding is expected to come from changes to make the Medicare system more efficient, the 2010 Health Care Reform Act imposes new taxes on high-earning individuals to create additional sources of funding.

The 2010 Health Care Reform Act amends the Hospital Insurance (HI) portion of the Federal Insurance Contributions Act (FICA) tax to increase the rate at which high-earning employees are taxed

---

[46] PPACA § 6301, adding new Subtitle D to 42 U.S.C. §§ 1301 *et seq.*

[47] 42 U.S.C. § 1181(a)(2).

[48] 42 U.S.C. § 1181(b).

[49] PPACA § 6301 (adding I.R.C. § 4375). The fee does not apply to policies where substantially all of the coverage is for excepted benefits, as defined in Section 9832(c) of the Code. I.R.C. § 4375(b)(2).

[50] I.R.C. § 4375(a).

[51] I.R.C. § 4375(a).

[52] I.R.C. § 4375(d).

[53] PPACA § 6301 (adding I.R.C. § 4376).

[54] I.R.C. § 4376(b).

[55] I.R.C. § 4376(c)(1); *see supra* **§ 4.04** for a discussion of the grandfathered health plan exception for collectively bargained insured plans and the statutory ambiguity regarding what constitutes an insured plan.

[56] I.R.C. §§ 4375(e), 4376(e).

from 1.45 percent of wages to 2.35 percent of wages—a 62 percent increase.[57] The increase applies only to annual wages in excess of $250,000 for taxpayers who are married filing jointly for federal income tax purposes, $125,000 for taxpayers who are married filing separately, or $200,000 for taxpayers with any other filing status.[58] For purposes of wage withholding, employers may assume that the additional tax applies to the employee's wages in excess of $200,000.[59] There is no corresponding additional HI tax assessed against employers.

The additional HI tax applies on the same basis to self-employed individuals who are subject to the Self-Employment Contributions Act (SECA) tax.[60] However, self-employed individuals are not permitted to deduct any portion of the additional HI tax.[61] Thus, a self-employed individual who is a high earner may continue to deduct one-half of the 2.9 percent HI tax imposed under SECA, but cannot deduct any portion of the additional 0.9 percent HI tax imposed on self-employment income in excess of $250,000, $125,000, or $200,000 as applicable.[62] The inability of self-employed individuals to deduct the additional 0.9 percent HI tax under SECA is consistent with the fact that the additional 0.9 percent HI tax under FICA applies only to employees and not employers.

The additional HI taxes will apply to taxable years beginning after December 31, 2012.[63]

[B] HI Tax on Unearned Income

In addition to the increase in the rate of the HI tax under both FICA and SECA, the 2010 Health Care Reform Act imposes a significant new tax on certain taxpayers who have unearned income.[64] The new tax is equal to 3.8 percent of the *lesser* of (1) the taxpayer's net investment income for the taxable year, or (2) the excess of the taxpayer's modified adjusted gross income for the taxable year over the threshold amount.[65] Because the threshold amount is equal to $250,000 for taxpayers who are married filing jointly for federal income tax purposes and for surviving spouses, or $200,000 for other filers, the new tax on unearned income applies only to high earners who have unearned income.[66]

"Net investment income" means, for this purpose, the sum of all income derived from interest, dividends, annuities, royalties, and rents (other than such income derived from the ordinary course of a trade or business); all income derived from the disposition of property other than property held in a trade or business; and all income derived from a trade or business that is a passive activity or the trading of financial instruments or commodities; over deductions allocable to such gross income or net gain.[67] Special rules apply to income on investments in working capital, certain active interests in partnerships and Subchapter S corporations, and self-employment income.[68] Finally, net investment income does not include distributions from qualified retirement plans under Section 401(a) of the Code, qualified annuities under Section 403(a), tax-sheltered annuities under Section 403(b), traditional or Roth individual retirement arrangements under Sections 408 and 408A, respectively, and eligible deferred compensation plans under Section 457(b).[69]

---

[57] PPACA § 9015 (amending I.R.C. § 3101(b)).

[58] I.R.C. § 3101(b)(2).

[59] PPACA § 9015(a)(2) (adding I.R.C. § 3102(f)).

[60] PPACA § 9015(b) (amending I.R.C. § 1401(b)).

[61] PPACA § 9015(b)(2) (amending I.R.C. § 164(f)).

[62] I.R.C. § 1402(a)(12).

[63] PPACA § 9015(c).

[64] HCERA § 1402(a) (adding new I.R.C. § 1411). The new tax does not apply to nonresident aliens. I.R.C. § 1411(e).

[65] I.R.C. § 1411(a)(1).

[66] I.R.C. § 1411(b).

[67] I.R.C. § 1411(c).

[68] I.R.C. §§ 1411(c)(3), (4) and (6).

[69] I.R.C. § 1411(c)(5). The existence of this exception for "qualified"-type retirement plans raises a question as to whether the new tax applies to distributions from nonqualified deferred compensation plans such as supplemental executive retirement plans and Section 401(k) excess plans.

"Modified adjusted gross income" is defined, for this purpose, as adjusted gross income increased by the excess of the taxpayer's foreign earned income and housing costs (as defined in Section 911(a)(1) of the Code) over the amount of any deductions or exclusions disallowed under Section 911(d)(6).[70]

The new tax on unearned income is extended to certain trusts and estates in addition to high-earning individual taxpayers. The tax on trusts and estates is equal to 3.8 percent of the lesser of (i) the undistributed net investment income for the taxable year, or (ii) the excess of the adjusted gross income for the taxable year over the dollar amount at which the highest tax bracket applicable to trusts and estates begins for such taxable year ($7,500 for 2010).[71]

The new tax on unearned income will apply to taxable years beginning after December 31, 2012.[72]

§ 12.06   Other Taxes

[A]   Tax on Charitable Hospitals

The 2010 Health Care Reform Act adds a new Section 501(r) to the Code, which imposes additional requirements on tax-exempt charitable hospitals relating to community health needs assessments, financial assistance policies, limits on charges, and billing and collections.[73] Charitable hospitals that fail to meet the requirements of Section 501(r) are subject to a tax on the organization equal to $50,000.[74] New reporting and monitoring mandates also apply.

[B]   Fees on Constituencies Participating in the U.S. Health System

The 2010 Health Care Reform Act imposes fees on several different constituencies that form the U.S. health system, including branded pharmaceutical manufacturers and importers,[75] medical device manufacturers and importers,[76] and health insurance providers.[77]

[C]   Increased Threshold for Itemized Medical Expense Deductions

Currently, taxpayers are permitted to deduct their unreimbursed medical expenses in excess of 7.5 percent of their adjusted gross income.[78] The 2010 Health Care Reform Act increases the threshold from 7.5 percent to 10 percent, effective for taxable years beginning after December 31, 2012.[79] However, for the 2013–2016 taxable years, if the taxpayer or the taxpayer's spouse has attained age 65 or older, the threshold remains at 7.5 percent for such taxable year.[80]

---

[70] I.R.C. § 1411(d).

[71] I.R.C. § 1411(a)(2). The new tax does not apply to a trust if all of the unexpired interests are devoted to charitable purposes. I.R.C. § 1411(e)(2) (referencing charitable interests described in Section 170(c)(2)(B) of the Code).

[72] HCERA § 1402(a)(4).

[73] PPACA § 9007 (adding I.R.C. § 501(r)).

[74] PPACA § 9007 (adding I.R.C. § 4959).

[75] PPACA § 9008, as amended by HCERA § 1404(a).

[76] HCERA § 1405(a) (adding I.R.C. § 4191). Section 1405(d) of the HCERA repealed the original version of the annual fee on medical device manufacturers and importers, as set forth in Section 9009 of the PPACA, as amended by Section 10904(a) of the PPACA.

[77] PPACA § 9010, as amended by PPACA § 10905 and HCERA § 1406.

[78] I.R.C. § 213.

[79] PPACA § 9013 (amending I.R.C. § 213).

[80] I.R.C. § 213(f).

[D] Limitation on Compensation Deduction for Health Insurance Executives

Section 162(m) of the Code generally limits an employer's deduction on annual compensation paid to certain covered employees to $1 million, subject to exceptions for commissions and certain performance-based compensation.[81] Section 162(m) is limited in that it applies only to the compensation paid by a publicly held corporation to its chief executive officer and the three other highest paid executives (other than the CEO) whose compensation for the year is required to be reported to shareholders.[82]

The 2010 Health Care Reform Act extends the Section 162(m) deduction limitation to *any* officer, director, or employee of a "covered health insurance provider," which is defined as any insurance company that issues health insurance coverage and receives premiums for such coverage.[83] For taxable years beginning after December 31, 2012, a health insurance issuer is subject to Section 162(m) only if at least 25 percent of its gross premiums from providing health insurance coverage is from minimum essential coverage.[84] The limitation also applies to any affiliated entity that is in the same controlled group as the covered health insurance provider.[85] For purposes of applying the Section 162(m) deduction limitation to covered health insurance providers, the limitation on annual compensation is reduced to $500,000, and annual compensation is determined without regard to the exceptions for commissions and performance-based compensation.[86] Also, deferred compensation attributable to a year in which the $500,000 limit is reached will be nondeductible, even if it is paid in a later year.[87]

The extension of a modified version of Section 162(m) applies to covered health insurance providers for taxable years beginning after December 31, 2009.[88]

[E] Tax on Indoor Tanning Services

The 2010 Health Care Reform Act imposes a tax equal to 10 percent of the amount paid for any indoor tanning services.[89] The tax is paid by the individual who receives the indoor tanning services, but it is collected at the point of sale by the party providing the services and remitted quarterly to the IRS.[90] If the tax is not paid at the point of sale and ultimately not collected from the individual who received the tanning services, the indoor tanning provider is secondarily liable for the tax.[91]

---

[81] I.R.C. § 162(m).

[82] I.R.C. § 162(m); *see* IRS Notice 2007-49, 2007-25 I.R.B. 1429 (providing that the chief financial officer of a publicly traded corporation generally is not subject to the Section 162(m) limitation).

[83] PPACA § 9014 (adding I.R.C. § 162(m)(6)).

[84] I.R.C. § 162(m)(6)(C)(i)(II); *see supra* **§ 10.01[B]** notes 4–8 and accompanying text for a discussion of minimum essential coverage.

[85] I.R.C. § 162(m)(6)(C)(ii).

[86] I.R.C. §§ 162(m)(6)(A)(i) and (D).

[87] I.R.C. § 162(m)(6)(A)(ii).

[88] PPACA § 9014(b).

[89] PPACA § 10907(b) (adding I.R.C. § 5000B). "Indoor tanning services" means a service employing an electronic product designed to incorporate one or more ultraviolet lamps and intended to irradiate the individual with ultraviolet radiation. I.R.C. § 5000B(a)(1). Section 10907(a) of the PPACA nullified an earlier PPACA provision, set forth in Section 9017 of the PPACA, that would have imposed an excise tax on certain elective cosmetic medical procedures.

[90] I.R.C. § 5000B(c).

[91] I.R.C. § 5000B(c)(3).

CHAPTER 13
ANALYZING THE IMPACT OF HEALTH CARE REFORM

As the first 12 chapters of this book describe in detail, health care reform will have a significant effect on the way employers provide health benefits and the way individuals obtain health coverage. As currently constructed, health care reform can make the delivery of health benefits very different in 2014 than in 2010. Going forward, employers of all sizes will have many difficult decisions to make. In this chapter, we will highlight some of the major differences in the 2010 Health Care Reform Act for different types of employers and employees.

§ 13.01 Difference Based on Employer Size

One of the recurring themes in the 2010 Health Care Reform Act is an effort to avoid imposing economic and administrative burdens on small businesses. The Act imposes far fewer restrictions on small employers, and even provides some cost-savings opportunities for small employers.

[A] Employers With Fewer Than 25 Full-Time Equivalent Employees

Perhaps the most significant difference between large employers and small employers is the manner in which the 2010 Health Care Reform Act encourages employers to provide coverage. For the smallest employers (i.e., those with fewer than 25 full-time equivalent employees and an average payroll of less than $50,000 per full-time equivalent employee), the Act creates a "reward," in the form of a tax credit, to incentivize employers to provide health insurance coverage to employees.[1] Note that the Act applies the controlled group rules in determining which entities are small employers. Thus, an employer cannot divide its workforce among separate related entities in order to fit under the 25-employee threshold to take advantage of the small employer tax credit.

For the 2010 through 2013 taxable years, the tax credit amount is 35 percent (25 percent for tax-exempt entities) of the aggregate amount of non-elective employer contributions made on behalf of employees to an insured health plan. For taxable years beginning on or after January 1, 2014, the amount of the tax credit increases to 50 percent (35 percent for tax-exempt entities) of the aggregate amount of non-elective employer contributions made on behalf of employees to a QHP. The tax credit is subject to a phase-out provision, so the full tax credit is only available for employers with 10 or fewer employees and that pay average annual wages of $25,000 or less.

If a small employer chooses not to provide health insurance to its employees, it does not qualify for the tax incentive "reward," but it is not subject to the tax penalties that might otherwise apply to larger employers beginning in 2014. In fact, the only "penalty" that appears to apply to employers of this size is the free choice voucher requirement, and that requirement only applies if the small employer offers minimum essential coverage to its employees, pays a portion of the costs of the plan, and employs a "qualified employee."[2]

[B] Employers With Fewer Than 50 Full-Time Equivalent Employees

Employers that employ at least 25, but fewer than 50, employees are still considered small employers for purposes of the 2010 Health Care Reform Act and are exempt from certain tax penalties, but they are not eligible for the tax incentive reward described in **Section 13.01[A]**. Significantly, these small employers are exempt from the pay-or-play penalty, which is one of the key elements of health care reform.[3]

Beginning January 1, 2014, a large employer will be required to offer full-time employees the chance to enroll in employment-based group health plan coverage that satisfies the definition of minimum essential coverage and is both adequate and affordable. Large employers that fail to provide such

---

[1] See **§ 6.03** for a full description of the small-employer tax credit.
[2] See **§ 10.03** for a full description of the free choice voucher requirement.
[3] See **§ 10.02** for a full description of the employer pay-or-play penalty.

coverage on these terms are subject to an annual penalty of either $2,000 per full-time employee (where the large employer fails to offer minimum essential coverage) or $3,000 per full-time employee who receives a premium tax credit or cost-sharing reduction related to enrollment in a QHP through an Exchange (where the large employer's coverage is either inadequate or unaffordable).

A "large employer," for this purpose, is one that employs, on average, 50 or more full-time equivalent employees on business days during the preceding calendar year. In determining the 50 employee threshold, full-time equivalent employees are counted, and the controlled group rules are applied to aggregate the employees of related employers. Thus, a small employer with fewer than 50 full-time equivalent employees that chooses not to provide employment-based health coverage to its employees is not subject to tax penalties (other than, potentially, the free choice voucher requirement described in **Section 13.01[A]**).

Small employers with fewer than 50 employees also may be exempt from the 2010 Health Care Reform Act's requirement to make certain accommodations for nursing mothers.[4] If a small employer can show that the requirement to provide a reasonable break time and a private location for nursing mothers to express breast milk would impose an undue hardship on the employer, than the employer may be exempt from the 2010 Health Care Reform Act's requirement (but not necessarily exempt from similar state law requirements).

[C]   Employers With 100 or Fewer Employees

Beginning on January 1, 2014, the 2010 Health Care Reform Act directs that the State Exchanges will make available health insurance for individuals and small employers.[5] Small employers, defined for this purpose as having at least one but not more than 100 employees during the preceding calendar year, will be able to purchase a group QHP through the Exchange for their employees. Purchasing a QHP through an Exchange allows a small employer to take advantage of a single, state-wide risk pool, Exchange-approval requirements for QHPs and a variety of options that can be compared on an apples-to-apples basis.

Beginning in 2016, each state has the option to reduce the 100-employee limit for Exchange access for small employers to 50 employees. Also, Exchanges may begin to provide access to large employers beginning in 2017. The controlled-group rules are applied to these limits for purposes of aggregating related employers.

[D]   Employers With Fewer Than 200 Full-Time Employees

The 2010 Health Care Reform Act makes one other major distinction between large and small employers, and the distinction relates to the automatic enrollment requirements.[6] The Act requires large employers that offer enrollment in one or more group health plans to automatically enroll new full-time employees in one of the plans (subject to any waiting periods authorized by law) and to continue the enrollment of current employees. A "large employer," for this purpose, is defined as an employer having more than 200 full-time employees. Such employers also must provide advance notice of the automatic enrollment feature, as well as an opportunity for employees to opt out of coverage. A "small" employer with at least 50 but less than 200 full-time employees will be exempt from the automatic enrollment requirement, but generally will be subject to all other aspects of health care reform.

---

[4] See **§ 11.05** for a full description of the nursing mother requirements.
[5] See **§ 10.04** for a full description of Exchanges.
[6] See **§ 11.03** for a full description of the automatic enrollment requirements.

[E] Cost-Benefit Analysis

[1] Large Employers

In the long run, large employers may have the most to gain from the 2010 Health Care Reform Act. For years, large employers have been expected to provide employment-based group health plans to their employees. When the Exchanges become operational on January 1, 2014, coverage will be available to all individuals, regardless of where they work, potentially freeing employers of the expectation to provide health care coverage. Large employers will need to engage in a cost-benefit analysis to determine whether they should continue to offer an employment-based group health plan to their employees or pay a penalty under pay-or-play. Because the penalty for not providing an employment-based group health plan is much less than the current cost of providing employees with such a plan, large employers will need to take a close look at the recruiting and retention advantages that a group health plan presents. See Tables 13-1 and 13-2 below for two sample cost-benefit analyses for large employers.

Sample Cost-Benefit Analyses for Large Employers
Table 13-1

Thinking About Providing a Plan?

Costs	Benefits
• Possibility of an annual $3,000 penalty for each full-time employee who receives a subsidy under an Exchange plan because the large employer has an employment-based group health plan that constitutes minimum essential coverage, but the plan is inadequate or unaffordable. • Increases in administrative costs due to compliance with new plan design requirements, a new administrative scheme and a multitude of additional regulation. • Increases in administrative costs related to navigating the free choice voucher system. • Beginning in 2018, possible exposure to the Cadillac tax.	• Potentially effective tool for recruiting and retaining employees. • If the Exchanges prove difficult to navigate or offer inadequate coverage networks, employees may put a premium on employment-based group health plans. • Continuity of benefits. • Large employers may face pressure from employees to keep employment-based group health plans in and beyond 2014. Many employees have become accustomed to obtaining coverage through a large employer and would rather interact with internal personnel on benefits matters than external representatives employed by insurance companies or Exchanges. • Prevents benefit selection burden from being placed on employees. • Sometimes having more choices is not always beneficial. While the Exchange concept is supposed to foster a system that promotes ease of use, individuals will have to analyze many competing options when it comes to picking an appropriate plan, a stark change from the current system where the typical employer offers employees just a few options. While some employees may see an opportunity to customize their desired level of benefits by purchasing coverage through an Exchange, this option will be much less appealing to those employees who are not interested in taking a more active role in the benefit selection process.

Table 13-2

Thinking About NOT Providing a Plan?

Costs	Benefits
• Annual penalty of $2,000 per full-time employee (in excess of 30 employees) per year.	• If large employers choose to discontinue employment-based group health plans, they could pass along the cost savings to employees in the form of salary increases. Employers can spend approximately $800–$1,200 per month per employee on health care coverage. This would translate into large employer annual savings of approximately $10,000–$15,000 per employee. These savings could be passed along to employees in the form of increased compensation and employees could, in turn, choose the level of coverage they desire through an Exchange. • Reduction in administrative costs because there is no need to comply with the Act's new administrative scheme and a multitude of additional regulation. This could result in the reduction of HR staff needed to operate group health plans and open enrollment procedures. • No administrative costs associated with navigating the free choice voucher system. • Employees can choose from a wide array of coverage options through an Exchange. • Lower-paid employees may be eligible for federal government subsidies and credits. If employers increased the wages of subsidy-eligible individuals, these individuals may get the best of both worlds—additional take-home pay and adequate health care coverage.

[2] Small Employers

Unlike large employers, small employers are not subject to the 2010 Health Care Reform Act's pay-or-play rules. However, small employers still have some decisions to make. Like large employers, small employers will need to engage in a cost-benefit analysis to determine whether they should provide employment-based group health plans to their employees, which could allow them to take advantage of tax credits. Small employers will need to consider a few factors. First, the household incomes of employees will determine how many may be eligible for federal subsidies and credits if they obtained health care coverage through the Exchange rather than through an employment-based group health plan. Second, competitors may be seeking to hire from the same labor market, and they may offer employment-based group health plans as an incentive. Small employers that provide an employment-based group health plan, even with a 25 percent to 50 percent tax credit from the federal government, are still likely to incur more health care–related costs than small employers who send employees directly to the Exchange for coverage. This will likely affect the amount of wages that small employers with employment-based group health plans could afford. Employees who value an employment-based group health plan may be more inclined to look for employment with small employers offering such a plan, while employees who place little value on health care coverage may elect to find an employer who offers higher compensation in exchange for not providing health care coverage. See Tables 13-3 and 13-4 below for two sample cost-benefit analyses for small employers.

Sample Cost-Benefit Analyses for Small Employers
Table 13-3

Thinking About Providing a Plan?

Costs	Benefits
Before January 1, 2014 • Increases in administrative costs due to compliance with new plan design requirements, a new administrative scheme, and a multitude of additional regulation. *January 1, 2014, and after* • Limited additional plan administrative costs if health care coverage is purchased through an Exchange (which is required for the tax credits). • Administrative costs related to navigating the free choice voucher system.	• Tax credits. • A valuable benefit prior to 2014 when health coverage is not yet available through an Exchange. • Prevents benefit selection burden from being placed on employees. • Sometimes having more choices is not always beneficial. While the Exchange concept is supposed to foster a system that promotes ease of use, individuals will have to analyze many competing options when it comes to picking an appropriate plan, a stark change from the current system where the typical employer offers employees just a few options. While some employees may see an opportunity to customize their desired level of benefits by purchasing coverage through an Exchange, this option will be much less appealing to those employees who are not interested in taking a more active role in the benefit selection process.

Table 13-4

Thinking About NOT Providing a Plan?

Costs	Benefits
• None (except possibly higher wages if offered by the small employer).	• If small employers choose to discontinue employer-sponsored coverage, they could pass along the cost savings to employees in the form of salary increases. Employers spend approximately $800–$1,200 per month per employee on health care coverage. This would translate into small-employer annual savings of approximately $10,000–$15,000 per employee. These savings could be passed along to employees in the form of increased compensation and employees could, in turn, choose the level of coverage they desire through an Exchange. • No need to comply with a new administrative scheme and a multitude of additional regulations. • No administrative costs associated with navigating the free choice voucher system. • Employees can choose from a wide array of coverage options through an Exchange. • Lower-paid employees may be eligible for federal government subsidies and credits. If employers increased the wages of subsidy-eligible individuals, these individuals may get the best of both worlds—additional take-home pay and adequate health care coverage.

§ 13.02   Differences Based on Full-Time vs. Part-Time Employees

Many employers provide employment-based group health plans for only their full-time employee workforce. As a result, part-time employees make up a significant percentage of the uninsured. One common question is whether the 2010 Health Care Reform Act mandates that employers provide coverage for part-time employees. Simply put, no such mandate exists.

Uninsured part-time employees do benefit from the 2010 Health Care Reform Act in the sense that they, like all other individuals, will be able to purchase health insurance in a QHP at group rates through an Exchange beginning on January 1, 2014. Until that time, those uninsured part-time employees who have pre-existing conditions may obtain health insurance coverage through the state-based temporary high-risk insurance pools.[7]

Employers that have significant part-time workforces will need to consider the part-timers in determining whether certain aspects of health care reform will apply. For example, part-time employees must be aggregated in determining the number of full-time equivalent employees for the following purposes:

- Determining eligibility for small employer tax incentives for providing employment-based group health plans to employees (must employ fewer than 25 FTEs);[8] and

- Determining whether an employer is a "large employer" subject to the pay-or-play rules (all employers with 50 or more FTEs are subject to pay-or-play).[9] Once it is established that an employer is subject to the pay-or-play rules, the penalties only apply with respect to the employer's full-time employees.

§ 13.03   Differences Based on Union vs. Non-Union Workforces

Employers with unionized workforces do not have any significant advantages or disadvantages over employers with non-union workforces when it comes to health care reform, except possibly in the timing of the health care reform changes. Employers that have "health insurance coverage maintained pursuant to one or more collective bargaining agreements . . . ratified before [March 23, 2010]" may be able to take advantage of the grandfathered health plan exemption.[10] The exemption would apply until the date on which the last of the collective bargaining agreements relating to the health coverage terminates.

Employers and unions that engage in collective bargaining, particularly in 2010 or 2011 in advance of regulatory guidance, will face a daunting task when it comes to health care reform. Employers that wish to take advantage of the grandfathered health plan exemption will not know for certain what it covers or the time frame to which it applies until further guidance is issued (if then). Also, employers and unions will need to estimate and allocate the expected costs arising from health care reform changes at a time when the impact of such changes is not well understood. Evaluating the impact of the Exchanges in 2014 on health care costs, for example, probably cannot be done with any confidence until each state gets a better idea of the structure of the Exchange and the degree of participation from health insurers.

---

[7] See § 6.02 for a full description of the temporary high-risk pools.

[8] See § 6.03 for a full description of the small-employer tax incentives.

[9] See § 10.02 for a full description of the pay-or-play rules.

[10] See § 4.02 for a full description of the grandfathered health plan exemption and its application to collectively bargained insured health plans.

§13.04 Looking Ahead

There is no doubt that the 2010 Health Care Reform Act will change the role employers currently play in providing access to health care coverage for employees and their families. But unless the tax laws eliminate the tax advantages of employer-provided welfare benefits, including health care, large employers and small employers with well-paid workforces probably will, at a minimum, continue to have a role in providing access to health care coverage for their employees. While the type of coverage may change, employers can still provide financing for health coverage and/or the coverage itself on a tax-preferred basis.

As health care reform evolves, and the universality, quality, and cost-effectiveness of the 2010 Health Care Reform Act's measures become better known, each employer will need to remain informed, maintain compliance with the immediate reforms and continue to analyze what course is best for it and its workforce. Maintaining focus and pressure on the reduction of costs, particularly by insurance issuers, will be as much or more of a challenge for employers than ever. Employers will also have larger communication and education roles with respect to employees as their options for coverage change.

We are confident that further changes and refinements to the 2010 Health Care Reform Act will be made prior to the roll out of the Exchanges. In the face of these seemingly overwhelming changes, we remind our readers that the trends prior to reform where unsustainable and that health care reform is a national imperative for our long-term economic stability. We are optimistic that the national dialogue will continue and that over time, these reforms will spur needed changes to the delivery and access to health care. We hope that the cost curve also will begin to improve.

A. 2010 Health Care Reform Act Provisions Applicable to Grandfathered Health Plans

- A "grandfathered plan" is defined as a group health plan (insured or self-insured) in which individuals were enrolled for coverage as of March 23, 2010.
  —New employees and their families may be enrolled in a grandfathered plan after 3/23/2010.
  —Family members of new employees and existing enrollees may be added after 3/23/2010.
  —A grandfathered plan may be renewed indefinitely.

SUBJECT	SECTION(S) OF PHSA (UNLESS NOTED)	EFFECTIVE DATE	APPLY TO GRANDFATHERED PLAN?
Extension of dependent coverage to age 26	2714	1st plan year after 9/23/2010	Yes
Pre-existing exclusions prohibited for children under age 19	2704	1st plan year after 9/23/2010	Yes
Prohibition on lifetime dollar maximum on benefits	2711	1st plan year after 9/23/2010	Yes
Prohibition on annual dollar limits on restricted benefits	2711	1st plan year after 9/23/2010	Yes
Rescissions of coverage for reasons other than fraud or non-payment	2712	1st plan year after 9/23/2010	Yes
Required preventive health services without cost-sharing	2713	1st plan year after 9/23/2010	No
Mandated appeals process with binding external review	2719	1st plan year after 9/23/2010	No
Nondiscrimination against health care providers	2706	1st plan year after 1/1/2014	No
Summary communication requirements for enrollees	2715	24 months after date of enactment	Yes
No discrimination based on salary permitted	2716	1st plan year after 9/23/2010	No
Insured plans must rebate prorated share of premiums if medical claims ratios too low	2718	1st plan year after 9/23/2010	Yes (insured plans only)
HHS reporting requirements (quality outcomes, etc.)	2717	24 months after date of enactment	No
Reinsurance for retirees	PPACA 1102	June 23, 2010	Yes
Adm. Simplification—amends HIPAA to add new transaction standards	PPACA 1104	1/1/2013–1/1/2014	Yes (electronic funds transfer standards)
All insured plans must guarantee eligibility and renewability	2702, 2703	1st plan year on or after 1/1/2014	No
All insured plans are subject to premium underwriting restrictions	2701, 1252	1st plan year on or after 1/1/2014	No
Prohibitions on health status discrimination	2704, 2705	1st plan year on or after 1/1/2014	No
Comprehensive health insurance—annual cost-sharing limits	2707	1st plan year on or after 1/1/2014	No
Nondiscrimination in health care coverage (provider)	2706	1st plan year on or after 1/1/2014	No

SUBJECT	SECTION(S) OF PHSA (UNLESS NOTED)	EFFECTIVE DATE	APPLY TO GRANDFATHERED PLAN?
No waiting period in excess of 90 days	2708	1st plan year on or after 1/1/2014	Yes
Coverage for clinical trials	2709 (Can be found in Title X)	1st plan year on or after 1/1/2014	No
Reinsurance for early retirees	PPACA 1101	6/23/2010 to 1/1/2014	Yes
Automatic enrollment for large employers	FLSA, 1511	1/1/2011	Yes, employer responsibility
Employee notice re: coverage options (FLSA amendment)	FLSA, 1512	3/1/2013	Yes, employer responsibility
Health insurance fee	PPACA 9010	Calendar year 2014	Yes, except it does not apply to self-insured or government plans

B. HHS Regulations on Grandfathered Health Plans

Thursday,
June 17, 2010

Part II

Department of the Treasury

Internal Revenue Service

26 CFR Parts 54 and 602

Department of Labor

Employee Benefits Security
Administration

29 CFR Part 2590

Department of Health and Human Services

45 CFR Part 147

Group Health Plans and Health Insurance Coverage Relating to Status as a Grandfathered Health Plan Under the Patient Protection and Affordable Care Act; Interim Final Rule and Proposed Rule

34538 Federal Register / Vol. 75, No. 116 / Thursday, June 17, 2010 / Rules and Regulations

DEPARTMENT OF THE TREASURY

Internal Revenue Service

26 CFR Parts 54 and 602

[TD 9489]

RIN 1545–BJ51

DEPARTMENT OF LABOR

Employee Benefits Security Administration

29 CFR Part 2590

RIN 1210–AB42

DEPARTMENT OF HEALTH AND HUMAN SERVICES

[OCIIO–9991–IFC]

45 CFR Part 147

RIN 0991–AB68

Interim Final Rules for Group Health Plans and Health Insurance Coverage Relating to Status as a Grandfathered Health Plan Under the Patient Protection and Affordable Care Act

AGENCY: Internal Revenue Service, Department of the Treasury; Employee Benefits Security Administration, Department of Labor; Office of Consumer Information and Insurance Oversight, Department of Health and Human Services.

ACTION: Interim final rules with request for comments.

SUMMARY: This document contains interim final regulations implementing the rules for group health plans and health insurance coverage in the group and individual markets under provisions of the Patient Protection and Affordable Care Act regarding status as a grandfathered health plan.

DATES: *Effective date.* These interim final regulations are effective on June 14, 2010, except that the amendments to 26 CFR 54.9815–2714T, 29 CFR 2590.715–2714, and 45 CFR 147.120 are effective July 12, 2010.

Comment date. Comments are due on or before August 16, 2010.

ADDRESSES: Written comments may be submitted to any of the addresses specified below. Any comment that is submitted to any Department will be shared with the other Departments. Please do not submit duplicates.

All comments will be made available to the public. *Warning:* Do not include any personally identifiable information (such as name, address, or other contact information) or confidential business information that you do not want

publicly disclosed. All comments are posted on the Internet exactly as received, and can be retrieved by most Internet search engines. No deletions, modifications, or redactions will be made to the comments received, as they are public records. Comments may be submitted anonymously.

Department of Labor. Comments to the Department of Labor, identified by RIN 1210–AB42, by one of the following methods:

• *Federal eRulemaking Portal: http:// www.regulations.gov.* Follow the instructions for submitting comments.

• *E-mail:* E-OHPSCA1251.EBSA@dol.gov.

• *Mail or Hand Delivery:* Office of Health Plan Standards and Compliance Assistance, Employee Benefits Security Administration, Room N–5653, U.S. Department of Labor, 200 Constitution Avenue, NW., Washington, DC 20210, *Attention:* RIN 1210–AB42.

Comments received by the Department of Labor will be posted without change to *http:// www.regulations.gov* and *http:// www.dol.gov/ebsa,* and available for public inspection at the Public Disclosure Room, N–1513, Employee Benefits Security Administration, 200 Constitution Avenue, NW., Washington, DC 20210.

Department of Health and Human Services. In commenting, please refer to file code OCIIO–9991–IFC. Because of staff and resource limitations, the Departments cannot accept comments by facsimile (FAX) transmission.

You may submit comments in one of four ways (please choose only one of the ways listed):

1. *Electronically.* You may submit electronic comments on this regulation to *http://www.regulations.gov.* Follow the instructions under the "More Search Options" tab.

2. *By regular mail.* You may mail written comments to the following address ONLY: Office of Consumer Information and Insurance Oversight, Department of Health and Human Services, Attention: OCIIO–9991–IFC, P.O. Box 8016, Baltimore, MD 21244–1850.

Please allow sufficient time for mailed comments to be received before the close of the comment period.

3. *By express or overnight mail.* You may send written comments to the following address ONLY: Office of Consumer Information and Insurance Oversight, Department of Health and Human Services, Attention: OCIIO–9991–IFC, Mail Stop C4–26–05, 7500 Security Boulevard, Baltimore, MD 21244–1850.

4. *By hand or courier.* If you prefer, you may deliver (by hand or courier) your written comments before the close of the comment period to either of the following addresses:

a. For delivery in Washington, DC—Office of Consumer Information and Insurance Oversight, Department of Health and Human Services, Room 445–G, Hubert H. Humphrey Building, 200 Independence Avenue, SW., Washington, DC 20201.

(Because access to the interior of the Hubert H. Humphrey Building is not readily available to persons without Federal government identification, commenters are encouraged to leave their comments in the OCIIO drop slots located in the main lobby of the building. A stamp-in clock is available for persons wishing to retain a proof of filing by stamping in and retaining an extra copy of the comments being filed.)

b. For delivery in Baltimore, MD—Centers for Medicare & Medicaid Services, Department of Health and Human Services, 7500 Security Boulevard, Baltimore, MD 21244–1850.

If you intend to deliver your comments to the Baltimore address, please call (410) 786–7195 in advance to schedule your arrival with one of our staff members.

Comments mailed to the addresses indicated as appropriate for hand or courier delivery may be delayed and received after the comment period.

Submission of comments on paperwork requirements. You may submit comments on this document's paperwork requirements by following the instructions at the end of the "Collection of Information Requirements" section in this document.

Inspection of Public Comments: All comments received before the close of the comment period are available for viewing by the public, including any personally identifiable or confidential business information that is included in a comment. The Departments post all comments received before the close of the comment period on the following Web site as soon as possible after they have been received: *http:// www.regulations.gov.* Follow the search instructions on that Web site to view public comments.

Comments received timely will also be available for public inspection as they are received, generally beginning approximately three weeks after publication of a document, at the headquarters of the Centers for Medicare & Medicaid Services, 7500 Security Boulevard, Baltimore, Maryland 21244, Monday through Friday of each week from 8:30 a.m. to 4 p.m. EST. To schedule an appointment to view public comments, phone 1–800–743–3951.

Internal Revenue Service. Comments to the IRS, identified by REG–118412–10, by one of the following methods:

• *Federal eRulemaking Portal: http:// www.regulations.gov.* Follow the instructions for submitting comments.

• *Mail:* CC:PA:LPD:PR (REG–118412–10), room 5205, Internal Revenue Service, P.O. Box 7604, Ben Franklin Station, Washington, DC 20044.

• *Hand or courier delivery:* Monday through Friday between the hours of 8 a.m. and 4 p.m. to: CC:PA:LPD:PR (REG–118412–10), Courier's Desk, Internal Revenue Service, 1111 Constitution Avenue, NW., Washington, DC 20224.

All submissions to the IRS will be open to public inspection and copying in room 1621, 1111 Constitution Avenue, NW., Washington, DC from 9 a.m. to 4 p.m.

FOR FURTHER INFORMATION CONTACT: Amy Turner or Beth Baum, Employee Benefits Security Administration, Department of Labor, at (202) 693–8335; Karen Levin, Internal Revenue Service, Department of the Treasury, at (202) 622–6080; Jim Mayhew, Office of Consumer Information and Insurance Oversight, Department of Health and Human Services, at (410) 786–1565.

Customer Service Information: Individuals interested in obtaining information from the Department of Labor concerning employment-based health coverage laws may call the EBSA Toll-Free Hotline at 1–866–444–EBSA (3272) or visit the Department of Labor's Web site (*http://www.dol.gov/ebsa*). In addition, information from HHS on private health insurance for consumers can be found on the Centers for Medicare & Medicaid Services (CMS) Web site (*http://www.cms.hhs.gov/ HealthInsReformforConsume/ 01_Overview.asp*) and information on health reform can be found at *http:// www.healthreform.gov.*

SUPPLEMENTARY INFORMATION:

I. Background

The Patient Protection and Affordable Care Act (the Affordable Care Act), Public Law 111–148, was enacted on March 23, 2010; the Health Care and Education Reconciliation Act (the Reconciliation Act), Public Law 111–152, was enacted on March 30, 2010. The Affordable Care Act and the Reconciliation Act reorganize, amend, and add to the provisions in part A of title XXVII of the Public Health Service Act (PHS Act) relating to group health plans and health insurance issuers in the group and individual markets. The

term "group health plan" includes both insured and self-insured group health plans.[1] The Affordable Care Act adds section 715(a)(1) to the Employee Retirement Income Security Act (ERISA) and section 9815(a)(1) to the Internal Revenue Code (the Code) to incorporate the provisions of part A of title XXVII of the PHS Act into ERISA and the Code, and make them applicable to group health plans, and health insurance issuers providing health insurance coverage in connection with group health plans. The PHS Act sections incorporated by this reference are sections 2701 through 2728. PHS Act sections 2701 through 2719A are substantially new, though they incorporate some provisions of prior law. PHS Act sections 2722 through 2728 are sections of prior law renumbered, with some, mostly minor, changes. Section 1251 of the Affordable Care Act, as modified by section 10103 of the Affordable Care Act and section 2301 of the Reconciliation Act, specifies that certain plans or coverage existing as of the date of enactment (that is, grandfathered health plans) are only subject to certain provisions.

The Affordable Care Act also adds section 715(a)(2) of ERISA, which provides that, to the extent that any provision of part 7 of ERISA conflicts with part A of title XXVII of the PHS Act with respect to group health plans or group health insurance coverage, the PHS Act provisions apply. Similarly, the Affordable Care Act adds section 9815(a)(2) of the Code, which provides that, to the extent that any provision of subchapter B of chapter 100 of the Code conflicts with part A of title XXVII of the PHS Act with respect to group health plans or group health insurance coverage, the PHS Act provisions apply. Therefore, although ERISA section 715(a)(1) and Code section 9815(a)(1) incorporate by reference new provisions, they do not affect preexisting sections of ERISA or the Code unless they cannot be read consistently with an incorporated provision of the PHS Act. For example, ERISA section 732(a) generally provides that part 7 of ERISA—and Code section 9831(a) generally provides that chapter 100 of the Code—does not apply to plans with less than two participants who are current employees (including retiree-only plans that cover less than two participants who are current employees). Prior to enactment of the

Affordable Care Act, the PHS Act had a parallel provision at section 2721(a). After the Affordable Care Act amended, reorganized, and renumbered most of title XXVII of the PHS Act, that exception no longer exists. Similarly, ERISA section 732(b) and (c) generally provides that the requirements of part 7 of ERISA—and Code section 9831(b) and (c) generally provides that the requirements of chapter 100 of the Code—do not apply to excepted benefits.[2] Prior to enactment of the Affordable Care Act, the PHS Act had a parallel section 2721(c) and (d) that indicated that the provisions of subparts 1 through 3 of part A of title XXVII of the PHS Act did not apply to excepted benefits. After the Affordable Care Act amended and renumbered PHS Act section 2721(c) and (d) as section 2722(b) and (c), that exception could be read to be narrowed so that it applies only with respect to subpart 2 of part A of title XXVII of the PHS Act, thus, in effect requiring excepted benefits to comply with subparts I and II of part A.

The absence of an express provision in part A of title XXVII of the PHS Act does not create a conflict with the relevant requirements of ERISA and the Code. Accordingly, the exceptions of ERISA section 732 and Code section 9831 for very small plans and certain retiree-only health plans, and for excepted benefits, remain in effect and, thus, ERISA section 715 and Code section 9815, as added by the Affordable Care Act, do not apply to such plans or excepted benefits.

Moreover, there is no express indication in the legislative history of an intent to treat issuers of group health insurance coverage or nonfederal governmental plans (that are subject to the PHS Act) any differently in this respect from plans subject to ERISA and the Code. The Departments of Health and Human Services, Labor, and the Treasury (the Departments) operate under a Memorandum of Understanding (MOU)[3] that implements section 104 of the Health Insurance Portability and Accountability Act of 1996 (HIPAA), enacted on August 21, 1996, and subsequent amendments, and provides that requirements over which two or more Secretaries have responsibility ("shared provisions") must be administered so as to have the same effect at all times. HIPAA section 104

---

[1] The term "group health plan" is used in title XXVII of the PHS Act, part 7 of ERISA, and chapter 100 of the Code, and is distinct from the term "health plan," as used in other provisions of title I of the Affordable Care Act. The term "health plan" does not include self-insured group health plans.

[2] Excepted benefits generally include dental-only and vision-only plans, most health flexible spending arrangements, Medigap policies, and accidental death and dismemberment coverage. For more information on excepted benefits, see 26 CFR 54.9831–1, 29 CFR 2590.732, 45 CFR 146.145, and 45 CFR 148.220.

[3] *See* 64 FR 70164 (December 15, 1999).

34540 Federal Register/Vol. 75, No. 116/Thursday, June 17, 2010/Rules and Regulations

also requires the coordination of policies relating to enforcing the shared provisions in order to avoid duplication of enforcement efforts and to assign priorities in enforcement.

There is no express statement of intent that nonfederal governmental retiree-only plans should be treated differently from private sector plans or that excepted benefits offered by nonfederal governmental plans should be treated differently from excepted benefits offered by private sector plans. Because treating nonfederal governmental retiree-only plans and excepted benefits provided by nonfederal governmental plans differently would create confusion with respect to the obligations of issuers that do not distinguish whether a group health plan is subject to ERISA or the PHS Act, and in light of the MOU, the Department of Health and Human Services (HHS) does not intend to use its resources to enforce the requirements of HIPAA or the Affordable Care Act with respect to nonfederal governmental retiree-only plans or with respect to excepted benefits provided by nonfederal governmental plans.

PHS Act section 2723(a)(2) (formerly section 2722(a)(2)) gives the States primary authority to enforce the PHS Act group and individual market provisions over group and individual health insurance issuers. HHS enforces these provisions with respect to issuers only if it determines that the State has "failed to substantially enforce" one of the Federal provisions. Furthermore, the PHS Act preemption provisions allow States to impose requirements on issuers in the group and individual markets that are more protective than the Federal provisions. However, HHS is encouraging States not to apply the provisions of title XXVII of the PHS Act to issuers of retiree-only plans or of excepted benefits. HHS advises States that if they do not apply these provisions to the issuers of retiree-only plans or of excepted benefits, HHS will not cite a State for failing to substantially enforce the provisions of part A of title XXVII of the PHS Act in these situations.

Subtitles A and C of title I of the Affordable Care Act amend the requirements of title XXVII of the PHS Act (changes to which are incorporated into ERISA section 715). The preemption provisions of ERISA section 731 and PHS Act section 2724[4] (implemented in 29 CFR 2590.731(a)

---

[4] Code section 9815 incorporates the preemption provisions of PHS Act section 2724. Prior to the Affordable Care Act, there were no express preemption provisions in chapter 100 of the Code.

and 45 CFR 146.143(a)) apply so that the requirements of part 7 of ERISA and title XXVII of PHS Act, as amended by the Affordable Care Act, are not to be "construed to supersede any provision of State law which establishes, implements, or continues in effect any standard or requirement solely relating to health insurance issuers in connection with group or individual health insurance coverage except to the extent that such standard or requirement prevents the application of a requirement" of the Affordable Care Act. Accordingly, State laws that impose on health insurance issuers requirements that are stricter than the requirements imposed by the Affordable Care Act will not be superseded by the Affordable Care Act.

The Departments are issuing regulations implementing the revised PHS Act sections 2701 through 2719A in several phases. The first publication in this series was a Request for Information relating to the medical loss ratio provisions of PHS Act section 2718, published in the **Federal Register** on April 14, 2010 (75 FR 19297). The second publication was interim final regulations implementing PHS Act section 2714 (requiring dependent coverage of children to age 26), published in the **Federal Register** on May 13, 2010 (75 FR 27122). This document contains interim final regulations implementing section 1251 of the Affordable Care Act (relating to grandfathered health plans), as well as adding a cross-reference to these interim final regulations in the regulations implementing PHS Act section 2714. The implementation of other provisions in PHS Act sections 2701 through 2719A will be addressed in future regulations.

II. Overview of the Regulations: Section 1251 of the Affordable Care Act, Preservation of Right To Maintain Existing Coverage (26 CFR 54.9815–1251T, 29 CFR 2590.715–1251, and 45 CFR 147.140)

A. Introduction

Section 1251 of the Affordable Care Act, as modified by section 10103 of the Affordable Care Act and section 2301 of the Reconciliation Act, provides that certain group health plans and health insurance coverage existing as of March 23, 2010 (the date of enactment of the Affordable Care Act), are subject only to certain provisions of the Affordable Care Act. The statute and these interim final regulations refer to these plans and health insurance coverage as grandfathered health plans.

The Affordable Care Act balances the objective of preserving the ability of individuals to maintain their existing coverage with the goals of ensuring access to affordable essential coverage and improving the quality of coverage. Section 1251 provides that nothing in the Affordable Care Act requires an individual to terminate the coverage in which the individual was enrolled on March 23, 2010. It also generally provides that, with respect to group health plans or health insurance coverage in which an individual was enrolled on March 23, 2010, various requirements of the Act shall not apply to such plan or coverage, regardless of whether the individual renews such coverage after March 23, 2010. However, to ensure access to coverage with certain particularly significant protections, Congress required grandfathered health plans to comply with a subset of the Affordable Care Act's health reform provisions. Thus, for example, grandfathered health plans must comply with the prohibition on rescissions of coverage except in the case of fraud or intentional misrepresentation and the elimination of lifetime limits (both of which apply for plan years, or in the individual market, policy years, beginning on or after September 23, 2010). On the other hand, grandfathered health plans are not required to comply with certain other requirements of the Affordable Care Act; for example, the requirement that preventive health services be covered without any cost sharing (which otherwise becomes generally applicable for plan years, or in the individual market, policy years, beginning on or after September 23, 2010).

A number of additional reforms apply for plan years (in the individual market, policy years) beginning on or after January 1, 2014. As with the requirements effective for plan years (in the individual market, policy years) beginning on or after September 23, 2010, grandfathered health plans must then comply with some, but not all of these reforms. See Table 1 in section II.D of this preamble for a list of various requirements that apply to grandfathered health plans.

In making grandfathered health plans subject to some but not all of the health reforms contained in the Affordable Care Act, the statute balances its objective of preserving the ability to maintain existing coverage with the goals of expanding access to and improving the quality of health coverage. The statute does not, however, address at what point changes to a group health plan or health insurance coverage in which an individual was enrolled on March 23, 2010 are significant enough to cause the plan or health insurance coverage to cease to be a grandfathered health plan, leaving that question to be addressed by regulatory guidance.

These interim final regulations are designed to ease the transition of the healthcare industry into the reforms established by the Affordable Care Act by allowing for gradual implementation of reforms through a reasonable grandfathering rule. A more detailed description of the basis for these interim final regulations and other regulatory alternatives considered is included in section IV.B later in this preamble.

B. Definition of Grandfathered Health Plan Coverage in Paragraph (a) of 26 CFR 54.9815–1251T, 29 CFR 2590.715–1251, and 45 CFR 147.140 of These Interim Final Regulations

Under the statute and these interim final regulations, a group health plan or group or individual health insurance coverage is a grandfathered health plan with respect to individuals enrolled on March 23, 2010. Paragraph (a)(1) of 26 CFR 54.9815–1251T, 29 CFR 2590.715–1251, and 45 CFR 147.140 of these interim final regulations provides that a group health plan or group health insurance coverage does not cease to be grandfathered health plan coverage merely because one or more (or even all) individuals enrolled on March 23, 2010 cease to be covered, provided that the plan or group health insurance coverage has continuously covered someone since March 23, 2010 (not necessarily the same person, but at all times at least one person). The determination under the rules of these interim final regulations is made separately with respect to each benefit package made available under a group health plan or health insurance coverage.

Moreover, these interim final regulations provide that, subject to the rules of paragraph (f) of 26 CFR 54.9815–1251T, 29 CFR 2590.715–1251, and 45 CFR 147.140 for collectively bargained plans, if an employer or employee organization enters into a new policy, certificate, or contract of insurance after March 23, 2010 (because, for example, any previous policy, certificate, or contract of insurance is not being renewed), then that policy, certificate, or contract of insurance is not a grandfathered health plan with respect to the individuals in the group health plan. Any policies sold in the group and individual health insurance markets to new entities or individuals after March 23, 2010 will not be grandfathered health plans even if the health insurance products sold to

those subscribers were offered in the group or individual market before March 23, 2010.

To maintain status as a grandfathered health plan, a plan or health insurance coverage (1) must include a statement, in any plan materials provided to participants or beneficiaries (in the individual market, primary subscribers) describing the benefits provided under the plan or health insurance coverage, that the plan or health insurance coverage believes that it is a grandfathered health plan within the meaning of section 1251 of the Affordable Care Act and (2) must provide contact information for questions and complaints.

Model language is provided in these interim final regulations that can be used to satisfy this disclosure requirement. Comments are invited on possible improvements to the model language of grandfathered health plan status. Some have suggested, for example, that each grandfathered health plan be required to list and describe the various consumer protections that do not apply to the plan or health insurance coverage because it is grandfathered, together with their effective dates. The Departments intend to consider any comments regarding possible improvements to the model language in the near term; any changes to the model language that may result from such comments could be published in additional administrative guidance other than in the form of regulations.

Similarly, under these interim final regulations, to maintain status as a grandfathered health plan, a plan or issuer must also maintain records documenting the terms of the plan or health insurance coverage that were in effect on March 23, 2010, and any other documents necessary to verify, explain, or clarify its status as a grandfathered health plan. Such documents could include intervening and current plan documents, health insurance policies, certificates or contracts of insurance, summary plan descriptions, documentation of premiums or the cost of coverage, and documentation of required employee contribution rates. In addition, the plan or issuer must make such records available for examination. Accordingly, a participant, beneficiary, individual policy subscriber, or State or Federal agency official would be able to inspect such documents to verify the status of the plan or health insurance coverage as a grandfathered health plan. The plan or issuer must maintain such records and make them available for examination for as long as the plan or issuer takes the position that the plan or

health insurance coverage is a grandfathered health plan.

Under the statute and these interim final regulations, if family members of an individual who is enrolled in a grandfathered health plan as of March 23, 2010 enroll in the plan after March 23, 2010, the plan or health insurance coverage is also a grandfathered health plan with respect to the family members.

C. Adding New Employees in Paragraph (b) of 26 CFR 54.9815–1251T, 29 CFR 2590.715–1251, and 45 CFR 147.140 of These Interim Final Regulations

These interim final regulations at 26 CFR 54.9815–1251T, 29 CFR 2590.715–1251, and 45 CFR 147.140 provide that a group health plan that provided coverage on March 23, 2010 generally is also a grandfathered health plan with respect to new employees (whether newly hired or newly enrolled) and their families who enroll in the grandfathered health plan after March 23, 2010. These interim final regulations clarify that in such cases, any health insurance coverage provided under the group health plan in which an individual was enrolled on March 23, 2010 is also a grandfathered health plan. To prevent abuse, these interim final regulations provide that if the principal purpose of a merger, acquisition, or similar business restructuring is to cover new individuals under a grandfathered health plan, the plan ceases to be a grandfathered health plan. The goal of this rule is to prevent grandfather status from being bought and sold as a commodity in commercial transactions. These interim final regulations also contain a second anti-abuse rule designed to prevent a plan or issuer from circumventing the limits on changes that cause a plan or health insurance coverage to cease to be a grandfathered health plan under paragraph (g) (described more fully in section II.F of this preamble). This rule in paragraph (b)(2)(ii) addresses a situation under which employees who previously were covered by a grandfathered health plan are transferred to another grandfathered health plan. This rule is intended to prevent efforts to retain grandfather status by indirectly making changes that would result in loss of that status if those changes were made directly.

D. Applicability of Part A of Title XXVII of the PHS Act to Grandfathered Health Plans Paragraphs (c), (d), and (e) of 26 CFR 54.9815–1251T, 29 CFR 2590.715–1251, and 45 CFR 147.140 of These Interim Final Regulations

A grandfathered health plan generally is not subject to subtitles A and C of title I of the Affordable Care Act, except as specifically provided by the statute and these interim final regulations. The statute and these interim final regulations provide that some provisions of subtitles A and C of title I of the Affordable Care Act continue to apply to all grandfathered health plans and some provisions continue to apply only to grandfathered health plans that are group health plans. These interim final regulations clarify that a grandfathered health plan must continue to comply with the requirements of the PHS Act, ERISA, and the Code that were applicable prior to the changes enacted by the Affordable Care Act, except to the extent supplanted by changes made by the Affordable Care Act. Therefore, the HIPAA portability and nondiscrimination requirements and the Genetic Information Nondiscrimination Act requirements applicable prior to the effective date of the Affordable Care Act continue to apply to grandfathered health plans. In addition, the mental health parity provisions, the Newborns' and Mothers' Health Protection Act provisions, the Women's Health and Cancer Rights Act, and Michelle's Law continue to apply to grandfathered health plans. The following table lists the new health coverage reforms in part A of title XXVII of the PHS Act (as amended by the Affordable Care Act) that apply to grandfathered health plans:

TABLE 1—LIST OF THE NEW HEALTH REFORM PROVISIONS OF PART A OF TITLE XXVII OF THE PHS ACT THAT APPLY TO GRANDFATHERED HEALTH PLANS

PHS Act statutory provisions	Application to grandfathered health plans
§ 2704 Prohibition of preexisting condition exclusion or other discrimination based on health status.	Applicable to grandfathered group health plans and group health insurance coverage. Not applicable to grandfathered individual health insurance coverage.
§ 2708 Prohibition on excessive waiting periods	Applicable.
§ 2711 No lifetime or annual limits	Lifetime limits: Applicable. Annual limits: Applicable to grandfathered group health plans and group health insurance coverage; not applicable to grandfathered individual health insurance coverage.
§ 2712 Prohibition on rescissions	Applicable.
§ 2714 Extension of dependent coverage until age 26	Applicable[5].
§ 2715 Development and utilization of uniform explanation of coverage documents and standardized definitions.	Applicable.
§ 2718 Bringing down cost of health care coverage (for insured coverage).	Applicable to insured grandfathered health plans.

[5] For a group health plan or group health insurance coverage that is a grandfathered health plan for plan years beginning before January 1, 2014, PHS Act section 2714 is applicable in the case of an adult child only if the adult child is not eligible for other employer-sponsored health plan coverage. The interim final regulations relating to PHS Act section 2714, published in 75 FR 27122 (May 13, 2010), and these interim final regulations clarify that, in the case of an adult child who is eligible for coverage under the employer-sponsored plans of both parents, neither parent's plan may exclude the adult child from coverage based on the fact that the adult child is eligible to enroll in the other parent's employer-sponsored plan.

E. Health Insurance Coverage Maintained Pursuant to a Collective Bargaining Agreement of Paragraph (f) of 26 CFR 54.9815–1251T, 29 CFR 2590.715–1251, and 45 CFR 147.140 of These Interim Final Regulations

In paragraph (f) of 26 CFR 54.9815–1251T, 29 CFR 2590.715–1251, and 45 CFR 147.140, these interim final regulations provide that in the case of health insurance coverage maintained pursuant to one or more collective bargaining agreements ratified before March 23, 2010, the coverage is a grandfathered health plan at least until the date on which the last agreement relating to the coverage that was in effect on March 23, 2010 terminates. Thus, before the last of the applicable collective bargaining agreement terminates, any health insurance coverage provided pursuant to the collective bargaining agreements is a grandfathered health plan, even if there is a change in issuers (or any other change described in paragraph (g)(1) of

26 CFR 54.9815–1251T, 29 CFR 2590.715–1251, and 45 CFR 147.140 of these interim final regulations) during the period of the agreement. The statutory language of the provision refers solely to "health insurance coverage" and does not refer to a group health plan; therefore, these interim final regulations apply this provision only to insured plans maintained pursuant to a collective bargaining agreement and not to self-insured plans. After the date on which the last of the collective bargaining agreements terminates, the determination of whether health insurance coverage maintained pursuant to a collective bargaining agreement is grandfathered health plan coverage is made under the rules of paragraph (g). This determination is made by comparing the terms of the coverage on the date of determination with the terms of the coverage that were in effect on March 23, 2010. A change in issuers during the period of the agreement, by itself, would not cause the plan to cease to be a grandfathered health plan at the termination of the agreement. However, for a change in issuers after the termination of the agreement, the rules of paragraph (a)(1)(ii) of 26 CFR 54.9815–1251T, 29 CFR 2590.715–1251, and 45 CFR 147.140 of these interim final regulations apply.

Similar language to section 1251(d) in related bills that were not enacted would have provided a delayed effective date for collectively bargained plans with respect to the Affordable Care Act requirements. Questions have arisen as to whether section 1251(d) as enacted in the Affordable Care Act similarly operated to delay the application of the Affordable Care Act's requirements to collectively bargained plans—specifically, whether the provision of section 1251(d) that exempts collectively bargained plans from requirements for the duration of the agreement effectively provides the plans with a delayed effective date with respect to all new PHS Act requirements (in contrast to the rules for grandfathered health plans which provide that specified PHS Act provisions apply to all plans, including grandfathered health plans). However, the statutory language that applies only to collectively bargained plans, as signed into law as part of the Affordable Care Act, provides that insured collectively bargained plans in which individuals were enrolled on the date of enactment are included in the definition of a grandfathered health plan. Therefore, collectively bargained plans (both insured and self-insured) that are grandfathered health plans are subject to the same requirements as other grandfathered health plans, and are not provided with a delayed effective date for PHS Act provisions with which other grandfathered health plans must comply. Thus, the provisions that apply to grandfathered health plans apply to collectively bargained plans before and after termination of the last of the applicable collective bargaining agreement.

F. Maintenance of Grandfather Status of Paragraph (g) of 26 CFR 54.9815–1251T, 29 CFR 2590.715–1251, and 45 CFR 147.140 of These Interim Final Regulations)

Questions have arisen regarding the extent to which changes can be made to a plan or health insurance coverage and still have the plan or coverage considered the same as that in existence on March 23, 2010, so as to maintain status as a grandfathered health plan. Some have suggested that any change would cause a plan or health insurance coverage to be considered different and thus cease to be a grandfathered health plan. Others have suggested that any degree of change, no matter how large, is irrelevant provided the plan or health insurance coverage can trace some continuous legal relationship to the plan or health insurance coverage that was in existence on March 23, 2010.

In paragraph (g)(1) of 26 CFR 54.9815–1251T, 29 CFR 2590.715–1251, and 45 CFR 147.140 of these interim final regulations, coordinated rules are set forth for determining when changes to the terms of a plan or health insurance coverage cause the plan or coverage to cease to be a grandfathered health plan. The first of those rules (in paragraph (g)(1)(i) constrains the extent to which the scope of benefits can be reduced. It provides that the elimination of all or substantially all benefits to diagnose or treat a particular condition causes a plan or health insurance coverage to cease to be a grandfathered health plan. If, for example, a plan eliminates all benefits for cystic fibrosis, the plan ceases to be a grandfathered

health plan (even though this condition may affect relatively few individuals covered under the plan). Moreover, for purposes of paragraph (g)(1)(i), the elimination of benefits for any necessary element to diagnose or treat a condition is considered the elimination of all or substantially all benefits to diagnose or treat a particular condition. An example in these interim final regulations illustrates that if a plan provides benefits for a particular mental health condition, the treatment for which is a combination of counseling and prescription drugs, and subsequently eliminates benefits for counseling, the plan is treated as having eliminated all or substantially all benefits for that mental health condition.

A second set of rules (in paragraphs (g)(1)(ii) through (g)(1)(iv)) limits the extent to which plans and issuers can increase the fixed-amount and the percentage cost-sharing requirements that are imposed with respect to individuals for covered items and services. Plans and issuers can choose to make larger increases to fixed-amount or percentage cost-sharing requirements than permissible under these interim final regulations, but at that point the individual's plan or health insurance coverage would cease to be grandfathered health plan coverage. A more detailed description of the basis for the cost-sharing requirements in these interim final regulations is included in section IV.B later in this preamble.

These interim final regulations provide different standards with respect to coinsurance and fixed-amount cost sharing. Coinsurance automatically rises with medical inflation. Therefore, changes to the level of coinsurance (such as moving from a requirement that the patient pay 20 percent to a requirement that the patient pay 30 percent of inpatient surgery costs) would significantly alter the level of benefits provided. On the other hand, fixed-amount cost-sharing requirements (such as copayments and deductibles) do not take into account medical inflation. Therefore, changes to fixed-amount cost-sharing requirements (for example, moving from a $35 copayment to a $40 copayment for outpatient doctor visits) may be reasonable to keep up with the rising cost of medical items and services. Accordingly, paragraph (g)(1)(ii) provides that any increase in a percentage cost-sharing requirement (such as coinsurance) causes a plan or health insurance coverage to cease to be a grandfathered health plan.

With respect to fixed-amount cost-sharing requirements, paragraph (g)(1)(iii) provides two rules: a rule for

cost-sharing requirements other than copayments and a rule for copayments. Fixed-amount cost-sharing requirements include, for example, a $500 deductible, a $30 copayment, or a $2,500 out-of-pocket limit. With respect to fixed-amount cost-sharing requirements other than copayments, a plan or health insurance coverage ceases to be a grandfathered health plan if there is an increase, since March 23, 2010, in a fixed-amount cost-sharing requirement that is greater than the maximum percentage increase. The maximum percentage increase is defined as medical inflation (from March 23, 2010) plus 15 percentage points. For this purpose, medical inflation is defined in these interim final regulations by reference to the overall medical care component of the Consumer Price Index for All Urban Consumers, unadjusted (CPI), published by the Department of Labor. For fixed-amount copayments, a plan or health insurance coverage ceases to be a grandfathered health plan if there is an increase since March 23, 2010 in the copayment that exceeds the greater of (A) the maximum percentage increase or (B) five dollars increased by medical inflation. A more detailed description of the basis for these rules relating to cost-sharing requirements is included in section IV.B later in this preamble.

With respect to employer contributions, these interim final regulations include a standard for changes that would result in cessation of grandfather status. Specifically, paragraph (g)(1)(v) limits the ability of an employer or employee organization to decrease its contribution rate for coverage under a group health plan or group health insurance coverage. Two different situations are addressed. First, if the contribution rate is based on the cost of coverage, a group health plan or group health insurance coverage ceases to be a grandfathered health plan if the employer or employee organization decreases its contribution rate towards the cost of any tier of coverage for any class of similarly situated individuals [6] by more than 5 percentage points below the contribution rate on March 23, 2010. For this purpose, contribution rate is defined as the amount of contributions made by an employer or employee organization compared to the total cost of coverage, expressed as a percentage. These interim final regulations provide that total cost of coverage is determined in the same manner as the applicable

---

[6] Similarly situated individuals are described in the HIPAA nondiscrimination regulations at 26 CFR 54.9802–1(d), 29 CFR 2590.702(d), and 45 CFR 146.121(d).

premium is calculated under the COBRA continuation provisions of section 604 of ERISA, section 4980B(f)(4) of the Code, and section 2204 of the PHS Act. In the case of a self-insured plan, contributions by an employer or employee organization are calculated by subtracting the employee contributions towards the total cost of coverage from the total cost of coverage. Second, if the contribution rate is based on a formula, such as hours worked or tons of coal mined, a group health plan or group health insurance coverage ceases to be a grandfathered health plan if the employer or employee organization decreases its contribution rate towards the cost of any tier of coverage for any class of similarly situated individuals by more than 5 percent below the contribution rate on March 23, 2010.

Finally, paragraph (g)(1)(vi) addresses the imposition of a new or modified annual limit by a plan, or group or individual health insurance coverage.[7] Three different situations are addressed:

• A plan or health insurance coverage that, on March 23, 2010, did not impose an overall annual or lifetime limit on the dollar value of all benefits ceases to be a grandfathered health plan if the plan or health insurance coverage imposes an overall annual limit on the dollar value of benefits.

• A plan or health insurance coverage, that, on March 23, 2010, imposed an overall lifetime limit on the dollar value of all benefits but no overall annual limit on the dollar value of all benefits ceases to be a grandfathered health plan if the plan or health insurance coverage adopts an overall annual limit at a dollar value that is lower than the dollar value of the lifetime limit on March 23, 2010.

• A plan or health insurance coverage that, on March 23, 2010, imposed an overall annual limit on the dollar value of all benefits ceases to be a grandfathered health plan if the plan or health insurance coverage decreases the dollar value of the annual limit (regardless of whether the plan or health insurance coverage also imposed an overall lifetime limit on March 23, 2010 on the dollar value of all benefits).

Under these interim final regulations, changes other than the changes

described in 26 CFR 54.9815–1251T(g)(1), 29 CFR 2590.715–1251(g)(1), and 45 CFR 147.140(g)(1) will not cause a plan or coverage to cease to be a grandfathered health plan. Examples include changes to premiums, changes to comply with Federal or State legal requirements, changes to voluntarily comply with provisions of the Affordable Care Act, and changing third party administrators, provided these changes are made without exceeding the standards established by paragraph (g)(1).

These interim final regulations provide transitional rules for plans and issuers that made changes after the enactment of the Affordable Care Act pursuant to a legally binding contract entered into prior to enactment, made changes to the terms of health insurance coverage pursuant to a filing before March 23, 2010 with a State insurance department, or made changes pursuant to written amendments to a plan that were adopted prior to March 23, 2010. If a plan or issuer makes changes in any of these situations, the changes are effectively considered part of the plan terms on March 23, 2010 even though they are not then effective. Therefore, such changes are not taken into account in considering whether the plan or health insurance coverage remains a grandfathered health plan.

Because status as a grandfathered health plan under section 1251 of the Affordable Care Act is determined in relation to coverage on March 23, 2010, the date of enactment of the Affordable Care Act, the Departments considered whether they should provide a good-faith compliance period from Departmental enforcement until guidance regarding the standards for maintaining grandfather status was made available to the public. Group health plans and health insurance issuers often make routine changes from year to year, and some plans and issuers may have needed to implement such changes prior to the issuance of these interim final regulations.

Accordingly, for purposes of enforcement, the Departments will take into account good-faith efforts to comply with a reasonable interpretation of the statutory requirements and may disregard changes to plan and policy terms that only modestly exceed those changes described in paragraph (g)(1) of 26 CFR 54.9815–1251T, 29 CFR 2590.715–1251, and 45 CFR 147.140 and that are adopted before June 14, 2010, the date the regulations were made publicly available.

In addition, these interim final regulations provide employers and issuers with a grace period within

which to revoke or modify any changes adopted prior to June 14, 2010, where the changes might otherwise cause the plan or health insurance coverage to cease to be a grandfathered health plan. Under this rule, grandfather status is preserved if the changes are revoked, and the plan or health insurance coverage is modified, effective as of the first day of the first plan or policy year beginning on or after September 23, 2010 to bring the terms within the limits for retaining grandfather status in these interim final regulations. For this purpose, and for purposes of the reasonable good faith standard changes will be considered to have been adopted before these interim final regulations are publicly available if the changes are effective before that date, the changes are effective on or after that date pursuant to a legally binding contract entered into before that date, the changes are effective on or after that date pursuant to a filing before that date with a State insurance department, or the changes are effective on or after that date pursuant to written amendments to a plan that were adopted before that date.

While the Departments have determined that the changes identified in paragraph (g)(1) of these interim final regulations would cause a group health plan or health insurance coverage to cease to be a grandfathered health plan, the Departments invite comments from the public on whether this list of changes is appropriate and what other changes, if any, should be added to this list. Specifically, the Departments invite comments on whether the following changes should result in cessation of grandfathered health plan status for a plan or health insurance coverage: (1) Changes to plan structure (such as switching from a health reimbursement arrangement to major medical coverage or from an insured product to a self-insured product); (2) changes in a network plan's provider network, and if so, what magnitude of changes would have to be made; (3) changes to a prescription drug formulary, and if so, what magnitude of changes would have to be made; or (4) any other substantial change to the overall benefit design. In addition, the Departments invite comments on the specific standards included in these interim final regulations on benefits, cost sharing, and employer contributions. The Departments specifically invite comments on whether these standards should be drawn differently in light of the fact that changes made by the Affordable Care Act may alter plan or issuer practices in the next several

---

[7] Independent of these rules regarding the impact on grandfather status of newly adopted or reduced annual limits, group health plans and group or individual health insurance coverage (other than individual health insurance policies that are grandfathered health plans) are required to comply with PHS Act section 2711, which permits restricted annual limits (as defined in regulations) until 2014. The Departments expect to publish regulations regarding restricted annual limits in the very near future.

years. Any new standards published in the final regulations that are more restrictive than these interim final regulations would only apply prospectively to changes to plans or health insurance coverage after the publication of the final rules.

Moreover, the Departments may issue, as appropriate, additional administrative guidance other than in the form of regulations to clarify or interpret the rules contained in these interim final regulations for maintaining grandfathered health plan status prior to the issuance of final regulations. The ability to issue prompt, clarifying guidance is especially important given the uncertainty as to how plans or issuers will alter their plans or policies in response to these rules. This guidance can address unanticipated changes by plans and issuers to ensure that individuals benefit from the Affordable Care Act's new health care protections while preserving the ability to maintain the coverage individuals had on the date of enactment.

III. Interim Final Regulations and Request for Comments

Section 9833 of the Code, section 734 of ERISA, and section 2792 of the PHS Act authorize the Secretaries of the Treasury, Labor, and HHS (collectively, the Secretaries) to promulgate any interim final rules that they determine are appropriate to carry out the provisions of chapter 100 of the Code, part 7 of subtitle B of title I of ERISA, and part A of title XXVII of the PHS Act, which include PHS Act sections 2701 through 2728 and the incorporation of those sections into ERISA section 715 and Code section 9815. The rules set forth in these interim final regulations govern the applicability of the requirements in these sections and are therefore appropriate to carry them out. Therefore, the foregoing interim final rule authority applies to these interim final regulations.

In addition, under Section 553(b) of the Administrative Procedure Act (APA) (5 U.S.C. 551 *et seq.*) a general notice of proposed rulemaking is not required when an agency, for good cause, finds that notice and public comment thereon are impracticable, unnecessary, or contrary to the public interest. The provisions of the APA that ordinarily require a notice of proposed rulemaking do not apply here because of the specific authority granted by section 9833 of the Code, section 734 of ERISA, and section 2792 of the PHS Act. However, even if the APA were applicable, the Secretaries have determined that it would be impracticable and contrary to the public

interest to delay putting the provisions in these interim final regulations in place until a full public notice and comment process was completed. As noted above, numerous provisions of the Affordable Care Act are applicable for plan years (in the individual market, policy years) beginning on or after September 23, 2010, six months after date of enactment. Grandfathered health plans are exempt from many of these provisions while group health plans and group and individual health insurance coverage that are not grandfathered health plans must comply with them. The determination of whether a plan or health insurance coverage is a grandfathered health plan therefore could substantially affect the design of the plan or health insurance coverage.

The six-month period between the enactment of the Affordable Care Act and the applicability of many of the provisions affected by grandfather status would not allow sufficient time for the Departments to draft and publish proposed regulations, receive and consider comments, and draft and publish final regulations. Moreover, regulations are needed well in advance of the effective date of the requirements of the Affordable Care Act. Many group health plans and health insurance coverage that are not grandfathered health plans must make significant changes in their provisions to comply with the requirements of the Affordable Care Act. Moreover, plans and issuers considering other modifications to their terms need to know whether those modifications will affect their status as grandfathered health plans. Accordingly, in order to allow plans and health insurance coverage to be designed and implemented on a timely basis, regulations must be published and available to the public well in advance of the effective date of the requirements of the Affordable Care Act. It is not possible to have a full notice and comment process and to publish final regulations in the brief time between enactment of the Affordable Care Act and the date regulations are needed.

The Secretaries further find that issuance of proposed regulations would not be sufficient because the provisions of the Affordable Care Act protect significant rights of plan participants and beneficiaries and individuals covered by individual health insurance policies and it is essential that participants, beneficiaries, insureds, plan sponsors, and issuers have certainty about their rights and responsibilities. Proposed regulations are not binding and cannot provide the necessary certainty. By contrast, the

interim final regulations provide the public with an opportunity for comment, but without delaying the effective date of the regulations.

For the foregoing reasons, the Departments have determined that it is impracticable and contrary to the public interest to engage in full notice and comment rulemaking before putting these regulations into effect, and that it is in the public interest to promulgate interim final regulations.

IV. Economic Impact and Paperwork Burden

A. Overview—Department of Labor and Department of Health and Human Services

As stated earlier in this preamble, these interim final regulations implement section 1251 of the Affordable Care Act, as modified by section 10103 of the Affordable Care Act and section 2301 of the Reconciliation Act. Pursuant to section 1251, certain provisions of the Affordable Care Act do not apply to a group health plan or health insurance coverage in which an individual was enrolled on March 23, 2010 (a grandfathered health plan).[8] The statute and these interim final regulations allow family members of individuals already enrolled in a grandfathered health plan to enroll in the plan after March 23, 2010; in such cases, the plan or coverage is also a grandfathered health plan with respect to the family members. New employees (whether newly hired or newly enrolled) and their families can enroll in a grandfathered group health plan after March 23, 2010 without affecting status as a grandfathered health plan.[9]

---

[8] The Affordable Care Act adds section 715(a)(1) to ERISA and section 9815(a)(1) to the Code to incorporate the provisions of part A of title XXVII of the PHS Act into ERISA and the Code, and make them applicable to group health plans, and health insurance issuers providing health insurance coverage in connection with group health plans. The PHS Act sections incorporated by this reference are sections 2701 through 2728. PHS Act sections 2701 through 2719A are substantially new, though they incorporate some provisions of prior law. PHS Act sections 2722 through 2728 are sections of prior law renumbered, with some, mostly minor, changes. Section 1251 of the Affordable Care Act, as modified by section 10103 of the Affordable Care Act and section 2301 of the Reconciliation Act, specifies that certain plans or coverage existing as of the date of enactment (that is, grandfathered health plans) are only subject to certain provisions.

[9] For individuals who have coverage through an insured group health plans subject to a collective bargaining agreement ratified before March 23, 2010, an individual's coverage is grandfathered at least until the date on which the last agreement relating to the coverage that was in effect on March 23, 2010, terminates. These collectively bargained plans may make any permissible changes to the benefit structure before the agreement terminates and remain grandfathered. After the termination

Continued

As addressed earlier in this preamble, and further discussed below, these interim final regulations include rules for determining whether changes to the terms of a grandfathered health plan made by issuers and plan sponsors allow the plan or health insurance coverage to remain a grandfathered health plan. These rules are the primary focus of this regulatory impact analysis.

The Departments have quantified the effects where possible and provided a qualitative discussion of the economic effects and some of the transfers and costs that may result from these interim final regulations.

B. Executive Order 12866—Department of Labor and Department of Health and Human Services

Under Executive Order 12866 (58 FR 51735), "significant" regulatory actions are subject to review by the Office of Management and Budget (OMB). Section 3(f) of the Executive Order defines a "significant regulatory action" as an action that is likely to result in a rule (1) having an annual effect on the economy of $100 million or more in any one year, or adversely and materially affecting a sector of the economy, productivity, competition, jobs, the environment, public health or safety, or State, local or tribal governments or communities (also referred to as "economically significant"); (2) creating a serious inconsistency or otherwise interfering with an action taken or planned by another agency; (3) materially altering the budgetary impacts of entitlement grants, user fees, or loan programs or the rights and obligations of recipients thereof; or (4) raising novel legal or policy issues arising out of legal mandates, the President's priorities, or the principles set forth in the Executive Order. OMB has determined that this regulation is economically significant within the meaning of section 3(f)(1) of the Executive Order, because it is likely to have an annual effect on the economy of $100 million in any one year. Accordingly, OMB has reviewed these rules pursuant to the Executive Order. The Departments provide an assessment of the potential costs, benefits, and transfers associated with these interim final regulations below. The Departments invite comments on this assessment and its conclusions.

date, grandfather status will be determined by comparing the plan, as it existed on March 23, 2010 to the changes that the plan made before termination under the rules established by these interim final regulations.

1. Need for Regulatory Action

As discussed earlier in this preamble, Section 1251 of the Affordable Care Act, as modified by section 10103 of the Affordable Care Act and section 2301 of the Reconciliation Act, provides that grandfathered health plans are subject only to certain provisions of the Affordable Care Act. The statute, however, is silent regarding changes plan sponsors and issuers can make to plans and health insurance coverage while retaining grandfather status. These interim final regulations are necessary in order to provide rules that plan sponsors and issuers can use to determine which changes they can make to the terms of the plan or health insurance coverage while retaining their grandfather status, thus exempting them from certain provisions of the Affordable Care Act and fulfilling a goal of the legislation, which is to allow those that like their healthcare to keep it. These interim final regulations are designed to allow individuals who wish to maintain their current health insurance plan to do so, to reduce short term disruptions in the market, and to ease the transition to market reforms that phase in over time.

In drafting this rule, the Departments attempted to balance a number of competing interests. For example, the Departments sought to provide adequate flexibility to plan sponsors and issuers to ease transition and mitigate potential premium increases while avoiding excessive flexibility that would conflict with the goal of permitting individuals who like their healthcare to keep it and might lead to longer term market segmentation as the least costly plans remain grandfathered the longest. In addition, the Departments recognized that many plan sponsors and issuers make changes to the terms of plans or health insurance coverage on an annual basis: Premiums fluctuate, provider networks and drug formularies change, employer and employee contributions and cost-sharing change, and covered items and services may vary. Without some ability to make some adjustments while retaining grandfather status, the ability of individuals to maintain their current coverage would be frustrated, because most plans or health insurance coverage would quickly cease to be regarded as the same group health plan or health insurance coverage in existence on March 23, 2010. At the same time, allowing unfettered changes while retaining grandfather status would also be inconsistent with Congress's intent to preserve coverage that was in effect on March 23, 2010.

Therefore, as further discussed below, these interim final regulations are designed, among other things, to take into account reasonable changes routinely made by plan sponsors or issuers without the plan or health insurance coverage relinquishing its grandfather status so that individuals can retain the ability to remain enrolled in the coverage in which they were enrolled on March 23, 2010. Thus, for example, these interim final regulations generally permit plan sponsors and issuers to make voluntary changes to increase benefits, to conform to required legal changes, and to adopt voluntarily other consumer protections in the Affordable Care Act.

2. Regulatory Alternatives

Section 6(a)(3)(C)(iii) of Executive Order 12866 requires an economically significant regulation to include an assessment of the costs and benefits of potentially effective and reasonable alternatives to the planned regulation, and an explanation of why the planned regulatory action is preferable to the potential alternatives. The alternatives considered by the Departments fall into two general categories: Permissible changes to cost sharing and benefits. The discussion below addresses the considered alternatives in each category.

The Departments considered allowing looser cost-sharing requirements, such as 25 percent plus medical inflation. However, the data analysis led the Departments to believe that the cost-sharing windows provided in these interim final regulations permit enough flexibility to enable a smooth transition in the group market over time, and further widening this window was not necessary and could conflict with the goal of allowing those who like their healthcare to keep it.

Another alternative the Departments considered was an annual allowance for cost-sharing increases above medical inflation, as opposed to the one-time allowance of 15 percent above medical inflation. An annual margin of 15 percent above medical inflation, for example, would permit plans to increase cost sharing by medical inflation plus 15 percent every year. The Departments concluded that the effect of the one-time allowance (15 percent of the original, date-of-enactment level plus medical inflation) would diminish over time insofar as it would represent a diminishing fraction of the total level of cost sharing with the cumulative effects of medical inflation over time. Accordingly, the one-time allowance would better reflect (i) the potential need of grandfathered health plans to make adjustments in the near term to reflect the requirement that they comply with the market reforms that apply to grandfathered health plans in the near term as well as (ii) the prospect that, for many plans and health insurance coverage, the need to recover the costs of compliance in other ways will diminish in the medium term, in part because of the changes that will become effective in 2014 and in part because of the additional time plan sponsors and issuers will have to make gradual adjustments that take into account the market reforms that are due to take effect in later years.

The Departments considered establishing an overall prohibition against changes that, in the aggregate, or cumulatively over time, render the plan or coverage substantially different than the plan or coverage that existed on March 23, 2010, or further delineating other examples of changes that could cause a plan to relinquish grandfather status. This kind of "substantially different" standard would have captured significant changes not anticipated in the interim final regulation. However, it would rely on a "facts and circumstances" analysis in defining "substantially different" or "significant changes," which would be less transparent and result in greater uncertainty about the status of a health plan. That, in turn, could hinder plan sponsor or issuer decisions as well as enrollee understanding of what protections apply to their coverage.

An actuarial equivalency standard was another considered option. Such a standard would allow a plan or health insurance coverage to retain status as a grandfathered health plan if the actuarial value of the coverage remains in approximately the same range as it was on March 23, 2010. However, under such a standard, a plan could make fundamental changes to the benefit design, potentially conflicting with the goal of allowing those who like their healthcare to keep it, and still retain grandfather status. Moreover, the complexity involved in defining and determining actuarial value for these purposes, the likelihood of varying methodologies for determining such value unless the Departments promulgated very detailed prescriptive rules, and the costs of administering and ensuring compliance with such rules led the Departments to reject that approach.

Another alternative was a requirement that employers continue to contribute the same dollar amount they were contributing for the period including March 23, 2010, plus an inflation component. However, the Departments were concerned that this approach would not provide enough flexibility to accommodate the year-to-year volatility in premiums that can result from changes in some plans' covered populations or other factors.

The Departments also considered whether a change in third party administrator by a self-insured plan should cause the plan to relinquish grandfather status. The Departments decided that such a change would not necessarily cause the plan to be so different from the plan in effect on March 23, 2010 that it should be required to relinquish grandfather status.

After careful consideration, the Departments opted against rules that would require a plan sponsor or issuer to relinquish its grandfather status if only relatively small changes are made to the plan. The Departments concluded that plan sponsors and issuers of grandfathered health plans should be permitted to take steps within the boundaries of the grandfather definition to control costs, including limited increases in cost-sharing and other plan changes not prohibited by these interim final regulations. As noted earlier, deciding to relinquish grandfather status is a one-way sorting process: after some period of time, more plans will relinquish their grandfather status. These interim final regulations will likely influence plan sponsors' decisions to relinquish grandfather status.

3. Discussion of Regulatory Provisions

As discussed earlier in this preamble, these interim final regulations provide that a group health plan or health insurance coverage no longer will be considered a grandfathered health plan if a plan sponsor or an issuer:

• Eliminates all or substantially all benefits to diagnose or treat a particular condition. The elimination of benefits for any necessary element to diagnose or treat a condition is considered the elimination of all or substantially all benefits to diagnose or treat a particular condition;

• Increases a percentage cost-sharing requirement (such as coinsurance)

above the level at which it was on March 23, 2010;

• Increases fixed-amount cost-sharing requirements other than copayments, such as a $500 deductible or a $2,500 out-of-pocket limit, by a total percentage measured from March 23, 2010 that is more than the sum of medical inflation and 15 percentage points.[10]

• Increases copayments by an amount that exceeds the greater of: a total percentage measured from March 23, 2010 that is more than the sum of medical inflation plus 15 percentage points, or $5 increased by medical inflation measured from March 23, 2010;

• For a group health plan or group health insurance coverage, an employer or employee organization decreases its contribution rate by more than five percentage points below the contribution rate on March 23, 2010; or

• With respect to annual limits (1) a group health plan, or group or individual health insurance coverage, that, on March 23, 2010, did not impose an overall annual or lifetime limit on the dollar value of all benefits imposes an overall annual limit on the dollar value of benefits; (2) a group health plan, or group or individual health insurance coverage, that, on March 23, 2010, imposed an overall lifetime limit on the dollar value of all benefits but no overall annual limit on the dollar value of all benefits adopts an overall annual limit at a dollar value that is lower than the dollar value of the lifetime limit on March 23, 2010; or (3) a group health plan, or group or individual health insurance coverage, that, on March 23, 2010, imposed an overall annual limit on the dollar value of all benefits decreases the dollar value of the annual limit (regardless of whether the plan or health insurance coverage also imposes an overall lifetime limit on the dollar value of all benefits).

Table 1, in section II.D of this preamble, lists the relevant Affordable Care Act provisions that apply to grandfathered health plans.

In accordance with OMB Circular A–4,[11] Table 2 below depicts an accounting statement showing the Departments' assessment of the benefits, costs, and transfers associated with this regulatory action. In accordance with Executive Order 12866, the Departments believe that the benefits of this regulatory action justify the costs.

---

[10] Medical inflation is defined in these interim regulations by reference to the overall medical care component of the CPI.

[11] Available at *http://www.whitehouse.gov/omb/circulars/a004/a-4.pdf.*

TABLE 2—ACCOUNTING TABLE

Benefits

Qualitative: These interim final regulations provide plans with guidance about the requirements for retaining grandfather status. Non-grandfathered plans are required to offer coverage with minimum benefit standards and patient protections as required by the Affordable Care Act, while grandfathered plans are required only to comply with certain provisions. The existence of grandfathered health plans will provide individuals with the benefits of plan continuity, which may have a high value to some. In addition, grandfathering could potentially slow the rate of premium growth, depending on the extent to which their current plan does not include the benefits and protections of the new law. It could also provide incentives to employers to continue coverage, potentially reducing new Medicaid enrollment and spending and lowering the number of uninsured individuals. These interim final regulations also provide greater certainty for plans and issuers about what changes they can make without affecting their grandfather status. As compared with alternative approaches, these regulations provide significant economic and noneconomic benefits to both issuers and beneficiaries, though these benefits cannot be quantified at this time.

Costs	Low-end estimate	Mid-range estimate	High-end estimate	Year dollar	Discount rate	Period covered
Annualized	22.0	25.6	27.9	2010	7%	2011–2013
Monetized ($millions/year)	21.2	24.7	26.9	2010	3%	2011–2013

Monetized costs are due to a requirement to notify participants and beneficiaries of a plan's grandfather status and maintain plan documents to verify compliance with these interim final regulation's requirements to retain grandfather status.

Qualitative: Limitations on cost-sharing increases imposed by these interim final regulations could result in the cost of some grandfathered health plans increasing more (or decreasing less) than they otherwise would. This increased cost may encourage some sponsors and issuers to replace their grandfathered health plans with new, non-grandfathered ones. Market segmentation (adverse selection) due to the decision of higher risk plans to relinquish grandfathering could cause premiums in the exchanges to be higher than they would have been absent grandfathering.

Transfers

Qualitative: Limits on the changes to cost-sharing in grandfathered plans and the elimination of cost-sharing for some services in non-grandfathered plans, leads to transfers of wealth from premium payers overall to individuals using covered services. Once pre-existing conditions are fully prohibited and other insurance reforms take effect, the extent to which individuals are enrolled in grandfathered plans could affect adverse selection, as higher risk plans relinquish grandfather status to gain new protections while lower risk grandfathered plans retain their grandfather status. This could result in a transfer of wealth from non-grandfathered plans to grandfathered health plans.

4. Discussion of Economic Impacts of Retaining or Relinquishing Grandfather Status

The economic effects of these interim final regulations will depend on decisions by plan sponsors and issuers, as well as by those covered under these plans and health insurance coverage. The collective decisions of plan sponsors and issuers over time can be viewed as a one-way sorting process in which these parties decide whether, and when, to relinquish status as a grandfathered health plan.

Plan sponsors and issuers can decide to:

1. Continue offering the plan or coverage in effect on March 23, 2010 with limited changes, and thereby retain grandfather status;

2. Significantly change the terms of the plan or coverage and comply with Affordable Care Act provisions from which grandfathered health plans are excepted; or

3. In the case of a plan sponsor, cease to offer any plan.

For a plan sponsor or issuer, the potential economic impact of the application of the provisions in the Affordable Care Act may be one consideration in making its decisions. To determine the value of retaining the health plan's grandfather status, each plan sponsor or issuer must determine whether the rules applicable to grandfathered health plans are more or less favorable than the rules applicable to non-grandfathered health plans. This determination will depend on such factors as the respective prices of grandfathered and non-grandfathered health plans, as well as on the preferences of grandfathered health plans' covered populations and their willingness to pay for benefits and patient protections available under non-grandfathered health plans. In making its decisions about grandfather status, a plan sponsor or issuer is also likely to consider the market segment (because different rules apply to the large and small group market segments), and the utilization pattern of its covered population.

In deciding whether to change a plan's benefits or cost sharing, a plan sponsor or issuer will examine its short-run business requirements. These requirements are regularly altered by, among other things, rising costs that result from factors such as technological changes, changes in risk status of the enrolled population, and changes in utilization and provider prices. As shown below, changes in benefits and cost sharing are typical in insurance markets. Decisions about the extent of changes will determine whether a plan retains its grandfather status. Ultimately, these decisions will involve a comparison by the plan sponsor or issuer of the long run value of grandfather status to the short-run need of that plan sponsor or issuer to adjust plan structure in order to control premium costs or achieve other business objectives.

Decisions by plan sponsors and issuers may be significantly affected by the preferences and behavior of the enrollees, especially a tendency among many towards inertia and resistance to change. There is limited research that has directly examined what drives this tendency—whether individuals remain with health plans because of simple inertia and procrastination, a lack of relevant information, or because they want to avoid risk associated with switching to new plans. One study that examined the extent to which premium changes influenced plan switching determined that younger low-risk employees were the most price-sensitive to premium changes; older, high-risk employees were the least price-sensitive. This finding suggests that, in particular, individuals with substantial health needs may be more apt to remain with a plan because of inertia as such or uncertainties associated with plan switching rather than quality per se—a phenomenon some behavioral economists have called "status quo bias,"[12] which can be found when people stick with the status quo even though a change would have higher expected value.

Even when an enrollee could reap an economic or other advantage from changing plans, that enrollee may not make the change because of inertia, a lack of relevant information, or because of the cost and effort involved in examining new options and uncertainty about the alternatives. Consistent with well-known findings in behavioral economics, studies of private insurance demonstrate the substantial effect of inertia in the behavior of the insured. One survey found that approximately 83 percent of privately insured individuals stuck with their plans in the year prior to the survey.[13] Among those who did change plans, well over half sought the same type of plan they had before. Those who switched plans also tended to do so for reasons other than preferring their new plans. For example, many switched because they changed jobs or their employer changed insurance offerings, compelling them to switch.

Medicare beneficiaries display similar plan loyalties. On average, only seven percent of the 17 million seniors on Medicare drug plans switch plans each year, according to the Centers for Medicare and Medicaid Services.[14] Researchers have found this comparatively low rate of switching is maintained whether or not those insured have higher quality information about plan choices, and that switching has little effect on the satisfaction of the insured with their health plans.[15]

The incentives to change are different for people insured in the individual market than they are for those covered by group health plans or group health insurance coverage. The median length of coverage for people entering the individual market is eight months.[16] In part, this "churn" stems from the individual market's function as a stopping place for people between jobs with employer-sponsored or other types of health insurance, but in part, the churn is due to the behavior of issuers. Evidence suggests that issuers often make policy changes such as raising deductibles as a means of attracting new, healthy enrollees who have few medical costs and so are little-concerned about such deductibles. There is also evidence that issuers use such changes to sort out high-cost enrollees from low-cost ones.[17]

Decisions about the value of retaining or relinquishing status as a grandfathered health plan are complex, and the wide array of factors affecting issuers, plan sponsors, and enrollees poses difficult challenges for the Departments as they try to estimate how large the presence of grandfathered health plans will be in the future and what the economic effects of their presence will be. As one example, these interim final regulations limit the extent to which plan sponsors and issuers can increase cost sharing and still remain grandfathered. The increases that are allowed provide plans and issuers with substantial flexibility in attempting to control expenditure increases. However, there are likely to be some plans and issuers that would, in the absence of these regulations, choose to make even larger increases in cost sharing than are specified here. Such plans will need to decide whether the benefits of maintaining grandfather status outweigh those expected from increasing cost sharing above the levels permitted in the interim final regulations.

A similar analysis applies to the provision that an employer's or employee organization's share of the total premium of a group health plan cannot be reduced by more than 5 percentage points from the share it was paying on March 23, 2010 without that plan or health insurance coverage relinquishing its grandfather status. Employers and employee organizations sponsoring group health plans or health insurance coverage may be faced with economic circumstances that would lead them to reduce their premium contributions. But reductions of greater than 5 percentage points would cause them to relinquish the grandfather status of their plans. These plan sponsors must decide whether the benefit of such premium reductions outweigh those of retaining grandfather status.

Market dynamics affecting these decisions change in 2014, when the Affordable Care Act limits variation in premium rates for individual and small group policies. Small groups for this purpose include employers with up to 100 employees (States may limit this threshold to 50 employees until 2016). The Affordable Care Act rating rules will not apply to grandfathered health plans, but such plans will remain subject to State rating rules, which vary widely and typically apply to employers with up to 50 employees. Based on the current State rating rules, it is likely that, in many States, no rating rules will apply to group health insurance policies that are grandfathered health plans covering employers with 51 to 100 employees.[18]

The interaction of the Affordable Care Act and State rating rules implies that, beginning in 2014, premiums can vary more widely for grandfathered plans than for non-grandfathered plans for employers with up to 100 employees in many States. This could encourage both plan sponsors and issuers to continue grandfathered health plans that cover lower-risk groups, because these groups will be isolated from the larger, higher-risk, non-grandfathered risk pool. On the other hand, this scenario likely will encourage plan sponsors and issuers that cover higher-risk groups to end grandfathered health plans, because the group would be folded into the larger, lower-risk non-grandfathered pool. Depending on the size of the grandfathered health plan market, such adverse selection by grandfathered health plans against non-grandfathered plans could cause premiums in the exchanges to be higher than they would have been absent grandfathering. To accommodate these changes in market dynamics in 2014, the Departments have structured a cost-sharing rule whose parameters enable greater flexibility in early years and less over time. It is likely that few plans will delay for many years before making changes that exceed medical inflation. This is because the cumulative increase in copayments from March 23, 2010 is compared to a maximum percentage increase that includes a fixed amount—15 percentage points—that does not increase annually with any type of inflator. This should help mitigate adverse selection and require plans and issuers that seek to maintain grandfather status to find ways other than increased

[12] http://www.nber.org/reporter/summer06/buchmueller.html. "Consumer Demand for Health Insurance" The National Bureau of Economic Research (Buchmueller, 2006).

[13] http://content.healthaffairs.org/cgi/reprint/19/3/158.pdf. "Health Plan Switching: Choice Or Circumstance?" (Cunningham and Kohn, 2000).

[14] http://www.kaiserhealthnews.org/Stories/2009/December/01/Medicare-Drug-Plan.aspx. "Seniors Often Reluctant To Switch Medicare Drug Plans" (2009, Kaiser Health News/Washington Post).

[15] http://www.ncbi.nlm.nih.gov/pubmed/16704882. "The effect of quality information on consumer health plan switching: evidence from the Buyers Health Care Action Group." (Abraham, Feldman, Carlin, and Christianson. 2006).

[16] Erika C. Ziller, Andrew F. Coburn, Timothy D. McBride, and Courtney Andrews. Patterns of Individual Health Insurance Coverage, 1996–2000. Health Affairs Nov/Dec 2004: 210–221.

[17] Melinda Beeuwkes Bustin, M. Susan Marquis, and Jill M. Yegian. The Role of the Individual Health Insurance Market and Prospects for Change. Health Affairs 2004; 23(6): 79–90.

[18] Kaiser Family Foundation State Health Facts (2010), http://www.statehealthfacts.org/comparetable.jsp?ind=351&cat=7.

34550   **Federal Register** / Vol. 75, No. 116 / Thursday, June 17, 2010 / Rules and Regulations

copayments to limit cost growth. As discussed in the preamble, the Departments are also soliciting comments to make any adjustments needed for the final rule prior to 2014. Therefore it is premature to estimate the economic effects described above in 2014 and beyond. In the following section, the Departments provide a range of estimates of how issuers and sponsors might respond to these interim final regulations, with the caveat that there is substantial uncertainty about actual outcomes, especially considering that available data are historical and so do not account for behavioral changes in plans and the insured as a result of enactment of the Affordable Care Act.

5. Estimates of Number of Plans and Employees Affected

The Affordable Care Act applies to group health plans and health insurance issuers in the group and individual markets. The large and small group markets will be discussed first, followed by a discussion of impacts on the individual market. The Departments have defined a large group health plan as a plan at an employer with 100 or more workers and a small group plan as a plan at an employer with less than 100 workers. Using data from the 2008 Medical Expenditure Survey—Insurance Component, the Departments estimated that there are approximately 72,000 large ERISA-covered health plans and 2.8 million small group health plans with an estimated 97.0 million participants and beneficiaries [19] in large group plans and 40.9 million participants and beneficiaries in small group plans. The Departments estimate that there are 126,000 governmental plans [20] with 36.1 million participants in large plans and 2.3 million participants in small plans. The Departments estimate there are 16.7 million individuals under age 65 covered by individually purchased policies.

a. Methodology for Analyzing Plan Changes Over Time in the Group Market

For the large and small group markets, the Departments analyzed three years of Kaiser-HRET data to assess the changes that plans made between plan years 2007 to 2008 and 2008 to 2009. Specifically, the Departments examined changes made to deductibles, out-of-pocket maximums, copayments, coinsurance, and the employer's share of the premium or cost of coverage. The

Departments also estimated the number of fully-insured plans that changed issuers.[21] The distribution of changes made within the two time periods were nearly identical and ultimately the 2008–2009 changes were used as a basis for the analyses.

As discussed previously, plans will need to make decisions that balance the value they (and their enrollees) place on maintaining grandfather status with the need to meet short run objectives by changing plan features including the various cost sharing requirements that are the subject of this rule. The 2008–2009 data reflect changes in plan benefit design that were made under very different market conditions and expectations than will exist in 2011 and beyond. Therefore, there is a significant degree of uncertainty associated with using the 2008–2009 data to project the number of plans whose grandfather status may be affected in the next few years. Because the level of uncertainty becomes substantially greater when trying to use this data to predict outcomes once the full range of reforms takes effect in 2014 and the exchanges begin operating, substantially changing market dynamics the Departments restrict our estimates to the 2011–2013 period and use the existing data and a range of assumptions to estimate possible outcomes based on a range of assumptions concerning how plans' behavior regarding cost sharing changes may change relative to what is reflected in the 2008–2009 data.

Deriving projections of the number of plans that could retain grandfather status under the requirements of these interim final regulations required several steps:

• Using Kaiser/HRET data for 2008–2009, estimates were generated of the number of plans in the large and small group markets that made changes in employer premium share or any of the cost-sharing parameters that were larger than permitted for a plan to retain grandfather status under these interim final regulations;

• In order to account for a range of uncertainty with regard to changes in plan behavior toward cost sharing changes, the Departments assumed that many plans will want to maintain grandfather status and will look for ways to achieve short run cost control and still maintain that status. One plausible assumption is that plans would look to a broader range of cost sharing strategies in order to achieve

cost containment and other objectives than they had in the past. In order to examine this possibility, the Departments carefully analyzed those plans that would have relinquished grandfather status based on a change they made from 2008–2009. The Departments then estimated the proportion of these plans that could have achieved similar cost control by using one or more other cost-sharing changes in addition to the one they made in a manner that would not have exceeded the limits set by these interim final regulations for qualifying as a grandfathered health plan. For example, if a plan was estimated to relinquish grandfather status because it increased its deductible by more than the allowed 15 percentage points plus medical inflation, the Departments analyze whether the plan could have achieved the same cost control objectives with a smaller change in deductible, but larger changes (within the limits set forth in these interim final regulations) in copayments, out-of-pocket maximums, and employer contributions to the premium or cost of coverage.

• Finally, the Departments examined the impact of alternative assumptions about sponsor behavior. For example, it is possible that some sponsors who made changes from 2008–2009 in plan parameters that were so large that they would have relinquished their grandfather status would not make similar changes in 2011–2013. It is also possible that even though a sponsor could make an equivalent change that conforms to the rules established in these interim final regulations to maintain grandfather status, it would decide not to.

The estimates in this example rely on several other assumptions. Among them: (1) The annual proportion of plans relinquishing grandfather status is the same throughout the period; (2) all group health plans existing at the beginning of 2010 qualify for grandfather status; (3) all changes during 2010 occur after March 23, 2010; (4) annual medical inflation is 4 percent (based on the average annual change in the medical CPI between 2000 and 2009); and (5) firms for which the Kaiser-HRET survey has data for both 2008 and 2009 are representative of all firms.[22] The assumption used for

---

[19] All participant counts and the estimates of individual policies are from the 2009 Current Population Survey (CPS).

[20] Estimate is from the 2007 Census of Government.

[21] Under the Affordable Care Act and these interim final regulations, if a plan that is not a collectively bargained plan changes issuers after March 23, 2010, it is no longer a grandfathered health plan.

[22] The analysis is limited to firms that responded to the Kaiser/HRET survey in both 2008 and 2009. Large firms are overrepresented in the analytic sample. New firms and firms that went out of business in 2008 or 2009 are underrepresented. The Departments present results separately for large firms and small firms, and weight the results to the number of employees in each firm-size category. Results are presented for PPO plans. The Kaiser/

estimating the effects of the limits on copayment increases does not take into account the greater flexibility in the near term than in the long term; the estimated increase in firms losing their grandfather status over time reflects cumulative effects of a constant policy. To the extent that the data reflect plans that are more likely to make frequent changes in cost sharing, the assumption that a constant share of plans relinquishing grandfather status throughout the period may underestimate the number of plans that will retain grandfather status through 2013. In addition, data on substantial benefit changes were not available and thus not included in the analysis. The survey data is limited, in that it covers only one year of changes in healthcare plans. The Departments' analysis employed data only on PPO plans, the predominant type of plan. In addition, the difficulties of forecasting behavior in response to this rule create uncertainties for quantitative evaluation. However, the analysis presented here is illustrative of the rule's goal of balancing flexibility with maintaining current coverage.

b. Impacts on the Group Market Resulting From Changes From 2008 to 2009

The Departments first estimated the percentage of plans that had a percent change in the dollar value of deductibles, copayments, or out-of-pocket maximums that exceeded 19 percent (the sum of medical inflation (assumed in these analyses to be four percent) plus 15 percentage points measured from March 23, 2010. Plans making copayment changes of five dollars or less were considered to have satisfied the copayment limit, even if that change exceeded 19 percent.[23] The Departments also estimated the number of plans for whom the percentage of

HRET survey gathers information about the PPO with the most enrollment in each year. If enrollment at a given employer shifted from one PPO to a different PPO between 2008 and 2009, then the PPO with the most enrollment in 2009 may be different than the PPO with the most enrollment in 2008. To the extent this occurred, the estimates presented here may overestimate the fraction of plans that will relinquish grandfather status. However, given the behavioral assumptions of the analysis and the need to present a range of results, the Departments believe that such overestimation will not have a noticeable effect on estimates presented here.

[23] The regulation allows plans to increase fixed-amount copayments by an amount that does not exceed $5 increased by medical inflation. In this analysis, the Departments used a threshold of $5, rather than the threshold of approximately $5.20 that would be allowed by these interim final regulations. There would have been no difference in the results if the Departments had used $5.20 rather than $5 as the threshold.

total premium paid by the employer declined by more than 5 percentage points. For fully-insured plans only, estimates were made of the proportion that switched to a different issuer.[24] This estimate does not take into account collectively bargained plans, which can change issuers during the period of the collective bargaining agreement without a loss of grandfather status, because the Departments could not quantify this category of plans. Accordingly, this estimate represents an upper bound.

Using the Kaiser/HRET data, the Departments estimated that 55 percent of small employers and 36 percent of large employers made at least one change in cost-sharing parameters above the thresholds provided in these interim final regulations. Similarly, 33 percent of small employers and 21 percent of large employers decreased the employer's share of premium by more than five percentage points. In total, approximately 66 percent of small employers and 48 percent of large employers made a change in either cost sharing or premium contribution during 2009 that would require them to relinquish grandfather status if the same change were made in 2011.[25]

The changes made by employers from 2008 to 2009 were possibly made in anticipation of the recession. As discussed previously, analysis of changes from 2007 to 2008 suggests that the 2007–08 changes were not much different from the 2008–09 changes. Nevertheless, as a result of improvements in economic conditions, it makes sense to think that the pressure on employers to reduce their contributions to health insurance will be smaller in 2011 than they were in 2009, and that the Department's analysis of changes in 2009 may overestimate the changes that should be expected in 2011.[26]

As discussed previously, it is highly unlikely that plans would continue to exhibit the same behavior in 2011 to 2013 as in 2008 to 2009. In order to guide the choice of behavioral assumptions, the Departments

[24] In contrast, for self-insured plans, a change in third party administrator in and of itself does not cause a group health plan to cease to be a grandfathered health plan, provided changes do not exceed the limits of paragraph (g)(1) of these interim final regulations.

[25] Some employers made changes which exceeded at least one cost-sharing threshold and decreased the employer's share of contribution by more than five percent.

[26] Employers who offer plans on a calendar year basis generally make decisions about health plan offerings during the preceding summer. Thus, decisions for calendar 2009 were generally made during the summer of 2008. At that time, the depth of the coming recession was not yet clear to most observers.

conducted further analyses of the 2008–2009 data. Many employers who made changes between 2008 and 2009 that would have caused them to relinquish grandfather status did so based on exceeding one of the cost-sharing limits. Assuming that the sponsor's major objective in implementing these changes was to restrain employer costs or overall premiums, the Departments examined whether the sponsor could have achieved the same net effect on employer cost or premiums by spreading cost sharing over two or more changes without exceeding the limits on any of these changes. For example, an employer that increased its deductible by 30 percent would have relinquished grandfather status. However, it is possible that the employer could have achieved the same cost control objectives by limiting the deductible increase to 19 percent, and, also increasing the out-of-pocket maximum or copayments, or decreasing the employer share of the premium.

The Departments estimate that approximately two-thirds of the employers that made changes in 2009 that would have exceeded the threshold implemented by this rule could have achieved the same cost-control objective and remained grandfathered by making changes in other cost-sharing parameters or in the employer share of the premium. Only 24 percent of small employers and 16 percent of large employers could not have reconfigured the cost-sharing parameters or employer contributions in such a manner that would have allowed them to stay grandfathered. If benefit changes that are allowed within the grandfathered health plan definition were also taken into account (not possible with available data), these percentages would be even lower.

For fully insured group health plans, another change that would require a plan to relinquish grandfather status is a change in issuer. Between 2008 and 2009, 15 percent of small employers and four percent of large employers changed insurance carriers.[27] However, it is likely that the incentive to stay grandfathered would lead some of these employers to continue with the same issuer, making the actual share of firms relinquishing grandfather status as a result of an issuer change lower than the percentage that switched in 2009. There appears to be no empirical evidence to

[27] Among the 76 percent of small employers and 84 percent of large employers who could have accommodated the cost-sharing changes they desired to make within the parameters of these interim final regulations, 13 percent of the small employers and three percent of the large employers changed issuers.

provide guidance on the proportion of employers that would choose to remain with their issuer rather than relinquish grandfather status. That being so, an assumption was made that 50 percent of employers that changed issuers in 2009 would not have made a similar change in 2011 in order to retain grandfather status. It is likely that fewer employers will elect to change carriers than in recent years given that some will prefer to retain grandfather status. But it is also likely that many employers will prefer to switch carriers given a change in the issuer's network or other factors. Because there is little empirical evidence regarding the fraction of firms that would elect to switch in response to the change in regulations, we take the midpoint of the plausible range of no switching carriers at one extreme and all switching carriers at the other extreme. We therefore assume that 50 percent of employers that changed issuers in 2009 would not make a similar change in 2011 to retain grandfather status.

Combining the estimates of the percentage of employers that would relinquish grandfather status because they chose to make cost-sharing, benefit or employer contribution changes beyond the permitted parameters with the estimates of the percentage that would relinquish grandfather status because they change issuers, the Departments estimate that approximately 31 percent of small employers and 18 percent of large employers would make changes that would require them to relinquish grandfather status in 2011. The Departments use these estimates as our mid-range scenario.

c. Sensitivity Analysis: Assuming That Employers Will Be Willing To Absorb a Premium Increase in Order To Remain Grandfathered

To the extent that a large number of plans placed a high value on remaining grandfathered, it is reasonable to assume that some would consider other measures to maintain that status. In addition to the adjustments that employers could relatively easily make by simply adjusting the full set of cost-sharing parameters rather than focusing changes on a single parameter, the Departments expect that further behavioral changes in response to the incentives created by the Affordable Care Act and these interim final regulations is possible. For instance, plans could alter other benefits or could decide to accept a slight increase in plan premium or in premium contribution. All of these options would further lower the percentage of firms that would relinquish grandfather status. There is

substantial uncertainty, however, about how many firms would utilize these other avenues.

To examine the impact of this type of behavior on the estimates on the number of plans that would not maintain grandfather status, the Departments examined the magnitude of additional premium increases plans would need to implement if they were to modify their cost-sharing changes to stay within the allowable limits. Among the 24 percent of small firms that would have relinquished grandfather status based on the changes they made in 2009, 31 percent would have needed to increase premiums by 3 percent or less in order to maintain grandfather status. The analogous statistic for the 16 percent of large firms that would have relinquished grandfather status is 41 percent. It is reasonable to think that employers that are facing only a relatively small premium increase might choose to remain grandfathered.

Using these estimates, if employers value grandfathering enough that they are willing to allow premiums to increase by three percent more than their otherwise intended level (or can make changes to benefits other than cost-sharing that achieve a similar result), then 14 percent of small employers and 11 percent of large employers would relinquish grandfather status if they made the same changes in 2011 as they had in 2009. Adding in the employers who would relinquish grandfather status because they change issuers, the Departments' lower bound estimate is that approximately 21 percent of small employers and 13 percent of large employers will relinquish grandfather status in 2011.

d. Sensitivity Analysis: Incomplete Flexibility To Substitute One Cost-Sharing Mechanism for Another

Although economic conditions may cause more plans to remain grandfathered in 2011 than might be expected from analysis of the 2009 data, there are other factors that may cause the Departments' estimates of the fraction of plans retaining grandfather status to be overestimates of the fraction that will retain grandfather status. The estimates are based on the assumption that all plans that could accommodate the 2009 change they made in a single cost-sharing parameter by spreading out those changes over multiple parameters would actually do so. However, some plans and sponsors may be concerned about the labor relations consequences of reducing the employer contribution to premium. For example, if a plan increases its out-of-pocket maximum from $3,000 to $5,000 in 2009, it could

choose to remain grandfathered by limiting the out-of-pocket maximum to $3,570, reducing the employer contribution and increasing the employee contribution to premium. It is not clear, however, that all plan sponsors would do so—some may see the costs in negative employee relations as larger than the benefits from remaining grandfathered. Moreover, because some plans may already nearly comply with all provisions of the Affordable Care Act, or because enrollees are of average to less favorable health status, some employers may place less value on retaining grandfather status.

With this in mind, the Departments replicated the analysis, but assumed that one-half of the employers who made a change in cost-sharing parameter that could not be accommodated without reducing the employer contribution will be unwilling to reduce the employer contribution as a share of premium. Under this assumption, the 24 percent and 16 percent estimates of the proportion of employers relinquishing grandfather status increases to approximately 37 percent and 28 percent among small and large employers, respectively. Adding in the number of employers that it is estimated will change issuers, the Departments' high-end estimate for the proportion that will relinquish grandfather status in 2011 is approximately 42 percent for small employers and 29 percent for large employers.

e. Estimates for 2011–2013

Estimates are provided above for the percentage of employers that will retain grandfather status in 2011. These estimates are extended through 2013 by assuming that the identical percentage of plan sponsors will relinquish grandfathering in each year. Again, to the extent that the 2008–2009 data reflect plans that are more likely to make frequent changes in cost sharing, this assumption will overestimate the number of plans relinquishing grandfather status in 2012 and 2013.

Under this assumption, the Departments' mid-range estimate is that 66 percent of small employer plans and 45 percent of large employer plans will relinquish their grandfather status by the end of 2013. The low-end estimates are for 49 percent and 34 percent of small and large employer plans, respectively, to have relinquished grandfather status, and the high-end estimates are 80 percent and 64 percent, respectively.

TABLE 3—ESTIMATES OF THE CUMULATIVE PERCENTAGE OF EMPLOYER PLANS RELINQUISHING THEIR GRANDFATHERED STATUS, 2011–2013

	2011	2012	2013
Low-end Estimate			
Small Employer Plans	20%	36%	49%
Large Employer Plans	13%	24%	34%
All Employer Plans	15%	28%	39%
Mid-range Estimate			
Small Employer Plans	30%	51%	66%
Large Employer Plans	18%	33%	45%
All Employer Plans	22%	38%	51%
High-end Estimate			
Small Employer Plans	42%	66%	80%
Large Employer Plans	29%	50%	64%
All Employer Plans	33%	55%	69%

Notes: Represents full-time employees. Small Employers=3 to 99 employees; Large Employers=100+ employees. All three scenarios assume that two percent of all large employer plans and six percent of small employer plans would relinquish grandfathered status due to a change in issuer. Estimates are based on enrollment in PPOs.
Source: Kaiser/RHET Employer Survey, 2008–2009

f. Impacts on the Individual Market

The market for individual insurance is significantly different than that for group coverage. This affects estimates of the proportion of plans that will remain grandfathered until 2014. As mentioned previously, the individual market is a residual market for those who need insurance but do not have group coverage available and do not qualify for public coverage. For many, the market is transitional, providing a bridge between other types of coverage. One study found a high percentage of individual insurance policies began and ended with employer-sponsored coverage.[28] More importantly, coverage on particular policies tends to be for short periods of time. Reliable data are scant, but a variety of studies indicate that between 40 percent and 67 percent of policies are in effect for less than one year.[29] Although data on changes in benefit packages comparable to that for the group market is not readily available, the high turnover rates described here would dominate benefit changes as the chief source of changes in grandfather status.

While a substantial fraction of individual policies are in force for less than one year, a small group of individuals maintain their policies over longer time periods. One study found that 17 percent of individuals maintained their policies for more than two years,[30] while another found that

nearly 30 percent maintained policies for more than three years.[31]

Using these turnover estimates, a reasonable range for the percentage of individual policies that would terminate, and therefore relinquish their grandfather status, is 40 percent to 67 percent. These estimates assume that the policies that terminate are replaced by new individual policies, and that these new policies are not, by definition, grandfathered. In addition, the coverage that some individuals maintain for long periods might lose its grandfather status because the cost-sharing parameters in policies change by more than the limits specified in these interim final regulations. The frequency of this outcome cannot be gauged due to lack of data, but as a result of it, the Departments estimate that the percentage of individual market policies losing grandfather status in a given year exceeds the 40 percent to 67 percent range that is estimated based on the fraction of individual policies that turn over from one year to the next.

g. Application to Extension of Dependent Coverage to Age 26

One way to assess the impact of these interim final regulations is to assess how they interact with other Affordable Care Act provisions. One such provision is the requirement that, in plan years on or after September 23, 2010, but prior to January 1, 2014, grandfathered group health plans are required to offer dependent coverage to a child under the age of 26 who is not eligible for employer-sponsored insurance. In the Regulatory Impact Assessment (RIA) for the regulation that was issued on May

13, 2010 (75 FR 27122), the Departments estimated that there were 5.3 million young adults age 19–25 who were covered by employer-sponsored coverage (ESI) and whose parents were covered by employer-sponsored insurance, and an additional 480,000 young adults who were uninsured, were offered ESI, and whose parents were covered by ESI. In that impact assessment, the Departments assumed that all parents with employer-sponsored insurance would be in grandfathered health plans, and that none of their 19–25 year old dependents with their own offer of employer-sponsored insurance would gain coverage as a result of that regulation.

As estimated here, approximately 80 percent of the parents with ESI are likely to be in grandfathered health plans in 2011, leaving approximately 20 percent of these parents in non-grandfathered health plans. Young adults under 26 with employer-sponsored insurance or with an offer of such coverage whose parents are in non-grandfathered plans potentially could enroll in their parents' coverage. The Departments assume that a large percentage of the young adults who are uninsured will enroll in their parents' coverage when given the opportunity. It is more difficult to model the choices of young adults with an offer of employer-sponsored insurance whose parents also have group coverage. One assumes these young adults will compare the amount that they must pay for their own employer's coverage with the amount that they (or their parents) would pay if they were covered under their parents' policies. Such a decision will incorporate the type of plan that the parent has, since if the parent already has a family plan whose premium does not vary by number of dependents, the

[28] Adele M. Kirk. The Individual Insurance Market: A Building Block for Health Care Reform? *Health Care Financing Organization Research Synthesis.* May 2008.

[29] Ibid.

[30] http://content.healthaffairs.org/cgi/content/full/23/6/210#R14. "Patterns of Individual Health Insurance Coverage" *Health Affairs* (Ziller et al, 2004).

[31] http://content.healthaffairs.org/cgi/content/full/hlthaff.25.w226v1/DC1. "Consumer Decision Making in the Individual Health Insurance Market" *Health Affairs* (Marquis et al., 2006).

34554   **Federal Register**/Vol. 75, No. 116/Thursday, June 17, 2010/Rules and Regulations

adult child could switch at no additional cost to the parents. A very rough estimate therefore is that approximately 25 percent of young adults with ESI will switch to their parents' coverage when their parents' coverage is not grandfathered. The Departments assume that 15 percent of young adults who are offered ESI but are uninsured and whose parents have non-grandfathered health plans will switch to their parents' plan. This latter estimate roughly corresponds to the assumption made in the low-take up rate scenario in the RIA for dependent coverage for young adults who are uninsured.

These assumptions imply that an additional approximately 414,000 young adults whose parents have non-grandfathered ESI will be covered by their parents' health coverage in 2011, of whom 14,000 would have been uninsured, compared with the dependent coverage regulation impact analysis that assumed that all existing plans would have remained grandfathered and none of these adult children would have been eligible for coverage under their parents' plans. By 2013, an estimated 698,000 additional young adults with ESI or an offer of ESI will be covered by their parent's non-grandfathered health policy, of which 36,000 would have been uninsured.

6. Grandfathered Health Plan Document Retention and Disclosure Requirements

To maintain grandfathered health plan status under these interim final regulations, a plan or issuer must maintain records that document the plan or policy terms in connection with the coverage in effect on March 23, 2010, and any other documents necessary to verify, explain or clarify is status as a grandfathered health plan. The records must be made available for examination by participants, beneficiaries, individual policy subscribers, or a State or Federal agency official.

Plans or health insurance coverage that intend to be a grandfathered health plan, also must include a statement, in any plan materials provided to participants or beneficiaries (in the individual market, primary subscriber) describing the benefits provided under the plan or health insurance coverage, and that the plan or coverage is intended to be a grandfathered health plan within the meaning of section 1251 of the Affordable Care Act. In these interim final regulations, the Departments provide a model statement plans and issuers may use to satisfy the disclosure requirement. The Department's estimate that the one time

cost to plans and insurance issuers of preparing and distributing the grandfathered health plan disclosure is $39.6 million in 2011. The one time cost to plans and insurance issuers for the record retention requirement is estimated to be $32.2 million in 2011. For a discussion of the grandfathered health plan document retention and disclosure requirements, see the Paperwork Reduction Act section later in this preamble.

C. Regulatory Flexibility Act— Department of Labor and Department of Health and Human Services

The Regulatory Flexibility Act (5 U.S.C. 601 *et seq.*) (RFA) imposes certain requirements with respect to federal rules that are subject to the notice and comment requirements of section 553(b) of the APA (5 U.S.C. 551 *et seq.*) and that are likely to have a significant economic impact on a substantial number of small entities. Under Section 553(b) of the APA, a general notice of proposed rulemaking is not required when an agency, for good cause, finds that notice and public comment thereon are impracticable, unnecessary, or contrary to the public interest. These interim final regulations are exempt from the APA, because the Departments made a good cause finding that a general notice of proposed rulemaking is not necessary earlier in this preamble. Therefore, the RFA does not apply and the Departments are not required to either certify that the regulations would not have a significant economic impact on a substantial number of small entities or conduct a regulatory flexibility analysis.

Nevertheless, the Departments carefully considered the likely impact of the regulations on small entities in connection with their assessment under Executive Order 12866. Consistent with the policy of the RFA, the Departments encourage the public to submit comments that suggest alternative rules that accomplish the stated purpose of section 1251 of the Affordable Care Act and minimize the impact on small entities.

D. Special Analyses—Department of the Treasury

Notwithstanding the determinations of the Department of Labor and Department of Health and Human Services, for purposes of the Department of the Treasury, it has been determined that this Treasury decision is not a significant regulatory action for purposes of Executive Order 12866. Therefore, a regulatory assessment is not required. It has also been determined that section 553(b) of the Administrative

Procedure Act (5 U.S.C. chapter 5) does not apply to these regulations. For the applicability of the RFA, refer to the Special Analyses section in the preamble to the cross-referencing notice of proposed rulemaking published elsewhere in this issue of the **Federal Register**. Pursuant to section 7805(f) of the Code, these temporary regulations have been submitted to the Chief Counsel for Advocacy of the Small Business Administration for comment on their impact on small businesses.

E. Paperwork Reduction Act

1. Department of Labor and Department of Treasury: Affordable Care Act Grandfathered Plan Disclosure and Record Retention Requirements

As part of their continuing efforts to reduce paperwork and respondent burden, the Departments conduct a preclearance consultation program to provide the general public and federal agencies with an opportunity to comment on proposed and continuing collections of information in accordance with the Paperwork Reduction Act of 1995 (PRA) (44 U.S.C. 3506(c)(2)(A)). This helps to ensure that requested data can be provided in the desired format, reporting burden (time and financial resources) is minimized, collection requirements on respondents can be properly assessed.

As discussed earlier in this preamble, if a plan or health insurance coverage intends to be a grandfathered health plan, it must include a statement in any plan materials provided to participants or beneficiaries (in the individual market, primary subscriber) describing the benefits provided under the plan or health insurance coverage, and that the plan or coverage is intended to be grandfathered health plan within the meaning of section 1251 of the Affordable Care Act ("grandfathered health plan disclosure"). Model language has been provided in these interim final regulations, the use of which will satisfy this disclosure requirement.

To maintain status as a grandfathered health plan under these interim final regulations, a plan or issuer must maintain records documenting the plan or policy terms in connection with the coverage in effect on March 23, 2010, and any other documents necessary to verify, explain, or clarify its status as a grandfathered health plan ("recordkeeping requirement"). In addition, the plan or issuer must make such records available for examination. Accordingly, a participant, beneficiary, individual policy subscriber, or State or Federal agency official would be able to inspect such documents to verify the status of the plan or health insurance coverage as a grandfathered health plan.

As discussed earlier in this preamble, grandfathered health plans are not required to comply with certain Affordable Care Act provisions. These interim regulations define for plans and issuers the scope of changes that they can make to their grandfathered health plans and policies under the Affordable Care Act while retaining their grandfathered health plan status.

The Affordable Care Act grandfathered health plan disclosure and recordkeeping requirements are information collection requests (ICR) subject to the PRA. Currently, the Departments are soliciting public comments for 60 days concerning these disclosures. The Departments have submitted a copy of these interim final regulations to OMB in accordance with 44 U.S.C. 3507(d) for review of the information collections. The Departments and OMB are particularly interested in comments that:

• Evaluate whether the collection of information is necessary for the proper performance of the functions of the agency, including whether the information will have practical utility;

• Evaluate the accuracy of the agency's estimate of the burden of the collection of information, including the validity of the methodology and assumptions used;

• Enhance the quality, utility, and clarity of the information to be collected; and

• Minimize the burden of the collection of information on those who are to respond, including through the use of appropriate automated, electronic, mechanical, or other technological collection techniques or other forms of information technology, for example, by permitting electronic submission of responses.

Comments should be sent to the Office of Information and Regulatory Affairs, Attention: Desk Officer for the Employee Benefits Security Administration either by fax to (202) 395–7285 or by e-mail to *oira_submission@omb.eop.gov*. A copy of the ICR may be obtained by contacting the PRA addressee: G. Christopher Cosby, Office of Policy and Research, U.S. Department of Labor, Employee Benefits Security Administration, 200 Constitution Avenue, NW., Room N–5718, Washington, DC 20210. Telephone: (202) 693–8410; Fax: (202) 219–2745. These are not toll-free numbers. E-mail: *ebsa.opr@dol.gov*. ICRs submitted to OMB also are available at reginfo.gov

(*http://www.reginfo.gov/public/do/ PRAMain*).

a. Grandfathered Health Plan Disclosure

In order to satisfy the interim final regulations' grandfathered health plan disclosure requirement, the Departments estimate that 2.2 million ERISA-covered plans will need to notify an estimated 56.3 million policy holders of their plans' grandfathered health plan status.[32] The following estimates, except where noted, are based on the mid-range estimates of the percent of plans retaining grandfather status. Because the interim final regulations provide model language for this purpose, the Departments estimate that five minutes of clerical time (with a labor rate of $26.14/hour) will be required to incorporate the required language into the plan document and ten minutes of an human resource professional's time (with a labor rate of $89.12/hour) will be required to review the modified language.[33] After plans first satisfy the grandfathered health plan disclosure requirement in 2011, any additional burden should be de minimis if a plan wants to maintain its grandfather status in future years. The Departments also expect the cost of removing the notice from plan documents as plans relinquish their grandfather status to be de minimis and therefore is not estimated. Therefore, the Departments estimate that plans will incur a one-time hour burden of 538,000 hours with an equivalent cost of $36.6 million to meet the disclosure requirement.

The Departments assume that only printing and material costs are associated with the disclosure requirement, because the interim final regulations provide model language that can be incorporated into existing plan documents, such as a summary plan description (SPD). The Departments estimate that the notice will require one-half of a page, five cents per page printing and material cost will be incurred, and 38 percent of the notices will be delivered electronically. This results in a cost burden of $873,000 ($0.05 per page* ½ pages per notice * 34.9 million notices*0.62).

[32] The Departments' estimate of the number of ERISA-covered health plans was obtained from the 2008 Medical Expenditure Panel Survey's Insurance component. The estimate of the number of policy holders was obtained from the 2009 Current Population Survey. The methodology used to estimate the percentage of plans that will retain their grandfathered plans was discussed above.

[33] EBSA estimates of labor rates include wages, other benefits, and overhead based on the National Occupational Employment Survey (May 2008, Bureau of Labor Statistics) and the Employment Cost Index June 2009, Bureau of Labor Statistics).

b. Record-Keeping Requirement

The Departments assume that most of the documents required to be retained to satisfy recordkeeping requirement of these interim final regulations already are retained by plans for tax purposes, to satisfy ERISA's record retention and statute of limitations requirements, and for other business reasons. Therefore, the Departments estimate that the recordkeeping burden imposed by this ICR will require five minutes of a legal professional's time (with a rate of $119.03/hour) to determine the relevant plan documents that must be retained and ten minutes of clerical staff time (with a labor rate of $26.14/hour) to organize and file the required documents to ensure that they are accessible to participants, beneficiaries, and Federal and State governmental agency officials.

With an estimated 2.2 million grandfathered plans in 2011, the Departments estimate an hour burden of approximately 538,000 hours with equivalent costs of $30.7 million. The Departments have estimated this as a one-time cost incurred in 2011, because after the first year, the Departments anticipate that any future costs will be de minimis.

Overall, for both the grandfathering notice and the recordkeeping requirement, the Departments expect there to be a total hour burden of 1.1 million hours and a cost burden of $291,000.

The Departments note that persons are not required to respond to, and generally are not subject to any penalty for failing to comply with, an ICR unless the ICR has a valid OMB control number.

These paperwork burden estimates are summarized as follows:

Type of Review: New Collection.

Agencies: Employee Benefits Security Administration, Department of Labor; Internal Revenue Service, U.S. Department of Treasury.

Title: Disclosure and Recordkeeping Requirements for Grandfathered Health Plans under the Affordable Care Act.

OMB Number: 1210–0140; 1545–2178.

Affected Public: Business or other for-profit; not-for-profit institutions.

Total Respondents: 2,151,000.

Total Responses: 56,347,000.

Frequency of Response: One time.

Estimated Total Annual Burden Hours: 538,000 (Employee Benefits Security Administration); 538,000 (Internal Revenue Service).

Estimated Total Annual Burden Cost: $437,000 (Employee Benefits Security Administration); $437,000 (Internal Revenue Service).

34556 **Federal Register** / Vol. 75, No. 116 / Thursday, June 17, 2010 / Rules and Regulations

2. Department of Health and Human Services: Affordable Care Act Grandfathered Plan Disclosure and Record Retention Requirements

As discussed above in the Department of Labor and Department of the Treasury PRA section, these interim final regulations contain a record retention and disclosure requirement for grandfathered health plans. These requirements are information collection requirements under the PRA.

a. Grandfathered Health Plan Disclosure

In order to satisfy the interim final regulations' grandfathered health plan disclosure requirement, the Department estimates that 98,000 state and local governmental plans will need to notify approximately 16.2 million policy holders of their plans' status as a grandfathered health plan. The following estimates except where noted are based on the mid-range estimates of the percent of plans retaining grandfather status. An estimated 490 insurers providing coverage in the individual market will need to notify an estimated 4.3 million policy holders of their policies' status as a grandfathered health plan.[34]

Because the interim final regulations provide model language for this purpose, the Department estimates that five minute of clerical time (with a labor rate of $26.14/hour) will be required to incorporate the required language into the plan document and ten minutes of a human resource professional's time (with a labor rate of $89.12/hour) will be required to review the modified language.[35] After plans first satisfy the grandfathered health plan disclosure requirement in 2011, any additional burden should be *de minimis* if a plan wants to maintain its grandfather status in future years. The Department also expects the cost of removing the notice from plan documents as plans relinquish their grandfather status to be de minimis and therefore is not estimated. Therefore, the Department estimates that plans and insurers will incur a one-time hour burden of 26,000 hours with an equivalent cost of $1.8

million to meet the disclosure requirement.

The Department assumes that only printing and material costs are associated with the disclosure requirement, because the interim final regulations provide model language that can be incorporated into existing plan documents, such as an SPD. The Department estimates that the notice will require one-half of a page, five cents per page printing and material cost will be incurred, and 38 percent of the notices will be delivered electronically. This results in a cost burden of $318,000 ($0.05 per page*½ pages per notice * 12.7 million notices*0.62).

b. Record-Keeping Requirement

The Department assumes that most of the documents required to be retained to satisfy the Affordable Care Act's recordkeeping requirement already are retained by plans for tax purposes, to satisfy ERISA's record retention and statute of limitations requirements, and for other business reasons. Therefore, the Department estimates that the recordkeeping burden imposed by this ICR will require five minutes of a legal professional's time (with a rate of $119.03/hour) to determine the relevant plan documents that must be retained and ten minutes of clerical staff time (with a labor rate of $26.14/hour) to organize and file the required documents to ensure that they are accessible to participants, beneficiaries, and Federal and State governmental agency officials.

With an estimated 98,000 grandfathered health plans and 7,400 grandfathered individual insurance products[36] in 2011, the Department estimates an hour burden of approximately 26,000 hours with equivalent costs of $1.5 million. The Department's have estimated this as a one-time cost incurred in 2011, because after the first year, the Department assumes any future costs will be *de minimis.*

Overall, for both the grandfathering notice and the recordkeeping requirement, the Department expects there to be a total hour burden of 53,000 hours and a cost burden of $318,000.

The Department notes that persons are not required to respond to, and generally are not subject to any penalty for failing to comply with, an ICR unless

the ICR has a valid OMB control number.

These paperwork burden estimates are summarized as follows:

Type of Review: New collection.

Agency: Department of Health and Human Services.

Title: Disclosure and Recordkeeping Requirements for Grandfathered Health Plans under the Affordable Care Act.

OMB Number: 0938–1093.

Affected Public: Business; State, Local, or Tribal Governments.

Respondents: 105,000.

Responses: 20,508,000.

Frequency of Response: One-time.

Estimated Total Annual Burden Hours: 53,000 hours.

Estimated Total Annual Burden Cost: $318,000.

If you comment on this information collection and recordkeeping requirements, please do either of the following:

1. Submit your comments electronically as specified in the **ADDRESSES** section of this proposed rule; or

2. Submit your comments to the Office of Information and Regulatory Affairs, Office of Management and Budget,

Attention: OCIIO Desk Officer, OCIIO–9991–IFC.

Fax: (202) 395–6974; or

E-mail:
OIRA_submission@omb.eop.gov.

F. Congressional Review Act

These interim final regulations are subject to the Congressional Review Act provisions of the Small Business Regulatory Enforcement Fairness Act of 1996 (5 U.S.C. 801 *et seq.*) and have been transmitted to Congress and the Comptroller General for review.

G. Unfunded Mandates Reform Act

The Unfunded Mandates Reform Act of 1995 (Pub. L. 104–4) requires agencies to prepare several analytic statements before proposing any rules that may result in annual expenditures of $100 million (as adjusted for inflation) by State, local and tribal governments or the private sector. These interim final regulations are not subject to the Unfunded Mandates Reform Act, because they are being issued as an interim final regulation. However, consistent with the policy embodied in the Unfunded Mandates Reform Act, these interim final regulations have been designed to be the least burdensome alternative for State, local and tribal governments, and the private sector, while achieving the objectives of the Affordable Care Act.

---

[34] The Department's estimate of the number of state and local governmental health plans was obtained from the 2007 Census of Governments. The estimate of the number of policy holders in the individual market were obtained from the 2009 Current Population Survey. The methodology used to estimate the percentage of state and local governmental plans and individual market policies that will retain their grandfathered health plan status was discussed above.

[35] EBSA estimates of labor rates include wages, other benefits, and overhead based on the National Occupational Employment Survey (May 2008, Bureau of Labor Statistics) and the Employment Cost Index June 2009, Bureau of Labor Statistics).

[36] The Department is not certain on the number of products offered in the individual market and requests comments. After reviewing the number of products offered by various insurers in the individual market the Department used an estimate of 15 which it believes is a high estimate.

H. Federalism Statement—Department of Labor and Department of Health and Human Services

Executive Order 13132 outlines fundamental principles of federalism, and requires the adherence to specific criteria by Federal agencies in the process of their formulation and implementation of policies that have "substantial direct effects" on the States, the relationship between the national government and States, or on the distribution of power and responsibilities among the various levels of government. Federal agencies promulgating regulations that have these federalism implications must consult with State and local officials, and describe the extent of their consultation and the nature of the concerns of State and local officials in the preamble to the regulation.

In the Departments' view, this regulation has federalism implications, because it has direct effects on the States, the relationship between the national government and States, or on the distribution of power and responsibilities among various levels of government. However, in the Departments' view, the federalism implications of the regulation is substantially mitigated because, with respect to health insurance issuers, the Departments expect that the majority of States will enact laws or take other appropriate action resulting in their meeting or exceeding the Federal standard.

In general, through section 514, ERISA supersedes State laws to the extent that they relate to any covered employee benefit plan, and preserves State laws that regulate insurance, banking, or securities. While ERISA prohibits States from regulating a plan as an insurance or investment company or bank, the preemption provisions of ERISA section 731 and PHS Act section 2724 (implemented in 29 CFR 2590.731(a) and 45 CFR 146.143(a)) apply so that the HIPAA requirements (including those of the Affordable Care Act) are not to be "construed to supersede any provision of State law which establishes, implements, or continues in effect any standard or requirement solely relating to health insurance issuers in connection with group health insurance coverage except to the extent that such standard or requirement prevents the application of a requirement" of a Federal standard. The conference report accompanying HIPAA indicates that this is intended to be the "narrowest" preemption of State laws. (See House Conf. Rep. No. 104–736, at 205, reprinted in 1996 U.S. Code Cong. & Admin. News 2018.) States may continue to apply State law requirements except to the extent that such requirements prevent the application of the Affordable Care Act requirements that are the subject of this rulemaking. State insurance laws that are more stringent than the federal requirements are unlikely to "prevent the application of" the Affordable Care Act, and be preempted. Accordingly, States have significant latitude to impose requirements on health insurance issuers that are more restrictive than the Federal law.

In compliance with the requirement of Executive Order 13132 that agencies examine closely any policies that may have federalism implications or limit the policy making discretion of the States, the Departments have engaged in efforts to consult with and work cooperatively with affected State and local officials, including attending conferences of the National Association of Insurance Commissioners and consulting with State insurance officials on an individual basis. It is expected that the Departments will act in a similar fashion in enforcing the Affordable Care Act requirements. Throughout the process of developing these regulations, to the extent feasible within the specific preemption provisions of HIPAA as it applies to the Affordable Care Act, the Departments have attempted to balance the States' interests in regulating health insurance issuers, and Congress' intent to provide uniform minimum protections to consumers in every State. By doing so, it is the Departments' view that they have complied with the requirements of Executive Order 13132.

Pursuant to the requirements set forth in section 8(a) of Executive Order 13132, and by the signatures affixed to these regulations, the Departments certify that the Employee Benefits Security Administration and the Office of Consumer Information and Insurance Oversight have complied with the requirements of Executive Order 13132 for the attached regulation in a meaningful and timely manner.

V. Statutory Authority

The Department of the Treasury temporary regulations are adopted pursuant to the authority contained in sections 7805 and 9833 of the Code.

The Department of Labor interim final regulations are adopted pursuant to the authority contained in 29 U.S.C. 1027, 1059, 1135, 1161–1168, 1169, 1181–1183, 1181 note, 1185, 1185a, 1185b, 1191, 1191a, 1191b, and 1191c; section 101(g), Public Law 104–191, 110 Stat. 1936; section 401(b), Public Law 105–200, 112 Stat. 645 (42 U.S.C. 651 note); section 512(d), Public Law 110–343, 122 Stat. 3881; section 1001, 1201, and 1562(e), Public Law 111–148, 124 Stat. 119, as amended by Public Law 111–152, 124 Stat. 1029; Secretary of Labor's Order 6–2009, 74 FR 21524 (May 7, 2009).

The Department of Health and Human Services interim final regulations are adopted pursuant to the authority contained in sections 2701 through 2763, 2791, and 2792 of the PHS Act (42 U.S.C. 300gg through 300gg–63, 300gg–91, and 300gg–92), as amended.

List of Subjects

26 CFR Part 54

Excise taxes, Health care, Health insurance, Pensions, Reporting and recordkeeping requirements.

26 CFR Part 602

Reporting and recordkeeping requirements.

29 CFR Part 2590

Continuation coverage, Disclosure, Employee benefit plans, Group health plans, Health care, Health insurance, Medical child support, Reporting and recordkeeping requirements.

45 CFR Part 147

Health care, Health insurance, Reporting and recordkeeping requirements, and State regulation of health insurance.

Steven T. Miller,
Deputy Commissioner for Services and Enforcement, Internal Revenue Service.

Approved: June 10, 2010.

Michael F. Mundaca,
Assistant Secretary of the Treasury (Tax Policy).

Signed this 4th day of June, 2010.

Phyllis C. Borzi,
Assistant Secretary, Employee Benefits Security Administration, Department of Labor.

Approved: June 8, 2010.

Jay Angoff,
Director, Office of Consumer Information and Insurance Oversight.

Approved: June 9, 2010.

Kathleen Sebelius,
Secretary.

DEPARTMENT OF THE TREASURY

Internal Revenue Service

26 CFR Chapter I

■ Accordingly, 26 CFR parts 54 and 602 are amended as follows:

PART 54—PENSION EXCISE TAXES

■ 1. The authority citation for part 54 is amended by adding entries for §§ 54.9815–1251T and 54.9815–2714T in numerical order to read in part as follows:

Authority: 26 U.S.C. 7805. * * *

Section 54.9815–1251T also issued under 26 U.S.C. 9833.

Section 54.9815–2714T also issued under 26 U.S.C. 9833. * * *

■ 2. Section 54.9815–1251T is added to read as follows:

§ 54.9815–1251T Preservation of right to maintain existing coverage (temporary).

(a) *Definition of grandfathered health plan coverage*—(1) *In general*—(i) *Grandfathered health plan coverage* means coverage provided by a group health plan, or a health insurance issuer, in which an individual was enrolled on March 23, 2010 (for as long as it maintains that status under the rules of this section). A group health plan or group health insurance coverage does not cease to be grandfathered health plan coverage merely because one or more (or even all) individuals enrolled on March 23, 2010 cease to be covered, provided that the plan or group health insurance coverage has continuously covered someone since March 23, 2010 (not necessarily the same person, but at all times at least one person). For purposes of this section, a plan or health insurance coverage that provides grandfathered health plan coverage is referred to as a grandfathered health plan. The rules of this section apply separately to each benefit package made available under a group health plan or health insurance coverage.

(ii) Subject to the rules of paragraph (f) of this section for collectively bargained plans, if an employer or employee organization enters into a new policy, certificate, or contract of insurance after March 23, 2010 (because, for example, any previous policy, certificate, or contract of insurance is not being renewed), then that policy, certificate, or contract of insurance is not a grandfathered health plan with respect to the individuals in the group health plan.

(2) *Disclosure of grandfather status*—(i) To maintain status as a grandfathered health plan, a plan or health insurance coverage must include a statement, in any plan materials provided to a participant or beneficiary describing the benefits provided under the plan or health insurance coverage, that the plan or coverage believes it is a grandfathered health plan within the meaning of

section 1251 of the Patient Protection and Affordable Care Act and must provide contact information for questions and complaints.

(ii) The following model language can be used to satisfy this disclosure requirement:

This [group health plan or health insurance issuer] believes this [plan or coverage] is a "grandfathered health plan" under the Patient Protection and Affordable Care Act (the Affordable Care Act). As permitted by the Affordable Care Act, a grandfathered health plan can preserve certain basic health coverage that was already in effect when that law was enacted. Being a grandfathered health plan means that your [plan or policy] may not include certain consumer protections of the Affordable Care Act that apply to other plans, for example, the requirement for the provision of preventive health services without any cost sharing. However, grandfathered health plans must comply with certain other consumer protections in the Affordable Care Act, for example, the elimination of lifetime limits on benefits.

Questions regarding which protections apply and which protections do not apply to a grandfathered health plan and what might cause a plan to change from grandfathered health plan status can be directed to the plan administrator at [insert contact information]. [For ERISA plans, insert: You may also contact the Employee Benefits Security Administration, U.S. Department of Labor at 1–866–444–3272 or *www.dol.gov/ebsa/ healthreform*. This website has a table summarizing which protections do and do not apply to grandfathered health plans.] [For individual market policies and nonfederal governmental plans, insert: You may also contact the U.S. Department of Health and Human Services at *www.healthreform.gov*.]

(3) *Documentation of plan or policy terms on March 23, 2010.* To maintain status as a grandfathered health plan, a group health plan, or group health insurance coverage, must, for as long as the plan or health insurance coverage takes the position that it is a grandfathered health plan—

(i) Maintain records documenting the terms of the plan or health insurance coverage in connection with the coverage in effect on March 23, 2010, and any other documents necessary to verify, explain, or clarify its status as a grandfathered health plan; and

(ii) Make such records available for examination upon request.

(4) *Family members enrolling after March 23, 2010.* With respect to an individual who is enrolled in a group health plan or health insurance coverage on March 23, 2010, grandfathered health plan coverage includes coverage of family members of the individual who enroll after March 23, 2010 in the grandfathered health plan coverage of the individual.

(5) *Examples.* The rules of this paragraph (a) are illustrated by the following examples:

Example 1. (i) *Facts.* A group health plan not maintained pursuant to a collective bargaining agreement provides coverage through a group health insurance policy from Issuer X on March 23, 2010. For the plan year beginning January 1, 2012, the plan enters into a new policy with Issuer Z.

(ii) *Conclusion.* In this *Example 1*, for the plan year beginning January 1, 2012, the group health insurance coverage issued by Z is not a grandfathered health plan under the rules of paragraph (a)(1)(ii) of this section because the policy issued by Z did not provide coverage on March 23, 2010.

Example 2. (i) *Facts.* A group health plan not maintained pursuant to a collective bargaining agreement offers three benefit packages on March 23, 2010. Option F is a self-insured option. Options G and H are insured options. Beginning July 1, 2013, the plan replaces the issuer for Option H with a new issuer.

(ii) *Conclusion.* In this *Example 2*, the coverage under Option H is not grandfathered health plan coverage as of July 1, 2013, consistent with the rule in paragraph (a)(1)(ii) of this section. Whether the coverage under Options F and G is grandfathered health plan coverage is determined under the rules of this section, including paragraph (g) of this section. If the plan enters into a new policy, certificate, or contract of insurance for Option G, Option G's status as a grandfathered health plan would cease under paragraph (a)(1)(ii) of this section.

(b) *Allowance for new employees to join current plan*—(1) *In general.* Subject to paragraph (b)(2) of this section, a group health plan (including health insurance coverage provided in connection with the group health plan) that provided coverage on March 23, 2010 and has retained its status as a grandfathered health plan (consistent with the rules of this section, including paragraph (g) of this section) is grandfathered health plan coverage for new employees (whether newly hired or newly enrolled) and their families enrolling in the plan after March 23, 2010.

(2) *Anti-abuse rules*—(i) *Mergers and acquisitions.* If the principal purpose of a merger, acquisition, or similar business restructuring is to cover new individuals under a grandfathered health plan, the plan ceases to be a grandfathered health plan.

(ii) *Change in plan eligibility.* A group health plan or health insurance coverage (including a benefit package under a group health plan) ceases to be a grandfathered health plan if—

(A) Employees are transferred into the plan or health insurance coverage (the transferee plan) from a plan or health insurance coverage under which the employees were covered on March 23, 2010 (the transferor plan);

(B) Comparing the terms of the transferee plan with those of the transferor plan (as in effect on March 23, 2010) and treating the transferee plan as if it were an amendment of the transferor plan would cause a loss of grandfather status under the provisions of paragraph (g)(1) of this section; and

(C) There was no bona fide employment-based reason to transfer the employees into the transferee plan. For this purpose, changing the terms or cost of coverage is not a bona fide employment-based reason.

(3) *Examples.* The rules of this paragraph (b) are illustrated by the following examples:

Example 1. (i) *Facts.* A group health plan offers two benefit packages on March 23, 2010, Options F and G. During a subsequent open enrollment period, some of the employees enrolled in Option F on March 23, 2010 switch to Option G.

(ii) *Conclusion.* In this *Example 1,* the group health coverage provided under Option G remains a grandfathered health plan under the rules of paragraph (b)(1) of this section because employees previously enrolled in Option F are allowed to enroll in Option G as new employees.

Example 2. (i) *Facts.* Same facts as *Example 1,* except that the plan sponsor eliminates Option F because of its high cost and transfers employees covered under Option F to Option G. If instead of transferring employees from Option F to Option G, Option F was amended to match the terms of Option G, then Option F would cease to be a grandfathered health plan.

(ii) *Conclusion.* In this *Example 2,* the plan did not have a bona fide employment-based reason to transfer employees from Option F to Option G. Therefore, Option G ceases to be a grandfathered health plan with respect to all employees. (However, any other benefit package maintained by the plan sponsor is analyzed separately under the rules of this section.)

Example 3. (i) *Facts.* A group health plan offers two benefit packages on March 23, 2010, Options H and I. On March 23, 2010, Option H provides coverage only for employees in one manufacturing plant. Subsequently, the plant is closed, and some employees in the closed plant are moved to another plant. The employer eliminates Option H and the employees that are moved are transferred to Option I. If instead of transferring employees from Option H to Option I, Option H was amended to match the terms of Option I, then Option H would cease to be a grandfathered health plan.

(ii) *Conclusion.* In this *Example 3,* the plan has a bona fide employment-based reason to transfer employees from Option H to Option I. Therefore, Option I does not cease to be a grandfathered health plan.

(c) *General grandfathering rule*—(1) Except as provided in paragraphs (d) and (e) of this section, subtitles A and C of title I of the Patient Protection and Affordable Care Act (and the amendments made by those subtitles,

and the incorporation of those amendments into section 9815 and ERISA section 715) do not apply to grandfathered health plan coverage. Accordingly, the provisions of PHS Act sections 2701, 2702, 2703, 2705, 2706, 2707, 2709 (relating to coverage for individuals participating in approved clinical trials, as added by section 10103 of the Patient Protection and Affordable Care Act), 2713, 2715A, 2716, 2717, 2719, and 2719A, as added or amended by the Patient Protection and Affordable Care Act, do not apply to grandfathered health plans. (In addition, *see* 45 CFR 147.140(c), which provides that the provisions of PHS Act section 2704, and PHS Act section 2711 insofar as it relates to annual limits, do not apply to grandfathered health plans that are individual health insurance coverage.)

(2) To the extent not inconsistent with the rules applicable to a grandfathered health plan, a grandfathered health plan must comply with the requirements of the Code, the PHS Act, and ERISA applicable prior to the changes enacted by the Patient Protection and Affordable Care Act.

(d) *Provisions applicable to all grandfathered health plans.* The provisions of PHS Act section 2711 insofar as it relates to lifetime limits, and the provisions of PHS Act sections 2712, 2714, 2715, and 2718, apply to grandfathered health plans for plan years beginning on or after September 23, 2010. The provisions of PHS Act section 2708 apply to grandfathered health plans for plan years beginning on or after January 1, 2014.

(e) *Applicability of PHS Act sections 2704, 2711, and 2714 to grandfathered group health plans and group health insurance coverage*—(1) The provisions of PHS Act section 2704 as it applies with respect to enrollees who are under 19 years of age, and the provisions of PHS Act section 2711 insofar as it relates to annual limits, apply to grandfathered health plans that are group health plans (including group health insurance coverage) for plan years beginning on or after September 23, 2010. The provisions of PHS Act section 2704 apply generally to grandfathered health plans that are group health plans (including group health insurance coverage) for plan years beginning on or after January 1, 2014.

(2) For plan years beginning before January 1, 2014, the provisions of PHS Act section 2714 apply in the case of an adult child with respect to a grandfathered health plan that is a group health plan only if the adult child is not eligible to enroll in an eligible employer-sponsored health plan (as

defined in section 5000A(f)(2)) other than a grandfathered health plan of a parent. For plan years beginning on or after January 1, 2014, the provisions of PHS Act section 2714 apply with respect to a grandfathered health plan that is a group health plan without regard to whether an adult child is eligible to enroll in any other coverage.

(f) *Effect on collectively bargained plans*—(1) *In general.* In the case of health insurance coverage maintained pursuant to one or more collective bargaining agreements between employee representatives and one or more employers that was ratified before March 23, 2010, the coverage is grandfathered health plan coverage at least until the date on which the last of the collective bargaining agreements relating to the coverage that was in effect on March 23, 2010 terminates. Any coverage amendment made pursuant to a collective bargaining agreement relating to the coverage that amends the coverage solely to conform to any requirement added by subtitles A and C of title I of the Patient Protection and Affordable Care Act (and the amendments made by those subtitles, and the incorporation of those amendments into section 9815 and ERISA section 715) is not treated as a termination of the collective bargaining agreement. After the date on which the last of the collective bargaining agreements relating to the coverage that was in effect on March 23, 2010 terminates, the determination of whether health insurance coverage maintained pursuant to a collective bargaining agreement is grandfathered health plan coverage is made under the rules of this section other than this paragraph (f) (comparing the terms of the health insurance coverage after the date the last collective bargaining agreement terminates with the terms of the health insurance coverage that were in effect on March 23, 2010) and, for any changes in insurance coverage after the termination of the collective bargaining agreement, under the rules of paragraph (a)(1)(ii) of this section.

(2) *Examples.* The rules of this paragraph (f) are illustrated by the following examples:

Example 1. (i) *Facts.* A group health plan maintained pursuant to a collective bargaining agreement provides coverage through a group health insurance policy from Issuer W on March 23, 2010. The collective bargaining agreement has not been amended and will not expire before December 31, 2011. The group health plan enters into a new group health insurance policy with Issuer Y for the plan year starting on January 1, 2011.

(ii) *Conclusion.* In this *Example 1,* the group health plan, and the group health insurance policy provided by Y, remains a grandfathered health plan with respect to existing employees and new employees and their families because the coverage is maintained pursuant to a collective bargaining agreement ratified prior to March 23, 2010 that has not terminated.

Example 2. (i) *Facts.* Same facts as *Example 1,* except the coverage with Y is renewed under a new collective bargaining agreement effective January 1, 2012, with the only changes since March 23, 2010 being changes that do not cause the plan to cease to be a grandfathered health plan under the rules of this section, including paragraph (g) of this section.

(ii) *Conclusion.* In this *Example 2,* the group health plan remains a grandfathered health plan pursuant to the rules of this section. Moreover, the group health insurance policy provided by Y remains a grandfathered health plan under the rules of this section, including paragraph (g) of this section.

(g) *Maintenance of grandfather status*—(1) *Changes causing cessation of grandfather status.* Subject to paragraph (g)(2) of this section, the rules of this paragraph (g)(1) describe situations in which a group health plan or health insurance coverage ceases to be a grandfathered health plan.

(i) *Elimination of benefits.* The elimination of all or substantially all benefits to diagnose or treat a particular condition causes a group health plan or health insurance coverage to cease to be a grandfathered health plan. For this purpose, the elimination of benefits for any necessary element to diagnose or treat a condition is considered the elimination of all or substantially all benefits to diagnose or treat a particular condition.

(ii) *Increase in percentage cost-sharing requirement.* Any increase, measured from March 23, 2010, in a percentage cost-sharing requirement (such as an individual's coinsurance requirement) causes a group health plan or health insurance coverage to cease to be a grandfathered health plan.

(iii) *Increase in a fixed-amount cost-sharing requirement other than a copayment.* Any increase in a fixed-amount cost-sharing requirement other than a copayment (for example, deductible or out-of-pocket limit), determined as of the effective date of the increase, causes a group health plan or health insurance coverage to cease to be a grandfathered health plan, if the total percentage increase in the cost-sharing requirement measured from March 23, 2010 exceeds the maximum percentage increase (as defined in paragraph (g)(3)(ii) of this section).

(iv) *Increase in a fixed-amount copayment.* Any increase in a fixed-amount copayment, determined as of the effective date of the increase, causes

a group health plan or health insurance coverage to cease to be a grandfathered health plan, if the total increase in the copayment measured from March 23, 2010 exceeds the greater of:

(A) An amount equal to $5 increased by medical inflation, as defined in paragraph (g)(3)(i) of this section (that is, $5 times medical inflation, plus $5), or

(B) The maximum percentage increase (as defined in paragraph (g)(3)(ii) of this section), determined by expressing the total increase in the copayment as a percentage.

(v) *Decrease in contribution rate by employers and employee organizations*—(A) *Contribution rate based on cost of coverage.* A group health plan or group health insurance coverage ceases to be a grandfathered health plan if the employer or employee organization decreases its contribution rate based on cost of coverage (as defined in paragraph (g)(3)(iii)(A) of this section) towards the cost of any tier of coverage for any class of similarly situated individuals (as described in § 54.9802–1(d)) by more than 5 percentage points below the contribution rate for the coverage period that includes March 23, 2010.

(B) *Contribution rate based on a formula.* A group health plan or group health insurance coverage ceases to be a grandfathered health plan if the employer or employee organization decreases its contribution rate based on a formula (as defined in paragraph (g)(3)(iii)(B) of this section) towards the cost of any tier of coverage for any class of similarly situated individuals (as described in § 54.9802–1(d)) by more than 5 percent below the contribution rate for the coverage period that includes March 23, 2010.

(vi) *Changes in annual limits*—(A) *Addition of an annual limit.* A group health plan, or group health insurance coverage, that, on March 23, 2010, did not impose an overall annual or lifetime limit on the dollar value of all benefits ceases to be a grandfathered health plan if the plan or health insurance coverage imposes an overall annual limit on the dollar value of benefits.

(B) *Decrease in limit for a plan or coverage with only a lifetime limit.* A group health plan, or group health insurance coverage, that, on March 23, 2010, imposed an overall lifetime limit on the dollar value of all benefits but no overall annual limit on the dollar value of all benefits ceases to be a grandfathered health plan if the plan or health insurance coverage adopts an overall annual limit at a dollar value that is lower than the dollar value of the lifetime limit on March 23, 2010.

(C) *Decrease in limit for a plan or coverage with an annual limit.* A group health plan, or group health insurance coverage, that, on March 23, 2010, imposed an overall annual limit on the dollar value of all benefits ceases to be a grandfathered health plan if the plan or health insurance coverage decreases the dollar value of the annual limit (regardless of whether the plan or health insurance coverage also imposed an overall lifetime limit on March 23, 2010 on the dollar value of all benefits).

(2) *Transitional rules*—(i) *Changes made prior to March 23, 2010.* If a group health plan or health insurance issuer makes the following changes to the terms of the plan or health insurance coverage, the changes are considered part of the terms of the plan or health insurance coverage on March 23, 2010 even though they were not effective at that time and such changes do not cause a plan or health insurance coverage to cease to be a grandfathered health plan:

(A) Changes effective after March 23, 2010 pursuant to a legally binding contract entered into on or before March 23, 2010;

(B) Changes effective after March 23, 2010 pursuant to a filing on or before March 23, 2010 with a State insurance department; or

(C) Changes effective after March 23, 2010 pursuant to written amendments to a plan that were adopted on or before March 23, 2010.

(ii) *Changes made after March 23, 2010 and adopted prior to issuance of regulations.* If, after March 23, 2010, a group health plan or health insurance issuer makes changes to the terms of the plan or health insurance coverage and the changes are adopted prior to June 14, 2010, the changes will not cause the plan or health insurance coverage to cease to be a grandfathered health plan if the changes are revoked or modified effective as of the first day of the first plan year (in the individual market, policy year) beginning on or after September 23, 2010, and the terms of the plan or health insurance coverage on that date, as modified, would not cause the plan or coverage to cease to be a grandfathered health plan under the rules of this section, including paragraph (g)(1) of this section. For this purpose, changes will be considered to have been adopted prior to June 14, 2010 if:

(A) The changes are effective before that date;

(B) The changes are effective on or after that date pursuant to a legally binding contract entered into before that date;

(C) The changes are effective on or after that date pursuant to a filing before that date with a State insurance department; or

(D) The changes are effective on or after that date pursuant to written amendments to a plan that were adopted before that date.

(3) *Definitions*—(i) *Medical inflation defined.* For purposes of this paragraph (g), the term *medical inflation* means the increase since March 2010 in the overall medical care component of the Consumer Price Index for All Urban Consumers (CPI–U) (unadjusted) published by the Department of Labor using the 1982–1984 base of 100. For this purpose, the increase in the overall medical care component is computed by subtracting 387.142 (the overall medical care component of the CPI–U (unadjusted) published by the Department of Labor for March 2010, using the 1982–1984 base of 100) from the index amount for any month in the 12 months before the new change is to take effect and then dividing that amount by 387.142.

(ii) *Maximum percentage increase defined.* For purposes of this paragraph (g), the term *maximum percentage increase* means medical inflation (as defined in paragraph (g)(3)(i) of this section), expressed as a percentage, plus 15 percentage points.

(iii) *Contribution rate defined.* For purposes of paragraph (g)(1)(v) of this section:

(A) *Contribution rate based on cost of coverage.* The term *contribution rate based on cost of coverage* means the amount of contributions made by an employer or employee organization compared to the total cost of coverage, expressed as a percentage. The total cost of coverage is determined in the same manner as the applicable premium is calculated under the COBRA continuation provisions of section 4980B(f)(4), section 604 of ERISA, and section 2204 of the PHS Act. In the case of a self-insured plan, contributions by an employer or employee organization are equal to the total cost of coverage minus the employee contributions towards the total cost of coverage.

(B) *Contribution rate based on a formula.* The term *contribution rate based on a formula* means, for plans that, on March 23, 2010, made contributions based on a formula (such as hours worked or tons of coal mined), the formula.

(4) *Examples.* The rules of this paragraph (g) are illustrated by the following examples:

Example 1. (i) *Facts.* On March 23, 2010, a grandfathered health plan has a coinsurance requirement of 20% for inpatient surgery. The plan is subsequently amended to increase the coinsurance requirement to 25%.

(ii) *Conclusion.* In this *Example 1*, the increase in the coinsurance requirement from 20% to 25% causes the plan to cease to be a grandfathered health plan.

Example 2. (i) *Facts.* Before March 23, 2010, the terms of a group health plan provide benefits for a particular mental health condition, the treatment for which is a combination of counseling and prescription drugs. Subsequently, the plan eliminates benefits for counseling.

(ii) *Conclusion.* In this *Example 2*, the plan ceases to be a grandfathered health plan because counseling is an element that is necessary to treat the condition. Thus the plan is considered to have eliminated substantially all benefits for the treatment of the condition.

Example 3. (i) *Facts.* On March 23, 2010, a grandfathered health plan has a copayment requirement of $30 per office visit for specialists. The plan is subsequently amended to increase the copayment requirement to $40. Within the 12-month period before the $40 copayment takes effect, the greatest value of the overall medical care component of the CPI–U (unadjusted) is 475.

(ii) *Conclusion.* In this *Example 3*, the increase in the copayment from $30 to $40, expressed as a percentage, is 33.33% (40 − 30 = 10; 10 ÷ 30 = 0.3333; 0.3333 = 33.33%). Medical inflation (as defined in paragraph (g)(3)(i) of this section) from March 2010 is 0.2269 (475 − 387.142 = 87.858; 87.858 ÷ 387.142 = 0.2269). The maximum percentage increase permitted is 37.69% (0.2269 = 22.69%; 22.69% + 15% = 37.69%). Because 33.33% does not exceed 37.69%, the change in the copayment requirement at that time does not cause the plan to cease to be a grandfathered health plan.

Example 4. (i) *Facts.* Same facts as *Example 3*, except the grandfathered health plan subsequently increases the $40 copayment requirement to $45 for a later plan year. Within the 12-month period before the $45 copayment takes effect, the greatest value of the overall medical care component of the CPI–U (unadjusted) is 485.

(ii) *Conclusion.* In this *Example 4*, the increase in the copayment from $30 (the copayment that was in effect on March 23, 2010) to $45, expressed as a percentage, is 50% (45 − 30 = 15; 15 ÷ 30 = 0.5; 0.5 = 50%). Medical inflation (as defined in paragraph (g)(3)(i) of this section) from March 2010 is 0.2527 (485 − 387.142 = 97.858; 97.858 ÷ 387.142 = 0.2527). The increase that would cause a plan to cease to be a grandfathered health plan under paragraph (g)(1)(iv) of this section is the greater of the maximum percentage increase of 40.27% (0.2527 = 25.27%; 25.27% + 15% = 40.27%), or $6.26 ($5 × 0.2527 = $1.26; $1.26 + $5 = $6.26). Because 50% exceeds 40.27% and $15 exceeds $6.26, the change in the copayment requirement at that time causes the plan to cease to be a grandfathered health plan.

Example 5. (i) *Facts.* On March 23, 2010, a grandfathered health plan has a copayment of $10 per office visit for primary care providers. The plan is subsequently amended to increase the copayment requirement to $15. Within the 12-month period before the $15 copayment takes effect, the greatest value of the overall medical care component of the CPI–U (unadjusted) is 415.

(ii) *Conclusion.* In this *Example 5*, the increase in the copayment, expressed as a percentage, is 50% (15 − 10 = 5; 5 ÷ 10 = 0.5; 0.5 = 50%). Medical inflation (as defined in paragraph (g)(3) of this section) from March 2010 is 0.0720 (415.0 − 387.142 = 27.858; 27.858 ÷ 387.142 = 0.0720). The increase that would cause a plan to cease to be a grandfathered health plan under paragraph (g)(1)(iv) of this section is the greater of the maximum percentage increase of 22.20% (0.0720 = 7.20%; 7.20% + 15% = 22.20), or $5.36 ($5 × 0.0720 = $0.36; $0.36 + $5 = $5.36). The $5 increase in copayment in this *Example 5* would not cause the plan to cease to be a grandfathered health plan pursuant to paragraph (g)(1)(iv) of this section, which would permit an increase in the copayment of up to $5.36.

Example 6. (i) *Facts.* The same facts as *Example 5*, except on March 23, 2010, the grandfathered health plan has no copayment ($0) for office visits for primary care providers. The plan is subsequently amended to increase the copayment requirement to $5.

(ii) *Conclusion.* In this *Example 6*, medical inflation (as defined in paragraph (g)(3)(i) of this section) from March 2010 is 0.0720 (415.0 − 387.142 = 27.858; 27.858 + 387.142 = 0.0720). The increase that would cause a plan to cease to be a grandfathered health plan under paragraph (g)(1)(iv)(A) of this section is $5.36 ($5 × 0.0720 = $0.36; $0.36 + $5 = $5.36). The $5 increase in copayment in this *Example 6* is less than the amount calculated pursuant to paragraph (g)(1)(iv)(A) of this section of $5.36. Thus, the $5 increase in copayment does not cause the plan to cease to be a grandfathered health plan.

Example 7. (i) *Facts.* On March 23, 2010, a self-insured group health plan provides two tiers of coverage—self-only and family. The employer contributes 80% of the total cost of coverage for self-only and 60% of the total cost of coverage for family. Subsequently, the employer reduces the contribution to 50% for family coverage, but keeps the same contribution rate for self-only coverage.

(ii) *Conclusion.* In this *Example 7*, the decrease of 10 percentage points for family coverage in the contribution rate based on cost of coverage causes the plan to cease to be a grandfathered health plan. The fact that the contribution rate for self-only coverage remains the same does not change the result.

Example 8. (i) *Facts.* On March 23, 2010, a self-insured grandfathered health plan has a COBRA premium for the 2010 plan year of $5000 for self-only coverage and $12,000 for family coverage. The required employee contribution for the coverage is $1000 for self-only coverage and $4000 for family coverage. Thus, the contribution rate based on cost of coverage for 2010 is 80% ((5000 − 1000)/5000) for self-only coverage and 67% ((12,000 − 4000)/12,000) for family coverage. For a subsequent plan year, the COBRA premium is $6000 for self-only coverage and $15,000 for family coverage. The employee contributions for that plan year are $1200 for self-only coverage and $5000 for family coverage. Thus, the contribution rate based on cost of coverage is

80% ((6000 − 1200)/6000) for self-only coverage and 67% ((15,000 − 5000)/15,000) for family coverage.

(ii) *Conclusion.* In this *Example 8*, because there is no change in the contribution rate based on cost of coverage, the plan retains its status as a grandfathered health plan. The result would be the same if all or part of the employee contribution was made pre-tax through a cafeteria plan under section 125 of the Internal Revenue Code.

Example 9. (i) *Facts.* Before March 23, 2010, Employer W and Individual B enter into a legally binding employment contract that promises B lifetime health coverage upon termination. Prior to termination, B is covered by W's self-insured grandfathered group health plan. B is terminated after March 23, 2010 and W purchases a new health insurance policy providing coverage to B, consistent with the terms of the employment contract.

(ii) *Conclusion.* In this *Example 9*, because no individual is enrolled in the health insurance policy on March 23, 2010, it is not a grandfathered health plan.

(h) *Expiration date.* This section expires on or before June 14, 2013.

■ 3. Section 54.9815–2714T is amended by revising paragraphs (h) and (i) to read as follows:

*   *   *   *   *

(h) *Applicability date.* The provisions of this section apply for plan years beginning on or after September 23, 2010. *See* § 54.9815–1251T for determining the application of this section to grandfathered health plans.

(i) *Expiration date.* This section expires on or before May 10, 2013.

PART 602—OMB CONTROL NUMBERS UNDER THE PAPERWORK REDUCTION ACT

■ 4. The authority citation for part 602 continues to read in part as follows:

Authority: 26 U.S.C. 7805. * * *

■ 5. Section 602.101(b) is amended by adding the following entry in numerical order to the table to read as follows:

§ 602.101   OMB Control numbers.

(b) * * *

CFR part or section where identified and described	Current OMB control No.
* * * * *	
54.9815–1251T	1545–2178
* * * * *	

DEPARTMENT OF LABOR

Employee Benefits Security Administration

29 CFR Chapter XXV

■ 29 CFR part 2590 is amended as follows:

PART 2590—RULES AND REGULATIONS FOR GROUP HEALTH PLANS

■ 1. The authority citation for part 2590 continues to read as follows:

Authority: 29 U.S.C. 1027, 1059, 1135, 1161–1168, 1169, 1181–1183, 1181 note, 1185, 1185a, 1185b, 1191, 1191a, 1191b, and 1191c; sec. 101(g), Pub. L. 104–191, 110 Stat. 1936; sec. 401(b), Pub. L. 105–200, 112 Stat. 645 (42 U.S.C. 651 note); sec. 512(d), Pub. L. 110–343, 122 Stat. 3881; sec. 1001, 1201, and 1562(e), Pub. L. 111–148, 124 Stat. 119, as amended by Pub. L. 111–152, 124 Stat. 1029; Secretary of Labor's Order 6–2009, 74 FR 21524 (May 7, 2009).

■ 2. Section 2590.715–1251 is added to subpart C to read as follows:

§ 2590.715–1251   Preservation of right to maintain existing coverage.

(a) *Definition of grandfathered health plan coverage*—(1) *In general*—(i) *Grandfathered health plan coverage* means coverage provided by a group health plan, or a health insurance issuer, in which an individual was enrolled on March 23, 2010 (for as long as it maintains that status under the rules of this section). A group health plan or group health insurance coverage does not cease to be grandfathered health plan coverage merely because one or more (or even all) individuals enrolled on March 23, 2010 cease to be covered, provided that the plan or group health insurance coverage has continuously covered someone since March 23, 2010 (not necessarily the same person, but at all times at least one person). For purposes of this section, a plan or health insurance coverage that provides grandfathered health plan coverage is referred to as a grandfathered health plan. The rules of this section apply separately to each benefit package made available under a group health plan or health insurance coverage.

(ii) Subject to the rules of paragraph (f) of this section for collectively bargained plans, if an employer or employee organization enters into a new policy, certificate, or contract of insurance after March 23, 2010 (because, for example, any previous policy, certificate, or contract of insurance is not being renewed), then that policy, certificate, or contract of insurance is not a grandfathered health plan with respect to the individuals in the group health plan.

(2) *Disclosure of grandfather status*— (i) To maintain status as a grandfathered health plan, a plan or health insurance coverage must include a statement, in any plan materials provided to a participant or beneficiary describing the benefits provided under the plan or health insurance coverage, that the plan or coverage believes it is a grandfathered health plan within the meaning of section 1251 of the Patient Protection and Affordable Care Act and must provide contact information for questions and complaints.

(ii) The following model language can be used to satisfy this disclosure requirement:

This [group health plan or health insurance issuer] believes this [plan or coverage] is a "grandfathered health plan" under the Patient Protection and Affordable Care Act (the Affordable Care Act). As permitted by the Affordable Care Act, a grandfathered health plan can preserve certain basic health coverage that was already in effect when that law was enacted. Being a grandfathered health plan means that your [plan or policy] may not include certain consumer protections of the Affordable Care Act that apply to other plans, for example, the requirement for the provision of preventive health services without any cost sharing. However, grandfathered health plans must comply with certain other consumer protections in the Affordable Care Act, for example, the elimination of lifetime limits on benefits.

Questions regarding which protections apply and which protections do not apply to a grandfathered health plan and what might cause a plan to change from grandfathered health plan status can be directed to the plan administrator at [insert contact information]. [For ERISA plans, insert: You may also contact the Employee Benefits Security Administration, U.S. Department of Labor at 1–866–444–3272 or *www.dol.gov/ebsa/ healthreform*. This Web site has a table summarizing which protections do and do not apply to grandfathered health plans.] [For individual market policies and nonfederal governmental plans, insert: You may also contact the U.S. Department of Health and Human Services at *www.healthreform.gov*.]

(3) *Documentation of plan or policy terms on March 23, 2010.* To maintain status as a grandfathered health plan, a group health plan, or group health insurance coverage, must, for as long as the plan or health insurance coverage takes the position that it is a grandfathered health plan—

(i) Maintain records documenting the terms of the plan or health insurance coverage in connection with the coverage in effect on March 23, 2010, and any other documents necessary to verify, explain, or clarify its status as a grandfathered health plan; and

(ii) Make such records available for examination upon request.

(4) *Family members enrolling after March 23, 2010.* With respect to an individual who is enrolled in a group health plan or health insurance coverage on March 23, 2010, grandfathered health plan coverage includes coverage of family members of the individual who

enroll after March 23, 2010 in the grandfathered health plan coverage of the individual.

(5) *Examples.* The rules of this paragraph (a) are illustrated by the following examples:

Example 1. (i) *Facts.* A group health plan not maintained pursuant to a collective bargaining agreement provides coverage through a group health insurance policy from Issuer *X* on March 23, 2010. For the plan year beginning January 1, 2012, the plan enters into a new policy with Issuer *Z*.

(ii) *Conclusion.* In this *Example 1,* for the plan year beginning January 1, 2012, the group health insurance coverage issued by *Z* is not a grandfathered health plan under the rules of paragraph (a)(1)(ii) of this section because the policy issued by *Z* did not provide coverage on March 23, 2010.

Example 2. (i) *Facts.* A group health plan not maintained pursuant to a collective bargaining agreement offers three benefit packages on March 23, 2010. Option *F* is a self-insured option. Options *G* and *H* are insured options. Beginning July 1, 2013, the plan replaces the issuer for Option *H* with a new issuer.

(ii) *Conclusion.* In this *Example 2,* the coverage under Option *H* is not grandfathered health plan coverage as of July 1, 2013, consistent with the rule in paragraph (a)(1)(ii) of this section. Whether the coverage under Options *F* and *G* is grandfathered health plan coverage is determined under the rules of this section, including paragraph (g) of this section. If the plan enters into a new policy, certificate, or contract of insurance for Option *G*, Option *G*'s status as a grandfathered health plan would cease under paragraph (a)(1)(ii) of this section.

(b) *Allowance for new employees to join current plan*—(1) *In general.* Subject to paragraph (b)(2) of this section, a group health plan (including health insurance coverage provided in connection with the group health plan) that provided coverage on March 23, 2010 and has retained its status as a grandfathered health plan (consistent with the rules of this section, including paragraph (g) of this section) is grandfathered health plan coverage for new employees (whether newly hired or newly enrolled) and their families enrolling in the plan after March 23, 2010.

(2) *Anti-abuse rules*—(i) *Mergers and acquisitions.* If the principal purpose of a merger, acquisition, or similar business restructuring is to cover new individuals under a grandfathered health plan, the plan ceases to be a grandfathered health plan.

(ii) *Change in plan eligibility.* A group health plan or health insurance coverage (including a benefit package under a group health plan) ceases to be a grandfathered health plan if—

(A) Employees are transferred into the plan or health insurance coverage (the

transferee plan) from a plan or health insurance coverage under which the employees were covered on March 23, 2010 (the transferor plan);

(B) Comparing the terms of the transferee plan with those of the transferor plan (as in effect on March 23, 2010) and treating the transferee plan as if it were an amendment of the transferor plan would cause a loss of grandfather status under the provisions of paragraph (g)(1) of this section; and

(C) There was no bona fide employment-based reason to transfer the employees into the transferee plan. For this purpose, changing the terms or cost of coverage is not a bona fide employment-based reason.

(3) *Examples.* The rules of this paragraph (b) are illustrated by the following examples:

Example 1. (i) *Facts.* A group health plan offers two benefit packages on March 23, 2010, Options *F* and *G*. During a subsequent open enrollment period, some of the employees enrolled in Option *F* on March 23, 2010 switch to Option *G*.

(ii) *Conclusion.* In this *Example 1,* the group health coverage provided under Option *G* remains a grandfathered health plan under the rules of paragraph (b)(1) of this section because employees previously enrolled in Option *F* are allowed to enroll in Option *G* as new employees.

Example 2. (i) *Facts.* Same facts as *Example 1,* except that the plan sponsor eliminates Option *F* because of its high cost and transfers employees covered under Option *F* to Option *G*. If instead of transferring employees from Option *F* to Option *G,* Option *F* was amended to match the terms of Option *G,* then Option *F* would cease to be a grandfathered health plan.

(ii) *Conclusion.* In this *Example 2,* the plan did not have a bona fide employment-based reason to transfer employees from Option *F* to Option *G.* Therefore, Option *G* ceases to be a grandfathered health plan with respect to all employees. (However, any other benefit package maintained by the plan sponsor is analyzed separately under the rules of this section.)

Example 3. (i) *Facts.* A group health plan offers two benefit packages on March 23, 2010, Options *H* and *I.* On March 23, 2010, Option *H* provides coverage only for employees in one manufacturing plant. Subsequently, the plant is closed, and some employees in the closed plant are moved to another plant. The employer eliminates Option *H* and the employees that are moved are transferred to Option *I.* If instead of transferring employees from Option *H* to Option *I,* Option *H* was amended to match the terms of Option *I,* then Option *H* would cease to be a grandfathered health plan.

(ii) *Conclusion.* In this *Example 3,* the plan has a bona fide employment-based reason to transfer employees from Option *H* to Option *I.* Therefore, Option *I* does not cease to be a grandfathered health plan.

(c) *General grandfathering rule*—(1) Except as provided in paragraphs (d)

and (e) of this section, subtitles A and C of title I of the Patient Protection and Affordable Care Act (and the amendments made by those subtitles, and the incorporation of those amendments into ERISA section 715 and Internal Revenue Code section 9815) do not apply to grandfathered health plan coverage. Accordingly, the provisions of PHS Act sections 2701, 2702, 2703, 2705, 2706, 2707, 2709 (relating to coverage for individuals participating in approved clinical trials, as added by section 10103 of the Patient Protection and Affordable Care Act), 2713, 2715A, 2716, 2717, 2719, and 2719A, as added or amended by the Patient Protection and Affordable Care Act, do not apply to grandfathered health plans. (In addition, *see* 45 CFR 147.140(c), which provides that the provisions of PHS Act section 2704, and PHS Act section 2711 insofar as it relates to annual limits, do not apply to grandfathered health plans that are individual health insurance coverage.)

(2) To the extent not inconsistent with the rules applicable to a grandfathered health plan, a grandfathered health plan must comply with the requirements of the PHS Act, ERISA, and the Internal Revenue Code applicable prior to the changes enacted by the Patient Protection and Affordable Care Act.

(d) *Provisions applicable to all grandfathered health plans.* The provisions of PHS Act section 2711 insofar as it relates to lifetime limits, and the provisions of PHS Act sections 2712, 2714, 2715, and 2718, apply to grandfathered health plans for plan years beginning on or after September 23, 2010. The provisions of PHS Act section 2708 apply to grandfathered health plans for plan years beginning on or after January 1, 2014.

(e) *Applicability of PHS Act sections 2704, 2711, and 2714 to grandfathered group health plans and group health insurance coverage*—(1) The provisions of PHS Act section 2704 as it applies with respect to enrollees who are under 19 years of age, and the provisions of PHS Act section 2711 insofar as it relates to annual limits, apply to grandfathered health plans that are group health plans (including group health insurance coverage) for plan years beginning on or after September 23, 2010. The provisions of PHS Act section 2704 apply generally to grandfathered health plans that are group health plans (including group health insurance coverage) for plan years beginning on or after January 1, 2014.

(2) For plan years beginning before January 1, 2014, the provisions of PHS Act section 2714 apply in the case of an

34564 **Federal Register**/Vol. 75, No. 116/Thursday, June 17, 2010/Rules and Regulations

adult child with respect to a grandfathered health plan that is a group health plan only if the adult child is not eligible to enroll in an eligible employer-sponsored health plan (as defined in section 5000A(f)(2) of the Internal Revenue Code) other than a grandfathered health plan of a parent. For plan years beginning on or after January 1, 2014, the provisions of PHS Act section 2714 apply with respect to a grandfathered health plan that is a group health plan without regard to whether an adult child is eligible to enroll in any other coverage.

(f) *Effect on collectively bargained plans*—(1) *In general.* In the case of health insurance coverage maintained pursuant to one or more collective bargaining agreements between employee representatives and one or more employers that was ratified before March 23, 2010, the coverage is grandfathered health plan coverage at least until the date on which the last of the collective bargaining agreements relating to the coverage that was in effect on March 23, 2010 terminates. Any coverage amendment made pursuant to a collective bargaining agreement relating to the coverage that amends the coverage solely to conform to any requirement added by subtitles A and C of title I of the Patient Protection and Affordable Care Act (and the amendments made by those subtitles, and the incorporation of those amendments into ERISA section 715 and Internal Revenue Code section 9815) is not treated as a termination of the collective bargaining agreement. After the date on which the last of the collective bargaining agreements relating to the coverage that was in effect on March 23, 2010 terminates, the determination of whether health insurance coverage maintained pursuant to a collective bargaining agreement is grandfathered health plan coverage is made under the rules of this section other than this paragraph (f) (comparing the terms of the health insurance coverage after the date the last collective bargaining agreement terminates with the terms of the health insurance coverage that were in effect on March 23, 2010) and, for any changes in insurance coverage after the termination of the collective bargaining agreement, under the rules of paragraph (a)(1)(ii) of this section.

(2) *Examples.* The rules of this paragraph (f) are illustrated by the following examples:

Example 1. (i) *Facts.* A group health plan maintained pursuant to a collective bargaining agreement provides coverage through a group health insurance policy from Issuer *W* on March 23, 2010. The collective bargaining agreement has not been amended and will not expire before December 31, 2011. The group health plan enters into a new group health insurance policy with Issuer *Y* for the plan year starting on January 1, 2011.

(ii) *Conclusion.* In this *Example 1,* the group health plan, and the group health insurance policy provided by *Y,* remains a grandfathered health plan with respect to existing employees and new employees and their families because the coverage is maintained pursuant to a collective bargaining agreement ratified prior to March 23, 2010 that has not terminated.

Example 2. (i) *Facts.* Same facts as *Example 1,* except the coverage with *Y* is renewed under a new collective bargaining agreement effective January 1, 2012, with the only changes since March 23, 2010 being changes that do not cause the plan to cease to be a grandfathered health plan under the rules of this section, including paragraph (g) of this section.

(ii) *Conclusion.* In this *Example 2,* the group health plan remains a grandfathered health plan pursuant to the rules of this section. Moreover, the group health insurance policy provided by *Y* remains a grandfathered health plan under the rules of this section, including paragraph (g) of this section.

(g) *Maintenance of grandfather status*—(1) *Changes causing cessation of grandfather status.* Subject to paragraph (g)(2) of this section, the rules of this paragraph (g)(1) describe situations in which a group health plan or health insurance coverage ceases to be a grandfathered health plan.

(i) *Elimination of benefits.* The elimination of all or substantially all benefits to diagnose or treat a particular condition causes a group health plan or health insurance coverage to cease to be a grandfathered health plan. For this purpose, the elimination of benefits for any necessary element to diagnose or treat a condition is considered the elimination of all or substantially all benefits to diagnose or treat a particular condition.

(ii) *Increase in percentage cost-sharing requirement.* Any increase, measured from March 23, 2010, in a percentage cost-sharing requirement (such as an individual's coinsurance requirement) causes a group health plan or health insurance coverage to cease to be a grandfathered health plan.

(iii) *Increase in a fixed-amount cost-sharing requirement other than a copayment.* Any increase in a fixed-amount cost-sharing requirement other than a copayment (for example, deductible or out-of-pocket limit), determined as of the effective date of the increase, causes a group health plan or health insurance coverage to cease to be a grandfathered health plan, if the total percentage increase in the cost-sharing requirement measured from March 23, 2010 exceeds the maximum percentage increase (as defined in paragraph (g)(3)(ii) of this section).

(iv) *Increase in a fixed-amount copayment.* Any increase in a fixed-amount copayment, determined as of the effective date of the increase, causes a group health plan or health insurance coverage to cease to be a grandfathered health plan, if the total increase in the copayment measured from March 23, 2010 exceeds the greater of:

(A) An amount equal to $5 increased by medical inflation, as defined in paragraph (g)(3)(i) of this section (that is, $5 times medical inflation, plus $5), or

(B) The maximum percentage increase (as defined in paragraph (g)(3)(ii) of this section), determined by expressing the total increase in the copayment as a percentage.

(v) *Decrease in contribution rate by employers and employee organizations*—(A) *Contribution rate based on cost of coverage.* A group health plan or group health insurance coverage ceases to be a grandfathered health plan if the employer or employee organization decreases its contribution rate based on cost of coverage (as defined in paragraph (g)(3)(iii)(A) of this section) towards the cost of any tier of coverage for any class of similarly situated individuals (as described in § 2590.702(d) of this part) by more than 5 percentage points below the contribution rate for the coverage period that includes March 23, 2010.

(B) *Contribution rate based on a formula.* A group health plan or group health insurance coverage ceases to be a grandfathered health plan if the employer or employee organization decreases its contribution rate based on a formula (as defined in paragraph (g)(3)(iii)(B) of this section) towards the cost of any tier of coverage for any class of similarly situated individuals (as described in section 2590.702(d) of this part) by more than 5 percent below the contribution rate for the coverage period that includes March 23, 2010.

(vi) *Changes in annual limits*—(A) *Addition of an annual limit.* A group health plan, or group health insurance coverage, that, on March 23, 2010, did not impose an overall annual or lifetime limit on the dollar value of all benefits ceases to be a grandfathered health plan if the plan or health insurance coverage imposes an overall annual limit on the dollar value of benefits.

(B) *Decrease in limit for a plan or coverage with only a lifetime limit.* A group health plan, or group health insurance coverage, that, on March 23, 2010, imposed an overall lifetime limit on the dollar value of all benefits but no overall annual limit on the dollar value of all benefits ceases to be a grandfathered health plan if the plan or health insurance coverage adopts an overall annual limit at a dollar value that is lower than the dollar value of the lifetime limit on March 23, 2010.

(C) *Decrease in limit for a plan or coverage with an annual limit.* A group health plan, or group health insurance coverage, that, on March 23, 2010, imposed an overall annual limit on the dollar value of all benefits ceases to be a grandfathered health plan if the plan or health insurance coverage decreases the dollar value of the annual limit (regardless of whether the plan or health insurance coverage also imposed an overall lifetime limit on March 23, 2010 on the dollar value of all benefits).

(2) *Transitional rules—*(i) *Changes made prior to March 23, 2010.* If a group health plan or health insurance issuer makes the following changes to the terms of the plan or health insurance coverage, the changes are considered part of the terms of the plan or health insurance coverage on March 23, 2010 even though they were not effective at that time and such changes do not cause a plan or health insurance coverage to cease to be a grandfathered health plan:

(A) Changes effective after March 23, 2010 pursuant to a legally binding contract entered into on or before March 23, 2010;

(B) Changes effective after March 23, 2010 pursuant to a filing on or before March 23, 2010 with a State insurance department; or

(C) Changes effective after March 23, 2010 pursuant to written amendments to a plan that were adopted on or before March 23, 2010.

(ii) *Changes made after March 23, 2010 and adopted prior to issuance of regulations.* If, after March 23, 2010, a group health plan or health insurance issuer makes changes to the terms of the plan or health insurance coverage and the changes are adopted prior to June 14, 2010, the changes will not cause the plan or health insurance coverage to cease to be a grandfathered health plan if the changes are revoked or modified effective as of the first day of the first plan year (in the individual market, policy year) beginning on or after September 23, 2010, and the terms of the plan or health insurance coverage on that date, as modified, would not cause the plan or coverage to cease to be a grandfathered health plan under the rules of this section, including paragraph (g)(1) of this section. For this purpose, changes will be considered to have been adopted prior to June 14, 2010 if:

(A) The changes are effective before that date;

(B) The changes are effective on or after that date pursuant to a legally binding contract entered into before that date;

(C) The changes are effective on or after that date pursuant to a filing before that date with a State insurance department; or

(D) The changes are effective on or after that date pursuant to written amendments to a plan that were adopted before that date.

(3) *Definitions—*(i) *Medical inflation defined.* For purposes of this paragraph (g), the term *medical inflation* means the increase since March 2010 in the overall medical care component of the Consumer Price Index for All Urban Consumers (CPI–U) (unadjusted) published by the Department of Labor using the 1982–1984 base of 100. For this purpose, the increase in the overall medical care component is computed by subtracting 387.142 (the overall medical care component of the CPI–U (unadjusted) published by the Department of Labor for March 2010, using the 1982–1984 base of 100) from the index amount for any month in the 12 months before the new change is to take effect and then dividing that amount by 387.142.

(ii) *Maximum percentage increase defined.* For purposes of this paragraph (g), the term *maximum percentage increase* means medical inflation (as defined in paragraph (g)(3)(i) of this section), expressed as a percentage, plus 15 percentage points.

(iii) *Contribution rate defined.* For purposes of paragraph (g)(1)(v) of this section:

(A) *Contribution rate based on cost of coverage.* The term *contribution rate based on cost of coverage* means the amount of contributions made by an employer or employee organization compared to the total cost of coverage, expressed as a percentage. The total cost of coverage is determined in the same manner as the applicable premium is calculated under the COBRA continuation provisions of section 604 of ERISA, section 4980B(f)(4) of the Internal Revenue Code, and section 2204 of the PHS Act. In the case of a self-insured plan, contributions by an employer or employee organization are equal to the total cost of coverage minus the employee contributions towards the total cost of coverage.

(B) *Contribution rate based on a formula.* The term *contribution rate based on a formula* means, for plans that, on March 23, 2010, made contributions based on a formula (such as hours worked or tons of coal mined), the formula.

(4) *Examples.* The rules of this paragraph (g) are illustrated by the following examples:

Example 1. (i) *Facts.* On March 23, 2010, a grandfathered health plan has a coinsurance requirement of 20% for inpatient surgery. The plan is subsequently amended to increase the coinsurance requirement to 25%.

(ii) *Conclusion.* In this *Example 1*, the increase in the coinsurance requirement from 20% to 25% causes the plan to cease to be a grandfathered health plan.

Example 2. (i) *Facts.* Before March 23, 2010, the terms of a group health plan provide benefits for a particular mental health condition, the treatment for which is a combination of counseling and prescription drugs. Subsequently, the plan eliminates benefits for counseling.

(ii) *Conclusion.* In this *Example 2*, the plan ceases to be a grandfathered health plan because counseling is an element that is necessary to treat the condition. Thus the plan is considered to have eliminated substantially all benefits for the treatment of the condition.

Example 3. (i) *Facts.* On March 23, 2010, a grandfathered health plan has a copayment requirement of $30 per office visit for specialists. The plan is subsequently amended to increase the copayment requirement to $40. Within the 12-month period before the $40 copayment takes effect, the greatest value of the overall medical care component of the CPI–U (unadjusted) is 475.

(ii) *Conclusion.* In this *Example 3*, the increase in the copayment from $30 to $40, expressed as a percentage, is 33.33% ($40 − 30 = 10$; $10 ÷ 30 = 0.3333$; $0.3333 = 33.33\%$). Medical inflation (as defined in paragraph (g)(3)(i) of this section) from March 2010 is 0.2269 ($475 − 387.142 = 87.858$; $87.858 ÷ 387.142 = 0.2269$). The maximum percentage increase permitted is 37.69% ($0.2269 = 22.69\%$; $22.69\% + 15\% = 37.69\%$). Because 33.33% does not exceed 37.69%, the change in the copayment requirement at that time does not cause the plan to cease to be a grandfathered health plan.

Example 4. (i) *Facts.* Same facts as *Example 3*, except the grandfathered health plan subsequently increases the $40 copayment requirement to $45 for a later plan year. Within the 12-month period before the $45 copayment takes effect, the greatest value of the overall medical care component of the CPI–U (unadjusted) is 485.

(ii) *Conclusion.* In this *Example 4*, the increase in the copayment from $30 (the copayment that was in effect on March 23, 2010) to $45, expressed as a percentage, is 50% ($45 − 30 = 15$; $15 ÷ 30 = 0.5$; $0.5 = 50\%$). Medical inflation (as defined in paragraph (g)(3)(i) of this section) from March 2010 is 0.2527 ($485 − 387.142 = 97.858$; $97.858 ÷ 387.142 = 0.2527$). The increase that would cause a plan to cease to be a grandfathered health plan under paragraph (g)(1)(iv) of this section is the greater of the maximum percentage increase of 40.27% ($0.2527 = 25.27\%$; $25.27\% + 15\% = 40.27\%$), or $6.26 ($5 × 0.2527 = 1.26; $1.26 + $5 = 6.26).

Because 50% exceeds 40.27% and $15 exceeds $6.26, the change in the copayment requirement at that time causes the plan to cease to be a grandfathered health plan.

Example 5. (i) *Facts.* On March 23, 2010, a grandfathered health plan has a copayment of $10 per office visit for primary care providers. The plan is subsequently amended to increase the copayment requirement to $15. Within the 12-month period before the $15 copayment takes effect, the greatest value of the overall medical care component of the CPI–U (unadjusted) is 415.

(ii) *Conclusion.* In this *Example 5,* the increase in the copayment, expressed as a percentage, is 50% ($15 − 10 = 5; 5 ÷ 10 = 0.5; 0.5 = 50%). Medical inflation (as defined in paragraph (g)(3) of this section) from March 2010 is 0.0720 (415.0 − 387.142 = 27.858; 27.858 ÷ 387.142 = 0.0720). The increase that would cause a plan to cease to be a grandfathered health plan under paragraph (g)(1)(iv) of this section is the greater of the maximum percentage increase of 22.20% (0.0720 = 7.20%; 7.20% + 15% = 22.20), or $5.36 ($5 x 0.0720 = $0.36; $0.36 + $5 = $5.36). The $5 increase in copayment in this *Example 5* would not cause the plan to cease to be a grandfathered health plan pursuant to paragraph (g)(1)(iv) of this section, which would permit an increase in the copayment of up to $5.36.

Example 6. (i) *Facts.* The same facts as *Example 5,* except on March 23, 2010, the grandfathered health plan has no copayment ($0) for office visits for primary care providers. The plan is subsequently amended to increase the copayment requirement to $5.

(ii) *Conclusion.* In this *Example 6,* medical inflation (as defined in paragraph (g)(3)(i) of this section) from March 2010 is 0.0720 (415.0 − 387.142 = 27.858; 27.858 ÷ 387.142 = 0.0720). The increase that would cause a plan to cease to be a grandfathered health plan under paragraph (g)(1)(iv)(A) of this section is $5.36 ($5 x 0.0720 = $0.36; $0.36 + $5 = $5.36). The $5 increase in copayment in this *Example 6* is less than the amount calculated pursuant to paragraph (g)(1)(iv)(A) of this section of $5.36. Thus, the $5 increase in copayment does not cause the plan to cease to be a grandfathered health plan.

Example 7. (i) *Facts.* On March 23, 2010, a self-insured group health plan provides two tiers of coverage—self-only and family. The employer contributes 80% of the total cost of coverage for self-only and 60% of the total cost of coverage for family. Subsequently, the employer reduces the contribution to 50% for family coverage, but keeps the same contribution rate for self-only coverage.

(ii) *Conclusion.* In this *Example 7,* the decrease of 10 percentage points for family coverage in the contribution rate based on cost of coverage causes the plan to cease to be a grandfathered health plan. The fact that the contribution rate for self-only coverage remains the same does not change the result.

Example 8. (i) *Facts.* On March 23, 2010, a self-insured grandfathered health plan has a COBRA premium for the 2010 plan year of $5000 for self-only coverage and $12,000 for family coverage. The required employee contribution for the coverage is $1000 for self-only coverage and $4000 for family coverage. Thus, the contribution rate based

on cost of coverage for 2010 is 80% ((5000−1000)/5000) for self-only coverage and 67% ((12,000−4000)/12,000) for family coverage. For a subsequent plan year, the COBRA premium is $6000 for self-only coverage and $15,000 for family coverage. The employee contributions for that plan year are $1200 for self-only coverage and $5000 for family coverage. Thus, the contribution rate based on cost of coverage is 80% ((6000−1200)/6000) for self-only coverage and 67% ((15,000−5000)/15,000) for family coverage.

(ii) *Conclusion.* In this *Example 8,* because there is no change in the contribution rate based on cost of coverage, the plan retains its status as a grandfathered health plan. The result would be the same if all or part of the employee contribution was made pre-tax through a cafeteria plan under section 125 of the Internal Revenue Code.

Example 9. (i) *Facts.* Before March 23, 2010, Employer *W* and Individual *B* enter into a legally binding employment contract that promises *B* lifetime health coverage upon termination. Prior to termination, *B* is covered by *W's* self-insured grandfathered group health plan. *B* is terminated after March 23, 2010 and *W* purchases a new health insurance policy providing coverage to *B,* consistent with the terms of the employment contract.

(ii) *Conclusion.* In this *Example 9,* because no individual is enrolled in the health insurance policy on March 23, 2010, it is not a grandfathered health plan.

■ 3. Section 2590.715–2714 is amended by revising paragraph (h) to read as follows:

§ 2590.715–2714 Eligibility of children until at least age 26.

*   *   *   *   *

(h) *Applicability date.* The provisions of this section apply for plan years beginning on or after September 23, 2010. *See* § 2590.715–1251 of this Part for determining the application of this section to grandfathered health plans.

DEPARTMENT OF HEALTH AND HUMAN SERVICES

45 CFR Chapter I

■ For the reasons stated in the preamble, the Department of Health and Human Services amends 45 CFR part 147 as follows:

PART 147—HEALTH INSURANCE REFORM REQUIREMENTS FOR THE GROUP AND INDIVIDUAL HEALTH INSURANCE MARKETS

■ 1. The authority citation for part 147 continues to read as follows:

Authority: Secs. 2701 through 2763, 2791, and 2792 of the Public Health Service Act (42 USC 300gg through 300gg–63, 300gg–91, and 300gg–92), as amended.

■ 2. Section 147.120 is amended by revising paragraph (h) to read as follows:

(h) *Applicability date.* The provisions of this section apply for plan years (in the individual market, policy years) beginning on or after September 23, 2010. *See* § 147.140 of this part for determining the application of this section to grandfathered health plans.

■ 3. Section 147.140 is added to read as follows:

§ 147.140 Preservation of right to maintain existing coverage.

(a) *Definition of grandfathered health plan coverage*—(1) *In general*—(i) *Grandfathered health plan coverage* means coverage provided by a group health plan, or a group or individual health insurance issuer, in which an individual was enrolled on March 23, 2010 (for as long as it maintains that status under the rules of this section). A group health plan or group health insurance coverage does not cease to be grandfathered health plan coverage merely because one or more (or even all) individuals enrolled on March 23, 2010 cease to be covered, provided that the plan or group health insurance coverage has continuously covered someone since March 23, 2010 (not necessarily the same person, but at all times at least one person). For purposes of this section, a plan or health insurance coverage that provides grandfathered health plan coverage is referred to as a grandfathered health plan. The rules of this section apply separately to each benefit package made available under a group health plan or health insurance coverage.

(ii) Subject to the rules of paragraph (f) of this section for collectively bargained plans, if an employer or employee organization enters into a new policy, certificate, or contract of insurance after March 23, 2010 (because, for example, any previous policy, certificate, or contract of insurance is not being renewed), then that policy, certificate, or contract of insurance is not a grandfathered health plan with respect to the individuals in the group health plan.

(2) *Disclosure of grandfather status*—(i) To maintain status as a grandfathered health plan, a plan or health insurance coverage must include a statement, in any plan materials provided to a participant or beneficiary (in the individual market, primary subscriber) describing the benefits provided under the plan or health insurance coverage, that the plan or coverage believes it is a grandfathered health plan within the meaning of section 1251 of the Patient Protection and Affordable Care Act and must provide contact information for questions and complaints.

(ii) The following model language can be used to satisfy this disclosure requirement:

This [group health plan or health insurance issuer] believes this [plan or coverage] is a "grandfathered health plan" under the Patient Protection and Affordable Care Act (the Affordable Care Act). As permitted by the Affordable Care Act, a grandfathered health plan can preserve certain basic health coverage that was already in effect when that law was enacted. Being a grandfathered health plan means that your [plan or policy] may not include certain consumer protections of the Affordable Care Act that apply to other plans, for example, the requirement for the provision of preventive health services without any cost sharing. However, grandfathered health plans must comply with certain other consumer protections in the Affordable Care Act, for example, the elimination of lifetime limits on benefits.

Questions regarding which protections apply and which protections do not apply to a grandfathered health plan and what might cause a plan to change from grandfathered health plan status can be directed to the plan administrator at [insert contact information]. [For ERISA plans, insert: You may also contact the Employee Benefits Security Administration, U.S. Department of Labor at 1–866–444–3272 or *www.dol.gov/ebsa/ healthreform*. This Web site has a table summarizing which protections do and do not apply to grandfathered health plans.] [For individual market policies and nonfederal governmental plans, insert: You may also contact the U.S. Department of Health and Human Services at *www.healthreform.gov.*]

(3) *Documentation of plan or policy terms on March 23, 2010.* To maintain status as a grandfathered health plan, a group health plan, or group or individual health insurance coverage, must, for as long as the plan or health insurance coverage takes the position that it is a grandfathered health plan—

(i) Maintain records documenting the terms of the plan or health insurance coverage in connection with the coverage in effect on March 23, 2010, and any other documents necessary to verify, explain, or clarify its status as a grandfathered health plan; and

(ii) Make such records available for examination upon request.

(4) *Family members enrolling after March 23, 2010.* With respect to an individual who is enrolled in a group health plan or health insurance coverage on March 23, 2010, grandfathered health plan coverage includes coverage of family members of the individual who enroll after March 23, 2010 in the grandfathered health plan coverage of the individual.

(5) *Examples.* The rules of this paragraph (a) are illustrated by the following examples:

Example 1. (i) *Facts.* A group health plan not maintained pursuant to a collective bargaining agreement provides coverage through a group health insurance policy from Issuer X on March 23, 2010. For the plan year beginning January 1, 2012, the plan enters into a new policy with Issuer Z.

(ii) *Conclusion.* In this *Example 1*, for the plan year beginning January 1, 2012, the group health insurance coverage issued by Z is not a grandfathered health plan under the rules of paragraph (a)(1)(ii) of this section because the policy issued by Z did not provide coverage on March 23, 2010.

Example 2. (i) *Facts.* A group health plan not maintained pursuant to a collective bargaining agreement offers three benefit packages on March 23, 2010. Option F is a self-insured option. Options G and H are insured options. Beginning July 1, 2013, the plan replaces the issuer for Option H with a new issuer.

(ii) *Conclusion.* In this *Example 2*, the coverage under Option H is not grandfathered health plan coverage as of July 1, 2013, consistent with the rule in paragraph (a)(1)(ii) of this section. Whether the coverage under Options F and G is a grandfathered health plan coverage is determined under the rules of this section, including paragraph (g) of this section. If the plan enters into a new policy, certificate, or contract of insurance for Option G, Option G's status as a grandfathered health plan would cease under paragraph (a)(1)(ii) of this section.

(b) *Allowance for new employees to join current plan*—(1) *In general.* Subject to paragraph (b)(2) of this section, a group health plan (including health insurance coverage provided in connection with the group health plan) that provided coverage on March 23, 2010 and has retained its status as a grandfathered health plan (consistent with the rules of this section, including paragraph (g) of this section) is grandfathered health plan coverage for new employees (whether newly hired or newly enrolled) and their families enrolling in the plan after March 23, 2010.

(2) *Anti-abuse rules*—(i) *Mergers and acquisitions.* If the principal purpose of a merger, acquisition, or similar business restructuring is to cover new individuals under a grandfathered health plan, the plan ceases to be a grandfathered health plan.

(ii) *Change in plan eligibility.* A group health plan or health insurance coverage (including a benefit package under a group health plan) ceases to be a grandfathered health plan if—

(A) Employees are transferred into the plan or health insurance coverage (the transferee plan) from a plan or health insurance coverage under which the employees were covered on March 23, 2010 (the transferor plan);

(B) Comparing the terms of the transferee plan with those of the transferor plan (as in effect on March 23, 2010) and treating the transferee plan as if it were an amendment of the transferor plan would cause a loss of grandfather status under the provisions of paragraph (g)(1) of this section; and

(C) There was no bona fide employment-based reason to transfer the employees into the transferee plan. For this purpose, changing the terms or cost of coverage is not a bona fide employment-based reason.

(3) *Examples.* The rules of this paragraph (b) are illustrated by the following examples:

Example 1. (i) *Facts.* A group health plan offers two benefit packages on March 23, 2010, Options F and G. During a subsequent open enrollment period, some of the employees enrolled in Option F on March 23, 2010 switch to Option G.

(ii) *Conclusion.* In this *Example 1*, the group health coverage provided under Option G remains a grandfathered health plan under the rules of paragraph (b)(1) of this section because employees previously enrolled in Option F are allowed to enroll in Option G as new employees.

Example 2. (i) *Facts.* Same facts as *Example 1*, except that the plan sponsor eliminates Option F because of its high cost and transfers employees covered under Option F to Option G. If instead of transferring employees from Option F to Option G, Option F was amended to match the terms of Option G, then Option F would cease to be a grandfathered health plan.

(ii) *Conclusion.* In this *Example 2*, the plan did not have a bona fide employment-based reason to transfer employees from Option F to Option G. Therefore, Option G ceases to be a grandfathered health plan with respect to all employees. (However, any other benefit package maintained by the plan sponsor is analyzed separately under the rules of this section.)

Example 3. (i) *Facts.* A group health plan offers two benefit packages on March 23, 2010, Options H and I. On March 23, 2010, Option H provides coverage only for employees in one manufacturing plant. Subsequently, the plant is closed, and some employees in the closed plant are moved to another plant. The employer eliminates Option H and the employees that are moved are transferred to Option I. If instead of transferring employees from Option H to Option I, Option H was amended to match the terms of Option I, then Option H would cease to be a grandfathered health plan.

(ii) *Conclusion.* In this *Example 3*, the plan has a bona fide employment-based reason to transfer employees from Option H to Option I. Therefore, Option I does not cease to be a grandfathered health plan.

(c) *General grandfathering rule*—(1) Except as provided in paragraphs (d) and (e) of this section, subtitles A and C of title I of the Patient Protection and Affordable Care Act (and the amendments made by those subtitles, and the incorporation of those amendments into ERISA section 715 and Internal Revenue Code section 9815) do not apply to grandfathered health plan coverage. Accordingly, the provisions of PHS Act sections 2701, 2702, 2703, 2705, 2706, 2707, 2709 (relating to coverage for individuals participating in approved clinical trials, as added by section 10103 of the Patient Protection and Affordable Care Act), 2713, 2715A, 2716, 2717, 2719, and 2719A, as added or amended by the Patient Protection and Affordable Care Act, do not apply to grandfathered health plans. In addition, the provisions of PHS Act section 2704, and PHS Act section 2711 insofar as it relates to annual limits, do not apply to grandfathered health plans that are individual health insurance coverage.

(2) To the extent not inconsistent with the rules applicable to a grandfathered health plan, a grandfathered health plan must comply with the requirements of the PHS Act, ERISA, and the Internal Revenue Code applicable prior to the changes enacted by the Patient Protection and Affordable Care Act.

(d) *Provisions applicable to all grandfathered health plans.* The provisions of PHS Act section 2711 insofar as it relates to lifetime limits, and the provisions of PHS Act sections 2712, 2714, 2715, and 2718, apply to grandfathered health plans for plan years (in the individual market, policy years) beginning on or after September 23, 2010. The provisions of PHS Act section 2708 apply to grandfathered health plans for plan years (in the individual market, policy years) beginning on or after January 1, 2014.

(e) *Applicability of PHS Act sections 2704, 2711, and 2714 to grandfathered group health plans and group health insurance coverage*—(1) The provisions of PHS Act section 2704 as it applies with respect to enrollees who are under 19 years of age, and the provisions of PHS Act section 2711 insofar as it relates to annual limits, apply to grandfathered health plans that are group health plans (including group health insurance coverage) for plan years beginning on or after September 23, 2010. The provisions of PHS Act section 2704 apply generally to grandfathered health plans that are group health plans (including group health insurance coverage) for plan years beginning on or after January 1, 2014.

(2) For plan years beginning before January 1, 2014, the provisions of PHS Act section 2714 apply in the case of an adult child with respect to a grandfathered health plan that is a group health plan only if the adult child is not eligible to enroll in an eligible employer-sponsored health plan (as defined in section 5000A(f)(2) of the Internal Revenue Code) other than a grandfathered health plan of a parent.

For plan years beginning on or after January 1, 2014, the provisions of PHS Act section 2714 apply with respect to a grandfathered health plan that is a group health plan without regard to whether an adult child is eligible to enroll in any other coverage.

(f) *Effect on collectively bargained plans*—(1) *In general.* In the case of health insurance coverage maintained pursuant to one or more collective bargaining agreements between employee representatives and one or more employers that was ratified before March 23, 2010, the coverage is grandfathered health plan coverage at least until the date on which the last of the collective bargaining agreements relating to the coverage that was in effect on March 23, 2010 terminates. Any coverage amendment made pursuant to a collective bargaining agreement relating to the coverage that amends the coverage solely to conform to any requirement added by subtitles A and C of title I of the Patient Protection and Affordable Care Act (and the amendments made by those subtitles, and the incorporation of those amendments into ERISA section 715 and Internal Revenue Code section 9815) is not treated as a termination of the collective bargaining agreement. After the date on which the last of the collective bargaining agreements relating to the coverage that was in effect on March 23, 2010 terminates, the determination of whether health insurance coverage maintained pursuant to a collective bargaining agreement is grandfathered health plan coverage is made under the rules of this section other than this paragraph (f) (comparing the terms of the health insurance coverage after the date the last collective bargaining agreement terminates with the terms of the health insurance coverage that were in effect on March 23, 2010) and, for any changes in insurance coverage after the termination of the collective bargaining agreement, under the rules of paragraph (a)(1)(ii) of this section.

(2) *Examples.* The rules of this paragraph (f) are illustrated by the following examples:

Example 1. (i) *Facts.* A group health plan maintained pursuant to a collective bargaining agreement provides coverage through a group health insurance policy from Issuer *W* on March 23, 2010. The collective bargaining agreement has not been amended and will not expire before December 31, 2011. The group health plan enters into a new group health insurance policy with Issuer *Y* for the plan year starting on January 1, 2011.

(ii) *Conclusion.* In this *Example 1,* the group health plan, and the group health insurance policy provided by *Y,* remains a

grandfathered health plan with respect to existing employees and new employees and their families because the coverage is maintained pursuant to a collective bargaining agreement ratified prior to March 23, 2010 that has not terminated.

Example 2. (i) *Facts.* Same facts as *Example 1,* except the coverage with *Y* is renewed under a new collective bargaining agreement effective January 1, 2012, with the only changes since March 23, 2010 being changes that do not cause the plan to cease to be a grandfathered health plan under the rules of this section, including paragraph (g) of this section.

(ii) *Conclusion.* In this *Example 2,* the group health plan remains a grandfathered health plan pursuant to the rules of this section. Moreover, the group health insurance policy provided by *Y* remains a grandfathered health plan under the rules of this section, including paragraph (g) of this section.

(g) *Maintenance of grandfather status*—(1) *Changes causing cessation of grandfather status.* Subject to paragraph (g)(2) of this section, the rules of this paragraph (g)(1) describe situations in which a group health plan or health insurance coverage ceases to be a grandfathered health plan.

(i) *Elimination of benefits.* The elimination of all or substantially all benefits to diagnose or treat a particular condition causes a group health plan or health insurance coverage to cease to be a grandfathered health plan. For this purpose, the elimination of benefits for any necessary element to diagnose or treat a condition is considered the elimination of all or substantially all benefits to diagnose or treat a particular condition.

(ii) *Increase in percentage cost-sharing requirement.* Any increase, measured from March 23, 2010, in a percentage cost-sharing requirement (such as an individual's coinsurance requirement) causes a group health plan or health insurance coverage to cease to be a grandfathered health plan.

(iii) *Increase in a fixed-amount cost-sharing requirement other than a copayment.* Any increase in a fixed-amount cost-sharing requirement other than a copayment (for example, deductible or out-of-pocket limit), determined as of the effective date of the increase, causes a group health plan or health insurance coverage to cease to be a grandfathered health plan, if the total percentage increase in the cost-sharing requirement measured from March 23, 2010 exceeds the maximum percentage increase (as defined in paragraph (g)(3)(ii) of this section).

(iv) *Increase in a fixed-amount copayment.* Any increase in a fixed-amount copayment, determined as of the effective date of the increase, causes a group health plan or health insurance coverage to cease to be a grandfathered health plan, if the total increase in the copayment measured from March 23, 2010 exceeds the greater of:

(A) An amount equal to $5 increased by medical inflation, as defined in paragraph (g)(3)(i) of this section (that is, $5 times medical inflation, plus $5), or

(B) The maximum percentage increase (as defined in paragraph (g)(3)(ii) of this section), determined by expressing the total increase in the copayment as a percentage.

(v) *Decrease in contribution rate by employers and employee organizations*—(A) *Contribution rate based on cost of coverage.* A group health plan or group health insurance coverage ceases to be a grandfathered health plan if the employer or employee organization decreases its contribution rate based on cost of coverage (as defined in paragraph (g)(3)(iii)(A) of this section) towards the cost of any tier of coverage for any class of similarly situated individuals (as described in section 146.121(d) of this subchapter) by more than 5 percentage points below the contribution rate for the coverage period that includes March 23, 2010.

(B) *Contribution rate based on a formula.* A group health plan or group health insurance coverage ceases to be a grandfathered health plan if the employer or employee organization decreases its contribution rate based on a formula (as defined in paragraph (g)(3)(iii)(B) of this section) towards the cost of any tier of coverage for any class of similarly situated individuals (as described in section 146.121(d) of this subchapter) by more than 5 percent below the contribution rate for the coverage period that includes March 23, 2010.

(vi) *Changes in annual limits*—(A) *Addition of an annual limit.* A group health plan, or group or individual health insurance coverage, that, on March 23, 2010, did not impose an overall annual or lifetime limit on the dollar value of all benefits ceases to be a grandfathered health plan if the plan or health insurance coverage imposes an overall annual limit on the dollar value of benefits.

(B) *Decrease in limit for a plan or coverage with only a lifetime limit.* A group health plan, or group or individual health insurance coverage, that, on March 23, 2010, imposed an overall lifetime limit on the dollar value of all benefits but no overall annual limit on the dollar value of all benefits ceases to be a grandfathered health plan if the plan or health insurance coverage adopts an overall annual limit at a dollar value that is lower than the dollar

value of the lifetime limit on March 23, 2010.

(C) *Decrease in limit for a plan or coverage with an annual limit.* A group health plan, or group or individual health insurance coverage, that, on March 23, 2010, imposed an overall annual limit on the dollar value of all benefits ceases to be a grandfathered health plan if the plan or health insurance coverage decreases the dollar value of the annual limit (regardless of whether the plan or health insurance coverage also imposed an overall lifetime limit on March 23, 2010 on the dollar value of all benefits).

(2) *Transitional rules*—(i) *Changes made prior to March 23, 2010.* If a group health plan or health insurance issuer makes the following changes to the terms of the plan or health insurance coverage, the changes are considered part of the terms of the plan or health insurance coverage on March 23, 2010 even though they were not effective at that time and such changes do not cause a plan or health insurance coverage to cease to be a grandfathered health plan:

(A) Changes effective after March 23, 2010 pursuant to a legally binding contract entered into on or before March 23, 2010;

(B) Changes effective after March 23, 2010 pursuant to a filing on or before March 23, 2010 with a State insurance department; or

(C) Changes effective after March 23, 2010 pursuant to written amendments to a plan that were adopted on or before March 23, 2010.

(ii) *Changes made after March 23, 2010 and adopted prior to issuance of regulations.* If, after March 23, 2010, a group health plan or health insurance issuer makes changes to the terms of the plan or health insurance coverage and the changes are adopted prior to June 14, 2010, the changes will not cause the plan or health insurance coverage to cease to be a grandfathered health plan if the changes are revoked or modified effective as of the first day of the first plan year (in the individual market, policy year) beginning on or after September 23, 2010, and the terms of the plan or health insurance coverage on that date, as modified, would not cause the plan or coverage to cease to be a grandfathered health plan under the rules of this section, including paragraph (g)(1) of this section. For this purpose, changes will be considered to have been adopted prior to June 14, 2010 if:

(A) The changes are effective before that date;

(B) The changes are effective on or after that date pursuant to a legally

binding contract entered into before that date;

(C) The changes are effective on or after that date pursuant to a filing before that date with a State insurance department; or

(D) The changes are effective on or after that date pursuant to written amendments to a plan that were adopted before that date.

(3) *Definitions*—(i) *Medical inflation defined.* For purposes of this paragraph (g), the term *medical inflation* means the increase since March 2010 in the overall medical care component of the Consumer Price Index for All Urban Consumers (CPI–U) (unadjusted) published by the Department of Labor using the 1982–1984 base of 100. For this purpose, the increase in the overall medical care component is computed by subtracting 387.142 (the overall medical care component of the CPI–U (unadjusted) published by the Department of Labor for March 2010, using the 1982–1984 base of 100) from the index amount for any month in the 12 months before the new change is to take effect and then dividing that amount by 387.142.

(ii) *Maximum percentage increase defined.* For purposes of this paragraph (g), the term *maximum percentage increase* means medical inflation (as defined in paragraph (g)(3)(i) of this section), expressed as a percentage, plus 15 percentage points.

(iii) *Contribution rate defined.* For purposes of paragraph (g)(1)(v) of this section:

(A) *Contribution rate based on cost of coverage.* The term *contribution rate based on cost of coverage* means the amount of contributions made by an employer or employee organization compared to the total cost of coverage, expressed as a percentage. The total cost of coverage is determined in the same manner as the applicable premium is calculated under the COBRA continuation provisions of section 604 of ERISA, section 4980B(f)(4) of the Internal Revenue Code, and section 2204 of the PHS Act. In the case of a self-insured plan, contributions by an employer or employee organization are equal to the total cost of coverage minus the employee contributions towards the total cost of coverage.

(B) *Contribution rate based on a formula.* The term *contribution rate based on a formula* means, for plans that, on March 23, 2010, made contributions based on a formula (such as hours worked or tons of coal mined), the formula.

(4) *Examples.* The rules of this paragraph (g) are illustrated by the following examples:

Example 1. (i) *Facts.* On March 23, 2010, a grandfathered health plan has a coinsurance requirement of 20% for inpatient surgery. The plan is subsequently amended to increase the coinsurance requirement to 25%.

(ii) *Conclusion.* In this *Example 1,* the increase in the coinsurance requirement from 20% to 25% causes the plan to cease to be a grandfathered health plan.

Example 2. (i) *Facts.* Before March 23, 2010, the terms of a group health plan provide benefits for a particular mental health condition, the treatment for which is a combination of counseling and prescription drugs. Subsequently, the plan eliminates benefits for counseling.

(ii) *Conclusion.* In this *Example 2,* the plan ceases to be a grandfathered health plan because counseling is an element that is necessary to treat the condition. Thus the plan is considered to have eliminated substantially all benefits for the treatment of the condition.

Example 3. (i) *Facts.* On March 23, 2010, a grandfathered health plan has a copayment requirement of $30 per office visit for specialists. The plan is subsequently amended to increase the copayment requirement to $40. Within the 12-month period before the $40 copayment takes effect, the greatest value of the overall medical care component of the CPI–U (unadjusted) is 475.

(ii) *Conclusion.* In this *Example 3,* the increase in the copayment from $30 to $40, expressed as a percentage, is 33.33% (40 − 30 = 10; 10 ÷ 30 = 0.3333; 0.3333 = 33.33%). Medical inflation (as defined in paragraph (g)(3)(i) of this section) from March 2010 is 0.2269 (475 − 387.142 = 87.858; 87.858 ÷ 387.142 = 0.2269). The maximum percentage increase permitted is 37.69% (0.2269 = 22.69%; 22.69% + 15% = 37.69%). Because 33.33% does not exceed 37.69%, the change in the copayment requirement at that time does not cause the plan to cease to be a grandfathered health plan.

Example 4. (i) *Facts.* Same facts as *Example 3,* except the grandfathered health plan subsequently increases the $40 copayment requirement to $45 for a later plan year. Within the 12-month period before the $45 copayment takes effect, the greatest value of the overall medical care component of the CPI–U (unadjusted) is 485.

(ii) *Conclusion.* In this *Example 4,* the increase in the copayment from $30 (the copayment that was in effect on March 23, 2010) to $45, expressed as a percentage, is 50% (45 − 30 = 15; 15 ÷ 30 = 0.5; 0.5 = 50%). Medical inflation (as defined in paragraph (g)(3)(i) of this section) from March 2010 is

0.2527 (485 − 387.142 = 97.858; 97.858 ÷ 387.142 = 0.2527). The increase that would cause a plan to cease to be a grandfathered health plan under paragraph (g)(1)(iv) of this section is the greater of the maximum percentage increase of 40.27% (0.2527 = 25.27%; 25.27% + 15% = 40.27%), or $6.26 ($5 × 0.2527 = $1.26; $1.26 + $5 = $6.26). Because 50% exceeds 40.27% and $15 exceeds $6.26, the change in the copayment requirement at that time causes the plan to cease to be a grandfathered health plan.

Example 5. (i) *Facts.* On March 23, 2010, a grandfathered health plan has a copayment of $10 per office visit for primary care providers. The plan is subsequently amended to increase the copayment requirement to $15. Within the 12-month period before the $15 copayment takes effect, the greatest value of the overall medical care component of the CPI–U (unadjusted) is 415.

(ii) *Conclusion.* In this *Example 5,* the increase in the copayment, expressed as a percentage, is 50% (15 − 10 = 5; 5 ÷ 10 = 0.5; 0.5 = 50%). Medical inflation (as defined in paragraph (g)(3) of this section) from March 2010 is 0.0720 (415.0 − 387.142 = 27.858; 27.858 ÷ 387.142 = 0.0720). The increase that would cause a plan to cease to be a grandfathered health plan under paragraph (g)(1)(iv) of this section is the greater of the maximum percentage increase of 22.20% (0.0720 = 7.20%; 7.20% + 15% = 22.20), or $5.36 ($5 × 0.0720 = $0.36; $0.36 + $5 = $5.36). The $5 increase in copayment in this *Example 5* would not cause the plan to cease to be a grandfathered health plan pursuant to paragraph (g)(1)(iv) this section, which would permit an increase in the copayment of up to $5.36.

Example 6. (i) *Facts.* The same facts as *Example 5,* except on March 23, 2010, the grandfathered health plan has no copayment ($0) for office visits for primary care providers. The plan is subsequently amended to increase the copayment requirement to $5.

(ii) *Conclusion.* In this *Example 6,* medical inflation (as defined in paragraph (g)(3)(i) of this section) from March 2010 is 0.0720 (415.0 − 387.142 = 27.858; 27.858 ÷ 387.142 = 0.0720). The increase that would cause a plan to cease to be a grandfathered health plan under paragraph (g)(1)(iv)(A) of this section is $5.36 ($5 × 0.0720 = $0.36; $0.36 + $5 = $5.36). The $5 increase in copayment in this *Example 6* is less than the amount calculated pursuant to paragraph (g)(1)(iv)(A) of this section of $5.36. Thus, the $5 increase in copayment does not cause the plan to cease to be a grandfathered health plan.

Example 7. (i) *Facts.* On March 23, 2010, a self-insured group health plan provides two

tiers of coverage—self-only and family. The employer contributes 80% of the total cost of coverage for self-only and 60% of the total cost of coverage for family. Subsequently, the employer reduces the contribution to 50% for family coverage, but keeps the same contribution rate for self-only coverage.

(ii) *Conclusion.* In this *Example 7,* the decrease of 10 percentage points for family coverage in the contribution rate based on cost of coverage causes the plan to cease to be a grandfathered health plan. The fact that the contribution rate for self-only coverage remains the same does not change the result.

Example 8. (i) *Facts.* On March 23, 2010, a self-insured grandfathered health plan has a COBRA premium for the 2010 plan year of $5000 for self-only coverage and $12,000 for family coverage. The required employee contribution for the coverage is $1000 for self-only coverage and $4000 for family coverage. Thus, the contribution rate based on cost of coverage for 2010 is 80% ((5000 − 1000)/5000) for self-only coverage and 67% ((12,000 − 4000)/12,000) for family coverage. For a subsequent plan year, the COBRA premium is $6000 for self-only coverage and $15,000 for family coverage. The employee contributions for that plan year are $1200 for self-only coverage and $5000 for family coverage. Thus, the contribution rate based on cost of coverage is 80% ((6000 − 1200)/6000) for self-only coverage and 67% ((15,000 − 5000)/15,000) for family coverage.

(ii) *Conclusion.* In this *Example 8,* because there is no change in the contribution rate based on cost of coverage, the plan retains its status as a grandfathered health plan. The result would be the same if all or part of the employee contribution was made pre-tax through a cafeteria plan under section 125 of the Internal Revenue Code.

Example 9. (i) *Facts.* Before March 23, 2010, Employer *W* and Individual *B* enter into a legally binding employment contract that promises *B* lifetime health coverage upon termination. Prior to termination, *B* is covered by *W*'s self-insured grandfathered group health plan. *B* is terminated after March 23, 2010 and *W* purchases a new health insurance policy providing coverage to *B,* consistent with the terms of the employment contract.

(ii) *Conclusion.* In this *Example 9,* because no individual is enrolled in the health insurance policy on March 23, 2010, it is not a grandfathered health plan.

[FR Doc. 2010–14488 Filed 6–14–10; 11:15 am]

BILLING CODE 4830–01–P, 4510–29–P, 4120–01–P

C. HHS Regulations on Web Portal Requirements

of the decision. The Secretary sends a written decision to the sponsor or the applicable Secretary's designee upon request.

Subpart G—Disclosure of Data Inaccuracies

§ 149.600   Sponsor's duty to report data inaccuracies.

A sponsor is required to disclose any data inaccuracies upon which a reimbursement determination is made, including inaccurate claims data and negotiated price concessions, in a manner and at a time specified by the Secretary in guidance.

§ 149.610   Secretary's authority to reopen and revise a reimbursement determination.

(a) The Secretary may reopen and revise a reimbursement determination upon the Secretary's own motion or upon the request of a sponsor:

(1) Within 1 year of the reimbursement determination for any reason.

(2) Within 4 years of a reimbursement determination for good cause.

(3) At any time, in instances of fraud or similar fault.

(b) For purposes of this section, the Secretary does not find good cause if the only reason for the revision is a change of legal interpretation or administrative ruling upon which the determination to reimburse was made.

(c) A decision by the Secretary not to revise a reimbursement determination is final and binding (unless fraud or similar fault is found) and cannot be appealed.

Subpart H—Change of Ownership Requirements

§ 149.700   Change of ownership requirements.

(a) *Change of ownership consists of:*
(1) *Partnership.* The removal, addition, or substitution of a partner, unless the partners expressly agree otherwise as permitted by applicable state law.

(2) *Asset sale.* Transfer of all or substantially all of the assets of the sponsor to another party.

(3) *Corporation.* The merger of the sponsor's corporation into another corporation or the consolidation of the sponsor's organization with one or more other corporations, resulting in a new corporate body.

(b) *Change of ownership; exception.* Transfer of corporate stock or the merger of another corporation into the sponsor's corporation, with the sponsor surviving, does not ordinarily constitute change of ownership.

(c) *Advance notice requirement.* A sponsor that has a sponsor agreement in effect under this part and is considering or negotiating a change in ownership must notify the Secretary at least 60 days before the anticipated effective date of the change.

(d) *Assignment of agreement.* When there is a change of ownership as specified in paragraph (a) of this section, and this results in a transfer of the liability for health benefits, the existing sponsor agreement is automatically assigned to the new owner.

(e) *Conditions that apply to assigned agreements.* The new owner to whom a sponsor agreement is assigned is subject to all applicable statutes and regulations and to the terms and conditions of the sponsor agreement.

(f) Failure to notify the Secretary at least 60 days before the anticipated effective date of the change may result in the Secretary recovering funds paid under this program.

Dated: April 29, 2010.

Jay Angoff,
Director, Office of Consumer Information and Insurance Oversight.

Dated: April 29, 2010

Kathleen Sebelius,
Secretary.

[FR Doc. 2010–10658 Filed 5–4–10; 8:45 am]
BILLING CODE 4150–03–P

DEPARTMENT OF HEALTH AND HUMAN SERVICES

Office of the Secretary

45 CFR Part 159

RIN 0991–AB63

Health Care Reform Insurance Web Portal Requirements

AGENCY: Office of the Secretary, HHS.
ACTION: Interim final rule with comment period.

SUMMARY: The Patient Protection and Affordable Care Act (the Affordable Care Act) was enacted on March 23, 2010. It requires the establishment of an internet Web site (hereinafter referred to as a Web portal) through which individuals and small businesses can obtain information about the insurance coverage options that may be available to them in their State. The Department of Health and Human Services (HHS) is issuing this interim final rule in order to implement this mandate. This interim final rule adopts the categories of information that will be collected and displayed as Web portal content, and the data we will require from issuers and request from States, associations, and high risk pools in order to create this content.

DATES: *Effective Date:* These regulations are effective on May 10, 2010.

Comment Date: To be assured consideration, comments must be received at the address provided below, no later than 5 p.m. on June 4, 2010.

ADDRESSES: In commenting, please refer to file code DHHS–9997–IFC. Because of staff and resource limitations, we cannot accept comments by facsimile (FAX) transmission.

You may submit comments in one of four ways (please choose only one of the ways listed):

• *Electronically.* You may submit electronic comments on this regulation to *http://www.regulations.gov.* Follow the instructions on the home page.

• *By regular mail.* You may mail written comments to the following address ONLY: Centers for Medicare & Medicaid Services, Department of Health and Human Services, Attention: DHHS–9997–IFC, P.O. Box 8014, Baltimore, MD 21244–8014.

Please allow sufficient time for mailed comments to be received before the close of the comment period.

• *By express or overnight mail.* You may send written comments to the following address ONLY: Centers for Medicare & Medicaid Services, Department of Health and Human Services, Attention: DHHS–9997–IFC, Mail Stop C4–26–05, 7500 Security Boulevard, Baltimore, MD 21244–1850.

• *By hand or courier.* If you prefer, you may deliver (by hand or courier) your written comments before the close of the comment period to either of the following addresses:

a. For delivery in Washington, DC— Centers for Medicare & Medicaid Services, Department of Health and Human Services, Room 445–G, Hubert H. Humphrey Building, 200 Independence Avenue, SW., Washington, DC 20201

(Because access to the interior of the Hubert H. Humphrey Building is not readily available to persons without Federal government identification, commenters are encouraged to leave their comments in the CMS drop slots located in the main lobby of the building. A stamp-in clock is available for persons wishing to retain a proof of filing by stamping in and retaining an extra copy of the comments being filed.)

b. For delivery in Baltimore, MD— Centers for Medicare & Medicaid Services, Department of Health and Human Services, 7500 Security Boulevard, Baltimore, MD 21244–1850.

If you intend to deliver your comments to the Baltimore address, please call telephone number (410) 786–9994 in advance to schedule your arrival with one of our staff members.

Comments mailed to the addresses indicated as appropriate for hand or courier delivery may be delayed and received after the comment period.

Submission of comments on paperwork requirements. You may submit comments on this document's paperwork requirements by following the instructions at the end of the "Collection of Information Requirements" section in this document.

For information on viewing public comments, see the beginning of the **SUPPLEMENTARY INFORMATION** section.

FOR FURTHER INFORMATION CONTACT:
Danielle Harris, (410) 786–1819.

SUPPLEMENTARY INFORMATION: *Inspection of Public Comments:* All comments received before the close of the comment period are available for viewing by the public, including any personally identifiable or confidential business information that is included in a comment. We post all comments received before the close of the comment period on the following Web site as soon as possible after they have been received: *http://regulations.gov.* Follow the search instructions on that Web site to view public comments.

Comments received timely will be also available for public inspection as they are received, generally beginning approximately 3 weeks after publication of a document, at the headquarters of the Centers for Medicare & Medicaid Services, 7500 Security Boulevard, Baltimore, Maryland 21244, Monday through Friday of each week from 8:30 a.m. to 4 p.m. To schedule an appointment to view public comments, phone 1–800–743–3951.

I. Background

The Patient Protection and Affordable Care Act (Pub. L. 111–148), hereinafter referred to as the Affordable Care Act, was enacted on March 23, 2010. Section 1103(a), as amended by section 10102(b) of the same act, directs the Secretary to immediately establish a mechanism, including an internet Web site, through which a resident of, or small business in, any State may identify affordable health insurance coverage options in that State.

In implementing these requirements, we seek to develop a Web site (hereinafter called the Web portal) that would empower consumers by increasing informed choice and promoting market competition. To achieve these ends, we intend to provide a Web portal that provides information to consumers in a clear,

salient, and easily navigated manner. We plan to minimize the use of technical language, jargon, or excessive complexity in order to promote the ability of consumers to understand the information and act in accordance with what they have learned. We will engage in careful consumer testing to identify the best methods to achieve these goals.

In obtaining information to populate the Web portal, we will be seeking all the statutorily required information from issuers, and we anticipate adopting electronic submission capabilities. As we develop the Web portal, and engage with consumers, this information will be used to create an effective consumer-friendly presentation of affordable health coverage option plans. In addition, we plan to provide information, consistent with applicable laws, in a format that is accessible for use by members of the public, allowing them to download and repackage the information, promoting innovation and the goal of consumer choice.

As we develop the Web portal, we are also seeking to balance the need to obtain information that will promote informed choice with the principles of the Paperwork Reduction Act and Executive Order 12866, which call for minimizing burdens and maximizing net benefits. To that end, we are seeking comments on how best to achieve that balance, and in particular how to reduce unnecessary burdens on the private sector.

This is an interim final rule that becomes effective May 10, 2010. We invite public comments on all relevant issues to make improvements.

A. Statutory Basis

As discussed above, Section 1103(a)of the Affordable Care Act, as amended by section 10102(b) of the same act, directs the Secretary to immediately establish a mechanism, including an internet Web site, through which a resident of, or small business in, any State may identify affordable health insurance coverage options in that State. To the extent practicable, the Web site (hereinafter called the Web portal) is to provide, at minimum, information on the following coverage options:

1. Health insurance coverage offered by health insurance issuers,

2. Medicaid coverage,

3. Children's Health Insurance Program (CHIP) coverage,

4. State health benefits high risk pool coverage,

5. Coverage under the high risk pool created by section 1101 of the Affordable Care Act, and

6. Coverage within the small group market for small businesses and their employees.

In order to provide this information in a standardized format, section 1103(b) requires the Secretary to develop a standardized format to present the coverage information described above. This format is to provide for, at a minimum, the inclusion of information on the percentage of total premium revenue expended on nonclinical costs (as reported under section 2718(a) of the Public Health Service Act), eligibility, availability, premium rates, and cost sharing with respect to such coverage options. The format must be consistent with the standards that are adopted for the uniform explanation of coverage under section 2715 of the Public Health Service Act. Defining the minimum content of the format required under section 1103(b) in effect defines what we will publish as the minimum content of the Web portal. This regulation, therefore, specifies the data that will be collected and disseminated through the Web portal in accordance with 1103(a) as amended by section 10102(b).

B. General Overview

Section 1103(a) of the Affordable Care Act, as amended by section 10102(b) of the same act, requires the establishment of a Web portal through which individuals can obtain information about the health insurance options that may be available to them in their "State." Section 1304(d) of the Affordable Care Act defines "State" to include the fifty states and the District of Columbia. The territories are not included in this definition. We therefore will interpret "State" in the Web portal context to mean the 50 States and the District of Columbia.

By statute, the Web portal must be available for public use no later than July 1, 2010. We will use the data collections and processes described in this rule to make the initial release of the Web portal available to the public on July 1, 2010, through a government sponsored Web site. We intend for the future development and updating of the Web portal to be an evolutionary process that involves all stakeholders, and we anticipate future updates, including annual and periodic revisions, to be released as the result of a continued refinement of the Web portal content.

In the July 1, 2010 release we will provide summary information about health insurance products that are available in the individual and small business markets including issuers of the products, types of products,

24472   Federal Register / Vol. 75, No. 86 / Wednesday, May 5, 2010 / Rules and Regulations

location, summaries of services offered, links to provider networks, and contact information (including Web site links and customer service telephone contact) to enable interaction with specific issuers. In addition, the Web portal will provide information on eligibility, coverage limitations and premium information for existing high risk pools operating in the States, to the extent that it is provided to us by the responding parties. It will also provide introductory information on eligibility and services for Medicaid and CHIP. We will include contact information and Web site links for the Medicaid and CHIP programs for individuals who believe that they or family members may meet eligibility criteria. In addition, we will provide information on coverage options for small businesses, including reinsurance for early retirees under section 1102 of the Affordable Care Act (which is being administered by HHS), and tax credits available under section 45R of the Internal Revenue Code, as added by section 1421 of the Affordable Care Act. We also will include Web site links to these programs so that small businesses can obtain further information.

We note that Section 1103(b)(1) requires the Secretary to present the Web portal information in a format that is consistent with the standards that are adopted for the uniform explanation of coverage under section 2715 of the Public Health Service Act (PHSA) as added by section 1001(a) of the Affordable Care Act. Section 2715 of the PHSA provides for the establishment of these standards within 12 months of the Affordable Care Act's enactment date. As a result, these standards will not be in place for the July 1, 2010 release of the Web portal. We will modify the format used to present the initial release of the Web portal to ensure Web portal consistency with these standards in accordance with the implementation schedule that is established for these standards.

In an effort to make the Web portal as comprehensive as possible, we will enhance the content over time to include more than the statutory minimum requirements that are discussed above. We will include any information that we have that we believe would be useful to consumers, such as medical loss ratios, quality and performance information, links to appropriate Web sites such as the Web site of the association that represents existing State health benefits high risk pools, and more State-specific information on Medicaid and CHIP eligibility and service coverage. Because of the complexity of pricing information and the need to incorporate pricing

engines into the Web site, detailed pricing and benefit information will be provided in the second release of the Web portal on October 1, 2010.

As we discuss in more detail in section III "Waiver of Proposed Rulemaking and the 30-Day Delay in the Effective Date," the statutory requirement for a July 1, 2010 Web portal release does not allow time for full notice and comment rulemaking. While this timeframe necessitates going directly to final, in order to maximize public input we are using an interim final rule with comment to establish the categories of information that we will collect for inclusion in the Web portal, including the data production requirements that we impose on health insurance issuers, and the data collection requests for States, associations, and high risk pools.

II. Provisions of the Interim Final Rule

A. Definitions

For any terms defined by the Affordable Care Act, including the definitions in section 1304, as well as any definitions in the Public Health Service Act that are incorporated by reference under sections 1301(b) or 1551 of the Affordable Care Act, we adopt those definitions. We discuss these definitions below. The regulatory text provides cross references to these provisions. We also explain here how we are defining the terms that are not defined in the Affordable Care Act or the PHSA. These terms are "State health benefits high risk pool," "section 1101 high risk pool," "health insurance product" and "portal plan."

Section 2791(b)(1) of the PHSA, as incorporated by reference into the Affordable Care Act, defines "health insurance coverage" as "benefits consisting of medical care (provided directly, through insurance or reimbursement, or otherwise and including items and services paid for as medical care) under any hospital or medical service policy or certificate, hospital or medical service plan contract, or health maintenance organization contract offered by a health insurance issuer." Section 2791(b)(2) in turn defines an insurance issuer (also referred to here as an "issuer") to be an entity "licensed to engage in the business of insurance in a State and which is subject to State law which regulates insurance" and specifies that it does not include a group health plan.

For purposes of the Affordable Care Act and the PHSA, a distinction is made between health insurance coverage sold to group health plans, and other health insurance coverage. The term "group

health plan," as defined in section 2791(a)(1) of the PHSA, exclusively refers to health coverage sold to group health plans. Section 1304(a)(2) of the Affordable Care Act, which adopts the identical definition as section 2791(e)(1)(A) of the PHSA, defines "individual market" as the "market for health insurance coverage offered to individuals other than in connection with a group health plan."

Section 2791(b)(5) of the PHSA in turn defines "individual health insurance coverage" as health insurance coverage "offered to individuals in the individual market, but does not include short-term limited duration insurance."

The Affordable Care Act and the PHSA further divide the group health insurance market into coverage sold to large employers (the "large group market," and coverage sold to small employers (the "small group market"). See section 1304(a)(3) of Affordable Care Act. Section 1304(b)(2) of the Affordable Care Act defines a "small employer" as, in connection with a group health plan with respect to a calendar year and a plan year, an employer who employed an average at least 1, but not more than 100 employees on business days during the preceding calendar year, and who employs at least 1 employee on the first day of the plan year. Section 1304(b)(3) of the Affordable Care Act allows for a State to elect the option to define "small employer" as an employer who employed on average at least 1, but not more than 50 employees on business days during the preceding calendar year in the case of plan years beginning before January 1, 2016. As such, for any State that elects this option, we would apply this alternate definition of "small employer" for their State for plan years beginning before January 1, 2016.

For purposes of this regulation, we will refer to health insurance coverage offered to employees of small employers in the small group market as "small group coverage."

Sections 1103(a)(2)(D) of the Affordable Care Act provides for Web portal reporting of "State health benefits high risk pools." For the purpose of this rule, we define "State health benefits high risk pools" as nonprofit organizations created by State law to offer comprehensive health coverage to individuals who otherwise would be unable to secure such coverage because of their health status. This language was adopted, with modification, from the National Association of Comprehensive Health Insurance Plans (NASCHIP) annual report. Our understanding is that this definition is generally understood to identify existing high risk pools.

Section 1103(a)(2)(E) provides for Web portal reporting of pools established pursuant to section 1101 of the Affordable Care Act. For purposes of this regulation, we define "section 1101 high risk pools" as any entity described in regulations implementing section 1101 of the Affordable Care Act.

The Affordable Care Act and the PHSA do not include the term "health insurance product." We are creating this term as a short hand reference to the information that we will publish in the first release of the Web portal. This term is needed in order to differentiate the information that will be collected for the July 1, 2010 release and the post-July 1, 2010 releases. We define "health insurance product" ("product") as a package of benefits that an issuer offers that is reported to State regulators in an insurance filing.

The Affordable Care Act and the PHSA also do not define the term "portal plan." We are creating this term to describe certain data that we will collect and disseminate in post-July 1, 2010 releases of the Web portal. We understand that consumers apply for coverage under individual health insurance products that issuers develop and market to offer a package of benefits. In applying for a package of benefits, we further understand that consumers are offered a range of cost-sharing arrangements, including deductibles and copayments but not including premium rates or premium rate quotes. As a result, each package of benefits can be paired with a multitude of cost sharing options. We will use the word "portal plan" to refer to the discrete pairing of a package of benefits with a particular cost-sharing option (not including premium rates or premium rate quotes). We will collect portal plan information for publication in post-July 1, 2010 releases of the Web portal. We believe that portal plan information is precise enough to provide a potential consumer with enough information to discern the relative costs and benefits of selecting a particular coverage option.

We welcome comments on the adequacy of these definitions, and, if applicable, suggestions to improve them.

B. Individual and Small Group Market Data Collection and Dissemination

In order to meet the mandate, we must collect information on individual and small group coverage from health insurance issuers and prepare the information to be presented publicly in a clear and concise fashion. We will have a two part rollout of the Web portal for 2010, and then annual and periodic updates to allow for the inclusion of updated data as well as consumer education content.

1. Data Submission Mandate

The Secretary currently regulates health insurance industry practices for private insurance plans offered through public programs such as Medicare, Medicaid, and CHIP. While she either has or has access to data on Federal government sponsored plans, we must issue regulations to mandate the production of the necessary information from issuers in order to fulfill the statutory mandate as it applies to private plans not offered through Federal government programs. To facilitate the development of a robust Web portal with comprehensive pricing and benefit information on individual and small group coverage, our current plan is to contract with a vendor that has a health insurance pricing engine and a related Web site with portal plan identification and comparison functionality through a full and open competition. The work on this contract will not be completed in time for the July 1, 2010 release of the Web portal. Accordingly, we will collect an initial set of data (health insurance product information) from issuers in order to present basic information on all issuers and health insurance products in the July 1, 2010 release of the Web portal. This release of the Web portal will only contain the basic information on issuers and their products in the individual and small group markets that was practicable to obtain in the constrained timeframe for meeting the statutory requirement that the Web portal be available for public use by July 1, 2010. We will provide a second release of the Web portal on October 1, 2010 with comprehensive pricing and benefit information for individual and small group coverage.

We will communicate to consumers through the Web portal and other public communication processes, such as presentations and reports to stakeholders, the names of those issuers who fail to timely meet the reporting requirements or who provide incomplete or inaccurate information.

a. July 1, 2010

To meet the July 1, 2010 deadline, we will require issuers to provide data that we will use to develop introductory information for consumers on the universe of issuers and health insurance products in their geographic area. By May 21, 2010 we will require issuers to submit corporate and contact information, such as corporate addresses and Web sites; administrative information, such as enrollment codes; enrollment data by product; product names and types, such as Preferred Provider Organization (PPO) or Health Maintenance Organization (HMO); whether enrollment is currently open for each product; geographic availability information, such as product availability by zip code or county; customer service phone numbers; Web site links to the issuer Web site, brochure documents such as benefit summaries, and provider networks; and financial ratings, such as those offered by financial rating firms including AM Best, Standard and Poor, and Moody's, if available.

We invite comment on whether enrollment information is considered by issuers to be confidential business information.

We are aware that some issuers are rated on their financial status and other performance measures. We considered excluding issuers with no or low financial ratings from firms such as AM Best, Standard and Poor, and Moody. However, it is our understanding that not all issuers seek financial ratings, and that the private firms that conduct them do not use standardized approaches. Therefore, we will instead require each issuer to submit information on whether they obtained a financial rating, from which firm, and what the rating is. We will use this information to help analyze whether such ratings are or could be useful in conveying meaningful differences to consumers. For the same purpose we will allow, but not require issuers to report other types of ratings they have received, such as ratings from The National Committee for Quality Assurance (NCQA) Accreditation.

Certain administrative information that we are collecting, such as an issuer's technical contact information (that is, the person who will work directly with us and our contractors to submit and validate data), tax identification number, and enrollment count in an issuer's products, will be used to support the structure of the database in which this information will be warehoused so that the data can be easily retrieved to support uploading information to the Web portal test site, and so that issuers and their portal plans can be reliably recognized by HHS and issuers and counted to support analyses for improving the Web portal. This information will also be used to support analysis necessary to improve the meaningfulness and usefulness of the Web portal in future releases. In addition, certain contact information will allow the Federal government and its contractors to provide useful updates and reminders to issuers and to provide technical support.

Data submitted under the requirements contained in this regulation must be submitted by issuers in accordance with instructions issued by the Secretary.

b. October 1, 2010

We will release a more comprehensive version of the Web portal on October 1, 2010. This version will include benefit and pricing information. Benefit and pricing information includes data such as premiums, cost-sharing options, types of services covered, coverage limitations, and exclusions.

We note that for States in which premiums are not community rated, the premium data that we intend to collect will include manual rates that represent only standard risks. As a result of medical underwriting, issuers may charge individuals rates that are above the manual rate based on the applicant's health status. We recognize that there is not a feasible method for collecting or displaying information on the rate that an individual who is underwritten might actually be charged, and in the absence of that are proposing to provide information on the manual rates with the understanding that they do not represent actual premium rates that an individual may be charged.

While the initial release of the Web portal will list all issuers and all health insurance products, we believe that it would confuse users if we were to display portal plans that are not open for enrollment. Furthermore, we believe that it is inappropriate to impose a pricing and benefits information reporting burden on issuers for products and portal plans that are not open for enrollment. Therefore, we will exempt issuers of products and portal plans that are not open to new enrollments from additional pricing and benefits reporting requirements. Such issuers will be required to provide the data defined under the May 21 collection to assure we have the universe of issuers and their health insurance products.

In the event that an issuer establishes new products or new portal plans under a product, or opens enrollment in products or portal plans under a product that was previously closed to enrollment, we will require the submission of the pricing and benefits information within 30 days of offering new, or newly re-opened to enrollment, products or portal plans.

We considered excluding issuers with minimal market share from the benefits and cost sharing data collection. However, we believe that some of the

portal plans offered by these issuers serve niche markets that would be particularly appealing to some consumers. At this time, we will include portal plans with minimal market share, but we will collect enrollment data for use in analyzing the effect, if any, of market share and our ability to meet consumer needs.

The intent of the Web portal is to present consumers with the full range of meaningful insurance options available to them. We believe this will be best accomplished through providing all plans that have a non-de minimus portion of the issuer's enrollment in an area and allowing for additional plans to be submitted based on the issuers perception of need. Our initial overview of the market indicates that most areas have coverage which is concentrated in a limited number of portal plans. One percent of an issuers' enrollment in the service area was seen as a reasonable cut off balancing the consumer's right to know with the burden imposed on issuers. Therefore, for each zip code, issuers will be required to submit information on at least all portal plans that are open for enrollment and that represent 1 percent or more of the issuer's total enrollment for the respective individual or small group market within that zip code.

We invite comments from the public on what information should be required from issuers to ensure consumer access to meaningful information about coverage options is included in the Web portal, and on the ways that information should be presented to allow for sorting and comparing portal plans. We are particularly interested in comments from consumers, to make certain that the Web portal meets the needs of those individuals who will use it as part of their health coverage decision making.

The data submissions for the October 1, 2010 Web portal release will be due by September 3, 2010. Data must be submitted by issuers in accordance with instructions issued by the Secretary.

c. Future Updates

After the initial data collection efforts described in the prior two subsections, we will require issuers to perform an annual verification and update of the data they submitted. In addition, we recognize that many issuers update pricing and benefit information for their portal plans more frequently than annually, and we therefore will require issuers to submit updated data whenever they change premiums, cost-sharing, types of services covered, coverage limitations, or exclusions for one or more of their individual or small group portal plans. Furthermore, we

will require issuers that develop new health insurance products between annual verifications to submit pricing and benefit information for the new product within 30 days of opening enrollment.

Finally, while not included in the statutory list of minimum requirements for the Web portal, we will collect from issuers and report on the Web portal in 2011 the following performance ratings: percent of individual market and small group market policies that are rescinded; the percent of individual market policies sold at the manual rate; the percent of claims that are denied under individual market and small group market policies; and the number and disposition of appeals on denials to insure, pay claims and provide required preauthorizations.

Updated data, including the required data updates previously discussed and annual verifications, must be submitted by issuers in accordance with instructions issued by the Secretary in a future Paperwork Reduction Act Package.

d. Data Validation

All data that is collected for the July 1, 2010, October 1, 2010, and future releases of the Web portal will be validated by the issuers to assure the information they provided is correct. We will require the issuer's CEO or CFO to electronically certify to the completeness and accuracy of the initial data collection for the October 1, 2010 release of the Web portal and for any future updates to these requirements. Following the submission of the data, we will provide issuers with access to preview the data that we will publish on the Web portal. They will also be provided with access to edit their data submissions to update or correct information.

2. Voluntary Data Submission by States

We are requesting that States submit data on issuer corporate and contact information for licensed issuers in their State, such as corporate addresses and Web sites; underwriting status, such as whether or not premium rates in the individual market are determined based on medical underwriting or community rating; and information on any public Web sites administered by the State that provide consumer guidance on individual and small group health insurance coverage in their State.

It is our understanding that States possess the issuer corporate and contact information we are requesting them to submit as a result of their filing requirements for regulated issuers. We are requesting that States voluntarily submit issuer corporate and contact information because we believe that it is incumbent upon us to ensure that we provide information on the entire universe of issuers and health insurance products. Gathering these data from both States and issuers will help us in determining the universe and ensure that we are not inadvertently excluding an issuer or product as a result of incomplete data collection.

The underwriting information and Web site links we are requesting from States will be included on the Web portal in an effort to develop consumer education content and incorporate (by way of linking) any State-developed information on insurance coverage options in a given State. We recognize that some States may have already developed Web portals that provide comprehensive information about health insurance coverage in their State, and we will link to that information if it is available.

In asking States to provide the data identified above, we note that the information would improve the accuracy and scope of the information we can provide to consumers in each of the States. We expect that States will want to ensure full access to information about issuers, health insurance products and portal plans to their residents. We believe that doing so would support consumer choice and a more robust marketplace for insurance. We therefore anticipate that States will be responsive to this request because the information requested will enhance the ability of the citizens of each State to identify affordable options for insurance.

3. Data Dissemination

We will disseminate the information collected as a result of our data submission mandates as described above, as well as other information about health insurance coverage in the individual and small group market that may be useful to the public.

a. July 1, 2010

On July 1, 2010 the Web portal will include information on the data collected as a result of the May 21, 2010 data submission mandate outlined above, including information for consumers on the issuers that sell individual and small group products in their area and links to benefit information for those products. In addition, we will provide some consumer education information on the individual market, including describing how it operates and why its offerings might be appropriate for a consumer, as well as information that will facilitate

health insurance coverage decision-making and increased understanding of how the Web portal operates in the context of the Affordable Care Act. We also will include information for small businesses on the small group market, including information on the reinsurance and tax credit programs discussed previously.

b. October 1, 2010

On October 1, 2010 the Web portal will include expanded content that will incorporate the data collected as a result of the September 3, 2010 data submission mandate outlined above with the data collected for the May 21, 2010 mandate previously discussed. Using the pricing and benefit information gathered as a result of the September 3rd collection, we will display portal plans as packages of benefits and cost sharing, with associated premiums, based on geographic availability.

The display of portal plans will be driven by interactive functionality that accounts for geographic and personal demographic information such as State and zip code of residence, sex, family composition, smoking status and other health indicators. We intend for the order and layering of search results to be based on consumer choice parameters such as range of premium, high and low deductibles, ranges of out-of-pocket maximums, provider network, and indicators of market interest in the product including enrollment. We intend that consumers will also have the ability to select on all available issuers and portal plans and view them alphabetically.

We invite comments on the sort and selection functionality of the Web portal, and on the order and layering of portal plans that we will display.

Certain administrative data collected for the October 1 Web portal release will not be displayed directly on the Web portal but these data are important to the functionality of a pricing engine, such as input data that defines the geographic and demographic variables that affect premium price and cost sharing that will be displayed on the Web portal.

We also will retain and enhance the consumer education content established for the July 1, 2010 Web portal release.

c. Future Updates

We will update the portal plan pricing and benefit information as frequently as monthly to reflect updates that issuers submit as a result of changes to their portal plans. As discussed previously, because issuers may update pricing and benefit information more frequently

than annually, we are requiring updated data submissions whenever an issuer changes the premiums, cost-sharing, types of services covered, coverage limitations, or exclusions for one or more of their individual or small group portal plans. Our monthly updates will also reflect these updates. Consumer education content will be updated periodically in the event that new and pertinent information about either of these markets becomes available that would be beneficial for a consumer to know.

In addition, we are required by section 1103(b)(1) to provide information on the percentage of total premium revenue expended on nonclinical costs, as reported under section 2718(a) of the Public Health Service Act (PHSA). We will report medical loss ratios to meet this requirement, which will provide more than the minimally required information and is believed to be more useful to the public. Section 2718 of the PHSA requires issuers to report this information to HHS beginning with plan years starting on or after September 23, 2010, and the Secretary is promulgating rules on these reporting requirements. After the regulations for this provision are implemented, we anticipate including medical loss ratio information on the Web portal.

As discussed previously, we anticipate including portal plan performance rating information, such as percent of individual market and small group market policies that are rescinded, the percent of individual market policies sold at the manual rate, the percent of claims that are denied under individual market and small group market policies, and the number and disposition of appeals, on the Web portal in the future.

We also anticipate posting information derived from standards and reporting obligations that will apply to insurance sold under the exchanges. For example, we might post information on issuers' financial stability, trends in enrollment and disenrollment, appeals and grievances, and other indicators of fiscal viability, customer service and policy-holder satisfaction.

The Affordable Care Act directs the Secretary to develop quality measures and standards to inform the public about quality of care and to drive improvements in the service delivery system. When such measures and standards become available they will be incorporated into the Web portal.

We invite comments on the content of futures updates to the Web portal, including the frequency of updates, the inclusion of performance rating information, and the incorporation of quality measures and standards.

C. Information to be Collected and Disseminated on High Risk Pool Coverage

Sections 1103(a)(2)(D) and (E) of the Affordable Care Act requires HHS to include information about State health benefits high risk pools and high risk pools established under section 1101 of the Affordable Care Act. In order to fulfill this mandate, HHS must establish a mechanism for collecting and preparing this information for public dissemination in a clear and concise fashion.

1. Data Submission Request

Pursuant to the requirement that the Web portal include information on coverage through these high risk pools, this rule requests that certain information on State health benefits high risk pools and high risk pools that will operate under authority established in section 1101 of the Affordable Care Act be reported.

a. July 1, 2010

We will ask the National Association of State Comprehensive Health Insurance Plans (NASCHIP) for information about State health benefit high risk pools. This information will include administrative and contact information, such as a customer service phone number and a Web site for pool information; pool eligibility information, such as state residency and health condition requirements; pool coverage limitations, such as restrictive riders; and pool premium information, such as rules and restrictions for premium subsidy programs. We understand that this information is currently collected and maintained by NASCHIP, and that all of the existing State health benefits high risk pools are members of NASCHIP. As such, we believe that NASCHIP is strategically equipped to work with the State health benefits high risk pools to gather and transmit data to HHS on behalf of State health benefits high risk pools. Therefore, we will ask NASCHIP to provide the data as discussed above by May 21, 2010.

b. Future Updates

We understand that coverage that is offered by State health benefits high risk pools is updated on an annual calendar-year basis. We will therefore ask NASCHIP to provide annual updates of the information that we will request for the May 21, 2010 data collection. If NASCHIP is unable to provide this information in the future, we will ask

State health benefits high risk pools to provide this information.

Because the initial release of the Web portal is July 1, 2010, which is in the middle of a calendar-year, we will initiate the annual update data submission requests in the fall of 2010.

In addition, we request that any State health benefits high risk pool that is established after May 21, 2010, including any high risk pool established pursuant to section 1101 of the Affordable Care Act, report the requested information within 30 days of when the pool begins accepting enrollment, and then annually thereafter.

2. Data Dissemination

a. July 1, 2010

The July 1, 2010 release of the Web portal will include eligibility, coverage limitations and premium information as collected under the request as described above, as well as consumer education content that would aid consumer understanding about high risk pools generally, and whether such pools might offer a potential source of coverage for them.

b. Future Updates

Future updates to the high risk pool content of the Web portal will include updates to the eligibility, coverage, and premium information requested above. These updates may include data for new high risk pools that are established subsequent to the July 1, 2010 release of the Web portal, including those established pursuant to section 1101 of the Affordable Care Act. We understand NASCHIP intends to build a Web site to contain detailed information that today is only available in NASCHIP's hard copy annual report. We will therefore also provide a link to a NASCHIP Web site in a future release in order to provide even more comprehensive information on those State health benefits high risk pools that are represented by NASCHIP.

D. Information to be Disseminated on Medicaid and CHIP

Sections 1103(a)(2)(B) and (C) of the Affordable Care Act require that Medicaid and CHIP information be included on the Web portal. Title XIX of the Social Security Act, the law governing the Medicaid program, has allowed States broad discretion over Medicaid eligibility policy and therefore, Medicaid eligibility varies widely across States. In general, Medicaid eligibility is dependent on categorical and income requirements. Title XXI of the Social Security Act outlines the eligibility rules in CHIP,

and such eligibility requirements are generally based on certain income requirements for children under age 19. There are instances where pregnant women and parents can be eligible for CHIP. The Affordable Care Act simplifies Medicaid and CHIP income eligibility rules for most populations beginning January 2014. In the meantime, individuals will need to directly contact their State programs for definitive determinations of their eligibility or for their family members. However, the Web portal can serve as a resource to educate potential beneficiaries that they or their family members may be eligible for Medicaid and CHIP and provide information about how they can contact their State programs to determine eligibility and services available to them. The portal will serve as a resource for understanding what their State Medicaid and CHIP programs generally cover and how to apply for benefits.

To implement sections 1103(a)(2)(B) and (C) we will provide information guiding consumers on general eligibility criteria for the individual State programs in an effort to assist them in assessing the need to pursue the application processes for these programs. There are no new reporting requirements to support implementation of this section. The data will come from existing Federal sources. The Web portal will also be designed to offer links to the various State Medicaid and CHIP agencies in order to facilitate consumers' submission of program applications.

For each eligibility category, the Web portal will present information regarding the services that are available to eligible applicants. General cost sharing requirements will also be presented on the Web portal, to the extent that they are permitted for the eligibility category in these programs.

In order to provide this information, data are being compiled within CMS across all Medicaid and CHIP eligibility categories regarding the services available under each program. This includes both mandatory and optional Medicaid services for which States receive Federal funding as defined in each State Medicaid plan and any waiver of such plan, as well as the services available under each State's CHIP plan and any waiver of such plan. Mandatory services are specific services States are required to cover for certain groups of Medicaid beneficiaries, both adults and children under the age of 21. Each required service is defined in Federal regulations 42 CFR part 440. Optional Medicaid services are defined as those services not required by Federal

Federal Register / Vol. 75, No. 86 / Wednesday, May 5, 2010 / Rules and Regulations   **24477**

law that States may elect to provide Medicaid beneficiaries. Optional services are also defined in Federal regulation at 42 CFR part 440. CHIP regulations define mandatory and optional services at 42 CFR part 457.

The portal will include data elements for mandatory services for each mandatory and optional categorical group defined in each Medicaid State plan, such as: Inpatient hospital care (excluding inpatient services in institutions for mental disease for working age adults); outpatient hospital care; physician's services; nurse midwife services; pediatric and family nurse practitioner services; laboratories and x-ray services; rural health clinic services including Federally qualified health centers ("FQHC") and if permitted by State law, rural health clinic and other ambulatory services provided by a rural health clinic which are otherwise included under a State Medicaid plan; prenatal care and family planning services, skilled nursing facility services for persons over age 21, home health care services for persons over 21 who are eligible for skilled nursing services (includes medical supplies and equipment), early and periodic screening, diagnosis, and treatment for persons under age 21 ("EPSDT"), necessary transportation services, and vaccines for children.

If States include optional services in their Medicaid State plan, they must be provided in a manner that is consistent with all Federal requirements. The Web portal will include data elements to reflect the availability of optional services such as home health therapy services, rehabilitative services, case management services, medical or remedial care services or other licensed practitioners (chiropractors, podiatrists, optometrist, psychologists and nurse anesthetists), smoking cessation services and palliative care for children in each State Medicaid plan. Additional program specific service information will be provided with regard to Demonstration programs designed by States under the authority of section 1115 of the Social Security Act as well as services provided through the Children's Health Insurance Program.

Appropriate information on a specific State's Demonstration programs, including variations in eligibility, coverage and service delivery systems used under the Demonstrations, will also be provided on the portal. Demonstrations that are Statewide or high impact, meaning that they have a significant penetration in the market and serve more than a narrow coverage group, will also be included in the initial release of the Web portal. Other

Demonstration programs in Medicaid and CHIP will be added in future releases.

Additionally, the Web portal will provide information to consumers on the Home and Community-Based Waiver program (Section 1915(c) of the Act), including a broad range of State defined services that enable independence in a consumer's own home.

All of the above data will be derived from sources internal to CMS and include Medicaid State Plan Amendments, CHIP State Plans, CHIP annual reports, home and community based waivers applications and renewals, 1115 Demonstration documents, and the contacts database used for *http://www.cms.gov* which includes consumer contacts to state Medicaid and CHIP program offices. We are not collecting any new data elements for the Medicaid and CHIP portions of the Web portal under the authorities that were granted to us under section 1103 of the Affordable Care Act. All information will come from data that CMS already collects for program management and administration purposes.

Certain State-based variations in Medicaid and CHIP programs, such as specific income and resource disregards, and variations in services, such as limits on the number of visits, cannot be presented with a high degree of detail in early releases of the Web portal. We expect to list the services and note that there are limitations, giving consumers enough information to ask questions of the State program if they pursue an application to enroll.

Finally, while a significant amount of data is being compiled to populate the Web portal, some of the data for the Medicaid and CHIP portion will be presented in an aggregated format to enhance public understanding. For example, eligibility categories may be collapsed together for purposes of maximizing public understanding. By way of example, there are several working disabled eligibility categories in Medicaid that inter-relate. We would expect, given the complexity of these definitions, that consumers may have difficulty fully understanding these categories. Therefore, we are presenting the public with summary-level information, such as collapsing information about the working disabled into one category.

III. Waiver of Proposed Rulemaking and the 30-Day Delay in the Effective Date

We ordinarily publish a notice of proposed rulemaking in the **Federal**

Register and invite public comment on the proposed rule in accordance with 5 U.S.C. 553(b) of the Administrative Procedure Act (APA). The notice of proposed rulemaking includes a reference to the legal authority under which the rule is proposed, and the terms and substances of the proposed rule or a description of the subjects and issues involved. This procedure can be waived, however, if an agency finds good cause for concluding that a notice-and-comment procedure is impracticable, unnecessary, or contrary to the public interest and incorporates a statement of the finding and its reasons in the rule issued. Section 1103(a), as amended by section 10102(b), and section 1103(b) of the Affordable Care Act provide for the establishment by July 1, 2010 of a Web portal through which a resident or small business of any State may identify affordable health insurance coverage options in that State. In order to meet this mandate, we have to collect and prepare for dissemination a broad array of data on issuers, health insurance products, and plans, including administrative and product information for the individual and small group markets; information on eligibility and coverage limits for high risk pools; and information on eligibility and services for Medicaid and CHIP. This cannot be accomplished unless issuers are made aware of the data submission requirements in short order and States, associations and high risk pools are made aware of opportunities to aide in this information dissemination effort within the established narrow timeframes. In order to allow sufficient time for data submission and validation prior to public presentation, we must be in possession of the data that is to be included on the Web portal in the July 1, 2010 release no later than May 21, 2010.

As a result of this data collection timeline, it is impracticable to issue a notice of proposed rulemaking prior to publishing a final rule that would implement these data production requirements. Therefore, we find good cause to waive notice and comment rulemaking, and we are proceeding with issuing this final rule on an interim basis. We are providing a 30-day public comment period.

In addition, we ordinarily provide a 30-day delay in the effective date of the provisions of an interim final rule. While the Administrative Procedures Act (5 U.S.C. 551 *et seq.*) generally requires the publication of a substantive rule not less than thirty days prior to its effective date, agencies may establish a shorter time frame based on good cause.

5 U.S.C. 553(d)(3). In accordance with the good cause basis explained below, these regulations are effective on May 10, 2010.

Section 1103(a) of the Affordable Care Act requires the public release of the Web portal on July 1, 2010. As shown below, a sequenced order of activities must be completed in order to meet this statutory deadline.

Data will be uploaded into the database supporting the Web portal to populate the Web portal test site, and based on observations adjustments to the actual Web site may be made. Any problems with the actual data would be adjusted as well. This is a four week iterative process that continues until the test site is functioning and presenting data output as expected, which begins with the first data upload on June 3 and ends with the release of the Web portal on July 1.

Prior to this, the data that is submitted must be formatted in preparation for upload to the database that supports the Web portal test site. First upload to the test site takes approximately two days, from June 1 to June 3. There can be subsequent uploads through June 14, as noted below.

Prior to this, beginning May 21, we must have time to view the submitted data to assure it is complete and clean. At this same time we believe that the regulated parties should be offered an opportunity to validate the data they submit and resubmit any erroneous data. We believe that the minimum time required to accomplish such work is three weeks, which brings us to June 14, 2010. There is a 10 day overlap between this process and the two processes described above.

Prior to this, we must afford those submitting the data with adequate time to gather and submit the data. We believe that the minimum time that should be provided for this work is 7 business days from May 12 through to May 21, 2010.

In order to submit that data, these parties will need to establish accounts that will allow secure data entry into the data collection tool. This will entail approximately 3 business days from May 10 to May 12.

Furthermore, we anticipate that these parties will need training and guidance on gathering data, obtaining an account and entering data. This will include a webinar on or about May 7 and other technical support through a help desk. This collection of activities would take at least 4 business days which brings us to May 12, 2010.

Thus, in order to meet the statutory deadline of July 1, 2010, the processes described above must commence no later than May 10, 2010.

Furthermore, certain activities had to occur within the agency prior to our being able to publish a rule to implement the Web portal requirements, or enter the contracts necessary to support work under this rule. The Affordable Care Act was enacted on March 23, 2010. We immediately established a workgroup to analyze policy options and the contractual and regulatory needs of the Web portal program. This work was completed on April 22. We then commenced task-specific workgroups to draft the necessary documents, including this regulation, and to procure the initial contractors. While these activities would usually take at least 6 months we have accomplished them in just under six weeks. It was impossible to have accomplished this work any faster, and the brief timeframe between the publication of this document and the effective date of its provisions could not have been avoided through more diligent use of time by the individuals working to implement this mandate.

To afford a full thirty days between publication and the effective date we would be have to hold the parties submitting the data and ourselves to inadequate timeframes in which to accomplish the necessary tasks. The timeframes and dates described above therefore establish good cause for an effective date that is fewer than thirty days after publication.

We will accept comments on the content of this regulation until June 4, 2010. This schedule will allow for a ten day comment period prior to the initial reporting requirement under these regulations.

IV. Collection of Information Requirements

In accordance with section 3507(j) of the Paperwork Reduction Act of 1995 (44 U.S.C. 3501 *et seq.*), the information collection included in this interim rule have been submitted for emergency approval to the Office of Management and Budget (OMB). OMB has assigned control number 0938–1086 to the information collection requirements.

Under the Paperwork Reduction Act of 1995, we are required to provide 60-day notice in the **Federal Register** and solicit public comment before a collection of information requirement is submitted to the Office of Management and Budget (OMB) for review and approval. In order to fairly evaluate whether an information collection should be approved by OMB, section 3506(c)(2)(A) of the Paperwork

Reduction Act of 1995 requires that we solicit comment on the following issues:

• The need for the information collection and its usefulness in carrying out the proper functions of our agency.
• The accuracy of our estimate of the information collection burden.
• The quality, utility, and clarity of the information to be collected.
• Recommendations to minimize the information collection burden on the affected public, including automated collection techniques.

We are soliciting public comment on each of these issues for the following sections of this document that contain information collection requirements (ICRs):

ICRs Regarding Data Submission for the Individual and Small Group Markets (§ 159.120)

Section 159.120(a) requires health insurance issuers (issuers), in accordance with guidance issued by the Secretary, to submit corporate and contact information; administrative information; enrollment data by health insurance product; health insurance product name and type; whether enrollment is currently open for each health insurance product; geographic availability information; customer service phone numbers; and Web site links to the issuer Web site, brochure documents, and provider networks; and financial ratings on or before May 21, 2010, and annually thereafter. The information must be submitted via a template furnished by the Secretary. The burden associated with these reporting requirements is both the time and effort necessary to review the regulations, analyze data, and train issuer staff and the time and effort necessary for an issuer to compile the necessary information, to download and complete the template, and to submit the required information. We estimate that this requirement affects 650 issuers. We believe it will take each issuer 30 hours to review the regulations, analyze data, and train its staff on how to comply with the requirements. The total one-time burden associated with this requirement is 19,500 hours. The estimated cost associated with complying with this part of the requirement is $1,950,000.

Based on our experience with Medicare Part C, we also estimate that each issuer will submit information on 9 of its portal plans and that it will take each issuer a total of 19 minutes to download the information submission template, complete the template, and submit the template. The estimated annual burden associated with the requirements in § 159.120 is 206 hours.

The estimate cost associated with complying with these requirements is $13,390.

Section 159.120(b) requires issuers, in accordance with the guidance issued by the Secretary, to submit pricing and benefit data for their portal plans on or before September 3, 2010, and annually thereafter. The information must be submitted via a template furnished by the Secretary. The burden associated with this requirement is the time and effort necessary for issuers to compile and submit pricing and benefit information. We estimate that it will take each of the 650 issuers 533 minutes to comply with these requirements. The total annual burden associated with these requirements is 51,968 hours. The estimated cost associated with complying with these requirements is $3,377,920.

Section 159.120(c) requires issuers to submit updated pricing and benefit data

for their portal plans whenever they change premiums, cost-sharing, types of services covered, coverage limitations, or exclusions for one or more of their individual or small group portal plans. Section 159.120(d) requires issuers to submit pricing and benefit data for portal plans associated with products that are newly open or reopened for enrollment within 30 days of opening for enrollment. Each submission would include a certification on the completeness and accuracy of the submission. The burden associated with these requirements is the time and effort necessary for an issuer to submit the aforementioned data. While these requirements are subject to the PRA, we do not have sufficient data to estimate the associated burden. We do not know the frequency with which issuers will make the aforementioned updates. For that reason, we are estimating a total burden of 1 hour for these requirements.

The estimate of one hour acknowledges that there is a burden associated with this requirement. The total estimated annual burden to industry associated with these updates is 13,000 hours, or 20 hours per issuer. This estimate is based on a three times a year, 19 minute per batch response update. The total cost associated with this requirement is $845,000.

Section 159.120(e) requires issuers to annually verify the data submitted under § 159.120(a) through (d). Section 159.120(f) requires issuers to submit administrative data on product and performance rating information for future releases of the Web portal in accordance with guidance issued by the Secretary. While these requirements are subject to the PRA, we will seek OMB approval at a later date under notice and comment periods separate from this interim final rule with comment.

TABLE 1—RECORDKEEPING AND REPORTING BURDEN

Regulation section(s)	OMB control No.	Respondents	Responses	Burden per response (hours)	Total annual burden (hours)	Hourly labor cost of reporting ($)	Total labor cost of reporting ($)	Total capital/maintenance costs ($)	Total cost ($)
§ 159.120(a)	0938–1086	650	650	30	19,500	100	1,950,000	0	1,950,000
	....	650	650	.317	206	65	13,390	0	13,390
§ 159.120(b)	0938–1086	650	650	4	52,000	65	3,380,000	....	3,380,000
§ 159.120(c) and (d)	0938–1086	650	13,000	1	13,000	65	845,000	0	845,000
Total	....	650	14,950	....	84,706	....	....	....	6,188,390

This interim final rule imposes information collection requirements as outlined in the regulation text and specified above. However, this interim final rule also makes reference to several associated information collections that are not discussed in the regulation text contained in this document. The following is a discussion of these information collections.

State Data Submissions

As previously stated in Section II.B.2 of the preamble of this interim final rule, we are requesting that States, in accordance with guidance issued by the Secretary, submit issuer corporate and contact information, underwriting status, and information on any State-administered Web sites that provide consumer information on health insurance coverage in their State by May 21, 2010. The information must be submitted via a template furnished by the Secretary.

The burden associated with these voluntary reporting requests is both the time and effort necessary to review the regulations, analyze data, and train issuer staff and the time and effort necessary for an issuer to compile the

necessary information, to download and complete the template, and to submit the required information. We estimate that this request affects all 50 States and the District of Columbia. We believe it will take each State 10 hours to review the preamble discussion, analyze data, and train its staff on how to comply with the request. The total one-time burden associated with this request is 500 hours. The total estimated cost associated with complying with this part of the requirement is $50,000.

We further estimate that it will take each State a total of 10 minutes to download the information submission template, complete the template, and submit the template. The estimated annual burden associated with this request is 8 hours. The estimated cost associated with complying with this request is $520.

Data Submissions for High Risk Pools

As discussed in section II.C.1 of the preamble of this interim final rule, we are asking the National Association of State Comprehensive Health Insurance Plans (NASCHIP) to provide data pertaining to the information listed in section II.C.1., in accordance with

guidance issued by the Secretary, no later than May 21, 2010. In the event that NSACHIP is unable to provide this information, State health benefits high risk pools have been asked to submit it to HHS. While this request is subject to the PRA, we anticipate that this information will be collected from NASCHIP. Therefore, we are not assigning any burden to these entities within the first year of this collection.

In section II.C.1, we also request that NASCHIP or State health benefits high risk pools submit annual updates on the aforementioned information. While these requests are subject to the PRA, we will seek OMB approval at a later date under notice and comment periods separate from this interim final rule with comment.

Similarly, in the case of a high risk pool established under section 1101 of the Affordable Care Act, we are requesting that the pool submit to HHS the aforementioned information within thirty days of accepting enrollment and then annually thereafter. While these requests are subject to the PRA, we will seek OMB approval at a later date under notice and comment periods separate from this interim final rule with comment.

All of the information collection requirements contained in this interim final rule were submitted to the Office of Management and Budget (OMB) for emergency review and approval as part of a single information collection request (ICR). As part of the emergency review and approval process, OMB waived the notification requirements. The ICR was approved under OMB control number 0938–1086 with an expiration date of October 31, 2010. However, we are still seeking public comments on the information collection requirements discussed in this interim final rule with comment. All comments will be considered as we continue to develop the ICR as we must resubmit the ICR to obtain a standard 3-year approval.

If you comment on these information collection and recordkeeping requirements, please do either of the following:

1. Submit your comments electronically as specified in the **ADDRESSES** section of this rule; or

2. Submit your comments to the Office of Information and Regulatory Affairs, Office of Management and Budget,

Attention: CMS Desk Officer, DHHS–9997–IFC.

Fax: (202) 395–6974; or *E-mail:* OIRA_submission@omb.eop.gov.

V. Response to Comments

Because of the large number of public comments we normally receive on **Federal Register** documents, we are not able to acknowledge or respond to them individually. We will consider all comments we receive by the date and time specified in the **DATES** section of this preamble, and, when we proceed with a subsequent document, we will respond to the comments in the preamble to that document.

VI. Regulatory Impact Statement

We have examined the impacts of this rule as required by Executive Order 12866 (September 1993, Regulatory Planning and Review), the Regulatory Flexibility Act (RFA) (September 19, 1980, Pub. L. 96–354), section 1102(b) of the Social Security Act, the Unfunded Mandates Reform Act of 1995 (Pub. L. 104–4), Executive Order 13132 on Federalism, and the Congressional Review Act (5 U.S.C. 804(2)).

Executive Order 12866 directs agencies to assess all costs and benefits of available regulatory alternatives and, if regulation is necessary, to select regulatory approaches that maximize net benefits (including potential

economic, environmental, public health and safety effects, distributive impacts, and equity). A regulatory impact analysis (RIA) must be prepared for major rules with economically significant effects ($100 million or more in any 1 year). As discussed below, we have concluded that this rule does not have economic impacts of $100 million or more or otherwise meet the definitions of "significant rule" under EO 12866.

Based primarily on data that we have obtained from the National Association of Insurance Commissioners (NAIC), we believe that there are about 650 insurance firms that sell insurance in the individual and small group markets and are hence subject to this interim final rule. This estimate is consistent with other data on the size of the health insurance industry estimated by HHS in previous rulemakings. In addition, about 50 States and other governmental entities will be encouraged to provide voluntarily administrative data on Medicaid and CHIP and (as applicable) data on high risk pool programs. We estimate that on average these approximately 700 respondents will spend 40 hours of time reading this rule, determining what information sources will be used to respond, determining how to provide that information in the newly required formats, and completing a certification on the completeness and accuracy of the information. Assuming that high level staff (for example, managers, attorneys, actuaries, and senior IT professionals) are involved in these efforts, at an average compensation cost of $100 an hour, total one-time costs will be approximately $3 million dollars. Actual provision of data we estimate to cost approximately $3 million a year both in the first year and annually thereafter. Federal government planning, oversight, preparation, and maintenance of the portal web site we estimate to cost $11 million in one-time costs in 2010, and $12 million to oversee and operate in 2011 and annually thereafter. In total, we estimate costs in calendar 2010 to be approximately $17 million, and annual costs thereafter to be approximately $15 million. Additional detail on these estimates can be found in the Paperwork Reduction Act section of this preamble and we welcome comment on them.

All or virtually all of the information needed for the Web portal is standard information that is already made available to individuals, insurance agents, or existing IT contractors with pricing engines and other entities that sell or otherwise provide health insurance to individuals and small groups. For example, information on

deductibles, coverage, cost-sharing, and catastrophic protection limits is routinely available on all or virtually all insurance available to individuals or small groups. Nothing in this rule requires preparation of entirely new information. In essence, we simply require that relatively comprehensive information be provided in standardized formats so that plan comparisons can be automated in ways that present comparable information in comparable levels of detail to facilitate consumer understanding of available choices. We believe that carriers that offer large numbers of plans will find that once they have determined how best to provide the data for a few of those plans, adding additional plans will involve very little if any additional cost. We have also limited the number of plans on which carriers will be required to provide data. Because we appreciate that the time schedule provided in the statute is extremely short, and because the Federal government itself needs time to prepare and populate its Web portal, we have provided for two data submissions in 2010, the first in May and a second more detailed collection in September. This will provide the Federal government with the time needed to competitively bid for a contractor that has a sophisticated pricing engine, as well as for issuers and States time to plan for and compile some of the more detailed information that we are deferring until later in the year.

Nothing in this interim final rule prevents other parties from aggregating and presenting similar information. For example, the State of Massachusetts already presents essentially the entire set of information we will obtain, and more, on its Connector Web site. Several online firms aggregate and present information for some of the policies sold in all or most States. Many insurance brokers and agents, and some consumer organizations, present information on subsets of plans available to their client target groups in their geographic areas. In fact, the Web portal we will provide may facilitate such efforts and improve the scope and accuracy of information provided by alternative sources.

As specified in the statute, our Web portal will include the range of insurance coverage options available to individuals or small businesses, including both public (for example, Medicaid, CHIP, and high risk pool) and private plans, and all types of plans including health maintenance organization, preferred provider organization and indemnity plans. To the best of our knowledge no web sites include such a broad range of health care coverage and specific plan information on a national scale, with the intent of serving such a broad range of consumers needing health insurance coverage. (There are, however, similarly broad portals for some specific population groups, such as Medicare beneficiaries and Federal employees).

It is difficult if not impossible to quantify the benefits of such a broad expansion of consumer information. Moreover, the benefits of this information will change over time, most importantly as State-specific insurance exchanges expand their presence. We do believe, however, that the benefits of improved information will facilitate informed consumer choices as well as benefit the insurance market more broadly. We expect that our Web portal will inform State decisions on the design of exchanges both by positive example and, doubtless, through ideas on ways to improve on the information and formats and tools we provide. Among the likely effects of this effort will be increased use of State high risk insurance pools, increased sale of private policies to uninsured individuals, increased enrollment in Medicaid and CHIP, and commensurate reductions in spending on care for the uninsured. We believe, however, that the most important effect of the Web portal will be to improve health insurance coverage choices. For example, private plans that offer better benefit packages at lower premium costs are likely to benefit from improved consumer information.

We have considered a range of alternatives to the Web portal approach we describe in this final rule with comment, including both more and less ambitious efforts. For example, we could provide less complete information on health insurance coverage choices, and rely on States and private efforts to provide more complete comparisons. In our view, however, costs would not be significantly less were we to require less plan-specific information. Moreover, the full range of information we specify is likely to facilitate other efforts. For example, we do not believe that any other service has been able to assemble in one source information on all insurance issuers and programs serving the individual and small group markets across a broad range of States. One specific alternative on which we request comment is on our proposal to limit the number of plan variations on which we present information for an issuer in a particular area to those that represent at least one percent of their total enrollment in that area (that is, never more than 100 variations, and usually far fewer). Without such a limitation, if

a particular issuer offers twenty or more possible products and twenty alternative cost sharing arrangements applied to the products in a particular geographic area, the combinations and permutations of offerings would be 400 for this one issuer alone. Our use of zip codes for plan service areas is an essential simplifying approach to reducing the number of alternative plans presented, by eliminating irrelevant plans, but does not solve this problem.

We welcome comments on the likely costs and benefits of this rule as presented, on alternatives that would improve the consumer and small business purchaser information to be provided, and on our quantitative estimates of burden. Comments are welcome to address both regulatory changes and changes that might be made through administrative decisions in planning and implementing the Web portal. Comments on ways to design our Internet portal to best meet consumer information needs are especially welcome.

The RFA requires agencies to analyze options for regulatory relief of small businesses, if a rule has a significant impact on a substantial number of small entities. For purposes of the RFA, small entities include small businesses, nonprofit organizations, and small government jurisdictions. Small businesses are those with sizes below thresholds established by the Small Business Administration (SBA). We examined the health insurance industry in depth in the Regulatory Impact Analysis we prepared for the proposed rule on establishment of the Medicare Advantage program (69 FR 46866, August 3, 2004). In that analysis we determined that there were few if any insurance firms underwriting comprehensive health insurance policies (in contrast, for example, to travel insurance policies or dental discount policies) that fell below the size thresholds for "small" business established by the SBA. In fact, then and even more so now, the market for health insurance is dominated by a relative handful of firms with substantial market shares. For example, nationally the approximately 40 Blue Cross and Blue Shield companies account for approximately half of all private insurance sold in the United States. A recent GAO study focused on the small business market and found that the five largest issuers in the small group market, when combined, represented three-quarters or more of the market in 34 of 39 States for which this information was available (GAO, February 27, 2009, *Private Health*

Insurance: 2008 Survey Results on Number and Market Share of Issuers in the Small Group Health Insurance Market). These firms included Blue Cross companies, and also other major insurers such as United HealthCare, Aetna, and Kaiser. Small government jurisdictions do not sell insurance in the individual or small business markets. There are, however, a number of health maintenance organizations (HMOs) that are small entities by virtue of their non-profit status, including Kaiser, even though few if any of them are small by SBA size standards. There are approximately one hundred such HMOs. These HMOs and those Blue Cross and Blue Shield plans that are non-profit organizations, like the other firms affected by this interim final rule, will be required to provide information on their insurance policies to the Department. Accordingly, this interim final rule will affect a "substantial number" of small entities.

We estimate, however, that the one-time costs of this interim final rule are approximately $5 thousand per covered entity (regardless of size or non-profit status) and about $5 thousand annually both in the first year and thereafter. Numbers of this magnitude do not remotely approach the amounts necessary to be a "significant economic impact" on firms with revenues of tens of millions of dollars (usually hundreds of millions or billions of dollars annually). Moreover, the Regulatory Flexibility Act only requires an analysis for those final rules for which a Notice of Proposed Rule Making was required. Accordingly, we have determined, and certify, that this rule will not have a significant economic impact on a substantial number of small entities and that a regulatory flexibility analysis is not required.

In addition, section 1102(b) of the Social Security Act requires us to prepare a regulatory impact analysis if a rule may have a significant economic impact on the operations of a substantial number of small rural hospitals. This analysis must conform to the provisions of section 604 of the RFA. This interim final rule would not affect small rural hospitals. Therefore, the Secretary has determined that this rule would not have a significant impact on the operations of a substantial number of small rural hospitals.

Section 202 of the Unfunded Mandates Reform Act of 1195 requires that agencies assess anticipated costs and benefits before issuing any rule that includes a Federal mandate that could result in expenditure in any one year by State, local or tribal governments, in the aggregate, or by the private sector, of

$100 million in 1995 dollars, updated annually for inflation. That threshold level is currently about $135 million. This interim final rule contains reporting mandates for private sector firms, but these will not cost more than the approximately $6 million that we have estimated. It includes no mandates on State, local, or tribal governments.

Executive Order 13132 establishes certain requirements that an agency must meet when it promulgates a proposed rule and subsequent final rule that imposes substantial direct requirement costs on State and local governments, preempts State law, or otherwise has Federalism implications. This interim final rule does not impose substantial direct requirement costs on State and local governments, preempt State law, or otherwise have Federalism implications.

In accordance with the provisions of Executive Order 12866, this interim final rule was reviewed by the Office of Management and Budget.

List of Subjects in 45 CFR Part 159

Administrative practice and procedure, Computer technology, Health care, Health facilities, Health insurance, Health records, Hospitals, Medicaid, Medicare, Penalties, Reporting and recordkeeping requirements.

■ For the reasons set forth in the preamble, the Department of Health and Human Services amends 45 CFR subtitle A, subchapter B, by adding a new part 159 to read as follows:

PART 159—HEALTH CARE REFORM INSURANCE WEB PORTAL

Sec.
159.100   Basis and Scope.
159.110   Definitions.
159.120   Data Submission for the individual and small group markets.

Authority: Section 1103 of the Patient Protection and Affordable Care Act (Pub. L. 111–148).

§ 159.100   Basis and scope.

This part establishes provisions governing a Web portal that will provide information on health insurance coverage options in each of the 50 States and the District of Columbia. It sets forth data submission requirements for health insurance issuers. It covers the individual market and the small group market.

§ 159.110   Definitions.

For purposes of part 159, the following definitions apply unless otherwise provided:

Health Insurance Coverage: We adopt the Public Health Service Act (PHSA)

definition of "health insurance coverage" found at section 2791(b)(1) of the Public Health Service Act (PHSA).

Health Insurance Issuer: We adopt the PHSA definition of "health insurance issuer" found at section 2791(b)(2) of the PHSA.

Health Insurance Product: Means a package of benefits that an issuer offers that is reported to State regulators in an insurance filing.

Individual Health Insurance Coverage: We adopt the PHSA definition of "individual health insurance coverage" found at section 2791(b)(5) of the PHSA.

Individual Market: We adopt the Affordable Care Act definition of "individual market" found at section 1304(a)(2) of the Affordable Care Act and 2791(e)(1)(A) of the PHSA.

Portal Plan: Means the discrete pairing of a package of benefits and a particular cost sharing option (not including premium rates or premium quotes).

Section 1101 High Risk Pools: We define section 1101 high risk pools as any entity described in regulations implementing section 1101 of the Affordable Care Act.

Small Employer: We adopt the Affordable Care Act definition of "small employer" found at section 1304(b)(2) and (3).

Small Group Coverage: Means health insurance coverage offered to employees of small employers in the small group market.

Small Group Market: We adopt the Affordable Care Act definition of "small group market" found at section 1304(a)(3).

State Health Benefits High Risk Pools: Means nonprofit organizations created by State law to offer comprehensive health insurance to individuals who otherwise would be unable to secure such coverage because of their health status.

§ 159.120   Data submission for the individual and small group markets.

(a) Health insurance issuers (hereinafter referred to as issuers) must, in accordance with guidance issued by the Secretary, submit corporate and contact information; administrative information; enrollment data by health insurance product; product names and types; whether enrollment is currently open for each health insurance product; geographic availability information; customer service phone numbers; and Web site links to the issuer Web site, brochure documents, and provider networks; and financial ratings on or before May 21, 2010, and annually thereafter.

(b) Issuers must, as determined by the Secretary, submit pricing and benefit information for their portal plans on or before September 3, 2010, and annually thereafter.

(c) Issuers must submit updated pricing and benefit data for their portal plans whenever they change premiums, cost-sharing, types of services covered, coverage limitations, or exclusions for one or more of their individual or small group portal plans.

(d) Issuers must submit pricing and benefit data for portal plans associated with products that are newly open or newly reopened for enrollment within 30 days of opening for enrollment.

(e) Issuers must annually verify the data submitted under paragraphs (a) through (d) of this section, and make corrections to any errors that are found.

(f) Issuers must submit administrative data on products and portal plans, and these performance ratings, percent of individual market and small group market policies that are rescinded; the percent of individual market policies sold at the manual rate; the percent of claims that are denied under individual market and small group market policies; and the number and disposition of appeals on denials to insure, pay claims and provide required preauthorizations, for future releases of the Web portal in accordance with guidance issued by the Secretary.

(g) The issuer's CEO or CFO must electronically certify to the completeness and accuracy of all data submitted for the October 1, 2010, release of the Web portal and for any future updates to these requirements.

Dated: April 29, 2010.

Jay Angoff,
Director, Office of Consumer Information and Insurance Oversight.

Dated: April 29, 2010.

Kathleen Sebelius,
Secretary.

[FR Doc. 2010–10504 Filed 4–30–10; 4:15 pm]

BILLING CODE 4150–03–P

DEPARTMENT OF COMMERCE

National Oceanic and Atmospheric Administration

50 CFR Part 660

[Docket No. 100218107–0199–01]

RIN 0648–AY60

Fisheries Off West Coast States; West Coast Salmon Fisheries; 2010 Management Measures

AGENCY: National Marine Fisheries Service (NMFS), National Oceanic and

D. HHS Regulations on Early Retiree Reinsurance Program

DEPARTMENT OF HEALTH AND HUMAN SERVICES

Office of the Secretary

45 CFR Part 149

RIN 0991–AB64

Early Retiree Reinsurance Program

AGENCY: Office of the Secretary, HHS.

ACTION: Interim final rule with comment period.

SUMMARY: This interim final rule with comment period (IFC) implements the Early Retiree Reinsurance Program, which was established by section 1102 of the Patient Protection and Affordable Care Act (the Affordable Care Act). The Congress appropriated funding of $5 billion for the temporary program. Section 1102(a)(1) requires the Secretary to establish this temporary program not later than 90 days after enactment of the statute, which is June 21, 2010. The program ends no later than January 1, 2014. The program provides reimbursement to participating employment-based plans for a portion of the cost of health benefits for early retirees and their spouses, surviving spouses and dependents. The Secretary will reimburse plans for certain claims between $15,000 and $90,000 (with those amounts being indexed for plan years starting on or after October 1, 2011). The purpose of the reimbursement is to make health benefits more affordable for plan participants and sponsors so that health benefits are accessible to more Americans than they would otherwise be without this program.

DATES: *Effective Date:* These regulations are effective on June 1, 2010.

Comment date: To be assured consideration, comments must be received at one of the addresses provided below, no later than 5 p.m. EST on June 4, 2010.

ADDRESSES: In commenting, please refer to file code DHHS–9996–IFC. Because of staff and resource limitations, we cannot accept comments by facsimile (FAX) transmission.

You may submit comments in one of four ways (please choose only one of the ways listed).

• *Electronically.* You may submit electronic comments on this regulation to *http://www.regulations.gov.* Follow the instructions on the home page.

• *By regular mail.* You may mail written comments to the following address only: Centers for Medicare & Medicaid Services, Department of Health and Human Services, Attention:

DHHS–9996–IFC, P.O. Box 8014, Baltimore, MD 21244–8014.

Please allow sufficient time for mailed comments to be received before the close of the comment period.

• *By express or overnight mail.* You may send written comments to the following address only: Centers for Medicare & Medicaid Services, Department of Health and Human Services, Attention: DHHS–9996–IFC, Mail Stop C4–26–05, 7500 Security Boulevard, Baltimore, MD 21244–1850.

• *By hand or courier.* If you prefer, you may deliver (by hand or courier) your written comments before the close of the comment period to either of the following addresses:

a. For delivery in Washington, DC— Centers for Medicare & Medicaid Services, Department of Health and Human Services, Room 445–G, Hubert H. Humphrey Building, 200 Independence Avenue, SW., Washington, DC 20201.

(Because access to the interior of the Hubert H. Humphrey Building is not readily available to persons without Federal government identification, commenters are encouraged to leave their comments in the CMS drop slots located in the main lobby of the building. A stamp-in clock is available for persons wishing to retain a proof of filing by stamping in and retaining an extra copy of the comments being filed.)

b. For delivery in Baltimore, MD— Centers for Medicare & Medicaid Services, Department of Health and Human Services, 7500 Security Boulevard, Baltimore, MD 21244–1850.

If you intend to deliver your comments to the Baltimore address, please call telephone number (410) 786– 9994 in advance to schedule your arrival with one of our staff members.

Comments mailed to the addresses indicated as appropriate for hand or courier delivery may be delayed and received after the comment period.

Submission of comments on paperwork requirements. You may submit comments on this document's paperwork requirements by following the instructions at the end of the "Collection of Information Requirements" section in this document.

For information on viewing public comments, see the beginning of the **SUPPLEMENTARY INFORMATION** section.

FOR FURTHER INFORMATION CONTACT: James Slade, (410) 786–1073, for information regarding the Purpose and Basis, Requirements for Eligible Employment-Based Plans, Use of Reimbursement Amounts, Appeals, and Disclosure of Data Inaccuracies.

David Mlawsky, (410) 786–6851, for information regarding the Definitions,

Reinsurance Amounts, Reimbursement Methods, Including Provision of Necessary Information, and Change of Ownership Requirements.

SUPPLEMENTARY INFORMATION: *Inspection of Public Comments.* All comments received before the close of the comment period are available for viewing by the public, including any personally identifiable or confidential business information that is included in a comment. We post all electronic comments received before the close of the comment period on the following public Web site as soon as possible after they have been received: *http:// www.regulations.gov.* Follow the search instructions on that Web site to view public comments.

Comments received timely will be available for public inspection as they are received, generally beginning approximately 3 weeks after publication of a document, at Room 445–G, Department of Health and Human Services, Hubert H. Humphrey Building, 200 Independence Avenue, SW., Washington, DC 20201, Monday through Friday of each week from 8:30 a.m. to 4 p.m. To schedule an appointment to view public comments, call 1–800–743–3951.

I. Background

A. Overview of the Early Retiree Reinsurance Program Enacted as Part of the Patient Protection and Affordable Care Act

On March 21, 2010, the Congress passed the Patient Protection and Affordable Care Act (the Affordable Care Act) (Pub. L. 111–148), which was signed into law on March 23, 2010. Included in this health insurance reform law is a provision that establishes the temporary Early Retiree Reinsurance Program. This provision addresses the recent erosion in the number of employers providing health coverage to early retirees. People in the early retiree age group often face difficulties obtaining insurance in the individual market because of advanced age or chronic conditions that make coverage unaffordable and inaccessible. The Early Retiree Reinsurance Program provides needed financial help for employer-based plans to continue to provide valuable coverage to plan participants, and provides financial relief to plan participants.

The Early Retiree Reinsurance Program provides reimbursement to participating sponsors for a portion of the costs of providing health coverage to early retirees (and eligible spouses, surviving spouses, and dependents of such retirees). Section 1102(a)(2)(B) of the Affordable Care Act defines "employment-based plan" to include a group benefits plan providing health benefits that is maintained by private employers, State or local governments, employee organizations, voluntary employees' beneficiary association, a committee or board of individuals appointed to administer such plan, or a multiemployer plan (as defined by Employee Retirement Income Security Act or ERISA). Section 1102 does not differentiate between health benefits provided by self-funded plans or through the purchase of insurance.

Section 1102(a)(1) requires the Secretary of HHS (the Secretary) to establish the program within 90 days of enactment of the law, which is June 21, 2010. We expect this program to be established by June 1, 2010. By law, the program will expire on January 1, 2014. Funding for the program is limited to $5 billion.

II. Provisions of the Interim Final Rule

This regulation establishes 45 CFR part 149, "Requirements for the Early Retiree Reinsurance Program." This part implements section 1102 of the Affordable Care Act, which requires the Secretary to provide reimbursement to sponsors with certified plans for a portion of the cost of health benefits for early retirees and their spouses, surviving spouses and dependents, provided funds remain available. In part 149, we established new subparts A through H. These new subparts set forth the framework for implementing the Early Retiree Reinsurance Program effective June 1, 2010 through January 1, 2014. We are implementing the statutory requirements of the program as follows:

A. General Provisions (Subpart A)

1. Purpose and Basis (§ 149.1)

In this section, we provide the statutory authority for promulgating the regulation.

2. Definitions (§ 149.2)

Section 1102(a) of the Affordable Care Act (also referred to as the "statute") provides definitions for three specific terms. One of these terms is the term "employment-based plan", which the statute defines as a "group benefits plan providing health benefits" that satisfies certain conditions. The statute at section 1102(a)(1) also specifies that under the program, the Secretary shall provide reimbursement to participating employment-based plans. However, a plan typically constitutes merely an arrangement to provide benefits, as opposed to a discrete entity to which

payments can be directly made or sent. Thus, the regulation interprets this provision to require reimbursement under the program to a "sponsor," and defines sponsor as that term is defined in regulations promulgated for the Retiree Drug Subsidy (RDS) Program at 42 CFR 423.882. That definition defines sponsor as a plan sponsor as defined in section 3(16)(B) of ERISA, 29 U.S.C. 1002(16)(B), except that, in the case of a plan maintained jointly by one employer and an employee organization and for which the employer is the primary source of financing, the term means the employer. By defining the term sponsor in the regulation, and by specifying that sponsors are the entities that apply for and get reimbursed under the program, we believe we are achieving two important objectives: (1) We are ensuring that program reimbursements can be made to actual existing entities, and (2) We are promoting consistency with the RDS Program. This second objective is critical, as we believe that many of the entities that will apply for the Early Retiree Reinsurance Program are entities that participate in the RDS Program, as these two programs have many similarities. Thus, the common use of terms across the two programs will minimize confusion, and we believe will help to maximize program participation.

Although we drafted the regulation to specify that a sponsor is the entity that would be directly paid under the program, there is still a need to use the term "employment-based plan" in the regulation. This is because the statute envisions that the entity receiving reimbursement have a benefits arrangement (that is, a plan) in place that satisfies certain criteria (for example, implements programs and procedures to generate cost-savings with respect to participants with chronic and high-cost conditions.) The statute provides a definition of "employment-based plan" as constituting a "group benefits plan" that has certain characteristics. Those characteristics (for example, must be maintained by one or more employers, can include a multiemployer plan as defined in section 3(37) of ERISA) borrow components of the ERISA definition of a "group health plan". For that reason, we define "employment-based plan" as meaning a "group health plan" as defined in the RDS regulations at 42 CFR 423.882 that provides health benefits to early retirees, but excludes Federal governmental plans. (Unlike the RDS statutory provisions, the Early Retiree Reinsurance Program's statutory

provisions do not expressly include Federal plans). The RDS regulatory definition of "group health plan" largely tracks the ERISA definition. For reasons previously stated, we believe it is beneficial to use the same or similar terminology, and have the same or similar requirements for the RDS Program and the Early Retiree Reinsurance Program, when appropriate. Because the RDS program requires a sponsor to have a benefits arrangement that constitutes a group health plan, we believe the benefits arrangement must be in place for purposes of the Early Retiree Reinsurance Program (that is, an employment-based plan), should also be a group health plan (that is, an employment-based plan, defined generally as group health plan). Generally, the regulation uses the term "sponsor" when referring to the entity that applies for and receives reimbursement under the program, and uses the term "employment-based plan" when discussing the health benefits arrangement the sponsor must offer.

In addition to introducing the definition of "sponsor", the regulation also defines other terms that are not defined in the statute, including the term "authorized representative." We define this term to mean an individual with legal authority to sign and bind a sponsor to the terms of a contract or agreement. This term is important in the regulatory provision relating to the program application and the plan sponsor agreement. The regulation requires an authorized representative to sign a plan sponsor agreement as part of the program application.

We use the term "benefit option" in the regulation when discussing the fact that there is only one cost threshold and cost limit per early retiree per plan, regardless of how many benefit options within that plan the early retiree is enrolled in, in a given plan year. We define "benefit option" as a particular benefit design, category of benefits, or cost-sharing arrangement offered within an employment-based plan.

The statute at section 1102(b) requires that an employment-based plan be certified by the Secretary, and submit an application for the program, before the plan can participate in the program. As stated above, under this regulation, the entity that participates in (that is, applies for) the program, is the plan sponsor. We will not approve an application unless the sponsor, and the employment-based plan, meet their respective requirements under the statute and the regulation. Therefore, we define the term "certified" as meaning that the sponsor and its employment-based plan or plans meet the requirements of this part and the sponsor's application to participate in the program has been approved by the Secretary. All elements of this requirement must be satisfied before a sponsor can participate in the program.

The statute at section 1102(b)(2) requires employment-based plans to have programs and procedures in place to generate cost savings for participants with chronic and high-cost conditions. We define the term "chronic and high-cost condition" to mean a condition for which $15,000 or more in health benefit claims are likely to be incurred during a plan year by any one participant. Sponsors participating in this program are likely to be sponsors that have offered the applicable plan in previous years. Sponsors, therefore, will recognize which conditions are likely to result in $15,000 in claims in a plan year for one participant. While we expect that the employment-based plans will have programs and procedures in place that have generated or have the potential to generate savings for participants with these conditions, which may vary across plans, geographic regions and due to other factors, we do not expect plans to have programs and procedures in place for all conditions for which claims are likely to exceed $15,000 in a plan year for a plan participant. To require that plans have programs and procedures in place to address all chronic and high-cost conditions could exclude many sponsors from participating in the program and could be overly restrictive. We expect sponsors to take a reasonable approach when identifying such conditions and selecting programs and procedures to lower the cost of care, as well as improve the quality of care, for such conditions.

We define "claim" or "medical claim" in order to lay out in more detail what is required on the claim to be reimbursed under this program, and to note that the terms "claim" or "medical claim" include medical, surgical, hospital, prescription drug and other types of claims as determined by the Secretary. The statute at section 1102(a)(2)(A) defines "health benefits" as medical, surgical, hospital, prescription drug, and such other benefits as shall be determined by the Secretary whether self-funded, or delivered through the purchase of insurance or otherwise. The regulatory definition of "health benefit" clarifies that such benefits include benefits for the diagnosis, cure, mitigation, or prevention of physical or mental disease or condition with respect to any structure or function of the body. (As

discussed below, health benefits do not include benefits specified at 45 CFR 146.145(c)(2) through (4)). Therefore, per the Secretary's authority to determine benefits for which claims may be submitted, the terms "claim" or "medical claim" include claims for the benefits set out in the definition of "health benefit." This list of benefits, for which the Secretary has the authority to determine are appropriate under the program, is not exhaustive.

The statute at section 1102(a)(2)(C) defines "early retirees" as individuals who are age 55 and older but are not eligible for coverage under Medicare, and who are not active employees of an employer maintaining, or currently contributing to, the employment-based plan or of any employer that has made substantial contributions to fund such plan. We have incorporated this definition into the regulation, and we clarified that spouses, surviving spouses, and dependents are also included in the definition of early retiree. This definition accommodates the language in section 1102(a)(1) of the statute, which states that reimbursement under the program is made to cover a portion of the costs of providing health coverage to early retirees and to the eligible spouses, surviving spouses, and dependents of such retirees. This definition accommodates the language in section 1102(a)(1) in such a way that reimbursement can be made under the program for the health benefit costs of eligible spouses, surviving spouses, and dependents of such retirees, even if they are under the age of 55, and/or are eligible for Medicare. We believe the statute can reasonably be interpreted to provide reimbursement for the health benefit costs of such individuals. This interpretation will provide additional assistance to sponsors, which will encourage them to continue to offer coverage to the spouses, surviving spouses, and dependents of early retirees.

The regulatory definition of early retiree also clarifies that the determination of whether an individual is not an active employee is made by the sponsor in accordance with the rules of its plan. However, an individual is presumed to be an active employee if, under the Medicare Secondary Payer (MSP) rules in 42 CFR 411.104 and related Centers for Medicare & Medicaid Services' (CMS) guidance, the person is considered to be receiving coverage by reason of current employment status. The presumption would apply whether or not the MSP rules actually apply to the sponsor. We also clarify that a sponsor may treat a person receiving coverage under its employment-based

plan as a dependent in accordance with the rules of its plan, regardless of whether that person constitutes a dependent for Federal or state tax purposes. These two clarifications are also found in the RDS regulation in the definition of "qualifying covered retiree," under which, as that term implies, an individual must be a retiree. As previously stated, we believe that regulatory terminology and concepts should be the same or similar between the RDS Program and the Early Retiree Reinsurance Program when appropriate, and we believe it is appropriate when determining whether an individual is a retiree under each program. Finally, in the regulatory definition of "early retiree," we also clarify that for purposes of this definition, the phrase "an employer maintaining or currently contributing to the employment-based plan or any employer that has made substantial contributions to fund such plan," which is also found in the statutory definition of "early retiree," means a plan sponsor. Under ERISA (and the RDS Program regulation), a plan sponsor is an entity (such as an employer) that establishes or maintains a group health plan. Thus, because this part of the statutory definition of early retiree in the Affordable Care Act speaks to the relationship between the sponsor (for example, the employer) and the employment-based plan, we believe this clarification is appropriate.

Section 149.610 of this regulation permits the Secretary to reopen and revise a reimbursement determination upon the Secretary's own motion or upon the request of a sponsor within 1 year of the reimbursement determination for any reason, within 4 years of the reimbursement determination for good cause, or at any time in instances of fraud or similar fault. These three standards are the same regulatory standards that apply with respect to CMS' ability to reopen or revise an initial or reconsidered determination under the RDS Program, at 42 CFR 423.890(d). The RDS regulatory provision provides examples of what constitutes "good cause," and again, because of the similarity between that program and the Early Retiree Reinsurance Program, we believe those examples would be appropriate for the latter. Therefore, similar to the RDS regulation, this regulation provides the following examples of good cause: (1) New and material evidence exists that was not readily available at the time the reimbursement determination was made, (2) A clerical error in the computation of the reimbursement determination was made, or (3) The evidence that was considered in making the reimbursement determination clearly shows on its face that an error was made. For example, if a sponsor receives a post-point-of-sale price concession that was not known at the time a reimbursement determination was made, good cause may be found and the reimbursement determination may be reopened and revised.

The statute at section 1102(a)(2)(A) defines "health benefits" as medical, surgical, hospital, prescription drug, and such other benefits as shall be determined by the Secretary, whether self-funded, or delivered through the purchase of insurance or otherwise. We clarify in the regulatory definition that such benefits include benefits for the diagnosis, cure, mitigation, or prevention of physical or mental disease or condition with respect to any structure or function of the body. This is not an exhaustive list. We also specify that health benefits do not include certain benefits designated as excepted benefits under the regulations implementing the health insurance portability provisions of the Health Insurance Portability and Accountability Act (HIPAA). Those provisions impose certain requirements on group health plans and group health insurance issuers, but do not apply those requirements to certain arrangements that typically are not part of a major medical plan (that is, excepted benefits). For example, long-term care benefits are excepted benefits. In the context of the Early Retiree Reinsurance Program, we do not believe it would be appropriate to consider health benefits as including benefits provided under such arrangements, as we believe the best read of the statutory phrase "medical, surgical, hospital, [and] prescription drug" means such major medical benefits.

In order to aid stakeholders in understanding when the Secretary will make reimbursement to a sponsor, we define the term "incurred" to mean the point in time when the sponsor, health insurance issuer, group health plan or plan participant, or a combination of these or similar stakeholders, become responsible for payment of the claim. In short, the Secretary will not pay a sponsor until a claim has been incurred and paid, as the statute at section 1102(c)(1)(B) specifies that claims "shall be based on the actual amount expended."

We define a "negotiated price concession" as any direct or indirect remuneration that would serve to decrease the costs incurred under the employment-based plan. We set out examples of what negotiated price

concessions are, which include discounts, rebates, coupons, and goods in kind. The list at § 149.2, "Definitions," describing what may constitute a negotiated price concession is not an exhaustive list.

Because the statute does not use the terms "early retiree" and "plan participant" interchangeably, we define the term "plan participant" to include all enrollees in a plan, including an early and other retiree, an early and other retiree's spouse, surviving spouse, and dependent, and an active employee and an active employee's spouse and dependent.

The statute at section 1102(c)(1)(B) specifies that claims submitted under the program "shall be based on the actual amount expended by the participating employment-based plan involved within the plan year" for the health benefits provided to early retirees and eligible spouses, surviving spouses, and dependents. This regulation includes a definition of plan year, and defines plan year as the year that is designated as the plan year in the plan document of an employment-based plan, except that if the plan document does not designate a plan year, if the plan year is not a 12-month plan year, or if there is no plan document, the plan year is: (1) The deductible or limit year used under the plan, (2) the policy year, if the plan does not impose deductibles or limits on a 12-month basis: (3) the sponsor's taxable year, if the plan does not impose deductibles or limits on a 12-month basis, and either the plan is not insured or the insurance policy is not renewed on a 12-month basis, or (4) the calendar year, in any other case. We define this term in such a way to give deference to the plan year the sponsor has already established for other purposes. However, we balance that deference with our belief that the intent of the statute is to calculate reimbursement amounts, and to apply the cost threshold and cost limit, to periods of time that are 12 months in duration. We believe most sponsors' plan years are in fact 12 months in duration.

The term "post point-of-sale negotiated price concession" is defined because not all negotiated price concessions occur at or before the point of sale. The statute requires negotiated price concessions to be excluded from the calculation of reimbursement, which causes reimbursement to be based on the actual amounts paid, not an inflated amount that may not reflect a price concession. When post point-of-sale negotiated price concessions occur they may cause data submitted for reimbursement to become inaccurate,

resulting in ultimately, an inaccurate reimbursement. Once these price concessions are accounted for, a sponsor's reimbursement determination may be reopened and revised.

For purposes of brevity, we defined the term "program" to mean the Early Retiree Reinsurance Program.

We define the term "Secretary" to mean the Secretary of the Department of Health & Human Services or the Secretary's designee. We include the Secretary's designee in the definition because the Secretary will not actually be performing the tasks set out in this regulation, but will designate an individual or entity to act on the Secretary's behalf.

The term "sponsor agreement" is based on the definition of the term in the RDS regulation. The sponsor agreement is basically used to ensure that the sponsor and Department are bound to comply with the details of the program that appear in the regulation and in other guidance, and to address any other points that must be addressed in order to implement this program.

B. Requirements for Eligible Employment-Based Plans (Subpart B)

1. General Requirement (§ 149.30)

In this section, we provide the requirements that allow a sponsor to be eligible to participate in the Early Retiree Reinsurance Program.

2. Requirements to Participate (§ 149.35)

Section 1102(b)(2)(A) of the Affordable Care Act requires that an employment-based plan implement programs and procedures to generate cost-savings with respect to participants with chronic and high-cost conditions. We interpret this to mean that a plan must have in place programs and procedures that have generated or have the potential to generate cost-savings for these participants in order to participate in the Early Retiree Reinsurance Program, not necessarily that the sponsor has to ensure that new programs and procedures are put in place just to participate in this program.

Proper management and treatment of chronic and high-cost conditions may be promoted by generating cost-savings for plan participants with these conditions because plan participants may be more apt to seek out proper and timely treatment and management before a condition becomes critical if treatment and management are financially manageable. As an example of a program and procedure to generate cost savings for a participant with a chronic condition, a sponsor may determine that diabetes, if not managed properly, is likely to lead to claims in excess of $15,000 for a plan year for one plan participant. The sponsor may ensure implementation of a diabetes management program that includes aggressive monitoring and behavioral counseling to prevent complications and unnecessary hospitalization. With respect to generating cost savings for a high-cost condition, a sponsor may determine that cancer is a high-cost condition for which it should generate cost savings. The sponsor may ensure that its plan covers all or a large portion of the participant's coinsurances or copayments, and/or it could eliminate or reduce the plan's deductible for treatment and visits related to the condition. Sponsors may choose other chronic and high-cost conditions to address, but upon audit the sponsor must be able to demonstrate that its programs and procedures have generated or had the potential to generate cost savings, consistent with the representations the sponsor made in its program application.

We considered various options of how best to implement this provision and developed several options. The first option was to further identify which specific conditions meet the chronic condition definition and which specific conditions meet the high-cost condition definition and identify these specific conditions in sub-regulatory guidance to be issued at the time of, or immediately after, the issuance of this regulation. Issues that arose with this option consisted of:

(1) How best to define the terms "chronic and high-cost conditions", which would likely involve a significant amount of data analysis. Chronic and high-cost conditions can vary significantly across geographic regions, age ranges, and due to other factors. We do not think that specifying the chronic and high-cost conditions to be addressed could effectively occur within the 90 days allowed for establishment of this program; and

(2) Our belief that the Congress intends this to be an inclusive program, not a program that excludes potential sponsors merely because they did not develop programs to address the specific conditions we might identify in our guidance. Had the Congress narrowly defined the types of plans for which sponsors might be reimbursed, we might have thought that this program is not an inclusive program. Instead Congress defined the term "employment-based plan" broadly in the statute at section 1102 (a)(2)(B). It defines the term as a "group benefits plan providing health benefits" as a plan that "is * * * maintained by one or

more current or former employers (including without limitation any State or local government or political subdivision thereof), employee organization, a voluntary employees' beneficiary association, or a committee or board of individuals appointed to administer such plan; or * * * a multiemployer plan * * *" Therefore the scope of sponsors eligible to receive this reimbursement is extremely broad, which shows intent on behalf of Congress to be inclusive.

The inclusive nature of the program is particularly important because this program will involve plans with plan years that began before the effective date of the program, as will be discussed below. This means that a plan may not have a program in place to address certain chronic and high-cost conditions that we may have identified after the plan year has started, which would then exclude the sponsor from participation in the program. In such cases, sponsors would, in effect, be penalized if we identified specific conditions. As stated above, chronic and high-cost conditions can vary significantly across geographic regions, age ranges, and due to other factors, so we expect that sponsors might focus cost-saving programs and procedures on conditions that effect enrollees in their plan or plans. Our intent is that the regulation takes into account these differences.

The approach we decided to take was to define the term "chronic and high-cost condition" as specified in § 149.2—Definitions. "Chronic and high-cost condition" means a condition for which $15,000 or more in applicable claims are likely to be incurred during a plan year by one participant. Therefore, a sponsor must have programs and procedures in place that generate or have the potential to generate cost savings for plan participants with conditions that are likely to generate $15,000 in claims for a plan year, in order to participate in this program. We do not require that a sponsor have programs and procedures in place to address all conditions that may result in claims exceeding $15,000 for one participant in a plan year. The sponsor must take a reasonable approach to identifying which conditions it must address. We believe this is a reasonable interpretation of the statute because it will promote cost savings for participants with chronic and high-cost conditions, but due to the approaches' flexibility (that is, the fact that sponsors may choose programs and procedures that meet this requirement that are applicable to their enrollees) will serve to allow as many of the types of sponsors referenced in the definition of "employment-based plan" as possible

to become certified to participate in the program. Of course, this requirement does not supersede requirements in other Federal laws that may apply to programs and procedures for chronic and high-cost conditions, such as the Americans with Disabilities Act.

In order to administer this program and to audit the program as required by section 1102(d), we are requiring the sponsor to make records available for these purposes. For example, when a sponsor is audited, the auditors may request a copy of the sponsor's (or the sponsor's health insurance issuer or group health plan's, as applicable) policies and procedures to detect fraud, waste and abuse, and data to substantiate the effectiveness of the policies and procedures. Under this provision, the sponsor is required to ensure that the applicable policies and procedures are produced.

We also require that the sponsor have a written agreement with its health insurance issuer (as defined in 45 CFR 160.103) or employment-based plan (as defined in 45 CFR 149.2), as applicable, requiring the health insurance issuer or employment-based plan to disclose information on behalf of the sponsor to the Secretary. This requirement in part exists to accommodate the HIPAA Privacy Rule at 45 CFR part 160 and subparts A and E of part 164 ("Privacy Rule"). This rule applies to "covered entities," which include group health plans (that is, employment-based plans) and health insurance issuers, as defined in 45 CFR 160.103. Third party administrators would be business associates, as defined in 45 CFR 160.103, of group health plans. Sponsors would not become covered entities by sponsoring a plan. Sponsors typically do not perform administrative activities for their group health plans and therefore do not have access to the claims information or similar protected health information (PHI) we require in this regulation to support program reimbursement. Much of the data that we would need to support program reimbursements, as outlined above, would be PHI held by group health plans, health insurance issuers, or third party administrators on behalf of group health plans. The requirement for health insurance issuers and employment-based plans to disclose information to the Secretary encompasses information created or held by Business Associates on behalf of the health insurance issuer or group health plan.

We believe that we have the authority to require the disclosure of the PHI in accordance with section 1102(c)(1)(A), which states that a participating plan "shall submit claims for reimbursement to the Secretary which shall contain documentation of the actual costs of the items and services for which each claim is being submitted." Additionally, section 1102(d) requires the Secretary to conduct audits of claims data submitted by, or on behalf of, sponsors participating in the program, to ensure that such plans are in compliance with the statute, and this simply cannot be done without mandating disclosure of PHI. Thus, covered entities can comply with the mandate (without first obtaining specific authorization from individuals) pursuant to "the required by law" provisions of the Privacy Rule (45 CFR 164.512(a)).

As noted above, typically group health plans and health insurance issuers or third party administrators acting on behalf of group health plans, have PHI that the Secretary requires for the submission of claims data for reimbursement under the program pursuant to the regulations. In these situations, it may be unlawful, under the Privacy Rule, for PHI to be shared with the sponsors. This regulation does not authorize disclosure of PHI to sponsors. Therefore, for purposes of this subpart, the sponsor must have a written agreement with the group health plan (that is, the employment-based plan) or health insurance issuer, as applicable, regarding disclosure of records, and the plan or issuer must disclose to us, on the sponsor's behalf, the information, data, documents, and records necessary for the sponsor to comply with this program, part, and guidance, at a time and in a manner specified by the Secretary. Sponsors of self-funded plans with legal access to such data will be able to either provide this data to us themselves or have a group health plan or insurer provide the data to us on their behalf.

Section 1102 (c)(6) of the Affordable Care Act requires the Secretary to establish procedures to protect against fraud, waste and abuse. In order to implement this provision, the Secretary will, for example, check the exclusions lists developed by the HHS' Office of the Inspector General and the U.S. General Services Administration before allowing an entity to participate, or play a role, in the program, and will take other steps such as verifying the identities of the early retirees for whom claims are being submitted. The Secretary may also verify the identities of the individuals associated with the sponsor and health insurance issuer, or group health plan, as applicable, and will examine claims before reimbursement is made, to ensure, among other things, that instances of fraud, waste and abuse are minimized.

Furthermore, the Secretary will perform audits per section 1102(d) of the Affordable Care Act. To aid the Secretary in detecting and reducing fraud, waste and abuse, we are requiring that sponsors ensure that there are policies and procedures in place to detect and reduce fraud, waste and abuse. While the policies and procedures may be maintained by the sponsor's health insurance issuer or group health plan, the sponsor will have to attest that these policies and procedures are in place in the application. The sponsor must comply with requests from the Secretary to produce the policies and procedures and any documents or data to substantiate the implementation, and the effectiveness, of the procedures. We believe we meet the requirements of the statute by taking actions to detect and reduce fraud, waste, and abuse, by requiring sponsors to have such policies and procedures in place, and by requiring a sponsor to produce the policies and procedures upon request (such as for the purposes of an audit). If it is found that a sponsor committed fraud, waste or abuse, or allowed fraud, waste, and abuse to occur under its plan or plans, the Secretary may recoup from the sponsor some or all of the reimbursements paid under the program, and/or may revoke a sponsor's certification to participate in the program. Of course, there are other laws relating to fraud, waste, and abuse, with which sponsors and their health insurance issuers or group health plans must comply.

3. Application (§ 149.40)

Section 1102(b)(1)(B) requires the sponsor to submit "an application for participation in the program, at such time, in such manner, and containing such information as the Secretary shall require." In order to implement this provision, a sponsor must submit one application per plan, and identify the plan year cycle for which the sponsor is applying (that is, starting month and day, and ending month and day; no year is required). One application must be filed for each plan. Filing a different application for each plan will aid in tracking the plan as this program progresses to ensure proper reimbursement and compliance with program requirements.

In order to verify the accuracy of the information contained in the application, the application will have to be signed by an authorized representative of the applicant and the authorized representative will have to certify that the information contained in the application is true and accurate to the best of the authorized representative's knowledge and belief, among other certifications. We use the term applicant in this section to refer to any sponsor that has filed an application that has not yet been certified under the program. The term applicant is used to clarify that the applicant is not entitled to the privileges of a certified sponsor, such as the ability to submit a reimbursement request or appeal a reimbursement determination. Before a sponsor may submit claims and make a reimbursement request, the sponsor's application must be approved by the Secretary. Applications will be processed in the order in which they are received. Because funding for this program is limited, we expect more requests for reimbursement than there are funds to pay the requests. Therefore we expect an applicant to perform its due diligence when applying, which should result in the submission of a complete application upon the first submission. Because it is important that applicants submit complete applications the first time, we will be providing assistance. If an application is incomplete, it will be denied and the applicant will have to submit a new application, which will be processed based on when the new application is received. If we were to allow an applicant to cure defects in the application, it would likely result in an extended application process, which would hinder the efficient implementation of this program. We must be prepared to exercise our authority under section 1102(f) to stop accepting applications based on the availability of the $5 billion appropriated for the program. It is therefore of paramount importance to applicants that they submit complete applications upon their first submission, otherwise there may not be an opportunity to submit a new and complete application.

An application for a given plan does not have to be submitted each year. To require a separate application for a plan each year would only complicate the process and would place unneeded burden on applicants and the Secretary. The application will request the plan year cycles (that is, the start month and day and the end month and day; no year required), which for our purposes will provide the information we need to calculate reimbursement based on reimbursement requests. We do not think that an annual application approval is required. Once a plan is certified, the application approved, and the sponsor continues to meet the requirements of the statute, this part, and applicable guidance, the plan and sponsor will continue to be certified and the application approved.

We set out in § 149.40 what we believe we will need in order to approve an application. The application must include the applicant's Tax Identification Number, the applicant's name and address, and contact information for the applicant. To ensure compliance with the requirements of the statute, an applicant must provide a summary in its application of how it will use the reimbursement to meet the requirements of the program, including how it will use the reimbursement to reduce plan participant or sponsor costs, or any combination of these costs, and its plans to implement programs and procedures to generate savings for plan participants with chronic and high-cost conditions. Because the statute requires that the funds dispersed under this program not be used as general revenue, we are requiring sponsors to maintain the level of effort in contributing to support their applicable plan or plans. Otherwise, sponsors might circumvent the prohibition on using the program funds as general revenue by using, dollar for dollar, sponsors' funds not otherwise used for health benefits due to the program reimbursement, as general revenue. We expect that sponsors will use the reimbursement to pay for increases in, for example, the sponsor's premium, or increases in other health benefit costs (or to reduce plan participants' costs). Therefore the sponsor's summary of how it will use the program's reimbursement must also explain how the reimbursement will be applied to maintain the sponsor's level of effort in contributing to support the applicable plan. We do not expect a sponsor to explain every detail of their programs and procedures and use of program funds but to give us an idea of how it will meet these requirements. We understand that these submissions may vary because applicants' situations with respect to their plans may vary widely. For example, reimbursements received in the first year that a sponsor participates may be applied the second year of participation because many plans will have already been negotiated, agreed to, and implemented upon the effective date of this regulation. Other sponsors may have more flexibility to use these reimbursements immediately to lower costs.

We will also require applicants to project their reimbursement amounts for the first two plan-year cycles in the application so that we can project total reimbursement amounts. To help us with our funding projections, we will need sponsors to identify specific projected reimbursement amounts for each of the two plan-year cycles. This assessment will help us determine if and when we should stop accepting applications due to funding limitations. We will also require applicants to identify all benefit options under the employment-based plan that any early retiree, for whom the applicant may receive program reimbursement, may be claimed. This is necessary for us to track where funds are being spent and to otherwise manage the program. We will also require sponsors to attest that there are fraud, waste and abuse policies and procedures in place.

As is required in the RDS program, as a condition of participation, the sponsor will be required to sign a plan sponsor agreement, which will include certain assurances made by the sponsor. Included in this agreement will be a provision stating that reimbursement is based on information and data submitted by the sponsor and if the information and data are found to be inaccurate, incomplete or otherwise incorrect, the Secretary may reopen and revise a reimbursement determination, including recouping reimbursement from the sponsor. The sponsor will be required to specifically agree to comply with the terms and conditions for participation in the program, and acknowledge that information in the application is being provided for the purpose of obtaining federal funds. This list of application requirements is not exhaustive. Due to the compressed timeline for implementing this program, we may need to request additional information in the application.

Finally, we allow the Secretary to reopen a determination under which an application had been approved or denied so that if it is later determined that a sponsor committed fraud or otherwise was untruthful in the application, the Secretary can revisit the determination.

4. Consequences of Non-Compliance, Fraud or Similar Fault (§ 149.41)

To clarify the actions the Secretary may take in instances when non-compliance, fraud, waste, and abuse, or similar fault are found, we include a regulation that states that failure to comply with the requirements of this part, or if fraud, waste, and abuse, or similar fault are found, the Secretary may recoup or withhold funds, terminate or deny an application, or take any combination of these actions. We include termination of an application because, depending upon the specific situation involved, if it is found that a sponsor committed fraud or otherwise was untruthful in the application, the determination to approve an application can be revised under § 149.40. We believe it is important to set out what actions the Secretary may take so that sponsors are aware of the ramifications of non-compliance, fraud, waste and abuse, or similar fault. This regulation does not, of course, supersede other Federal laws or consequences of non-compliance fraud, waste and abuse, or similar fault.

5. Funding Limitation (§ 149.45)

Section 1102(f) authorizes the Secretary to stop accepting applications based on the availability of funds. We clarify that a reimbursement request made on behalf of a certified plan may also be denied, in whole or in part, due to limitation of funds. Determinations based on funding limitations are final, binding and cannot be appealed, because any appeal, even if a sponsor is successful, would not result in reimbursement to a sponsor. Once the program funds are exhausted there will be no funds to reimburse a sponsor that may have been successful upon appeal.

C. Reinsurance Amounts (Subpart C)

1. Amount of Reimbursement (§ 149.100)

The statute at section 1102(c) requires the Secretary, upon receipt of a valid claim for health benefits, to make reimbursement in an amount of 80 percent of the portion of the health benefit costs (net of negotiated price concessions) attributable to the claims that exceed $15,000, but are below $90,000. We interpret the statute to mean that cumulative health benefits incurred in a given plan year and paid for a given early retiree, as defined in § 149.2, that fall between those amounts will receive reimbursement, rather than reimbursement being made only for discrete health benefit items or services whose reimbursement total falls between those amounts. This interpretation will get much needed program funds to plan sponsors more quickly. The statute also specifies that in determining the amount of claims, the costs paid by the early retiree (or his or her spouse, surviving spouse, or dependent) in the form of deductibles, copayments, or coinsurance shall be included in the amounts paid by the participating employment-based plan. As an initial matter, we clarify in the regulation that reimbursement will be made under the program only for claims that are incurred during the applicable plan year, and paid.

The regulation refers to the $15,000 lower limit and the $90,000 ceiling as the "cost threshold" and "cost limit", respectively, and indicates that reimbursement under the program is calculated by first determining the costs for health benefits net of negotiated price concessions, within the applicable plan year for each early retiree, and then subtracting amounts below the cost threshold and above the cost limit within the applicable plan year for each early retiree. We also clarify that for purposes of determining the amounts below the cost threshold and above the cost limit for any given early retiree, all costs for health benefits paid by the plan or by the early retiree for all benefit options the early retiree is enrolled in with respect to a given certified employment-based plan for a given plan year, will be combined. We make this clarification because the statute, at section 1102(c)(3), specifies that "a claim submitted by a participating employment-based plan shall not be less than $15,000 nor greater than $90,000" (emphasis added). For example, an early retiree is simultaneously enrolled in two different benefit options within one group health plan—Option 1 as a retiree, and Option 2 as a spouse of a retiree. For purposes of determining when the early retiree satisfies the cost threshold, all claims incurred and paid for that early retiree by both benefit options within the applicable plan year, will be counted. The claims for that early retiree under each benefit option will not be separately counted. For purposes of determining if and when the early enrollee has satisfied the cost limit, the same principle applies. In other words, within one employment-based plan for a given plan year, there is one threshold limit, and one cost limit, per early retiree.

We also indicate that the reimbursement formula specified in the regulation applies to insured plans as well as self-funded plans, and that with respect to insured plans, costs for health benefits means costs the insurer and the early retiree pay for health benefits net of negotiated price concessions the insurer receives for health benefits. Thus, for insured plans, the amount of premium the sponsor pays (and the amount of premium contribution the early retiree pays) is irrelevant for purposes of calculating reimbursement under the program. We believe this is the correct interpretation because section 1102(c)(1)(A) states that claims for reimbursement must "contain documentation of actual costs of items and services * * *." Premiums are not costs for items and services.

2. Transition (§ 149.105)

The program becomes effective June 1, 2010. We carefully considered whether to allow sponsors to participate in the program for plan years that ended before the program's effective date, but decided that such an approach would seem inconsistent with the program's effective date. We also considered whether to permit sponsors to participate only for plan years that start on or after the program's effective date, but decided that such an approach would arbitrarily favor sponsors with plan years that start soon after June 1, 2010. Therefore, we decided to allow sponsors to apply for plan years that start before June 1, 2010, provided they end after that date (for example, calendar year 2010 plans).[1] This raised the question of how claims incurred during such a plan year, but before June 1, 2010, would be dealt with under the program. Under one approach considered, any such claims would count toward the cost threshold, and any such claims exceeding the threshold, but below the cost limit, would be eligible for program reimbursement. We did not adopt that approach, as it arguably would unfairly favor sponsors with plan years that started significantly before the program's effective date, especially in light of the program's limited funding.

We decided upon the following approach. For claims incurred before June 1, 2010, the amount of such claims up to $15,000 count toward the cost threshold and the cost limit. The amount of claims incurred before June 1, 2010 that exceed $15,000 are not eligible for reimbursement and do not count toward the cost limit. The reinsurance amount to be paid is based solely on claims incurred on and after June 1, 2010, and that fall between the cost threshold and cost limit for the plan year. As an example, for a plan with a plan year that began July 1, 2009, with an end date of June 30, 2010, with an early retiree for which it has spent $120,000 in health benefit claims before June 1, 2010, and it then spends another $30,000 in health benefit claims on the early retiree between June 1, 2010 and June 30, 2010, the sponsor would receive credit for $15,000 in claims incurred before June 1 and receive reimbursement of 80 percent of the $30,000 (for the claims incurred after June 1, 2010), or $24,000. We believe this is a reasonable approach because it provides as much relief as possible as soon as possible to sponsors, while

---

[1] Sponsors can also apply for plan years that start after June 1, 2010.

giving meaning to the effective date of the program. A sponsor should therefore not submit claims above the $15,000 cost threshold that were incurred before June 1, 2010, for reimbursement, as submission of such claims is outside the scope of the regulation. Also, to submit these claims for reimbursement will make the reimbursement process more complex than it needs to be.

3. Negotiated Price Concessions (§ 149.110) and Cost Threshold and Cost Limit (§ 149.115)

Section 1102(c)(1)(B) states that any negotiated price concessions obtained by an employment-based plan with respect to a health benefit must be reflected in claims submitted for program reimbursement. We recognize that sponsors and insurers sometimes do not receive certain negotiated price concessions until after payment is made, and in many cases, after the plan year during which the claim is incurred and paid, has ended. For example, this is typically the case with prescription drug rebates. Thus, we specify in the regulation that sponsors must disclose such "post-point-of-sale" negotiated price concessions, in a form and manner to be specified by the Secretary. We expect to specify the form and manner of such disclosures in future guidance. This will ensure that sponsors ultimately submit accurate claims data, and thus ultimately receive accurate reimbursement.

Finally, the statute indicates that the $15,000 and $90,000 figures shall be adjusted each fiscal year based on the percentage increase in the Medical Care Component of the Consumer Price Index for all urban consumers (rounded to the nearest multiple of $1,000) for the year involved. We specify in the regulations that for plan years starting on or after October 1, 2011, the figures will be so adjusted.

D. Use of Reimbursements (Subpart D)

Use of Reimbursements (§ 149.200)

Section 1102(c)(4) requires that the reimbursement "shall be used to lower costs for the plan. Such payments may be used to reduce premium costs for an entity" receiving a reimbursement or to reduce premium contributions, co-payments, deductibles, co-insurance, or other out-of-pocket costs for plan participants. We encourage sponsors to use their reimbursement under the program for both of the following purposes: (1) To reduce the sponsor's health benefit premiums or health benefit costs, and (2) To reduce health benefit premium contributions, co-payments, deductibles, coinsurance, or other out-of-pocket costs, or any combination of these costs, for plan participants. We expect that sponsors will continue to provide at least the same level of contribution to support the applicable plan, as it did before this program. For example, for a sponsor that pays a premium to an insurer, if the premium increases, program funds may be used to pay the sponsor's share of the premium increase from year to year, which reduces the sponsor's premium costs. Section 1102(c)(4) sets forth the requirements for use of reimbursements under this section and envisions a role for the Secretary in developing a mechanism to monitor the appropriate use of such reimbursements. Additional information about this mechanism will be disseminated as it is developed.

The statute does not appear to use the terms "early retiree" and "plan participants" interchangeably. Therefore, we interpret this provision to mean that a sponsor may only receive program funds for claims of early retirees or their spouses, surviving spouses or dependents, but the funds may be used to lower health benefit costs for all participants in the plan, including retirees, and their spouses and dependents, and active employees and their spouses and dependents. At § 149.200 (b), we clarify the statutory prohibition on using the funds as general revenue of the sponsor.

E. Reimbursement Methods (Subpart E)

1. General Reimbursement Rules (§ 149.300), Timing (§ 149.310), Reimbursement Conditioned Upon Available Funds (§ 149.315), Universe of Claims That Must Be Submitted (§ 149.320), Requirements for Eligibility of Claims (§ 149.325), and Content of Claims (§ 149.330)

Section 1102(c)(1) of the Affordable Care Act states that a participating employment-based plan shall submit claims for reimbursement to the Secretary which shall contain documentation of the actual costs of the items and services for which each claim is being submitted. As noted above, we define "claim" as documentation specifying the health benefit provided, the provider or supplier, the incurred date, the individual for whom the health benefit was provided, the date and amount of payment net any known negotiated price concessions, and the employment-based plan and benefit option under which the health benefit was provided. The terms "claim" or "medical claim" include medical, surgical, hospital, prescription drug and other such claims as determined by the Secretary. We clarify in the regulation

that claims for benefits for the diagnosis, cure, mitigation, or prevention of physical or mental disease or condition with respect to any structure or function of the body, may be filed. This clarification is not an exhaustive list of claims that the Secretary may determine are appropriate.

The regulation also specifies that claims cannot be submitted for a given plan year until the application that is associated with the claim and that references the applicable plan year cycle has been approved. With respect to a given early retiree, claims cannot be submitted until the early retiree's total paid costs for health benefits incurred for the plan year exceed the applicable cost threshold. Once that threshold has been reached, claims can be submitted, but they must include all claims below the applicable cost threshold for the plan year in order to verify that the cost threshold has been met. Claims must be submitted based on the amounts actually paid, which may include the amounts paid by the early retiree. Once the cumulative claims of an early retiree, as defined in § 149.2, exceed $90,000 for a plan year, a sponsor should not submit claims above this claims limit for that early retiree because no reimbursement will be paid on these claims.

2. Documentation of the Actual Cost of Medical Claims Involved (§ 149.335), Rule for Insured Plans (§ 149.340), and Use of Information Provided (§ 149.345)

All claims submissions must include a list of early retirees for whom claims are being submitted. Both the documentation of actual costs of claims and the list of early retirees must be submitted in a form and manner to be specified by the Secretary. Claims submissions will be processed on a first-in, first-out basis until program funding is expended.

We also specify that with respect to insured plans, the claims and the list of early retirees can be submitted directly to the Secretary by the insurer.

In order for a sponsor to receive credit for the cost-sharing amounts paid by the early retiree or the early retiree's spouse, surviving spouse or dependent, the sponsor must provide prima facie evidence that the early retiree or the early retiree's spouse, surviving spouse or dependent, paid his or her portion of the costs. Such evidence may include an actual payment receipt. If a sponsor cannot provide prima facie evidence, it may receive credit under the program only for the portion of the claim the sponsor actually paid.

There may be instances when a sponsor contracts with, for example, a

staff-model health maintenance organization, that either has its own provider(s) on-staff or pays providers a capitated payment to care for plan participants. In these instances, claims might not ordinarily be produced. However, in order for the Secretary to calculate reimbursement under this program for such sponsors, the sponsor will be required to ensure that the insurer submit the information required in a claim as specified in § 149.330 and § 149. 335. The information submitted by the insurer must be reasonable in light of the specific market that the insurer is serving.

3. Maintenance of Records (§ 149.350)

The regulations also specify how the Secretary may use the information collected for purposes of the program, and the records maintenance requirements that apply to the sponsor. The specified records must be maintained for 6 years after the expiration of the plan year in which the costs were incurred, or longer if otherwise required by law. The sponsor must require its health insurance issuer or employment-based health plan, as applicable, to maintain and produce upon request records to satisfy the maintenance of records requirements.

F. Appeals (Subpart F)

1. Appeals (§ 149.500)

Section 1102(c)(6) of the Affordable Care Act requires the Secretary to establish an appeals process to permit sponsors to appeal a determination made by the Secretary with respect to claims submitted under the program. Due to the limited funding and temporary nature of the program, we have established a one-step appeal process. A sponsor may appeal directly to the Secretary within 15 calendar days of receipt of the determination at issue. Section 149.500 sets out what we consider to be an adverse reimbursement determination, which is a determination relating to the amount of reimbursement paid under the program.

2. Content of Request for Appeal (§ 149.510)

The request for appeal must specify the findings or issues with which the sponsor disagrees and the reasons for the disagreements. The request for appeal may include supporting documentary evidence the sponsor wishes the Secretary to consider. Essentially the sponsor must provide the Secretary with its issues and arguments and any supporting documentation that it has to support its arguments. The Secretary may accept subsequent supporting documentation if, for example, the sponsor did not have time during the 15-day window to perform a comprehensive data analysis of the issue. It would be helpful in the request for appeal if the sponsor notes that further information will be provided to support the request for appeal and a date by which the information will be received by the Secretary.

3. Review of Appeals (§ 149.520)

The regulation sets out generally the process the Secretary will use when reviewing the appeal and clarifies that the Secretary's decision will be final and binding, unless fraud or similar fault are involved. The Secretary will not accept oral argument or oral testimony, either in person or on the telephone.

If all or part of a reimbursement request is denied based on the unavailability of funds, the sponsor may not appeal because an appeal would serve no purpose. If funds are exhausted, there will be no funds to reimburse a sponsor if it is found that the sponsor should otherwise be eligible for reimbursement. Allowing an appeal when funds are exhausted only serves to add burden to sponsors that have received an adverse determination, because, if we allow such an appeal, an aggrieved sponsor may feel that it must appeal in order to exhaust its remedies and to protect its interests. Once the funds for the program are exhausted, there is no interest for the sponsor to protect because there will be no chance of reimbursement, even upon a successful appeal. It will also serve to increase the Secretary's burden because the Secretary will have to process and respond to each of these appeals, when there would be no possibility of a reimbursement adjustment in favor of the sponsor.

The Secretary will inform the sponsor and the applicable HHS designee of the Secretary's decision. Because time is of the essence with respect to funding, we do not specify how the Secretary will inform these stakeholders of the decision because it may be in writing, via electronic means or orally. The response process will be further reviewed to ensure that stakeholders receive appropriate notice of a decision. Of course, we do specify that if the sponsor requests a written response, the Secretary will provide a written response.

G. Disclosure of Data Inaccuracies (Subpart G)

1. Sponsor's Duty To Report Data Inaccuracies (§ 149.600)

Claims submitted for reimbursement may change after the 15-day appeal-request period has expired. For example, if a provider reverses a claim after the appeal-request period has expired, data would need to be updated to reflect the reversal. However, in order to make accurate reimbursements (reopen and revise reimbursement determinations that have already been made), sponsors are required to submit accurate data for reimbursement purposes. We understand that claims may be reversed or otherwise altered and that data that was accurate when submitted for reimbursement under the program may become inaccurate. Furthermore, reimbursement under this program is based on claims that are net of negotiated price concessions. Because negotiated price concessions include post-point-of-sale price concessions, data submitted for reimbursement may become inaccurate once the price concessions are finalized for a given plan year.

We do not believe it is necessary to require a sponsor to submit a formal appeal under § 149.500 to the Secretary merely because data changes due to the natural course of business. Also, we realize that certain changes in data due to the normal course of business might not become evident to a sponsor within 15 days after a reimbursement determination. Therefore, we are establishing a process that will give sponsors the ability to update us on any data inaccuracies and will allow us to reopen and revise a reimbursement determination as necessary, based on the updated data. We believe this would be the most efficient way to administer this program, particularly because of the limited nature of the program funds and the uncertain length of time that an appeal to the Secretary may involve.

2. Secretary's Authority To Reopen and Revise Reimbursement Determination Amounts (§ 149.610)

While the details of this process will be developed in sub-regulatory guidance, we state that the Secretary may reopen and revise a reimbursement determination upon its own motion or upon the request of a sponsor, within 1 year of a reimbursement determination, for any reason, within 4 years of a reimbursement determination for good cause, or at any time in instances fraud or similar fault. We define the term "good cause" in § 149.2, and discuss in the regulation what we believe is not

good cause for revising the reimbursement. This regulation tracks the language in the RDS and Part D reconciliation reopening regulations at § 423.890 and § 423.346, respectively.

We specify in this section that the Secretary may reopen and revise a reimbursement determination on the Secretary's own motion. If the Secretary becomes aware that a reimbursement determination was made based upon inaccurate data, this will allow the Secretary to reopen and revise the reimbursement determination without the sponsor having to make a request. Reimbursement determinations may be reopened and revised to pay out more funds to a sponsor assuming such funds exist or to recoup funds that were already paid, or to withhold funds from a future reimbursement to offset a sponsor's liability.

H. Change of Ownership Requirements (Subpart H)

1. Change of Ownership Requirements (§ 149.700)

We include in this regulation requirements for a sponsor to provide the Secretary with advance notice of any change of ownership of the sponsor. Complying with this requirement is critically important, as it helps to ensure that program reimbursement is being made only to legitimate entities, and only to such entities that are actually complying with the requirements of the program. The requirements mirror the change of ownership requirements that are found in the RDS regulation, which we believe are appropriate for the Early Retiree Reinsurance Program, in light of the fact that we expect many sponsors to participate in both programs. Complying with the change of ownership requirements is especially critical with respect to the Early Retiree Reinsurance Program, in light of the program's limited funding.

The regulations define a change of ownership as any of the following:

(1) The removal, addition, or substitution of a partner, unless the partners expressly agree otherwise as permitted by applicable state law.

(2) Transfer of all or substantially all of the assets of the sponsor to another party.

(3) The merger of the sponsor's corporation into another corporation or the consolidation of the sponsor's organization with one or more other corporations, resulting in a new corporate body.

Transfer of corporate stock or the merger of another corporation into the sponsor's corporation, with the sponsor surviving, does not ordinarily constitute change of ownership.

A sponsor that has a sponsor agreement in effect and is considering or negotiating a change in ownership must notify the Secretary at least 60 days before the anticipated effective date of the change. When there is a change of ownership that results in a transfer of the liability for health benefit costs, the existing sponsor agreement is automatically assigned to the new owner. This requirement is necessary because there may be obligations under the plan sponsor agreement that do not surface until some time after the change of ownership. The Secretary must ensure that there is a party to the plan sponsor agreement that can satisfy those obligations, which may include the return of program reimbursement. The new owner to whom a sponsor agreement is assigned is subject to all applicable statutes, regulations, and guidance, and to the terms and conditions of the sponsor agreement. Failure to notify the Secretary at least 60 days before the anticipated effective date of the change may result in the Secretary recovering funds paid under the program.

III. Waiver of Proposed Rulemaking and Delay in Effective Date

A. Waiver of Notice-and-Comment Procedure

We ordinarily publish a notice of proposed rulemaking in the **Federal Register** and invite public comment on the proposed rule. The notice of proposed rulemaking includes a reference to the legal authority under which the rule is proposed, and the terms and substances of the proposed rule or a description of the subjects and issues involved. This procedure can be waived under section 553(b)(3)(B) of the Administrative Procedure Act, however, if an agency finds good cause that notice-and-comment procedure is impracticable, unnecessary, or contrary to the public interest and incorporates a statement of the finding and its reasons in the rule issued. Below, we discuss our reasons for the waiver of notice-and-comment procedure.

Section 1102(a)(1) of the Affordable Care Act requires the Secretary, not later than 90 days after enactment of the Act, to establish a temporary Early Retiree Reinsurance Program. The Affordable Care Act was enacted on March 23, 2010, which means that the Secretary must implement the Early Retiree Reinsurance Program by June 21, 2010. We believe this is insufficient time for notice-and-comment rulemaking. The 90 days Congress specified does not

allow for development of the rule, a meaningful public comment period, and agency analysis of, and response to, those comments before this rule can be made final. Moreover, we need to actually establish a temporary Early Retiree Reinsurance Program—not simply issue this interim final rule—by June 1, 2010, in order to align the effective date of the program with some sponsors' plan year start dates and to simplify accounting for sponsors and the Secretary, as is discussed below. We must finalize this rule in order to take the multiple other steps necessary to establish the program. Within the time frame contemplated in the statute, we need to have regulations effective in time for applicants to be able to review them and begin to put together their information so that they can apply (once the application process is finalized). The application process cannot be finalized until the regulations are close to being finalized in this Interim Final Rule. Furthermore, the Secretary needs to have established the rules by which she is going to implement this program so that she can move forward with actually administering it, which includes contracting with a contractor to aid with administering the program. The regulations have to be close to finalized before the Secretary can draft a comprehensive scope of work for the contract that will be issued to aid the Secretary with administering this program.

Therefore, we find good cause to waive the notice of proposed rulemaking and to issue this final rule on an interim basis without prior comment. While we are not providing prior comment, we are providing a 30-day public comment period.

B. Waiver of Delay of Effective Date

In addition, section 553(d) of the APA ordinarily requires that a regulation be effective no earlier than 30 days after publication. Under section 553(d)(3) this requirement can be waived for good cause.

As explained above, Section 1102(a)(1) of the Affordable Care Act requires the Secretary to establish the Early Retiree Reinsurance Program by June 21, 2010. In order to better align the effective date of some sponsors' plan and/or fiscal years with the effective date of the program, to allow sponsors to be credited for claims starting at the beginning of a month in order to simplify accounting for sponsors and the Secretary, and to allow sponsors to be credited for claims incurred before June 21, 2010, we need to actually establish the program—not simply issue this Interim Final Rule—by June 1,

2010, as opposed to June 21, 2010. As a result, we find good cause to waive the 30-day delay in effective date that would otherwise apply under section 553(d) of the Administrative Procedure Act (APA) for this rule implementing the Early Retiree Reinsurance Program. This Interim Final Rule will become effective on June 1, 2010.

In addition, 5 U.S.C. 801 generally requires that agencies submit major rules to the Congress 60 days before the rules are scheduled to become effective. This delay does not apply, however, when there has been a finding of good cause for waiver of prior notice and comment as set forth above.

IV. Collection of Information Requirements

Under the Paperwork Reduction Act of 1995, we are required to provide 30-day notice in the **Federal Register** and solicit public comment before a collection of information requirement is submitted to the Office of Management and Budget (OMB) for review and approval. In order to fairly evaluate whether an information collection should be approved by OMB, section 3506(c)(2)(A) of the Paperwork Reduction Act of 1995 requires that we solicit comment on the following issues:

• The need for the information collection and its usefulness in carrying out the proper functions of our agency.
• The accuracy of our estimate of the information collection burden.
• The quality, utility, and clarity of the information to be collected.
• Recommendations to minimize the information collection burden on the affected public, including automated collection techniques.

We are soliciting public comment on each of these issues for the following sections of this document that contain information collection requirements (ICRs).

A. ICRs Regarding Requirements To Participate (§ 149.35)

Section 149.35(b)(1) requires plan sponsors to make available documentation, data, and other information related to this part and any other records specified by the Secretary, as stated in § 149.350. The burden associated with this requirement is detailed in our discussion of § 149.350.

Section 149.35(b)(2) states that a plan sponsor must have a written agreement with its health insurance issuer (as defined in 45 CFR 160.103) or employment-based plan (as applicable) regarding disclosure of information, data, documents, and records to the Secretary, and the health insurance issuer or employment-based plan must disclose to the Secretary, on behalf of the sponsor, the information necessary for the sponsor to comply with the program, this part, and program guidance. The burden associated with this requirement is the time and effort necessary for a plan sponsor to develop, sign, and maintain the aforementioned written agreement with its health insurance issuer or employment-based plan. We estimate that it will take 1 hour to develop, sign, and maintain one such written agreement. We also estimate that each plan sponsor on average will need to maintain and sign 3 such agreements. Using the RDS Program as a baseline, we estimate that 4,500 Early Retiree Reinsurance Program plan sponsors must comply with this requirement. The estimated annual burden associated with this requirement is 13,500 hours. The estimate cost of compliance with this requirement is $1,005,885, for the first year of the program. For the subsequent four years, we estimate that roughly one-quarter of the 4,500 sponsors (1,125) will contract with one different entity each year to disclose information, data, etc., to the Secretary. For each of those years, the estimated cost of compliance with this requirement is $83,824.

Section 149.35(b)(3) requires plan sponsors to have procedures to protect against fraud, waste and abuse under this program, and must comply timely with requests from the Secretary to produce the procedures and any documents or data to substantiate the implementation of the procedures and their effectiveness. Additionally, § 149.35(b)(5) requires plan sponsors to comply timely with requests from the Secretary to produce the procedures and any documents or data to substantiate the implementation of the procedures and their effectiveness. The burden associated with the requirements in § 149.35(b)(3) is the time and effort necessary to develop, implement, and maintain procedures to protect against fraud, waste and abuse under this program. There is also burden associated with producing the procedures and any supporting documentation up request by the Secretary. We estimate that it will take 20 hours for each plan sponsor or designee to develop, implement and maintain one set of such policies and procedures. We also estimate that with respect to each plan sponsor, an average of three separate sets of policies and procedures will have to be developed, implemented and maintained, to account for the fact that many sponsors will have multiple benefit options, each

using a different entity that is submitting claims to the program on their behalf. However, we estimate that one-third of the 4,500 expected plan sponsors will be contracting with entities that submit claims to the program that already have fraud, waste and abuse programs and procedures in place. Therefore, we estimate that 3,000 plan sponsors will have to newly develop, implement, and maintain such program and procedures. The estimated annual burden for these requirements is 20 hours per set of fraud, waste and abuse procedures. The estimated cost associated with this requirement is $9,982,800 for the first year of the program. For the subsequent four years of the program, we estimate that roughly one quarter of the estimated 4,500 sponsors (roughly 1,125) will contract with one new entity each year, to submit claims to the program on the sponsor's behalf. For each of those years, the estimated annual burden associated with this burden is 1,125 sponsors multiplied by 20 hours, or 22,500 hours, with estimated costs equal to $1,247,850.

Section 149.35(b)(4) also requires plan sponsors to submit an application to the Secretary in the manner, and at the time, required by the Secretary, as specified in § 149.40. The burden associated with this requirement is detailed in our discussion of § 149.40.

B. ICRs Regarding Application (§ 149.40)

Section 149.40 discusses the application process for the early retiree reinsurance program. As stated in § 149.40(a) requires an applicant to submit an application to participate in this program to the Secretary, which is signed by an authorized representative of the applicant who certifies that the information contained in the application is true and accurate to the best of the authorized representative's knowledge and belief. Section 149.40(e) states that an applicant must submit an application for each plan for which it will submit a reimbursement request. Furthermore, as part of the application process, every application must be accompanied by the information listed in § 149.40(f).

The burden associated with the requirements in this section is the time and effort necessary for a plan sponsor or its designee to complete an application for each plan for which it will submit a reimbursement request. In addition, there is burden associated with compiling and submitting the required ancillary information listed in § 149.40(f). We estimate that the program will receive an average of 1

application each, from 4,500 plan sponsors or their designees. We further estimate that it will take 35 hours for a plan sponsor or designee to complete one application package. The total estimated annual burden associated with this requirement is 157,500 hours. The total estimated annual cost associated with this requirement is $8,820,675. This is a one-time burden, as sponsors are not required to submit a new application for each plan year.

C. ICRs Regarding Documentation of Actual Costs of Medical Claims Involved (§ 149.335)

Section § 149.335 requires that sponsors must submit claims, with each submission consisting of a list of early retirees for whom claims are being submitted, and documentation of the actual costs of the items and services for each claim being submitted. These material must be submitted in a form and manner specified by the Secretary. Additionally, in order for a sponsor to receive reimbursement for the portion of a claim that an early retiree paid, the sponsor must submit prima facie evidence that the early enrollee paid his or her portion of the claim. The burden associated with the requirements in this section is the time and effort necessary for sponsors to assemble and submit the aforementioned information. We estimate that it will take each sponsor an average of 45 hours to comply with these requirements, with the number of hours varying based upon the number of early retirees for whom claims are submitted, the number of claims, the technology used to generate the required information, etc. We estimate that each of the 4,500 participating sponsors will make two submissions annually. The total estimated annual burden associated with this requirement is 405,000 hours. The total estimated annual cost associated with these requirements is $15,758,550.

D. ICRs Regarding Maintenance of Records (§ 149.350)

Section 149.350(a) requires the sponsor of the certified plan (or a subcontractor, as applicable) must maintain and furnish to the Secretary, or its designee, upon request the records as specified in § 149.350(b). The records must be maintained for 6 years after the expiration of the plan year in which the costs were incurred, or longer if otherwise required by law. Similarly, as required by § 149.350(d), the sponsor must require its health insurance issuer or employment-based plan, as applicable, to maintain and produce upon request records to satisfy subparagraph (c) of this regulation. The burden associated with the requirements in this section is the time and effort necessary to retain the specified records. We estimate that each of the estimated 4,500 sponsors will require 6 hours to retain the records. The total estimated annual burden associated with this requirement is 27,000 hours. The total estimated annual cost associated with this requirement is $1,050,570.

E. ICRs Regarding Appeals (§ 149.500 and § 149.510)

Section 149.500(d) states that if a sponsor appeals an adverse reimbursement determination, the sponsor must submit the appeal in writing to the Secretary within 15 days of receipt of the determination. Section 149.510 requires a request for appeal to specify the findings or issues with which the sponsor disagrees and the reasons for the disagreements. In addition, the request for appeal may include supporting documentary evidence the sponsor wishes the Secretary to consider. The burden associated with the aforementioned requirements is the time and effort necessary for a sponsor to draft and submit an appeal, including supporting documentation. While this requirement is subject to the PRA, we believe the associated burden is exempt under 5 CFR 1320.4. In this case, the information associated with an appeal would be collected subsequent to an administrative action, that is, an adverse reimbursement determination or an application denial.

F. ICRs Regarding Sponsor's Duty To Report Data Inaccuracies (§ 149.600)

Section 149.600 requires a sponsor to disclose any data inaccuracies on which a reimbursement request has been made, including inaccurate claims data and negotiated price concessions, in a manner and at a time specified by the Secretary in guidance. The burden associated with this requirement is the time and effort necessary for a sponsor to comply with the reporting requirement. We estimate that 1,500 sponsors annually will be subject to this requirement, and that burden associated with this requirement is 32 hours per sponsor (two disclosures per year per sponsor, each disclosure having an estimated burden of 16 hours). The estimated annual burden associated with this requirement is 48,000 hours. The total estimated annual cost associated with this burden is $1,867,680.

G. ICRs Regarding Change of Ownership Requirements (§ 149.700)

Section 149.700(c) requires a sponsor that has a sponsor agreement in effect under this part and is considering or negotiating a change in ownership to notify the Secretary at least 60 days before the anticipated effective date of the change. The burden associated with the requirement is the time and effort necessary for a sponsor to comply with the reporting requirement. Based on our experience with the RDS Program, we estimate that it will take each sponsor an average of 1 hour to comply with these requirements, and that 50 sponsors per year will be subject to this requirement. The total estimated annual burden associated with this requirement is 50 hours. The total estimated annual cost associated with these requirements is $2,773.

All of the information collection requirements containing burden were submitted to the Office of Management and Budget (OMB) for emergency review and approval as part of a single information collection request (ICR). As part of the emergency review and approval process, OMB waived the notification requirements. The ICR was approved under OMB control number 0938–1087 with an expiration date of October 31, 2010. However, we are still seeking public comments on the information collection requirements discussed in this interim final rule with comment. All comments will be considered as we continue to develop the ICR as we must resubmit the ICR to obtain a standard 3-year approval.

TABLE 1—ANNUAL RECORDKEEPING AND REPORTING BURDEN

Regulation section	OMB Control No.	Respondents	Responses	Time per response (hours)	Total burden (hours)	Hourly labor cost ($)	Total labor cost ($)	Total capital/ maintenance cost ($)	Total cost ($)
§ 149.35(b)(2)	0938–1087	4,500	13,500	1	13,500	74.51	1,005,885	0	1,005,885
		1,125	1,125	1	1,125	74.51	83,824	0	83,824
§ 149.35(b)(3)	0938–1087	3,000	9,000	20	180,000	55.46	9,982,800	0	9,982,800
		1,125	1,125	20	22,500	55.46	1,247,850	0	1,247,850
§ 149.40	0938–1087	4,500	4,500	35	157,500	**	8,820,675	0	8,820,675
§ 149.335	0938–1087	4,500	9,000	45	405,000	38.91	15,758,550	0	15,758,550
§ 149.350	0938–1087	4,500	4,500	6	27,000	38.91	1,050,570	0	1,050,570
§ 149.600	0938–1087	1,500	3,000	16	48,000	38.91	1,867,680	0	1,867,680
§ 149.700(c)	0938–1087	50	50	1	50	55.46	2,773	0	2,773
Total	....	11,300	45,800	....	854,675	....	....	....	39,820,607

**$74.51 per hour for 1 hour per response, $55.46 per hour for 34 hours per response.

If you comment on these information collection and recordkeeping requirements, please do either of the following:

1. Submit your comments electronically as specified in the **ADDRESSES** section of this proposed rule; or

2. Submit your comments to the Office of Information and Regulatory Affairs, Office of Management and Budget, Attn: CMS Desk Officer, CMS– 9996–IFC, fax (202) 395–6974, or via email *OIRA_submission@omb.eop.gov*.

V. Response to Comments

Because of the large number of public comments we normally receive on **Federal Register** documents, we are not able to acknowledge or respond to them individually. We will consider all comments we receive by the date and time specified in the **DATES** section of this preamble, and, when we proceed with a subsequent document, we will respond to the comments in the preamble to that document.

VI. Regulatory Impact Analysis

A. Overall Impact

We have examined the impacts of this rule as required by Executive Order 12866 on Regulatory Planning and Review (September 30, 1993), the Regulatory Flexibility Act (RFA) (September 19, 1980, Pub. L. 96–354), section 1102(b) of the Social Security Act, section 202 of the Unfunded

Mandates Reform Act of 1995 (Pub. L. 104–4), Executive Order 13132 on Federalism (August 4, 1999), and the Congressional Review Act (5 U.S.C. 804(2)).

Executive Order 12866 directs agencies to assess all costs and benefits of available regulatory alternatives and, if regulation is necessary, to select regulatory approaches that maximize net benefits (including potential economic, environmental, public health and safety effects, distributive impacts, and equity). A regulatory impact analysis (RIA) must be prepared for major rules with economically significant effects ($100 million or more in any 1 year). This rule will be economically significant because it sets out the requirements that sponsors will need to meet in order to participate in the Early Retiree Reinsurance Program and obtain a portion of the $5 billion the Congress appropriated for this program. While a small portion of the funds will be used to administer the program, the remainder of the $5 billion will be paid to eligible sponsors over the life of the program, resulting in economically significant net positive transfers to sponsors. We believe that the costs imposed on sponsors that want to receive the early retiree reimbursement will not be significant relative to the payments received. The costs will consist of staff or contractor time to complete the application to participate, to file claims for reimbursement, and to comply with program requirements such as any requests related to an audit, as well as any supplies necessary to perform these tasks summarized in Table 1 above. As a result this rulemaking is "economically significant" as measured by the $100 million threshold, and hence also a major rule under the Congressional Review Act. Accordingly, we have prepared a regulatory impact analysis that to the best of our ability presents the costs and benefits of the rulemaking.

The RFA requires agencies to analyze options for regulatory relief of small businesses, if a rule has a significant impact on a substantial number of small entities. According to the Kaiser Family Foundation and Health Research & Educational Trust's 2009 Employer Health Benefits Survey, 5 percent of surveyed businesses with 3 to 199 workers offered retiree health benefits. See pg. 166 of the Survey. *http:// ehbs.kff.org/pdf/2009/7936.pdf.* It is unclear how many offered health benefits to early retirees, but since there were about 3.3 million such firms (page 15 of the survey), even if only 5 percent provided such benefits, over 150,000 such firms would be eligible for the

program. However, we estimate that the number of sponsors that will actually participate in the Early Retiree Reinsurance Program, will be similar to the number that participate in the Retiree Drug Subsidy Program. For purposes of the RFA, we estimate that 5 percent of sponsors are small entities as that term is used in the RFA (including small businesses, nonprofit organizations, and small governmental jurisdictions). Ultimately, the number of small businesses affected will depend upon how many small businesses apply for the reimbursement, which we do not currently know. What we do know is that we have made, and will make, the application and claims submission processes as simple as possible, while still protecting the integrity of the program. Therefore, if small businesses want to participate, they may do so.

Turning to small business providers, the great majority of hospitals and most other health care providers and suppliers are small entities, either by being nonprofit organizations or by meeting the Small Business Administration (SBA) definition of a small business (having revenues of less than $7.0 million to $34.5 million in any 1 year). While this rule does not directly impact providers (unless they apply to be sponsors), it does increase access to health insurance, which may then cause more individuals to be able to afford health care and therefore be able to utilize providers' services and products more often. Therefore, health care providers may see an increase in patients and may not be required to deliver health care free of charge or at reduced rates in as many instances as they may currently do.

Because much of the effect on health care providers depends upon where plan participants choose to receive these services, which must be from a provider that accepts the plan participant's coverage, the term "health care provider" is likely to include health care entities operated by small governmental entities such as counties or towns. Small governmental health care entities may include county hospitals, clinics or other such entities. Regardless of the entity, we expect a positive effect on these entities. For purposes of the RFA, a significant number of health care providers indirectly affected by the program are considered small businesses according to the SBA's size standards with total revenues of $7 million to $34.5 million or less in any 1 year and an undetermined percent are nonprofit organizations. Individuals and States are not included in the definition of a small entity. Uncertainty arises because we do not know how many

small businesses or other small entities will apply to participate in the Early Retiree Reinsurance Program, nor do we know how the increased access to health insurance will affect small businesses that provide health care services and products to the participants affected by the program. We believe, however, that this interim final rule will have a significant positive economic effect on a substantial number of small businesses. The HHS interpretation of the Regulatory Flexibility Act has historically been that it does not trigger a regulatory flexibility analysis as a result of positive economic impacts (the statute requires that economic impacts be minimized, which makes no sense when applied to positive effects). The Department nonetheless usually prepares a voluntary regulatory flexibility analysis in such circumstances. In addition, because a regulatory flexibility analysis is only required for rules for which an NPRM must be prepared, there is an additional exemption that applies to this rule. Accordingly, we conclude that a regulatory flexibility analysis is not required. Nonetheless, we believe that this regulatory impact section, together with the remainder of the preamble, constitutes a voluntary analysis that meets the requirements that would otherwise be applicable.

In addition, section 1102(b) of the Act requires us to prepare a regulatory impact analysis if a rule may have a significant impact on the operations of a substantial number of small rural hospitals. For purposes of section 1102(b) of the Act, we define a small rural hospital as a hospital that is located outside of a metropolitan statistical area and has fewer than 100 beds. We do not believe this rule will have a significant impact on the operations of a substantial number of small rural hospitals because the increased access to health insurance, while positively affecting small rural hospitals' ability to collect payment for services rendered to plan participants affected by the program, will be unlikely to increase revenues in an economically significant amount. Therefore, the Secretary has determined that this interim final rule will not have a significant impact on the operations of a substantial number of small rural hospitals. In addition, such an analysis is not required when an NPRM is not required, as in this case.

Section 202 of the Unfunded Mandates Reform Act of 1995 (UMRA) also requires that agencies assess anticipated costs and benefits before issuing any rule whose mandates required spending in any 1 year of $100 million in 1995 dollars, updated annually for inflation. In 2010, that threshold is approximately $135 million. This rule does not mandate any spending by State, local, or tribal governments in the aggregate, or by the private sector. In fact, participation in the program is voluntary and for all sponsors participating, we expect in the aggregate that sponsors will receive $5 billion in reimbursement, less administrative costs.

Executive Order 13132 establishes certain requirements that an agency must meet when it promulgates a proposed rule (and subsequent final rule) that imposes substantial direct requirement costs on State and local governments, preempts State law, or otherwise has Federalism implications. This rule will not have a substantial direct effect on State or local governments, preempt State laws, or otherwise have a Federalism implication.

B. Need for Regulatory Action

As previously discussed, the Affordable Care Act, includes this provision that establishes the temporary Early Retiree Reinsurance Program. Section 1102(a)(1) requires the Secretary to establish the program within 90 days of enactment of the law, which is June 21, 2010. This interim final rule is necessary to implement this program by the statutory deadline. The program is designed to assist people in the early retiree age group who often face difficulties obtaining insurance in the individual market because of advanced age or chronic conditions that make coverage unaffordable and inaccessible. The Early Retiree Reinsurance Program will provide financial help for employer-based plans to continue to provide coverage to plan participants, and provides financial relief to plan participants.

C. Anticipated Effects

1. Effects on Plan Sponsors

This rule will positively affect employers and employee organizations that self-fund health benefits or pay premiums to insure their early retirees' health benefits. The amount of the effects depends upon the sponsors' determination of the use of the reimbursement. Thus the positive effect will range from negligible if they use the reimbursement almost exclusively for plan participants' costs to just under $5 billion, minus the administrative costs of this program if they maximize the amount of reimbursement used to lower plan costs.

2. Effects on Plan Participants

We believe that this rule will have a positive effect on plan participants. We believe that the program will encourage sponsors to maintain coverage that they might not otherwise maintain, and will lower health benefit costs for plan participants and sponsors. With access to insurance, we believe, that plan participants will access health care as needed, instead of delaying a health care encounter until the condition progresses to a point when an encounter is unavoidable (and then more severe and expensive). Furthermore, we believe plan participants will not incur as much debt due to health care costs. The amount of the effects depends upon the sponsors' determination of the use of the reimbursement. Thus, the positive effect will range from moderate if sponsors use almost all of the reimbursement for sponsors' costs (in this case, the lower costs to the sponsor encourages continued provision of retiree coverage, which is of benefit to the retiree) to nearly $5 billion, minus administrative costs, if sponsors use the reimbursement almost exclusively to lower plan participants' costs.

3. Effects on Other Providers

We expect this rule to have an indirect positive effect on providers because more individuals will have access to health insurance, which will cause these individuals to seek health care when needed, as may not be the case currently, and health care providers will be able to receive payment for services provided. It is a two-fold benefit. Providers may have more patients and more of the patients will be able to pay for the services or products provided, whether directly (for example, co-insurance or co-payment) or via their insurance.

4. Effects on the Medicare and Medicaid Programs

This rule does not impose any consequential costs on Medicare or Medicaid. While sponsors may only submit claims for reimbursement for early retirees and early retirees' spouses, surviving spouses or dependents, the reimbursements paid to a sponsor must be used to lower costs for all plan participants, which may include enrollees who also have Medicare coverage. Other than increased utilization of health care services or products for plan participants that are covered by a certified plan, we do not expect any notable impact on Medicare. We expect the impact due to increased utilization to be minimal.

This rule may in fact lessen the number of individuals on Medicaid, or slow any growth in numbers of individuals eligible for Medicaid, because sponsors that are considering dropping health insurance for early retirees or plan participants may decide otherwise, once the sponsor becomes eligible for the program. Furthermore, it is possible that employers may decide to offer health insurance to early retirees because of the program.

D. Alternatives Considered

With respect to implementing this program, there is no alternative. The Congress requires that the program be in effect not later than 90 days after the enactment of the bill. The statute was enacted March 23, 2010. With respect to the application process, we considered numerous requirements as to what we would need in order to protect the integrity of the program, but ultimately settled on the requirements in the regulation. We had originally considered requiring an attestation from a qualified actuary, certifying that the sponsor's estimate of projected costs is reasonable. We decided against this requirement because the projection was merely for the purpose of letting us know if and when we should stop taking applications. Weighing the expense of requiring a sponsor to pay an actuary to make the certification against the benefit the certification would provide, we decided not to require this because we want this program to be as inclusive as possible.

We also considered how best to implement the provision relating to participants with chronic and high-cost conditions. We considered identifying specific conditions in sub-regulatory guidance but decided that such a policy would ultimately work against the goals of the program because we would not be able to do a comprehensive analysis to identify them in the time allotted to implement this program. Furthermore, because many sponsors' plans were initiated before the effective date of the statute and any guidance we may have developed, sponsors that covered what they think are chronic and high-cost conditions, but which we did not identify as such, would have been penalized. Because this is supposed to be an inclusive program, we defined the term "chronic and high-cost conditions" to be any condition for which the plan is likely to incur health benefits costs of at least $15,000 for any one plan participant in a plan year. If a sponsor has programs and procedures that have generated or have the potential to generate cost savings in place to address any such conditions, it will meet the requirement.

Ultimately, the approach we took in these regulations is intended to balance the need to protect the integrity of the program with the inclusive nature of the program.

E. Accounting Statement and Table

Whenever a rule is considered an economically significant rule under Executive Order 12866, we are required to develop an Accounting Statement. We have prepared an accounting statement below (Table 2) showing the classification of the expenditures associated with the provisions of this interim final rule.

The terminology from this table may be interpreted as follows:

1. Annualized—means to determine cost/benefits on a yearly basis as opposed to quarterly. This would include both start-up and ongoing costs amortized over the number of years used in the RIA. Due to the uncertainty in estimating these costs/benefits we have estimated the amortization equally over the 4 years 2010 through 2013.

2. Monetized—means to develop quantitative estimates and convert them to dollar amounts, if possible.

3. Qualitative Benefits and Costs— means to categorize or rank the qualitative effects in terms of their importance (for example, certainty, likely magnitude, and reversibility).

4. Effects—means the effects on Medicare/Medicaid program, beneficiaries, and health care facilities, taken from the impact analysis. (We note that regulations with annual costs that are less than one billion dollars are likely to have a minimal effect on economic growth.)

5. All quantitative estimates must be presented as discounted flows using 3 percent and 7 percent factors.

TABLE 2—ACCOUNTING STATEMENT

Category	Primary estimate	Year dollars	Discount rate	Period covered	Source citation (RIA, preamble, etc.)
BENEFITS					
Annualized monetized benefits (in millions of dollars per year).	Not estimated.				
COSTS					
Annualized monetized costs (in millions of dollars per year).	39.8	2010	7%	2010–2013	Paperwork Reduction Act Burden in Preamble.
	39.8	2010	3%		
TRANSFERS					
Annualized monetized transfers: "on budget" (in millions of dollars per year).	$1,250	2010	7%	2010–2013	Statute.
From whom to whom? ..	$1,250 From the Federal Government to eligible sponsors and for administration of the program including to contractors.	2010 From the Federal Government to eligible sponsors and for administration of the program including to contractors.	3% From the Federal Government to eligible sponsors and for administration of the program including to contractors.		

Category	Effects				*Source Citation (RIA, preamble, etc.).
Effects on State, local, and/or tribal governments.	Positive, but currently unable to be determined.				RIA.
Effects on small businesses.	Positive, but currently unable to be determined.				RIA.

E. Conclusion

We used statistics from the RDS Program as a model because it has similar characteristics to the characteristics of this new Early Retiree Reinsurance Program, and, based on this model, we expect that approximately 4,500 sponsors will apply to participate in the Early Retiree Reinsurance Program. Of those sponsors, we expect approximately 3,000 will be private entities and 1,500 will be State and local governments. Alternatively, the number of applicants could be substantially higher if small or other employers participate in this program in higher numbers than they did in the Retiree Drug Subsidy Program. Regardless, total spending cannot exceed the $5 billion appropriated for this program over the four-year period. While some of the funds allotted for the program are required to be used to implement the program, we anticipate an overall positive transfer of $5 billion to eligible sponsors (and indirectly a portion of those funds will be transferred for the benefit of plan participants), less administrative costs. The analysis above, together with the remainder of this preamble, provides a regulatory impact analysis and meets the requirements for a Final Regulatory Flexibility Analysis.

In accordance with the provisions of Executive Order 12866 the Office of Management and Budget reviewed this regulation.

List of Subjects in 45 CFR Part 149

Administrative practice and procedure, Health care, Health insurance, Penalties, Reporting and recordkeeping requirements.

■ For the reasons set forth in the preamble, the Department of Health and Human Services amends 45 CFR subtitle A, subchapter B, by adding a new part 149 to read as follows:

PART 149—REQUIREMENTS FOR THE EARLY RETIREE REINSURANCE PROGRAM

Subpart A—General Provisions

Subpart B—Requirements for Eligible Employment-based Plans

Subpart C—Reinsurance Amounts

Subpart D—Use of Reimbursements

Subpart E—Reimbursement Methods

Subpart F—Appeals

Subpart G—Disclosure of Inaccurate Data

Subpart H—Change of Ownership Requirements

Authority: Section 1102 of the Patient Protection and Affordable Care Act (Pub. L. 111–148).

Subpart A—General Provisions

§ 149.1   Purpose and basis.

This part implements the Early Retiree Reinsurance Program, as required by section 1102 of the Patient Protection and Affordable Care Act (Pub. L. 111–148).

§ 149.2   Definitions.

For purposes of this part, the following definitions apply:

Authorized representative means an individual with legal authority to sign and bind a sponsor to the terms of a contract or agreement.

Benefit option means a particular benefit design, category of benefits, or cost-sharing arrangement offered within an employment-based plan.

Certified means that the sponsor and its employment-based plan or plans meet the requirements of this part and the sponsor's application to participate in the program has been approved by the Secretary.

Chronic and high-cost condition means a condition for which $15,000 or more in health benefit claims are likely to be incurred during a plan year by one plan participant.

Claim or *medical claim* means documentation, in a form and manner to be specified by the Secretary, indicating the health benefit provided, the provider or supplier, the incurred date, the individual for whom the health benefit was provided, the date and amount of payment net any known negotiated price concessions, and the employment-based plan and benefit option under which the health benefit was provided. The terms *claim* or *medical claim* include medical, surgical, hospital, prescription drug and other such claims as determined by the Secretary.

Early retiree means a plan participant who is age 55 and older who is enrolled for health benefits in a certified employment-based plan, who is not eligible for coverage under title XVIII of the Act, and who is not an active employee of an employer maintaining, or currently contributing to, the employment-based plan or of any employer that has made substantial contributions to fund such plan. In this part, the term *early retiree* also includes the enrolled spouse, surviving spouse, and dependents of such individuals. The determination of whether an individual is not an active employee is made by the sponsor in accordance with the rules of its plan. For purposes of this subpart, however, an individual is presumed to be an active employee if, under the Medicare Secondary Payer rules in 42 CFR 411.104 and related guidance published by the Centers for Medicare & Medicaid Services, the person is considered to be receiving coverage by reason of current employment status. This presumption applies whether or not the Medicare Secondary Payer rules actually apply to the sponsor. For this purpose, a sponsor may also treat a person receiving coverage under its employment-based plan as a dependent in accordance with the rules of its plan, regardless of whether that individual is considered a dependent for Federal or state tax purposes. For purposes of this definition of early retiree, an employer maintaining, or currently contributing to, the employment-based plan or any employer that has made substantial contributions to fund such plan, means a plan sponsor (as defined in this section).

Employment-based plan means a group health plan as defined in this section of the regulation.

Good cause means:

(1) New and material evidence exists that was not readily available at the time the reimbursement determination was made;

(2) A clerical error in the computation of the reimbursement determination was made by the Secretary; or

(3) The evidence that was considered in making the reimbursement determination clearly shows on its face that an error was made.

Group health plan means group health plan as defined in 42 CFR 423.882 that provides health benefits to early retirees, but excludes Federal governmental plans.

Health benefits means medical, surgical, hospital, prescription drug, and other benefits that may be specified by the Secretary, whether self-funded or delivered through the purchase of health insurance or otherwise. Such benefits include benefits for the diagnosis, cure, mitigation, or prevention of physical or mental disease or condition with respect to any structure or function of the body. Health benefits do not include benefits specified at 45 CFR 146.145(c)(2) through (4).

Incurred means the point in time when the sponsor, health insurance issuer (as defined in 45 CFR 160.103), employment-based plan, plan participant, or a combination of these or similar stakeholders, become responsible for payment of the claim.

Negotiated price concession means any direct or indirect remuneration (including discounts, direct or indirect subsidies, charge backs or rebates, cash discounts, free goods contingent on a purchase agreement, up-front payments, coupons, goods in kind, free or reduced-price services, grants, or other price concessions or similar benefits) offered to some or all purchasers, which may include a sponsor, a health insurance issuer, or an employment-based plan) that would serve to decrease the costs incurred under the employment-based plan.

Plan participant means anyone enrolled in an applicable plan including an early retiree, as defined in this section, a retiree, a retiree's spouse and dependent, an active employee and an active employee's spouse and dependent.

Plan year means the year that is designated as the plan year in the plan document of an employment-based plan, except that if the plan document does not designate a plan year, if the plan year is not a 12-month plan year, or if there is no plan document, the plan year is:

(1) The deductible or limit year used under the plan;

(2) The policy year, if the plan does not impose deductibles or limits on a 12-month basis;

(3) The sponsor's taxable year, If the plan does not impose deductibles or limits on a 12-month basis, and either the plan is not insured or the insurance policy is not renewed on a 12-month basis, or;

(4) The calendar year, in any other case.

Post point-of-sale negotiated price concession means any negotiated price concession that an employment-based plan or insurer receives with respect to a given health benefit, after making payment for that health benefit.

Program means the Early Retiree Reinsurance Program established in section 1102 of the Patient Protection and Affordable Care Act.

Secretary means the Secretary of the United States Department of Health & Human Services or the Secretary's designee.

Sponsor means a plan sponsor as defined in section 3(16)(B) of the Employee Retirement Income Security Act of 1974 (ERISA), 29 U.S.C. 1002(16)(B), except that in the case of a plan maintained jointly by one employer and an employee organization and for which the employer is the primary source of financing, the term means the employer.

Sponsor agreement means an agreement between the sponsor and the United States Department of Health & Human Services, or its designee, which is made to comply with the provisions of this part.

Subpart B—Requirements for Eligible Employment-Based Plans

§ 149.30   General requirements.

A sponsor is eligible to participate in the program if it meets the requirements of section 1102 of the Patient Protection and Affordable Care Act, this part, and guidance developed by the Secretary.

§ 149.35   Requirements to participate.

(a) A sponsor's employment-based plan must—

(1) Be certified by the Secretary.

(2) Include programs and procedures that have generated or have the potential to generate cost-savings with respect to plan participants with chronic and high-cost conditions.

(b) A sponsor must—

(1) Make available information, data, documents, and records as specified in § 149.350.

(2) Have a written agreement with its health insurance issuer (as defined in 45 CFR 160.103) or employment-based plan (as applicable) regarding disclosure of information, data, documents, and records, to the Secretary, and the health insurance issuer or employment-based plan must disclose to the Secretary, on behalf of the sponsor, at a time and in a manner specified by the Secretary in guidance, the information, data, documents and records necessary for the sponsor to comply with the program, this part, and program guidance.

(3) Ensure that policies and procedures to protect against fraud, waste and abuse under this program are in place, and must comply timely with requests from the Secretary to produce the policies and procedures and any documents or data to substantiate the implementation of the policies and procedures and their effectiveness.

(4) Submit an application to the Secretary in the manner, and at the time, required by the Secretary as specified in § 149.40.

§ 149.40   Application.

(a) The applicant must submit an application to participate in this program to the Secretary, which is signed by an authorized representative of the applicant who certifies that the information contained in the application is true and accurate to the best of the authorized representative's knowledge and belief.

(b) Applications will be processed in the order in which they are received.

(c) An application that fails to meet all the requirements of this part will be denied and the applicant must submit another application if it wishes to participate in the program. The new application will be processed based on when the new submission is received.

(d) An applicant need not submit a separate application for each plan year but must identify in its application the plan year start and end date cycle (starting month and day, and ending month and day) for which it is applying.

(e) An applicant must submit an application for each plan for which it will submit a reimbursement request.

(f) In connection with each application the applicant must submit the following:

(1) Applicant's Tax Identification Number.

(2) Applicant's name and address.

(3) Contact name, telephone number and email address.

(4) Plan sponsor agreement signed by an authorized representative, which includes—

(i) An assurance that the sponsor has a written agreement with its health insurance issuer (as defined in 45 CFR 160.103) or employment-based plan, as applicable, regarding disclosure of information to the Secretary, and the health insurance issuer or employment-based plan must disclose to the Secretary, on behalf of the sponsor, at a time and in a manner specified by the Secretary in guidance, information, data, documents, and records necessary for the sponsor to comply with the requirements of the program.

(ii) An acknowledgment that the information in the application is being provided to obtain Federal funds, and that all subcontractors acknowledge that information provided in connection with a subcontract is used for purposes of obtaining Federal funds.

(iii) An attestation that policies and procedures are in place to detect and reduce fraud, waste, and abuse, and that the sponsor will produce the policies and procedures, and necessary information, records and data, upon request by the Secretary, to substantiate existence of the policies and procedures and their effectiveness.

(iv) Other terms and conditions required by the Secretary.

(5) A summary indicating how the applicant will use any reimbursement received under the program to meet the requirements of the program, including:

(i) How the reimbursement will be used to reduce premium contributions, co-payments, deductibles, coinsurance, or other out-of-pocket costs for plan participants, to reduce health benefit or health benefit premium costs for the sponsor, or to reduce any combination of these costs;

(ii) What procedures or programs the sponsor has in place that have generated or have the potential to generate cost savings with respect to plan participants with chronic and high-cost conditions; and

(iii) How the sponsor will use the reimbursement to maintain its level of contribution to the applicable plan.

(6) Projected amount of reimbursement to be received under the program for the first two plan year cycles with specific amounts for each of the two cycles.

(7) A list of all benefit options under the employment-based plan that any early retiree for whom the sponsor receives program reimbursement may be claimed.

(8) Any other information the Secretary requires.

(g) An application must be approved, and the plan and the sponsor certified, by the Secretary before a sponsor may request reimbursement under the program.

(h) The Secretary may reopen a determination under which an application had been approved or denied:

(1) Within 1 year of the determination for any reason;

(2) Within 4 years of the determination if the evidence that was considered in making the determination shows on its face that an error was made; or

(3) At any time in instances of fraud or similar fault.

§ 149.41 Consequences of Non-Compliance, Fraud, or Similar Fault.

Upon failure to comply with the requirements of this part, or if fraud, waste, and abuse, or similar fault are found, the Secretary may recoup or withhold funds, terminate or deny a sponsor's application, or take a combination of these actions.

§ 149.45 Funding limitation.

(a) Based on the projected or actual availability of program funding, the Secretary may deny applications that otherwise meet the requirements of this part, and if an application is approved, may deny all or part of a sponsor's reimbursement request.

(b) The Secretary's decision to stop accepting applications or satisfying reimbursement requests based on the availability of funding is final and binding, and is not appealable.

Subpart C—Reinsurance Amounts

§ 149.100 Amount of reimbursement.

(a) For each early retiree enrolled in a certified plan in a plan year, the sponsor receives reimbursement in the amount of 80 percent of the costs for health benefits (net of negotiated price concessions for health benefits) for claims incurred during the plan year that are attributed to health benefits costs between the cost threshold and cost limit, and that are paid by the employment-based plan or by the insurer (if an insured plan), and by the early retiree.

(b) Costs are considered paid by an early retiree, if paid by that individual or another person on behalf of the early retiree, and the early retiree (or person paying on behalf of the early retiree) is not reimbursed through insurance or otherwise, or other third party payment arrangement.

(c) Reimbursement is calculated by first determining the costs for health benefits net of negotiated price concessions, within the applicable plan year for each early retiree, and then subtracting amounts below the cost threshold and above the cost limit within the applicable plan year for each such individual.

(d) For purposes of determining amounts below the cost threshold and above the cost limit for any given early retiree, all costs for health benefits paid by the employment-based plan (or by the insurer, if applicable), or by or on behalf of, an early retiree, for all benefit options the early retiree is enrolled in with respect to a given certified employment-based plan for a given plan year, will be combined. For each early retiree enrolled in an employment-based plan, there is only one cost threshold and one cost limit per plan year regardless of the number of benefit options the early retiree is enrolled in during that plan year.

§ 149.105 Transition provision.

For a certified plan that has a plan year that begins before June 1, 2010 and ends on any date thereafter, the reinsurance amount for the plan year must be determined as follows:

(a) With respect to claims incurred before June 1, 2010, the amount of such claims up to $15,000 count toward the cost threshold and the cost limit. The amount of claims incurred before June 1, 2010 that exceed $15,000 are not eligible for reimbursement and do not count toward the cost limit.

(b) The reinsurance amount to be paid is based only on claims incurred on and after June 1, 2010, that fall between the

cost threshold and cost limit for the plan year.

§ 149.110 Negotiated price concessions.

(a) The amount of negotiated price concessions that will be taken into account in determining the reinsurance amount will reflect negotiated price concessions that have already been subtracted from the amount the employment-based plan or insurer paid for the cost of health benefits and the amount of post-point-of-sale negotiated price concessions received.

(b) At a time specified by the Secretary, sponsors are required to disclose the amount of post-point-of-sale price concessions that were received but not accounted for in their submitted claims.

§ 149.115 Cost threshold and cost limit.

The following cost threshold and cost limits apply individually, to each early retiree as defined in § 149.2:

(a) The cost threshold is equal to $15,000 for plan years that start on any date before October 1, 2011.

(b) The cost limit is equal to $90,000 for plan years that start on any date before October 1, 2011.

(c) The cost threshold and cost limit specified in paragraphs (a) and (b) of this section, for plan years that start on or after October 1, 2011, will be adjusted each fiscal year based on the percentage increase in the Medical Care Component of the Consumer Price Index for all urban consumers (rounded to the nearest multiple of $1,000) for the year involved.

Subpart D—Use of Reimbursements

§ 149.200 Use of reimbursements.

(a) A sponsor must use the proceeds under this program:

(1) To reduce the sponsor's health benefit premiums or health benefit costs,

(2) To reduce health benefit premium contributions, copayments, deductibles, coinsurance, or other out-of-pocket costs, or any combination of these costs, for plan participants, or

(3) To reduce any combination of the costs in (a)(1) and (a)(2) of this section.

(b) Proceeds under this program must not be used as general revenue for the sponsor.

Subpart E—Reimbursement Methods

§ 149.300 General reimbursement rules.

Reimbursement under this program is conditioned on provision of accurate information by the sponsor or its designee. The information must be submitted, in a form and manner and at the times provided in this subpart and other guidance specified by the Secretary. A sponsor must provide the information specified in section § 149.335.

§ 149.310   Timing.

(a) An employment-based plan and a sponsor must be certified by the Secretary before claims can be submitted and a reimbursement request may be made. Reimbursement will be made with respect to submitted claims for health benefits at a time and in a manner to be specified by the Secretary, after the sponsor or its designee submits the claims to the Secretary. Claims must satisfy the requirements of this subpart in order to be eligible for reimbursement.

(b) Claims for health benefits may be submitted for a given plan year only upon the approval of an application that references that plan year cycle. Claims for an early retiree for a plan year cannot be submitted until the total paid costs for health benefits for that early retiree incurred for that plan year exceed the applicable cost threshold.

(c) For employment-based plans for which a provider in the normal course of business does not produce a claim, such as a staff-model health maintenance organization, the information required in a claim must be produced and provided to the Secretary, as set out in this regulation and applicable guidance.

§ 149.315   Reimbursement conditioned upon available funds.

Notwithstanding a sponsor's compliance with this part, reimbursement is conditioned upon the availability of program funds.

§ 149.320   Universe of claims that must be submitted.

(a) Claims submitted for an early retiree, as defined in § 149.2, must include claims below the applicable cost threshold for the plan year.

(b) Claims must not be submitted until claims are submitted for amounts that exceed the applicable cost threshold for the plan year for the early retiree.

(c) Sponsors must not submit claims for health benefits for an early retiree to the extent the sponsor has already submitted claims for the early retiree that total more than the applicable cost limit for the applicable plan year.

§ 149.325   Requirements for eligibility of claims.

A claim may be submitted only if it represents costs for health benefits for an early retiree, as defined in § 149.2, has been incurred during the applicable plan year, and has been paid.

§ 149.330   Content of claims.

Each claim on its face must include the information specified in, and meet, the definition of claim or medical claim found at § 149.2.

§ 149.335   Documentation of costs of actual claims involved.

(a) A submission of claims consists of a list of early retirees for whom claims are being submitted, and documentation of the actual costs of the items and services for claims being submitted, in a form and manner specified by the Secretary.

(b) In order for a sponsor to receive reimbursement for the portion of a claim that an early retiree paid, the sponsor must submit prima facie evidence that the early enrollee paid his or her portion of the claim.

§ 149.340   Rule for insured plans.

With respect to insured plans, the claims and data specified in the subpart may be submitted directly to the Secretary by the insurer.

§ 149.345   Use of information provided.

The Secretary may use data and information collected under this section only for the purpose of, and to the extent necessary in, carrying out this part including, but not limited to, determining reimbursement and reimbursement-related oversight and program integrity activities, or as otherwise allowed by law. Nothing in this section limits the Office of the Inspector General's authority to fulfill the Inspector General's responsibilities in accordance with applicable Federal law.

§ 149.350   Maintenance of records.

(a) The sponsor of the certified plan (or a subcontractor, as applicable) must maintain and furnish to the Secretary, upon request the records enumerated in paragraph (b) of this section. The records must be maintained for 6 years after the expiration of the plan year in which the costs were incurred, or longer if otherwise required by law.

(b) The records that must be retained are as follows—

(1) All documentation, data, and other information related to this part.

(2) Any other records specified by the Secretary.

(c) The Secretary may issue additional guidance addressing recordkeeping requirements, including (but not limited to) the use of electronic media.

(d) The sponsor must require its health insurance issuer or employment-based plan, as applicable, to maintain and produce upon request records to satisfy subparagraph (a) of this regulation.

(e) The sponsor is responsible for ensuring that the records are maintained and provided according to this subpart.

Subpart F—Appeals

§ 149.500   Appeals.

(a) An adverse reimbursement determination is final and binding unless appealed pursuant to paragraph (e) of this section.

(b) Except as provided in paragraph (c) of this section, a sponsor may request an appeal of an adverse reimbursement determination.

(c) A sponsor may not appeal an adverse reimbursement determination if the denial is based on the unavailability of funds.

(d) An adverse reimbursement determination is a determination constituting a complete or partial denial of a reimbursement request.

(e) If a sponsor appeals an adverse reimbursement determination, the sponsor must submit the appeal in writing to the Secretary within 15 calendar days of receipt of the determination pursuant to guidance issued by the Secretary.

§ 149.510   Content of request for appeal.

The request for appeal must specify the findings or issues with which the sponsor disagrees and the reasons for the disagreements. The request for appeal may include supporting documentary evidence the sponsor wishes the Secretary to consider.

§ 149.520   Review of appeals.

(a) In conducting review of the appeal, the Secretary reviews the appeal, the evidence and findings upon which the adverse reimbursement determination was made, and any other written evidence submitted by the sponsor or the Secretary's designee and will provide a ruling on the appeal request.

(b) In conducting the review, the Secretary reviews the determination at issue, the evidence and findings upon which it was based, any written documents submitted to the Secretary by the sponsor and the Secretary's designee, and determines whether to uphold, reverse or modify the Secretary's initial reimbursement determination.

(c) A decision by the Secretary under this provision is final and binding.

(d) Regardless of the Secretary's decision, additional reimbursement is contingent upon the availability of funds at the time of the Secretary's determination.

(e) The Secretary informs the sponsor and the applicable Secretary's designee of the decision. The Secretary sends a written decision to the sponsor or the applicable Secretary's designee upon request.

Subpart G—Disclosure of Data Inaccuracies

§ 149.600   Sponsor's duty to report data inaccuracies.

A sponsor is required to disclose any data inaccuracies upon which a reimbursement determination is made, including inaccurate claims data and negotiated price concessions, in a manner and at a time specified by the Secretary in guidance.

§ 149.610   Secretary's authority to reopen and revise a reimbursement determination.

(a) The Secretary may reopen and revise a reimbursement determination upon the Secretary's own motion or upon the request of a sponsor:

(1) Within 1 year of the reimbursement determination for any reason.

(2) Within 4 years of a reimbursement determination for good cause.

(3) At any time, in instances of fraud or similar fault.

(b) For purposes of this section, the Secretary does not find good cause if the only reason for the revision is a change of legal interpretation or administrative ruling upon which the determination to reimburse was made.

(c) A decision by the Secretary not to revise a reimbursement determination is final and binding (unless fraud or similar fault is found) and cannot be appealed.

Subpart H—Change of Ownership Requirements

§ 149.700   Change of ownership requirements.

(a) *Change of ownership consists of:*
(1) *Partnership.* The removal, addition, or substitution of a partner, unless the partners expressly agree otherwise as permitted by applicable state law.

(2) *Asset sale.* Transfer of all or substantially all of the assets of the sponsor to another party.

(3) *Corporation.* The merger of the sponsor's corporation into another corporation or the consolidation of the sponsor's organization with one or more other corporations, resulting in a new corporate body.

(b) *Change of ownership; exception.* Transfer of corporate stock or the merger of another corporation into the sponsor's corporation, with the sponsor surviving, does not ordinarily constitute change of ownership.

(c) *Advance notice requirement.* A sponsor that has a sponsor agreement in

effect under this part and is considering or negotiating a change in ownership must notify the Secretary at least 60 days before the anticipated effective date of the change.

(d) *Assignment of agreement.* When there is a change of ownership as specified in paragraph (a) of this section, and this results in a transfer of the liability for health benefits, the existing sponsor agreement is automatically assigned to the new owner.

(e) *Conditions that apply to assigned agreements.* The new owner to whom a sponsor agreement is assigned is subject to all applicable statutes and regulations and to the terms and conditions of the sponsor agreement.

(f) Failure to notify the Secretary at least 60 days before the anticipated effective date of the change may result in the Secretary recovering funds paid under this program.

Dated: April 29, 2010.

Jay Angoff,

Director, Office of Consumer Information and Insurance Oversight.

Dated: April 29, 2010

Kathleen Sebelius,

Secretary.

[FR Doc. 2010–10658 Filed 5–4–10; 8:45 am]

BILLING CODE 4150–03–P

DEPARTMENT OF HEALTH AND HUMAN SERVICES

Office of the Secretary

45 CFR Part 159

RIN 0991–AB63

Health Care Reform Insurance Web Portal Requirements

AGENCY: Office of the Secretary, HHS.

ACTION: Interim final rule with comment period.

SUMMARY: The Patient Protection and Affordable Care Act (the Affordable Care Act) was enacted on March 23, 2010. It requires the establishment of an internet Web site (hereinafter referred to as a Web portal) through which individuals and small businesses can obtain information about the insurance coverage options that may be available to them in their State. The Department of Health and Human Services (HHS) is issuing this interim final rule in order to implement this mandate. This interim final rule adopts the categories of information that will be collected and displayed as Web portal content, and the data we will require from issuers and request from States, associations,

and high risk pools in order to create this content.

DATES: *Effective Date:* These regulations are effective on May 10, 2010.

Comment Date: To be assured consideration, comments must be received at the address provided below, no later than 5 p.m. on June 4, 2010.

ADDRESSES: In commenting, please refer to file code DHHS–9997–IFC. Because of staff and resource limitations, we cannot accept comments by facsimile (FAX) transmission.

You may submit comments in one of four ways (please choose only one of the ways listed):

• *Electronically.* You may submit electronic comments on this regulation to *http://www.regulations.gov.* Follow the instructions on the home page.

• *By regular mail.* You may mail written comments to the following address ONLY: Centers for Medicare & Medicaid Services, Department of Health and Human Services, Attention: DHHS–9997–IFC, P.O. Box 8014, Baltimore, MD 21244–8014.

Please allow sufficient time for mailed comments to be received before the close of the comment period.

• *By express or overnight mail.* You may send written comments to the following address ONLY: Centers for Medicare & Medicaid Services, Department of Health and Human Services, Attention: DHHS–9997–IFC, Mail Stop C4–26–05, 7500 Security Boulevard, Baltimore, MD 21244–1850.

• *By hand or courier.* If you prefer, you may deliver (by hand or courier) your written comments before the close of the comment period to either of the following addresses:

a. For delivery in Washington, DC— Centers for Medicare & Medicaid Services, Department of Health and Human Services, Room 445–G, Hubert H. Humphrey Building, 200 Independence Avenue, SW., Washington, DC 20201

(Because access to the interior of the Hubert H. Humphrey Building is not readily available to persons without Federal government identification, commenters are encouraged to leave their comments in the CMS drop slots located in the main lobby of the building. A stamp-in clock is available for persons wishing to retain a proof of filing by stamping in and retaining an extra copy of the comments being filed.)

b. For delivery in Baltimore, MD— Centers for Medicare & Medicaid Services, Department of Health and Human Services, 7500 Security Boulevard, Baltimore, MD 21244–1850.

If you intend to deliver your comments to the Baltimore address,

E. Application and Instructions for Early Retiree Reinsurance Program

OMB Approval 0938-1087

ERRP

Early Retiree Reinsurance Program Application

U.S. Department of Health and Human Services

HHS Form # CMS-10321

Please note that if any information in this Application changes or if the sponsor discovers that any information is incorrect, the sponsor is required to promptly report the change or inaccuracy.

An asterisk (*) identifies a required field.

PART I: Plan Sponsor and Key Personnel Information

A. Plan Sponsor Information

1) *Organization's Name (Must correspond with the information associated with the Federal Employer Tax Identification Number (EIN): _____

2) *Type of Organization (Check the one category that best describes your organization):
    ___ Government
    ___ Union
    ___ Religious
    ___ Commercial
    ___ Non-profit

3) *Organization's Employer Identification Number (EIN): _____

4) *Organization's Telephone Number: ____ ext._____
5) Organization's FAX Number _____

6) *Organization's Address (must be the address associated with the EIN provided above):
* Street Line 1: _____
Street Line 2: _____
*City: _____
 *State/US Territory: _____
*Zip Code: _____

7) Organization's Website Address:_____

B. Authorized Representative Information

1) *First Name: _____ Middle Initial (optional): ____ *Last Name: _____

2) *Job Title: _____

3) *Date of Birth(Month/Day/Year):_____

4) *Social Security Number: _____

5) *Email Address: _____

6) *Telephone Number: _____ext_____

7) FAX Number:_____

OMB Approval 0938-1087

---

8) *Employer Name: _____

9) * Authorized Representative Business Address:

* Street Line 1: _____

Street Line 2: _____

*City: _____

*State/US Territory: _____

*Zip Code: _____

C. Account Manager Information

1) *First Name: _____ Middle Initial (optional): ____ *Last Name: _____

2) *Job Title: _____

3) *Date of Birth(Month/Day/Year):_____

4) *Social Security Number: _____

5) *Email Address: _____

6) *Telephone Number: _____ext_____

7) FAX Number:_____

8) *Employer Name: _____

9) *Account Manager Business Address:

* Street Line 1: _____

Street Line 2: _____

*City: _____

*State/US Territory: _____

*Zip Code: _____

HHS Form #CMS-10321

OMB Approval 0938-1087

PART II: Plan Information

A. Plan Information

1) *Plan Name:

2) *Plan Year Cycle: Start Month/Day:_____   End Month/Day: _____

B. Benefit Option(s) Provided Under This Plan (If the plan has more than one benefit option for which you intend to seek program reimbursement, please include the information below for each benefit option, on a separate copy of the Attachment below.

1a) *Benefit Option Name: _____

1b) *Unique Benefit Option Identifier: _____

1c) *Benefit Option Type: Self-Funded _____ Insured _____ Both _____

1d) *Benefit Administrator Company Name: _____

C. *Programs and Procedures for Chronic and High-Cost Conditions

A sponsor cannot participate in the Early Retiree Reinsurance Program unless, as of the date of its application for the program is submitted, its employment-based plan has in place programs and procedures that have generated or have the potential to generate cost savings with respect to plan participants with chronic and high cost conditions. The program regulations define "chronic and high cost condition" as a condition for which $15,000 or more in health benefit claims are likely to be incurred during a plan year by one plan participant. Please identify the chronic and high cost conditions for which the employment-based plan has such programs and procedures in place, and summarize those programs and procedures, including how it was determined that the identified conditions satisfy the $15,000 threshold. If necessary to provide a complete response, the sponsor may submit additional pages as an attachment to the application. Please reference such attachment in this space.

D. *Estimated Amount of Early Retiree Reinsurance Program Reimbursements

Please estimate the projected amount of proceeds you expect to receive under the Early Retiree Reinsurance Program for the plan identified in this application, for each of the first two plan year cycles identified in this application. If you wish, you may provide a range of expected program proceeds that includes: (1) a low-end estimate of expected program proceeds, (2) an estimate that represents your most likely amount of program proceeds, and (3) a high-end estimate of expected program proceeds. For purposes of this estimate only, please assume for each of those plan year cycles that there will be sufficient program funds to cover all claims submitted by the Plan Sponsor that comply with program requirements. If necessary to provide a complete response, the sponsor may submit additional pages as

OMB Approval 0938-1087

an attachment to the application. Please reference such attachment in this space.

E. *Intended Use of Early Retiree Reinsurance Program Reimbursements

1) Please summarize how your organization will use the reimbursement under the Early Retiree Reinsurance Program to reduce health benefit or health benefit premium costs for the sponsor of the employment-based plan (i.e., to offset increases in such costs); or reduce premium contributions, copayments, deductibles, coinsurance, or other out-of-pocket costs (or combination of these) for plan participants; or reduce a combination of any of these costs (whether offsetting increases in sponsor costs or offsetting or reducing plan participants' costs). If necessary to provide a complete response, the sponsor may submit additional pages as an attachment to the application. Please reference such attachment in this space.

2) If a sponsor decides to apply the reimbursement for its own use, it may only use the reimbursement to offset increases in its health benefit premium costs, if an insured plan, or its health benefit costs, if it is self-funded. If any amount of the reimbursement is used to offset increases in health benefit premium or health benefit costs of your organization (as opposed to offsetting increases to, or reducing, plan participants' costs), please summarize how program funds, as a result of being used by your organization for such purposes, will relieve your organization of using its own funds to subsidize such increases, thereby allowing your organization to instead use its own funds to maintain its level of financial contribution to the employment-based plan. (In other words, please explain how your organization will continue to maintain the level of support for this plan, and if it applies the reimbursement for its own use, will use the program reimbursement to pay for increases in health benefit premium costs or health benefit costs, as applicable). If necessary to provide a complete response, the sponsor may submit additional pages as an attachment to the application. Please reference such attachment in this space.

HHS Form #CMS-10321

OMB Approval 0938-1087

PART III: Banking Information for Electronic Funds Transfer

1) *Bank Name: _____

2) *Bank Address:

*Street Line 1: _____
Street Line 2: _____
*City: _____
 *State/US Territory: _____
*Zip Code: _____

3) *Account Number: _____

4) *Name of Organization Associated with Account: _____

5) *Account type: (Checking or Savings Account) _____

6) *Bank Routing Number: _____

7) *Bank Contact First Name: _____ Middle Initial (optional): ___ *Last Name: _____

8) *Email address: _____

9) *Telephone Number: _____

OMB Approval 0938-1087

PART IV. Plan Sponsor Agreement

1.	**Compliance:** In order to receive program reimbursement(s), Plan Sponsor agrees to comply with all of the terms and conditions of Section 1102 of the Patient Protection Act (P.L. 111-148) and 45 C.F.R .Part 149 and in other guidance issued by the Secretary of the U.S. Department of Health & Human Services (the Secretary), including, but not limited to, the conditions for submission of data for obtaining reimbursement and the record retention requirements.
2.	**Reimbursement-Related and Other Representations Made by Designees:** Plan Sponsor may be given the opportunity to identify one or more Designees (i.e., individuals the Sponsor will authorize to perform certain functions on behalf of the Sponsor related to the Early Retiree Reinsurance Program, such as individual(s) who will be involved in making program reimbursement requests). Plan Sponsor certifies that all individuals that will be identified as Designees will have first been given authority by the Plan Sponsor to perform those respective functions on behalf of the Plan Sponsor. Plan Sponsor understands that it is bound by any representations such individuals make with respect to the Sponsor's involvement in the Early Retiree Reinsurance Program, including but not limited to the Sponsor's reimbursement under, the program.
3.	**Written Agreement:** Plan Sponsor certifies that, prior to submitting a Reimbursement Request, it has executed a written agreement with its health insurance issuer or employment-based plan regarding disclosure of information, data, documents, and records to HHS, and the issuer or plan agrees to disclose to HHS, on behalf of the Plan Sponsor, at a time and in a manner specified by the HHS Secretary in guidance, the information, data, documents, and records necessary for the Plan Sponsor to comply with the requirements of the Early Retiree Reinsurance Program, as specified in 45 C.F.R. 149.35.
4.	**Use of Records:** Plan Sponsor understands and agrees that the Secretary may use data and information collected under the Early Retiree Reinsurance Program only for the purposes of, and to the extent necessary in, carrying out Section 1102 of the Patient Protection Act (P.L. 111-148) and 45 C.F.R. Part 149 including, but not limited to, determining reimbursements and reimbursement-related oversight and program integrity activities, or as otherwise allowed by law. Nothing in this section limits the U.S. Department of Health & Human Services' Office of the Inspector General's authority to fulfill the Inspector General's responsibilities in accordance with applicable Federal law.
5.	**Obtaining Federal Funds:** Plan Sponsor acknowledges that the information furnished in its Plan Sponsor application is being provided to obtain Federal funds. Plan Sponsor certifies that it requires all subcontractors, including plan administrators, to acknowledge that information provided in connection with a subcontract is used for purposes of obtaining Federal funds. Plan Sponsor acknowledges that reimbursement of program funds is conditioned on the submission of accurate information. Plan Sponsor agrees that it will not knowingly present or cause to be presented a false or fraudulent claim. Plan Sponsor acknowledges that any excess reimbursement made to the Plan Sponsor under the Early Retiree Reinsurance Program, or any debt that arises from such excess reimbursement, may be recovered by the Secretary. Plan Sponsor will promptly update any changes to the information submitted in its Plan Sponsor application. If Plan Sponsor becomes aware that information in this application is not (or is no longer) true, accurate and

Page 7

OMB Approval 0938-1087

complete, Plan Sponsor agrees to notify the Secretary promptly of this fact.

6.	**Data Security:** Plan Sponsor agrees to establish and implement proper safeguards against unauthorized use and disclosure of the data exchanged under this Plan Sponsor application. Plan Sponsor recognizes that the use and disclosure of protected health information (PHI) is governed by the Health Insurance Portability and Accountability Act (HIPAA) and accompanying regulations. Plan Sponsor certifies that its employment-based plan(s) has established and implemented appropriate safeguards in compliance with 45 C.F.R. Parts 160 and 164 (HIPAA administrative simplification, privacy and security rule) in order to prevent unauthorized use or disclosure of such information. Sponsor also agrees that if it participates in the administration of the plan(s), then it has also established and implemented appropriate safeguards in regard to PHI. Any and all Plan Sponsor personnel interacting with PHI shall be advised of: (1) the confidential nature of the information; (2) safeguards required to protect the information; and (3) the administrative, civil and criminal penalties for noncompliance contained in applicable Federal laws.
7.	**Depository Information:** Plan Sponsor hereby authorizes the Secretary to initiate reimbursement, credit entries and other adjustments, including offsets and requests for reimbursement, in accordance with the provisions of Section 1102 of the Patient Protection Act (P.L. 111-148) and 45 C.F.R Part 149 and applicable provisions of 45 C.F.R. Part 30, to the account at the financial institution (hereinafter the "Depository") indicated under the Electronic Funds Transfer (EFT) section of the Plan Sponsor application. Plan Sponsor agrees to immediately pay back any excess reimbursement or debt upon notification from the Secretary of the excess reimbursement or debt. Plan Sponsor agrees to promptly update any changes in its Depository information.
8.	**Policies and Procedures to Detect Fraud, Waste and Abuse**. The Plan Sponsor attests that, as of the date this Application is submitted, has in place policies and procedures to detect and reduce fraud, waste, and abuse related to the Early Retiree Reinsurance Program. The Plan Sponsor will produce the policies and procedures, and necessary information, records and data, upon request by the Secretary, to substantiate existence of the policies and procedures and their effectiveness, as specified in 45 C.F.R. Part 149.
9.	**Change of Ownership:** The Plan Sponsor shall provide written notice to the Secretary at least 60 days prior to a change in ownership, as defined in 45 C.F.R, 149.700. When a change of ownership results in a transfer of the liability for health benefits costs, this Plan Sponsor Agreement is automatically assigned to the new owner, who shall be subject to the terms and conditions of this Plan Sponsor Agreement.
	Signature of Plan Sponsor Authorized Representative I, the undersigned Authorized Representative of Plan Sponsor, declare that I have legal authority to sign and bind the Plan Sponsor to the terms of this Plan Sponsor Agreement, and I have or will provide evidence of such authority. I declare that I have examined this Plan Sponsor Application and Plan Sponsor Agreement. My signature legally and financially binds the Plan Sponsor to the statutes, regulations, and other guidance applicable to the Early Retiree Reinsurance Program including, but not limited to Section 1102 of the Patient Protection Act (P.L. 111-148) and 45 C.F.R. Part 149 and applicable provisions of 45 C.F.R. Part 30 and all other applicable statutes and

OMB Approval 0938-1087

regulations. I certify that the information contained in this Plan Sponsor Application and Plan Sponsor Agreement is true, accurate and complete to the best of my knowledge and belief, and I authorize the Secretary to verify this information. I understand that, because program reimbursement will be made from Federal funds, any false statements, documents, or concealment of a material fact is subject to prosecution under applicable Federal and/or State law.

Signature

HHS Form #CMS-10321

OMB Approval 0938-1087

Attachment: Additional Benefit Options

(Complete this form for each unique benefit option)

1a) *Benefit Option Name: _____

1b) *Unique Benefit Option Identifier: _____

1c) *Benefit Option Type: Self-Funded _____ Insured _____ Both _____

1d) *Benefit Administrator Company Name: _____

OMB Approval # 0938-1087

ERRP

Early Retiree Reinsurance Program

Plan Sponsor Application Instructions

U.S. Department of Health and Human Services

HHS Form #CMS-10321

OMB Approval # 0938-1087

Early Retiree Reinsurance Program (ERRP) Plan Sponsor Instructions for Completing an Application

U.S. DEPARTMENT OF HEALTH & HUMAN SERVICES

Overview

The Early Retiree Reinsurance Program (ERRP) was established by section 1102 of the Patient Protection and Affordable Care Act (the Affordable Care Act), P.L. 111-148, enacted on March 23, 2010. The Congress appropriated funding of $5 billion for the temporary program. Section 1102(a)(1) requires the Secretary to establish this temporary program not later than 90 days after enactment of the statute, which is June 21, 2010. The program ends no later than January 1, 2014. The program provides reimbursement to participating employment-based plans for a portion of the cost of health benefits for early retirees and their spouses, surviving spouses and dependents. The Secretary will reimburse plans for certain claims between $15,000 and $90,000 (with those amounts being indexed for plan years starting on or after October 1, 2011). The purpose of the reimbursement is to make health benefits more affordable for plan participants and sponsors so that health benefits are accessible to more Americans than they would otherwise be without this program.

The program addresses the recent erosion in the number of employers providing health benefits to early retirees. People in the early retiree age group often face difficulties obtaining insurance in the individual market because of advanced age or chronic conditions that make coverage unaffordable and inaccessible. The program provides needed financial help for employer-based plans to continue to provide valuable coverage to plan participants, and provides financial relief to plan participants.

The program provides reimbursement to participating sponsors of employment-based plans for a portion of the costs of providing health benefits to early retirees (and eligible spouses, surviving spouses, and dependents of such retirees). The program regulation at 45 C.F.R. Part 149 defines the term "sponsor", "employment-based plan", "health benefits," and "early retiree," as well as many other important terms that are relevant to the program. The regulation also sets forth the requirements of the program, including the requirements discussed in these instructions.

This document provides general instructions with respect to completing a program application (see ERRP regulation at 45 C.F.R. §149.40). Please note that if any information in the Application changes or if the sponsor discovers that any information is incorrect, the sponsor is required to promptly report the change or inaccuracy.

It is critical for program applicants and participants to read the regulation in order to fully understand which organizations qualify for the program, how to apply for the program, what costs are eligible for reimbursement under the program, how to submit a request for reimbursement under the program, and sponsors' obligations under the program.

OMB Approval # 0938-1087

HHS Form #CMS-10321

OMB Approval # 0938-1087

Application Information

General Instructions for Completing and Submitting the ERRP Application

The ERRP application has been designed by the U.S. Department of Health & Human Services (HHS) to assist in the efficient administration of the ERRP in compliance with Federal regulatory requirements at 45 C.F.R. Part 149. HHS will make an announcement on the applicable HHS webpage when applicants can begin submitting applications, with information on how applications must be submitted. We encourage interested parties to regularly monitor www.hhs.gov/ociio/ for this and other program information.

The following is an overview of the application process:

1. The Account Manager or Authorized Representative completes ALL parts of the application, including the Plan Sponsor Agreement which must be signed by the Plan Sponsor's Authorized Representative.

2. The completed application is submitted.

3. Plan Sponsors will be notified about the status of their application.

.An applicant must submit an application for each plan for which it will submit a reimbursement request. The application must be completed in its entirety (and reviewed and approved by HHS) in order to participate in the ERRP. HHS will certify the sponsor and the plan when the application is approved. Even if the submitted application satisfies all criteria specified in the program regulation, it may be denied, depending on the availability of limited ERRP funds.

Complete the items in Parts I through IV. Responses to all items marked with an asterisk (*) are required. The following are specific instructions for each Part for each item that is not self explanatory.

APPLICATION PART I: Plan Sponsor and Key Personnel Information

A. Plan Sponsor Information

Complete the required information in items 1-7.

Item 1: The Plan Sponsor Organization Name must be the same as that associated with its Federal Employer Tax Identification Number (EIN).

Item 2: This item is self-selected by the Plan Sponsor. Please choose the one category that best describes the Plan Sponsor's type of organization.

OMB Approval # 0938-1087

Item 6: Organization address must be the address associated with the EIN.

B. Authorized Representative Information

An Authorized Representative is an individual with legal authority to sign and bind a sponsor to the terms of a contract or agreement. Examples of the Authorized Representative include the Sponsor's general partner, CFO, CEO, President, Human Resource Director, or an individual who holds a position of similar status and authority within the Plan Sponsor's organization. Only one individual at a time can serve in the role of Authorized Representative. For multi-employer plans, the Authorized Representative does not have to be an employee of the Plan Sponsor, but may be a member of the jointly appointed board of trustees, which includes both labor and management trustees. An Authorized Representative of the requesting Plan Sponsor must sign the Plan Sponsor Agreement in the completed application and certify that the information contained in the application is true and accurate to the best of the Plan Sponsor's knowledge and belief.

The Authorized Representative is responsible for the completion of the required information in Items 1-9.

Item 4: The Authorized Representative's Social Security Number must be provided in order to verify the individual's identity, and therefore help maintain the integrity of the Early Retiree Reinsurance Program.

C. Account Manager Information

The Account Manager is generally the individual who coordinates the application process for the Plan Sponsor, and is the Sponsor's primary contact with HHS with respect to the application. An Account Manager may be an employee of the Plan Sponsor, or a non-employee, such as a consultant, with whom the Plan Sponsor has an arrangement to assist with the application process. There can be only one Account Manager per ERRP application at a time.

Complete the required information in Items 1-9 for the Account Manager Information.

Item 4: The Account Manager's Social Security Number must be provided in order to verify the individual's identity, and therefore help maintain the integrity of the Early Retiree Reinsurance Program.

APPLICATION PART II: Plan Information

A. Plan Information

Complete the required information in Items 1-2 for the employment-based plan for which you are requesting ERRP payments.

Page 5

HHS Form #CMS-10321

OMB Approval # 0938-1087

Item 2: For ERRP purposes, your plan year cycle start (MM/DD) and end (MM/DD) are determined as follows: The plan year as the year that is designated as the plan year in the plan document of an employment-based plan, except that if the plan document does not designate a plan year, if the plan year is not a 12-month plan year, or if there is no plan document, the plan year is: (1) the deductible or limit year used under the plan; (2) the policy year, if the plan does not impose deductibles or limits on a 12-month basis: (3) the sponsor's taxable year, if the plan does not impose deductibles or limits on a 12-month basis, and either the plan is not insured or the insurance policy is not renewed on a 12-month basis, or (4) the calendar year, in any other case. (See the program regulation at 45 C.F.R. §149.2).

B. Benefit Option(s) Provided Under This Plan

Complete the required information in items 1a-d for each benefit option in the plan for which you are requesting reimbursement under the program.

Item 1b: Unique Benefit Option Identifier uniquely identifies each benefit option under the plan. If a Group Number uniquely identifies each option under the plan, then that number may be used. If a Group Number does not uniquely identify each benefit option, then the Plan Sponsor should assign an identifier to each option. Plan Sponsors may use existing internal identifiers, or can develop one specifically for purposes of completing the ERRP application.

Item 1d: Specify the name of the insurer, third-party administrator, or other entity that is administering the benefit option.

If the plan has more than one benefit option for which the sponsor intends to seek program reimbursement, please indicate the information in Items 1a-d for each such benefit option, with each benefit option listed in a separate copy of the attachment that appears at the end of this application.

C. Programs and Procedures for Chronic and High-Cost Conditions

In completing this item, please follow the instructions in the application. Please be aware that the ERRP regulation defines "chronic and high-cost condition" as a condition for which $15,000 or more in health benefit claims are likely to be incurred during a plan year by one plan participant. (See the ERRP regulation at 45 C.F.R. §149.2). Therefore, you should make clear in your summary that the conditions for which you have programs and procedures in place, have resulted in $15,000 or more in health benefit claims, or likely would result in such amount of claims, absent the programs and procedures, for one plan participant, during a plan year.

D. Estimated Amount of Early Retiree Reinsurance Program Proceeds

In completing this item, please follow the instructions in the application.

E. Intended Use of Early Retiree Reinsurance Program Proceeds

OMB Approval # 0938-1087

In completing this item, please be aware that the ERRP regulation specifies that the sponsor must use the proceeds under this program for the following purposes: (1) To reduce the sponsor's health benefit premiums or health benefit costs, or (2) To reduce health benefit premium contributions, copayments, deductibles, coinsurance, or other out-of-pocket costs, or any combination of these costs, for plan participants, or (3) To reduce any combination of the costs in (1) and (2). Proceeds under this program must not be used as general revenue for the sponsor. (See the ERRP regulation at 45 C.F.R. §149.200). In completing this item, please follow the instructions in the application.

APPLICATION PART III: Banking Information for Electronic Funds Transfer

All ERRP payments will be paid via electronic funds transfer. In order to receive payments, all information in this section must be provided.

Please provide the required information for Items 1-9 for the Plan Sponsor's bank and related information.

APPLICATION PART IV: Plan Sponsor Agreement

The Authorized Representative of the Plan Sponsor must read the Plan Sponsor Agreement, and if the terms are accepted, must indicate acceptance by providing his or her signature.

Attachment: Additional Benefit Options
If the plan has more than one benefit option for which the sponsor intends to seek program reimbursement, please indicate the information in PART II, B, items 1a through 1d, for each such benefit option, with each benefit option listed on a separate copy of this attachment.

Page 7

F. IRS Notice 2010-44
(Small-Employer Tax Credit)

Internal Revenue Bulletin: 2010-22

June 1, 2010

Notice 2010-44

Tax Credit for Employee Health Insurance Expenses of Small Employers

Table of Contents

I. PURPOSE AND BACKGROUND

Section 45R of the Internal Revenue Code (Code) offers a tax credit to certain small employers that provide health insurance coverage to their employees. It is effective for taxable years beginning in 2010. Both taxable employers and employers that are organizations described in section 501(c) that are exempt from tax under section 501(a) (tax-exempt employers) may be eligible for the section 45R credit. Employers that satisfy the requirements for the credit are referred to in this notice as "eligible small employers."

Section 45R was added to the Code by section 1421 of the Patient Protection and Affordable Care Act (Affordable Care Act), enacted March 23, 2010, Pub. L. No. 111-148. This notice provides guidance on section 45R as in effect for taxable years beginning before January 1, 2014, and also includes transition relief for taxable years beginning in 2010 with respect to the requirements for a qualifying arrangement under section 45R.

II. EMPLOYERS ELIGIBLE FOR THE CREDIT

A. Overview of Requirements for Eligibility

In order to be an eligible small employer, (1) the employer must have fewer than 25 full-time equivalent employees (FTEs) for the taxable year; (2) the average annual wages of its employees for the year must be lessthan $50,000 per FTE; and (3) the employer must maintain a "qualifying arrangement."[30] A qualifying arrangement is an arrangement under which the employer pays premiums for each employee enrolled in health insurance coverage offered by the employer in an amount equal to a uniform percentage (not less than 50 percent) of the premium cost of the coverage (but see section V of this notice for transition relief for taxable years beginning in 2010 with respect to the requirements for a qualifying arrangement). An employer that is an agency or instrumentality of the federal government, or of a State, local or Indian tribal government, is not an eligible small employer for purposes of section 45R unless it is an organization described in section 501(c) that is exempt from tax under section 501(a).

The following steps must be followed to determine whether an employer is eligible for a credit under section 45R:

1. Determine the employees who are taken into account for purposes of the credit.

2. Determine the number of hours of service performed by those employees.

3. Calculate the number of the employer's FTEs.

4. Determine the average annual wages paid per FTE.

5. Determine the premiums paid by the employer that are taken into account for purposes of the credit. Specifically, the premiums must be paid by an employer under a qualifying arrangement and must be paid for health insurance that meets the requirements of section 45R.

The remainder of this section II explains the steps involved in determining whether an employer is eligible for the credit. Section III of this notice explains how to calculate the credit, and section IV explains how to claim the credit. Finally, section V provides transition relief for taxable years beginning in 2010 with respect to certain requirements for qualifying arrangements.

B. Determining the Employees Taken into Account

In general, employees who perform services for the employer during the taxable year are taken into account in determining the employer's FTEs, average wages, and premiums paid, with certain individuals excluded and with employees of certain related employers included. This section describes these rules.

Partners in a business and certain owners are not taken into account as employees for purposes of section 45R. Specifically, sole proprietors, partners in a partnership, shareholders owning more than two percent of an S corporation, and any owners of more than five percent of other businesses are not taken into account as employees for purposes of the credit. Family members of these owners and partners are also not taken into account as employees. For purposes of section 45R, a family member is defined

---

[30] Although the term "eligible small employer" is defined in section 45R(d)(1) to include employers with "no more than" 25 FTEs and average annual wages that "do not exceed" $50,000, the phaseout of the credit amount under section 45R(c) operates in such a way that an employer with exactly 25 FTEs or with average annual wages exactly equal to $50,000 is not in fact eligible for the credit.

as a child (or descendant of a child); a sibling or step-sibling; a parent (or ancestor of a parent); a step-parent; a niece or nephew; an aunt or uncle; or a son-in-law, daughter-in-law, father-in-law, mother-in-law, brother-in-law or sister-in-law. Finally, any other member of the household of these owners and partners who qualifies as a dependent under section 152(d)(2)(H) is not taken into account as an employee for purposes of section 45R.

Accordingly, the wages and hours of these business owners and partners, and of their family members and dependent members of their household, are disregarded in determining FTEs and average annual wages, and the premiums paid on their behalf are not counted in determining the amount of the section 45R credit.

Seasonal workers are disregarded in determining FTEs and average annual wages unless the seasonal worker works for the employer on more than 120 days during the taxable year, although premiums paid on their behalf may be counted in determining the amount of the section 45R credit.

All employers treated as a single employer under section 414(b), (c), (m) or (o) are treated as a single employer for purposes of section 45R. Thus, all employees of a controlled group under section 414(b) or (c), or an affiliated service group under section 414(m) (except employees not taken into account as described above), and all wages paid to, and premiums paid for, employees by the members of the controlled group or affiliated service group (except employees not taken into account as described above), are taken into account in determining whether any member of the controlled group or affiliated service group is an eligible small employer.

C. Determining the Number of Hours of Service Worked by Employees for the Taxable Year

An employee's hours of service for a year include the following: (1) each hour for which an employee is paid, or entitled to payment, for the performance of duties for the employer during the employer's taxable year; and (2) each hour for which an employee is paid, or entitled to payment, by the employer on account of a period of time during which no duties are performed due to vacation, holiday, illness, incapacity (including disability), layoff, jury duty, military duty or leave of absence (except that no more than 160 hours of service are required to be counted for an employee on account of any single continuous period during which the employee performs no duties).

In calculating the total number of hours of service which must be taken into account for an employee for the year, the employer may use any of the following methods: (1) determine actual hours of service from records of hours worked and hours for which payment is made or due (payment is made or due for vacation, holiday, illness, incapacity, etc., as described above); (2) use a days-worked equivalency whereby the employee is credited with 8 hours of service for each day for which the employee would be required to be credited with at least one hour of service under rule (1) or (2) in the preceding paragraph; or (3) use a weeks-worked equivalency whereby the employee is credited with 40 hours of service for each week for which the employee would be required to be credited with at least one hour of service under rule (1) or (2) in the preceding paragraph.

Examples. In all of the examples in this notice, none of the employees is an owner, partner in a business or otherwise excluded from being taken into account under section 45R.

Example 1— Counting hours of service by hours actually worked or for which payment is made or due. (i) For the 2010 taxable year, an employer's payroll records indicate that Employee A worked 2,000 hours and was paid for an additional 80 hours on account of vacation, holiday and illness. The employer counts hours actually worked.

(ii) Under this method of counting hours, Employee A must be credited with 2,080 hours of service (2,000 hours worked and 80 hours for which payment was made or due).

Example 2— Counting hours of service under weeks-worked equivalency. (i) For the 2010 taxable year, Employee B worked 49 weeks, took 2 weeks of vacation with pay, and took 1 week of leave without pay. The employer uses the weeks-worked equivalency.

(ii) Under this method of counting hours, Employee B must be credited with 2,040 hours of service (51 weeks multiplied by 40 hours per week).

D. Determining the Number of an Employer's FTEs

The number of an employer's FTEs is determined by dividing (1) the total hours of service, determined in accordance with section II.C of this notice, credited during the year to employees taken into account under section II.B of this notice (but not more than 2,080 hours for any employee) by (2) 2,080. The result, if not a whole number, is then rounded to the next lowest whole number. In some circumstances, an employer with 25 or more employees may qualify for the credit if some of its employees work part-time. For example, an employer with 46 half-time employees (meaning they are paid wages for 1,040 hours) has 23 FTEs and, therefore, may qualify for the credit.

Example 3— Determining the number of FTEs. (i) For the 2010 taxable year, an employer pays 5 employees wages for 2,080 hours each, 3 employees wages for 1,040 hours each, and 1 employee wages for 2,300 hours. The employer does not use an equivalency method to determine hours of service for any of these employees.

(ii) The employer's FTEs would be calculated as follows:

(1) Total hours of service not exceeding 2,080 per employee is the sum of:

a. 10,400 hours of service for the 5 employees paid for 2,080 hours each (5 × 2,080)

b. 3,120 hours of service for the 3 employees paid for 1,040 hours each (3 × 1,040), and

c. 2,080 hours of service for the 1 employee paid for 2,300 hours (lesser of 2,300 and 2,080).

d. The sum of a, b and c equals 15,600 hours of service.

(2) FTEs equal 7 (15,600 divided by 2,080 = 7.5, rounded to the next lowest whole number).

Example 4— Determining the number of FTEs: (i) For the 2010 taxable year, an employer has 26 FTEs with average annual wages of $23,000 per FTE. Only 20 of the employer's employees are enrolled in the employer's health insurance plan.

(ii) The hours of service and wages of all employees are taken into consideration in determining whether the employer is an eligible small employer for purposes of the credit. Because the employer does not have fewer than 25 FTEs for the taxable year, the employer is not an eligible small employer for purposes of the credit.

E. Determining the Employer's Average Annual Wages for the Taxable Year

The average annual wages paid by an employer for a taxable year is determined by dividing (1) the total wages paid by the employer during the employer's taxable year to employees taken into account under section II.B of this notice by (2) the number of the employer's FTEs for the year. The result is then rounded down to the nearest $1,000 (if not otherwise a multiple of $1,000). For purposes of determining the employer's average annual wages for the taxable year, only wages that are paid for hours of service determined under section II.C of this notice are taken into account. Wages for this purpose means wages as defined under section 3121(a) for purposes of the Federal Insurance Contributions Act (FICA), determined without regard to the wage base limitation under section 3121(a)(1).

Example 5— Determining the amount of average annual wages. (i) For the 2010 taxable year, an employer pays $224,000 in wages and has 10 FTEs.

(ii) The employer's average annual wages is: $22,000 ($224,000 divided by 10 = $22,400, rounded down to the nearest $1,000).

F. Premium Payments by the Employer for the Taxable Year

Only premiums paid by the employer for health insurance coverage are counted in calculating the credit. If an employer pays only a portion of the premiums for the coverage provided to employees (with employees paying the rest), only the portion paid by the employer is taken into account. For example, if an employer pays 80 percent of the premiums for employees' coverage (with employees paying the other 20 percent), the 80 percent paid by the employer is taken into account in calculating the credit. For purposes of this credit, any premium paid pursuant to a salary reduction arrangement under a section 125 cafeteria plan is not treated as paid by the employer. In calculating the credit for a taxable year beginning in 2010, an employer may count all premiums paid by the employer in the 2010 tax year, including premiums that were paid in the 2010 tax year before the Affordable Care Act was enacted.

G. Premiums for Health Insurance Coverage under a Qualifying Arrangement

An employer's premium payments are not taken into account for purposes of the section 45R credit unless they are paid for health insurance coverage under a qualifying arrangement. As noted in section II.A of this notice, a qualifying arrangement is an arrangement under which the employer pays premiums for each employee enrolled in health insurance coverage offered by the employer in an amount equal to a uniform percentage (not less than 50 percent) of the premium cost of the coverage (but see section V of this notice for transition relief for taxable years beginning in 2010 with respect to certain requirements for a qualifying arrangement).

For years prior to 2014, health insurance coverage for purposes of the credit means benefits consisting of medical care (provided directly, through insurance or reimbursement, or otherwise) under any hospital or medical service policy or certificate, hospital or medical service plan contract, or health maintenance organization contract offered by a health insurance issuer. See section 9832(b)(1). Health insurance coverage for purposes of the section 45R credit also includes the following plans described in section 9832(c)(2), (3) and (4): limited scope dental or vision; long-term care, nursing home care, home health care, community-based care, or any combination thereof; coverage only for a specified disease or illness; hospital indemnity or other fixed indemnity insurance; and Medicare supplemental health insurance; certain other supplemental coverage, and similar supplemental coverage provided to coverage under a group health plan. Health insurance coverage does not include the benefits listed in section 9832(c)(1).[31] If an eligible small employer offers any of the plans described in section

---

[31] Section 9832(c)(1) includes the following benefits: (A) coverage only for accident, or disability income insurance, or any combination thereof; (B) coverage issued as a supplement to liability insurance; (C) liability insurance, including general liability insurance and automobile liability insurance; (D) worker's compensation or similar insurance; (E) automobile medical payment insurance; (F)

9832(b)(1) or 9832(c)(2), (3) or (4), the premiums paid by the employer for that plan can be counted in calculating the credit if the premiums are paid under a qualifying arrangement.

Different types of health insurance plans are not aggregated for purposes of meeting the qualifying arrangement requirement. So, for example, if an employer offers a major medical insurance plan and a stand-alone vision plan, the employer must separately satisfy the requirements for a qualifying arrangement with respect to each type of coverage.

The amount of an employer's premium payments that are taken into account in calculating the credit is limited to the premium payments the employer would have made under the same arrangement if the average premium for the small group market in the State (or an area within the State) in which the employer offers coverage were substituted for the actual premium. For example, if an eligible small employer pays 80 percent of the premiums for coverage provided to employees (and employees pay the other 20 percent), the premiums taken into account for purposes of the credit are the lesser of 80 percent of the total actual premiums paid or 80 percent of the premiums that would have been paid for the coverage if the average premium for the small group market in the State (or an area within the State) were substituted for the actual premium. See Rev. Rul. 2010-13, 2010-21 I.R.B. 691, for the average premium for the small group market in a State for the 2010 taxable year.

The average premium for the small group market in the State does not apply separately to each type of coverage described in section 9832(b)(1), (c)(2), (c)(3) and (c)(4), but rather provides an overall cap for all health insurance coverage provided by an eligible small employer.

Example 6— Determining amount of premium payments for purposes of the credit. (i) For the 2010 taxable year, an eligible small employer offers a health insurance plan with single and family coverage. Employer has 9 FTEs with average annual wages of $23,000 per FTE. Four employees are enrolled in single coverage and 5 are enrolled in family coverage.

(ii) The employer pays 50% of the premiums for all employees enrolled in single coverage and 50% of the premiums for all employees enrolled in family coverage (and the employee is responsible for the remainder in each case). The premiums are $4,000 a year for single coverage and $10,000 a year for family coverage. The average premium for the small group market in employer's State is $5,000 for single coverage and $12,000 for family coverage.

(iii) The employer's premium payments for each FTE ($2,000 for single coverage and $5,000 for family coverage) do not exceed 50% of the average premium for the small group market in employer's State ($2,500 for single coverage and $6,000 for family coverage).

(iv) Thus, the amount of premiums paid by the employer for purposes of computing the credit equals $33,000 ((4 × $2,000) plus (5 × $5,000)).

Example 7— Premium payments exceeding average premium for small group market. (i) Same facts as *Example 6*, except that the premiums are $6,000 for single coverage and $14,000 for family coverage.

(ii) The employer's premium payments for each employee ($3,000 for single coverage and $7,000 for family coverage) exceed 50% of the average premium for the small group market in the employer's State ($2,500 for single coverage and $6,000 for family coverage).

---

credit-only insurance; (G) coverage for on-site medical clinics; and (H) other similar insurance coverage, specified in regulations, under which benefits for medical care are secondary or incidental to other insurance benefits.

(iii) Thus, the amount of premiums paid by the employer for purposes of computing the credit equals $40,000 ((4 × $2,500) plus (5 × $6,000)).

Example 8— Offering health insurance plan and dental plan. (i) For the 2010 taxable year, an eligible small employer offers a major medical plan and a dental plan. The employer pays 50% of the premium cost for single coverage for all employees enrolled in the major medical plan and 50% of the premium cost for single coverage for all employees enrolled in the dental plan.

(ii) For purposes of calculating the credit, the employer can take into consideration the premiums paid by the employer for both the major medical plan and the dental plan, but only up to 50% of the amount of the average premium for single coverage for the small group market in the employer's State.

Example 9— Meeting qualifying arrangement requirement. (i) Same facts as *Example 8*, except that the employer pays 40% of the premium cost for single coverage for all employees enrolled in the dental plan.

(ii) For purposes of calculating the credit, the employer can take into consideration only the premiums paid by the employer for the major medical plan, and only up to 50% of the amount of the average premium for single coverage for the small group market in the employer's State. The employer cannot take into consideration premiums paid for the dental plan.

III. CALCULATING THE CREDIT

A. In General

The following steps are followed to calculate the section 45R credit:

1. Calculate the maximum amount of the credit (section III.B);

2. Reduce the maximum credit in step 1 in accordance with the phaseout rule (section III.C), if necessary; and

3. For employers receiving a State credit or subsidy for health insurance, determine the employer's actual premium payment (section III.D).

B. Maximum Credit

For taxable years beginning in 2010 through 2013, the maximum credit is 35 percent of a taxable eligible small employer's premium payments taken into account for purposes of the credit. For a tax-exempt eligible small employer for those years, the maximum credit is 25 percent of the employer's premium payments taken into account for purposes of the credit. However, for a tax-exempt employer, the amount of the credit cannot exceed the total amount of income tax under section 3402 and Medicare (*i.e.*, Hospital Insurance) tax under section 3101(b) that the employer is required to withhold from employees' wages for the year and the employer share of Medicare tax under section 3111(b) on employees' wages for the year.

C. Credit Phaseout

The credit phases out gradually (but not below zero) for eligible small employers if the number of FTEs exceeds 10 or if the average annual wages exceed $25,000. If the number of FTEs exceeds 10, the reduction is determined by multiplying the otherwise applicable credit amount by a fraction, the numerator of which is the number of FTEs in excess of 10 and the denominator of which is 15. If average annual wages exceed $25,000, the reduction is determined by multiplying the otherwise applicable credit amount by a fraction, the numerator of which is the amount by which average annual wages exceed $25,000 and the denominator of which is $25,000. In both cases, the result of the calculation is subtracted from the otherwise applicable credit to determine the credit to which the employer is entitled. For an employer with both more than 10 FTEs and average annual wages exceeding $25,000, the total reduction is the sum of the two reductions. This may reduce the credit to zero for some employers with fewer than 25 FTEs and average annual wages of less than $50,000.

Example 10— Calculating the maximum credit for a taxable eligible small employer. (i) For the 2010 taxable year, a taxable eligible small employer has 9 FTEs with average annual wages of $23,000 per FTE. The employer pays $72,000 in health insurance premiums for those employees (which does not exceed the average premium for the small group market in the employer's State) and otherwise meets the requirements for the credit.

(ii) The credit for 2010 equals $25,200 (35% × $72,000).

Example 11— Calculating the maximum credit for a tax-exempt eligible small employer. (i) For the 2010 taxable year, a tax-exempt eligible small employer has 10 FTEs with average annual wages of $21,000 per FTE. The employer pays $80,000 in health insurance premiums for its employees (which does not exceed the average premium for the small group market in the employer's State) and otherwise meets the requirements for the credit. The total amount of the employer's income tax and Medicare tax withholding plus the employer's share of the Medicare tax equals $30,000 in 2010.

(ii) The credit is calculated as follows:

(1) Initial amount of credit determined before any reduction: (25% × $80,000) = $20,000

(2) Employer's withholding and Medicare taxes: $30,000

(3) Total 2010 tax credit equals $20,000 (the lesser of $20,000 and $30,000).

Example 12— Calculating the credit phase-out if the number of FTEs exceeds 10 or average annual wages exceed $25,000. (i) For the 2010 taxable year, a taxable eligible small employer has 12 FTEs and average annual wages of $30,000. The employer pays $96,000 in health insurance premiums for its employees (which does not exceed the average premium for the small group market in the employer's State) and otherwise meets the requirements for the credit.

(ii) The credit is calculated as follows:

(1) Initial amount of credit determined before any reduction: (35% × $96,000) = $33,600

(2) Credit reduction for FTEs in excess of 10: ($33,600 × 2/15) = $4,480

(3) Credit reduction for average annual wages in excess of $25,000: ($33,600 × $5,000/$25,000) = $6,720

(4) Total credit reduction: ($4,480 + $6,720) = $11,200

(5) Total 2010 tax credit equals $22,400 ($33,600 − $11,200).

D. State Credits and State Subsidies for Health Insurance

Some States offer tax credits to certain small employers that provide health insurance to their employees. Some of these are refundable credits and others are nonrefundable credits. In addition, some States offer premium subsidy programs for certain small employers under which the State makes a payment equal to a portion of the employees' health insurance premiums under the employer-provided health insurance plan. Generally, the State pays this premium subsidy either directly to the employer or to the employer's insurance company (or another entity licensed under State law to engage in the business of insurance). If the employer is entitled to a State tax credit (whether refundable or nonrefundable) or a premium subsidy that is paid directly to the employer, the premium payment made by the employer is not reduced by the credit or subsidy for purposes of determining whether the employer has satisfied the "qualifying arrangement" requirement to pay an amount equal to a uniform percentage (not less than 50 percent) of the premium cost. Also, except as described below in this section III.D, the maximum amount of the section 45R credit is not reduced by reason of a State tax credit (whether refundable or nonrefundable) or by reason of payments by a State directly to an employer.

Generally, if a State makes payments directly to an insurance company (or another entity licensed under State law to engage in the business of insurance) to pay a portion of the premium for coverage of an employee under employer-provided health insurance (State direct payments), the State is treated as making these payments on behalf of the employer for purposes of determining whether the employer has satisfied the "qualifying arrangement" requirement to pay an amount equal to a uniform percentage (not less than 50 percent) of the premium cost of coverage. Also, except as described below in this section III.D, these premium payments by the State are treated as an employer contribution under section 45R for purposes of calculating the credit.

Although State tax credits and payments to an employer generally do not reduce an employer's otherwise applicable credit under section 45R, and although State direct payments are generally treated as paid on behalf of an employer, in no event may the amount of the section 45R credit exceed the amount of the employer's net premium payments. In the case of a State tax credit for an employer or a State subsidy paid directly to an employer, the employer's net premium payments are calculated by subtracting the State tax credit or subsidy from the employer's actual premium payments. In the case of a State payment directly to an insurance company (or another entity licensed under State law to engage in the business of insurance), the employer's net premium payments are the employer's actual premium payments.

If a State-administered program (such as Medicaid or another program that makes payments directly to a health care provider or insurance company on behalf of individuals and their families who meet certain eligibility guidelines) makes payments that are not contingent on the maintenance of an employer-provided group health plan, those payments are not taken into account in determining the credit under section 45R.

Example 13— State premium subsidy paid directly to employer. (i) Employer's State provides a health insurance premium subsidy of up to 40% of the health insurance premiums for each eligible employee. The State pays the subsidy directly to the employer.

(ii) Employer has one employee, Employee D. Employee D's health insurance premiums are $100 per month and are paid as follows: $80 by the employer and $20 by Employee D through salary reductions to a cafeteria plan. The State pays Employer $40 per month as a subsidy for Employer's payment of insurance premiums on behalf of Employee D. Employer is otherwise an eligible small employer that meets the requirements for the section 45R credit.

(iii) For purposes of the requirements for a qualifying arrangement, and for purposes of calculating the amount of the section 45R credit, the amount of premiums paid by the employer is $80 per month (the premium payment by the Employer without regard to the subsidy from the State).

Example 14— State premium subsidy paid directly to employer's insurance company. (i) Employer's State provides a health insurance premium subsidy of up to 50% for each eligible employee. The State pays the premium directly to the employer's health insurance provider.

(ii) Employer has one employee, Employee E. Employee E is enrolled in single coverage under Employer's health insurance plan.

(iii) Employee E's health insurance premiums are $100 per month and are paid as follows: $30 by the employer; $50 by the State and $20 by the employee. The State pays the $50 per month directly to the insurance company and the insurance company bills the employer for the employer and employee's share, which equal $50 per month. Employer is otherwise an eligible small employer that meets the requirements for the section 45R credit.

(iv) For purposes of the requirements for a qualifying arrangement, and for purposes of calculating the amount of the section 45R credit, the amount of premiums paid by the employer is $80 per month (the sum of the employer's payment and the State's payment).

Example 15— Credit limited by employer's net premium payment. (i) Employer's State provides a health insurance premium subsidy of up to 50% for each eligible employee. The State pays the premium directly to the employer's health insurance provider. Employer has one employee, Employee F. Employee F is enrolled in single coverage under Employer's health insurance plan. Employee F's health insurance premiums are $100 per month and are paid as follows: $20 by the employer; $50 by the State and $30 by the employee. The State pays the $50 per month directly to the insurance company and the insurance company bills the employer for the employer's and employee's shares, which total $50 per month. Employer is otherwise an eligible small employer that meets the requirements for the section 45R credit.

(ii) The amount of premiums paid by the employer for purposes of determining whether the employer meets the qualifying arrangement requirement (the sum of the employer's payment and the State's payment) is $70 per month, which is more than 50% of the $100 monthly premium payment. The amount of the premium for calculating the maximum section 45R credit is also $70 per month. The maximum credit is $24.50 ($70 × 35%).

(iii) The employer's net premium payment is $20 (the amount actually paid by the employer excluding the State subsidy). After applying the limit for the employer's net premium payment, the section 45R credit is $20 per month, (the lesser of $24.50 or $20).

IV. CLAIMING THE CREDIT AND EFFECT ON ESTIMATED TAX, ALTERNATIVE MINIMUM TAX AND DEDUCTIONS

The section 45R credit is claimed on an eligible small employer's annual income tax return and offsets an employer's actual tax liability for the year. For a tax-exempt eligible small employer, the IRS will provide further information on how to claim the credit. For an eligible small employer that is not a tax-exempt employer, the credit is a general business credit and, thus, any unused credit amount can be carried back one year and carried forward 20 years (however, because an unused credit amount cannot be carried back to a year before the effective date of the credit, any unused credit amounts for taxable years beginning in 2010 can only be carried forward). For a tax-exempt eligible small employer, the credit is a refundable credit, so that even if the employer has no taxable income, the employer may receive a refund (so long as it does not exceed the tax-exempt eligible small employer's total income tax withholding and Medicare tax liability for the year).

The credit can be reflected in determining estimated tax payments for the year in which the credit applies in accordance with regular estimated tax rules. The credit can also be used to offset an employer's alternative minimum tax (AMT) liability for the year, subject to certain limitations based on the amount of an employer's regular tax liability, AMT liability and other allowable credits. See section 38(c)(1), as modified by section 38(c)(4)(B)(vi). However, because the credit applies against income tax, an employer may not reduce employment tax (*i.e.*, withheld income tax, social security tax under sections 3101(a) and 3111(a), and Medicare tax) deposits and payments during the year in anticipation of the credit. Finally, no deduction is allowed for the employer under section 162 for that portion of the health insurance premiums which is equal to the amount of the section 45R credit.

V. TRANSITION RELIEF FOR TAXABLE YEARS BEGINNING IN 2010

Because the section 45R credit applies to taxable years beginning in 2010 (including the period in 2010 before enactment of the Affordable Care Act), an employer that satisfies the requirements for the transition relief in this section V will be deemed to satisfy the requirement for a qualifying arrangement that the employer pay a uniform percentage (not less than 50 percent) of the premium cost of the health insurance coverage (uniformity requirement). Specifically, for taxable years beginning in 2010, an employer that pays an amount equal to at least 50 percent of the premium for single (employee-only) coverage for each employee enrolled in coverage offered to employees by the employer will be deemed to satisfy the uniformity requirement for a qualifying arrangement, even if the employer does not pay the same percentage of the premium for each such employee. Thus, an employer will be deemed to satisfy the uniformity requirement for a qualifying arrangement if it pays at least 50 percent of the premium for single coverage for each employee receiving single coverage, and, if the employer offers coverage that is more expensive than single coverage (such as family or self-plus-one coverage), if it pays an amount for each employee receiving that more expensive coverage that is no less than 50 percent of the premium for single coverage for that employee (even if it is less than 50 percent of the premium for the more expensive coverage the employee is actually receiving).

Example 16— Transition relief rule for a qualifying arrangement. (i) For the 2010 taxable year, an eligible small employer has 9 FTEs with average annual wages of $23,000 per FTE. Six employees are enrolled in single coverage and 3 employees are enrolled in family coverage.

(ii) The premiums are $8,000 for single coverage for the year and $14,000 for family coverage for the year (which do not exceed the average premiums for the small group market in the employer's State). The employer pays 50% of the premium for single coverage for each employee enrolled in single or family coverage (50% × $8,000 = $4,000 for each employee).

(iii) Thus, the employer pays $4,000 of the premium for each of the 6 employees enrolled in single coverage and $4,000 of the premium for each of the 3 employees enrolled in family coverage.

(iv) The employer is deemed to satisfy the uniformity requirement for a qualifying arrangement under the transition relief rule.

Example 17— Arrangement that does not satisfy requirement for transition relief. (i) Same facts as *Example 16*, except that the employer pays 50% of the premium for employees enrolled in single coverage ($4,000 for each of those 6 employees) but pays none of the premium for employees enrolled in family coverage.

(ii) The employer does not satisfy the uniformity requirement for a qualifying arrangement.

VI. EFFECTIVE DATE

Section 45R is effective for taxable years beginning after December 31, 2009.

VI. REQUEST FOR COMMENTS

The IRS and Treasury intend to issue future guidance that will address additional issues under section 45R, including the application of the uniformity requirement and the 50-percent requirement for taxable years beginning after 2010. Comments are requested on issues that should be addressed in that future guidance.

Comments should be submitted on or before September 1, 2010, and should include a reference to Notice 2010-44. Send submissions to CC:PA:LPD:PR (Notice 2010-44), Room 5203, Internal Revenue Service, P.O. Box 7604, Ben Franklin Station, Washington, DC 20044. Submissions may be hand delivered **Monday through Friday** between the hours of 8 a.m. and 4 p.m. to CC:PA:LPD:PR (Notice 2010-44), Courier's Desk, Internal Revenue Service, 1111 Constitution Avenue, NW, Washington, DC 20044, or sent electronically, via the following e-mail address: *Notice.comments@irscounsel.treas.gov*. Please include "Notice 2010-44" in the subject line of any electronic communication. All material submitted will be available for public inspection and copying.

VI. DRAFTING INFORMATION

The principal author of this notice is Mireille Khoury of the Office of Division Counsel/Associate Chief Counsel (Tax Exempt and Government Entities). For further information regarding this notice, contact Ms. Khoury at (202) 622-6080 (not a toll-free call).

G. Recommended Immunization Schedules

Recommended Immunization Schedule for Persons Aged 0 Through 6 Years—United States • 2010
For those who fall behind or start late, see the catch-up schedule

Vaccine ▼ Age ►	Birth	1 month	2 months	4 months	6 months	12 months	15 months	18 months	19-23 months	2-3 years	4-6 years	
Hepatitis B[1]	HepB	HepB			Hep B							Range of recommended ages for all children except certain high-risk groups
Rotavirus[2]			RV	RV	RV[2]							
Diphtheria, Tetanus, Pertussis[3]			DTaP	DTaP	DTaP	see footnote[3]	DTaP				DTaP	
Haemophilus influenzae type b[4]			Hib	Hib	Hib[4]	Hib						
Pneumococcal[5]			PCV	PCV	PCV	PCV					PPSV	Range of recommended ages for certain high-risk groups
Inactivated Poliovirus[6]			IPV	IPV		IPV					IPV	
Influenza[7]						Influenza (Yearly)						
Measles, Mumps, Rubella[8]						MMR		see footnote[8]			MMR	
Varicella[9]						Varicella		see footnote[9]			Varicella	
Hepatitis A[10]						HepA (2 doses)					HepA Series	
Meningococcal[11]											MCV	

This schedule includes recommendations in effect as of December 15, 2009. Any dose not administered at the recommended age should be administered at a subsequent visit, when indicated and feasible. The use of a combination vaccine generally is preferred over separate injections of its equivalent component vaccines. Considerations should include provider assessment, patient preference, and the potential for adverse events.

1. **Hepatitis B vaccine (HepB).** (Minimum age: birth)
   At birth:
   - Administer monovalent HepB to all newborns before hospital discharge.
   - If mother is hepatitis B surface antigen (HBsAg)-positive, administer HepB and 0.5 mL of hepatitis B immune globulin (HBIG) within 12 hours of birth.
   - If mother's HBsAg status is unknown, administer HepB within 12 hours of birth. Determine mother's HBsAg status as soon as possible and, if HBsAg-positive, administer HBIG (no later than age 1 week).
   After the birth dose:
   - The HepB series should be completed with either monovalent HepB or a combination vaccine containing HepB. The second dose should be administered at age 1 or 2 months. Monovalent HepB vaccine should be used for doses administered before age 6 weeks. The final dose should be administered no earlier than age 24 weeks.
   - Infants born to HBsAg-positive mothers should be tested for HBsAg and antibody to HBsAg 1 to 2 months after completion of at least 3 doses of the HepB series, at age 9 through 18 months (generally at the next well-child visit).
   - Administration of 4 doses of HepB to infants is permissible when a combination vaccine containing HepB is administered after the birth dose. The fourth dose should be administered no earlier than age 24 weeks.
2. **Rotavirus vaccine (RV).** (Minimum age: 6 weeks)
   - Administer the first dose at age 6 through 14 weeks (maximum age: 14 weeks 6 days). Vaccination should not be initiated for infants aged 15 weeks 0 days or older.
   - The maximum age for the final dose in the series is 8 months 0 days
   - If Rotarix is administered at ages 2 and 4 months, a dose at 6 months is not indicated.
3. **Diphtheria and tetanus toxoids and acellular pertussis vaccine (DTaP).** (Minimum age: 6 weeks)
   - The fourth dose may be administered as early as age 12 months, provided at least 6 months have elapsed since the third dose.
   - Administer the final dose in the series at age 4 through 6 years.
4. **Haemophilus influenzae type b conjugate vaccine (Hib).** (Minimum age: 6 weeks)
   - If PRP-OMP (PedvaxHIB or Comvax [HepB-Hib]) is administered at ages 2 and 4 months, a dose at age 6 months is not indicated.
   - TriHiBit (DTaP/Hib) and Hiberix (PRP-T) should not be used for doses at ages 2, 4, or 6 months for the primary series but can be used as the final dose in children aged 12 months through 4 years.
5. **Pneumococcal vaccine.** (Minimum age: 6 weeks for pneumococcal conjugate vaccine [PCV]; 2 years for pneumococcal polysaccharide vaccine [PPSV])
   - PCV is recommended for all children aged younger than 5 years. Administer 1 dose of PCV to all healthy children aged 24 through 59 months who are not completely vaccinated for their age.

- Administer PPSV 2 or more months after last dose of PCV to children aged 2 years or older with certain underlying medical conditions, including a cochlear implant. See MMWR 1997;46(No. RR-8).

The Recommended Immunization Schedules for Persons Aged 0 through 18 Years are approved by the Advisory Committee on Immunization Practices (http://www.cdc.gov/vaccines/recs/acip), the American Academy of Pediatrics (http://www.aap.org), and the American Academy of Family Physicians (http://www.aafp.org).
Department of Health and Human Services • Centers for Disease Control and Prevention

Providers should consult the relevant Advisory Committee on Immunization Practices statement for detailed recommendations: http://www.cdc.gov/vaccines/pubs/acip-list.htm. Clinically significant adverse events that follow immunization should be reported to the Vaccine Adverse Event Reporting System (VAERS) at http://www.vaers.hhs.gov or by telephone, 800-822-7967.

6. **Inactivated poliovirus vaccine (IPV)** (Minimum age: 6 weeks)
   - The final dose in the series should be administered on or after the fourth birthday and at least 6 months following the previous dose.
   - If 4 doses are administered prior to age 4 years a fifth dose should be administered at age 4 through 6 years. See MMWR 2009;58(30):829-30.

7. **Influenza vaccine (seasonal).** (Minimum age: 6 months for trivalent inactivated influenza vaccine [TIV]; 2 years for live, attenuated influenza vaccine [LAIV])
   - Administer annually to children aged 6 months through 18 years.
   - For healthy children aged 2 through 6 years (i.e., those who do not have underlying medical conditions that predispose them to influenza complications), either LAIV or TIV may be used, except LAIV should not be given to children aged 2 through 4 years who have had wheezing in the past 12 months.
   - Children receiving TIV should receive 0.25 mL if aged 6 through 35 months or 0.5 mL if aged 3 years or older.
   - Administer 2 doses (separated by at least 4 weeks) to children aged younger than 9 years who are receiving influenza vaccine for the first time or who were vaccinated for the first time during the previous influenza season but only received 1 dose.
   - For recommendations for use of influenza A (H1N1) 2009 monovalent vaccine see MMWR 2009;58(No. RR-10).

8. **Measles, mumps, and rubella vaccine (MMR).** (Minimum age: 12 months)
   - Administer the second dose routinely at age 4 through 6 years. However, the second dose may be administered before age 4, provided at least 28 days have elapsed since the first dose.

9. **Varicella vaccine.** (Minimum age: 12 months)
   - Administer the second dose routinely at age 4 through 6 years. However, the second dose may be administered before age 4, provided at least 3 months have elapsed since the first dose.
   - For children aged 12 months through 12 years the minimum interval between doses is 3 months. However, if the second dose was administered at least 28 days after the first dose, it can be accepted as valid.

10. **Hepatitis A vaccine (HepA).** (Minimum age: 12 months)
    - Administer to all children aged 1 year (i.e., aged 12 through 23 months). Administer 2 doses at least 6 months apart.
    - Children not fully vaccinated by age 2 years can be vaccinated at subsequent visits
    - HepA also is recommended for older children who live in areas where vaccination programs target older children, who are at increased risk for infection, or for whom immunity against hepatitis A is desired.

11. **Meningococcal vaccine.** (Minimum age: 2 years for meningococcal conjugate vaccine [MCV4] and for meningococcal polysaccharide vaccine [MPSV4])
    - Administer MCV4 to children aged 2 through 10 years with persistent complement component deficiency, anatomic or functional asplenia, and certain other conditions placing tham at high risk.
    - Administer MCV4 to children previously vaccinated with MCV4 or MPSV4 after 3 years if first dose administered at age 2 through 6 years. See MMWR 2009;58:1042-3.

Recommended Immunization Schedule for Persons Aged 7 Through 18 Years—United States • 2010
For those who fall behind or start late, see the schedule below and the catch-up schedule

Vaccine ▼ Age ►	7-10 years	11-12 years	13-18 years	
Tetanus, Diphtheria, Pertussis[1]		Tdap	Tdap	Range of recommended ages for all children except certain high-risk groups
Human Papillomavirus[2]	*see footnote 2*	HPV (3 doses)	HPV series	
Meningococcal[3]	MCV	MCV	MCV	
Influenza[4]	Influenza (Yearly)			
Pneumococcal[5]	PPSV			Range of recommended ages for catch-up immunization
Hepatitis A[6]	HepA Series			
Hepatitis B[7]	Hep B Series			
Inactivated Poliovirus[8]	IPV Series			Range of recommended ages for certain high-risk groups
Measles, Mumps, Rubella	MMR Series			
Varicella[10]	Varicella Series			

This schedule includes recommendations in effect as of December 15, 2009. Any dose not administered at the recommended age should be administered at a subsequent visit, when indicated and feasible. The use of a combination vaccine generally is preferred over separate injections of its equivalent component vaccines. Considerations should include provider assessment, patient preference, and the potential for adverse events.

Providers should consult the relevant Advisory Committee on Immunization Practices statement for detailed recommendations: http://www.cdc.gov/vaccines/pubs/acip-list.htm. Clinically significant adverse events that follow immunization should be reported to the Vaccine Adverse Event Reporting System (VAERS) at http://www.vaers.hhs.gov or by telephone, 800-822-7967.

1. **Tetanus and diphtheria toxoids and acellular pertussis vaccine (Tdap).** (Minimum age: 10 years for Boostrix and 11 years for Adacel)
   - Administer at age 11 or 12 years for those who have completed the recommended childhood DTP/DTaP vaccination series and have not received a tetanus and diphtheria toxoid (Td) booster dose.
   - Persons aged 13 through 18 years who have not received Tdap should receive a dose.
   - A 5-year interval from the last Td dose is encouraged when Tdap is used as a booster dose; however, a shorter interval may be used if pertussis immunity is needed.
2. **Human papillomavirus vaccine (HPV).** (Minimum age: 9 years)
   - Two HPV vaccines are licensed: a quadrivalent vaccine (HPV4) for the prevention of cervical, vaginal and vulvar cancers (in females) and genital warts (in females and males), and a bivalent vaccine (HPV2) for the prevention of cervical cancers in females.
   - HPV vaccines are most effective for both males and females when given before exposure to HPV through sexual contact.
   - HPV4 or HPV2 is recommended for the prevention of cervical precancers and cancers in females.
   - HPV4 is recommended for the prevention of cervical, vaginal and vulvar precancers and cancers and genital warts in females.
   - Administer the first dose to females at age 11 or 12 years.
   - Administer the second dose 1 to 2 months after the first dose and the third dose 6 months after the first dose (at least 24 weeks after the first dose).
   - Administer the series to females at age 13 through 18 years if not previously vaccinated.
   - HPV4 may be administered in a 3-dose series to males aged 9 through 18 years to reduce their likelihood of acquiring genital warts.
3. **Meningococcal conjugate vaccine (MCV4).**
   - Administer at age 11 or 12 years, or at age 13 through 18 years if not previously vaccinated.
   - Administer to previously unvaccinated college freshmen living in a dormitory.
   - Administer MCV4 to children aged 2 through 10 years with persistent complement component deficiency, anatomic or functional asplenia, or certain other conditions placing them at high risk.
   - Administer to children previously vaccinated with MCV4 or MPSV4 who remain at increased risk after 3 years (if first dose administered at age 2 through 6 years) or after 5 years (if first dose administered at age 7 years or older). Persons whose only risk factor is living in on-campus housing are not recommended to receive an additional dose. See MMWR 2009;58:1042-3.

4. **Influenza vaccine (seasonal).**
   - Administer annually to children aged 6 months through 18 years.
   - For healthy nonpregnant persons aged 7 through 18 years (i.e., those who do not have underlying medical conditions that predispose them to influenza complications), either LAIV or TIV may be used.
   - Administer 2 doses (separated by at least 4 weeks) to children aged younger than 9 years who are receiving influenza vaccine for the first time or who were vaccinated for the first time during the previous influenza season but only received 1 dose.
   - For recommendations for use of influenza A (H1N1) 2009 monovalent vaccine. See MMWR 2009;58(No. RR-10).
5. **Pneumococcal polysaccharide vaccine (PPSV).**
   - Administer to children with certain underlying medical conditions, including a cochlear implant. A single revaccination should be administered after 5 years to children with functional or anatomic asplenia or an immunocompromising condition. See MMWR 1997;46(No. RR-8).
6. **Hepatitis A vaccine (HepA).**
   - Administer 2 doses at least 6 months apart.
   - HepA is recommended for children aged older than 23 months who live in areas where vaccination programs target older children, who are at increased risk for infection, or for whom immunity against hepatitis A is desired.
7. **Hepatitis B vaccine (HepB).**
   - Administer the 3-dose series to those not previously vaccinated.
   - A 2-dose series (separated by at least 4 months) of adult formulation Recombivax HB is licensed for children aged 11 through 15 years.
8. **Inactivated poliovirus vaccine (IPV).**
   - The final dose in the series should be administered on or after the fourth birthday and at least 6 months following the previous dose.
   - If both OPV and IPV were administered as part of a series, a total of 4 doses should be administered, regardless of the child's current age.
9. **Measles, mumps, and rubella vaccine (MMR).**
   - If not previously vaccinated, administer 2 doses or the second dose for those who have received only 1 dose, with at least 28 days between doses.
10. **Varicella vaccine.**
   - For persons aged 7 through 18 years without evidence of immunity (see MMWR 2007;56[No. RR-4]), administer 2 doses if not previously vaccinated or the second dose if only 1 dose has been administered.
   - For persons aged 7 through 12 years, the minimum interval between doses is 3 months. However, if the second dose was administered at least 28 days after the first dose, it can be accepted as valid.
   - For persons aged 13 years and older, the minimum interval between doses is 28 days.

The Recommended Immunization Schedules for Persons Aged 0 through 18 Years are approved by the Advisory Committee on Immunization Practices (http://www.cdc.gov/vaccines/recs/acip), the American Academy of Pediatrics (http://www.aap.org), and the American Academy of Family Physicians (http://www.aafp.org). Department of Health and Human Services • Centers for Disease Control and Prevention

Catch-up Immunization Schedule for Persons Aged 4 Months Through 18 Years Who Start Late or Who Are More Than 1 Month Behind—United States • 2010

The table below provides catch-up schedules and minimum intervals between doses for children whose vaccinations have been delayed. A vaccine series does not need to be restarted, regardless of the time that has elapsed between doses. Use the section appropriate for the child's age.

Vaccine	Minimum Age for Dose 1	Minimum Interval Between Doses			
		Dose 1 to Dose 2	Dose 2 to Dose 3	Dose 3 to Dose 4	Dose 4 to Dose 5
PERSONS AGED 4 MONTHS THROUGH 6 YEARS					
Hepatitis B[1]	Birth	**4 weeks**	**8 weeks** (and at least 16 weeks after first dose)		
Rotavirus[2]	6 wks	**4 weeks**	**4 weeks**[2]		
Diphtheria, Tetanus, Pertussis[3]	6 wks	**4 weeks**	**4 weeks**	**6 months**	**6 months**[3]
Haemophilus influenza type b[4]	6 wks	**4 weeks** if first dose administered at younger than age 12 months **8 weeks (as final dose)** if first dose administered at age 12-14 months **No further doses needed** if first dose administered at age 15 months or older	**4 weeks**[4] if current age is younger than 12 months **8 weeks (as final dose)**[4] if current age is 12 months or older and first dose administered at younger than age 12 months and second dose administered at younger than 15 months **No further doses needed** if previous dose administered at age 15 months or older	**8 weeks (as final dose)** This dose only necessary for children aged 12 months through 59 months who received 3 doses before age 12 months	
Pneumococcal[5]	6 wks	**4 weeks** if first dose administered at younger than age 12 months **8 weeks (as final dose for healthy children)** if first dose administered at age 12 months or cider or current age 24 through 59 months **No further doses needed** for healthy children if first dose administered at age 24 months or older	**4 weeks** if current age is younger than 12 months **8 weeks (as final dose for healthy children)** if current age is 12 months or older **No further doses needed** for healthy children if previous dose administered at age 24 months or older	**8 weeks (as final dose)** This dose only necessary for children aged 12 months through 59 months who received 3 doses before age 12 months or for high-risk children who received 3 doses at any age	
Inactivated Poliovirus[6]	6 wks	**4 weeks**	**4 weeks**		
Measles, Mumps Rubella[7]	12 mos	**4 weeks**		**6 months**	
Varicella[8]	12 mos	**3 months**			
Hepatitis A[8]	12 mos	**6 months**			
PERSONS AGED 7 THROUGH 18 YEARS					
Tetanus, Diphtheria/ Tetanus, Diphtheria, Pertussis[10]	7yrs[10]	**4 weeks**	**4 weeks** if first dose administered at younger than age 12 months **6 months** if first dose administered at 12 months or older	**6 months** if first dose administered at younger than age 12 months	
Human Papillomavirus[11]	9 yrs		Routine dosing Intervals are recommended[11]		
Hepatitis A[9]	12 mos	**6 months**			
Hepatitis B[1]	Birth	**4 weeks**	**8 weeks** (and at least 16 weeks after first dose)		
Inactivated Poliovirus[6]	6 wks	**4 weeks**	**4 weeks**		
Measles, Mumps, Rubella[7]	12 mos	**4 weeks**		**6 months**	
Varicella[9]	12 mos	**3 months** if person is younger than age 13 years **4 weeks** if person is aged 13 years or older			

1. **Hepatitis B vaccine (HepB).**
   - Administer the 3-dose series to those not previously vaccinated.
   - A 2-dose series (separated by at least 4 months) of adult formulation Recombivax HB is licensed for children aged 11 through 15 years.
2. **Rotavirus vaccine (RV).**
   - The maximum age for the first dose is 14 weeks 6 days. Vaccination should not be initiated for infants aged 15 weeks 0 days or older.
   - The maximum age for the final dose in the series is 8 months 0 days.
   - If Rotarix was administered for the first and second doses, a third dose is not indicated.
3. **Diphtheria and tetanus toxoids and acellular pertussis vaccine (DTaP).**
   - The fifth dose is not necessary if the fourth dose was administered at age 4 years or older.
4. **Haemophilus influenzae type b conjugate vaccine (Hib).**
   - Hib vaccine is not generally recommended for persons aged 5 years or older. No efficacy data are available on which to base a recommendation concerning use of Hib vaccine for older children and adults. However, studies suggest good immunogenicity in persons who have sickle cell disease, leukemia, or HIV infection, or who have had a splenectomy; administering 1 dose of Hib vaccine to these persons who have not previously received Hib vaccine is not contraindicated.
   - If the first 2 doses were PRP-OMP (PedvaxHIB or Comvax), and administered at age 11 months or younger, the third (and final) dose should be administered at age 12 through 15 months and at least 8 weeks after the second dose.
   - If the first dose was administered at age 7 through 11 months, administer the second dose at least 4 weeks later and a final dose at age 12 through 15 months.
5. **Pneumococcal vaccine.**
   - Administer 1 dose of pneumococcal conjugate vaccine (PCV) to all healthy children aged 24 through 59 months who have not received at least 1 dose of PCV on or after age 12 months.
   - For children aged 24 through 59 months with underlying medical conditions, administer 1 dose of PCV if 3 doses were received previously or administer 2 doses of PCV at least 8 weeks apart if fewer than 3 doses were received previously.
   - Administer pneumococcal polysaccharide vaccine (PPSV) to children aged 2 years or older with certain underlying medical conditions, including a cochlear implant, at least 8 weeks after the last dose of PCV. See MMWR 1997; 46(No. RR-8).

6. **Inactivated poliovirus vaccine (IPV).**
   - The final dose in the series should be administered on or after the fourth birthday and at least 6 months following the previous dose.
   - A fourth dose is not necessary if the third dose was administered at age 4 years or older and at least 6 months following the previous dose.
   - In the first 6 months of life, minimum age and minimum intervals are only recommended if the person is at risk for imminent exposure to circulating poliovirus (i.e., travel to a polio-endemic region or during an outbreak).
7. **Measles, mumps, and rubella vaccine (MMR).**
   - Administer the second dose routinely at age 4 through 6 years. However, the second dose may be administered before age 4, provided at least 28 days have elapsed since the first dose.
   - If not previously vaccinated, administer 2 doses with at least 28 days between doses.
8. **Varicella vaccine.**
   - Administer the second dose routinely at age 4 through 6 years. However, the second dose may be administered before age 4, provided at least 3 months have elapsed since the first dose.
   - For persons aged 12 months through 12 years, the minimum interval between doses is 3 months. However, if the second dose was administered at least 28 days after the first dose, it can be accepted as valid.
   - For persons aged 13 years and older, the minimum interval between doses is 28 days.
9. **Hepatitis A vaccine (HepA).**
   - HepA is recommended for children aged older than 23 months who live in areas where vaccination programs target older children, who are at increased risk for infection, or for whom immunity against hepatitis A is desired.
10. **Tetanus and diphtheria toxoids vaccine (Td) and tetanus and diphtheria toxoids and acellular pertussis vaccine (Tdap).**
    - Doses of DTaP are counted as part of the Td/Tdap series
    - Tdap should be substituted for a single dose of Td in the catch-up series or as a booster for children aged 10 through 18 years; use Td for other doses.
11. **Human papillomavirus vaccine (HPV).**
    - Administer the series to females at age 13 through 18 years if not previously vaccinated.
    - Use recommended routine dosing intervals for series catch-up (i.e., the second and third doses should be administered at 1 to 2 and 6 months after the first dose). The minimum interval between the first and second doses is 4 weeks. The minimum interval between the second and third doses is 12 weeks, and the third dose should be administered at least 24 weeks after the first dose.

The Recommended Immunization Schedules for Persons Aged 0 through 18 Years are approved by the Advisory Committee on Immunization Practices (**http://www.cdc.gov/vaccines/recs/acip**), the American Academy of Pediatrics (**http://www.aap.org**), and the American Academy of Family Physicians (**http://www.aafp.org**).
Department of Hearth and Human Services • Centers for Disease Control and Prevention

H. Tri-Agency Regulations on Extended Coverage for Adult Children

Thursday,
May 13, 2010

Part II

Department of the Treasury
Internal Revenue Service
26 CFR Parts 54 and 602

Department of Labor
Employee Benefits Security
Administration

29 CFR Part 2590

Department of Health and Human Services

45 CFR Parts 144, 146, and 147

Group Health Plans and Health Insurance Issuers Relating to Dependent Coverage of Children to Age 26 Under the Patient Protection and Affordable Care Act; Interim Final Rule and Proposed Rule

27122 Federal Register / Vol. 75, No. 92 / Thursday, May 13, 2010 / Rules and Regulations

DEPARTMENT OF THE TREASURY

Internal Revenue Service

26 CFR Parts 54 and 602

[TD 9482]

RIN 1545–BJ46

DEPARTMENT OF LABOR

Employee Benefits Security Administration

29 CFR Part 2590

RIN 1210–AB41

DEPARTMENT OF HEALTH AND HUMAN SERVICES

Office of the Secretary

[OCIIO–4150–IFC]

45 CFR Parts 144, 146, and 147

RIN 0991–AB66

Interim Final Rules for Group Health Plans and Health Insurance Issuers Relating to Dependent Coverage of Children to Age 26 Under the Patient Protection and Affordable Care Act

AGENCY: Internal Revenue Service, Department of the Treasury; Employee Benefits Security Administration, Department of Labor; Department of Health and Human Services.

ACTION: Interim final rules with request for comments.

SUMMARY: This document contains interim final regulations implementing the requirements for group health plans and health insurance issuers in the group and individual markets under provisions of the Patient Protection and Affordable Care Act regarding dependent coverage of children who have not attained age 26.

DATES: *Effective date.* These interim final regulations are effective on July 12, 2010.

Comment date. Comments are due on or before August 11, 2010.

Applicability date. These interim final regulations generally apply to group health plans and group health insurance issuers for plan years beginning on or after September 23, 2010. These interim final regulations generally apply to individual health insurance issuers for policy years beginning on or after September 23, 2010.

ADDRESSES: Written comments may be submitted to any of the addresses specified below. Any comment that is submitted to any Department will be shared with the other Departments. Please do not submit duplicates.

All comments will be made available to the public. *Warning:* Do not include any personally identifiable information (such as name, address, or other contact information) or confidential business information that you do not want publicly disclosed. All comments are posted on the Internet exactly as received, and can be retrieved by most Internet search engines. No deletions, modifications, or redactions will be made to the comments received, as they are public records. Comments may be submitted anonymously.

Department of Labor. Comments to the Department of Labor, identified by RIN 1210–AB41, by one of the following methods:

• *Federal eRulemaking Portal: http:// www.regulations.gov.* Follow the instructions for submitting comments.

• *E-mail: E-OHPSCA.EBSA@dol.gov.*

• *Mail or Hand Delivery:* Office of Health Plan Standards and Compliance Assistance, Employee Benefits Security Administration, Room N–5653, U.S. Department of Labor, 200 Constitution Avenue NW., Washington, DC 20210, *Attention:* RIN 1210–AB41.

Comments received by the Department of Labor will be posted without change to *http:// www.regulations.gov* and *http:// www.dol.gov/ebsa,* and available for public inspection at the Public Disclosure Room, N–1513, Employee Benefits Security Administration, 200 Constitution Avenue, NW., Washington, DC 20210.

Department of Health and Human Services. In commenting, please refer to file code OCIIO–4150–IFC. Because of staff and resource limitations, we cannot accept comments by facsimile (FAX) transmission.

You may submit comments in one of four ways (please choose only one of the ways listed):

1. *Electronically.* You may submit electronic comments on this regulation to *http://www.regulations.gov.* Follow the instructions under the "More Search Options" tab.

2. *By regular mail.* You may mail written comments to the following address only: Office of Consumer Information and Insurance Oversight, Department of Health and Human Services, Attention: OCIIO–4150–IFC, P.O. Box 8016, Baltimore, MD 21244– 1850.

Please allow sufficient time for mailed comments to be received before the close of the comment period.

3. *By express or overnight mail.* You may send written comments to the following address only: Office of Consumer Information and Insurance Oversight, Department of Health and

Human Services, Attention: OCIIO– 4150–IFC, Mail Stop C4–26–05, 7500 Security Boulevard, Baltimore, MD 21244–1850.

4. *By hand or courier.* If you prefer, you may deliver (by hand or courier) your written comments before the close of the comment period to either of the following addresses:

a. For delivery in Washington, DC— Office of Consumer Information and Insurance Oversight, Department of Health and Human Services, Room 445– G, Hubert H. Humphrey Building, 200 Independence Avenue, SW., Washington, DC 20201 (Because access to the interior of the Hubert H. Humphrey Building is not readily available to persons without Federal government identification, commenters are encouraged to leave their comments in the OCIIO drop slots located in the main lobby of the building. A stamp-in clock is available for persons wishing to retain a proof of filing by stamping in and retaining an extra copy of the comments being filed.).

b. For delivery in Baltimore, MD— Centers for Medicare & Medicaid Services, Department of Health and Human Services, 7500 Security Boulevard, Baltimore, MD 21244–1850.

If you intend to deliver your comments to the Baltimore address, please call (410) 786–7195 in advance to schedule your arrival with one of our staff members.

Comments mailed to the addresses indicated as appropriate for hand or courier delivery may be delayed and received after the comment period.

Submission of comments on paperwork requirements. You may submit comments on this document's paperwork requirements by following the instructions at the end of the "Collection of Information Requirements" section in this document.

Inspection of Public Comments: All comments received before the close of the comment period are available for viewing by the public, including any personally identifiable or confidential business information that is included in a comment. We post all comments received before the close of the comment period on the following Web site as soon as possible after they have been received: *http:// www.regulations.gov.* Follow the search instructions on that Web site to view public comments.

Comments received timely will also be available for public inspection as they are received, generally beginning approximately three weeks after publication of a document, at the headquarters of the Centers for Medicare & Medicaid Services, 7500 Security

Boulevard, Baltimore, Maryland 21244, Monday through Friday of each week from 8:30 a.m. to 4 p.m. EST. To schedule an appointment to view public comments, phone 1–800–743–3951.

Internal Revenue Service. Comments to the IRS, identified by REG–114494–10, by one of the following methods:

• *Federal eRulemaking Portal: http:// www.regulations.gov.* Follow the instructions for submitting comments.

• *Mail:* CC:PA:LPD:PR (REG–114494–10), room 5205, Internal Revenue Service, P.O. Box 7604, Ben Franklin Station, Washington, DC 20044.

• *Hand or courier delivery:* Monday through Friday between the hours of 8 a.m. and 4 p.m. to: CC:PA:LPD:PR (REG–114494–10), Courier's Desk, Internal Revenue Service, 1111 Constitution Avenue, NW., Washington DC 20224.

All submissions to the IRS will be open to public inspection and copying in room 1621, 1111 Constitution Avenue, NW., Washington, DC from 9 a.m. to 4 p.m.

FOR FURTHER INFORMATION CONTACT: Amy Turner or Beth Baum, Employee Benefits Security Administration, Department of Labor, at (202) 693–8335; Karen Levin, Internal Revenue Service, Department of the Treasury, at (202) 622–6080; Jim Mayhew, Office of Consumer Information and Insurance Oversight, Department of Health and Human Services, at (410) 786–1565.

Customer Service Information: Individuals interested in obtaining information from the Department of Labor concerning employment-based health coverage laws may call the EBSA Toll-Free Hotline at 1–866–444–EBSA (3272) or visit the Department of Labor's Web site (*http://www.dol.gov/ebsa*). In addition, information from HHS on private health insurance for consumers can be found on the Centers for Medicare & Medicaid Services (CMS) Web site (*http://www.cms.hhs.gov/ HealthInsReformforConsume/ 01_Overview.asp*).

SUPPLEMENTARY INFORMATION:

I. Background

The Patient Protection and Affordable Care Act (the Affordable Care Act), Public Law 111–148, was enacted on March 23, 2010; the Health Care and Education Reconciliation Act (the Reconciliation Act), Public Law 111–152, was enacted on March 30, 2010. The Affordable Care Act and the Reconciliation Act reorganize, amend, and add to the provisions of part A of title XXVII of the Public Health Service Act (PHS Act) relating to group health plans and health insurance issuers in

the group and individual markets. The term "group health plan" includes both insured and self-insured group health plans.[1] The Affordable Care Act adds section 715 to the Employee Retirement Income Security Act (ERISA) and section 9815 to the Internal Revenue Code (the Code) to make the provisions of part A of title XXVII of the PHS Act applicable under ERISA and the Code to group health plans, and health insurance issuers providing health insurance coverage in connection with group health plans, as if those provisions of the PHS Act were included in ERISA and the Code. The PHS Act sections incorporated by this reference are sections 2701 through 2728. PHS Act sections 2701 through 2719A are substantially new, though they incorporate some provisions of prior law. PHS Act sections 2722 through 2728 are sections of prior law renumbered with some, mostly minor, changes. Section 1251 of the Affordable Care Act, as modified by section 10103 of the Affordable Care Act and section 2301 of the Reconciliation Act, specifies that certain plans or coverage existing as of the date of enactment (*i.e.,* grandfathered health plans) are subject to only certain provisions.

Subtitles A and C of title I of the Affordable Care Act amend the requirements of title XXVII of the PHS Act (changes to which are incorporated into ERISA section 715). The preemption provisions of ERISA section 731 and PHS Act section 2724[2] (implemented in 29 CFR 2590.731(a) and 45 CFR 146.143(a)) apply so that the requirements of the Affordable Care Act are not to be "construed to supersede any provision of State law which establishes, implements, or continues in effect any standard or requirement solely relating to health insurance issuers in connection with group or individual health insurance coverage except to the extent that such standard or requirement prevents the application of a requirement" of the Affordable Care Act. Accordingly, State laws that impose on health insurance issuers stricter requirements than those imposed by the Affordable Care Act will not be superseded by the Affordable Care Act.

---

[1] The term "group health plan" is used in title XXVII of the PHS Act, part 7 of ERISA, and chapter 100 of the Code, and is distinct from the term "health plan", as used in other provisions of title I of the Affordable Care Act. The term "health plan" does not include self-insured group health plans.

[2] Code section 9815 incorporates the preemption provisions of PHS Act section 2724. Prior to the Affordable Care Act, there were no express preemption provisions in chapter 100 of the Code.

The Departments of Health and Human Services, Labor, and the Treasury (the Departments) expect to issue regulations implementing the revised PHS Act sections 2701 through 2719A in several phases. The first publication in this series was a Request for Information relating to the medical loss ratio provisions of PHS Act section 2718, published in the **Federal Register** on April 14, 2010 (75 FR 19297). These interim final regulations are being published to implement PHS Act section 2714 (requiring dependent coverage of children to age 26). PHS Act section 2714 generally is effective for plan years (in the individual market, policy years) beginning on or after September 23, 2010, which is six months after the March 23, 2010 date of enactment of the Affordable Care Act.[3] The implementation of other provisions of PHS Act sections 2701 through 2719A and section 1251 of the Affordable Care Act will be addressed in future regulations.

Because subtitles A and C of title I of the Affordable Care Act contain requirements that are applicable to both the group and individual health insurance markets, it would be duplicative to insert the requirements into both the existing 45 CFR part 146 (Requirements for the Group Health Insurance Market) and 45 CFR part 148 (Requirements for the Individual Health Insurance Market). Accordingly, these interim final regulations create a new part 147 in subchapter B of 45 CFR to implement the provisions of the Affordable Care Act. The provisions of the Affordable Care Act, to the extent that they apply to group health plans and group health insurance coverage, are also implemented under new regulations added to 29 CFR part 2590 and 26 CFR part 54.

II. Overview of the Regulations

A. PHS Act Section 2714, Continued Eligibility of Children Until Age 26 (26 CFR 54.9815–2714, 29 CFR 2590.715–2714, 45 CFR 147.120)

Section 2714 of the PHS Act, as added by the Affordable Care Act (and amended by the Reconciliation Act), and these interim final regulations provide that a plan or issuer that makes available dependent coverage[4] of children must make such coverage available for children until attainment

---

[3] *See* section 1004 of the Affordable Care Act.

[4] For purposes of these interim final regulations, dependent coverage means coverage of any individual under the terms of a group health plan, or group or individual health insurance coverage, because of the relationship to a participant (in the individual market, primary subscriber).

of 26 years of age. The statute also requires the issuance of regulations to "define the dependents to which coverage shall be made available" under this rule.

Many group health plans that provide dependent coverage limit the coverage to health coverage excludible from employees' gross income for income tax purposes. Thus, dependent coverage is limited to employees' spouses and employees' children that qualify as dependents for income tax purposes. Consequently, these plans often condition dependent coverage, in addition to the age of the child, on student status, residency, and financial support or other factors indicating dependent status. However, with the expansion of dependent coverage required by the Affordable Care Act to children until age 26, conditioning coverage on whether a child is a tax dependent or a student, or resides with or receives financial support from the parent, is no longer appropriate in light of the correlation between age and these factors. Therefore, these interim final regulations do not allow plans or coverage to use these requirements to deny dependent coverage to children. Because the statute does not distinguish between coverage for minor children and coverage for adult children under age 26, these factors also may not be used to determine eligibility for dependent coverage for minor children.

Accordingly, these interim final regulations clarify that, with respect to children who have not attained age 26, a plan or issuer may not define dependent for purposes of eligibility for dependent coverage of children other than in terms of the relationship between the child and the participant (in the individual market, the primary subscriber). Examples of factors that cannot be used for defining dependent for purposes of eligibility (or continued eligibility) include financial dependency on the participant or primary subscriber (or any other person), residency with the participant or primary subscriber (or any other person), student status, employment, eligibility for other coverage, or any combination of these. These interim final regulations also provide that the terms of the plan or policy for dependent coverage cannot vary based on the age of a child, except for children age 26 or older. Examples illustrate that surcharges for coverage of children under age 26 are not allowed except where the surcharges apply regardless of the age of the child (up to age 26) and that, for children under age 26, the plan cannot vary benefits based on the age of the child. The Affordable Care Act, as

originally enacted, required plans and issuers to make dependent coverage available only to a child "who is not married." This language was struck by section 2301(b) of the Reconciliation Act. Accordingly, under these interim final regulations, plans and issuers may not limit dependent coverage based on whether a child is married. (However, a plan or issuer is not required under these interim final regulations to cover the spouse of an eligible child).

The statute and these interim final regulations provide that nothing in PHS Act section 2714 requires a plan or issuer to make available coverage for a child of a child receiving dependent coverage.

Under section 1004(d) of the Reconciliation Act and IRS Notice 2010–38 (released to the public on April 27, 2010 and scheduled to be published in 2010–20 Internal Revenue Bulletin, May 17, 2010), employers may exclude from the employee's income the value of any employer-provided health coverage for an employee's child for the entire taxable year the child turns 26 if the coverage continues until the end of that taxable year. This means that if a child turns 26 in March, but stays on the plan past December 31st (the end of most people's taxable year), the health benefits up to December 31st can be excluded for tax purposes.

Application to grandfathered health plans. Under the statute and these interim final regulations, the requirement to make available dependent coverage for children who have not attained age 26 generally applies to all group health plans and health insurance issuers offering group or individual health insurance coverage whether or not the plan or health insurance coverage qualifies as a grandfathered health plan [5] under section 1251 of the Affordable Care Act, for plan years (in the individual market, policy years) beginning on or after September 23, 2010. However, in accordance with section 2301(a) of the Reconciliation Act, for plan years beginning before January 1, 2014, these interim final regulations provide that a grandfathered health plan that is a group health plan that makes available dependent coverage of children may exclude an adult child who has not attained age 26 from coverage only if the child is eligible to enroll in an employer-sponsored health plan (as

defined in section 5000A(f)(2) of the Code) other than a group health plan of a parent. In the case of an adult child who is eligible for coverage under the plans of the employers of both parents, neither plan may exclude the adult child from coverage based on the fact that the adult child is eligible to enroll in the plan of the other parent's employer.

Regulations relating to grandfathered health plans under section 1251 of the Affordable Care Act are expected to be published in the very near future. The Departments anticipate that the regulations will make clear that changes to plan or policy terms to comply with PHS Act section 2714 and these interim final regulations, including voluntary compliance before plan years (in the individual market, policy years) beginning on or after September 23, 2010, will not cause a plan or health insurance coverage to lose grandfathered health plan status for any purpose under the Affordable Care Act, as amended.

Transitional Rule. Prior to the applicability date of PHS Act section 2714, a child who was covered under a group health plan or health insurance coverage as a dependent may have lost eligibility under the plan (or coverage) due to age prior to age 26. Moreover, if, when a parent first became eligible for coverage, a child was under age 26 but older than the age at which the plan (or coverage) stopped covering children, the child would not have become eligible for the plan (or coverage). When the provisions of section 2714 become applicable, a plan or issuer can no longer exclude coverage for the child prior to age 26 irrespective of whether or when that child was enrolled in the plan (or coverage). Also, a child of a primary subscriber with family coverage in the individual market may be entitled to an opportunity to enroll if the child previously lost coverage due to age while other family members retained the coverage.[6]

Accordingly, these interim final regulations provide transitional relief for a child whose coverage ended, or who was denied coverage (or was not

---

[5] Section 1251 of the Affordable Care Act, as modified by section 10103 of the Affordable Care Act and section 2301 of the Reconciliation Act, specifies that certain plans or coverage existing as of the March 23, 2010 date of enactment (*i.e.,* grandfathered health plans) are subject to only certain provisions.

[6] In the group market, section 9802(a) of the Code, section 702(a) of ERISA, and section 2705 of the PHS Act provide that a plan or issuer cannot impose any rule for eligibility for benefits (including any rule excluding coverage) based on a health factor, including a preexisting condition. These rules were added by HIPAA and generally became applicable for group health plans for plan years beginning on or after July 1, 1997. Similar guidance regarding re-enrollment rights for individuals previously denied coverage due to a health factor was issued by the Departments of the Treasury, Labor, and HHS on December 29, 1997, at 62 FR 67689 and on January 8, 2001 at 66 FR 1378, 1403, 1410, 1418.

eligible for coverage) under a group health plan or health insurance coverage because, under the terms of the plan or coverage, the availability of dependent coverage of children ended before the attainment of age 26.

These interim final regulations require a plan or issuer to give such a child an opportunity to enroll that continues for at least 30 days (including written notice of the opportunity to enroll), regardless of whether the plan or coverage offers an open enrollment period and regardless of when any open enrollment period might otherwise occur. This enrollment opportunity (including the written notice) must be provided not later than the first day of the first plan year (in the individual market, policy year) beginning on or after September 23, 2010. Thus, many plans can use their existing annual enrollment periods (which commonly begin and end before the start of the plan year) to satisfy the enrollment opportunity requirement. If the child is enrolled, coverage must begin not later than the first day of the first plan year (in the individual market, policy year) beginning on or after September 23, 2010, even if the request for enrollment is made after the first day of the plan year. In subsequent years, dependent coverage may be elected for an eligible child in connection with normal enrollment opportunities under the plan or coverage.

Under these interim final regulations, the notice may be provided to an employee on behalf of the employee's child (in the individual market, to a primary subscriber on behalf of the primary subscriber's child). In addition, for a group health plan or group health insurance coverage, the notice may be included with other enrollment materials that a plan distributes to employees, provided the statement is prominent. For a group health plan or group health insurance coverage, if a notice satisfying these requirements is provided to an employee whose child is entitled to an enrollment opportunity, the obligation to provide the notice of enrollment opportunity with respect to that child is satisfied for both the plan and the issuer.

Any child enrolling in group health plan coverage pursuant to this enrollment right must be treated as a special enrollee, as provided under the regulations interpreting the HIPAA portability provisions.[7] Accordingly, the child must be offered all the benefit

---

[7] HIPAA is the Health Insurance Portability and Accountability Act of 1996 (Public Law 104–191). Regulations regarding the treatment of HIPAA special enrollees are included at 26 CFR 54.9801–6(d), 29 CFR 2590.701–6(d), and 45 CFR 146.117(d).

packages available to similarly situated individuals who did not lose coverage by reason of cessation of dependent status. The child also cannot be required to pay more for coverage than similarly situated individuals who did not lose coverage by reason of cessation of dependent status.

The Departments have been informed that many health insurance issuers have announced that they will allow continued coverage of adult children before such coverage is required by the Affordable Care Act. A plan or issuer that allows continued coverage of adult children before being required to do so by the Affordable Care Act is not required to provide the enrollment opportunity with respect to children who do not lose coverage.

Examples in these interim final regulations illustrate the application of these transitional rules. One example illustrates that, if a child qualifies for an enrollment opportunity under this section and the parent is not enrolled but is otherwise eligible for enrollment, the plan must provide an opportunity to enroll the parent, in addition to the child. Similarly, another example illustrates that, if a plan has more than one benefit package option, a child qualifies for enrollment under this section, and the parent is enrolled in one benefit package option, the plan must provide an opportunity to enroll the child in any benefit package option for which the child is otherwise eligible (thus allowing the parent to switch benefit package options). Another example illustrates that a child who qualifies for an enrollment opportunity under this section and who is covered under a COBRA continuation provision must be given the opportunity to enroll as a dependent of an active employee (*i.e.*, other than as a COBRA-qualified beneficiary). In this situation, if the child loses eligibility for coverage due to a qualifying event (including aging out of coverage at age 26), the child has another opportunity to elect COBRA continuation coverage. (If the qualifying event is aging out, the COBRA continuation coverage could last 36 months from the loss of eligibility that relates to turning age 26.) The final example in this section illustrates that an employee who joined a plan prior to the applicability date of PHS Act section 2714, and has a child who never enrolled because the child was too old under the terms of the plan but has not yet turned 26, must be provided an opportunity to enroll the child under this section even though the child was not previously covered under the plan. If the parent is no longer eligible for coverage under the plan (for example, if

the parent has ceased employment with the plan sponsor) as of the first date on which the enrollment opportunity would be required to be given, the plan would not be required to enroll the child.

B. Conforming Changes Under the PHS Act

1. References to the Public Health Service Act

Conforming changes to references to sections of title XXVII of the PHS Act are made throughout parts 144 and 146 of title 45 of the Code of Federal Regulations to reflect the renumbering of certain sections by the Affordable Care Act.

2. Definitions (45 CFR 144.103)

These interim final regulations define "policy year" as the 12-month period that is designated in the policy documents of individual health insurance coverage. If the policy document does not designate a policy year (or no such document is available), then the policy year is the deductible or limit year used under the coverage. If deductibles or other limits are not imposed on a yearly basis, the policy year is the calendar year. The Affordable Care Act uses the term "plan year" in referring to the period of coverage in both the individual and group health insurance markets. The term "plan year", however, is generally used in the group health insurance market. Accordingly, these interim final regulations substitute the term "policy year" for "plan year" in defining the period of coverage in the individual health insurance market.

III. Interim Final Regulations and Request for Comments

Section 9833 of the Code, section 734 of ERISA, and section 2792 of the PHS Act authorize the Secretaries of the Treasury, Labor, and HHS (collectively, the Secretaries) to promulgate any interim final rules that they determine are appropriate to carry out the provisions of chapter 100 of the Code, part 7 of subtitle B of title I of ERISA, and part A of title XXVII of the PHS Act, which include PHS Act sections 2701 through 2728 and the incorporation of those sections into ERISA section 715 and Code section 9815.

In addition, under Section 553(b) of the Administrative Procedure Act (APA) (5 U.S.C. 551 *et seq.*) a general notice of proposed rulemaking is not required when an agency, for good cause, finds that notice and public comment thereon are impracticable, unnecessary, or contrary to the public interest. The provisions of the APA that ordinarily require a notice of proposed rulemaking do not apply here because of the specific authority granted by section 9833 of the Code, section 734 of ERISA, and section 2792 of the PHS Act. However, even if the APA was applicable, the Secretaries have determined that it would be impracticable and contrary to the public interest to delay putting the provisions in these interim final regulations in place until a full public notice and comment process is completed. The statutory requirement implemented in these interim final regulations was enacted on March 23, 2010, and applies for plan years (in the individual market, policy years) beginning on or after September 23, 2010. Having a binding rule in effect is critical to ensuring that individuals entitled to the new protections being implemented have these protections uniformly applied.

Moreover, the provisions in these interim final regulations require lead time for implementation. These interim final regulations require that an enrollment period be provided no later than the first day the obligation to allow dependent children to enroll until attainment of age 26 takes effect. Preparations presumably would have to be made to put such an enrollment process in place. Group health plans and health insurance issuers also would have to take the cost associated with this new obligation into account in establishing their premiums, and in making other changes to the designs of plan or policy benefits, and any such premiums and changes would have to receive necessary approvals in advance of the plan or policy year in question.

For the foregoing reasons, the Departments have determined that it is essential to provide certainty about what will be required of group health plans and health insurance issuers under the statutory requirements implemented in binding regulations as far in advance of September 23, 2010 as possible. This makes it impracticable to engage in full notice and comment rulemaking before putting regulations into effect, and in the public interest to do so through interim final regulations under which the public will have an opportunity for comment, but that opportunity will not delay putting rules in effect (a delay that could possibly last past September 23, 2010).

Issuance of proposed regulations would not be sufficient because the proposed regulations would not be binding, and different group health plans or health insurance issuers could interpret the statutory language in different ways. Had the Departments published a notice of proposed rulemaking, provided for a 60-day comment period, and only then prepared final regulations, which would be subject to a 60-day delay in effective date, it is unlikely that it would have been possible to have final regulations in effect before late September, when these requirements could be in effect for some plans or policies. It therefore is in the public interest that these interim final regulations be in effect and apply when the statutory protections being implemented apply.

IV. Economic Impact and Paperwork Burden

A. Summary—Department of Labor and Department of Health and Human Services

As stated earlier in this preamble, these interim final regulations implement PHS Act section 2714, which requires plans or issuers that make dependent coverage available for children to continue to make such coverage available for an adult child until the attainment of age 26. The regulation also provides an enrollment opportunity to individuals who lost or were not eligible for dependent coverage before age 26.[8] This provision generally is effective for plan years (in the individual market, policy years) beginning on or after September 23, 2010, which is six months after the March 23, 2010 date of enactment of the Affordable Care Act.

The Departments have crafted these interim final regulations to secure the protections intended by Congress in the most economically efficient manner possible. The Departments have quantified costs where possible and provided a qualitative discussion of the economic benefits and some of the transfers and costs that may stem from these interim final regulations.

B. Executive Order 12866—Department of Labor and Department of Health and Human Services

Under Executive Order 12866 (58 FR 51735), this regulatory action has been determined "significant" and therefore subject to review by the Office of

---

[8] The Affordable Care Act adds section 715 and Code section to make the provisions of part A of title XXVII of the PHS Act applicable to group health plans, and health insurance issuers providing health insurance coverage in connection with group health plans, under ERISA and the Code as if those provisions of the PHS Act were included in ERISA and the Code. The PHS Act sections incorporated by this reference are sections 2701 through 2728. Section 1251 of the Affordable Care Act provides rules for grandfathered health plans, and these rules are further clarified in section 10103 of the Affordable Care Act and section 2301 of the Reconciliation Act.

Management and Budget (OMB). Section 3(f) of the Executive Order defines a "significant regulatory action" as an action that is likely to result in a rule (1) having an annual effect on the economy of $100 million or more in any one year, or adversely and materially affecting a sector of the economy, productivity, competition, jobs, the environment, public health or safety, or State, local or tribal governments or communities (also referred to as "economically significant"); (2) creating a serious inconsistency or otherwise interfering with an action taken or planned by another agency; (3) materially altering the budgetary impacts of entitlement grants, user fees, or loan programs or the rights and obligations of recipients thereof; or (4) raising novel legal or policy issues arising out of legal mandates, the President's priorities, or the principles set forth in the Executive Order. OMB has determined that this regulation is economically significant within the meaning of section 3(f)(1) of the Executive Order, because it is likely to have an annual effect on the economy of $100 million in any one year. Accordingly, OMB has reviewed these rules pursuant to the Executive Order. The Departments provide an assessment of the potential costs, benefits, and transfers associated with the regulatory provision below. The Departments invite comments on this assessment and its conclusions.

1. Need for Regulatory Action

PHS Act section 2714, as added by the Affordable Care Act and amended by the Reconciliation Act requires group health plans and health insurance issuers offering group or individual health insurance coverage that make dependent coverage available for children to continue to make coverage available to such children until the attainment of age 26. With respect to a child receiving dependent coverage, coverage does not have to be extended to a child or children of the child or a spouse of the child. In addition, as provided by the Reconciliation Act, grandfathered group health plans are not required to offer dependent coverage to a child under 26 who is otherwise eligible for employer-sponsored insurance other than a group health plan of a parent for plan years beginning before January 1, 2014. PHS Act section 2714 generally is effective for plan years (in the individual market, policy years) beginning on or after September 23, 2010. Thus, these interim final regulations are necessary to amend the Departments' existing regulations to implement these statutorily mandated changes.

2. *Summary of Impacts*

In this section, the Departments estimate the number of individuals affected by these interim final regulations, and the impact of the regulations on health insurance premiums in the group and individual markets. Beginning with the population of individuals age 19–25, the number of individuals potentially affected is estimated by applying several criteria including whether their parents have existing employer-sponsored insurance (ESI) or an individual market policy; and whether the individuals are themselves uninsured, have ESI, individual market policies or other forms of coverage. A range of assumptions concerning the percentage of the potentially affected individuals that will accept the offer of new dependent coverage—"take-up" rates— is then applied to estimate the number of newly covered individuals. The premium impact is calculated by using an estimated incremental insurance cost per newly-covered individual as a percent of average family premiums.

In accordance, with OMB Circular A–4,[9] Table 1 below depicts an accounting statement showing the Departments' assessment of the benefits, costs, and transfers associated with this regulatory action.

TABLE 1—ACCOUNTING TABLE

Benefits:

Annualized Quantified: low estimate | 0.19 million previously uninsured individuals gain coverage in 2011.
mid-range estimate .... | 0.65 million previously uninsured individuals gain coverage in 2011.
high estimate .... | 1.64 million previously uninsured individuals gain coverage in 2011.

Qualitative: Expanding coverage options of the 19–25 population should decrease the number uninsured, which in turn should decrease the cost-shifting of uncompensated care onto those with insurance, increase the receipt of preventive health care and provide more timely access to high quality care, resulting in a healthier population. Allowing extended dependent coverage will also permit greater job mobility for this population as their insurance coverage will no longer be tied to their own jobs or student status. Dependents aged 19–25 that have chronic or other serious health conditions would still be able to continue their current coverage through a parent's plan. To the extent there is an increase in beneficial utilization of healthcare, health could improve.

Costs[10]	Low estimate	Mid-range estimate	High estimate	Year dollar	Discount rate percent	Period covered[11]
Annualized Monetized ($millions/year)	11.2	11.2	11.2	2010	7	2011–2013
	10.4	10.4	10.4	2010	3	2011–2013

A one-time notice of right to enroll must be sent to those affected.

Qualitative: To the extent additional coverage increases utilization of health care services, there will be additional costs incurred to achieve the health benefits.

Transfer: [12]

	Low estimate	Mid-range estimate	High estimate	Year dollar	Discount rate percent	Period covered
Annualized Monetized ($millions/year)	3,459.3	5,250.2	6,893.9	2010	7	2011–2013
	3,482.5	5,274.5	6,895.4	2010	3	2011–2013

Qualitative: If the rule causes family health insurance premiums to increase, there will be a transfer from individuals with family health insurance coverage who do not have dependents aged 19–25 to those individuals with family health insurance coverage that have dependents aged 19–25. To the extent that these higher premiums result in lower profits or higher prices for the employer's product, then the higher premiums will result in a transfer either from stockholders or consumers.

[10] The cost estimates are annualize across the years 2011–2013, and reflects a single point estimate of the cost to send out a notice in the first year only.

[11] The Departments limited the period covered by the RIA to 2011–2013, because it only has reliable data to make projections over this period due to the fact that in 2014, things will change drastically when the subsidies and tax credits to offset premium increases and the exchanges are in effect.

[12] The estimates in this table reflect the annualized discounted value in 2010 of the additional premium costs for family policies calculated as the product of the newly covered dependents in each year from 2011–2013 (see below) and an incremental cost per newly-covered person in those years (see below).

3. *Estimated Number of Affected Individuals*

The Departments' estimates in this section are based on the 2004–2006 Medical Expenditure Panel Survey Household Component (MEPS–HC) which was projected and calibrated to 2010 to be consistent with the National Health Accounts projections. The Departments estimate that in 2010, there are approximately 29.5 million individuals aged 19–25 (young adults) in the United States. Of those individuals, 9.3 million young adults (of whom 3.1 million are uninsured) do not have a parent who has either ESI or non-group insurance, and thus they have no access to dependent coverage. As shown in Table 2, among the remaining 20.2 million young adults whose parents are covered either by ESI or by non-group insurance:

- 3.44 million are currently uninsured,
- 2.42 million are covered by their own non-group insurance,
- 5.55 million are covered by their own ESI,
- 5.73 million are already on their parent's or spouse's ESI, and
- 3.01 million have some other form of coverage such as Medicaid or TRICARE.

[9] Available at *http://www.whitehouse.gov/omb/ circulars/a004/a-4.pdf*.

TABLE 2—YOUNG ADULTS AGED 19–25 BY INSURANCE STATUS

	Uninsured*	Non-group	Own ESI	ESI as a dependent	Other	Total
Total U.S. Population Aged 19–25	**6.59**	**2.69**	6.98	5.75	7.5	29.5
All Young Adults in U.S. with a Parent with a Policy by Young Adult Insurance Status						
Parents have ESI	**3.28**	**2.03**	5.32	5.73	2.91	19.27
Parents have non-group	**0.16**	**0.40**	0.23	....	0.10	0.88
Subtotal A	**3.44**	**2.42**	5.55	5.73	3.01	20.15

*The **bolded** numbers are potentially affected by the regulation.

Source: MEPS 2004–2006 HC Surveys, controlled to 2010 consistent with the National Health Accounts. Note: Total number of young adults, age 19–25 is 29.5 million; the 20.15 million in this Table are the subset whose parents have either ESI or non-group coverage.

Initially, the subset of this group of young adults that will be affected by these interim final regulations are those who are either uninsured (3.44 million) or covered by individual coverage (2.42 million). The statute does not require grandfathered group health plans to offer coverage to young adults who currently have their own ESI or an offer of an ESI. For the purposes of this analysis, it is assumed that all plans begin 2011 with grandfathered status. These impacts could change if plans lose their Grandfathered status.

Of these 5.86 million young adults, as shown in Table 3, 3.49 million are also unlikely to switch to their parents' coverage because:

• They are already allowed to enroll in extended dependent coverage for young adults through their State's existing laws, but have chosen not to

(2.61 million). Thirty-seven states already have requirements concerning dependent coverage in the group market, although most of these are substantially more restrictive than those contained in this regulation.[13] Using information about State laws obtained from the Kaiser Family Foundation,[14] a State by State profile of State required coverage based on a person's State of residence, age, student status, and living situation was developed. This profile was then overlaid on MEPS data to obtain an estimate of the number of individuals that would newly become eligible for coverage due to these interim final regulations.

• They have an offer of ESI and have parents who are covered by ESI (0.48 million). For the purposes of this regulatory impact statement, the Departments assume that the parents of

these young adults will be in grandfathered group health plans, and thus that these young adults will not be affected by the provisions of these interim final regulations. To the extent that some of the coverage in which these parents are enrolled is not grandfathered, the effect of these interim final regulations will be larger than the estimates provided here.

• Finally, there are 0.40 million young adults who have non-group coverage and whose parents have non-group coverage. Because the parents' non-group coverage is underwritten, there is not likely to be any financial benefit to the family in moving the young adult onto the parents' coverage, and the Departments assume that these young adults will not be affected by the regulation.

TABLE 3—"UNINSURED" AND "NON-GROUP" YOUNG ADULTS UNLIKELY TO BE AFFECTED BY EXTENDING DEPENDENT COVERAGE TO AGE 26

	Uninsured	Non-Group coverage	Total
(1) Young adults potentially covered by parent ESI due to state law	1.30	1.31	2.61
(2) Young adults with an offer of ESI whose parents have ESI	0.31	0.17	0.48
(3) Young adults with non-group coverage whose parents have non-group coverage	....	0.40	0.40
Subtotal B	1.61	1.88	3.49

As shown in Table 4, this leaves approximately 2.37 million young adults who might be affected by this provision, or approximately eight percent of the 29.5 million young adults

in the age group. Among the approximately 2.37 million young adults who are estimated to be potentially affected by this provision, approximately 1.83 million are

currently uninsured, and 0.55 million are currently covered by their own non-group coverage.

TABLE 4—YOUNG ADULTS POTENTIALLY AFFECTED BY EXTENDING DEPENDENT COVERAGE TO AGE 26

	Uninsured	Non-group coverage	Total
Parents have ESI	1.67	0.55	2.21
Parents have non-group	0.16	....	0.16

---

[13] Restrictions include requirements for financial dependency, student status, and age limits.

[14] As described in Kaiser Family Foundation, *Definition of Dependency by Age, 2010*, KFF State Health Facts, *at http://www.statehealthfacts.org/ comparetable.jsp?ind=601&cat=7.*

TABLE 4—YOUNG ADULTS POTENTIALLY AFFECTED BY EXTENDING DEPENDENT COVERAGE TO AGE 26—Continued

	Uninsured	Non-group coverage	Total
Total (Subtotal A–Subtotal B)*	1.83	0.55	2.37

Source: MEPS 2004–2006 HC Surveys, controlled to 2010 consistent with projections of the National Health Accounts.
*Subtotal A is in Table 2 and Subtotal B is in Table 3.

It is difficult to estimate precisely what fraction of the 2.37 million young adults who might potentially be affected by the provision will actually enroll on their parents' coverage. A study by Monheit and Cantor of the early experience in States that have extended coverage to dependents suggests that few uninsured children in these States shift to their parents' policy.[15] However, data and methodological difficulties inevitably lead to substantial uncertainty about the finding.

The Departments considered two other points of reference to estimate take-up rates. One is the work that has analyzed take-up rates among people made newly eligible for public coverage by Medicaid expansions. These studies suggest take-up rates in the range of 10–34 percent.[16] However, the populations eligible for these expansions have different socio-demographic compositions than those eligible for the dependent coverage provisions covered under these interim final regulations, and the decision to take-up Medicaid is clearly different than the decision to cover a child on a parent's private insurance policy. A second point of reference are estimates from the Kaiser/HRET Employer Health benefits Survey[17] which suggest that, depending on the size of the worker contribution, between 77 percent and 90 percent of employees accept offers of family

policies. Again, these estimates would be based on a group that differs in characteristics from those eligible for new dependent coverage. These concerns notwithstanding, the analyses of Medicaid expansions and employee take-up of employer sponsored coverage provide useful points of reference.

Recognizing the uncertainty in the area, the Departments produced a range of assumptions concerning take-up rates. In developing the range of take-up rates, the Departments assume that these rates will vary by the following factors: (1) The young adult's current health coverage status (uninsured young adults are less likely to take advantage of the dependent coverage option than young adults already covered by non-group insurance, because young adults who have purchased non-group insurance have shown a strong preference for coverage, and can almost always save money and get better coverage by switching to their parents' policy); (2) the young adult's health status (young adults in fair or poor health are more likely to take advantage of the option than those in excellent, very good or good health), and (3) the young adult's living situation (those living with their parents are more likely to take up the option than those not living with their parents).

The almost fully covered or "high" take-up rate scenario assumes that

regardless of health or insurance status, 95 percent of young adults living at home and 85 percent of those not living at home would move to dependent coverage. For the mid-range scenario, the Departments assume that relative to the high take-up rate scenario, 90 percent of the uninsured whose health status was fair or poor health and 50 percent of those in good to excellent health would move to dependent coverage. In the low take-up rate scenario, the Departments adjusted the percentages to 80 percent and 10 percent of the high take-up rate scenario. In all three scenarios, the same assumptions apply to individuals with non-group policies whose parents have ESI—95 percent of those living at home and 85 percent of those living elsewhere would move to dependent coverage.

In the low take-up rate scenario, the assumptions lead to the result that approximately 30 percent of eligibles will enroll in dependent coverage. In the mid-range scenario, they result in an approximate 50 percent take-up rate, and in the high take-up scenario, they result in an approximate 90 percent take-up rate. The Departments are uncertain regarding which of these scenarios is most likely but are confident that they bracket the expected outcome.

TABLE 5—NUMBER OF INDIVIDUALS WITH NEW DEPENDENT COVERAGE AND IMPACT ON GROUP INSURANCE PREMIUMS, 2011–2013

	Low estimate			Mid-range estimate			High estimate		
	2011	2012	2013	2011	2012	2013	2011	2012	2013
Individuals with New Dependent Coverage (millions)	0.68	0.97	1.08	1.24	1.60	1.65	2.12	2.07	1.98
From Uninsured (millions)	0.19	0.29	0.33	0.65	0.94	0.91	1.64	1.42	1.21
Incremental Premium Cost Per Individual Coverage	$3,670	$3,800	$4,000	$3,380	$3,500	$3,690	$3,220	$3,340	$3,510
Impact on Group Insurance Premiums (%)	0.5	0.7	0.7	0.7	1.0	1.0	1.2	1.2	1.1

[15] Monheit, A., J. Cantor, et al, "State Policies Expanding Dependent Coverage to Young Adults in Private Health Insurance Plans," presented at the Academy Health State Health Research and Policy Interest Group Meeting, Chicago IL, June 27, 2009.

[16] Bansak, Cynthia and Steven Raphael. "The Effects of State Policy Design Features on Take-Up and Crowd-out Rates fro the State Children's Health Insurance Program." Journal of Policy Analysis and Management, Vol. 26, No. 1, 149–175. 2006. Find that for the time period 1998–2002 take-up rates for SCHIP were about 10 percent.

Currie, Janet and Jonathan Gruber. "Saving babies: The Efficacy and Cost of Recent Changes in Medicaid Eligibility of Pregnant Women." The Journal of Political Economy, Vol. 104, No. 6, Dec. 1996, pp. 1263–1296. Find for Medicaid expansions during the 1979–1992 period the take-up rate for eligible pregnant women was 34 percent.

Cutler, David and Jonathan Gruber. "Does Public Insurance Crowd Out Private Insurance?" The Quarterly Journal of Economics, Vol. 111, No. 2, May 1996, pp. 391–430. Find that for the Medicaid expansions from 1987–1992 the take-up rate for the

uninsured is close to 30 percent, while for pregnant women it was seven percent.

Gruber, Jonathan and Kosali Simon. "Crowd-Out Ten years Later: Have Recent Public Insurance Expansions Crowded Out Private Health Insurance?" NBER Working Paper 12858. January 2007. Find that for the Medicaid expansions during 1996–2002 the take-up rate was 7 percent across all children, but nearly one-third for uninsured children.

[17] Found at http://www.kff.org/insurance/snapshot/chcm020707oth.cfm.

27130   **Federal Register** / Vol. 75, No. 92 / Thursday, May 13, 2010 / Rules and Regulations

These take-up rate assumptions are then applied to the number of potentially affected individuals displayed in Table 3. The resulting number of individuals with new dependent coverage is summarized in Table 5. Under the mid-range take-up rate assumption, the Departments estimate that in 2011, 1.24 million young adults will newly be covered by their parents' ESI or non-group market policies, of whom 0.65 million were previously uninsured, and 0.6 million were previously covered by non-group coverage. The number of individuals newly covered by their parents' plans would be 0.7 and 2.12 million under the high and low take-up rate assumptions respectively, with 0.2 and 1.64 million of these individuals being previously uninsured. Relative to the individuals covered under the high take-up rate assumption, higher proportions of the low- and mid-range assumption groups are accounted for by people who previously had non-group coverage (72 percent and 48 percent respectively in contrast to 23 percent for the high take-up rate group). This difference is a result of the Departments' assumption for the low- and mid-range take-up rates that people with non-group coverage will be more likely than healthy people who were uninsured to take advantage of the dependent coverage option.

Under the mid-range take-up rate assumptions, the estimated number of young adults covered by their parents' plans in 2012 increases somewhat over the 2011 estimate to 1.6 million in total, of whom approximately 0.9 million would have been uninsured. The increase in the estimate for 2012 results from the assumption that as children reach the age that would have caused them to be excluded from their parents' policy before the implementation of these interim final regulations, a large fraction of them now will remain on their parents' policy. Similarly, the estimated number of young adults enrolling in their parents' non-group policy increases from just under 75,000 in 2011 to approximately 100,000 in 2012, and 120,000 in 2013.

4. Benefits

The benefits of these interim final regulations are expected to outweigh the costs to the regulated community. In the mid-range take-up rate assumption, the Departments estimate that in 2011, 0.65 million previously uninsured individuals will now be covered on their parent's policies due to these interim final regulations and 1.24 million individuals total will now be covered on their parent's coverage. Expanding coverage options for the

19–25 population should decrease the number uninsured, which in turn should decrease the cost-shifting of uncompensated care onto those with coverage, increase the receipt of preventive health care and provide more timely access to high quality care, resulting in a healthier population. In particular, children with chronic conditions or other serious health issues will be able to continue coverage through a parent's plan until age 26. Allowing extended dependent coverage also will permit greater job mobility for this population as their health coverage will no longer be tied to their own jobs or student status.

5. Costs and Transfers Associated With the Rule

Estimates for the incremental annual premium costs for the newly covered individuals are developed based on expenditure data from MEPS and vary based on the take-up rate assumptions. These incremental costs are lowest for the high take-up rate assumption since the newly covered group would contain a relatively high percentage of individuals whose health status was good to excellent. Conversely, the low take-up rate assumption results in the highest incremental costs because a higher percentage of the newly covered individuals would be those whose health status was fair to poor. For those enrolling in their parents' ESI, the expected annual premium cost under the mid-range take-up rate assumption would be $3,380 in 2011, $3,500 in 2012 and $3,690 in 2013. If these costs were distributed among all family ESI plans, family premiums would be expected to rise by 0.7 percent in 2011, 1.0 percent in 2012, and 1.0 percent in 2013 due to these interim final regulations.[18] The comparable incremental costs and premium effects for the low and high take-up rate assumptions are summarized in Table 5. To the extent that these increases are passed on to workers in the form of higher premiums for all workers purchasing family policies or in the form of lower wages for all workers, there will be a transfer from workers who do not have newly covered dependents to those who do. To the extent that these higher premiums result in lower profits or higher prices for the employer's product, the higher premiums will result in a transfer either from stockholders or consumers.

In addition, to the extent that these interim final regulations result in a decrease in the number of uninsured,

the Departments expect a reduction in uncompensated care, and a reduction in liability for those who fund uncompensated care, including public programs (primarily Medicaid and State and local general revenue support for public hospitals), as well as the portion of uncompensated care that is paid for by the cost shift from private premium payers. Such effects would lead to lower premiums for the insured population, both with or without newly covered children.

For the small number of children (75,000 in 2011) enrolling in their parents' non-group insurance policy under the mid-range take-up assumption, the Departments expect estimated annual premium cost to be $2,360 in 2011, $2,400 in 2012 and $2,480 in 2013. To a large extent, premiums in the non-group market are individually underwritten, and the Departments expect that most of the premium cost will be borne by the parents who are purchasing the policy to which their child is added. If, instead, these costs were distributed over the entire individual market (as would be the case in a pure community-rated market), then individual premiums would be expected to rise 0.7 percent in 2011, 1.0 percent in 2012, and 1.2 percent in 2013 due to these interim final regulations. However, the Departments expect the actual increase across the entire individual market, if any, will be much smaller than these estimates, because they expect that the costs largely will be borne by the subscribers who are directly affected rather than distributed across the entire individual market.

6. Enrollment Opportunity

These interim final regulations provide an enrollment opportunity for children excluded from coverage because of age before the effective date of the rule. The Departments estimate that this information collection request will result in approximately 105,000,000 notices being distributed with an hour burden of approximately 1,100,000 hours and cost burden of approximately $2,010,500. For a discussion of this enrollment opportunity, see the Paperwork Reduction Act section later in this preamble.

7. Regulatory Alternatives

Section 6(a)(3)(C)(iii) of Executive Order 12866 requires an economically significant regulation to include an assessment of the costs and benefits of potentially effective and reasonable alternatives to the planned regulation, and an explanation of why the planned

---

[18] For purposes of this regulatory impact analysis, the Departments assume that there would be no effect on premiums for employee-only policies.

regulatory action is preferable to the potential alternatives. The Departments carefully considered limiting the flexibility of plans and policies to define who is a child. However, the Departments concluded, as they have in other regulatory contexts, that plan sponsors and issuers should be free to determine whether to cover children or which children should be covered by their plans and policies (although they must comply with other applicable Federal or State law mandating coverage, such as ERISA section 609). Therefore, these interim final regulations have not limited a plan's or policy's flexibility to define who is a child for purposes of the determination of children to whom coverage must be made available.

C. Regulatory Flexibility Act— Department of Labor and Department of Health and Human Services

The Regulatory Flexibility Act (5 U.S.C. 601 *et seq.*) (RFA) imposes certain requirements with respect to Federal rules that are subject to the notice and comment requirements of section 553(b) of the APA (5 U.S.C. 551 *et seq.*) and that are likely to have a significant economic impact on a substantial number of small entities. Under Section 553(b) of the APA, a general notice of proposed rulemaking is not required when an agency, for good cause, finds that notice and public comment thereon are impracticable, unnecessary, or contrary to the public interest. These interim final regulations are exempt from APA, because the Departments made a good cause finding that a general notice of proposed rulemaking is not necessary earlier in this preamble. Therefore, the RFA does not apply and the Departments are not required to either certify that the regulations would not have a significant economic impact on a substantial number of small entities or conduct a regulatory flexibility analysis.

Nevertheless, the Departments carefully considered the likely impact of the regulations on small entities in connection with their assessment under Executive Order 12866. Consistent with the policy of the RFA, the Departments encourage the public to submit comments that suggest alternative rules that accomplish the stated purpose of PHS Act section 2714 and minimize the impact on small entities.

D. Special Analyses—Department of the Treasury

Notwithstanding the determinations of the Department of Labor and Department of Health and Human Services, for purposes of the Department

of the Treasury, it has been determined that this Treasury decision is not a significant regulatory action for purposes of Executive Order 12866. Therefore, a regulatory assessment is not required. It has also been determined that section 553(b) of the APA (5 U.S.C. chapter 5) does not apply to these interim final regulations. For the applicability of the RFA, refer to the Special Analyses section in the preamble to the cross-referencing notice of proposed rulemaking published elsewhere in this issue of the **Federal Register.** Pursuant to section 7805(f) of the Code, these temporary regulations have been submitted to the Chief Counsel for Advocacy of the Small Business Administration for comment on their impact on small businesses.

E. Paperwork Reduction Act

1. Department of Labor and Department of the Treasury: Affordable Care Act Enrollment Opportunity Notice Relating to Extended Dependent Coverage

As part of their continuing efforts to reduce paperwork and respondent burden, the Departments conduct a preclearance consultation program to provide the general public and federal agencies with an opportunity to comment on proposed and continuing collections of information in accordance with the Paperwork Reduction Act of 1995 (PRA) (44 U.S.C. 3506(c)(2)(A)). This helps to ensure that requested data can be provided in the desired format, reporting burden (time and financial resources) is minimized, collection instruments are clearly understood, and the impact of collection requirements on respondents can be properly assessed.

As discussed earlier in this preamble, prior to the applicability date of PHS Act section 2714, a child who was covered under a group health plan (or group health insurance coverage) may have lost eligibility for coverage under the plan due to age before age 26. Moreover, if a child was under age 26 when a parent first became eligible for coverage, but older than the age at which the plan stopped covering children, the child would not have become eligible for coverage. When the provisions of PHS Act section 2714 become applicable to the plan (or coverage), the plan or coverage can no longer exclude coverage for the individual until age 26.

Accordingly, these interim final regulations require plans to provide a notice of an enrollment opportunity to individuals whose coverage ended, or who were denied coverage (or were not eligible for coverage) under a group health plan or health insurance coverage

because, under the terms of the plan or coverage, the availability of dependent coverage of children ended before the attainment of age 26. The enrollment opportunity must continue for at least 30 days, regardless of whether the plan or coverage offers an open enrollment period and regardless of when any open enrollment period might otherwise occur. This enrollment opportunity must be presented not later than the first day of the first plan year (in the individual market, policy year) beginning on or after September 23, 2010 (which is the applicability date of PHS Act section 2714). Coverage must begin not later than the first day of the first plan year (in the individual market, policy year) beginning on or after September 23, 2010.[19]

The Affordable Care Act dependent coverage enrollment opportunity notice is an information collection request (ICR) subject to the PRA. Currently, the Departments are soliciting public comments for 60 days concerning these disclosures. The Departments have submitted a copy of these interim final regulations to OMB in accordance with 44 U.S.C. 3507(d) for review of the information collections. The Departments and OMB are particularly interested in comments that:

• Evaluate whether the collection of information is necessary for the proper performance of the functions of the agency, including whether the information will have practical utility;

• Evaluate the accuracy of the agency's estimate of the burden of the collection of information, including the validity of the methodology and assumptions used;

• Enhance the quality, utility, and clarity of the information to be collected; and

• Minimize the burden of the collection of information on those who are to respond, including through the use of appropriate automated, electronic, mechanical, or other technological collection techniques or other forms of information technology, for example, by permitting electronic submission of responses.

Comments should be sent to the Office of Information and Regulatory Affairs, Attention: Desk Officer for the Employee Benefits Security

---

[19] Any individual enrolling in coverage pursuant to this enrollment right must be treated as a special enrollee, as provided under HIPAA portability rules. Accordingly, the individual must be offered all the benefit packages available to similarly situated individuals who did not lose coverage by reason of cessation of dependent status. The individual also cannot be required to pay more for coverage than similarly situated individuals who did not lose coverage by reason of cessation of dependent status.

Administration either by fax to (202) 395–7285 or by e-mail to *oira_submission@omb.eop.gov.* A copy of the ICR may be obtained by contacting the PRA addressee: G. Christopher Cosby, Office of Policy and Research, U.S. Department of Labor, Employee Benefits Security Administration, 200 Constitution Avenue, NW., Room N–5718, Washington, DC 20210. Telephone: (202) 693–8410; Fax: (202) 219–4745. These are not toll-free numbers. E-mail: *ebsa.opr@dol.gov.* ICRs submitted to OMB also are available at reginfo.gov (*http://www.reginfo.gov/public/do/ PRAMain*).

The Departments assume that 2,800,000 ERISA covered plans will send the enrollment opportunity notice to all 79,573,000 employees eligible for group health insurance coverage. The Departments estimate that preparing the enrollment notice will require 30 minutes of legal professional time at a labor rate of $119 per hour [20] and one minute of clerical time at $26 per hour per paper notice to distribute the notices.[21] This results in an hour burden of nearly 822,000 hours and an associated equivalent cost of nearly $21,513,000.

The Departments estimate that the cost burden associated with distributing the approximately 79,573,000 notices will be approximately $2,467,000 based on one minute of clerical time, and $.05 per page for material and printing costs. The Departments assumed that 38 percent of the notices would be sent electronically.[22] In addition, plans can send these notices with other plan documents, such as open enrollment materials. Therefore, the Departments have not included postage costs in this estimate. The Departments note that persons are not required to respond to, and generally are not subject to any penalty for failing to comply with, an ICR unless the ICR has a valid OMB control number.[23]

These paperwork burden estimates are summarized as follows:

Type of Review: New collection.

Agencies: Employee Benefits Security Administration, Department of Labor; Internal Revenue Service, U.S. Department of the Treasury.

Title: Affordable Care Act Enrollment Opportunity Notice Relating to Extended Dependent Coverage.

OMB Number: 1210–0139; 1545–2172.

Affected Public: Business or other for-profit; not-for-profit institutions.

Total Respondents: 2,800,000.

Total Responses: 79,573,000.

Frequency of Response: One-time.

Estimated Total Annual Burden Hours: 411,000 hours (Employee Benefits Security Administration); 411,000 hours (Internal Revenue Service).

Estimated Total Annual Burden Cost: $1,233,500 (Employee Benefits Security Administration); $1,233,500 (Internal Revenue Service).

2. Department of Health and Human Services: Affordable Care Act Enrollment Opportunity Notice Relating to Extended Dependent Coverage

We are soliciting public comment on the following sections of this document that contain information collection requirements (ICR) regarding the Affordable Care Act—ICR Relating to Enrollment Opportunity Notice—Dependent Coverage. As discussed earlier in this preamble, the Affordable Care Act and these interim final regulations require issuers in the individual market and group health plans sponsored by State and local governments to notify participants regarding an enrollment opportunity related to the extension of dependent coverage. Prior to the applicability date of PHS Act section 2714, a child who was covered under a group health plan (or group health insurance coverage) as a dependent may have lost eligibility for coverage under the plan due to age before age 26. Moreover, if, when a parent first became eligible for coverage, a child was under age 26 but older than the age at which the plan stopped covering children, the child would not have become eligible for coverage.

When the provisions of PHS Act section 2714 become applicable to the plan (or coverage), the plan or coverage can no longer exclude coverage for the individual until age 26.

Accordingly, these interim final regulations require issuers in the individual insurance market and group health plans sponsored by State and local governments to provide a notice of an enrollment opportunity to individuals whose coverage ended, or who was denied coverage (or was not eligible for coverage) under a group health plan or group health insurance coverage because, under the terms of the plan or coverage, the availability of dependent coverage of children ended before the attainment of age 26. The enrollment opportunity must continue for at least 30 days, regardless of whether the plan or coverage offers an open enrollment period and regardless of when any open enrollment period might otherwise occur. This enrollment opportunity must be presented not later than the first day of the first plan year (in the individual market, policy year) beginning on or after September 23, 2010 (which is the applicability date of PHS Act section 2714). Coverage must begin not later than the first day of the first plan year (in the individual market, policy year) beginning on or after September 23, 2010.[24]

The Department estimates that 126,000 State and local governmental plans would have to send 19,627,000 notices to eligible employees and 490 insurers in the individual market would have to send approximately 5,444,000 notices to individuals with policies covering dependents.[25] For purposes of this estimate, the Department assumes that it will take a legal professional, on average, 30 minutes to prepare the notice at a labor rate of $119 per hour,[26] and one minute, on average, of a clerical professional's time at $26 per hour to copy and mail the notice.[27] While plans could prepare their own notice, the

---

[20] Hourly wage estimates are based on data from the Bureau of Labor Statistics Occupational Employment Survey (May 2008) and the Bureau of Labor Statistics Employment Cost Index (June 2009). All hourly wage rates include wages and benefits. Clerical wage and benefits estimates are based on metropolitan wage rates for executive secretaries and administrative assistants. Legal professional wage and benefits estimates are based on metropolitan wage rates for lawyers.

[21] While plans could prepare their own notice, the Departments assume that the notices will be prepared by service providers. The Departments have previously estimated that there are 630 health insurers (460 providing coverage in the group market, and 490 providing coverage in the individual market.). These estimates are from NAIC 2007 financial statements data and the California Department of Managed Healthcare (2009), *at http://wpso.dmhc.ca.gov/hpsearch/viewall.aspx.* Because the hour and cost burden is shared between the Departments of Labor/Treasury and the Department of Health and Human Services, the burden to prepare the notices is calculated using half the number of insurers (315).

[22] For purposes of this burden estimate, the Departments assume that 38 percent of the disclosures will be provided through electronic means in accordance with the Department of Labor's standards for electronic communication of required information provided under 29 CFR 2520.104b–1(c).

[23] 5 CFR 1320.1 through 1320.18.

[24] Any individual enrolling in coverage pursuant to this enrollment right must be treated as a special enrollee, as provided under HIPAA portability rules. Accordingly, the individual must be offered all the benefit packages available to similarly situated individuals who did not lose coverage by reason of cessation of dependent status. The individual also cannot be required to pay more for coverage than similarly situated individuals who did not lose coverage by reason of cessation of dependent status.

[25] The number of individual insurance notices was based on the number of individual policy holders with dependents on that policy according to the 2009 March Current Population Survey (CPS).

[26] Estimates of labor rates include wages, other benefits, and overhead based on the National Occupational Employment Survey (May 2008, Bureau of Labor Statistics) and the Employment Cost Index June 2009, Bureau of Labor Statistics).

Department assumes that the notices will be prepared by service providers. The Department has previously estimated that there are 630 health insurers [28] (460 providing coverage in the group market, and 490 providing coverage in the individual market). Because the hour and cost burden is shared among the Departments of Labor/Treasury and the Department of Health and Human Services, the burden to prepare the notices is calculated using half the number of insurers (315). The Department assumes that 38 percent of the notices would be sent electronically.[29] Notices that are sent electronically do not require any of the clerical worker's time to mail the notice. This results in an hour burden of approximately 259,000 hours and an associated equivalent cost of about $6,791,000 to prepare and distribute 25,071,000 notices. The Department estimates that the cost burden associated with distributing the notices will be approximately $777,000.[30] The Department assumes that 38 percent of the notices would be sent electronically.[31] In addition, plans and issuers can send these notices with other plan documents (for example, during open enrollment for the government plans, or other communication at reenrollment in the individual market). Therefore, the Department did not include postage costs in this estimate. The Department notes that persons are not required to respond to, and generally are not subject to any penalty for failing to comply with, an ICR unless the ICR has a valid OMB control number.[32]

These paperwork burden estimates are summarized as follows:

Type of Review: New collection.

Agency: Department of Health and Human Services.

Title: Notice of Special Enrollment Opportunity under the Affordable Care Act Relating to Dependent Coverage.

OMB Number: 0938–1089.

Affected Public: Business; State, Local, or Tribal Governments.

Respondents: 126,000.

---

[28] These estimates are from NAIC 2007 financial statements data and the California Department of Managed Healthcare (2009), *at http://wpso.dmhc.ca.gov/hpsearch/viewall.aspx.*

[29] For purposes of this burden estimate, the Department assumes that 38 percent of the disclosures will be provided through electronic means.

[30] This estimate is based on an average document size of one page and $.05 cents per page for material and printing costs.

[31] For purposes of this burden estimate, the Department assumes that 38 percent of the disclosures will be provided through electronic means.

[32] 5 CFR 1320.1 through 1320.18.

Responses: 25,071,000.

Frequency of Response: One-time.

Estimated Total Annual Burden Hours: 259,000 hours.

Estimated Total Annual Burden Cost: $777,000.

If you comment on this information collection and recordkeeping requirements, please do either of the following:

1. Submit your comments electronically as specified in the **ADDRESSES** section of this proposed rule; or

2. Submit your comments to the Office of Information and Regulatory Affairs, Office of Management and Budget,

   Attention: CMS Desk Officer, 4140–IFC

   Fax: (202) 395–6974; or

   E-mail: OIRA_submission@omb.eop.gov

F. Congressional Review Act

These interim final regulations are subject to the Congressional Review Act provisions of the Small Business Regulatory Enforcement Fairness Act of 1996 (5 U.S.C. 801 *et seq.*) and have been transmitted to Congress and the Comptroller General for review.

G. Unfunded Mandates Reform Act

The Unfunded Mandates Reform Act of 1995 (Pub. L. 104–4) requires agencies to prepare several analytic statements before proposing any rules that may result in annual expenditures of $100 million (as adjusted for inflation) by State, local and tribal governments or the private sector. These interim final regulations are not subject to the Unfunded Mandates Reform Act, because they are being issued as an interim final regulation. However, consistent with the policy embodied in the Unfunded Mandates Reform Act, these interim final regulations have been designed to be the least burdensome alternative for State, local and tribal governments, and the private sector, while achieving the objectives of the Affordable Care Act.

H. Federalism Statement—Department of Labor and Department of Health and Human Services

Executive Order 13132 outlines fundamental principles of federalism, and requires the adherence to specific criteria by Federal agencies in the process of their formulation and implementation of policies that have "substantial direct effects" on the States, the relationship between the national government and States, or on the distribution of power and responsibilities among the various

levels of government. Federal agencies promulgating regulations that have these federalism implications must consult with State and local officials, and describe the extent of their consultation and the nature of the concerns of State and local officials in the preamble to the regulation.

In the Departments' view, these interim final regulations have federalism implications, because they have direct effects on the States, the relationship between the national government and States, or on the distribution of power and responsibilities among various levels of government. However, in the Departments' view, the federalism implications of these interim final regulations are substantially mitigated because, with respect to health insurance issuers, the Departments expect that the majority of States will enact laws or take other appropriate action resulting in their meeting or exceeding the Federal standard.

In general, through section 514, ERISA supersedes State laws to the extent that they relate to any covered employee benefit plan, and preserves State laws that regulate insurance, banking, or securities. While ERISA prohibits States from regulating a plan as an insurance or investment company or bank, the preemption provisions of ERISA section 731 and PHS Act section 2724 (implemented in 29 CFR 2590.731(a) and 45 CFR 146.143(a)) apply so that the HIPAA requirements (including those of the Affordable Care Act) are not to be "construed to supersede any provision of State law which establishes, implements, or continues in effect any standard or requirement solely relating to health insurance issuers in connection with group health insurance coverage except to the extent that such standard or requirement prevents the application of a requirement" of a federal standard. The conference report accompanying HIPAA indicates that this is intended to be the "narrowest" preemption of State laws. (See House Conf. Rep. No. 104–736, at 205, reprinted in 1996 U.S. Code Cong. & Admin. News 2018.) States may continue to apply State law requirements except to the extent that such requirements prevent the application of the Affordable Care Act requirements that are the subject of this rulemaking. State insurance laws that are more stringent than the Federal requirements are unlikely to "prevent the application of" the Affordable Care Act, and be preempted. Accordingly, States have significant latitude to impose requirements on health insurance issuers that are more restrictive than the Federal law.

In compliance with the requirement of Executive Order 13132 that agencies examine closely any policies that may have federalism implications or limit the policy making discretion of the States, the Departments have engaged in efforts to consult with and work cooperatively with affected State and local officials, including attending conferences of the National Association of Insurance Commissioners and consulting with State insurance officials on an individual basis. It is expected that the Departments will act in a similar fashion in enforcing the Affordable Care Act requirements. Throughout the process of developing these interim final regulations, to the extent feasible within the specific preemption provisions of HIPAA as it applies to the Affordable Care Act, the Departments have attempted to balance the States' interests in regulating health insurance issuers, and Congress' intent to provide uniform minimum protections to consumers in every State. By doing so, it is the Departments' view that they have complied with the requirements of Executive Order 13132.

Pursuant to the requirements set forth in section 8(a) of Executive Order 13132, and by the signatures affixed to these regulations, the Departments certify that the Employee Benefits Security Administration and the Office of Consumer Information and Insurance Oversight have complied with the requirements of Executive Order 13132 for the attached regulation in a meaningful and timely manner.

V. Statutory Authority

The Department of the Treasury temporary regulations are adopted pursuant to the authority contained in sections 7805 and 9833 of the Code.

The Department of Labor interim final regulations are adopted pursuant to the authority contained in 29 U.S.C. 1027, 1059, 1135, 1161–1168, 1169, 1181–1183, 1181 note, 1185, 1185a, 1185b, 1191, 1191a, 1191b, and 1191c; sec. 101(g), Pub. L. 104–191, 110 Stat. 1936; sec. 401(b), Pub. L. 105–200, 112 Stat. 645 (42 U.S.C. 651 note); sec. 512(d), Pub. L. 110–343, 122 Stat. 3881; sec. 1001, 1201, and 1562(e), Pub. L. 111–148, 124 Stat. 119, as amended by Pub. L. 111–152, 124 Stat. 1029; Secretary of Labor's Order 6–2009, 74 FR 21524 (May 7, 2009).

The Department of Health and Human Services interim final regulations are adopted pursuant to the authority contained in sections 2701 through 2763, 2791, and 2792 of the PHS Act (42

USC 300gg through 300gg–63, 300gg–91, and 300gg–92), as amended.

List of Subjects

26 CFR Part 54

Excise taxes, Health care, Health insurance, Pensions, Reporting and recordkeeping requirements.

26 CFR Part 602

Reporting and recordkeeping requirements.

29 CFR Part 2590

Continuation coverage, Disclosure, Employee benefit plans, Group health plans, Health care, Health insurance, Medical child support, Reporting and recordkeeping requirements.

45 CFR Parts 144, 146, and 147

Health care, Health insurance, Reporting and recordkeeping requirements, and State regulation of health insurance.

Steven T. Miller,

Deputy Commissioner for Services and Enforcement, Internal Revenue Service.

Approved: May 7, 2010.

Michael F. Mundaca,

Assistant Secretary of the Treasury (Tax Policy).

Signed this 6th day of May 2010.

Phyllis C. Borzi,

Assistant Secretary, Employee Benefits Security Administration, Department of Labor.

Approved: May 4, 2010.

Jay Angoff,

Director, Office of Consumer Information and Insurance Oversight.

Approved: May 7, 2010.

Kathleen Sebelius,

Secretary, Department of Health and Human Services.

Internal Revenue Service

26 CFR Chapter 1

■ Accordingly, 26 CFR Parts 54 and 602 are amended as follows:

PART 54—PENSION EXCISE TAXES

■ **Paragraph 1.** The authority citation for part 54 continues to read in part as follows:

Authority: 26 U.S.C. 7805. * * *

■ **Par. 2.** Section 54.9815–2714T is added to read as follows:

§ 54.9815–2714T   Eligibility of children until at least age 26 (temporary).

(a) *In general*—(1) A group health plan, or a health insurance issuer offering group health insurance coverage, that makes available dependent coverage of children must

make such coverage available for children until attainment of 26 years of age.

(2) The rule of this paragraph (a) is illustrated by the following example:

Example. (i) *Facts.* For the plan year beginning January 1, 2011, a group health plan provides health coverage for employees, employees' spouses, and employees' children until the child turns 26. On the birthday of a child of an employee, July 17, 2011, the child turns 26. The last day the plan covers the child is July 16, 2011.

(ii) *Conclusion.* In this *Example,* the plan satisfies the requirement of this paragraph (a) with respect to the child.

(b) *Restrictions on plan definition of dependent.* With respect to a child who has not attained age 26, a plan or issuer may not define dependent for purposes of eligibility for dependent coverage of children other than in terms of a relationship between a child and the participant. Thus, for example, a plan or issuer may not deny or restrict coverage for a child who has not attained age 26 based on the presence or absence of the child's financial dependency (upon the participant or any other person), residency with the participant or with any other person, student status, employment, or any combination of those factors. In addition, a plan or issuer may not deny or restrict coverage of a child based on eligibility for other coverage, except that paragraph (g) of this section provides a special rule for plan years beginning before January 1, 2014 for grandfathered health plans that are group health plans. (Other requirements of Federal or State law, including section 609 of ERISA or section 1908 of the Social Security Act, may mandate coverage of certain children.)

(c) *Coverage of grandchildren not required.* Nothing in this section requires a plan or issuer to make coverage available for the child of a child receiving dependent coverage.

(d) *Uniformity irrespective of age.* The terms of the plan or health insurance coverage providing dependent coverage of children cannot vary based on age (except for children who are age 26 or older).

(e) *Examples.* The rules of paragraph (d) of this section are illustrated by the following examples:

Example 1. (i) *Facts.* A group health plan offers a choice of self-only or family health coverage. Dependent coverage is provided under family health coverage for children of participants who have not attained age 26. The plan imposes an additional premium surcharge for children who are older than age 18.

(ii) *Conclusion.* In this *Example 1,* the plan violates the requirement of paragraph (d) of this section because the plan varies the terms for dependent coverage of children based on age.

Example 2. (i) *Facts.* A group health plan offers a choice among the following tiers of health coverage: self-only, self-plus-one, self-plus-two, and self-plus-three-or-more. The cost of coverage increases based on the number of covered individuals. The plan provides dependent coverage of children who have not attained age 26.

(ii) *Conclusion.* In this *Example 2,* the plan does not violate the requirement of paragraph (d) of this section that the terms of dependent coverage for children not vary based on age. Although the cost of coverage increases for tiers with more covered individuals, the increase applies without regard to the age of any child.

Example 3. (i) *Facts.* A group health plan offers two benefit packages—an HMO option and an indemnity option. Dependent coverage is provided for children of participants who have not attained age 26. The plan limits children who are older than age 18 to the HMO option.

(ii) *Conclusion.* In this *Example 3,* the plan violates the requirement of paragraph (d) of this section because the plan, by limiting children who are older than age 18 to the HMO option, varies the terms for dependent coverage of children based on age.

(f) *Transitional rules for individuals whose coverage ended by reason of reaching a dependent eligibility threshold*—(1) *In general.* The relief provided in the transitional rules of this paragraph (f) applies with respect to any child—

(i) Whose coverage ended, or who was denied coverage (or was not eligible for coverage) under a group health plan or group health insurance coverage because, under the terms of the plan or coverage, the availability of dependent coverage of children ended before the attainment of age 26 (which, under this section, is no longer permissible); and

(ii) Who becomes eligible (or is required to become eligible) for coverage under a group health plan or group health insurance coverage on the first day of the first plan year beginning on or after September 23, 2010 by reason of the application of this section.

(2) *Opportunity to enroll required.* (i) If a group health plan, or group health insurance coverage, in which a child described in paragraph (f)(1) of this section is eligible to enroll (or is required to become eligible to enroll) is the plan or coverage in which the child's coverage ended (or did not begin) for the reasons described in paragraph (f)(1)(i) of this section, and if the plan, or the issuer of such coverage, is subject to the requirements of this section, the plan and the issuer are required to give the child an opportunity to enroll that continues for at least 30 days (including written notice of the opportunity to enroll). This

opportunity (including the written notice) must be provided beginning not later than the first day of the first plan year beginning on or after September 23, 2010.

(ii) The written notice must include a statement that children whose coverage ended, or who were denied coverage (or were not eligible for coverage), because the availability of dependent coverage of children ended before attainment of age 26 are eligible to enroll in the plan or coverage. The notice may be provided to an employee on behalf of the employee's child. In addition, the notice may be included with other enrollment materials that a plan distributes to employees, provided the statement is prominent. If a notice satisfying the requirements of this paragraph (f)(2) is provided to an employee whose child is entitled to an enrollment opportunity under this paragraph (f), the obligation to provide the notice of enrollment opportunity under this paragraph (f)(2) with respect to that child is satisfied for both the plan and the issuer.

(3) *Effective date of coverage.* In the case of an individual who enrolls under paragraph (f)(2) of this section, coverage must take effect not later than the first day of the first plan year beginning on or after September 23, 2010.

(4) *Treatment of enrollees in a group health plan.* Any child enrolling in a group health plan pursuant to paragraph (f)(2) of this section must be treated as if the child were a special enrollee, as provided under the rules of § 54.9801–6(d). Accordingly, the child (and, if the child would not be a participant once enrolled in the plan, the participant through whom the child is otherwise eligible for coverage under the plan) must be offered all the benefit packages available to similarly situated individuals who did not lose coverage by reason of cessation of dependent status. For this purpose, any difference in benefits or cost-sharing requirements constitutes a different benefit package. The child also cannot be required to pay more for coverage than similarly situated individuals who did not lose coverage by reason of cessation of dependent status.

(5) *Examples.* The rules of this paragraph (f) are illustrated by the following examples:

Example 1. (i) *Facts.* Employer Y maintains a group health plan with a calendar year plan year. The plan has a single benefit package. For the 2010 plan year, the plan allows children of employees to be covered under the plan until age 19, or until age 23 for children who are full-time students. Individual B, an employee of Y, and Individual C, B's child and a full-time student, were enrolled in Y's group health

plan at the beginning of the 2010 plan year. On June 10, 2010, C turns 23 years old and loses dependent coverage under Y's plan. On or before January 1, 2011, Y's group health plan gives B written notice that individuals who lost coverage by reason of ceasing to be a dependent before attainment of age 26 are eligible to enroll in the plan, and that individuals may request enrollment for such children through February 14, 2011 with enrollment effective retroactively to January 1, 2011.

(ii) *Conclusion.* In this *Example 1,* the plan has complied with the requirements of this paragraph (f) by providing an enrollment opportunity to C that lasts at least 30 days.

Example 2. (i) *Facts.* Employer Z maintains a group health plan with a plan year beginning October 1 and ending September 30. Prior to October 1, 2010, the group health plan allows children of employees to be covered under the plan until age 22. Individual D, an employee of Z, and Individual E, D's child, are enrolled in family coverage under Z's group health plan for the plan year beginning on October 1, 2008. On May 1, 2009, E turns 22 years old and ceases to be eligible as a dependent under Z's plan and loses coverage. D drops coverage but remains an employee of Z.

(ii) *Conclusion.* In this *Example 2,* not later than October 1, 2010, the plan must provide D and E an opportunity to enroll (including written notice of an opportunity to enroll) that continues for at least 30 days, with enrollment effective not later than October 1, 2010.

Example 3. (i) *Facts.* Same facts as *Example 2,* except that D did not drop coverage. Instead, D switched to a lower-cost benefit package option.

(ii) *Conclusion.* In this *Example 3,* not later than October 1, 2010, the plan must provide D and E an opportunity to enroll in any benefit package available to similarly situated individuals who enroll when first eligible.

Example 4. (i) *Facts.* Same facts as *Example 2,* except that E elected COBRA continuation coverage.

(ii) *Conclusion.* In this *Example 4,* not later than October 1, 2010, the plan must provide D and E an opportunity to enroll other than as a COBRA qualified beneficiary (and must provide, by that date, written notice of the opportunity to enroll) that continues for at least 30 days, with enrollment effective not later than October 1, 2010.

Example 5. (i) *Facts.* Employer X maintains a group health plan with a calendar year plan year. Prior to 2011, the plan allows children of employees to be covered under the plan until the child attains age 22. During the 2009 plan year, an individual with a 22-year old child joins the plan; the child is denied coverage because the child is 22.

(ii) *Conclusion.* In this *Example 5,* notwithstanding that the child was not previously covered under the plan, the plan must provide the child, not later than January 1, 2011, an opportunity to enroll (including written notice to the employee of an opportunity to enroll the child) that continues for at least 30 days, with enrollment effective not later than January 1, 2011.

(g) *Special rule for grandfathered group health plans*—(1) For plan years beginning before January 1, 2014, a group health plan that qualifies as a grandfathered health plan under section 1251 of the Patient Protection and Affordable Care Act and that makes available dependent coverage of children may exclude an adult child who has not attained age 26 from coverage only if the adult child is eligible to enroll in an eligible employer-sponsored health plan (as defined in section 5000A(f)(2)) other than a group health plan of a parent.

(2) For plan years beginning on or after January 1, 2014, a group health plan that qualifies as a grandfathered health plan under section 1251 of the Patient Protection and Affordable Care Act must comply with the requirements of paragraphs (a) through (f) of this section.

(h) *Applicability date.* The provisions of this section apply for plan years beginning on or after September 23, 2010.

(i) *Expiration date.* This section expires on or before May 13, 2013.

PART 602—OMB CONTROL NUMBERS UNDER THE PAPERWORK REDUCTION ACT

■ **Par. 5.** The authority citation for part 602 continues to read as follows:

Authority: 26 U.S.C. 7805.

■ **Par. 6.** In § 602.101, paragraph (b) is amended by adding the following entry in numerical order to the table:

§ 602.101 OMB Control numbers.

*   *   *   *   *

(b) * * *

CFR part or section where identified and described	Current OMB control No.
* * * * *	
54.9815–2714T	1545–2172
* * * * *	

Employee Benefits Security Administration

29 CFR Chapter XXV

■ 29 CFR Part 2590 is amended as follows:

PART 2590—RULES AND REGULATIONS FOR GROUP HEALTH PLANS

■ 1. The authority citation for Part 2590 is revised to read as follows:

Authority: 29 U.S.C. 1027, 1059, 1135, 1161–1168, 1169, 1181–1183, 1181 note, 1185, 1185a, 1185b, 1191, 1191a, 1191b, 1191c; sec. 101(g), Pub. L.104–191, 110 Stat. 1936; sec. 401(b), Pub. L. 105–200, 112 Stat.

645 (42 U.S.C. 651 note); sec. 512(d), Pub. L. 110–343, 122 Stat. 3881; sec. 1001, 1201, and 1562(e), Pub. L. 111–148, 124 Stat. 119, as amended by Pub. L. 111–152, 124 Stat. 1029; Secretary of Labor's Order 6–2009, 74 FR 21524 (May 7, 2009).

■ 2. Section 2590.715–2714 is added to Subpart C to read as follows:

§ 2590.715–2714 Eligibility of children until at least age 26.

(a) *In general*—(1) A group health plan, or a health insurance issuer offering group health insurance coverage, that makes available dependent coverage of children must make such coverage available for children until attainment of 26 years of age.

(2) The rule of this paragraph (a) is illustrated by the following example:

Example. (i) *Facts.* For the plan year beginning January 1, 2011, a group health plan provides health coverage for employees, employees' spouses, and employees' children until the child turns 26. On the birthday of a child of an employee, July 17, 2011, the child turns 26. The last day the plan covers the child is July 16, 2011.

(ii) *Conclusion.* In this *Example,* the plan satisfies the requirement of this paragraph (a) with respect to the child.

(b) *Restrictions on plan definition of dependent.* With respect to a child who has not attained age 26, a plan or issuer may not define dependent for purposes of eligibility for dependent coverage of children other than in terms of a relationship between a child and the participant. Thus, for example, a plan or issuer may not deny or restrict coverage for a child who has not attained age 26 based on the presence or absence of the child's financial dependency (upon the participant or any other person), residency with the participant or with any other person, student status, employment, or any combination of those factors. In addition, a plan or issuer may not deny or restrict coverage of a child based on eligibility for other coverage, except that paragraph (g) of this section provides a special rule for plan years beginning before January 1, 2014 for grandfathered health plans that are group health plans. (Other requirements of Federal or State law, including section 609 of ERISA or section 1908 of the Social Security Act, may mandate coverage of certain children.)

(c) *Coverage of grandchildren not required.* Nothing in this section requires a plan or issuer to make coverage available for the child of a child receiving dependent coverage.

(d) *Uniformity irrespective of age.* The terms of the plan or health insurance coverage providing dependent coverage of children cannot vary based on age

(except for children who are age 26 or older).

(e) *Examples.* The rules of paragraph (d) of this section are illustrated by the following examples:

Example 1. (i) *Facts.* A group health plan offers a choice of self-only or family health coverage. Dependent coverage is provided under family health coverage for children of participants who have not attained age 26. The plan imposes an additional premium surcharge for children who are older than age 18.

(ii) *Conclusion.* In this *Example 1,* the plan violates the requirement of paragraph (d) of this section because the plan varies the terms for dependent coverage of children based on age.

Example 2. (i) *Facts.* A group health plan offers a choice among the following tiers of health coverage: self-only, self-plus-one, self-plus-two, and self-plus-three-or-more. The cost of coverage increases based on the number of covered individuals. The plan provides dependent coverage of children who have not attained age 26.

(ii) *Conclusion.* In this *Example 2,* the plan does not violate the requirement of paragraph (d) of this section that the terms of dependent coverage for children not vary based on age. Although the cost of coverage increases for tiers with more covered individuals, the increase applies without regard to the age of any child.

Example 3. (i) *Facts.* A group health plan offers two benefit packages—an HMO option and an indemnity option. Dependent coverage is provided for children of participants who have not attained age 26. The plan limits children who are older than age 18 to the HMO option.

(ii) *Conclusion.* In this *Example 3,* the plan violates the requirement of paragraph (d) of this section because the plan, by limiting children who are older than age 18 to the HMO option, varies the terms for dependent coverage of children based on age.

(f) *Transitional rules for individuals whose coverage ended by reason of reaching a dependent eligibility threshold*—(1) *In general.* The relief provided in the transitional rules of this paragraph (f) applies with respect to any child—

(i) Whose coverage ended, or who was denied coverage (or was not eligible for coverage) under a group health plan or group health insurance coverage because, under the terms of the plan or coverage, the availability of dependent coverage of children ended before the attainment of age 26 (which, under this section, is no longer permissible); and

(ii) Who becomes eligible (or is required to become eligible) for coverage under a group health plan or group health insurance coverage on the first day of the first plan year beginning on or after September 23, 2010 by reason of the application of this section.

(2) *Opportunity to enroll required*—(i) If a group health plan, or group health

insurance coverage, in which a child described in paragraph (f)(1) of this section is eligible to enroll (or is required to become eligible to enroll) is the plan or coverage in which the child's coverage ended (or did not begin) for the reasons described in paragraph (f)(1)(i) of this section, and if the plan, or the issuer of such coverage, is subject to the requirements of this section, the plan and the issuer are required to give the child an opportunity to enroll that continues for at least 30 days (including written notice of the opportunity to enroll). This opportunity (including the written notice) must be provided beginning not later than the first day of the first plan year beginning on or after September 23, 2010.

(ii) The written notice must include a statement that children whose coverage ended, or who were denied coverage (or were not eligible for coverage), because the availability of dependent coverage of children ended before attainment of age 26 are eligible to enroll in the plan or coverage. The notice may be provided to an employee on behalf of the employee's child. In addition, the notice may be included with other enrollment materials that a plan distributes to employees, provided the statement is prominent. If a notice satisfying the requirements of this paragraph (f)(2) is provided to an employee whose child is entitled to an enrollment opportunity under this paragraph (f), the obligation to provide the notice of enrollment opportunity under this paragraph (f)(2) with respect to that child is satisfied for both the plan and the issuer.

(3) *Effective date of coverage.* In the case of an individual who enrolls under paragraph (f)(2) of this section, coverage must take effect not later than the first day of the first plan year beginning on or after September 23, 2010.

(4) *Treatment of enrollees in a group health plan.* Any child enrolling in a group health plan pursuant to paragraph (f)(2) of this section must be treated as if the child were a special enrollee, as provided under the rules of § 2590.701–6(d) of this Part. Accordingly, the child (and, if the child would not be a participant once enrolled in the plan, the participant through whom the child is otherwise eligible for coverage under the plan) must be offered all the benefit packages available to similarly situated individuals who did not lose coverage by reason of cessation of dependent status. For this purpose, any difference in benefits or cost-sharing requirements constitutes a different benefit package. The child also cannot be required to pay more for coverage than similarly situated individuals who did not lose

coverage by reason of cessation of dependent status.

(5) *Examples.* The rules of this paragraph (f) are illustrated by the following examples:

Example 1. (i) *Facts.* Employer Y maintains a group health plan with a calendar year plan year. The plan has a single benefit package. For the 2010 plan year, the plan allows children of employees to be covered under the plan until age 19, or until age 23 for children who are full-time students. Individual B, an employee of Y, and Individual C, B's child and a full-time student, were enrolled in Y's group health plan at the beginning of the 2010 plan year. On June 10, 2010, C turns 23 years old and loses dependent coverage under Y's plan. On or before January 1, 2011, Y's group health plan gives B written notice that individuals who lost coverage by reason of ceasing to be a dependent before attainment of age 26 are eligible to enroll in the plan, and that individuals may request enrollment for such children through February 14, 2011 with enrollment effective retroactively to January 1, 2011.

(ii) *Conclusion.* In this *Example 1,* the plan has complied with the requirements of this paragraph (f) by providing an enrollment opportunity to C that lasts at least 30 days.

Example 2. (i) *Facts.* Employer Z maintains a group health plan with a plan year beginning October 1 and ending September 30. Prior to October 1, 2010, the group health plan allows children of employees to be covered under the plan until age 22. Individual D, an employee of Z, and Individual E, D's child, are enrolled in family coverage under Z's group health plan for the plan year beginning on October 1, 2008. On May 1, 2009, E turns 22 years old and ceases to be eligible as a dependent under Z's plan and loses coverage. D drops coverage but remains an employee of Z.

(ii) *Conclusion.* In this *Example 2,* not later than October 1, 2010, the plan must provide D and E an opportunity to enroll (including written notice of an opportunity to enroll) that continues for at least 30 days, with enrollment effective not later than October 1, 2010.

Example 3. (i) *Facts.* Same facts as *Example 2,* except that D did not drop coverage. Instead, D switched to a lower-cost benefit package option.

(ii) *Conclusion.* In this *Example 3,* not later than October 1, 2010, the plan must provide D and E an opportunity to enroll in any benefit package available to similarly situated individuals who enroll when first eligible.

Example 4. (i) *Facts.* Same facts as *Example 2,* except that E elected COBRA continuation coverage.

(ii) *Conclusion.* In this *Example 4,* not later than October 1, 2010, the plan must provide D and E an opportunity to enroll other than as a COBRA qualified beneficiary (and must provide, by that date, written notice of the opportunity to enroll) that continues for at least 30 days, with enrollment effective not later than October 1, 2010.

Example 5. (i) *Facts.* Employer X maintains a group health plan with a calendar year plan year. Prior to 2011, the plan allows children

of employees to be covered under the plan until the child attains age 22. During the 2009 plan year, an individual with a 22-year old child joins the plan; the child is denied coverage because the child is 22.

(ii) *Conclusion.* In this *Example 5,* notwithstanding that the child was not previously covered under the plan, the plan must provide the child, not later than January 1, 2011, an opportunity to enroll (including written notice to the employee of an opportunity to enroll the child) that continues for at least 30 days, with enrollment effective not later than January 1, 2011.

(g) *Special rule for grandfathered group health plans*—(1) For plan years beginning before January 1, 2014, a group health plan that qualifies as a grandfathered health plan under section 1251 of the Patient Protection and Affordable Care Act and that makes available dependent coverage of children may exclude an adult child who has not attained age 26 from coverage only if the adult child is eligible to enroll in an eligible employer-sponsored health plan (as defined in section 5000A(f)(2) of the Internal Revenue Code) other than a group health plan of a parent.

(2) For plan years beginning on or after January 1, 2014, a group health plan that qualifies as a grandfathered health plan under section 1251 of the Patient Protection and Affordable Care Act must comply with the requirements of paragraphs (a) through (f) of this section.

(h) *Applicability date.* The provisions of this section apply for plan years beginning on or after September 23, 2010.

Department of Health and Human Services

45 CFR Subtitle A

■ For reasons set forth in the preamble, the Department of Health and Human Services is amending 45 CFR Subtitle A, Subchapter B as follows:

PART 144—REQUIREMENTS RELATING TO HEALTH INSURANCE COVERAGE

Subpart A—General Provisions

■ 1. Section 144.101 is amended by-
■ A. Revising paragraph (a).
■ B. Redesignating paragraphs (b), (c) and (d) as paragraphs (c), (d) and (e), respectively.
■ C. Adding a new paragraph (b).
■ D. Revising the first sentence of newly redesignated paragraph (c).
■ E. Amending newly redesignated paragraph (d) by removing "2722" and adding in its place "2723".

The revisions and additions read as follows:

§ 144.101   Basis and purpose.

(a) Part 146 of this subchapter implements requirements of Title XXVII of the Public Health Service Act (PHS Act, 42 U.S.C. 300gg, *et seq.*) that apply to group health plans and group health insurance issuers.

(b) Part 147 of this subchapter implements the provisions of the Patient Protection and Affordable Care Act that apply to both group health plans and health insurance issuers in the Group and Individual Markets.

(c) Part 148 of this subchapter implements Individual Health Insurance Market requirements of the PHS Act.

*   *   *

*   *   *   *   *

■ 2. Section 144.103 is amended by adding the definition of "Policy Year" to read as follows:

§ 144.103   Defintions.

*   *   *   *   *

Policy Year means in the individual health insurance market the 12-month period that is designated as the policy year in the policy documents of the individual health insurance coverage. If there is no designation of a policy year in the policy document (or no such policy document is available), then the policy year is the deductible or limit year used under the coverage. If deductibles or other limits are not imposed on a yearly basis, the policy year is the calendar year.

*   *   *   *   *

PART 146—REQUIREMENTS FOR THE GROUP HEALTH INSURANCE MARKET

■ 3. Section 146.101 is amended by—
■ A. Revising the first sentence of paragraph (a).
■ B. Revising paragraph (b)(4).
The revisions read as follows:

§ 146.101   Basis and Scope.

(a) Statutory basis. This part implements the Group Market requirements of the PHS Act.* * *
(b) * * *
(4) *Subpart E.* Subpart E of this part implements requirements relating to group health plans and issuers in the Group Health Insurance Market.

*   *   *   *   *

§ 146.115   [Amended]

■ 4. Section 146.115 is amended by removing "2721(b)" wherever it appears in paragraph (a)(6) and adding in its place "2722(a)".

§ 146.130   [Amended]

■ 5. Section 146.130 is amended by—
■ A. Removing "2704" wherever it appears in paragraphs (e) and (f),

including the examples in paragraph (e)(4), and adding in its place "2725".
■ B. Removing "2723" wherever it appears in paragraph (e)(3), including the paragraph heading, and adding in its place "2724".

■ 6. A new Part 147 is added to read as follows:

PART 147—HEALTH INSURANCE REFORM REQUIREMENTS FOR THE GROUP AND INDIVIDUAL HEALTH INSURANCE MARKETS

Authority: Secs 2701 through 2763, 2791, and 2792 of the Public Health Service Act (42 USC 300gg through 300gg–63, 300gg–91, and 300gg–92), as amended.

§ 147.100   Basis and scope.

Part 147 of this subchapter implements the requirements of the Patient Protection and Affordable Care Act that apply to group health plans and health insurance issuers in the Group and Individual markets.

§ 147.120   Eligibility of children until at least age 26.

(a) *In general*—(1) A group health plan, or a health insurance issuer offering group or individual health insurance coverage, that makes available dependent coverage of children must make such coverage available for children until attainment of 26 years of age.

(2) The rule of this paragraph (a) is illustrated by the following example:

Example. (i) *Facts.* For the plan year beginning January 1, 2011, a group health plan provides health coverage for employees, employees' spouses, and employees' children until the child turns 26. On the birthday of a child of an employee, July 17, 2011, the child turns 26. The last day the plan covers the child is July 16, 2011.

(ii) *Conclusion.* In this *Example,* the plan satisfies the requirement of this paragraph (a) with respect to the child.

(b) *Restrictions on plan definition of dependent.* With respect to a child who has not attained age 26, a plan or issuer may not define dependent for purposes of eligibility for dependent coverage of children other than in terms of a relationship between a child and the participant (in the individual market, the primary subscriber). Thus, for example, a plan or issuer may not deny or restrict coverage for a child who has not attained age 26 based on the presence or absence of the child's financial dependency (upon the participant or primary subscriber, or any other person), residency with the participant (in the individual market, the primary subscriber) or with any other person, student status, employment, or any combination of

those factors. In addition, a plan or issuer may not deny or restrict coverage of a child based on eligibility for other coverage, except that paragraph (g) of this section provides a special rule for plan years beginning before January 1, 2014 for grandfathered health plans that are group health plans. (Other requirements of Federal or State law, including section 609 of ERISA or section 1908 of the Social Security Act, may mandate coverage of certain children.)

(c) *Coverage of grandchildren not required.* Nothing in this section requires a plan or issuer to make coverage available for the child of a child receiving dependent coverage.

(d) *Uniformity irrespective of age.* The terms of the plan or health insurance coverage providing dependent coverage of children cannot vary based on age (except for children who are age 26 or older).

(e) *Examples.* The rules of paragraph (d) of this section are illustrated by the following examples:

Example 1. (i) *Facts.* A group health plan offers a choice of self-only or family health coverage. Dependent coverage is provided under family health coverage for children of participants who have not attained age 26. The plan imposes an additional premium surcharge for children who are older than age 18.

(ii) *Conclusion.* In this *Example 1,* the plan violates the requirement of paragraph (d) of this section because the plan varies the terms for dependent coverage of children based on age.

Example 2. (i) *Facts.* A group health plan offers a choice among the following tiers of health coverage: Self-only, self-plus-one, self-plus-two, and self-plus-three-or-more. The cost of coverage increases based on the number of covered individuals. The plan provides dependent coverage of children who have not attained age 26.

(ii) *Conclusion.* In this *Example 2,* the plan does not violate the requirement of paragraph (d) of this section that the terms of dependent coverage for children not vary based on age. Although the cost of coverage increases for tiers with more covered individuals, the increase applies without regard to the age of any child.

Example 3. (i) *Facts.* A group health plan offers two benefit packages—an HMO option and an indemnity option. Dependent coverage is provided for children of participants who have not attained age 26. The plan limits children who are older than age 18 to the HMO option.

(ii) *Conclusion.* In this *Example 3,* the plan violates the requirement of paragraph (d) of this section because the plan, by limiting children who are older than age 18 to the HMO option, varies the terms for dependent coverage of children based on age.

(f) *Transitional rules for individuals whose coverage ended by reason of reaching a dependent eligibility threshold*—(1) *In general.* The relief provided in the transitional rules of this paragraph (f) applies with respect to any child—

(i) Whose coverage ended, or who was denied coverage (or was not eligible for coverage) under a group health plan or group or individual health insurance coverage because, under the terms of the plan or coverage, the availability of dependent coverage of children ended before the attainment of age 26 (which, under this section, is no longer permissible); and

(ii) Who becomes eligible (or is required to become eligible) for coverage under a group health plan or group or individual health insurance coverage on the first day of the first plan year (in the individual market, the first day of the first policy year) beginning on or after September 23, 2010 by reason of the application of this section.

(2) *Opportunity to enroll required*—(i) If a group health plan, or group or individual health insurance coverage, in which a child described in paragraph (f)(1) of this section is eligible to enroll (or is required to become eligible to enroll) is the plan or coverage in which the child's coverage ended (or did not begin) for the reasons described in paragraph (f)(1)(i) of this section, and if the plan, or the issuer of such coverage, is subject to the requirements of this section, the plan and the issuer are required to give the child an opportunity to enroll that continues for at least 30 days (including written notice of the opportunity to enroll). This opportunity (including the written notice) must be provided beginning not later than the first day of the first plan year (in the individual market, the first day of the first policy year) beginning on or after September 23, 2010.

(ii) The written notice must include a statement that children whose coverage ended, or who were denied coverage (or were not eligible for coverage), because the availability of dependent coverage of children ended before attainment of age 26 are eligible to enroll in the plan or coverage. The notice may be provided to an employee on behalf of the employee's child (in the individual market, to the primary subscriber on behalf of the primary subscriber's child). In addition, for a group health plan or group health insurance coverage, the notice may be included with other enrollment materials that a plan distributes to employees, provided the statement is prominent. For a group health plan or group health insurance coverage, if a notice satisfying the requirements of this paragraph (f)(2) is provided to an employee whose child is entitled to an enrollment opportunity

under this paragraph (f), the obligation to provide the notice of enrollment opportunity under this paragraph (f)(2) with respect to that child is satisfied for both the plan and the issuer.

(3) *Effective date of coverage.* In the case of an individual who enrolls under paragraph (f)(2) of this section, coverage must take effect not later than the first day of the first plan year (in the individual market, the first day of the first policy year) beginning on or after September 23, 2010.

(4) *Treatment of enrollees in a group health plan.* For purposes of this Part, any child enrolling in a group health plan pursuant to paragraph (f)(2) of this section must be treated as if the child were a special enrollee, as provided under the rules of 45 CFR 146.117(d). Accordingly, the child (and, if the child would not be a participant once enrolled in the plan, the participant through whom the child is otherwise eligible for coverage under the plan) must be offered all the benefit packages available to similarly situated individuals who did not lose coverage by reason of cessation of dependent status. For this purpose, any difference in benefits or cost-sharing requirements constitutes a different benefit package. The child also cannot be required to pay more for coverage than similarly situated individuals who did not lose coverage by reason of cessation of dependent status.

(5) *Examples.* The rules of this paragraph (f) are illustrated by the following examples:

Example 1. (i) *Facts.* Employer *Y* maintains a group health plan with a calendar year plan year. The plan has a single benefit package. For the 2010 plan year, the plan allows children of employees to be covered under the plan until age 19, or until age 23 for children who are full-time students. Individual *B*, an employee of *Y*, and Individual *C*, *B*'s child and a full-time student, were enrolled in *Y*'s group health plan at the beginning of the 2010 plan year. On June 10, 2010, *C* turns 23 years old and loses dependent coverage under *Y*'s plan. On or before January 1, 2011, *Y*'s group health plan gives *B* written notice that individuals who lost coverage by reason of ceasing to be a dependent before attainment of age 26 are eligible to enroll in the plan, and that individuals may request enrollment for such children through February 14, 2011 with enrollment effective retroactively to January 1, 2011.

(ii) *Conclusion.* In this *Example 1*, the plan has complied with the requirements of this paragraph (f) by providing an enrollment opportunity to *C* that lasts at least 30 days.

Example 2. (i) *Facts.* Employer *Z* maintains a group health plan with a plan year beginning October 1 and ending September 30. Prior to October 1, 2010, the group health plan allows children of employees to be

covered under the plan until age 22. Individual *D*, an employee of *Z*, and Individual *E*, *D*'s child, are enrolled in family coverage under *Z*'s group health plan for the plan year beginning on October 1, 2008. On May 1, 2009, *E* turns 22 years old and ceases to be eligible as a dependent under *Z*'s plan and loses coverage. *D* drops coverage but remains an employee of *Z*.

(ii) *Conclusion.* In this *Example 2*, not later than October 1, 2010, the plan must provide *D* and *E* an opportunity to enroll (including written notice of an opportunity to enroll) that continues for at least 30 days, with enrollment effective not later than October 1, 2010.

Example 3. (i) *Facts.* Same facts as *Example 2*, except that *D* did not drop coverage. Instead, *D* switched to a lower-cost benefit package option.

(ii) *Conclusion.* In this *Example 3*, not later than October 1, 2010, the plan must provide *D* and *E* an opportunity to enroll in any benefit package available to similarly situated individuals who enroll when first eligible.

Example 4. (i) *Facts.* Same facts as *Example 2*, except that *E* elected COBRA continuation coverage.

(ii) *Conclusion.* In this *Example 4*, not later than October 1, 2010, the plan must provide *D* and *E* an opportunity to enroll other than as a COBRA qualified beneficiary (and must provide, by that date, written notice of the opportunity to enroll) that continues for at least 30 days, with enrollment effective not later than October 1, 2010.

Example 5. (i) *Facts.* Employer *X* maintains a group health plan with a calendar year plan year. Prior to 2011, the plan allows children of employees to be covered under the plan until the child attains age 22. During the 2009 plan year, an individual with a 22-year old child joins the plan; the child is denied coverage because the child is 22.

(ii) *Conclusion.* In this *Example 5*, notwithstanding that the child was not previously covered under the plan, the plan must provide the child, not later than January 1, 2011, an opportunity to enroll (including written notice to the employee of an opportunity to enroll the child) that continues for at least 30 days, with enrollment effective not later than January 1, 2011.

(g) *Special rule for grandfathered group health plans*—(1) For plan years beginning before January 1, 2014, a group health plan that qualifies as a grandfathered health plan under section 1251 of the Patient Protection and Affordable Care Act and that makes available dependent coverage of children may exclude an adult child who has not attained age 26 from coverage only if the adult child is eligible to enroll in an eligible employer-sponsored health plan (as defined in section 5000A(f)(2) of the Internal Revenue Code) other than a group health plan of a parent.

(2) For plan years beginning on or after January 1, 2014, a group health plan that qualifies as a grandfathered

27140   **Federal Register** / Vol. 75, No. 92 / Thursday, May 13, 2010 / Rules and Regulations

health plan under section 1251 of the Patient Protection and Affordable Care Act must comply with the requirements of paragraphs (a) through (f) of this section.

(h) *Applicability date.* The provisions of this section apply for plan years (in the individual market, policy years) beginning on or after September 23, 2010.

[FR Doc. 2010–11391 Filed 5–10–10; 4:15 pm]

BILLING CODE 4830–01–P; 4510–29–P; 4120–01–P

I. IRS Notice 2010-38 (Exclusions from Income for Adult Children Coverage)

Internal Revenue Bulletin: 2010-20

May 17, 2010

Notice 2010-38

Tax Treatment of Health Care Benefits Provided With Respect to Children Under Age 27

Table of Contents

I. PURPOSE

This notice provides guidance on the tax treatment of health coverage for children up to age 27 under the Affordable Care Act. (In this notice, the "Affordable Care Act" refers to the Patient Protection and Affordable Care Act, Public Law No. 111-148 (PPACA), and the Health Care and Education Reconciliation Act of 2010, Public Law No. 111-152 (HCERA), signed into law by the President on March 23 and 30, 2010, respectively.)

The Affordable Care Act requires group health plans and health insurance issuers that provide dependent coverage of children to continue to make such coverage available for an adult child until age 26. The Affordable Care Act also amends the Internal Revenue Code (Code) to give certain favorable tax treatment to coverage for adult children. This notice addresses a number of questions regarding the tax treatment of such coverage.

Specifically, this notice provides guidance on the Affordable Care Act's amendment of § 105(b) of the Code, effective March 30, 2010, to extend the general exclusion from gross income for reimbursements for medical care under an employer-provided accident or health plan to any employee's child who has not attained age 27 as of the end of the taxable year. (See § 1004(d) of HCERA.) The Affordable Care Act also makes parallel amendments, effective March 30, 2010, to § 401(h) for retiree health accounts in pension plans, to § 501(c)(9) for voluntary employees' beneficiary associations (VEBAs), and to § 162(l) for deductions by self-employed individuals for medical care insurance. (See § 1004(d) of HCERA.)

The Affordable Care Act amended the Public Health Service Act (PHS Act) to add § 2714, which requires group health plans and health insurance issuers that provide dependent coverage of children to continue to make such coverage available for an adult child until age 26. (See § 1001 of PPACA.)

Section 2714 of the PHS Act is incorporated into § 9815 of the Code by § 1562(f) of PPACA. In certain respects, the rules of § 2714 of the PHS Act extending coverage to an adult child do not parallel the gross income exclusion rules provided by the Affordable Care Act's amendments of §§ 105(b), 401(h), 501(c)(9), and 162(l) of the Code. For example, § 2714 of the PHS Act applies to children under age 26 and is effective for the first plan year beginning on or after September 23, 2010, while, as noted above, the amendments to the Code addressed in this notice apply to children who have not attained age 27 as of the end of the taxable year and are effective March 30, 2010.

II. EXCLUSION OF EMPLOYER-PROVIDED MEDICAL CARE REIMBURSEMENTS FOR EMPLOYEE'S CHILD UNDER AGE 27

Section 105(b) generally excludes from an employee's gross income employer-provided reimbursements made directly or indirectly to the employee for the medical care of the employee, employee's spouse or employee's dependents (as defined in § 152 (determined without regard to § 152(b)(1), (b)(2) or (d)(1)(B)). As amended by the Affordable Care Act, the exclusion from gross income under § 105(b) is extended to employer-provided reimbursements for expenses incurred by the employee for the medical care of the employee's child (within the meaning of § 152(f)(1)) who has not attained age 27 as of the end of the taxable year. (The Affordable Care Act does not alter the existing definitions of spouse or dependent for purposes of § 105(b).) Under § 152(f)(1), a child is an individual who is the son, daughter, stepson, or stepdaughter of the employee, and a child includes both a legally adopted individual of the employee and an individual who is lawfully placed with the employee for legal adoption by the employee. Under § 152(f)(1), a child also includes an "eligible foster child," defined as an individual who is placed with the employee by an authorized placement agency or by judgment, decree, or other order of any court of competent jurisdiction.

As amended by the Affordable Care Act, the exclusion from gross income under § 105(b) applies with respect to an employee's child who has not attained age 27 as of the end of the taxable year, including a child of the employee who is not the employee's dependent within the meaning of § 152(a). Thus, the age limit, residency, support, and other tests described in § 152(c) do not apply with respect to such a child for purposes of § 105(b).

The exclusion applies only for reimbursements for medical care of individuals who are not age 27 or older at any time during the taxable year. For purposes of §§ 105(b) and 106, the taxable year is the employee's taxable year; employers may assume that an employee's taxable year is the calendar year; a child attains age 27 on the 27th anniversary of the date the child was born (for example, a child born on April 10, 1983 attained age 27 on April 10, 2010); and employers may rely on the employee's representation as to the child's date of birth.

III. EXCLUSION OF EMPLOYER-PROVIDED ACCIDENT OR HEALTH COVERAGE FOR EMPLOYEE'S CHILD UNDER AGE 27

Section 106 excludes from an employee's gross income coverage under an employer-provided accident or health plan. The regulations under § 106 provide that the exclusion applies to employer-provided coverage for an employee and the employee's spouse or dependents (as defined in § 152, determined without regard to § 152(b)(1), (b)(2) or (d)(1)(B)). See Prop. Treas. Reg. § 1.106-1. Prior to the Affordable Care Act, the exclusion for employer-provided accident or health plan coverage under § 106 paralleled the exclusion for reimbursements under § 105(b). There is no indication that Congress intended to provide a broader exclusion in § 105(b) than in § 106. Accordingly, IRS and Treasury intend to amend the regulations under § 106, retroactively to March 30, 2010, to provide that coverage for an employee's child under age 27 is excluded from gross income. Thus, on and after

March 30, 2010, both coverage under an employer-provided accident or health plan and amounts paid or reimbursed under such a plan for medical care expenses of an employee, an employee's spouse, an employee's dependents (as defined in § 152, determined without regard to § 152(b)(1), (b)(2) or (d)(1)(B)), or an employee's child (as defined in § 152(f)(1)) who has not attained age 27 as of the end of the employee's taxable year are excluded from the employee's gross income.

The following examples illustrate this rule. In these examples, any reference to a "dependent" means a dependent as defined in § 152, determined without regard to § 152(b)(1), (b)(2) or (d)(1)(B). Also, in these examples, it is assumed that none of the individuals are disabled.

Example (1). (i) Employer X provides health care coverage for its employees and their spouses and dependents and for any employee's child (as defined in § 152(f)(1)) who has not attained age 26. For the 2010 taxable year, Employer X provides coverage to Employee A and to A's son, C. C will attain age 26 on November 15, 2010. During the 2010 taxable year, C is not a full-time student. C has never worked for Employer X. C is not a dependent of A because prior to the close of the 2010 taxable year C had attained age 19 (and was also not a student who had not attained age 24).

(ii) C is a child of A within the meaning of § 152(f)(1). Accordingly, and because C will not attain age 27 during the 2010 taxable year, the health care coverage and reimbursements provided to him under the terms of Employer X's plan are excludible from A's gross income under §§ 106 and 105(b) for the period on and after March 30, 2010 through November 15, 2010 (when C attains age 26 and loses coverage under the terms of the plan).

Example (2). (i) Employer Y provides health care coverage for its employees and their spouses and dependents and for any employee's child (as defined in § 152(f)(1)) who has not attained age 27 as of the end of the taxable year. For the 2010 taxable year, Employer Y provides health care coverage to Employee E and to E's son, G. G will not attain age 27 until after the end of the 2010 taxable year. During the 2010 taxable year, G earns $50,000 per year, and does not live with E. G has never worked for Employer Y. G is not eligible for health care coverage from his own employer. G is not a dependent of E because G does not live with E and E does not provide more than one half of his support.

(ii) G is a child of E within the meaning of § 152(f)(1). Accordingly, and because G will not attain age 27 during the 2010 taxable year, the health care coverage and reimbursements for G under Employer Y's plan are excludible from E's gross income under §§ 106 and 105(b) for the period on and after March 30, 2010 through the end of the 2010 taxable year.

Example (3). (i) Same facts as *Example (2)*, except that G's employer offers health care coverage, but G has decided not to participate in his employer's plan.

(ii) G is a child of E within the meaning of § 152(f)(1). Accordingly, and because G will not attain age 27 during the 2010 taxable year, the health care coverage and reimbursements for G under Employer Y's plan are excludible from E's gross income under §§ 106 and 105(b) for the period on and after March 30, 2010 through the end of the 2010 taxable year.

Example (4). (i) Same facts as *Example (3)*, except that G is married to H, and neither G nor H is a dependent of E. G and H have decided not to participate in the health care coverage offered by G's employer, and Employer Y provides health care coverage to G and H.

(ii) G is a child of E within the meaning of § 152(f)(1). Accordingly, and because G will not attain age 27 during the 2010 taxable year, the health care coverage and reimbursements for G under Employer Y's plan are excludible from E's gross income under §§ 106 and 105(b) for the period on and after

March 30, 2010 through the end of the 2010 taxable year. The fair market value of the coverage for H is includible in E's gross income for the 2010 taxable year.

Example (5). (i) Employer Z provides health care coverage for its employees and their spouses and dependents. Effective May 1, 2010, Employer Z amends the health plan to provide coverage for any employee's child (as defined in § 152(f)(1)) who has not attained age 26. Employer Z provides coverage to Employee F and to F's son, K, for the 2010 taxable year. K will attain age 22 in 2010. During the 2010 taxable year, F provides more than one half of K's support. K lives with F and graduates from college on May 15, 2010 and thereafter is not a student. K has never worked for Employer Z. Prior to K's graduation from college, K is a dependent of F. Following graduation from college, K is no longer a dependent of F.

(ii) For the 2010 taxable year, the health care coverage and reimbursements provided to K under the terms of Employer Z's plan are excludible from F's gross income under §§ 106 and 105(b). For the period through May 15, 2010, the reimbursements and coverage are excludible because K was a dependent of F. For the period on and after March 30, 2010, the coverage is excludible because K is a child of F within the meaning of § 152(f)(1) and because K will not attain age 27 during the 2010 taxable year. (Thus, for the period from March 30 through May 15, 2010, there are two bases for the exclusion.)

IV. CAFETERIA PLANS, FLEXIBLE SPENDING ARRANGEMENTS, AND HEALTH REIMBURSEMENT ARRANGEMENTS

Section 125 allows employees to elect between cash and certain qualified benefits, including accident or health plans (described in § 106) and health flexible spending arrangements (health FSAs) (described in § 105(b)). Section 125(f) defines "qualified benefit" as any benefit which, with the application of § 125(a), is not includible in the gross income of the employee by reason of an express provision of chapter 1 of the Code (other than §§ 106(b) (which applies to Archer MSAs), 117, 127, or 132). Accordingly, the exclusion of coverage and reimbursements from an employee's gross income under §§ 106 and 105(b) for an employee's child who has not attained age 27 as of the end of the employee's taxable year carries forward automatically to the definition of qualified benefits for § 125 cafeteria plans, including health FSAs. Thus, a benefit will not fail to be a qualified benefit under a cafeteria plan (including a health FSA) merely because it provides coverage or reimbursements that are excludible under §§ 106 and 105(b) for a child who has not attained age 27 as of the end of the employee's taxable year.

A cafeteria plan may permit an employee to revoke an election during a period of coverage and to make a new election only in limited circumstances, such as a change in status event. See Treas. Reg. § 1.125-4(c). A change in status event includes changes in the number of an employee's dependents. The regulations under § 1.125-4(c) currently do not permit election changes for children under age 27 who are not the employee's dependents. IRS and Treasury intend to amend the regulations under § 1.125-4, effective retroactively to March 30, 2010, to include change in status events affecting non-dependent children under age 27, including becoming newly eligible for coverage or eligible for coverage beyond the date on which the child otherwise would have lost coverage.

In general, a health reimbursement arrangement (HRA) is an arrangement that is paid for solely by an employer (and not through a § 125 cafeteria plan) which reimburses an employee for medical care expenses up to a maximum dollar amount for a coverage period. Notice 2002-45, 2002-2 C.B. 93. The same rules that apply to an employee's child under age 27 for purposes of §§ 106 and 105(b) apply to an HRA.

V. FICA, FUTA, RRTA, AND INCOME TAX WITHHOLDING TREATMENT

Coverage and reimbursements under an employer-provided accident and health plan for employees generally and their dependents (or a class or classes of employees and their dependents) are excluded from wages for Federal Insurance Contributions Act (FICA) and Federal Unemployment Tax Act (FUTA) tax purposes under §§ 3121(a)(2) and 3306(b)(2), respectively. For these purposes, a child of the employee is a dependent. Treas. Reg. §§ 31.3121(a)(2)-1(c) and 31.3306(b)(2)-1(c). No age limit, residency, support, or other test applies for these purposes. Thus, coverage and reimbursements under a plan for employees and their dependents that are provided for an employee's child under age 27 are not wages for FICA or FUTA purposes. For this purpose, child has the same meaning as in § 152(f)(1), as discussed in the first paragraph in Section II of this notice. A similar exclusion applies for Railroad Retirement Tax Act (RRTA) tax purposes under § 3231(e)(1)(i) and Treas. Reg. § 31.3231(e)-1(a)(1).

Such coverage and reimbursements are also exempt from income tax withholding. See Rev. Rul. 56-632, 1956-2 C.B. 101.

VI. VEBAS, SECTION 401(h) ACCOUNTS, AND SECTION 162(l) DEDUCTIONS

A VEBA is a tax-exempt entity described in § 501(c)(9) providing for the payment of life, sick, accident, or other benefits to members of the VEBA or their dependents or designated beneficiaries. The regulations provide that, for purposes of § 501(c)(9), "dependent" means the member's spouse; any child of the member or the member's spouse who is a minor or a student (within the meaning of § 151(e)(4) (now § 152(f)(2)); any other minor child residing with the member; and any other individual who an association, relying on information furnished to it by a member, in good faith believes is a person described in § 152(a). Treas. Reg. § 1.501(c)(9)-3. As amended by the Affordable Care Act, § 501(c)(9) provides that, for purposes of providing for the payment of sick and accident benefits to members of the VEBA and their dependents, the term dependent includes any individual who is a member's child (as defined in § 152(f)(1)) and who has not attained age 27 as of the end of the calendar year.

Section 401(h) provides that a pension or annuity plan can establish and maintain a separate account to provide for the payment of benefits for sickness, accident, hospitalization, and medical expenses of retired employees, their spouses and their dependents if certain enumerated conditions are met ("401(h) Account"). The regulations provide that, for purposes of § 401(h) and § 1.401-14, the term "dependent" shall have the same meaning as that assigned to it by § 152. Treas. Reg. § 1.401-14(b)(4)(i). As amended by the Affordable Care Act, § 401(h) provides that the term dependent includes any individual who is a retired employee's child (within the meaning of § 152(f)(1)) and who has not attained age 27 as of the end of the calendar year.

Section 162(l) generally allows a self-employed individual to deduct, in computing adjusted gross income, amounts paid during the taxable year for insurance that constitutes medical care for the taxpayer, his or her spouse, and dependents, if certain requirements are satisfied. As amended by the Affordable Care Act, § 162(l) covers medical insurance for any child (within the meaning of § 152(f)(1)) who has not attained age 27 as of the end of the taxable year.

VII. TRANSITION RULE FOR CAFETERIA PLAN AMENDMENTS

Cafeteria plans may need to be amended to include employees' children who have not attained age 27 as of the end of the taxable year. Pursuant to § 1.125-1(c) of the proposed regulations, cafeteria plan amendments may be effective only prospectively. Notwithstanding this general rule, as of March 30,

2010, employers may permit employees to immediately make pre-tax salary reduction contributions for accident or health benefits under a cafeteria plan (including a health FSA) for children under age 27, even if the cafeteria plan has not yet been amended to cover these individuals. However, a retroactive amendment to a cafeteria plan to cover children under age 27 must be made no later than December 31, 2010, and must be effective retroactively to the first date in 2010 when employees are permitted to make pre-tax salary reduction contributions to cover children under age 27 (but in no event before March 30, 2010).

VIII. EFFECT ON OTHER DOCUMENTS

IRS and Treasury intend to amend the regulations at §§ 1.105-1, 1.105-2, 1.106-1, 1.125-1, 1.125-4, 1.125-5, and 1.401-14 to include children (as defined in § 152(f)(1)) who are under age 27. Additionally, IRS and Treasury intend to amend the regulations at § 1.501(c)(9)-3 to include children (as defined in § 152(f)(1)) who are under age 27, with respect to sick and accident benefits. Taxpayers may rely on this notice pending the issuance of the amended regulations.

IX. EFFECTIVE DATES

The changes relating to §§ 105(b), 106, 501(c)(9), 401(h) and 162(l) are effective on March 30, 2010.

H. DRAFTING INFORMATION

The principal author of this notice is Karen Levin of the Office of Division Counsel/Associate Chief Counsel (Tax Exempt and Government Entities). For further information regarding this notice, contact Ms. Levin at (202) 622-6080 (not a toll-free call).

J. Information to Be Posted on a Web Site by HHS

INFORMATION TO BE POSTED ON A WEB SITE BY HHS

INFORMATION	WHEN AVAILABLE	PPACA CITATION
List of HHS authorities under the Act	April 23, 2010	1552
State health insurance options (To include health insurance offering, Medicaid programs, state high risk pool options)	July 1, 2010	1103
Standard hospital charges		
Insurer reports on ratio of claims vs. non-claim costs and premium revenue rebates		PHSA 2718
GAO report on denial of coverage and benefits by plans and insurers		1562
Reports from GHP and HIC re: reimbursement structures that encourage quality of care	March, 2012	PHSA 2717
Health Care Quality Website (to report national priorities for health care quality and agency strategic plans)	January 1, 2011	3011
Interagency Work Group on Health Care Quality (annual report and recommendations)	December 31, 2010	3012
Quality of inpatient care, hospital-acquired infections, medical errors, etc.	2015	3008
Reports on quality measures for inpatient care at long term hospitals, psychiatric hospitals, rehabilitation facilities and hospices (to be posted on CMS Web site)	2014	3004
Hospital Compare Web site —readmission rates —hospital acquired illnesses		3001, 3025
Nursing Home Compare to report on quality and data on nursing homes with a link to state sites (on CMS Web site)	March 1, 2011	6103
Physician Compare to report performance an efficiency data (on CMS Web site)	Plan to be developed no later than January 1, 2013	10331
Triennial report on development of quality measures and gaps in available quality measures		PHSA 931
Provider performance reports based on quality measures	Funds to develop authorized for years 2010–2014	PHSA
Prevention Information —Science-based information on guidelines for nutrition, regular exercise, obesity reduction, smoking cessation, and specific chronic disease prevention —Personalized prevention plan tool		4004
Report on data and analysis of health disparities from federal health care programs and public health clinics	2012	3101
Reports on physician-owned hospitals (to be posted on CMS Web site)		6001
Reports on payments to physicians by, and physician ownership in, manufacturers and group purchasing organizations	September 30, 2013	6002

INFORMATION	WHEN AVAILABLE	PPACA CITATION
Research results of Patient-Centered Outcomes Research Institute (to assist patients, clinicians, purchasers, and policymakers in making informed health decisions by advancing the quality and relevance of evidence concerning the manner in which diseases, disorders, and other health conditions can effectively and appropriately be prevented, diagnosed, treated, monitored, and managed through research and evidence synthesis that considers variations in patient subpopulations, and the dissemination of research findings with respect to the relative health outcomes, clinical effectiveness, and appropriateness of the medical treatments, services, and items)	Funding begins in 2010	6301

INDEX

References are to chapters (Ch.), section numbers, and appendices.